Enhancing Knowledge Discovery and Innovation in the Digital Era

Miltiadis D. Lytras
The American College of Greece, Greece

Linda Daniela
University of Latvia, Latvia

Anna Visvizi
The American College of Greece, Greece

A volume in the Advances in Knowledge Acquisition, Transfer, and Management (AKATM) Book Series

IGI Global
DISSEMINATOR OF KNOWLEDGE

Published in the United States of America by
IGI Global
Information Science Reference (an imprint of IGI Global)
701 E. Chocolate Avenue
Hershey PA, USA 17033
Tel: 717-533-8845
Fax: 717-533-8661
E-mail: cust@igi-global.com
Web site: http://www.igi-global.com

Library of Congress Cataloging-in-Publication Data

Names: Lytras, Miltiadis D., 1973- editor. | Daniela, Linda, 1967- editor. | Visvizi, Anna, 1976- editor.
Title: Enhancing knowledge discovery and innovation in the digital era / Miltiadis D. Lytras, Linda Daniela, and Anna Visvizi, editors.
Description: Hershey, PA : Information Science Reference, [2018] | Includes bibliographical references.
Identifiers: LCCN 2017030378| ISBN 9781522541912 (h/c) | ISBN 9781522541929 (eISBN)
Subjects: LCSH: Big data--Social aspects. | Knowledge economy. | Information commons. | Data mining.
Classification: LCC QA76.9.C66 E555 2018 | DDC 005.7--dc23 LC record available at https://lccn.loc.gov/2017030378

This book is published in the IGI Global book series Advances in Knowledge Acquisition, Transfer, and Management (AKATM) (ISSN: 2326-7607; eISSN: 2326-7615)

British Cataloguing in Publication Data
A Cataloguing in Publication record for this book is available from the British Library.

All work contributed to this book is new, previously-unpublished material. The views expressed in this book are those of the authors, but not necessarily of the publisher.

For electronic access to this publication, please contact: eresources@igi-global.com.

Advances in Knowledge Acquisition, Transfer, and Management (AKATM) Book Series

Murray E. Jennex
San Diego State University, USA

ISSN:2326-7607
EISSN:2326-7615

Mission

Organizations and businesses continue to utilize knowledge management practices in order to streamline processes and procedures. The emergence of web technologies has provided new methods of information usage and knowledge sharing.

The **Advances in Knowledge Acquisition, Transfer, and Management (AKATM) Book Series** brings together research on emerging technologies and their effect on information systems as well as the knowledge society.**AKATM** will provide researchers, students, practitioners, and industry leaders with research highlights surrounding the knowledge management discipline, including technology support issues and knowledge representation.

Coverage

- Cognitive Theories
- Cultural Impacts
- Information and Communication Systems
- Knowledge acquisition and transfer processes
- Knowledge management strategy
- Knowledge Sharing
- Organizational learning
- Organizational Memory
- Small and Medium Enterprises
- Virtual communities

IGI Global is currently accepting manuscripts for publication within this series. To submit a proposal for a volume in this series, please contact our Acquisition Editors at Acquisitions@igi-global.com or visit: http://www.igi-global.com/publish/.

The Advances in Knowledge Acquisition, Transfer, and Management (AKATM) Book Series (ISSN 2326-7607) is published by IGI Global, 701 E. Chocolate Avenue, Hershey, PA 17033-1240, USA, www.igi-global.com. This series is composed of titles available for purchase individually; each title is edited to be contextually exclusive from any other title within the series. For pricing and ordering information please visit http://www.igi-global.com/book-series/advances-knowledge-acquisition-transfer-management/37159. Postmaster: Send all address changes to above address.

Titles in this Series

For a list of additional titles in this series, please visit: www.igi-global.com/book-series

Techniques for Coding Imagery and Multimedia Emerging Research and Opportunities
Shalin Hai-Jew (Kansas State University, USA)
Information Science Reference • copyright 2018 • 483pp • H/C (ISBN: 9781522526797) • US $235.00 (our price)

Cross-Disciplinary Approaches to Action Research and Action Learning
Tome Awshar Mapotse (University of South Africa, South Africa)
Information Science Reference • copyright 2018 • 380pp • H/C (ISBN: 9781522526421) • US $215.00 (our price)

Cross-Cultural Analysis of Image-Based Assessments Emerging Research and Opportunities
Lisa Keller (University of Massachusetts Amherst, USA) Robert Keller (Measured Progress, USA) and Michael Nering (Measured Progress, USA)
Information Science Reference • copyright 2018 • 166pp • H/C (ISBN: 9781522526919) • US $130.00 (our price)

Social Media for Knowledge Management Applications in Modern Organizations
Francesca Di Virgilio (University of Molise, Italy)
Business Science Reference • copyright 2018 • 384pp • H/C (ISBN: 9781522528975) • US $215.00 (our price)

Philosophical Perceptions on Logic and Order
Jeremy Horne (International Institute of Informatics and Systemics, USA)
Information Science Reference • copyright 2018 • 402pp • H/C (ISBN: 9781522524434) • US $225.00 (our price)

Handbook of Research on Tacit Knowledge Management for Organizational Success
Dhouha Jaziri-Bouagina (University of Sousse, Tunisia) and George Leal Jamil (Informações em Rede Consultoria e Treinamento Ltda, Brazil)
Information Science Reference • copyright 2017 • 542pp • H/C (ISBN: 9781522523949) • US $275.00 (our price)

Bio-Inspired Computing for Information Retrieval Applications
D.P. Acharjya (School of Computing Science and Engineering, VIT University, India) and Anirban Mitra (Vignan Institute of Technology and Management, India)
Information Science Reference • copyright 2017 • 388pp • H/C (ISBN: 9781522523758) • US $205.00 (our price)

Managing Knowledge Resources and Records in Modern Organizations
Priti Jain (University of Botswana, Botswana) and Nathan Mnjama (University of Botswana, Botswana)
Business Science Reference • copyright 2017 • 280pp • H/C (ISBN: 9781522519652) • US $185.00 (our price)

IGI Global
DISSEMINATOR OF KNOWLEDGE

701 East Chocolate Avenue, Hershey, PA 17033, USA
Tel: 717-533-8845 x100 • Fax: 717-533-8661
E-Mail: cust@igi-global.com • www.igi-global.com

To all who put smiles on our faces and inspire our souls to dream of a better world for all, a world based on trust, peace, respect, and collaboration.

Table of Contents

Detailed Table of Contents

In the increasingly interconnected world, the relationship among learning and teaching, innovation and innovativeness, entrepreneurship, business development, as well as sustainable and inclusive socio-economic growth and development, requires a multidimensional interdisciplinary analysis. Importantly, information systems and advancements in sophisticated information and communication technologies (ICTs) are consequential for the potential inherent in education to be exploited. This edited volume opens discussion on ways and strategies of exploiting opportunities and synergies, which the maturing relationship between smart education and information systems offers. In this context, the objective of this chapter is to suggest how to (re)define smart education and how to reap its benefits in view of promoting dynamic education and information systems conducive to the emergence of innovation networks in socially, politically and economically trying times.

Innovation is a key source of new products, benefit and fresh growth in revenues. In developed economies, the private sector is the engine of innovation and growth, accounting for between half and two-thirds of total spending on research and development in some countries. On the other hand, increasing access to technology will be a critical driver of economic growth in emerging economies, but it will require private sector leaders and the public sector to work together to make their respective programs more impactful. At the same time, the rapid advances and pervasive diffusion of information and communication technology (ICT), combined with the growth of the Internet have led to deep transformations in economic, social and institutional structures. ICT applications affect the performance of businesses and the efficiency of markets, foster the empowerment of citizens and communities as well as their access to knowledge, and contribute to strengthening and redefining governance processes at all institutional levels.

In this chapter are shared experiences in educative innovation by using Information Communication and Technologies in higher education. The objective of this contribution is to provide a view related to the curricular integration of ICT, highlighting by practical examples of implementation, which include their impact in cognitive processes and in the development of personal and interpersonal abilities in students. In the distribution, it is incorporated a description in planning activities and their application in the classroom, methodological aspects and assessing strategies selected for each experience are detailed. In addition, it is delivered a reflexive view related to the teacher role in the educative act. Finally, it is discussed the relevance of an active role in higher education institutions, referring to improve permanent training programs in educative innovation and to generate communicational spaces between teachers as well as different formation areas in the sense of strengthening the educative process and improve the quality of education.

This research assesses the education quality factors in secondary schools using a business intelligence approach. We operationalize each layer of the business intelligence framework to identify the stakeholders and components relevant to education quality. The resulting Education Quality Indicator (EQI) framework consists of seven Critical Success Factors (CSFs) and is measured through twenty-eight Key Performance Indicators (KPIs). The EQI framework was evaluated through expert interviews and a survey, and uncovers that the most important factor in assuring education quality is a teacher's ability to communicate with students. Furthermore, a feasibility analysis was conducted in a Dutch student monitoring information system. The results pave the way towards attainable and data-driven innovation in secondary education towards personalized student and teacher performance management using business intelligence technologies, which may ultimately integrate a wide variety of data sources from environmental sensors to wearables to optimally understand each individual student and teacher.

The objective of this study is to investigate the impact of accreditation on engineering education including student learning outcomes and innovation based on two accreditation bodies the NCAAA in KSA, and the ABET in USA. The article explores the approach of constructionism with emphasis to makerspace by delivering engineering and design courses with opportunities for innovation, creativity, and the ability to design a system, component, or process to meet desired needs. This innovative approach shifts the active learning strategies from Do-It-Yourself to Do-It-With-Others culture. Makerspace is one of the integral parts of modern education system that brings together and facilitates the community of interdisciplinary individuals. Results from courses in engineering and design shows the benefit of the accreditation in terms of enhancing the overall program quality and the importance of re-evaluating strategies and methodologies of learning which help in delivering innovative solutions and educating tomorrow's leaders to address the most pressing issues facing our societies.

The main purpose of this research was to find relations between activities in Dees (Digital Electronics Education and Design Suite) and student performance in an undergraduate course of Digital Electronics. In our case of study, we used a dataset which contains examples of students using Dees toolkit. Firstly, we performed an analysis of the attributes of the dataset, to find correlations between student performance and activities developed during six sessions of the course. Secondly, we performed clustering using the algorithm k-means. Then, we concluded that, there is a relation between Dees activities performed by a student and student performance. This result opens the possibility of further analysis and perhaps the use of similar software toolkit in different courses of the Engineering curricula.

In the fourth revolution era talking innovation is not only necessary for improving and forwarding all social and economic activities, but also is it an exigence of those who are demanding high-quality goods or services. This is important for knowledge services, and becomes a core issue for educative issues designed for the millennials or digital natives. Sometimes, these exigencies are no shown directly, but it is possible assessing them by means of the analysis of sentiments, which reflects a range of feelings which are not clearly verbalized and even self-recognized. This paper analyzes sentiments for assessing the importance of innovative procedures in higher education, from the point of view of the students. A prototype architecture – LADEL (Learning Analytics Dashboard for E-Learning) - is introduced, for dealing with the diverse e-learning domains. Some experiments are conducted. This demonstrated the necessity of innovative procedures in higher education, since it is a widespread, multidisciplinary and transversal demand, even it is not always explicit.

This paper presents the development of a virtual campus named DeepThink designed to support a postgraduate program named MPhil (Master in Philosophy) at The Open University. The MPhil is a formal Open University degree delivered to a distance. The virtual campus integrates second life, moodle and several Web 2.0 technologies like elluminate (online conferencing tool), MyStuff (e-Portfolio), Skype and Ning (Social network). This integration between second life and web 2.0 technologies has caused enthusiasm in tutors at the Open University who saw the benefit of using DeepThink in their courses. This campus is an innovative project which brings new ways of supervision. Our campus DeepThink in general promotes higher Education using technologies like second life, which has shown to be useful in supervision and teaching undergraduate courses. Finally, we discuss our experiences on second life and its limitations.

The use of electronic presentations in the classroom has become a controversial subject, as the innovative educational value of electronic presentation tools such as MS-PowerPoint or Prezi is being questioned. This study uses the participatory research approach to investigate how college instructors feel about the use of PowerPoint presentations when teaching an introductory course of computer information systems. Nine college instructors participated in this research project by exchanging their views through an online discussion forum. The findings revealed that PowerPoint presentations are perceived by instructors as valuable only when combined with other teaching techniques. Moreover, it became evident that the instructors perceived that although students' attention and participation is affected by the use of electronic presentations, their actual performance is not.

Massive Open Online Courses (MOOC) is a model of educational delivery that is, to varying degrees, massive, with theoretically no limit to enrollment; open, allowing anyone to participate, usually at no cost; online, with learning activities typically taking place over the web; and a course, structured around a set of learning goals in a defined area of study. The MOOCs (Massive Online Open Course) are online courses, which are mainly for higher education level. These courses present an interesting evolution in the distance learn methods. The MOOCs do not replace the current universities, but they can be an innovative proposal to the curriculum. In this chapter, the authors present the algorithm they are creating. The main purpose of this algorithm is to create automatic mechanisms as the recommendation system to give such assistance and personalized guidance to students. They will also discuss the integration of this algorithm in MOOCMAROC which is a MOOC platform powred by Open edX.

Innovative knowledge discovery comes through collaboration of knowledge in educational systems. In a collaborative educational system the heterogeneity of data in different learning management systems presents many difficulties for data sharing; some of these difficulties are how to integrate data, produce

Preface

As the pace of change in our shared socio-economic environment seems to increase, the premise and promise inherent in the onset of the digital era suggest ways of dealing with the change-inflicted uncertainty besetting our societies. The digital era implies two distinct, and yet mutually reinforcing each other, ways of dealing with change and uncertainty, i.e., ceaseless knowledge discovery and continuous innovation. These two imperatives of knowledge discovery and innovation form the thrust of the discussion in this edited volume. Applying a variety of methodological approaches and research perspectives, the chapters included in this collection address specific issues pertinent to enhancing knowledge creation, knowledge discovery and boosting innovation in a sustainable manner. This edited volume recognizes that change is taking place, thus transforming the way our societies function, incl. our political and economic systems. This volume derives from the recognition that education and education-enabled innovation are the key factors that condition inclusive and sustainable socio-economic growth and development. Moreover, this volume is founded on the understanding that values and principles defining the functioning of liberal open societies are an integral part of education and education-enabled innovation. All things considered, this edited volume highlights how – if skillfully managed – education and education-enabled innovation can assist our societies in growing and developing in a sustainable, inclusive and peaceful manner.

The volume opens with a chapter that dwells on the role of education in boosting innovation in our societies. By (re)defining smart education and by introducing the concept of innovation networks, in Chapter 1, Visvizi, Lytras, and Daniela make a case for the centrality of education in boosting and exploiting the inherent in our societies potential to innovate. As the authors argue, the emergence and functioning of innovation networks is only possible if a certain set of fundamental values and principles is endorsed by the members of the society. The key role of education in instilling these values and principles in successive generations of agents is emphasized.

Taking the discussion on innovation networks as a point of departure, in Chapter 2, Danilo and Piagesi uphold the centrality of innovation for the development of our societies. They add to the argument introduced in the previous chapter by conceptualizing and exploring the complex relationship that unfolds among public research, business and governments. As they argue, rapid advancements in and diffusion of Information and Communication Technologies (ICTs) trigger dramatic changes in how our societies function. Importantly, while creating several challenges, ICTs bear several opportunities as well.

Indeed, as Badilla Quantana and Basso Aránguiz highlight in Chapter 3, efficient use of ICTs might advance teaching and learning process and hence might lead to dramatic positive transformation of the higher education system in Chile. As the authors explain, nevertheless, several obstacles and challenges exist that beset the prospect of improving the quality of education in Chile.

In Chapter 4, Spruit and Adriana uphold the notion of factors influencing the quality of education. By focusing explicitly on secondary education, they make a powerful case for employing business intelligence technologies to transforming secondary education. As the authors argue, as a result, a much more personalized student and teacher performance management environment would be created, thus enhancing the performance of teachers and students and, in turn, the efficacy of the teaching and learning process.

Brahimi et al., in Chapter 5, join the discussion on efficacy of the teaching and learning process and, overall, on boosting the performance of higher education institutions, by exploring the mechanism of accreditation. They argue, that accreditation supports innovation in both the delivery and the content of engineering education. Moreover, it offers insights into how to deal with specific challenges that contemporary higher education institutions confront.

Changing the level of analysis, Chapter 6 grapples with the question of how sophisticated ICTs' enhanced teaching and learning tools, such as Dees (Digital Electronics Education and Design Suite) may enhance undergraduate students' performance in Digital Electronics course. To prove her case, Vargas-Vera, the author, employs an impressive sample of more than 29 thousand. The sophisticated methodology behind the outcomes of the study presented in this chapter deserves particular attention.

In the following chapter, D'Avanzo et al. address the question of students' satisfaction with the EU co-funded Erasmus program. While the benefits of student mobility, seen as a mechanism of knowledge transfer, cannot be denied, the value added of this chapter consists in the methodology that the authors apply to conduct sentiment analysis of Erasmus' students.

Chapter 8 takes this discussion from the EU-wide mobility to virtual reality. Vargas-Vera explains how the development of a virtual campus named DeepThink, designed to support a postgraduate program in philosophy, brought about substantial transformation in the way of thinking about the nature of the teaching and learning process and the specific modes of delivery.

In Chapter 9, Stefanou and Kotsovolou explore the implications of the use of PowerPoint and how it redefines the role of the teacher, how it reshapes the interaction between the teacher and the student and how it forces them to adapt to different, respectively teaching and learning strategies.

In Chapter 10, Jdidou and Khaldi direct the discussion to Massive Online Open Courses (MOOCs) to argue that they role is not replace traditional modes of teaching and learning, but rather to enhance the learning process and enable students to improve their performance. To this end, however, as the Authors argue, it is necessary that students are offered assistance and personalized guidance. To this end, appropriate algorithms embedded in MOOCs might do just that.

In Chapter 11, Masud explores the challenges inherent in maintaining and updating the knowledge base upon which collaborative knowledge sharing systems are built. This highly interesting, albeit quite technical discussion, reminds us that ICTs-enhanced teaching and learning is a two-way street, which requires an equal focus on the uses of technology in education and the infrastructure that makes the use of technology feasible in the first place.

In the following three chapters, the level of analysis changes. Consequently, the conceptualization of education, especially its spatial and temporal dimensions, is extended. It is brought beyond the class room or a university setting, to entail cities and urban spaces. These, in turn, are conceived as modern *agora* where teaching and learning establish themselves a part of day-to-day interaction through which community and society is constructed and re-constructed over time. Specifically, in Chapter 12, Alides Rezende examines how ICTs' enhanced infrastructure enables citizens' access to information and knowledge about the urban space they inhabit. By exploring the cases of Chicago (USA) and Curitiba (Brazil),

Rezende makes a distinctive case for the value added of investing in ICTs' enhanced infrastructure. As the author demonstrates, this infrastructure, by facilitating access to information and services, improves citizens' well-being.

Another aspect defining the functioning of urban space seen as *agora*, is the rapid growth and evolution of this space. The challenge, thus, is how to ensure citizens' well-being given the speed of change. As Hipolito et al. demonstrate, if information about that space is skilfully collected, processed and fed-back into the policy-making process, it is possible to keep en par with the evolution of the urban space and ensure citizens' well-being. By focusing on the problem of noise pollution in urban space, in their discussion (Chapter 13), Hipolito et al. explain how user-generated content may constitute a key source of information in the process of monitoring and addressing environmental noise in cities. One of the arguments that Chapters 12 and 13 bring to the surface of the discussion on ICTs' enhanced infrastructure – seen as a means of facilitating the distribution of information and knowledge about the public space and services available to its inhabitants – is the question of how to ensure a form of active engagement of citizens with that infrastructure. In other words, if urban space is seen as an agora, the value of ICTs' enhanced infrastructure can be exploited only if that that infrastructure derives from citizens' feedback and, hence, mirrors citizens' needs. In Chapter 14, Hartman et al. grapple with the challenge of mobilizing citizens' participation by exploring the – as they argue – increasingly successful practice of 'innovation contests'.

In Chapter 16, the focus of the analysis presented in this volume narrows. By returning to MOOCs, this chapter explores the question of how to exploit the content generated in a voluntary manner by MOOCs' through their engagement with online MOOC-related communities. As Luna et al. argue, this spontaneous and voluntarily shared information bears great educational potential, which, nevertheless, only rarely is recognized and exploited. The discussion in the volume concludes with a chapter that explores the notion of internal branding seen as a function of communication and an organization's business strategy. As Matiatou outlines, communication practices are vital for companies to be able to fulfil their vision, mission, and goals. Implicitly, Matiatou's chapter reminds us that, ultimately, students already are, or are bound to become, members of organizations. In this view, knowledge discovery is a perpetual process that needs to be strengthened and enhanced. The promise of the digital era is that we can do it effectively. This edited volume attests to that.

Miltiadis Lytras
The American College of Greece, Greece

Linda Daniela
University of Latvia, Latvia

Anna Visvizi
The American College of Greece, Greece

Introduction

In a period of time when individuals and society are frequently helpless and unable to grapple with the speed and implications of rapid change, education based on the belief in the transformative power of the individual as a member of the society and founded on the principles of freedom, liberty, and respect for each other, has remained the most important constant. This edited volume recognizes that change indeed is taking place, thus transforming the way our societies function, incl. our political and economic systems. This edited volume recognizes that socio-economic sustainability is at stake as the world is swept by political upheavals, civil wars, and armed conflicts, and while soft risks to safety and security have risen to global concerns. Against all odds, this edited volume offers a way of navigating these challenges. It highlights how—if skillfully managed—education and education-enabled innovation can assist our societies in growing and developing in a sustainable, inclusive and peaceful manner.

By exploring a variety of perspectives, i.e. macro, mezzo and micro, this edited volume outlines how creative approaches to teaching and learning, sensitive to the use of information technology can in fact steer a bigger process leading to the emergence of innovation networks. The value and promise of innovation networks, as the Editors argue, is that they encourage both individual and collaborative efforts of knowledge creation. Simultaneously, by exploiting synergies that emerge between and among diverse and distinct clusters of innovation, innovation networks foster new knowledge production. Incorporating the fundamental set of values and principles—which define open, liberal, and inclusive society—innovation networks promote innovation for sustainable and inclusive growth and development locally, regionally, and globally. As the Authors contributing to this edited volume demonstrate, a lot of work conditioning the emergence of innovation network is being done at diverse levels of the society, tools exist and are being enhanced; and yet much more needs to be done. Individually and collectively, this edited volume sets the vision and draws the corresponding roadmap. As the developed world struggles with maintaining its competitiveness and so the question of innovation and innovativeness is bound to define the political debate any time soon, the emerging players on the global and regional scenes offer an alternative. Indeed, the Editors of this volume have already embarked on a new research project that ties the issues discussed in this volume with the developments in China and the Arab World.

It is our distinct pleasure to present a volume, which is the outcome of the most amazing collaboration spanning several continents, involving accomplished scholars and educators, all of whom thought it was worthwhile to engage in a debate on the future of our societies, while stressing the role of education and education-enabled innovation. We take this opportunity to express our gratitude and say ‘thank you’ to all of the contributing authors individually for embracing our idea, joining the project aimed at the development of this edited volume, and sharing the outcomes of their research with us and the readers of this volume. This volume would not be possible without the support and encouragement of Prof.

Chien-wen Mark Shen, from National Central University of Taiwan, who tirelessly discussed with us the topic of this work. We feel privileged to have gained his friendship throughout the process. We would also like to thank you, Ms Mara Gruber for the patience she showed in re-reading the subsequent drafts of the chapters included in this volume. Ms Gruber was always available to serve as the most patient interlocutor in our scientific discussions, even the most abstract. We are also obliged, to an exceptional researcher and scientist, Kwok Tai Chui, Department of Electronic Engineering, City University of Hong Kong, Hong Kong SAR, China, for his professional, top quality management of the complex communication process with the contributors and publishers. We are grateful to the Publisher for the opportunity to open the important debate and reach the international audience. Last but not least, we would like to thank our families and friends who were the witnesses of our work on this project. Any likely mistakes in the text are our own.

Miltiadis Lytras
The American College of Greece, Greece

Linda Daniela
University of Latvia, Latvia

Anna Visvizi
The American College of Greece, Greece

Chapter 1
(Re)Defining Smart Education:
Towards Dynamic Education and Information Systems for Innovation Networks

Anna Visvizi
The American College of Greece, Greece

Miltiadis D. Lytras
The American College of Greece, Greece

Linda Daniela
University of Latvia, Latvia

ABSTRACT

In the increasingly interconnected world, the relationship among learning and teaching, innovation and innovativeness, entrepreneurship, business development, as well as sustainable and inclusive socio-economic growth and development, requires a multidimensional interdisciplinary analysis. Importantly, information systems and advancements in sophisticated information and communication technologies (ICTs) are consequential for the potential inherent in education to be exploited. This edited volume opens discussion on ways and strategies of exploiting opportunities and synergies, which the maturing relationship between smart education and information systems offers. In this context, the objective of this chapter is to suggest how to (re)define smart education and how to reap its benefits in view of promoting dynamic education and information systems conducive to the emergence of innovation networks in socially, politically and economically trying times.

INTRODUCTION

In the increasingly interconnected world, the relationship among learning and teaching, innovation and innovativeness, entrepreneurship, business development, as well as sustainable and inclusive socio-economic growth and development, requires a multidimensional interdisciplinary analysis. Education stands at the heart of this multifaceted relationship and so is the key to understand and explain the chal-

DOI: 10.4018/978-1-5225-4191-2.ch001

lenges contemporary societies are confronted with and how to address them. Considering the plethora of social, political, economic and environmental problems that define the reality today, effective ways of anticipating, precepting and navigating those problems are needed. To this end, the development of enabling infrastructures, processes and systems, capable of transforming knowledge, creativity, skills and competencies of individuals and groups into meaningful services, products, effective policies, strategies, and finally cultural artefacts must be the priority of all stakeholders involved. Education plays a critical role in this context. Importantly, information systems and advancements in sophisticated information and communication technologies (ICTs) are consequential for the potential inherent in education to be exploited. This edited volume opens discussion on ways and strategies of exploiting opportunities and synergies, which the maturing relationship between smart education and information systems offers. In this context, the objective of this chapter is to suggest how to (re)define smart education and how to reap its benefits in view of promoting dynamic education and information systems conducive to the emergence of innovation networks in socially, politically and economically trying times. The discussion is structured as follows: First, the linkage between innovation and education is outlined. In the next two parts, the relationship between open information and innovation and teaching and learning and innovation is examined. In the following section of this chapter, the concepts of smart education and innovation networks are brought together in a discussion on a vision of open, inclusive, sustainable society of tomorrow. Conclusions follow.

THE INNOVATION-EDUCATION NEXUS

In 2010 Gassman et al. (2010) stated that an era of open innovations had just began. By 2017, an array of concepts converging around the promise of innovation, i.e. innovative businesses, innovative education, innovative medicine etc. populated the debate across diverse disciplines of social and natural sciences. This chapter offers a brief insight into the concept of innovation as seen from the perspective of education. In this sense, arguments introduced here represent a prequel of a larger research project devoted to the intrinsic relationship among education, innovation, growth and development and policy-making. From the perspective of education and education systems the key questions that need to be posed in this context are: What are the challenges related to innovation and how to employ innovation in view of building and exploiting innovation networks?

Some researchers state that there is no place for innovation if innovative education is not provided to everyone. Others insist that political decisions are prior to any discussion on innovation in education as it is the political decision that will eventually provide space for innovation. In this context, it is argued that influencing S (structural) theory parameters might require policy interventions, whereas F (functional) theory conditions often require managerial action (Jenson et al, 2016). From a different angle, innovation and the capacity to innovate are associated with technologies and smart solutions. From a different vantage point, in the burgeoning literature on innovation, the concept of *social innovation* (Sabato, Vanhercke & Verschraegen, 2017; Pohoryles, 2017) has also been employed, even if little consensus about its precise meaning exists. As Visvizi (2013: 77) argues, "social innovation is about changing the way things are done and social needs are conceptualised"; therefore, social innovation is about stimulating new approaches and promoting new responses to problems and challenges our societies face. It is beyond the scope of this chapter to explore the rich debate on social innovation and innovation as they unfold in social sciences today. The key lesson to be drawn from those debates is as follows.

Innovation is a broad multifaceted process geared toward transforming certain aspects of the functioning of the society. The specific fields of innovation (clusters) and specific items of innovation are correlated even if the linkages among them are not observable at first. These clusters and items of innovation nevertheless form a coherent multidimensional dynamic socio-economic and political phenomenon, i.e. an innovation network. To steer and boost the dynamics behind this complex innovation network, the connections and feedback effects among the clusters need to be nurtured and exploited if the next stage of innovations is to be attained. We argue that the success of this endeavour requires four factors (Figure 1). These include: appropriate approaches to learning and teaching; sustainable and inclusive socio-economic growth and development; entrepreneurship and business development; and information networks. What fuels the connections among these four factors are distributed knowledge resources and personal experience of individuals (talents, skills, attitude etc.). We argue that the innovation network model introduced here bears the promising of generating output at among diverse clusters of the innovation network, thus contributing to the next era of innovation.

OPEN INFORMATION AND INNOVATION

To develop new knowledge and to advance the process of creating new ideas and ways of addressing social needs, the society needs to have access to information. Simultaneously, the members of the society must have the capacity to understand information and to examine it critically if new knowledge is to be created and lessons from prior mistakes to be drawn. In this chapter, it is suggested that information on developments and trends concerning the entire society and its functioning, including the entire spectre

Figure 1. The dynamics steering the functioning of the innovation network

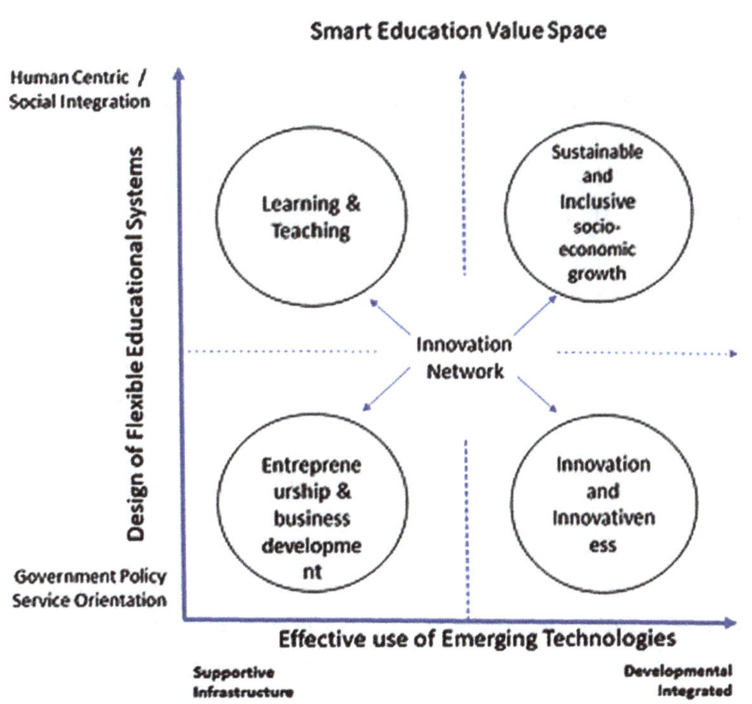

of policies, frameworks, risks, challenges in the fields of economics, health, education, environment, politics etc., must be open for everyone. This is what good governance, transparency and accountability in liberal socio-economic systems stand for.

Information is the key source enabling knowledge production. For this reason, it is fundamental in the process of fostering innovation. Indeed, innovation is a function of the opportunity to access information and data gathered earlier and of the ability of an individual or a group of people, to see and employ that piece of information in a new context. Nevertheless, information is a contentious good in that never all of it will be available to everyone. Information is not distributed evenly and access it may be deliberately denied by those who behold it. In this view any discussion on information must make a clear distinction between information that ought to be publicly shared and publicly available and knowledge, to which access -- due to national and international intellectual and industrial property rights regimes -- will be restricted. The discussion in this chapter focuses on the first field of information availability, i.e. information about, generated and granted by national governments and international organizations.

As Hartman et.al stress, by opening access to their data, governments aim at fostering participation, collaboration and transparency as well as economic and social values as citizens and companies can or will use the data to produce innovative products and services (Hartman et all, 2016; Albano, 2013; European Commission, 2011). Moreover, Yannoukakoua and Arakab (2014) state that access to government information has been directly linked with the history of the Right to Information movement, i.e. the RTI movement. The right to information springs from the right of expression under the notion that for an individual to be able to freely express ideas, opinions and thoughts, he/she should be able to freely formulate them, hence to be very well informed. According to Cuillier and Piotrowski (2009) there are four (4) primary ways of accessing government information (Cuillier & Piotrowski, 2009, p. 442):

- Reactive dissemination, when government information is released upon request
- Proactive dissemination, when government information is being released voluntarily by government bodies
- Leaks for whistle-blowers, e.g. WikiLeaks
- Open public meeting, where information is discussed and released in a public venue, i.e. real-time streaming of municipal council meeting etc.

Certainly, in today's debate on knowledge and education and their role in the process of enhancing inclusive sustainable growth and development, another important question that needs to be addressed is: May education and knowledge prove useful about the delivery of public goods? This issue is particularly salient given the fact that knowledge, similarly as information behind it, is neither freely available nor neutral (Visvizi, 2015). This sheds new light on the big debate on the availability of information and highlights the big challenge inherent in knowledge and information management that contemporary society faces.

These emerging questions about open information and the possibility to retrieve data, require that the users of that information, i.e. members of the society, have the skills necessary to critically examine it. Only in this way, creative use of that information will lead to knowledge production, rather than bubbles of quasi-knowledge, and decision by reference to it will generate common good. From the educational perspective, it means that the individual members of the society are prepared to connect different pieces of information together and – considering the diversity of information -- to construct their own knowledge (Vygotsky, 1962).

TEACHING AND LEARNING AND INNOVATION

In the transformative processes underpinning the functioning of knowledge society, education is a means to empower people, to be active agents of their learning, to equip them with knowledge, values and attitudes deemed conducive to sustainable development of that knowledge society. Education in this view enables individuals to live in the society, to create, to think, and to be innovative for the sake of future generations. There are several ways by means of which access to education can be facilitated to more and more people in an ever-greater spectre of locations. The question is how the use of smart solutions could be helpful in this regard? How to provide smart competencies and, simultaneously, how to ensure the development of metacognitive processes? How to develop soft skills etc. in this new innovation-facilitated context of teaching and learning?

New reality brings changes not only in everyday life of the society members but also in education, including the way how people learn, the way how they acquire knowledge, and how they use that knowledge. In this context, the pedagogy science undergoes deep transformation today in that a clear shift is taking place away from local teaching toward more trans local teaching. Specifically, advances in information and communication technologies (ICTs) open several opportunities that did not exist before, e.g. technological advances in the field of virtual reality (VR), and the smart use of virtual reality in the teaching and learning process, create the opportunity of detaching the teaching process from the physical environment (Maggio, Saltarelli, & Stranack, 2016). The use of VR-enhanced approaches to teaching and learning changes the meaning of the socialization process in that the very environment in which the act of teaching used to be performed moves from the traditional 'here and now' to the virtual 'anywhere & anytime'. What follows is that virtual communities are formed. Overall, new challenges to the teaching and learning process are generated. For instance, competencies which were necessary for the acquisition of knowledge in the 20th century are not as relevant as they used to be today in the advent of VR-enabled or augmented reality-enabled teaching and learning process. The evolution of the pedagogy science has changed direction from the situation where educators provided new ideas and worked to develop the knowledge of students, to a situation where students can acquire knowledge freely and pedagogy must find a way of teaching students how to identify and evaluate sources of information, critically assess the information and use it responsibly. Notably, this is an issue that forms the thrust of the debate on the need to teach students news literacy (Hornik, 2016).

Overall, the maturing of the education-information technologies linkage highlights the importance of critical thinking and, depending on the level of analysis, of the role of the teacher and/or the role of the pedagogy science in the process of developing a sustainable inclusive knowledge society. From this perspective, the initial question that this section sought to address, i.e. the relationship between learning and teaching and innovation acquires an interesting angle. In other words, it underlines the role of higher education as the gate for educated society to reach out to innovation (Aranguiz & Quintana, 2016).

Higher education internationally undergoes deep transformation also because of the paradigm shift from teacher- and content-oriented learning to student- and competence development-oriented learning (Taylor, 2012). Basso and Badilla (2016) explore innovative solutions in higher education and suggest that since technologies- brought paradigm shift in the learning process, it is imperative that new methodologies, approaches and strategies in need to be introduced in educational practice to creatively embrace the identified above shift in paradigm (Basso & Badilla, 2016; Aranguiz & Quintana, 2016). It is also pointed out that educational quality matters in this new paradigm, especially that students can access information everywhere (Basso & Badilla, 2016). This overwhelming amount of information opens new discussions, new ideas for problem solutions and new innovations, but at the same time the information which is open can be fake it can be misinterpreted, it can be useless etc. To have the ability to analyse retrieved information, there should be developed competence of critical thinking (Rubene, 2006; Walters, 1994) and it must be developed during the learning process, otherwise people can be manipulated and mislead by the information obtained.

Another issue related to the transformation of higher education which can be associated with smart education in modern higher educational setting is the development of Massive Open Online Courses (MOOCs). Essentially, MOOCs offer the opportunity for people to access knowledge from everywhere if they have internet connection. The growing popularity of MOOCs suggests that people are thirsty for open information, for open knowledge (Adinolfi et al., 2016; Jdidou & Khaldi, 2016; Moissa, Gasparini, & Kemczinski, 2015). At the same time there are educational challenges, which must be analysed to address them; the academic debate devoted to these issues has only began. For instance, Jdidou and Khaldi (2016) examine the emergence and popularity of MOOCs and point out risks, which MOOCs bear and which must be considered. They argue that the measure of the quality of a recommendation system in learning is one of the main research challenges as it is not limited to technical calculations, but that it is necessary to consider the context in which it is carried out by the teaching-learning process. Similarly, research conducted by Daniela et al. (2017) demonstrates that evidence obtained and described in recent studies emphasize more the benefits of use of technologies and technological solutions in the structure of the teaching/learning process and rarely the benefits of the learning outcomes. Vargas-Vera (2016) elaborates on the experiences gained while constructing a virtual campus. Named *Deep Think*, the campus was designed to support a postgraduate program. In other words, the future is already present in education and as such is a source of new ideas (Rapanotti & Hall 2010; Minocha & Hardy 2011).

(RE)DEFINING SMART EDUCATION: OUR VISION

The debate on smart education has only began but smart education systems are being implemented in some countries. The process of integrating smart solutions in educational systems is accelerated as the business environment and technology developers exert considerable pressure on potential users of technological advances they produce; education and education systems are one of the key users.

The debate on smart education and related developments have become a new popular trend in the field of education globally. Interestingly, although ideas developed in this context and solutions provided are well developed from the technological point of view, several non-technical questions still need to be addressed. These include, questions of competencies and skills needed to create and re-create knowledge, to develop metacognition, to develop creativity. The concept of smart education entails all these concerns even if they have remained implicit in the debate. In this chapter, we make a first attempt of bringing the otherwise bracketed items of the debate to the fore to stress the centrality of soft components, such as approaches to teaching and learning, the relationship between the teacher and the student, the role of the teacher, the objective of the teaching and learning process and its specific outcomes, and finally the relationship between the (re)defined education and increasingly sophisticated technology.

The concept of smart education presupposes that learners are partners of teachers, that both learners and teachers embrace the value of the use of technologies, and ultimately the goad of education is to turn today's learners in to engaged and responsible members of open, inclusive, sustainable society. From a different angle, at the heart of smart education lies the following dilemma: Given the changed nature of access to information discussed earlier, he role of the teacher changed and to many seems redundant, especially in the hype of the discussion on new technologies, on-line learning opportunities etc. Yet, at the same time, the society, more than ever, needs good education to instil in the students not only knowledge and skills but also values, attitudes and worldviews. What follows is that smart education as a concept and a growing trend in education is also about the recognition that education is not only about the transfer of knowledge or about equipping students with certain skills to effectively deal with that knowledge. Smart education is also about instilling certain values and attitudes that, in turn, will allow them to use the knowledge responsibly, i.e. to the benefit and to the harm of the society.

There is substantial evidence proving that technological solutions fascinate learners, that virtual reality provides the ability to look in the past and in the future, that it is possible to promote the development of an inclusive society and lessen the risks of social exclusion by implementing learning technologies in the learning process. At the same time, the acquired information gets fragmented, promoting the development of short-term memory, which could influence the development of cognitive processes in the future, thus influencing readiness for new innovations. To launch discussions on these emerging issues on how to use all sorts of smart education solutions in the context of already existing learning theories, on how to apply innovative solutions to reduce the marginalization of different groups in society.

Researchers are working on ideas how to keep students learning in context of SMART education (social; motivated; anywhere, anytime; resource enriched; technology embedded) and some of ideas are found in *active learning strategies* (Misseyanni et al., 2017) *gamification in learning* (Zhuhadar, Coleman & Marklin, 2016) *development of motivation* (Huitt, 2011; Ames, 1990), *adaptive learning* (Lavieri, 2014), *personalised learning* (Fiedler, Väljataga 2011), *blended learning* (Lothridge, 2013) etc., and all these concepts are well connectable with ideas of smart education to keep learners not only attracted by new, innovative solutions but to be responsible partners in process of knowledge construction.

It is proposed to apply learning strategies to promote the development of knowledge in a technologically enriched environment, but there are many unanswered questions which need to be answered by pedagogy science. For example, what sort of pedagogical principles should be applied to promote the learner's interest, motivation and cognitive development? How to promote creativity and innovation in a transformed educational environment that stretches beyond the borders of space and time? What is the teacher's role in a technologically enriched environment?

Endowed with a unique capacity, i.e. the 21st century smart education must permeate in an anticipatory manner the multiplicity of multidimensional processes and causal feedback effects that unfold at the intersection of learning and teaching, innovation and innovativeness, entrepreneurship and business development, and finally policies, policy-strategies and regulatory frameworks that bring them together (see Figure 2).

Smart Education becomes the top imperative for our societies. We have argued that smart education needs to equip students with knowledge, understanding, skills and certain capacities that eventually will enable them to contribute to the fostering of knowledge and innovation and, through their engagement in collaborative frameworks, to the emerging innovation networks. The implicit argument that this chapter made was that today greater emphasis than ever needs to be placed on instilling in students the fundamental values, attitudes and worldviews that form the foundations of liberal societies, open to innovation and collaboration (Visvizi, 2015).

In the virtual world, the role of the teacher is changed from the person who knows the content to the person who knows how to organize the learning process and to ensure that students become responsible active agents of their learning. But there comes another challenge for educators, i.e. how to evaluate suc-

Figure 2. Vision of smart education

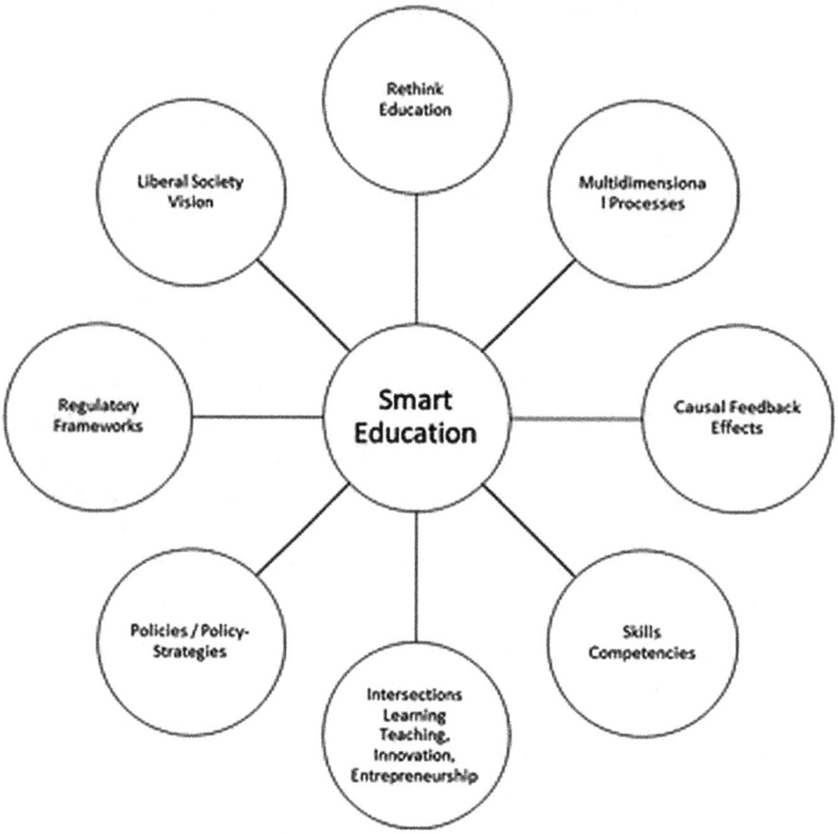

cess in so defined the learning process? How to assess the degree of the acquisition of knowledge? There are some valuable ideas on evaluation of teaching performance by use of sentiment analyses (Adinolfi et al., 2016), to evaluate the competence to solve real life problems. If we come to that end that result of teaching process is ability to use these knowledge in real situations to learn by hands-on principle and stop the evolution of knowledge development, then we produce generation which can reproduce the same knowledge which already exists, but will they be ready for next step of *Relativity theory* or any other big discoveries? This shows the importance of pedagogy as science of promoting creativity (Rhodes, 1961; Kaufman et al., 2011), critical thinking, metacognitive processes etc.

CONCLUSION: POLICY IMPLICATIONS AND RECOMMENDATIONS

The objective of this chapter was to suggest how to (re)define smart education and to explore the prospect of reaping the benefits of smart education to promote dynamic education and information systems conducive to the emergence of innovation networks in socially, politically and economically trying times. Having outlined the relationship between access to information and innovation as well as between education and innovation, we elaborated the concept of innovation network. Against this backdrop a revamped approach to smart education was presented. It was argued that the two concepts, i.e. innovation networks and smart education, offer a very useful multidimensional framing to the issues discussed in this volume by its contributing authors. The key line of argumentation that this chapter advanced was that, considering the increasing velocity of interactions and the shrinking of time and space in today's world, the role of education, education systems and education strategies needs to be rethought. In other words, if our objective as society today is to contribute to the development of inclusive sustainable society of tomorrow, education ought to acquire a unique capacity, i.e. the 21st century smart education has to permeate in an anticipatory manner the multiplicity of multidimensional processes and causal feedback effects that unfold at the intersection of learning and teaching, innovation and innovativeness, entrepreneurship and business development, and finally policies, policy-strategies and regulatory frameworks that bring them together. Seen in this way, smart education becomes the top imperative for our societies. We have argued that smart education needs to equip students with knowledge, understanding, skills and certain capacities that eventually will enable them to contribute to the fostering of knowledge and innovation and, through their engagement in collaborative frameworks, to the emerging innovation networks. The implicit argument that this chapter made was that today greater emphasis than ever needs to be placed on instilling in students the fundamental values, attitudes and worldviews that form the foundations of liberal societies, open to innovation and collaboration (Visvizi, 2015). This human-centred approach is inherent in the concept of smart education that this chapter introduced.

From a different angle, by introducing the concept of innovation networks we have opened a discussion on the vision that our societies want to follow. The key assumption upon which the concept of innovation networks builds is that we need to strive to build open inclusive and sustainable society. Innovation networks, as we argued in this chapter, offer the promise of the best use of the resources our societies have. Innovation networks offer the prospect of creating synergies and exploiting feedback effects that emerge across policy-fields, issue-areas, and industries. Innovation networks draw from the advances in sophisticated information and communication technologies (ICTs). Therefore, they are oblivious of the constraints of time and space and, hence, are more inclusive than the traditional modes and structures of collaborative arrangements. We have also suggested that the emergence and functioning of innovation networks is only possible if a certain set of fundamental values and principles is endorsed by the members of the society and if emphasis is placed on instilling these values and principles in successive generations of agents that contribute to the development of our society. In this view, innovation networks require smart education. This volume makes an explicit case for the direct connection that exists among smart anticipatory human-centred education, innovation networks and the possibility of developing open, inclusive, sustainable society.

In this chapter, similarly as several authors contributing to this volume, we highlighted the centrality of enabling policies, policy-strategies and regulatory frameworks conducive to the implementation of ideas and ideals underpinning smart education and innovation networks. It goes beyond the scope of the analysis in this volume to explore the intricacies of the policy-making process in connection to the concepts of smart education and innovation networks. Suffice it to say, as the findings of our forthcoming journal article suggests, that inter- and multi-disciplinary approaches to policy-making and policy-design are needed if the promise inherent in smart education is to be exploited (see Figure 3). We need a comprehensive take on the spectre of policies and regulatory frameworks implemented at national, regional and global levels so that the connections and positive feedback effects among the diverse policy-strategies and instruments are exploited. It is fundamental that the debate on smart education and its promise involves a variety of stakeholders located at the multiple levels of the policy-making and policy-design process. Moreover, even if some work in this domain has been done on the forum of the

Figure 3. The Integrative Smart Education-Innovation Networks technology enabled framework

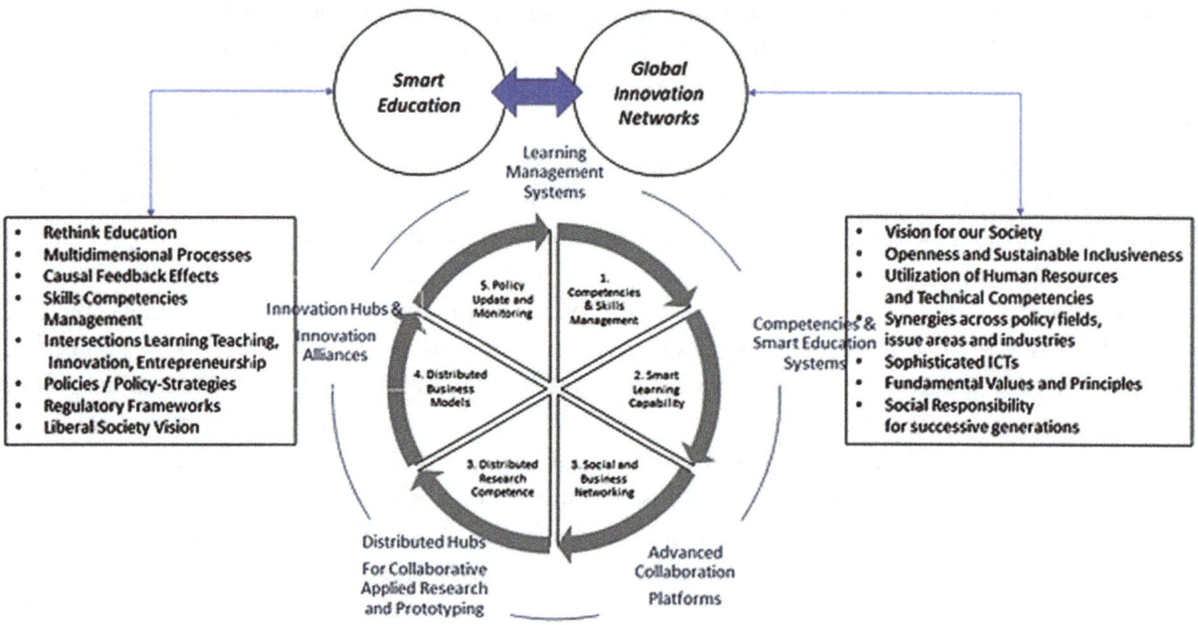

Organization for Economic Co-operation and Development (OECD), more effort needs to be invested to spread the best practices beyond the OECD members. It is imperative that novel approaches to education, seen as the key lever enhancing the vision of innovation networks, are emulated to countries, regions, areas otherwise deprived of the opportunity to benefit from the advances attained in other parts of the world. The concepts of smart education and innovation networks set the framework as to how to attain it. The remaining contributions in this volume elaborate the details. Overall, the discussion has just begun. More work needs to be done if effective ways of enhancing smart education and innovation for the sake of open, inclusive, sustainable society are to be negotiated at national, regional and global levels.

REFERENCES

Adinolfi, P., DAvanzo, E., Lytras, M. D., Novo-Corti, I., & Picatoste, J. (2016). Sentiment Analysis to Evaluate Teaching Performance. *International Journal of Knowledge Society Research*, *4*(7), 86–107. doi:10.4018/IJKSR.2016100108

Ames, C. (1990). Motivation: What teachers need to know. *Teachers College Record*, *91*(3), 409–421.

Aranguiz, M. S., & Quintana, M. G. (2016). ICT Resources to Improve Learning in Higher Education. *International Journal of Knowledge Society Research*, *4*(7), 1–11. doi:10.4018/IJKSR.2016100101

Basso, M., & Badilla, M.G. (2016a). ICT resources to improve learning in Higher Education. *International Journal of Knowledge Society Research, 7*(4), 1-11. doi: 104018/IJKSR.2016100101

Cuillier, D., & Piotrowski, S. J. (2009). Internet information seeking and its relation to support for access to government record. *Government Information Quarterly*, *26*(3), 441–449. doi:10.1016/j.giq.2009.03.001

Daniela, L., Kalniņa, D., & Strods, R. (2017). An overview on effectiveness of technology-enhanced learning (TEL). *International Journal of Knowledge Society Research, 8*(1).

Fiedler, S., & Väljataga, T. (2011). Personal learning environments: Concept or technology? *International Journal of Virtual and Personal Learning Environments*, *2*(4), 1–11. doi:10.4018/jvple.2011100101

Hartmann, S., Mainka, A., & Stock, W. G. (2016). Opportunities and challenges for civic engagement: A global investigation of innovation competitions. *International Journal of Knowledge Society Research, 7*(3), 1–15. doi:10.4018/IJKSR.2016070101

Hornik, R. (2016). A strategy to counter propaganda in the digital era. *Yearbook of the Institute of East-Central Europe*, *14*(2), 61–74.

Huitt, W. (2011). *Motivation to learn: An overview. Edu. Psychol. Interactive*. Valdosta, GA: Valdosta State University Univ. Available http: //www.edpsycinteractive.org/topics/motivation/motivate.html

Jdidou, Y., & Khaldi, M. (2016). Increasing the Profitability of Students in MOOCs using Recommendation Systems. *International Journal of Knowledge Society Research, 4*(7), 75–85. doi:10.4018/IJKSR.2016100107

Jenson, I., Leith, P., Doyle, R., West, J., & Miles, M. P. (2016, November). Innovation system problems: Causal configurations of innovation failure. *Journal of Business Research, 69*(11), 5408–5412. doi:10.1016/j.jbusres.2016.04.146

Kaufman, J. C., Kaufman, S. B., & Lichtenberger, E. O. (2011). Finding creativity on intelligence tests via divergent production. *Canadian Journal of School Psychology, 26*(2), 83–106. doi:10.1177/0829573511406511

Lavieri, E. (2014). *A Study of Adaptive Learning for Educational Game Design*. ProQuest UMI.

Lothridge, K., Fox, J., & Fynan, E. (2013). Blended learning: Efficient, timely, and cost effective. *Journal of Forensic Sciences, 45*(4), 407–416. doi:10.1080/00450618.2013.767375

Maggio, L., Saltarelli, A., & Stranack, K. (2016). *Crowdsourcing the Curriculum: A MOOC for Personalized, Connected Learning EDUCAUSE Learning Initiative*. ELI.

Minocha, S., & Hardy, C. L. (2011). Designing navigation and wayfinding in 3D virtual learning spaces. *Proceedings of OZCHI*, 211-220. doi:10.1145/2071536.2071570

Misseyanni, A., Daniela, L., Lytras, M., Papadopoulou, P., & Marouli, C. (2017) Analyzing Active Learning Strategies in Greece and Latvia: Lessons Learnt and the Way Ahead. *INTED 11th International Technology, Education and Development Conference*. doi:10.21125/inted.2017.0940

Moissa, B., Gasparini, I., & Kemczinski, A. (2015). A Systematic Mapping on the Learning Analytics Field and Its Analysis in the Massive Open Online Courses Context. *International Journal of Distance Education Technologies, 13*(3), 1–24. doi:10.4018/IJDET.2015070101

Pohoryles, R. J. (2017). Social Innovation – a complex subject to deal with, Innovation. *The European Journal of Social Science Research, 30*(2), 141–143. doi:10.1080/13511610.2017.1297019

Rapanotti, L., & Hall, J. (2010). *Lessons Learned in Developing a Second Life Educational Environment.* Valencia, Spain: CSEDU.

Rhodes, M. (1961). An Analysis of Creativity. *Phi Delta Kappan*, *42*(7), 306–307.

Rubene, Z. (2006). *Topicality of Critical Thinking in the Context of Higher Education Reform in Pedagogy and Teacher Education.* University of Latvia.

Sabato, S., Vanhercke, B., & Verschraegen, G. (2017). Connecting entrepreneurship with policy experimentation? The EU framework for social innovation, Innovation. *The European Journal of Social Science Research*, *30*(2), 147–167. doi:10.1080/13511610.2017.1282308

Taylor, E. W., & Cranton, P. (2012). *The Handbook of Transformative Learning. Theory, Research, and Practice.* San Francisco: Jossey-Bass Inc., Publishers.

Vargas-Vera, M. (2016). Reflections on the Second Life Platform used in the Development of a Virtual University Campus. *International Journal of Knowledge Society Research*, *4*(7), 12–23. doi:10.4018/IJKSR.2016100102

Visvizi, A. (2013). *Social Innovation in the EU and the Black Sea Region: Trends, challenges and opportunities.* Xenophon Paper no. 13. International Centre for Black Sea Studies (ICBSS).

Visvizi, A. (2015). Education, (the production of) knowledge and progress in context of the global public goods debate. In E. Latoszek et al. (Eds.), *Facing the Challenges in European Union: Re-thinking EU Education and Research for Smart and Inclusive Growth* (pp. 661–674). Warsaw: Warsaw University Press.

Vygotsky, L. S. (1962). Thought and language. Cambridge, MA: MIT Press. doi:10.1037/11193-000

Walters, K. (1994). *Re-Thinking Reason: New Perspectives in Critical Thinking Albany.* State University of New York Press.

Yannoukakoua, A., & Arakab, I. (2014). Access to Government Information: Right to Information and Open Government Data Synergy. *Procedia: Social and Behavioral Sciences*, *147*, 332–340. doi:10.1016/j.sbspro.2014.07.107

Zhuhadar, L., Coleman, P., & Marklin, S. (2016). Applicative Personalized Learning: How Gamification is Driving Learning. *International Journal of Knowledge Society Research*, *4*(7), 24–37. doi:10.4018/IJKSR.2016100103

Chapter 2
An Innovation-Based and Sustainable Knowledge Society:
The Triple Helix Approach

Danilo Piaggesi
FRAmericas, International Knowledge Economy Program (IKEP), USA

ABSTRACT

Innovation is a key source of new products, benefit and fresh growth in revenues. In developed economies, the private sector is the engine of innovation and growth, accounting for between half and two-thirds of total spending on research and development in some countries. On the other hand, increasing access to technology will be a critical driver of economic growth in emerging economies, but it will require private sector leaders and the public sector to work together to make their respective programs more impactful. At the same time, the rapid advances and pervasive diffusion of information and communication technology (ICT), combined with the growth of the Internet have led to deep transformations in economic, social and institutional structures. ICT applications affect the performance of businesses and the efficiency of markets, foster the empowerment of citizens and communities as well as their access to knowledge, and contribute to strengthening and redefining governance processes at all institutional levels.

1. INFORMATION AND COMMUNICATION TECHNOLOGY (ICT)

Numerous studies have focused on the direct contribution of ICT to socioeconomic development and, while their findings and conclusions vary according to the context and application, there is an overall agreement that access to information and its transformation into knowledge can augment production processes, increase income potential, and improve the living conditions of the poor. ICT is an effective tool that, when supplemented by investments in connectivity and other factors such as innovation, education, health and infrastructure, increases competitiveness and contributes to economic growth, social development and poverty reduction.

ICT solutions can facilitate the participation of lower income populations in the development process by directly tackling relevant aspects, which precisely hinder their integration into social and economic

DOI: 10.4018/978-1-5225-4191-2.ch002

development. In particular: (a) limited knowledge and literacy which impairs access to skills and jobs (education); (b) poor health and sanitary conditions limiting employability and risk-taking attitudes (health); (c) active involvement in civic life and strengthening of democratic process; and (d) economic opportunities.

In this respect, the evolution of modern ICT brings about concrete opportunities for enhanced provision of social services and poverty reduction through, among others, distance education and telemedicine solutions, connectivity, and strengthened and more transparent government operations (i.e. e-government). It also provides for the modernization and expansion of the micro-finance sector to effectively reach marginalized and less favored populations through effective technology-based solutions and innovative financial services and, thereby, creating economic opportunities at the local level.

Inequalities in access to education--especially high-quality education that prepares young people for employment opportunities in an inclusive knowledge society and to become active citizens in complex, market-driven, democratic societies--are a critical barrier to reducing poverty and increasing economic growth. Near-universal access to the Internet via low-cost networks enables teacher training, enhances student access to traditional teaching materials via Internet distribution, and allows the introduction and use of new and advanced multi-media resources and learning tools. The young generation takes readily to computers and such resources, and there is evidence that classroom access to ICT tools can improve learning and help motivate students to stay in school. At the same time, there is evidence that informal learning outside the classroom is strongly enhanced by affordable access to the Internet. This informal learning is driven, in part, by the growing availability of information on the Internet and the increasing organization of such information by search engines, but also by the growing use of interactive systems--from "chat" systems to e-mail and text-messaging to web logs and other interactive web-based systems--.

The improvement in the delivery of health care services in geographically remote and rural areas is one of the most promising and clearly demonstrated applications of ICT in social development. In particular, ICT is being used in many developing countries and communities to facilitate: (a) remote consultation, diagnosis and treatment through the use of digital cameras to download images onto a computer and transfer them to doctors in nearby towns; (b) collaboration and information exchange among physicians; (c) ICT-based medical research through the use a network of satellites and ground stations to submit data for clinical trials; (d) medical training through ICT-enabled delivery mechanisms; and (e) access to centralized data repositories connected to ICT networks that enable remote healthcare professionals to keep abreast of medical knowledge. Moreover, the Internet is an effective means to disseminate public health messages and disease prevention techniques in developing countries. It also enables better monitoring and response mechanisms. Also, ICT is helping improve the efficiency of public health systems and medical facilities by, for example, streamlining medical procurement or creating and managing patient records.

ICT tools can drive down transactions costs for financial services such as microfinance and a widening range of banking, insurance, and other services for low-income groups, particularly as their delivery expands beyond nonprofit groups and becomes more widespread. For example, the expanded use of ICT and the Internet can reduce the transaction costs of remittances in a way that brings higher social benefits for all parties involved in these transactions. Moreover, ICT technology offers several approaches to expanding access to electronic transactions and banking services via remote transaction devices for microfinance that work over mobile phone networks; smart cards that can store account balances, transaction histories, and positive IDs such as a fingerprints. The next generation of mobile phones may be capable of conducting transactions automatically via very short-range radio, potentially turning phones into electronic wallets.

Largely for reasons of cost, most rural communities and many low-income urban communities lack effective and affordable local phone systems, whereas a low-cost local phone system can make universal access a reality in many communities. The technological potential to solve the problem has now emerged via local Wireless Fidelity Networks (WiFi) and Voice-Over-Internet (VOIP) telephony using peer-to-peer systems that enable access to a great variety of Internet services and information via a computer or other converged device. Voice-driven or voice-accessible services -especially if also made available in indigenous languages- can help overcoming literacy and computer skill barriers. Other benefits also include ending rural isolation, enhanced family solidarity, increased access to information and services, improved ability to find employment and, at a community level, higher economic capacity and productivity and wider citizen participation in democratic processes.

A recent study by the London Business School found that, in a typical developing country, an increase of ten mobile phones per 100 people boosts GDP growth by 0.6 percentage points. The study concludes that wireless solutions are concrete examples of "technologies that help people help themselves."

It becomes clear that the poor can benefit from the effective deployment of ICT and the development of a knowledge economy when such interventions match the local conditions and meet the following four requirements. First, promote a multi-stakeholder partnership framework delineating the effective participation of the public sector and civil society, while creating the incentives for socially responsible private investment. Second, strengthen the provision of ICT-based public social services and promote social inclusion, while maintaining the role of the private sector as the main source of innovation. Third, stimulate macroeconomic growth by facilitating access to knowledge and information through increased connectivity and appropriate ICT solutions for marginalized and lower-income populations, thereby tapping a strong market potential. And fourth, design and adopt long-term ICT investment frameworks in human development (i.e. education, health and environment), along with the design and implementation of cost-effective technologies aimed at increasing the market access, efficiency and competitiveness of the poor (connectivity, knowledge centers, etc.).

As all major and wide-ranging technological advances, the ICT revolution is at the same time creating enormous opportunities and posing daunting challenges. On one hand, it has the potential to increase productivity and wealth, generate new activities, products and services, and improve the well being of the population, notably in regard to education, government and health levels. On the other hand, the uneven distribution of such opportunities can lead to further alienation of marginalized communities and an exacerbation of existing socioeconomic inequalities. Thereby, a balanced access and effective use of ICT tools and networks in the new global knowledge economy, along with an integrated process of technological innovation are critical for reducing poverty, increasing social inclusion and improving living conditions for all.

The "digital divide" (a phrase coined in the 1990s) described the perceived growing gap between those who have access to and the skills to use information and communication technologies and those who, for socioeconomic and/or geographical reasons, have limited or no access. In particular, it is used to raise the concern that the emergence of ICT could exacerbate existing inequalities in the access to information and that, thereby, certain groups could face additional disadvantages because of their geographic location, age, gender, culture, and social and economic status, among others. Moreover, the phrase reflects the prevalence of socioeconomic and structural inequalities at the regional, national and local levels, which are characterized by insufficient infrastructure, relatively high access costs, inappropriate or weak policy regimes, inefficiencies in the provision of telecommunication networks and services, lack of local content, and uneven ability to derive economic and social benefits from information-intensive activities.

The United Nations Millennium Declaration notes that efforts to make access available to all and harness the power of ICT can contribute toward the achievement of the Millennium Development Goals (MDGs) by 2020 now replaced by the SDGs, thereby creating "digital opportunities" in development.

Yet, these opportunities cannot be effectively and fully realized if left to market forces alone, and require the active participation of the public, private and civil society sectors under integrated efforts towards the development of an inclusive knowledge society. This is where a Triple Helix approach can be more beneficial; in fact, a model of knowledge society, is one that the results from the convergence and crossing-over of three worlds which were previously separated: public research, business and governments; this convergence also represents the Triple Helix model. This model refers to a spiral model of innovation that captures multiple reciprocal relationships among institutional settings (public, private and academic) at different stages in the capitalization of knowledge.

2. FOSTERING SUSTAINABLE DEVELOPMENT THROUGH ICT

The evolution of modern ICT within the broader scheme of a knowledge society, brings about concrete opportunities for enhanced provision of social services and inclusion and poverty reduction through, among others, strengthened and more transparent government operations, distance education, telemedicine and e-governance solutions. It also provides for the modernization and expansion of the micro-finance sector to effectively reach marginalized and less favored populations through effective technology-based solutions and innovative financial services and, thereby, creating economic opportunities at the local level triggering a knowledge economy.

In the past years in the developing countries many experiences have already been implemented that address the problems mentioned above, although most often they have been limited to local level without reaching a complete national or even regional coverage. This rises the problem of how to spread the benefits of ICT based development programs within and across the countries and how coordinated ICT based development programs can be implemented across different countries to foster development goals at the regional level, in order to facilitate south-south cooperation.

In this paper we address both problems by proposing to share and implement at the regional level, an action-oriented strategy based on four pillars:

- ICT and education
- ICT and health
- ICT and government services
- ICT and financial services

This paper refers to concrete examples of pilot and investment initiatives concerning the pillars above, as well as to similar experiences from other regions of the world, that are showing the ICT's favorable support to the social and economic growth of the developing regions.

Pillar 1: ICT and Education

Over the past years, three parallel ICT revolutions have begun to transform educational quality for the majority of children in the developing countries.

First and most important was near universal access to the Internet for every school, catalyzed in large part by efforts to extend wireless networks to low-income urban neighborhoods and even remote rural locations, and with the concrete effort to encourage extensive teacher training in computer-based instruction, and to support new curricula development (see (Barbosa 2010) for the case of the Brazilian schools). Under a policy reform that allowed "social use" exemptions from telecom monopolies in low-income communities, many of the schools also functioned as WiFi "hotspots" for community access as well (Mace 2007; Bhaskaran 2004; Hosman 2010), providing low-cost voice-over-Internet phone service and access to local-language voice-based e-government services (Heimer and Brewer 2010; Ho, Smyth, Karm and Dearden 2009).

Second, Universal access and teacher training allowed new curricula to benefit from the "Google" revolution of rapidly-expanding:

- Free knowledge resources on the Internet;
- New software tools to enable trusted networks of approved educational resources;
- Interactive discussions among students across a Region that created a more active and participatory learning environment;
- New multimedia courseware resources that engaged student interest.

Third, inexpensive technologies, like those described in (Brewer et al. 2005), introduced by pilot initiatives, began to make the new knowledge resources affordable to schools. These included less-expensive computers, although the goal of a computer for every child was far from being met, but more importantly included inexpensive screens for classroom displays, low-cost projectors to display information even on school walls, and inexpensive i-Pad-like hand-held devices that allowed classroom student access to knowledge and multi-media lessons (Patra et al. 2007; Vota 2010).

ICT innovations outside the school also had a marked impact on education. The proliferation of very low-cost solar-powered LED lighting made it possible for many low-income families to benefit from more productive use of evenings and for students to read and do homework (Bhusal et al. 2007). This transformation was driven by private-sector investments and innovative financing schemes, but public-private partnerships in addition to the implementation of pilot and demonstrative projects speeded their adoption by the countries of the Region. Additionally, the encouragement of reduced import duties and local manufacturing capacity speeded such process. Likewise, broadened access to communications and information via the community hotspots and inexpensive WiFi phones improved productivity and job creation in low-income communities, raising family incomes and enabling more children to stay in school.

LAC Governments, invested heavily in on-line as well as voice-accessible information tools in local languages, borrowing on global best practices for disseminating public health information, weather and agricultural extension services, disaster warnings and relief information, and a wide array of government services (World Bank 2004; UNESCO 2005). The private sector provided similar information sources for many commercial services.

In order to foster sustainable development, it is recommended that the following further actions take place:

- Support extension of wireless broadband connectivity to all schools, especially in rural areas;
- Support curriculum development and extensive teacher training to make effective use of expanding on-line knowledge resources;
- Encourage, facilitate and support policy reforms enabling school-based community "hotspot" networks, and support pilot undertakings to demonstrate their utility in facilitating local economic and social development;
- Support pilot projects demonstrating new, low-cost computer, projector, and handheld display technology options for educational use and encourage local manufacturing or lowered import duties for such equipment;
- Support pilot projects demonstrating low-cost lighting technologies that can enable expanded home learning opportunities;
- Support development of easily accessible knowledge bases and e-services as, for instance, the initiatives supported by the Inter America Development Bank (the largest lending development Bank in the LAC Region) including, among others, the "Latin American Network of Education Portals (http://www.relpe.org), the "International Virtual Education Network" (http://rived.proinfo.mec.gov.br/), and the "Education Connectivity Pilot Project" (http://www.iadb.org/en/projects/project,1303.html?id=tc0104012)

Pillar 2: ICT and Health

Over the past years, distribution of healthcare services improved, in part by extension of wireless connections to hospitals, clinics, pharmacies, and even front-line health workers, through expanding mobile networks and newer broadband wireless networks and solutions. That allowed real-time monitoring of diseases, rapid response to disasters and health emergencies, more extensive support for front-line health workers, and timely restocking of medicines. Also, software tools initially pioneered in Peru (Casas and Lajoie 2006) became widely adopted by the countries of the Region. These national health networks (which increasingly integrated private clinics and hospitals and new franchised clinics and pharmacies) not only increased the operational efficiency of the health care system, but also enabled:

- Expanded telemedicine efforts through both, remote screening and diagnosis and live consultations with national or international experts on particular cases and, thereby, improving the standard of care in many smaller towns and remote villages;
- Inexpensive digital distribution of public health information, including easily-updated video and audio segments on inexpensive devices in every clinic and in many schools and communities centers, allowing for private viewing and listening for such sensitive issues as HIV/AIDS or drug addiction, reinforcing public TV and radio campaigns, and providing basic information on maternal health (Kimani 2008), infant nutrition, and other common health needs;
- Expanded training of health workers at all levels through on-line courses and testing (HfALA 2007).

A second wave of improvements followed the increasing sophistication of mobile phone and other "smart" mobile devices. These next-generation mobile devices had "smart card" capabilities built in, as well as the ability to automatically update stored information via short-range wireless techniques (Anta,

El-Wahab and Giuffrida 2009). As a result of the wide promotion of encryption standards and support for a cooperative effort between health ministries and mobile phone companies, people now carry their medical records and health insurance information in their phones, updated with every clinic or pharmacy visit. This support ensured that doctors, nurses and other health workers carried more sophisticated devices or phones that could access secure databases; frontline health workers even had handheld devices that contained diagnostic or procedural scripts and diagrams to guide their procedures. The combined result of these smart mobile devices and supporting databases included:

- Improved patient management and records while maintaining confidentiality;
- Simplified administration and billing that determines considerable cost savings and represents an opportunity to leapfrog ahead on a problem that confronts every healthcare system.
- Improved emergency treatment of patients, since even ambulances carried the equipment to "read out" a patient's cell phone records;
- Increased efficiency for medical personal and enhanced capacity for frontline health workers, even when dealing with non-routine problems.

These changes improved health care at all levels, but amounted to a revolution in the access to and quality of care, especially for low-income populations. Improved health, in turn, eliminated one of the causes of persistent poverty.

In order to foster sustainable development, it is recommended that the following further actions take place:

- Support network extension to connect all healthcare facilities and mobile access for all health workers, including frontline (rural) workers, and support software development and applications to enable real-time reporting;
- Support pilot projects for public health information dissemination via clinics and community centers using new and inexpensive handheld display devices;
- Contribute to the establishment of public-private partnerships with telecom carriers, health ministries and other organizations towards the implementation of encryption standards and privacy policies, and to enable next-generation "smart" mobile devices to encode and manage personal health records;
- When possible, support pilot projects for electronic billing models and emergency system use of mobile personal health records.

Pillar 3: ICT and E-Government Services

Over the past years, extension of wireless connections to schools, healthcare facilities, and local government offices, especially in rural or underserved areas, provided the infrastructure foundation for e-government services. The policy reform that allowed "social purpose" community WiFi hotspots based in schools, clinics and community centers, and low-cost voice-over-internet phones (or mobile phones with WiFi capability built-in) connected via those hot spots, broadened access to the majority of the population (ITU 2011). However, the real transformation occurred as governments began to reshape their administrative processes and public services for the Knowledge Society.

The initial wave consisted mostly of voice-enabled databases, in all relevant local languages, accessed by toll-free calls from mobile or voice-over-internet phones. These information services initially provided public health information on HIV-AIDS or other health issues, information about agricultural extension services for an area, disaster reporting and relief information, guidance about availability of government programs, and a few simple voice-based transactions. But as the modernization of the state and government restructuring efforts based on global ICT best practices began to pay off, more sophisticated transactions (obtaining a passport, registering a land title) and one-stop integrated services spanning multiple agencies began to appear (Castillo Lòpez 2011). Use of low-cost software that allowed citizens to comment on or query government agencies, and for agencies to explain their policies, began to spread.

A powerful indirect benefit of expanding access to connectivity and to government services via Internet or phone links was increasing transparency (Casasbuenas 2011). Virtually all agencies now felt obliged to report budgets, expenditures, contracts and winning bidders, and related information on line. Businesses large and small, and citizens groups, tracked performance of government and were quick to question discrepancies. Some governments now required ministers and heads of agencies to disclose income and bank accounts. As a result, corruption declined significantly (Lidman 2011).

Moreover, with widespread connectivity, citizen participation and activism increased. Local discussions and organization via phone and text-messaging networks became more common. Governments found it increasingly important to explain their actions and seek consensus on potentially controversial policy issues, often via e-government networks. The result, even if sometimes chaotic, was more accountability and more active democracy throughout the developing countries.

In order to foster sustainable development, it is recommended that the following further actions take place:

- Support extension of wireless networks to rural areas, especially connectivity to schools, clinics, and local government offices;
- Encourage and support policy reform aimed at enabling local community wireless networks or hotspots under a "social use" exemption, where low-cost networks are not supported by legacy carriers;
- Support pilot projects for voice-accessible and Internet-based information bases, as a first wave of e-government services;
- Support re-engineering integration of government processes to enable sophisticated, one-stop e-government services;
- Support the use of interactive tools on e-government web sites and, thereby, encouraging transparency and government responsiveness.

Pillar 4: ICT and Financial Services

Compared to six year ago, the transformation of the economies from cash to cashless transactions is already well advanced. The primary stimulus for this change has been the increasing sophistication of mobile phones and other "smart" mobile devices with "smart card" capabilities built in. Equally, however, the business models incorporated lessons learned from earlier mobile financial services. As a result, smart mobile devices increasingly became portable banking terminals, electronic wallets, and the payment system of choice (stored account balances or credit status were updated with every transaction, usually by simply swiping the phone near the retail terminal). With encryption and often thumbprint or pass-code protection, the devices were more secure than cash or old-fashioned credit cards. This revolution was largely driven by the private sector, but efforts catalyzed early adoption of standards and modernization of financial regulations to facilitate the transformation, as well as encouraging extension of wireless networks to rural areas.

Mobile electronic transactions, instant banking, and cashless commerce were a great convenience. However, for the majority of the population, especially those with low incomes, the impact was more profound (Tejerina and Westley 2007) and included such benefits as:

- Extension of modern financial services including credit to the majority of the population, with much greater ease of access (no need to get to a bank branch, available at all hours of the day);
- Cheaper and faster means of transferring remittances from abroad. This derived in an accelerated modernization and capitalization of the micro-credit financial system fed by growing financial remittances and the resulting mobilization of credit resources and modern financial services;
- Greater safety, because not carrying large amounts of cash meant less risk of robbery; thieves quickly learned that stolen phones not only would deny access, but also automatically alerted police to the theft and to their location;
- Transaction and credit records were created automatically, empowering many low-income participants in informal occupations with the evidence of credit-worthiness or purchasing power required to obtain loans or life insurance, buy on credit, or otherwise interact with the formal economy;
- Even small transactions, and small amounts of credit, could be done electronically, via text-messaging or short-range wireless transfer, facilitating even the informal economy but linking it more closely to the banking system;
- With automation came reductions of transaction costs, more affordable financial services, and expansion of both credit and pre-paid commercial transactions.

The result was the inclusion of most of the population in the formal financial systems and, thereby, increasing equality of access to services (Tejerina, Bouillon and Demaestri 2006). Microfinance became a fully commercial activity, effectively providing similar services traditionally provided by all major financial entities. Such transformation also reduced informality and markedly increased the efficiency of local economies, stimulating investment and accelerating growth. These initiatives aim at reducing the transactions costs of international remittances to the Region and tying such cash flows to the development of the micro-credit sector. The deployment of ICT solutions is instrumental in meeting the objectives of such initiatives.

Equally important, with electronic systems and record keeping incorporated in most small and medium enterprises, large financial institutions and special venture funds increasingly began to provide finance for previously neglected enterprises. As this "meso-finance" expanded, small and medium sized enterprises (SMEs) began to fulfill their potential as growth engines for economies.

In order to foster sustainable development, it is recommended that the following further actions take place:

- Support wireless network extensions to rural areas as appropriate;
- Promote and facilitate the establishment of public-private partnerships with telecom carriers, bank regulatory agencies and private sector, among others, to catalyze the adoption of common stan-

dards for mobile transactions and updated banking regulations to enable financial transactions and banking services via next-generation "smart" mobile devices, and Internet-based applications;
- Finance and implement demonstrative and pilot projects to promote best practices and accelerate adoption.

Contributing to the development of less developed economies requires an environment that facilitates the deployment of ICT, its dissemination and use in various institutional, business and social settings.

An effective environment conducive to the promotion and use of ICT to foster development requires a number of concrete actions at the strategic level under a multi-sector approach that is transversal to all the initiatives described above:

- Strengthening of the institutional capacity with the participation of the public, private and civil society sectors, in order to promote and foster the dissemination and use of ICT through programs and initiatives that build a participatory knowledge society;
- Raising awareness and creating the conditions for the design and implementation of pilot initiatives and the replication of best practices in the priority areas discussed in this paper;
- Creating the organizational conditions for the identification of concrete and comprehensive national ICT investment plans which effectively delineate the participation of the various sectors and stakeholders;
- Implementing and/or strengthening national and regional regulatory frameworks to promote competition and loosen restrictions on the telecommunications market, allow for the expansion of media convergence, and promote and facilitate research and technological innovation.

All the above requires not only a concrete delineation of the responsibilities that the public, private sector and civil society should assume, but also the promotion and establishment of partnerships based on their mandates, responsibilities, purpose and competitive advantages. Experience shows that these partnerships allow for addressing multiple issues that cannot be resolved without the concerted efforts of diverse constituents, while also allowing for synergies, coordination and sharing of priority investments, and ultimately leading to a more efficient and sustainable process of economic and social development and inclusion through the deployment of appropriate and innovative technologies.

With respect to the public sector, experience shows that ICT-based programs aimed at enhancing the reach and impact of social development and inclusion programs not only strengthen the capacity of the public administration, at the national, local and regional levels, to deliver public services, but also contribute to building public trust while enhancing citizen participation.

With respect to the private sector, active participation of the technology-based private sector represents a pivotal source of innovation for promoting social development, and creating local jobs, income opportunities and wealth. This can be achieved:

- Through the effective implementation of market, regulatory and institutional conditions to create the incentives necessary to balance social responsibility with profit motives (blended strategy);
- By promoting the participation of the private sector through ICT and connectivity investments and technical assistance in priority social sectors while, at the same time, creating value-added opportunities and the expansion of ICT-based social and financial services to underserved communities;

- Tapping the profit potential that can be realized from efforts aimed at improving the social and economic conditions of the socially excluded vulnerable groups, national governments should pursue actions that facilitate financial and technical assistance instruments to effectively adapt to the demand of its citizens, and support activities to provide and facilitate access to efficient ICT tools for the exchange of information, ideas and knowledge, and the deployment of ICT.

ICT offers many opportunities to also improve the ageing process in the pillars above (Lehmann, Giacini and Davis 2012). Along with a major role for ICT in the public health arena (e.g., mobile technology) comes the ability to offer health interventions, and education and preventive strategies that can address the global challenges of the digital divide. To date, efforts to include the aging population in the Knowledge Society have been limited. Research indicates that when ICT is used as an enabling tool, all generations benefit and quality of life improves.

Mobile ICT is also promoting economic growth by helping communities compete in local and global marketplaces (e-commerce). Improving socio-economic development, particularly in developing countries, is due, in large part, to improved access to timely information (easing the burden of information seeking which is extremely difficult in remote locations). With mobile technology, literally in-hand, farmers negotiate crop prices (e-agriculture); fishermen locate rich fishing spots (via satellite mapping), migrant workers use mobile banking (e-banking) and governments offer citizens the ability to register land, and educational, health, and voting opportunities (e-government). ICT can also increase jobs opportunities by reducing the need for unnecessary travel to better perform one's job,particularly in the case of disability (see, for instance, the case of the Sao Paulo "Center of Excellence for Technology and Innovation in Favor of Persons with Disabilities" in Brazil (CETID 2011))

Finally, with respect to the civil society, adequate organizational arrangements must be in place to facilitate the participation of civil society organizations in the promotion and implementation of community-based development programs and, thereby, complement public sector investments in connectivity, ICT solutions in health care facilities, schools, and neighborhoods, the development of local content and, overall, the delivery of social targeted actions at the local level.

3. A TRIPLE HELIX APPROACH

The International Council for Caring Communities (ICCC) is a not-for-profit organization that has Special Consultative Status with the Economic and Social Council of the United Nations. It was founded in 1994 to stimulate and showcase innovative concepts that deal creatively with the challenges of global longevity. ICCC acts as a bridge linking government, civil society organizations, the private sector, universities and the United Nations in their efforts at sparking new ways of viewing an integrated society for all ages.

In 2006 ICCC launched its "Windsor Format" that involves input from international decision-makers, world leaders and futurists, representing business, design, architecture, education, health, research and technology, along with local and central government and United Nations officials. The success of the "Windsor Format" is due to its non-traditional gathering of developing and developed country government officials, private sector decision-makers and related experts focused on 21st Century issues of global impact. From this point of view the "Windsor Format" can be considered as an example of a Triple Helix approach in action.

The Windsor Consultations Series takes place at St. George's House within Windsor Castle itself, so chosen to build upon it origins dating back to 1384 when it was established as a place where people of influence and responsibility could come together to explore and develop ideas, and possible solutions, to the problems of the day. The basic approach is to discuss, reexamine, rethink, redefine, and identify viable recommendations, up-scale successful projects and concrete plan of actions on existing and future programs.

These cross-sectoral Consultations have included: Age of Connectivity: Citizenship and Care for Cities of the Future; Knowledge Management: Modern Innovations & Technology towards the Knowledge Society; Government Training Revisited, and a three part series: Confronting the Diseases of Poverty; Technology and Innovation for Equity; Digital Health in the Age of AIDS; Climate Change, Health Systems &The Digital Revolution; Digital Health & The Orphans of Global Health: Child Mortality & Maternal Health, Chronic Non-Communicable Disease & Neglected Tropical Disease.

The ICCC's Triple Helix approach in action of the Windsor Consultations Series can be best appreciated by considering some particularly successful initiatives, namely: the "Citizenship and Care for Cities of the Future" Consultation, the "Knowledge Management: Modern Innovations & Technology towards the Knowledge Society; Government Training Revisited" Consultation and the "Age of Connectivity: Cities of Hope" initiative.

ICCC realized that "a sleeping giant" is awakening, "the agequake", as every month around the world over 1 million people turn 60 years old, with the fastest growth in developing countries. To address this challenging topic not yet on the "radar" of most governments, the first Windsor Consultation "Citizenship and Care for Cities of the Future" was held in October 2007 to stimulate awareness and action. The session addressed current and future trends with special attention to demographic shifts, rapid urbanization, migration, the increasing burden of chronic disease and changes in work and education. It explored new possibilities in information and communication technologies and the design of dwellings and cities, as well as, the increasing role of citizens providing the majority of care and support to family and friends who are ill, frail or disabled. Also, reviewed the potential impact of a number of worldwide trends on caring relationships and the provision of care present and future requirements.

The Consultation participants proposed launching an international initiative to support those involved in care as a contribution to the pursuit of the achievement of the Millennium Development Goals (MDGs) and the work of UN Habitat in cooperation with other related UN partners. Their recommendations focused on coordinating and leading public and private sector partners and contributors in activities that would:

- Demonstrate the possibilities open to policy makers and regulators in government, business and community and stimulate the design of products and services;
- Encourage and in practical terms release the potential of caregivers and strengthen their contribution and involvement in local economies and communities;
- Promote cross-disciplinary research and development programs by coordinating good practices and ideas from business, design, construction, employment, education, leisure and the arts to design and develop care-friendly living and working environments in developing and developed countries;
- Establish an international mentoring expert group and a virtual academy with global and local capacity to support urban and rural development initiatives that sustain caring relationships within and across ages and generations;

- Integrate the use of Mobile-health (M-health) and Mobile-learning (M-learning) technologies presently being used and developed for both developing (Africa) and developed countries;
- Encourage application of the Community Carte System (CCS), a Triple Helix approach, using a web-based system to collect, analyze and disseminate information on people's wellbeing, which can be easily incorporated in the websites of local authorities. People can use the web-based self-diagnostic tool to better understand their strength and vulnerabilities in the pursuit of wellbeing.

The Windsor Consultation's unique contribution to the "health and environment" dialogue drew on research experience in Europe and Africa, as well as the outstanding related work of UN Habitat and the newly launched WHO Age-Friendly Cities Project. It benefited from the insights and practical knowledge of experts[1] who reached the brief broadly stated conclusions and insights which included:

1. The economic and social contribution made by family and friend caregivers is highly significant and often equates or exceeds the contribution of services provided by government, non-governmental organizations and the private sector. Caregivers underwrite state provision and are an important but often unrecognized feature of national life.
2. Increasing longevity, population ageing and the rapid growth of non-communicable diseases mean that increasing numbers of people worldwide will become caregivers and will juggle work, education, care and other family responsibilities. People may become caregivers at any stage of life.
3. The provision of care and the ability to support a close relative or friend can add to and bring meaning to life. But, when the demands go beyond a certain level, caring can draw people out of work and community life altogether. The loss to individuals, local economies and communities is almost incalculable.
4. Worldwide trends such as urbanization and migration will exert an influence on patterns of care alongside increasing longevity and changing patterns of health and illness. Rapid urbanization can disrupt caring relationships just as it can create poverty, damage health and lead to economic and social hardship.
5. A focus on caring must be addressed and can offer a new dimension to urban planning. It offers the potential to contribute to the building of common agendas between different age groups and between the old and new communities who share urban space.
6. Over 10% of the population is likely to be involved in caring at any one time. It makes social and economic sense to work with citizens to strengthen caring, make it more possible for caregivers to remain in employment, take part in education and participate in urban governance which is enabled with the use of ICT. Policymakers' indifference will squander a precious resource for cohesion, integration and the improvement of lives in slums and throughout society generally.
7. For all these reasons, one of the key Windsor recommendations is that support for caregivers should be just as much a part of the everyday infrastructure of cities and settlements as roads, hospitals and schools.

In the Windsor tradition the "Knowledge Management: Modern Innovations & Technology towards the Knowledge Society; Government Training Revisited" Consultation, that was held in 2007, broke new ground by gathering for the first time a "non-traditional" group of dignitaries, senior decision-makers, donors, and leading experts including government officials from selected developing and developed countries directly involved in designing and implementing Knowledge Management programs.[2] This convergence and crossing-over of public research, business and governments which were previously separated represented a good example of the Triple Helix model in action.

The Consultation stimulated practical recommendations, reviewed up-scale successful projects and developed a concrete plan of actions related to how existing and future training packages under the United Nations Public Administration Network (UNPAN) platform can be managed and developed effectively in an effort to ensure that the basic objectives of government and civil society organizations are enhanced. It established the essential building blocks for productive sharing of experiences and future actions; recommendations evolved from a Triple Helix approach:

- Presentation of the UNPAN training program on areas of assistance and cooperation, namely, improving the content of the exiting modules, increasing accessibility to the UNPAN training modules for potential participants from the developing countries by providing an opportunity to free internet access, and translation of training modules;
- Presentation of the existing training programs in the area of e-governance and knowledge management;
- Presentation of developing country projects in the area of new technologies including the mobile technology (M-Technologies) such as M-Education and M-Health;
- Exploring partnership opportunities and needed actions to support the UNPAN training program as well training programs of the participating institutions through strengthening cooperation and collaboration among the participants of the Consultation.

Results encouraged "Partnership in Practice," another typical aspect of the Triple Helix approach, using ICT to spearhead rethinking of priority actions and strengthen the effectiveness of existing institutional frameworks and implementation mechanisms between developed and developing countries as well as between developing countries using South-South cooperation as an effective modality for social and economic development, as well as, enhancing regional and interregional Knowledge Management (KM) cooperation and integration for accelerated socio-economic development in the globalized environment.

The ICCC initiative "Age of Connectivity: Cities of Hope", another example of a Triple Helix in action approach, seeks to create an open network, which leads to international planning and advisory groups seeking to involve public and private sector organizations in a range of activities supporting the overall goals.

In its first stages the initiative will bring the proceedings of Windsor and New York and later developments to a worldwide audience as the first step in the formation of an international mentoring group and academy and seek partnerships, alliances, regional hubs and interest groups to create and disseminate ideas and bring the products to local and national attention by taking the following steps:

- Draw up a business plan
- Set targets
- Secure the agreements necessary to acquire the resources
- Build an organization capable of contributing to the achievement of the Millennium Development Goals in the period to 2015.

This proposal is based on the recommendations of the Windsor Consultation 'Citizenship and Care in Cities and Settlements of the Future' and formulated by Consultation members following a High Level Working Session held at UN Headquarters in New York on February 8, 2008.

4. CONCLUSION

ICT is changing the way people live and do business globally, and is creating new social and economic development opportunities especially for lower-income populations, by enlarging markets and facilitating greater access to information, public services and economic activity. The effective deployment of ICT can create or expand economic and social opportunities for a growing share of the population in the developing countries and bring unprecedented opportunities to tackle the challenges faced by lower-income populations in their efforts to participate in and benefit from the growth of the knowledge economy. Yet, these opportunities to be effectively and fully realized require the active participation of the public, private and civil society sectors under integrated efforts towards the development of an inclusive knowledge society. This makes the Triple Helix model an interesting new paradigm of development and inclusion that, when applied along with a good ICT infrastructure, could help achieving a more fair distribution of digital dividends to developing countries, reducing the digital divide and helping attaining the Sustainable Development Goals (SDGs).

In this paper we described a number of sustainable development scenarios for the developing countries based on these principles. In discussing those scenarios, we aimed to contribute to the articulation of a best-practices manifesto that regional, national and local governments may want to pursue in fostering a socially inclusive knowledge society in which the "digital dividends" can flow to the majority at the base of the population's pyramid, empowered through the deployment of ICT.

In particular, we described some of the International Council for Caring Communities' best "Triple Helix approach" practices that have stimulated new avenues for discussion/dialogues and policy development that bring to the fore the role that innovation can play in the economic growth and well-being in developing countries. ICCC acts as a bridge linking government, civil society organizations, the private sector, universities and the United Nations in their efforts to devise new ways of building an integrated society. From this point of view, the ICCC's approach can be considered as a "Triple Helix in action" approach.

The ICCC gatherings composed of a non-traditional group of decision makers and experts from government, international organizations, local authorities, the private sector, academia, health organizations and related industries, have been ICCC's centerpiece for addressing social and economic issues. This format, in our opinion, represents a good model for tackling development issues and deploying new development strategies. Altogether, the ICCC model, considered as a "Triple Helix in action" approach, represents the "breaking" of the old approach to international development, and the onset of a new effective one.

The results of the gatherings in fact, have been a series of practical recommendations and promotion of a "Call for Action!" agenda. The method stimulated "fast-track" awareness of information "gaps", directly and indirectly promoted collaboration, and enhanced cost-effective use of limited funds to be used for international development. It also added an important element that focused and fostered the "connecting the dots" mindset to enhance community, health, well being and the quality of life and that supported the attainment of the MDGs and the post-2015 sustainable development agenda.

REFERENCES

Anta, R., El-Wahab, S., & Giuffrida, A. (2009). *Mobile Health: The potential of mobile telephony to bring health care to the majority. IDB Publications 8600*. Inter-American Development Bank.

Assolombarda. (1994). *Ricerca ed innovazione tecnologica: Analisi del fabbisogno delle aziende*. Milano.

Barbosa, F. A. (Ed.). (2011). *ICT EDUCATION 2010 - Survey on the use of Information and Communication Technologies in Brazilian Schools*. Sao Paulo: Brazilian Network Information Center.

Bellavista, J. (1997). The Barcelona Science Park: a triple helix model in the Catalan and Spanish Research System. In H. Leydesdorff & H. Etzkowitz (Eds.), *A Triple Helix of University-Industry-Government relations. The future location of research*. Academic Press.

Belsey, A. M. (2005). *AIDS and the Family: Policy Options for a Crisis in Family Capital*. UN Department of Economic and Social Affairs.

Bhaskaran, R. (2004). *Digital Gangetic Plains (DGP): 802.11-based Low-Cost Networking for Rural Areas - 2001-2004: A Report*. The DGP Media Labs Asia Team. Available: http://www.cse.iitk.ac.in/users/braman/papers/dgp-report.pdf

Bhusal, P., Zahnd, A., Eloholma, M., & Halonen, L. (2007). Energy-efficient innovative lighting and energy supply solutions in developing countries. *International Review of Electrical Engineering, 2*(5), 665-670.

Brewer, E., Demmer, M., Du, B., Fall, K., Ho, M., Kam, M., & Surana, S. et al. (2005). The Case for Technology for Developing Regions. *IEEE Computer, 38*(6), 25–38. doi:10.1109/MC.2005.204

Buckner, L., & Yeandle, S. (2011). *Valuing Carers*. Carers; doi:10.4018/IJKSR.2015070103

Bush-Brown, A., & Davis, D. (1992). *Hospitable Design for Healthcare and Senior Communities*. Van Nostrand Reinhold.

Campodall'Orto, S., & Ghiglione, B. (1997). The Technology Transfer Process within the New Innovation Models, in Managing Technological Knowledge Transfer. EC-Social Sciences COST, A3 (Vol. 4). EC Directorate General, Science, research and Development, Brussels.

Casas, C., & Lajoie, W. C. (2006). *The Fortune at the Bottom of the Pyramid. The Voxiva Story*. Wharton School Publishing.

Casasbuenas, G. J. (2011). The contribution of Colombian Civil Society Organizations to e-government for the Improvement of Transparency through the Use of Information and Communication Technologies. In D. Piaggesi, K. J. Sund, & W. Castelnovo (Eds.), *Global Strategy and Practice of E-Governance: Examples from Around the World* (pp. 324–337). New York: IGI Global. doi:10.4018/978-1-60960-489-9.ch018

Castillo, R. L. (2011). Municipal Mobile SMS Services: An e-Government Initiative of the Municipality of La Paz, Bolivia. In D. Piaggesi, K. J. Sund, & W. Castelnovo (Eds.), *Global Strategy and Practice of E-Governance: Examples from Around the World* (pp. 24–33). New York: IGI Global.

CESPRI. (1997). *Cambiamenti nella struttura industriale lombarda e politiche regionali per l'innovazione tecnologica, Rapporto di ricerca*. Milan: University Bocconi.

CETID. (2011). *The Center of Excellence for Technology and Innovation in Favor of Persons with Disabilities (CETID)*. Available: http://www.sedpcd.sp.gov.br

DOT-Force. (2001). *Digital Opportunities for All, Report of the G8 Digital Opportunities Task Force*. DOT-Force.

Dzidonu, C. (2010). *An analysis of the role of ICTs to achieving the MDGs*. UNDESA. Available: unpan1.un.org

Ericsson and Digital Health Initiative. (2011). *Challenges and Opportunities in Scaling UP Digital Health*. Author.

Etzkowitz, H. (1994). Academic-Industry Relations: A Sociological Paradigm for Economic Development. In H. Leydesdorff & P. Van den Besselaar (Eds.), *Evolutionary Economics and Chaos Theory: New directions in technology studies*. London: Pinter.

Etzkowitz, H. (1997). The Triple Helix: Academy-industry-governement relations and the growth of neo-corporatist industrial policy in the U.S. In S. Campodall'Orto (Ed.), Managing Technological Knowledge Transfer. EC Social Sciences COST A3 (Vol. 4). EC Directorate General, Science, Research and Development.

Eurofound. (2004). *Health and care in an enlarged Europe*. European Foundation for the Improvement of Living and Working Conditions.

Eurofound. (2006). *Employment in social care in Europe*. European Foundation for the Improvement of Living and Working Conditions.

Fondazione Rosselli-CES&T. (1995). *Analysis of the regional science & technology policies in Europe* (CE-DG XII, Grant Contract: PSS*0819). Fondazione Rosselli.

Gebhardt, C., & Etzkowitz, H. (1996). Regional innovation Organiser: a quasi-public role for transational corporations and universities. Management and New Technology, COST A3.

Heimerl, K., & Brewer, E. (2010). The Village Base Station. *Proceedings of the 4th ACM Workshop on Networked Systems for Developing Regions*. doi:10.1145/1836001.1836015

HfALA. (2007). *The Health for All in Latin America Project. Reference manual, theoretical and methodological framework, experiences and directory of best practices*. Perugia, Italy: Fondazione Angelo Celli.

HM Government UK. (2004). *Carers (Equal Opportunities) Act 2004*. London: The Stationary Office.

Ho, M. R., Smyth, T. N., Kam, M., & Dearden, A. (2009). Human-Computer Interaction for Development: The Past, Present, and Future. *Information Technologies and International Development*, *5*(3), 1–18.

Hosman, L. (2010). A National ICT-in-Education Initiative: Macedonia Connects. In *E-Strategies for Technological Diffusion and Adoption: National ICT Approaches for Socioeconomic Development* (pp. 1–18). New York: IGI Global. doi:10.4018/978-1-60566-388-3.ch001

ICCC. (2002, April). Ageing Dialogues 2020: the Future of Ageing. *Proceedings of the Second World Assembly on Ageing*, 131-132.

ICCC. (n.d.). *International Student Design Competitions Retrospective – 1994-2005*. Retrieved from http://www.unpan.org/Regions/Global/Directories/Resources/tabid/456/ItemID/1836/language/en-US/Default.aspx

ICCC. (n.d.). *Music As A Natural Resource: Solutions for Social and Economic Issues – Compendium*. Retrieved from http://www.unpan.org/Regions/Global/Directories/Resources/tabid/456/ItemID/1836/language/en-US/Default.aspx

International Longevity Center-USA and Schmieding Center for Senior Health and Education. (2006). *Caregiving in America*. International Longevity Center.

ITU. (2011). *Measuring the Information Society 2011*. Geneva, Switzerland: International Telecommunication Union.

ITU and UNESCO. (2010). *A 2010 Leadership Imperative: The future built on BROADBAND*. A Report of the Broadband Commission.

Jones-Evans, D. (1997). Entrepreneurial Universities - Cases of Good Practices from the Republic of Ireland. *Proceedings of the International Conference: Technology Policy and Less Developed Research and Development Systems in Europe*.

Kimani, M. (2008). Better health at the click of a button: Information helps Rwandan clinics reach out. *Africa Renewal*, *22*(1), 5. doi:10.18356/48f5cee5-en

Kusakabe, M. (2012). *Measuring Wellbeing for the City of Liverpool*. Open City Foundation Wellbeing Survey Series.

Lane, D., Malerba, F., Maxfield, R., & Orsenigo, L. (1991). Choice and Action. *Journal of Evolutionary Economics*.

Lehmann, C. A., Giacini, J. M., & Davis, D. (2012). *Innovative and Technology for the Ageing*. U.N. *Publications*.

Leydesdorff, H., & Etzkowitz, H. (1996). Emergence of a Triple Helix of University-Industry-Government Relations. *Science & Public Policy*.

Leydesdorff, H., & Etzkowitz, H. (Eds.). (1997). *A triple Helix of University-Industry-Government relations. The future location of Research, Book of Abstracts*. Science Policy Institute, State University of New York.

Leydesdorff, H., & Van den Besselaar, P. (Eds.). (1994). *Evolutionary Economics and Chaos Theory: New directions in technology studies*. London: Pinter.

Lidman, R. (2011). Is the Internet Mightier than the Sword: An Anti-Corruption Perspective. In D. Piaggesi, K. J. Sund, & W. Castelnovo (Eds.), *Global Strategy and Practice of E-Governance: Examples from Around the World* (pp. 340–358). New York: IGI Global. doi:10.4018/978-1-60960-489-9.ch019

Mace, J. C. (2007). *Powering up: Information Technology for Rural Schools in Latin America and the Caribbean*. Enersol Associates. Available: http://www.enersol.org/programs/docs/EduSol-Paper_Dec2007.pdf

Patra, R., Pal, J., Nedevschi, S., Plauche, M., & Pawar, U. (2007). Usage Models of Classroom Computing in Developing Regions. *Proceedings of International Conference on Information Technologies and Development (ICTD2007)*, 158-167. doi:10.1109/ICTD.2007.4937401

Piaggesi, D., & Davis, D. (2015). The Triple Helix Approach for the Creation of a Knowledge Society. *International Journal of Knowledge Society Research*, *6*(3).

Prahalad, C. K. (2005). *The fortune at the bottom of the pyramid*. Wharton School Publishing.

Tejerina, L., Bouillon, C., & Demaestri, E. (Eds.). (2006). *Financial Services and Poverty Reduction in Latin America and the Caribbean*. Washington, DC: Inter-American Development Bank.

Tejerina, L., & Westley, D. G. D. (2007). Financial services for the poor: household survey sources and gaps in borrowing and saving. Sustainable Development Department - Technical Papers Series, Inter-American Development Bank.

Teknova. (1995). *Sistema di monitoraggio della ricerca scientifica e dellíinnovazione tecnologica in Lombardia*. Ricerca IRER cod. 93.64.

The Royal Society. (2006). *Digital Healthcare: The Impact of Information and Communication Technologies on Health and Healthcare*. The Royal Society.

UNDESA. (2007, October). *Intergenerational Solidarity: Strengthening Economic and Social Ties*. Expert Group Meeting and Background Paper, UN Department of Economic and Social Affairs, Division of Social Policy and Development.

UNESCO. (2005). *E-government toolkit for developing countries*. UNESCO. Available: http://unesdoc.unesco.org/images/0013/001394/139418e.pdf

Venne, R. (2005). *Mainstreaming the concerns of older people into the social development agenda*. United Nations Secretariat: Division for Social Policy and Development.

Viale, R. (1998, March 4). *Tripla elica in Lombardia: evoluzione nel raccordo tra ricerca, impresa e governo*. Conferenza Regionale della Lombardia - Scenari dello Sviluppo, Milano, Italy.

Viale, R., & Ghiglione, B. (2005). *The Triple Helix model: a Tool for the Study of European Regional Socio Economic Systems*. Fondazione Rosselli Publication.

Vota, W. (2010). Updated Quick Guide to Low-Cost ICT Devices for Educational Systems in the Developing World. infoDev, the World Bank.

Wilson, M., & Warnock, K. (2007). *At the heart of change: the role of communication in sustainable development & the case for communication in sustainable development*. Panos Publications.

World Bank. (2004). Building blocks of e-government: lessons from developing countries. PREMnote, number 91, the World Bank.

Yeandle, S., Buckner, L. (2007). *Carers, Employment and Services: Time for a new social contract?* Carers, Employment and Services Report Series, 6.

ENDNOTES

1 Awarded 501.c.3 status by US-IRS in March 2013.

2 See our Website www.FRAmericas.org.

APPENDIX: ON-GOING RESEARCH AT FRAMERICAS

FRAmericas is a US-incorporated non-for-profit, charitable[1] organization, devoted to applying latest knowledge and technology achievements to improve living conditions and enhance income generation among low-income groups. FRAmericas was originally established in 2010, to cover the American continent as a branch of Fondazione Rosselli (FR), a prestigious Italian Foundation devoted to research and study of public policy as it relates to major societal and economic issues, seeking answers to the complex questions faced today by governments and citizens alike through the application of behavioral and cognitive science. FR works in coordination with the Organization for Economic Cooperation and Development (OECD) and it is host to its library in the subjects of expertise of the FR. FRAmericas has evolved naturally from this beginning, to acquire an individual identity and a more focused mission that emphasizes application of research for social purposes with a global reach. In 2015 FRAmericas has been awarded the United Nations consultative status.

Scope and Programs of FRAmericas

Outlook

FRAmericas is built on the concept that all social phenomena are inter-connected and global in nature, and on the belief that investing in human knowledge would maximize the benefit of this inter-connection. Economic stability in the poorest parts of the world reduces pressure on the richest regions; control of environmental degradation in developing countries amount to sustained ecosystem services locally, but also to reduced risks of climate change impacts for the rest of the world; knowledge generated in one region of the planet can be hugely useful and consequential in another.

FRAmericas also believes that new technologies bid great promise to allow countries to leapfrog to better, more inclusive and democratic futures, as technology innovation can multiply the reach and benefits of development investment, and touch wider audiences that could not have been easily reached by more conventional means. The accelerated pace at which technology innovation grows must be harnessed to put it to use to improve the conditions of all humanity, not only of the privileged few. Societies based on technology innovation and knowledge products are societies with the potential to become more egalitarian, more equitable and more prosperous in a sustainable way.

While large international organizations such as the United Nations and Multi-Lateral Development Banks work to create this balance at a macro scale, there is ample room and need for interventions at the local level, where citizens on both sides of the spectrum can act directly to positively affect one another. This is the realm of non-for-profits such as FRAmericas: the creation of bridges between citizens and private organizations worldwide, who believe in the value of individual actions to achieve global impacts. FRAmericas aims to give individuals a choice in the way their tax dollars are used: through the central government accounts, or in clearly identified, transparently managed, and directly beneficial projects and actions that benefit many while at the same time generate global public goods such as social stability and a sustainable environment.

FRAmericas' global vocation is reflected in its own history: born in Italy and acting in Europe; incorporated in the USA and working for developing countries in the three continents it also fosters south-south cooperation among them. FRAmericas uses all possible connections and networks to maximize the impact of its activities. Through FRAmericas, citizens of all countries gain a window to other realities and other perspectives. Through FRAmericas, individuals and private organizations are empowered to take action locally and achieve results globally[2].

Objectives

FRAmericas' objective is to promote socio-economic development by contributing to the creation of knowledge societies, capable of enhancing income opportunities and quality of life for low-income groups.

To achieve this objective, FRAmericas has concentrated its efforts initially in two areas: promoting *innovation* in the scope and means of development assistance, and advising on *public policies* needed to support such innovation. To support innovation FRAmericas promotes technological and organizational innovation projects applied to the search for solutions and alternatives for humanity to cope with today's most pressing global issues, such as social inclusion, climate change, alternative energy sources, and urban growth, among others. To foster corresponding changes in public policy FRAmericas promotes the discussion and analysis of areas which are perceived to hold the greatest potential for changing significantly the future of humanity, such as converging technologies, Web Democracy, the use of information and communication technologies (ICT) applied to development purposes, the growth of Knowledge Economies and the creation of Knowledge Societies.

Priority Areas of Interest and Work

FRAmericas works through three main programs:

1. Design and implementation of development projects through its International Knowledge Economy Program (IKEP).

IKEP provides technical assistance to Governments and direct financial assistance to practitioners for the development and application of technology innovation to development strategies, tools and products. IKEP utilizes the latest information and communication technologies to foster the creation and expansion of the Knowledge Society in developing countries.

At the country or "macro" level, IKEP fosters planning tools that exploit a country's comparative advantage through investment in sectors whose growth is based on the capture and dissemination of knowledge, as a tradable good. Typically, these projects will seek to identify where the knowledge capital of a given country lays, whether it is in the wealth of traditional knowledge accumulated by local communities; or new knowledge derived from original research; or knowledge adapted from other sources to conform to the needs of a certain client group. At the organization or "micro" level, IKEP fosters growth strategies aimed at increasing effectiveness, efficiency or coverage, by fostering improved management of existing or newly acquired knowledge available to the organization.

To promote the expansion of Knowledge Societies whether at the macro or micro levels, IKEP fosters the application of an architecture which includes the simultaneous and coordinated implementation of action in five areas: research in technology innovation; investment in education; social inclusion; expansion of ICT infrastructure; and the establishment of enabling government policies, including intellectual property rights. It is the simultaneity of the intervention in several fields that distinguishes IKEP's approach to development from other --more conventional-- methods, which are typically sector-specific; IKEP's approach bears greater promise to achieve durable solutions to the complex problems faced by low-income communities and developing countries in general.

FRAmericas develops strategic project ideas in favor of developing countries with active participation of potential beneficiaries. IKEP projects also promote south-south cooperation to multiply the impact of project financing.

2. Life-long education through the ICT4DEVIS program.

FRAmericas' Information and Communication Technology for Development International School (ICT4DEVIS) provides life-long learning opportunities for those interested in bridging internet-related applications to development needs. ICT4DEVIS offers formal education and training opportunities for students and practitioners of any age interested in furthering their education in the fields of technology and innovation for international development.

FRAmericas uses this program to prepare the future "change agents" in the field of ICT and all technology innovation applications for development. Sessions are organized and hosted by prestigious Universities worldwide offering conceptual and practical contents to bridge technology to development. Sessions involve in-person participation as well as simultaneous distance learning facilities. Students and interested parties –individually or in groups—of all ages and from different backgrounds are encouraged to participate. Previous sessions have been organized and hosted by the University of Insubria, Como, Italy; and by the Interactive Robots and Media Lab & the Software & Knowledge Engineering Lab at NCSR "Demokritos", in Athens, Greece, in collaboration with the ARCOMEM and SOCIALSENSOR FP7 ICT research projects of the European Union.

3. Networking, advocacy, and open fora through the AKNOS program.

Using the platform "Academy for Knowledge Society" (AKNOS) FRAmericas disseminates best practices in worldwide efforts to foster knowledge-based economic growth and local action of global significance, through networks, fora, advocacy and publications. FRAmericas acts as a hub for current, former and future development practitioners interested in pursuing the promise of new technologies to achieve development objectives at an accelerated rate and with a wider reach. FRAmericas aims to build a strong network of experts, decision-makers, researchers, opinion leaders and regular citizens and it provides a forum where each can have a voice and express an opinion on the topics on the table. To do this, FRAmericas makes use of state-of-the-art Web-based information and the latest telecommunications technology to host Webinars where this discussion can take place. Observations derived from these virtual and in-person meetings are immediately available to the public. Special briefings and short summary documents are prepared for target audiences.

Chapter 3
Use of ICT to Innovate in Teaching and Learning Processes in Higher Education:
Case Examples of Universities in Chile

María Graciela Badilla Quintana
Universidad Católica de la Santísima Concepción, Chile

Matilde Susana Basso Aránguiz
Universidad Católica de la Santísima Concepción, Chile

ABSTRACT

In this chapter are shared experiences in educative innovation by using Information Communication and Technologies in higher education. The objective of this contribution is to provide a view related to the curricular integration of ICT, highlighting by practical examples of implementation, which include their impact in cognitive processes and in the development of personal and interpersonal abilities in students. In the distribution, it is incorporated a description in planning activities and their application in the classroom, methodological aspects and assessing strategies selected for each experience are detailed. In addition, it is delivered a reflexive view related to the teacher role in the educative act. Finally, it is discussed the relevance of an active role in higher education institutions, referring to improve permanent training programs in educative innovation and to generate communicational spaces between teachers as well as different formation areas in the sense of strengthening the educative process and improve the quality of education.

INTRODUCTION

One of the main distinctive features of the society is that assemblies through TICs as a nuclear element. This has being a fundamental motor of growth and reaching insertion in every social sector, especially in education. According to this, in the last years there are efforts to integrate TICs in higher education as a strategic tool for development of new training scenarios, generating new perspectives of analyses

DOI: 10.4018/978-1-5225-4191-2.ch003

related to learning bases and generator of innovative learning environments. In this sense, the introduction of technologies in learning processes, and especially in university learning processes, has been a challenge in relation to pedagogical strategies that have to be developed. Moreover, the same situation presents a great opportunity for innovation and renovation of academic offers related to these institutions.

In this context, all international given data in reports are relevant. This has been evident relate to that there are more mobile devices than humans in the world, numbers in 2016 were around 8.0 million (Cisco, 2017; Ditrendia, 2016). The importance of considering this data was given during the mobile learning week, celebrated in Paris during March in 2017, where was highlighted the fact of using new technologies and the digital empowerment. These two ideas were highlighted to be important because they not only promote learning; otherwise, they transmit social values, norms and development electronic abilities needed for nowadays.

United Nations Educational, Scientific and Cultural Organization (UNESCO) and ACNUR (2017) stated that even having telecommunications this has been a challenge for some countries that are not developed, consequently having access to wireless and mobile devices for teachers and students can be a positive development for the environment. Due to this, it is important invest in acquisition of e-abilities to promote equality in opportunities in digital world.

For this perspective, is undeniable that higher education institutions should contribute to form professionals for future, adding to this, they have to form for knowledge and management of technical competences and digital abilities that would allow them to develop and compete in the working world in this century. In this sense, there are many evidences of ICT incorporations in Higher Education (Heflin, Shewmaker & Nguyen, 2017; Tur, Marín & Carpenter, 2017; Badilla & Meza, 2015; Garcia-Cabot, De-Marcos, & Garcia-Lopez, 2015; Sepúlveda, Badilla, & Careaga, 2014; Badilla, Carrasco, & Prats, 2014; Silva & Salinas, 2014, Cataldi, Méndez, Dominighini, & Lage, 2012).

This chapter was developed based on the information published by authors in previous works (Basso & Badilla, 2016a). Content was updated and expanded including new strategies and tools, with the idea to explore the curricular integration of different technologies in Higher Education, highlighting, through practical examples of implementation, its impact on cognitive processes and the development of students' personal and interpersonal skills.

Universities, as academic institutions should generate knowledge, updating and training on human resources in order to improve their competences and professional development. This will be to ensure an adequate teacher training that it is essential to unchain an educational process that can answer current trends. This would prepare future professionals in the domain and management of skills, the development of comprehensive learning strategies in the training of students and strengthening the knowledge, skills, attitudes and abilities inherent of their profession.

TEACHING HIGHER EDUCATION STUDENTS WITH ICT SUPPORT

The professional formation in XXI century has trigger a reconsideration about the entire educational act, since innovation, encouraging an inter relationship between different environments which are face-to-face and virtual learning trough ICT.

Nevertheless, virtualization of education goes beyond of the use of instrumental technology in educational practices, improving ICTs in the representation or creation of knowledge and in the regulation of required interactions for learning (Chan, 2016).

There is evidence that has been development in public policies to encourage the use of technology in education (Alderete & Formichella, 2016). For instance, in countries such as Chile (UNESCO, 2013a) Government supports an educational website for students that use massively to prepare a standard test to enter to university (PSU) and this one facilitates the content for mobile devices and other cases, such as in Argentina in universities (Sanz et al., 2007). However, these policies are not massive yet, therefore, are defined to have access to new learning scenarios, which led, connect students in ICT's contexts to improve study programs and their development as professionals at the end of the college.

There is now consensus on the importance of the use of ICT in the teaching-learning process even in different educational settings (Durall, Gros, Maina, Johnson, & Adams, 2012) and how they have been allow a challenge in the view related to learning from different dimensions. As Adell and Castaneda point out (2010) learning does not only occur in the school inside the classrrom (formal learning), but also outside of it (informal learning). López (2013) affirm the necessity to change roles between teachers (guide) and students (lead) in the educational process. Burbules (2012), and Ogata, Matsuka, El-Bishouty, and Yano (2009) refers to the ubiquitous learning concept, as an opportunity to cross the space and time boundaries. Authors like Garcia (2010) and Reynolds, Barnhill, Sias, Young, and Greer (2014) also highlight the relevance to consider real-time evaluation and visual response of learner performance, focused on the process, with a reflective component and an opportune feedback. To rate the creation of collaborative workspaces enhancing learning with others (López, 2013; Chih-Hung & Hwang, 2017).

Additionally, for UNESCO (2013b) and Marqués (2013), the curricular integration of ICT ensures quality of education, from different dimensions. As means of access to various sources of information and as a tool to build new knowledge (learning to know); As means of expression and participation with emphasis on respect and ethical use of technology (learning to be); As means for developing creations and construction solutions or problem solving (learning to do); As space for social participation and cooperative work (learning to live together); Encouraging diversification teaching-learning; Expanding time and space for learning (Ubiquity learning; Burbules, 2012); Providing countless educational resources; and allowing the permanent monitoring of the progress and achievements in learning outcomes.

In spite of, the omnipresence of mobile technologies and their massive use in educational environments, Wagner, Castillo, Murphy, Crofton, and Zahra (2014) reflect the less empiric evidence that supports their use for learning, demonstrating in their literature review descriptions of its use at an anecdotal level that not necessarily indicate real profits in learning or wider contextual impacts.

Despite the last idea, mobile technologies constitute an excellent way to expand educational opportunities. This is the reason why UNESCO (2013a) details advantages of their use, such as: how easy is it to learn according to the necessities of each student, answers and evaluations simplified and immediately, learning in every situation reinforcing essential information, well use of time inside the classroom, which it is more effective and creation of new student' communities.

Woodwill (2011) identifies other potential benefits of learning, based on the use of mobile technology. For instance, it improves content retention, efficiency, saving expenses, because the necessity of space decreases inside the classroom and saving time, because learning is a process almost immediately.

By reflexing the theoretical background exposed the relevance of incorporating ICT through the creation of virtual learning environments to encourage meaningful learning and foster both, autonomous and self-monitoring of the student as collaborative work is shown (López, 2013; Rodríguez, Escribano, & Lara, 2009).

At the same time to achieve the goal of inclusive and equitable quality education and lifelong learning by 2030 the Qingdao Declaration (1st global declaration on ICT in Education) indicates that ICT must be harnessed to strengthen education systems, knowledge, dissemination, information access, quality and effective learning, and more efficient service provision (UNESCO, 2015).

As WTIS (2015) affirm, Information and Communication Technologies are recognized as an extremely potential driver of sustainable development. Which means in Reimers (2015) words that could make education systems not only more accessible, but more relevant.

CASE EXAMPLES OF ICT INTEGRATION IN UNIVERSITIES IN CHILE

This section provides case examples of innovative educational experiences applied in higher education using technology into the curriculum of three careers: Teacher of Primary Education, Civil-Geological Engineering UCSC (both at Universidad Católica de la Santísima Concepción –UCSC); and Engineering in Construction, at the Universidad del Bío Bío, in Chile.

In the next pages, six examples are presented. These practices were developed by teachers who were inclined to integrate technology into the classroom, who have been received ICT training and who feel comfortable using innovative strategies to enhance their teaching processes. These proposals including aspects such as: methodology, curricular activity, contextualization and its implementation according to the learning outcomes, lesson plans, strategies and teachers' reflections.

Flipped Classroom: Optimizing Time Inside the Traditional Classroom

As an innovative methodology, Flipped Classroom is a pedagogical model that considers learning as the center of the educational process, where the student has an active role, and teacher is the learning facilitator who use different active methodologies to promote the integration of different knowledge.

It is characterized by transferring individual learning outside the classroom, by diverse technological resources, such as videos and the development of interactive activities in the class, which allow to improve the acquisition and practice of theoretical knowledge (Tourón & Santiago, 2015; Lee, Lim, & Kim, 2017).

This methodology was used at the Civil-Geological Engineering career, specifically in the theme unit *Sedimentary Petrology in the subject Fundamentals of Petrology.* Its implementation considered the use of four videos with their respective on site class per week. At the end of the unit, it is expected that students will be able to recognize the processes of formation of sedimentary rocks and its mineral and associated textures.

The planning and its post implementation considered each week, to lead the video in disposition for students in YouTube one week before on site class. Through virtual learning platform given by the university (Ev@ platform) it was available extra material, such as scientific articles, other videos, notes, between others, and through forum resource it was promoted asynchronous communication between students, teacher and virtual tutor (see Figure 1).

Within teaching mediation in face-to-face session, students worked collaboratively in the development of interactive activities designed under the objective to improve what was virtually learned and collaboratively, achieving meaningful learning (see Figure 2).

At the beginning and at the end of every on-site session short formative tests were taken, through Google Form. The use of this platform was to show if students did the previous work after class (videos) and if they achieve learning after post work inside the classroom.

Figure 1. Screen on Ev@Platform. Session 1 at the subject Fundamentals of Petrology

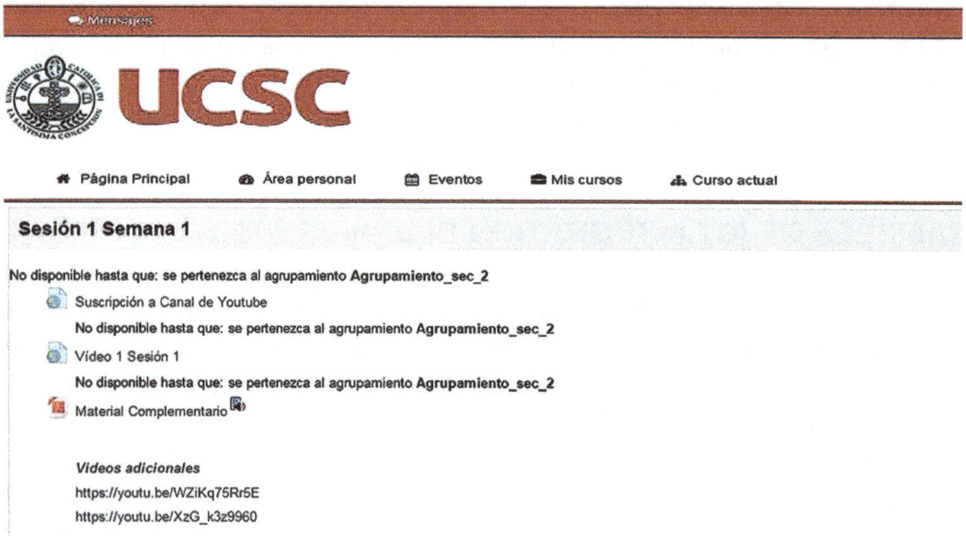

Figure 2. Panoramic view of classroom studio with students working

The use of this strategy allowed promoting the use and articulation of diverse technological resources in favor of the process of students' learning. This promoted autonomous work and pair learning, enhancing noticeably how students were aware and allowed to learn and be conscious about their achievements and progress.

Edmodo: Free Educational Web 2.0 Platform

Virtual environments have as a main goal to manage virtual learning communities by tools' systems that support educational actions to be on site, semi on site and or virtual (López, 2013). Edmodo is a free platform designed especially for education and in the last years it became popular because it was created to be a social networking service based on micro blogging created for educational purposes. It is available as an application for computers or mobile devices, and its main objective is to allow communication between teachers and students (https://www.edmodo.com).

In the experience it is presented, Edmodo was used to train future teachers (in Initial Teacher Training) and teachers who were in training as a long life learning. The emphasis in the creation of didactic activities by the platform uses, and not just for the instrumental use of the resource. This activity belongs to the subject Information and Communication Technology, assigned to first year for Initial Teacher

Training (major in Education: Elementary Level); and to the subject Use of ICT in educational management (master degree in education)

From a methodological point of view, the strategy was the access to an academic and virtual space of private use, in which teacher invite his or her students to be part of the community, manages communication with students through messages, files and links, as well as to share a class schedule, teacher proposes activities and homework (Garrido, 2013).

The expected learning outcomes of the thematic unit workshops were: a) To develop practical activities to show the importance of ICT for pedagogical innovation in various educational settings for students of Elementary Education; and b) To prepare a set of methodological strategies using ICT as a resource to support the teaching-learning processes and activities created autonomously and collaboratively to be applied with students of Elementary Education.

Regarding to its implementation in classroom, in one hand it was presented to students a course created in Edmodo (see Figure 3). It was introduced, invitations from teacher were made, profiles were created and edited by each student, and at the end the whole class reflected regarding its main possibilities.

Several of the functionalities highlighted were creation of a private space for communication between teachers, students and/or parent with restricted access, the possibility to share multimedia resources, files, links or videos, manage class schedule and grades, to generate homework and assessing questioners and to promote teamwork management through the creation of sub teams. It is highlighted its access through mobile devices (iPhone and Android).

During the first phase, it is required to each student to register in Edmodo as a teacher, to set a hypothetical course objective and to organize the available material on the platform according to the educational needs that were established. The student must design the welcome to the course, organize folders by subject or sessions, and upload files for reading and / or videos to introduce topics or reflect on certain contents, to create forms for feedback or evaluations, to create portfolios from each student of for him/herself, to generate a community of practice at school, among others. In a second phase in the workshop, it is required to each teacher to manage the learning community by inviting at least two teachers, which in this case corresponds to fellow workshop classmates. It is suggested to block the course once they have enrolled students, in order to prevent free access of people outside the group.

Figure 3. Screen of a message sent to the student in a course created in Edmodo

This sort of activity enhance participants to play different roles, and act as a teacher, student, and parents or representatives. In this sense, they are able to having a critical view related to effective use of this virtual educational environment.

The main virtues of this platform are being focused on how easy it is to use without professional knowledge in programming and its restricted access, allowing pedagogy students and ins-service teachers to develop free and restricted activities for their students (K-12 and/or higher education). Additionally, living different roles during the workshop, allow them to visualize potentialities of generating flexible learning environments that support collaborative work and communication among different actor from the educational community, as well as to create a community of practice inviting other teachers within the school.

Another relevant aspect to stand out, it is the fact of relevance of training for future teachers and teachers in training as a long life learning, based on innovation through the use of ICT, being contextualized and oriented to create diverse didactic activities, related to anticipated learning and not restricted to the use of technologies.

Google Drive: A Shared-Knowledge Manager

Drive is an extended and popular free Google application, constituted by a series of tools that allow to store information, to create and share files, excel documents, presentations, among others. All of this, enable collaborative with others in real time, augmenting participation and learning in a safer way (https://www.google.cl/drive/).

Drive was used as a collaborative experience by teachers in two careers: Civil-Geological Engineering, at the Mineral Systematics unit, of the subject Fundamentals of Mineralogy, in the third semester; and at the major in Education: Elementary Level, in the second and third semester in Initial teacher training. In the first career it is expected that students will be able to identify and describe minerals by their diagnostic properties through the application of systematic and determined classification. In the second one, it is expected that students to know and use information and communication technologies in an appropriate way in pedagogical context, and to know at the user level technological tools to develop academic work to their future professional performance. From methodological point of view, the expected tasks were developed in team works, in order to improve collaborative work and collaborative learning (De Miguel, 2005).

The implementation of the activity associates the development of sessions in the mineral laboratory of the subject, in which students in team works describe different groups of minerals. With the objective to demonstrate, assess progress and achievements, students based on mineral descriptions, are requested to create Digital Mineral Atlas using tools for design and creation of presentations available on Drive (https://www.google.cl/slides/about/). One student per group, should go to their Gmail account, get access to Google Applications, select Drive and create a Google Presentation. Having created this file, the student should send an invitation to the teacher and their classmates, in order to edit the file through the sharing option. Students then will receive in their email an invitation.

The tool Google presentation accomplishes the same functions that Power Point, but including numerous advantages, such as expands spaces for learning, allows to work simultaneously in real time, it possesses having control in changes or comments made by every user automatically (see Figure 4). The last idea, allows the user managing its knowledge easily and expressing ideas in one document.

Figure 4. Digital Mineralogical Atlas created by students

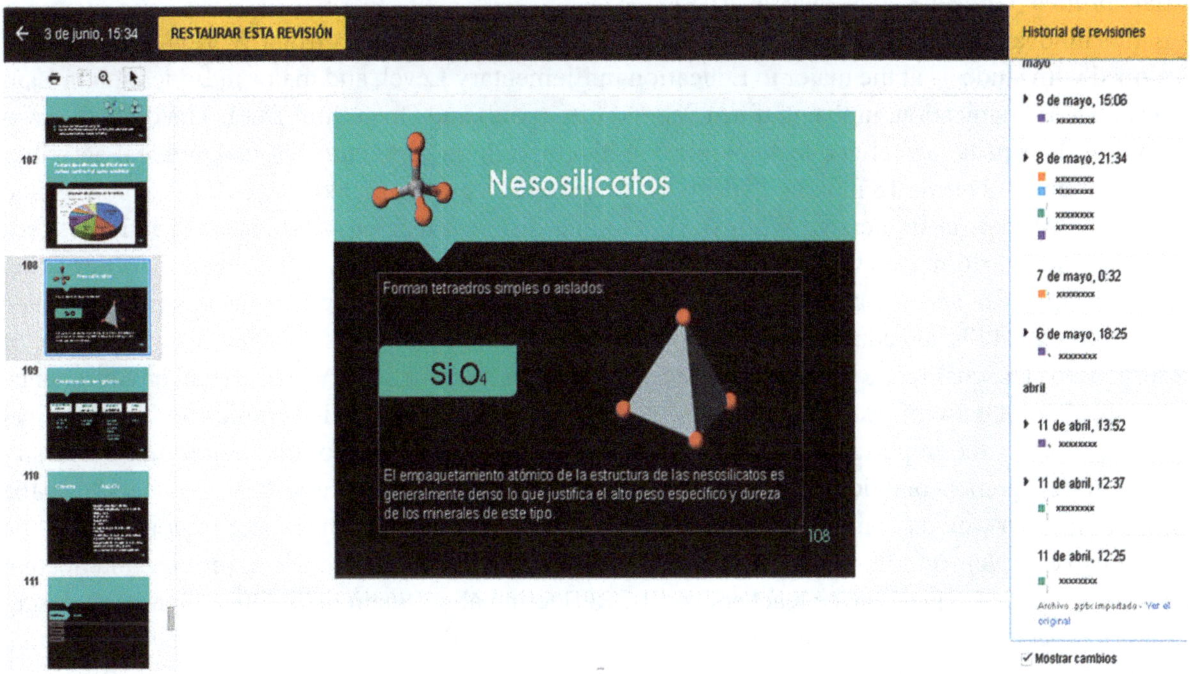

Google presentations, such as Document and other Google Applications, permit working with just one document version, because the shared document is saved automatically every time that changes or comments are made.

It is evident that the use of this sort of free tolls, in different educational areas, contributes to encourage students to have an active participation in the process of tasks in team works, because this allows them to interact synchronous or asynchronous, overcoming the fact to have a specific physical space. Additionally, there are evidences of individual contributions, in this sense, students assume agreement with the task and the process of feedback guided by the teacher it is easier, in order to improve the final task. From an evaluative perspective, it allows to make formative, in process and summative evaluations.

Immersive Virtual Worlds: Tool for the Development of Space Ability

Immersive Virtual Worlds (IVWs) are simulation places that offer new environments to interact, focusing on the users themselves, their identity and the actions they can perform (Díaz, 2014). IVWs offer real-life experiences and the ability to collaborate and create content in 3D simulated environments such as Second Life (SL), Open Simulator (OS), Active Worlds, Wonderland, Reaction Grid, and Olive, which run on Linux, Macintosh and Windows; and which certainly have a huge number of followers (Badilla, Vera, & Lytras, 2017).

Immersive environments, also called 3D virtual worlds, facilitate designing didactic activities that improve interaction between agents that participate in the educational area, providing a sense of on-site interaction (Badilla, Vera, Carripán, & Quilodrán, 2015; Sattolo et al., 2016). In this way, the developments of three-dimensional virtual worlds enrich online educational proposals and contribute to develop spatial abilities (Granados & Mendoza, 2014).

In this innovation were used, created and implemented two Immersive Virtual Worlds. First one was developed with students at the major in Education in Elementary Level, and major in Education in Language and Communication, in the platform Second Life (paid) and Open Sim (free). The objective was to enhance their pedagogical and technological skills through the simulation of pedagogical activities called Challenges. During 18 months students participated in a project called TYMMI (Technology and Pedagogical Models in Immersive Worlds), developing different teaching and learning activities (see Figure 5). Their performance was evaluated through various instruments of data collection: observation grids, questionnaires and Personal Log Book from each student. Results show that the students improved their technology skills and educational aspects about good practices in classes, regardless of the type of platform used. The qualitative analysis reported a positive assessment of the use of virtual environments, especially about the use of teaching strategies. Some of the highlights of this complex and longitudinal experience reflect the importance of peer assessment about teaching performance through university teachers of pedagogical practice, pedagogical moderator, technical support given by engineers from the technical staff, as well as comments given by their peers. Another relevant aspect to comment is the complexity of implement role-plays as a relevant and meaningful experience which propose intellectual challenges to enhance pre-service teachers' skills. Reflecting about main difficulties identified during the development of the activities it is necessary to have in mind that technical issues were reporting, regarding hardware and connectivity.

Second experience it is been developed with students of the Engineering in Construction career, in a platform with an open code called Open Simulator in order to develop space ability in students. Particularly, this educational innovation is oriented to analyze the effect of incorporating activities in immersive virtual worlds to promote the development of the ability to separate 3D objects in the subject *Technical Draw Workshop*. In order to assess this educational innovation, it was developed a pilot study with teachers and ex-students of the same subject. They had participate in an initial training about how to use the avatar into the virtual world, as well to pass successfully learning activities like to create object in three dimensions, and complete test about different views of an object in 3D.

It was applied a questionnaire to appreciate the perception of teachers and students, related to theoretical, pedagogical and technological aspects of the proposal. Preliminary results showed, in the theoretical aspects, that teachers and students are 'highly agree' in the sense that the activities have an educational approach based on competences, which improve self-adjustment in learning and which have as a main guiding point a Constructivist approach. Referring to pedagogical assessed aspects, spatial view and pedagogical design, activities were considered comprehensible, enabling understanding and/or practicing different views of an object that facilitate 3D object views.

Additionally, as a result using this IVW allow the teacher to observe which aspects are sensible to acquire by students, mainly associated to technological component, in which, external agents could affect the correct implementation of this curricular activity.

Both experiences allow to recommend the use of MVI as an educational innovation through ICT, which improve professional skills in higher education students. The main virtues of both platform, are being focused on how easy is to access them, and manipulate avatars, as walk, talk, as well to interact with the environment and tools available. Main disadvantages are related to cost and development. To

Figure 5. Teaching scenario in platform Second Life in TYMMI Project

use Second Life, is needed to create an account and monthly payments to have access to a very well developed infrastructure. To use Open Simulator, is needed to have some sort of technical knowledge in programming to install and create one personal island.

Socrative: Easy Tool to Assess Through Mobile Devices in Classroom

Socrative is an application available for mobile devices for free. It was designed especially for formative evaluations, in the sense of to obtain information in real time about student learning process (http://www.socrative.com/) (Sprague, 2016). To use it this application includes a teacher and student version, in which, users can enter by email account or by social platform networks, such as Facebook. In teacher version, Socrative allows to compose a test with different types of questions (true/false, alternatives and short answers) and spatial race.

Students ought to install the application in the mobile devices, logging in as students with the class code given by the teacher, and then, they had to answer the survey. As soon as the students answer the survey, Socrative starts the qualification process immediately, adding the results up and giving their individual visual results per group, facilitating the analysis and the reflection. Another good possibility is that can be downloaded those results in spreadsheets (see Figure 6).

On one side, it is suggested the utilization of Socrative to promote a procedural evaluation of students' learning in a quick and opportune way. On the other side, it is necessary to motivate students to improve their disposition to work inside the classroom.

This application was used in two different context. First one, was the Master in Educational Informatics and Knowledge Management at the Universidad Católica de la Santísima Concepción. It was expected that students were able to 'identify practices of innovation and educational change with the use of ICT', and 'to design a proposal for evaluation using ICT aimed at evaluating classroom learning or management of the educational institution'. With those students methodology was focused on knowing different tools which can be used in evaluation processes. It was socialized Socrative, its characteristics, access, strengths and weaknesses. Students had the opportunity to interact with it playing roles as a student and as a teacher. In this last role, they were motivated to create different test to be applied in their real teaching contexts.

Figure 6. Screen of the results displayed in Socrative

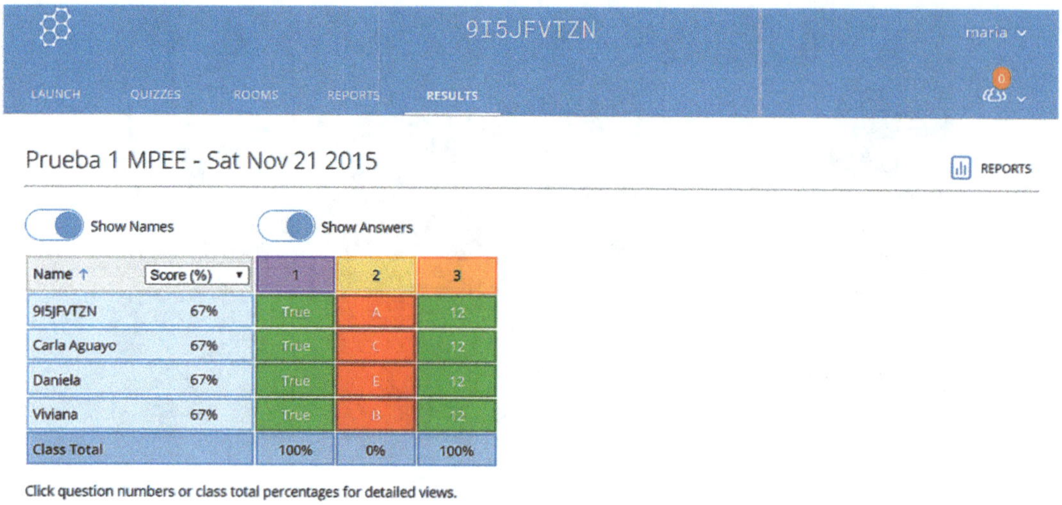

Second one, was the Sedimentary Petrology Unit of the Fundamentals of Petrology subject of second year in the major Civil-Geological Engineering. In this unit it was expected students will be able to recognize processes of rock formation of sediment, their former minerals and associated textures. As a methodological strategy, it was consider a reference suggestion by De Miguel (2005), related to methodologies in teaching oriented to learning.

It was applied the methodology of study and group work in which collaborative work and learning with others was promoted. Regarding the development of the activity, in first place the teacher composed a formative evaluation in Socrative, which is applied at the end of the topic of Sedimentary Petrology. The experience was carried out in a face-to-face session, in which students answered the test, using their mobile devices (cellphones and tablets are not highly used, when they already entered to student version by a code given to the class. In the first instance, students answered the evaluation individually and then they were analyzing and answering the given questions in groups of three. At the end of the activity, obtained results are shared individually and in groups. This corresponds to the fact to compare, in order to facilitate reflection in the process of learning.

As a final reflection, the incorporation of Socrative mobile application as a formative assessment instrument in higher education, allows the integration of the assessment process to daily educative activity, in this sense to give key information to students and teachers about the learning process. From the two experience exposed, it is highlighted the process of learning generated by answering for second time the test in small groups of three students, since it was promoted a discussion instance and transferring knowledge between pairs. These facilitate reflexive and metacognitive processes of students. On the other hand, authors believe that it contributes to motivate students and improve their willingness to work in the classroom.

Moreover, following to Ahumada (2001) it fosters the formative assessment focused on the students advances and achievements, as a permanent monitoring student' learning process in real time. It also allows a reflection by the teacher and students regarding his or her practice, and facilitates to make adjustments in the educative process (García, 2010; Hansen, 2005).

Symbaloo: Personal Learning Environment to Organize and Categorize

Symbaloo is known to be a free application, which allows easly to users to organize and categorize webpages, hyperlinks, and which enable users to establish their own resources network according to their interests. According to Adell and Castañeda (2010; 2013) it is considerate a Personal Learning Environments (PLE), which could be used by any device (www.symbaloo.com) or place, facilitating the access to personal resources and online markers.

This tool was implemented in the Geological Hazards subject, which corresponds to the ninth semester in the Geological Civil Engineering major and it joins all thematic units declare in the subject program. The objective of the pedagogical activity was to improve autonomous work and digital skills in students, oriented to search sources of information, which allow them to interpret geological processes associated to natural risks and to propose acceptable solutions to problems in society related to geological threats.

From a methodological point of view, teacher incorporated autonomous work to students, with the aim of acquiring a main role in the determination of their own learning process and self-regulation (De Miguel, 2005; Díaz-Barriga & Hernández, 2002), encouraging students proactivity in the search of efficient information, prioritizing and analyzing, letting them to establish their own network of resources. In addition, students work collaboratively in the creation of a summary and poster, socialization of their advances and results. They use the institutional virtual platform (Ev@ Platform), specifically Pedagogical Forum and Tasks, which were useful as means of registration of the process or learning plan, through evidences of advances in the process of sociability and feedback made by teacher and pairs (Basso & Badilla, 2016b).

During the implementation, students were encourage to start their process of searching, selection and prioritization of information sources for each thematic unit in some aspect that they are interested in. Once relevant information were found, every student created their own webmix and registered online markers (see Figure 7).

Figure 7. Symbaloo webmix display

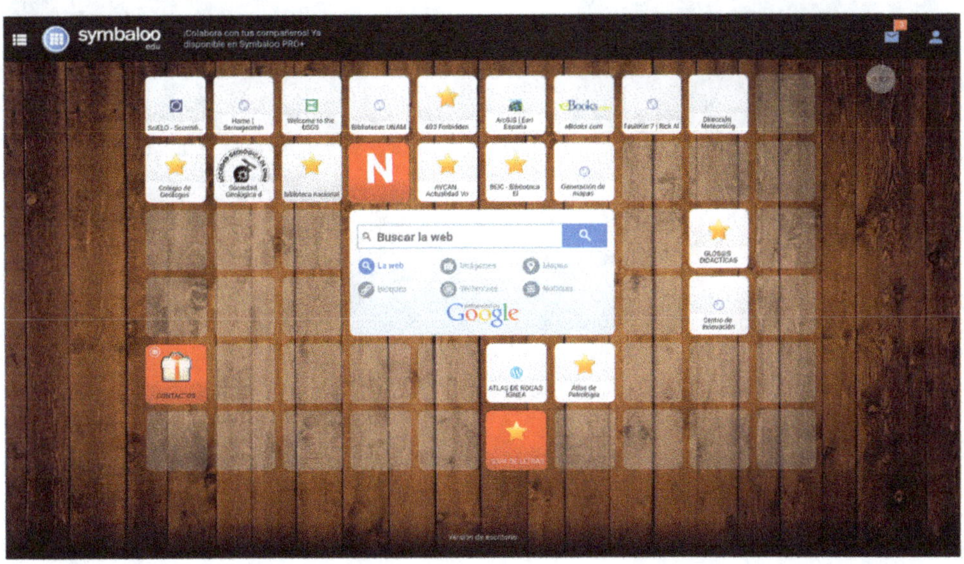

Webmix are individuals, thus, they differ from one to another, in function of articulation of information necessities and searching strategies. Teacher indicated to students the relevance of using valid and reliable information, hence it is given the instance to use the database from the Library of university (http://www.sibucsc.cl/). As much as there is progress in the unit program, every student supplies his or her each webmix, which it is shared in the intranet (Ev@ Platform). During the whole process, permanent feedback was given by the teacher, promoting adequate searching strategies and the appropriateness of chosen sources.

Once relevant information were located and selected, students worked in dyads creating a summary and a poster, referring to one selected area that called their attention. For the creation of the summary and poster, it was given a guideline with editorial norms, which indicate how to refer information according to American Psychological Association (APA).

Therefore, progress as final versions were shared by intranet, in order to receive teacher and pair feedback. Final version of posters were shared in the entrance Hall of the Engineering Faculty in the context of the Geological Risks Seminar, organized by Engineering Civil Department of that Faculty (see Figure 8).

Haworth (2016) highlight that using Personal Learning Environments (PLE) facilitates and promotes student autonomy in his or her process of learning; and depending the methodology used, it could be proposed collaborative work to reach common aims (Marín, Negre, & Pérez, 2014; Barroso, Cabero, & Vázquez, 2012; Cabero & Vázquez, 2013). In addition, Vázquez, Martín and Castrillo (2016) affirm that the use of those environments can promote the development of digital abilities in students, specifically related to searching strategies, selection and articulation in information according to their necessities. In addition, all of these enable to observe student-learning plan in every moment and place, facilitating opportune feedback by the teacher and classmates.

Figure 8. Socialization of the posters in entrance Hall of the Faculty of Engineering, UCSC

OVERALL REFLEXION

In this article is presented by contextualized examples, curricular integrative experiences of diverse resources of ICT in higher education, providing ideas to improve process of educational innovation and showing a vision related to the effect of the process of learning in students. All of these not from the cognitive point of view, but also in the process of developing personal and interpersonal abilities. In addition, precedents are delivered related to the positive perception by students and teachers reference to promote spatial abilities by using ICT validating theoretical, pedagogical and technological aspect of this proposal.

Practice proposals presented include experiences in diverse subjects with graduate and postgraduate students, proving that educative innovation processes in higher education are cross and they do not depend on the formation area. In this sense, they give a universal characteristic to the multiple resources in ICT. Even though, technology can be used in different educational areas, as it was exposed in this research, their integration should consider previous planning before activities, select methodological strategy, taking into consideration expected learning results and the type of instrument to assess, that allows seeing achievements reached by students.

In the processes of educative innovation, evaluation is one of the weakest aspects, because it is consider changes or improvements in the formative process just since utilization of ICT resources without relating with rating the process of teaching learning (García, 2014). In this context, it is relevant what it is argue by Brincones and Blázquez (2008) in terms of defining the concept of evaluation, considered as an essential element in curricular design, in such way that methodological changes should be linked to changes in evaluation, which it is consistent to what Leclercq and Cabrera (2014). For García (2014) one of the reasons of why teachers do not incorporate changes in assessing practices in innovation processes, it is related to the doubt that generate this processes and their lack of comprehensive vision of evaluation. As Barberá (2006) and García (2014) stated, it is relevant to increase fields and dimensions of evaluation, mainly to incorporate evaluation inside and outside the classroom. It is necessary value not just cognitive aspects, but at the same time attitudinal and social abilities and comprehend this as a constant process with emphasis in feedback (Ahumada, 2001).

Even when in this article there is not quantitative data presented related to the impact of the integration of ICT in the expected students learning, the presentation of the use of each ICT resource, show by a reflexive perspective their potentiality, emphasizing the generation of spaces of flexible learning in collaborative work and synchronous and asynchronous by different agents that at in the educative act. Likewise, analyzing diverse experiences showed, it is possible to understand from comprehensible view evaluation and visualize their effects in the metacognitive processes in students.

Considering these last two ideas, it is necessary that teachers of higher education should have a comprehensible view of evaluation and use diverse technological resources to improve processes of implementation curricular through activities with ICT. In this context it is expected they use them to collect information about progress in learning in their students (evaluation in process) as well as design and administration of evaluation tools.

The described advantages in the last paragraphs required a reflexive, flexible and creative teacher. Reflexive in terms of his or her teacher practice, flexible related to establish adjustments or improvements in the teaching learning process. Creative in the generation of innovative ideas to improve learning or adequate previous described experiences in other educative fields. In this sense, it is relevant to acquire improvement in communicational spaces between teachers in different levels and knowledge areas that allow sharing ideas and experiences related to the use of ICT in formative processes, not just implicated advantages, which have been discussed in this search, but also difficulties faced.

This last aspect, it is very important, because it allows to other teachers to take into consideration these issues and introduce adjustments in the implementation as previous planning before experience, which will improve formative processes, promote a reflexive teaching and increase better quality of education.

From a point of view of higher education institutions, it is needed to focus efforts on contribution of Teaching Communities related to innovative projects of their own educative practices and to generate space to reflect in curricular integration of ICT.

CONCLUSION

The incorporation of ICT in education in recent decades has produced a significant change in the teaching-learning processes, not only by the massive provision of computers and internet in universities and schools, but also by the exploration and introduction of new methodological strategies in educational practices. In addition to this, the massive access to information through internet, has generated the need to rethink the teacher's work as a facilitator or guide learning, and has resulted in enhancing students' proactivity, creativity, decision making and autonomy, among others. Moreover, ICT has created and expanded learning spaces, making them more flexible, without time and space barriers, creating greater access and participation for students in their educational process.

Within this context, the different experiences described in this article regarding the use of technologies in higher education, allow us to provide a glimpse of what learning is from a holistic perspective. This means, that ICT energizes the knowledge, skills and personal and interpersonal attitudes; thus, it contributes to training future professionals with the needed skills to thrive in a society and to work on an environment increasingly demanding, in which technologies play a fundamental role.

Considering the above, it is a great importance that tertiary educational institutions enhance and/or strengthen the curricular integration of ICT in the teaching-learning process. In this case, students not only know how to use technology, but also how to integrate them and its uses, which allow them to generate knowledge, build solutions, solve problems, among others. In this context, these institutions have a major role in the training of professionals in different subject areas. However, this task becomes increasingly important in terms of initial teacher training (ITT), fostering a substantial impact on new teachers that will guide the learning goals of students and; therefore, contributing on improving the quality of education.

On one hand, the work that higher-level institutions do must be highlighted, as a mean of that they are permanent training centers for teachers, especially when discussing the development of innovative learning strategies through the incorporation of ICT has had. In this regard, it is important that these trainings give an emphasis on the use of ICT not as an end, but as a tool to facilitate and enhance the educational process and to guide the design of educational activities mediated by technologies, which are coherent with both, learning outcomes and assessment instruments.

On the other hand, teachers must be trained to getting on as learning facilitators, whose educational activities allow them to create more flexible learning spaces generating greater access and participation of students in their educational process. Finally, it is a challenge for tertiary level institutions, in terms of expanding coverage and bandwidth of Internet to enhance the incorporation of ICT in the classroom and in the acquisition of mobile devices that allow the participation of all students on equal terms.

ACKNOWLEDGMENT

This chapter has been written thanks to the support of the National Commission for Scientific and Technological Research, CONICYT, Ministry of Education, Chile, through the Postdoctoral Scholarships Abroad (Becas de Postdoctorado en el Extranjero), Becas Chile, granted to Dr. María Graciela Badilla Quintana [Project No. 74160087].

REFERENCES

Adell, J., & Castañeda, L. (2010). Los entornos Personales de Aprendizaje (PLEs): una nueva manera de entender el aprendizaje. In R. Roig Vila, & M. Fiorucci (Eds.), *Claves para la investigación en innovación y calidad educativas. La integración de las Tecnologías de la Información y la Comunicación y la Interculturalidad en las aulas*. Alcoy: Marfil–Roma TRE Universita degli studi. Retrieved from https://digitum.um.es/jspui/bitstream/10201/17247/1/Adell%26Casta%C3%B1eda_2010.pdf

Adell, J., & Castañeda, L. (2013). La anatomía de los PLEs. In L. Castañeda & J. Adell (Eds.), *Entornos Personales de Aprendizaje: Claves para el ecosistema educativo en red* (pp. 11–27). Alcoy: Marfil. Retrieved from https://digitum.um.es/xmlui/bitstream/10201/30408/1/capitulo1.pdf

Ahumada, P. (2001). *La Evaluación una concepción de aprendizaje significativo*. Chile: Ediciones Universitarias de Valparaíso de la Universidad Católica de Valparaíso.

Alderete, M., & Formichella, M. (2016). Efecto de las TIC en el rendimiento educativo: el Programa Conectar Igualdad en la Argentina. *Revista CEPAL, 119*, 89-107. Retrieved from http://repositorio.cepal.org/handle/11362/40404

Badilla, M. G., Carrasco, J. L., & Prats, M. A. (2014). Use of PLE-Portfolio to Assess the Competency-Based Learning through Web 2.0 in Technical Engineering Education. *International Journal of Engineering Education, 30*(3), 675–682.

Badilla, M. G., & Meza, S. (2015). A pedagogical model to develop teaching skills. The collaborative learning experience in the Immersive Virtual World TYMMI. *Computers in Human Behavior, 51*, 594–603. doi:10.1016/j.chb.2015.03.016

Badilla, M. G., Vera, A., Carripán, C., & Quilodrán, J. (2015). Experiencias y reflexiones sobre el aporte de los mundos virtuales inmersivos en las habilidades pedagógicas y tecnológicas de alumnos en Formación Inicial Docente: la experiencia del proyecto TYMMI en OpenSim. *Encuentro Internacional Virtual Educa*. Retrieved from http://reposital.cuaed.unam.mx:8080/jspui/handle/123456789/4073

Badilla, M. G., Vera, A., & Lytras, M. (2017). Pre-service teachers skills and perceptions about the use of virtual learning environments to improve teaching and learning. *Behaviour & Information Technology, 36*(6), 575–588. doi:10.1080/0144929X.2016.1266388

Barberá, E. (2006). Aportaciones de la tecnología a la e-Evaluación, RED: Revista de Educación a Distancia. *Monograph, VI*, 1–13.

Barroso, J., Cabero, J., & Vázquez, A. (2012). Formación desde la perspectiva de los entornos personales de aprendizaje. *Revista Apertura, 4*(1), 1-12. Retrieved from http://www.udgvirtual.udg.mx/apertura/num16/1_formacion.html

Basso, M., & Badilla, M.G. (2016a). ICT resources to improve learning in Higher Education. *International Journal of Knowledge Society Research, 7*(4), 1-11. doi: 104018/IJKSR.2016100101

Basso, M., & Badilla, M. G. (2016b). Propuesta de modelo de innovación en evaluación con uso de TIC. *Proceedings of the IX Congreso Internacional y XV Nacional Investigadores en Educación (INVEDUC).*

Briscones, I., & Blázquez, J. (2008). Evaluación de los aprendizajes en la formación con TIC. *Tarbiya, Revista de Investigación e Innovación Educativa,* (39), 41-59. Retrieved from https://revistas.uam.es/tarbiya/article/view/7192

Burbules, N. (2012). El aprendizaje ubicuo y el futuro de la enseñanza. *Encounters on Education, 13,* 3–14. Retrieved from https://ojs.library.queensu.ca/index.php/encounters/article/view/4472/4498

Cabero, J., & Vázquez, A. (2013). Los Entornos Personales de Aprendizaje: uniendo lo formal, informal y no formal para la construcción del conocimiento. In *Los Entornos Personales de Aprendizaje. Visiones y retos para la formación* (pp. 9-26). Editorial de la Universidad Metropolitana de Caracas. Retrieved from http://tecnologiaedu.us.es/tecnoedu/images/stories/ples_2014.pdf

Cataldi, Z., Méndez, P., Dominighini, C., & Lage, F. (2012). *Dispositivos móviles en educación superior y entornos personalizados de aprendizaje.* WICC 2012. Retrieved from http://sedici.unlp.edu.ar/bitstream/handle/10915/19437/Documento_completo.pdf?sequence=1

Chan, M. E. (2016). La virtualización de la educación superior en América Latina: entre tendencias y paradigmas. *Revista de Educación a Distancia, 48*(1). Retrieved from http://www.um.es/ead/red/48/chan.pdf

Chih-Hung, C., & Hwang, G. (2017). Effects of the Team Competition-Based Ubiquitous Gaming Approach on Students' Interactive Patterns, Collective Efficacy and Awareness of Collaboration and Communication. *Journal of Educational Technology & Society, 20*(1), 87–98.

Cisco. (2017). *Cisco Visual Networking Index: Global Mobile Data Traffic Forecast Update, 2016–2021 White Paper.* Retrieved from http://www.cisco.com/c/en/us/solutions/collateral/service-provider/visual-networking-index-vni/mobile-white-paper-c11-520862.pdf

De Miguel, M. (2005). *Modalidades de enseñanza centradas en el desarrollo de competencias. Orientaciones para promover el cambio metodológico en el Espacio Europeo de Educación Superior.* Oviedo: Universidad de Oviedo.

Díaz, S. (2014). Desarrollo de una ficha de observación para el análisis y evaluación de experiencias educativas en mundo virtuales. *Revista Internacional de Investigación e Innovación Educativa, 2,* 69–82. Retrieved from http://www.upo.es/revistas/index.php/IJERI/article/view/1088

Díaz-Barriga, F., & Hernández, G. (2002). *Estrategias docentes para un aprendizaje significativo. Una interpretación constructivista.* Editorial Macgraw-Hill.

Ditrendia. (2016). *Informe Mobile en España y en el Mundo 2016*. Retrieved from http://www.amic.media/media/files/file_352_1050.pdf

Durall, E., Gros, B., Maina, M., Johnson, L., & Adams, S. (2012). *Perspectivas tecnológicas: educación superior en Iberoamérica 2012-2017*. Austin, TX: The New Media Consortium.

García, B. (2010). Modelos teóricos e indicadores de evaluación educativa. *Sinéctica, 35*, 1-17. Retrieved from http://www.scielo.org.mx/scielo.php?pid=S1665-109X2010000200005&script=sci_arttext&tlng=pt

García, L. M. (2014). Evaluación Formativa de los Aprendizajes en el Contexto Universitario: Resistencias y Paradojas del Profesorado. *Educación XX1, 17*(2), 35-54. Retrieved from http://revistas.uned.es/index.php/educacionXX1/article/view/11478/11418

García-Cabot, A., De-Marcos, L., & García-Lopez, E. (2015). An empirical study on m-learning adaptation: Learning performance and learning contexts. *Computers & Education, 82,* 450-459. 10.1016/j.compedu.2014.12.007

GarridoA. (2013). *Edmodo*. Retrieved from http://edmodo.antoniogarrido.es/

Granados, L., & Mendoza, J. (2014). Construcción de Mundos Virtuales para el Desarrollo de Destrezas de Lateralidad basado en Web3D. *Revista Educación en Ingeniería, 9*(17), 13-25. Retrieved from https://www.educacioneningenieria.org/index.php/edi/article/view/352

Hansen, H. (2005). Choosing evaluation models. A discussion on evaluation design. *Evaluation*, *11*(4), 447–462. doi:10.1177/1356389005060265

Haworth, R. (2016). Personal learning environments: A solution for self-directed learners. *TechTrends*, *60*(4), 359–364. doi:10.1007/s11528-016-0074-z

Heflin, H., Shewmaker, J., & Nguyense, J. (2017). Impact of mobile technology on student attitudes, engagement, and learning. *Computers & Education, 107*, 91-99. 10.1016/j.compedu.2017.01.006

Leclercq, D., & Cabrera, A. (2014). *Ideas e Innovaciones. Dispositivos de evaluación de los aprendizajes en la educación*. Editorial Universitaria.

Lee, J., Lim, C., & Kim, H. (2017). Development of an instructional design model for flipped learning in higher education. *Educational Technology Research and Development*, *65*(2), 427–453. doi:10.1007/s11423-016-9502-1

López, M. (2013). *Aprendizajes, Competencias y TIC*. Editorial Pearson.

Marín, V., Negre, F., & Pérez, A. (2014). Construction of the foundations of the PLE and PLN for collaborative learning. *Comunicar*, *21*(42), 35–43. doi:10.3916/C42-2014-03

Marqués, P. (2013). Impacto de las TIC en la educación: funciones y limitaciones. *3 c TIC: cuadernos de desarrollo aplicados a las TIC, 2*(1), 1-15. Retrieved from https://www.3ciencias.com/wp-content/uploads/2013/01/impacto-de-las-tic.pdf

Ogata, H., Matsuka, Y., El-Bishouty, M. M., & Yano, Y. (2009). LORAMS: Linking physical objects and videos for capturing and sharing learning experiences towards ubiquitous learning. *International Journal of Mobile Learning and Organisation*, *3*(4), 337–350. doi:10.1504/IJMLO.2009.027452

Reimers, F. M. (2015). Taking Action on Global Education. *Proceedings of the Special seminar at UNESCO Bangkok*. Retrieved from www.unescobkk.org/news/article/taking-action-on-global-education

Reynolds, K., Barnhill, D., Sias, J., Young, A., & Greer, F. (2014). Use of the QR Reader to Provide Real-Time Evaluation of Residents Skills Following Surgical Procedures. *Journal of Graduate Medical Education*, *6*(4), 738–741. doi:10.4300/JGME-D-13-00349.1 PMID:26140128

Rodríguez, R., Escribano, J., & Lara, P. (2009). Las TIC como herramienta para desarrollar competencias transversales en el aula. In A. Blanco (Ed.), Desarrollo y Evaluación de Competencias en Educación Superior (pp. 159-178). Madrid: Ediciones Narcea S.A.

Sanz, C. V., Cukierman, U. R., Zangara, M. A., González, A. H., Santángelo, H. N., Rozenhauz, J. C., . . . Ibañez, E. (2007). Integración de la tecnología móvil a los entornos virtuales de enseñanza y de aprendizaje. *II Congreso de Tecnología en Educación y Educación en Tecnología*. Universidad Nacional de La Plata. Retrieved from http://sedici.unlp.edu.ar/handle/10915/19120

Sattolo, I., Lipera, L., Romero, J. C., Cos, S., Figueroa, S., Cisneros, J. A., & Minutella, D. (2016). Elementos interactivos en los mundos virtuales 3 D. *XVIII Workshop de Investigadores en Ciencias de la Computación*. Retrieved from http://sedici.unlp.edu.ar/bitstream/handle/10915/53406/Documento_completo.pdf-PDFA.pdf?sequence=1

Sepúlveda, E., Badilla, M. G., & Careaga, M. (2014). Mobile devices for teaching English as a second–language in Higher Education, the case of DUOC in Chile. *Journal of Mobile Multimedia*, *10*(3 & 4), 234–243.

Silva, J., & Salinas, J. (2014). *Innovando con TIC en la formación inicial docente: aspectos teóricos y casos concretos*. Santiago: Enlaces. Retrieved from http://www.grupotecnologiaeducativa.es/images/LIBROS/ticfid_2014.pdf

Sprague, A. (2016). Improving the ESL Graduate Writing Classroom Using Socrative: (Re) Considering Exit Tickets. *TESOL Journal*, *7*(4), 989–998. doi:10.1002/tesj.295

Tourón, J., & Santiago, R. (2015). Flipped Learning model and the development of talent at school. *Revista de Educación*, *368*, 176-208. Retrieved from http://goo.gl/KYL3TX

Tur, G., Marín, V. I., & Carpenter, J. (2017). Using Twitter in Higher Education in Spain and the USA. *Comunicar*, *25*(51), 19-27. 10.3916/C51-2017-02

United Nations Educational, Scientific and Cultural Organization (UNESCO). (2006). *Using ICT to Develop Literacy. UNESCO ICT in Education Programme*. Bangkok: Phongwarin Printing Ltd. Retrieved from http://unesdoc.unesco.org/images/0014/001464/146426e.pdf

United Nations Educational, Scientific and Cultural Organization (UNESCO). (2013a). *Directrices de la UNESCO para las políticas de aprendizaje móvil*. Retrieved from http://unesdoc.unesco.org/images/0021/002196/219662S.pdf

United Nations Educational, Scientific and Cultural Organization (UNESCO). (2013b). *Enfoques estratégicos sobre las TICS en educación en América Latina y el Caribe*. Santiago, Chile: UNESCO. Retrieved from http://www.unesco.org/new/fileadmin/MULTIMEDIA/FIELD/Santiago/images/ticsesp.pdf

United Nations Educational, Scientific and Cultural Organization (UNESCO). (2015). QINGDAO Declaration. *International conference on ICT and post-2015 education. Seize digital opportunities, lead education transformation*. Retrieved from http://unesdoc.unesco.org/images/0023/002333/233352E.pdf

United Nations Educational, Scientific and Cultural Organization (UNESCO) & ACNUR. (2017). *Mobile learning Week Policy Forum*. Retrieved from http://www.unesco.org/new/fileadmin/MULTIMEDIA/HQ/ED/pdf/mlw2017_PolicyForumOutcomes.pdf

Vázquez, E., Martín, E., & Castrillo, M. (2016). Analysis of PLEs' Implementation under OER Design as a Productive Teaching-Learning Strategy in Higher Education. A Case Study at Universidad Nacional de Educación a Distancia. *Digital Education Review, 29*, 62-85. Retrieved from https://eric.ed.gov/?id=EJ1106187

Wagner, D., Castillo, N., Murphy, K., Crofton, M., & Tuz, F. (2014). Mobiles for literacy in developing countries: An effectiveness framework. *Prospects*, *44*(1), 119–132. doi:10.1007/s11125-014-9298-x

Woodill, G. (2011). *The mobile learning edge. Tools and Technologies for Developing your Teams*. EBSCO Publishing, Inc.

WTIS. (2015). *World Telecommunication/ICT Indicators Symposium*. Retrieved from http://www.itu.int/en/ITU-D/Statistics/Pages/events/wtis2015/default.aspx

KEY TERMS AND DEFINITIONS

Flipped Classroom: Pedagogical model that considers learning as the center of the educational process, where the student has an active role, and teacher is the learning facilitator who use different active methodologies to promote the integration of different knowledge.

ICT: The forms of technology that are used to transmit, store, create, share or exchange information (UNESCO, 2006).

Immersive Virtual Worlds: Simulation places that offer new environments to interact, focusing on the users themselves, their identity and the actions they can perform (Díaz, 2014).

Intranet: A private network accessible only to an organization's staff.

Personal Learning Environments (PLE): The tools, communities, and services that constitute the individual educational platforms learners use to direct their own learning and pursue educational goals.

Ubiquitous Learning: Learning anywhere, anytime and is therefore closely associated with mobile technologies.

Web 2.0: Knowing also as Social Web, comprises those websites that facilitate information sharing, interoperability, user-centered design and collaboration on the World Wide Web.

Chapter 4
Business Intelligence in Secondary Education:
Data-Driven Innovation by Quality Measurement

Marco Spruit
Utrecht University, The Netherlands

Tiffany Adriana
Utrecht University, The Netherlands

ABSTRACT

This research assesses the education quality factors in secondary schools using a business intelligence approach. We operationalize each layer of the business intelligence framework to identify the stakeholders and components relevant to education quality. The resulting Education Quality Indicator (EQI) framework consists of seven Critical Success Factors (CSFs) and is measured through twenty-eight Key Performance Indicators (KPIs). The EQI framework was evaluated through expert interviews and a survey, and uncovers that the most important factor in assuring education quality is a teacher's ability to communicate with students. Furthermore, a feasibility analysis was conducted in a Dutch student monitoring information system. The results pave the way towards attainable and data-driven innovation in secondary education towards personalized student and teacher performance management using business intelligence technologies, which may ultimately integrate a wide variety of data sources from environmental sensors to wearables to optimally understand each individual student and teacher.

1. INTRODUCTION

Even though many research works have been conducted to assess quality in education, there is no standard on how to measure quality of education (Becket & Brookes, 2005). In the Netherlands, there exists a protocol for measuring education quality in schools, which is conducted by the Education Inspectorate by investigating various aspects that affect the education process. However, this inspection is conducted

DOI: 10.4018/978-1-5225-4191-2.ch004

on a yearly basis. This means that the measurement of a school's strategy can only be done on a yearly basis, which is not ideal for schools as they cannot see whether their operational activities are conducted towards the right direction. Our research aims to provide a 'traffic light' which warns when school activities are not going toward the desired goal. This is done by employing a business intelligence framework and process model as first proposed by Spruit & Adriana (2015) to help schools direct their policy. We aim to answer the following research question: 'how can a business intelligence process be developed to assess the quality of education in secondary schools?'

2. RESEARCH METHODS

This research follows the Design Science research model by Hevner, March, Park, & Ram (2004) to create a framework that encompasses all the important components and stakeholders of the education process. As a first step of this research, a literature study is conducted in both the topic of education quality and business intelligence. In addition, we review the Dutch education system as this will be the exemplary environment for our research. Next, a semi-structured interview method (Longhurst, 2010; DiCicco-Bloom & Crabtree, 2006) is employed to gather data from experts in the field of education. The interviewees involved in this research include policy advisors of a school group, quality assurance personnel of a school group, independent researchers on education management and quality, and one founder of an education quality assessment organization. After conducting interviews, we develop our initial framework, which is then validated through a questionnaire survey to secondary school directors in the Netherlands. The questionnaires handed out in this research are online and aimed for school directors of the different level of secondary schools in the Netherlands.

3. THEORY

3.1. The Dutch Education System

In the Netherlands, the education system is divided into three parts: primary, secondary, and tertiary education, as shown in Figure 1 (Scheerens, Luyten, & Ravens, 2011; Dutch Eurydice Unit, 2007). The focus of this research is on secondary education, which starts at the age of twelve. After finishing primary education, students will enter one of the three types of secondary education, namely VMBO (pre-vocational secondary education), HAVO (senior general secondary education), and VWO (pre-university education). Pupils move after primary education to one of the type of schools described above on the basis of their achievement levels within primary education (Scheerens et al., 2011).

VMBO (*Voorbereidend Middelbaar Beroepsonderwijs*) or pre-vocational secondary education combines vocational training with theoretical education in languages, mathematics, history, arts, and sciences. VMBO lasts for four years and has four different levels, based on the combination portion of practical vocational training and theoretical education (School Choice International, 2008) which students should choose at the end of the second year for the continuation after *basisvorming*. The different levels are:

1. Theoretische Leerweg (VMBO-t), or theoretical learning path, is the most theoretical program of the pre-vocational education.

Figure 1. The Dutch education system
Based on Scheerens et al. (2011).

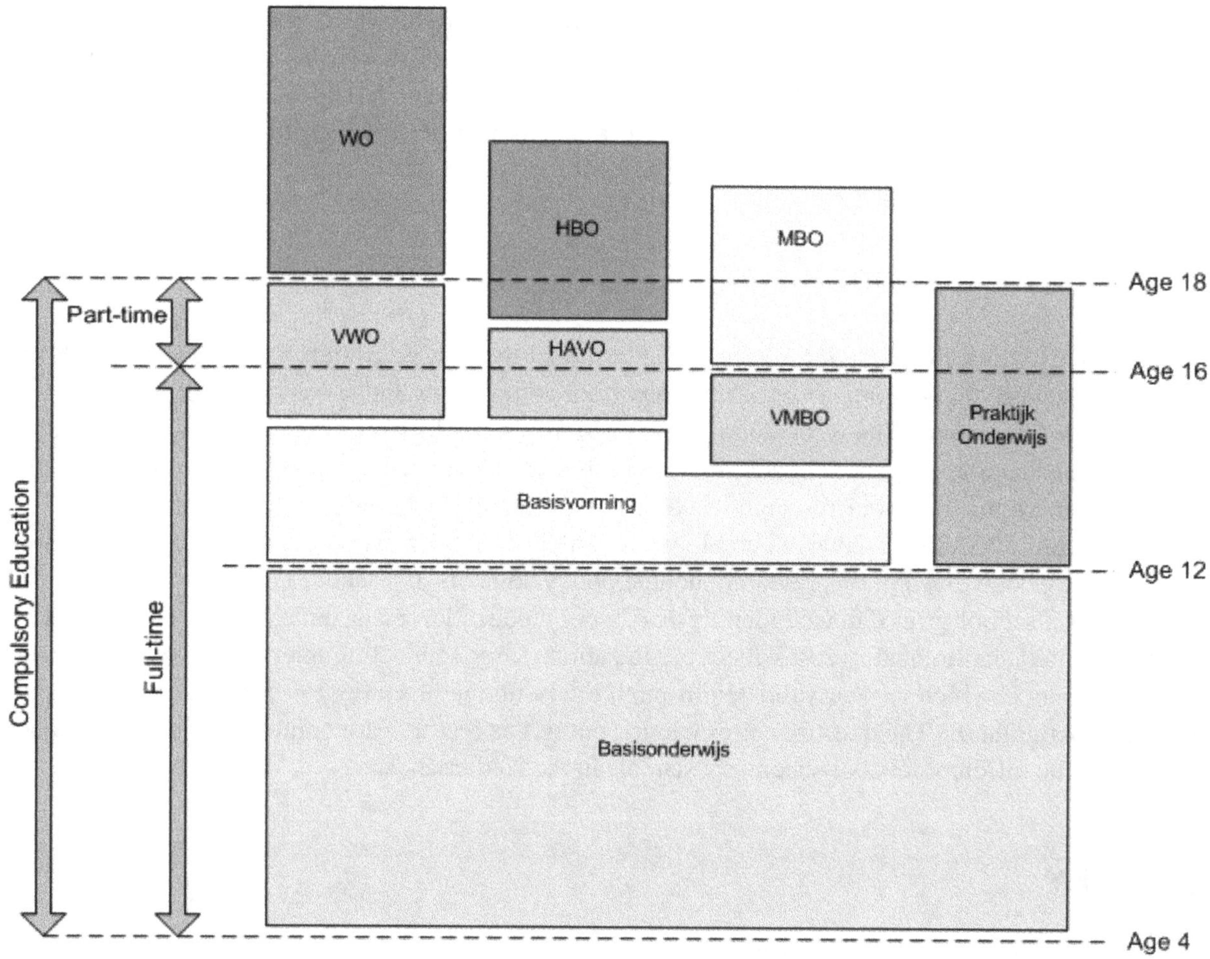

2. Kaderberoepsgerichte Leerweg (VMBO-k), or middle management-oriented learning path, is a middle-management program which teaches theory and vocational education equally.
3. Gemengde Leerweg (VMBO-g), or combined learning path, is a mixed program whose focus is between the theoretical and the middle management-oriented paths. In practice, the existence of this learning path is very small as not many schools with this path exist.
4. Basisberoepsgerichte Leerweg (VMBO-b), or basic profession-oriented learning path, equips and prepares students for vocational training in the higher level of education.

HAVO or *Hoger Algemeen Voortgezet Onderwijs* which literally means senior general secondary education is the secondary education which is intended to prepare students for professional higher education. This type of secondary education has a duration of five years. After finishing education in HAVO, students may continue to professional higher education (HBO), also known as the polytechnic level.

VWO stands for *Voorbereidend Wetenschappelijk Onderwijs*, which means pre-university secondary education, is the secondary educational system which prepares the students for academic higher education (WO) or generally known as the university level. This education lasts for six years and is attended by students from the age of 12-18. There are three different types of VWO available, namely *Atheneum*, *Gymnasium*, and TVWO. TVWO stands for *Tweetalig* VWO, where lectures are given in two languages: Dutch and a different language.

In both HAVO and VWO, after completing the *basisvorming* in their first three years of school, HAVO and VWO students should choose one of the four profiles which they find most suitable. The four profiles that they could choose from are as follows:

1. C&M (*Cultuur en Maatschappij*) or culture and society emphasizes on arts and foreign languages. The mathematics classes focus on statistics and stochastic.
2. E&M (*Economie en Maatschappij*) or economics and society emphasizes on social sciences, economy, and history. The mathematics classes focus on statistics and stochastics.
3. N&G (*Natuur en Gezondheid*) or science and health emphasizes on biology and natural sciences. The mathematic classes focus on algebra and geometry.
4. N&T (*Natuur en Techniek*) or science and technology emphasizes on the natural sciences. The mathematics classes focus on algebra and geometry.

3.2. Education Quality

Many research works have been done in the topic of educational quality, both in defining what quality in education means and in the effort for measuring the quality in education sector. This research uses the definition and differentiation of education quality by Harvey and Green (1993), which groups the concept of quality into five discrete but interrelated ways of thinking, as follows:

1. **Quality as Exceptional:** The term exceptional means that quality is something special, which has three variations. The first one is the traditional notion of quality as distinctive, where quality is apodictic and there is no benchmark to measure quality. This is useless in term of assessing quality in education, because it doesn't provide definable measure. Secondly, quality is viewed as embodied in excellence which is exceeding very high standards that are almost unattainable. The final view of quality as exceptional dilutes the notion of excellence, as quality product is defined as one that has passed a set of quality checks based on attainable criteria that are designed to reject 'defective' items. In this view it could be said that quality is the result of scientific quality control, and quality is improved if standards are raised.
2. **Quality as Perfection or Consistency:** This concept of quality focuses on processes and sets specifications that it aims to meet perfectly. The term 'zero defects' is used in this concept, and defines quality by the ability to conform to a particular specification perfectly and consistently. Furthermore, this view accentuates on prevention rather than inspection and always tries to ensure that things are done right the first time. It is by promoting a quality culture that zero defects could be achieved, where everybody in the organization is responsible for quality, and not just the quality controllers.
3. **Quality as Fitness for Purpose:** In this concept, quality is judged in terms of the extent to which the product or service fits its purpose. However, this view raises many questions such as the relativity of whose purpose should be fulfilled, and how fitness itself is assessed. This view is differentiated into two sub-concepts, which are fitness for purpose based on customer specification and fitness for

purpose based on mission or target. The customer itself is not clear in the education sector, whether it is the service user (i.e. student), or those who pay for the service (e.g. government, employers, parents), or whether other stakeholders (e.g. academic staff) should be included as the customer.

4. **Quality as Value for Money:** When quality is related to value for money, the main consideration is effectiveness. There are two ways to measure quality in terms of value for money: performance indicators which provide a measure of accountability for the treasury, and customer charters which encapsulate accountability to the customers.
5. **Quality as Transformative:** The transformative view of quality is rooted in the notion of 'qualitative change', a fundamental change of form. Education is not a service for a customer but an ongoing process of transformation of the participant, be it student or researcher. This leads to two notions of transformative quality in education, enhancing the participant and empowering the participant. Enhancing the participant values the quality of education as the one that effects changes on the participants through added-value and, thereby, presumably enhances them. Empowerment of participants involves giving power to participants to influence their own transformation, which means the ability for them to make decisions.

3.3. Business Intelligence

3.3.1. Business Intelligence Definition

Many research works propose different definitions of business intelligence (Negash & Gray, 2008; Power, 2007; Lönnqvist and Pirttimäki, 2006; Ranjan, 2009; Gangadharan & Swami, 2004; Watson and Wixom, 2007). From these definitions there are differences in defining business intelligence based on the point of view. In general it could be grouped into two broad patterns, the managerial and technical viewpoints (Ghazanfari, Rouhani, Jafari, & Akhavan; 2011). From the managerial approach, business intelligence is viewed as a process in which data gathered from inside and outside the enterprise are integrated in order to generate information relevant to the decision-making process. In contrast, the technical approach considers business intelligence as a set of tools that support the process in the managerial approach, focusing more on the technologies, algorithms, and tools, instead of on the process (e.g. Spruit, Vroon, and Batenburg; 2014).

From the various definitions and different views there is one underlying common concept, which is the purpose of business intelligence: to facilitate management with information that supports better decision-making. Business intelligence controls, manages, and delivers abundant business information – around and within an organization – about an organization and its business process.

Further, Ghazanfari et al. (2011) added a third approach to business intelligence definitions, namely the system enabler approach. This third approach focuses on value-added capabilities in supporting shared information (Rouhani, Asgari, Mirhosseini; 2012).

As for the purpose of this research, the managerial view of business intelligence is followed. We define Business intelligence as

... the process and methods used to improve the timeliness and quality of inputs to the decision process by first identifying and then processing information into condensed and useful managerial knowledge and intelligence. (Roekel, Linders, Raja, Reboullet, & Ommerborn, 2009; Lönnqvist & Pirttimäki, 2006; Negash, 2004)

3.3.2. Business Intelligence Framework

Wasmann and Spruit (2012) followed Roekel et al. (2009) in proposing a business intelligence framework which consists of several layers as shown in Figure 2. These layers are important in implementing business intelligence as it connects the vision of an organization with measurable data in the form of scorecards and dashboards. Every layer is connected to each other in a way that could be summarized as follows:

- Mission and vision statements lead to business goals and strategy. Critical Success Factors (CSFs) define the prerequisite to reach the goals, while strategy states how the goals should be reached.
- Business goals and imposed strategy lead to objectives and a policy (business plan). Key Performance Indicators (KPIs) define how the objectives will be measured, and the imposed policy will be stated with business rules.
- KPIs will be presented by scorecards and dashboards, among others. Business rules may be enforced by logic in the operational systems but may also be applied within the business intelligence environment.

3.3.3. Business Intelligence Process

The objective of a business intelligence process is to refine business data and information into useful and valuable knowledge and intelligence for decision making (Pirttimäki, 2007; Sangar & Iahad, 2013). Many researches proposed different process steps and models in implementing business intelligence. Literature analysis shows that the theoretical process models proposed by academics and consultants in business intelligence field (e.g., Gilad & Gilad, 1985; Herring, 1999; Vleugel, Spruit & Daal, 2010) are quite similar to each other (Pirttimäki, 2007; Sangar & Iahad, 2013). In general, the business intelligence process model could be summarized in the cyclical model proposed by Salonen & Pirttimaki (2005) as shown in Figure 3. The cyclical model starts with planning based on corporate needs, where goals, targets, and priorities are defined in order to identify what information is relevant to those goals and will help direct the choice of sources; then ethically collecting reliable information from valid sources, then analyzing the data to form intelligence in conjunction with strategic planning and market research. Finally, if the intelligence is to have value, it must be disseminated in a form that's clear and understandable, and will then be utilized by decision-maker.

Figure 2. BI framework
By Wasmann and Spruit (2012).

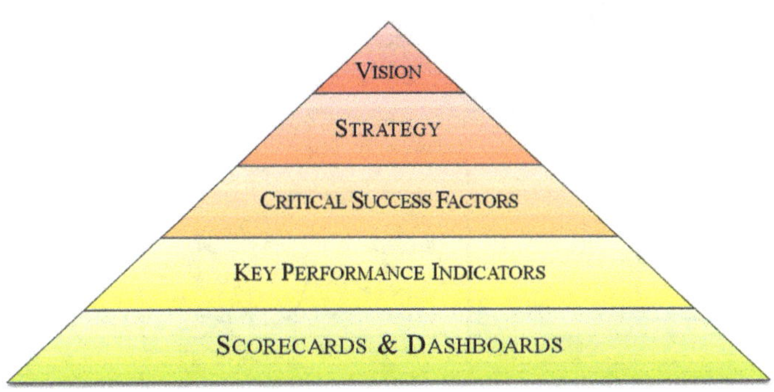

Figure 3. BI process
By Salonen & Pirttimaki (2005).

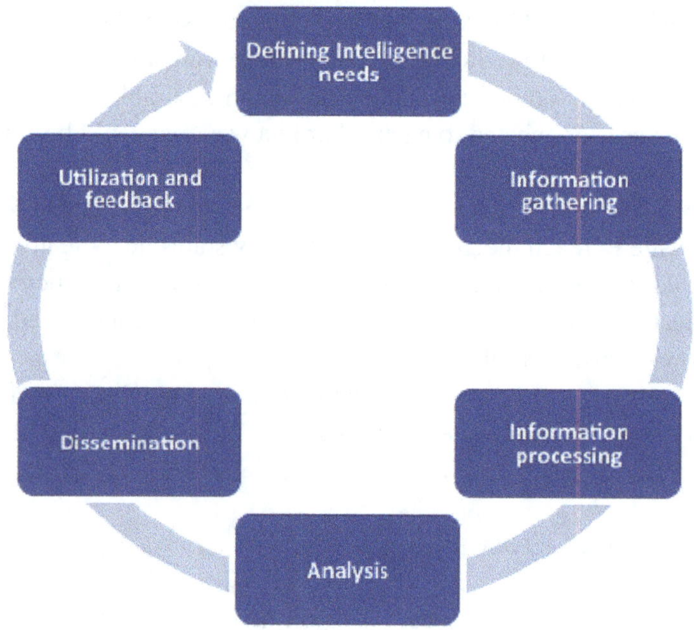

3.3.4. Business Intelligence Architecture

In their book, Sharda & Delen (2013) introduced a high-level architecture of business intelligence as depicted in Figure 4. They explain that a business intelligence system has four major components, namely a data warehouse, business analytics, business performance management, and user interface. The data warehouse environment has its own data source, which is "the cornerstone of any medium-to-large BI

Figure 4. BI architecture
By Sharda & Delen (2013).

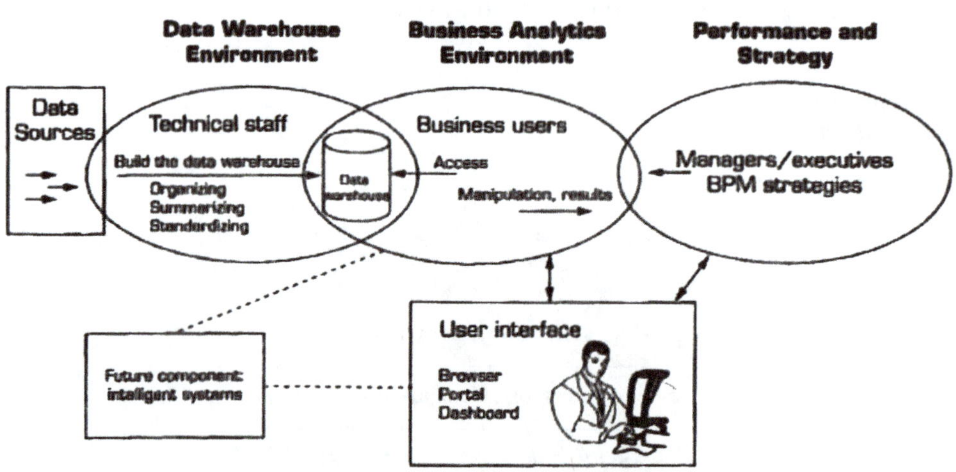

system" and is managed by the technical staff. The business analytics environment allows business users to work and manipulate the data and information in a data warehouse using variety of tools and techniques. Performance and strategy environment which includes business performance management allows a top-down enforcement of corporate-wide strategy, so that the BI system includes forecasting and planning based on specific organization need. The fourth component, user interface, is represented by an information broadcasting tool such as a dashboard, corporate portal, digital cockpits, and other visualization tools. It presents at-a-glance view of the organization's health, as information from multiple areas is integrated here.

3.4. Implementation in This Research

This research follows the six step business intelligence process model by Salonen & Pirttimäki (Figure 3), in putting into practice and translating the business intelligence framework (Figure 2). Correlation between the process model and the layers of business intelligence framework is summarized in Table 1.

4. RESULTS

4.1. Interviews

As an initial step for this research, semi-structured interviews were conducted with interviewees that have expertise in education sector. The number of interviews conducted was not predetermined, but instead interviews were conducted until a so-called theoretical saturation was achieved. Glaser and Strauss (as cited in Guest, Bunce, & Johnson, 2006) defined theoretical saturation as the point at which no addi-

Table 1. Our research operationalization which connects the BI framework and BI process model

<table>
<tr><th>BI Process Model Step</th><th>Explanation</th><th>BI Framework Layer</th><th>Research Activity</th><th>Deliverable</th></tr>
<tr><td>Defining intelligence needs</td><td>This step involves identification of the quality definition, which will direct the focus of this research</td><td>Vision, strategy</td><td>Literature study, Initial expert interview</td><td>Literature review</td></tr>
<tr><td>Information gathering</td><td>• Analyze previous research works in education quality about factors that affect education quality
• Investigate factors that affect education quality based on best practice</td><td rowspan="2">CSF, KPI</td><td rowspan="2">Literature study, Expert interview, Questionnaire</td><td rowspan="2">Education quality framework</td></tr>
<tr><td>Information processing</td><td>Connect the gathered information and translate into measurable way of communicating them</td></tr>
<tr><td>Analysis</td><td>Identify available (and not-available) measurement data relevant to identified CSF and KPI</td><td></td><td rowspan="3">Feasibility analysis through expert interview</td><td>IS data model</td></tr>
<tr><td>Dissemination</td><td>Connect data to components of the framework</td><td rowspan="2">Dashboard</td><td rowspan="2">Dashboard mockup</td></tr>
<tr><td>Utilization and feedback</td><td>Translate data into a practical way of communicating information gathered</td></tr>
</table>

tional data are being found that could develop properties of the category, or in another word, where no new information could be added. For this research, seven were found to be sufficient to reach theoretical saturation in the initial interview as a starting point for this research. The overview of interviewees involved is summarized in Table 2.

There were no strict guidelines and lists of questions for the interviews, but they did cover a predetermined list of topics. Because they were initial interviews, the topics prepared included:

1. Understanding how education quality could be best described in the field of secondary education.
2. Discovering the important stakeholders that should be taken into consideration in measuring education quality.
3. The important components in education process that affect quality of education.

At the end of each interview, interviewees were left with a long list of indicators about education quality which we gathered from previous research works on education quality. Interviewees were asked to give a rating and choose what indicators they consider important and relevant in the context of secondary education in the Netherlands. The results have been used in building the framework.

From the interviews conducted, the largest portion of discussion about education quality definition directs towards the fifth dimension of quality as transformation. All interviewees mentioned the importance of enhancing students with knowledge and preparing them for education continuation through empowerment. Aside from cognitive development of students, it is also very important to focus on the social development of students. Students should be able to function well in society, and school should help students to identify their potential and make the best out of each student. Based on these empirical findings, this research continues by focusing on the fifth dimension of education quality which is quality as transformation.

With regards to stakeholder selection, there are variations in the identified stakeholders with four overlapping stakeholders that all interviewees listed as the important stakeholders. The four stakeholders are (1) Students (2) Teachers (3) School management (4) External stakeholder, which includes parents

Table 2. Overview of interviewees

Expert	Description
1	Senior policy advisor in a secondary school group in the Netherlands, is responsible for education quality assurance
2	Senior policy advisor in a secondary school group in the Netherlands, is responsible for education quality assurance
3	Independent education management professional, a researcher and advisor in education quality, and has published number of papers about education quality in the Netherlands
4	Director of accreditation services in the council of international schools, has been actively involved in setting up guidelines and conducting accreditation of secondary schools around the world
5	Co-founder of an education quality assessment organization in the Netherlands, has been actively involved in projects for assessing schools' education quality. Currently, quality assessment projects conducted are focused in the higher education level
6	Expert in performance management, co-creator of a well-known dashboard to measure education quality in primary schools which supports the PDCA cycle
7	Advisor in education governance board. Interviewee has a coaching and consultancy firm that helps school leaders monitor education quality through an educational scorecard (which is based on the balanced scorecard). Interviewee is the co-creator of a well-known dashboard to monitor education quality in primary school which supports the PDCA cycle

and future employers; with the emphasis mostly on teacher. Note that the term future employer in this context is not limited to only people from the labor market that will employ graduates of school, but also the continuation level of education related. As the focus of this research is on secondary education, therefore the continuation level of education would be the higher education (university level). Aside from these stakeholders, some interviewee also listed government, non-teaching staff, alumni, and society as stakeholders that should be included in assuring education quality.

Furthermore, discussion about the education quality component ended with a conclusion that there are generally four components that could be identified and taken into consideration in assuring good quality of education. These components are (1) Curriculum, (2) Student, (3) Teacher, and (4) Circumstances. Circumstances include the organization factor of the school, the environment where the school is, government, and other components affecting education process. All interviewees agree that teachers are the heart of education and play the most important part in education process.

4.2. Education Quality Success Factors

Many research studies have been conducted in the topic of education quality and how to improve it by identifying the characteristics of a good education quality. This research tries to synthesize and compare components from previous research works that are considered relevant, and identify success factors that should be included in assuring education quality at the secondary school level. Selection of the previous works is based on the identification made in the expert interviews, with regards to the definition of quality, component of education, and stakeholders.

Table 3 shows a comparison and grouping of the characteristics based on previous research and education quality guidelines used by different organizations. Based on this characteristic grouping, critical success factors for this research are generated.

4.2.1. Curriculum Organization

Curriculum organization is a very important success factor for schools in the Netherlands, because the Dutch government only sets a certain target that schools have to achieve. As to the process of achieving those targets, every school has complete independence in using any approach they see fit. Therefore, in assuring education quality in the Netherlands, curriculum organization plays a very important role. Aligned with the interview result, our literature review also showed that curriculum is considered important as it is included in all previous researches and guidelines used for this research. Curriculum organization includes design of curriculum, content of curriculum and its philosophy. In their work, Gatfield, Barker, & Graham (1999) include 'academic instruction' as a factor. This factor consists of 10 variables which includes course content, intellectual stimulation, and variety of courses.

4.2.2. Delivery Method

As found from the interviews, the ability of the teacher to connect with a student is very crucial in assuring good education quality. This is supported by literature, where all literature used also include this as a characteristic of a good school. Different terms are identified from the literature, where some also include it in a more general factor such as teaching and learning as seen in CIS and QAA Guideline. As suggested by Horsburgh (1999), a student's learning experience is highly impacted by how teachers teach.

Table 3. Education quality success factors

Owlia & Aspinwall (1996)	Gatfield, Barker, & Graham (1999)	Horsburgh (1999)	CIS Guide	QAA	Chua (2004)	Excellente Scholen	This Research
Attitude	Guidance	Teaching staff and how they teach and assess	Faculty and Support Staff	Student Support and Guidance	Concern for Students	Organization of the Educational Process	Teacher Attitude
Competence					Professor's Knowledgeability		Teacher Competence
Delivery	Academic Instruction		Teaching and Learning	Teaching, learning	Teaching and Learning		Delivery Method
					Instruction Medium		
					Content and		
		The curriculum intent and philosophy			Delivery of Course Units		Curriculum Organization
Content				Curriculum Design, Content, and Organization	Accuracy of Curriculum Content		
Tangibles	Guidance		School Guiding Statements	Learning Resources			School Infrastructure
	Campus Life	Resource Issues	Operational Systems				
			School Culture and Partnerships for Learning	Quality Management and Enhancement	Social Activities		Organizational Support
	Academic Instruction	Teaching staff and the environment which they teach	Access to Teaching and Learning			The Circumstances in which the School Works	
		Program Specific Internal Quality Monitoring				Relation Between the Organization of the Educational Process and Result	
	Recognition					School Excellence Policy	
Reliability		Leadership	Governance and Leadership				
		Student Expectations		Student Progression and Achievement	Financially Rewarding Job		Student Achievement
					Placement		
					Academic	Exam Result	
				Assessment	Performance		
					Assessments		

Clarity of explanation, the level at which the learning material is pitched, and clear teaching organization and goals (Ramsden, 1991) are very important and could determine the quality of the teaching process. Other aspects viewed relevant for this CSF include 'instruction medium' (Chua, 2004), the extent to which a course is offered in a proper sequence (Mergen, Grant, &Widrick, 2000), and 'effective presentation' (Owlia & Aspinwall, 1996). However, our study found that there is no single instructional strategy that is successful, teachers who are able to use a broad repertoire of approaches skillfully are typically most successful (Darling-Hammond, 1999). Students should also be given an opportunity to become involved in taking responsibility for their own learning (Borahan & Ziarati, 2002). This is relevant to the fifth dimension of education quality by Harvey & Green (1993).

4.2.3. Organizational Support

In the context of this research, organizational support includes all policy and regulations made by school management – both school and school group level. Support from the organization is very important, with regards to quality control and assuring that regulations are set to support the education process fully (Scheerens et al., 2011; UNESCO, 2004). Recognition of school and having a good reputation is also included here, as it is considered one of the characteristics of good school according to Gatfield, Barker, & Graham (1999) and the guideline of *Excellente Scholen* (i.e. 'excellent schools'). Organizational support also includes quality management policies applied to teachers, non-teaching staff, and students; which will assure a good school climate for education process (Expert 6). Furthermore, schools should pay attention to students with low-ability by allocating additional resources for those students, as it will help improve their performance (de Haan, 2012; Card & Payne, 2002).

4.2.4. School Infrastructure

Tangibles also play an important role in having a smoothly conducted learning process. Student would be able to have a more optimal learning experience when there are sufficient facilities supporting the education process. This includes availability of classrooms, required equipment such as a computer and laboratory access, and also a clear guideline for students (UNESCO, 2004).

The condition of the school building itself has the effect on teaching and learning effectiveness. Comfortable classroom temperature and noise level are very important in efficient student performance; as students attending schools in better condition outperforms students in substandard buildings (Earthman, 2002). Furthermore, facility with good quality affects the school climate which impacted student achievement (Uline & Tschannen-Moran, 2008).

4.2.5. Student Achievement

The quality of education could clearly be seen from what the students achieve after undergoing the education process. This is a very interesting subject as it is currently being a political highlight in the Netherlands (Experts 6, 7). Literature study also shows that this is a very important aspect to highlight as it shows the product of education process, which could be seen through student academic result, transition from school to work (e.g., youth unemployment and employment by level of education attainment), and the social and labor-market outcomes of education (Scheerens et al., 2011; Gibbs, 2010). Other terms used in different research works include student progression, performance and degree classification, and retention and persistence.

Aside from the study result, the preliminary assessment of student's knowledge is seen to be important, which includes creating an admission requirement and appropriate faculty qualifications to filter selection of students (Chua, 2004; Mergen et al., 2000).

4.2.6. Teacher Attitude

Teachers are the heart of education, therefore it is very crucial for teachers to have a positive attitude. As discovered from interviews, teachers should be able to communicate and connect emotionally with students as their behavior in classroom affects how student receive education (Darling-Hammond, 1999). They should be able to motivate, understand, and give guidance to their students. As seen in Table 4, all research includes this factor as one of the characteristics of a good school.

This includes having teachers that could connect emotionally with student, have empathy, and are open to students (Experts 1, 2, 3, 5; Ramsden, 1991; UNESCO, 2004). Several ways could be used in measuring teacher effectiveness and attitude including student, peer, alumni, employer, and/or administrator ratings, self evaluation, and student interviews (Berk, 2005); but it is proven that alumni and student ratings evidence substantially greater validity than self-evaluation, colleague, and trained observer ratings (Howard, Conway, & Maxwell, 1985).

4.2.7. Teacher Competence

As solicited from interviews, a teacher plays a key role in assuring the education quality as they are the heart of education, as stated by Experts 1 and 2. Therefore, it is very important to assure the competency of the teacher. Expert 3 explains that the teacher's qualification, in terms of the level of the teacher's previous education, is an important aspect to focus on to assure the quality of the teacher. This is also supported by literature as stated in Owlia & Aspinwall (1996) which includes competence as one of the required factors for education quality, while Chua (2004) identifies this characteristic with the term 'Professor's Knowledgeability'.

Darling-Hammond (1999) in her research shows that differential teacher effectiveness is a strong determinant of difference in student learning, far outweighing the effects of differences in class size. Variables that affect a teacher's competence include measures of academic ability, years of education, years of teaching experience, and certification status. Furthermore, she concluded that "when student characteristics are held constant, the relationship of teachers' qualifications to student achievement is even more pronounced … [as study] found that differences in teacher qualifications (educational degrees, certification status, and experience) accounted for approximately 90% of the total variation in average school-level student achievement."

In the Netherlands itself, the teacher qualification system is already in use in secondary schools to differentiate their competence. The qualifications include 1st degree teacher, 2nd degree teacher, under qualified, and unqualified teacher. This differentiation is determined based on the education that they have received, with 1st degree teacher being the highest qualification.

4.3. Initial Framework

As explained in section 4.1., the interviewees were asked to give ratings on a list of indicators gathered from previous research work on education quality. The selection of research publications selected includes Becket & Brookes (2005); Borahan & Ziarati (2002); Chua (2004); Gatfield, Barker, & Graham (1999); Gibbs (2010); Horsburgh (1999); Owlia & Aspinwall (1998); Tam (2001); and Widrick et al. (2002). The ratings given were based on a 5-points Likert scale according to their importance, with 1 being very unimportant and 5 being very important. Furthermore, they were also asked to add other indicators that they find relevant in this context but not yet included in the list. The aim of this process is to see what indicators are considered important by the experts, which is used as a base for creating the initial framework.

The information gathered about the importance of indicators is then combined with the identified CSFs to create a framework constructed with a list of performance indicators. Each performance indicator is linked to a suitable critical success factor. These performance indicators are listed along with the possible measurement and potential data source needed, attached in Appendix A.

4.4. Validation of Framework

For the validation of framework, an online survey was conducted on secondary school directors through a questionnaire. In the questionnaire, respondents are provided with the CSF and KPI list from the initial framework. For each KPI they were asked to give a rating using 5 points Likert-scale with regards to the importance, where 1 being very unimportant and 5 is very important. Furthermore, respondents were asked to submit additional KPIs if necessary. The goal of this online survey is two folds: (1) to check if the framework created are found to be suitable in the daily school activity environment; and (2) to see the prioritization of the KPI and CSF components in practice in assuring a good education quality.

4.4.1. Survey Respondents

An invitation was sent out to 244 directors from all types of secondary schools. Schools were chosen based on their rank given by the so-called Elsevier rank of good schools, by focusing on schools that get a good review. In 2013 Elsevier published a rank of good quality secondary schools in the Netherlands, titled *Beste Scholen*, i.e. 'best schools'. From the invitation sent out, 35 responses were received from directors of different school types. In general, one respondent manages more than one school type. But there is one respondent who manages only one school type. Furthermore, there were also two respondents who are a director of a so-called *Praktijkonderwijs School* which is out of the scope of this research. But since he also manages other type of schools which are relevant to this research, the response is still included in the analysis. The list of respondents' school type and the related information are summarized in Table 4.

In the questionnaire, respondents are requested to add other relevant KPIs that are not included in the initial framework for each CSF. From the feedback received, only two respondents added three extra KPIs (in total) to the list. When analyzed, all three indicators are already represented by another KPI in the list and are a rephrasing of the same purpose. Therefore it is not necessary to add extra KPIs to the existing list, and it is considered complete.

Table 4. Respondents of the online survey

School Type Directed	Number of Students	Province	School Area
HAVO, VWO	1326	Limburg	South
HAVO, VWO	1571	Limburg	South
VMBO-t, VMBO-k, VMBO-b, HAVO	334	Zeeland	South
VMBO-t, VMBO-k, VMBO-b, HAVO, VWO, Praktijkonderwijs	3100	Zeeland	South
VMBO-t, HAVO, VWO	615	Groningen	North
VMBO-t, VMBO-k, VMBO-b, HAVO, VWO,	265	Friesland	North
HAVO, VWO	722	Groningen	North
VMBO-t, VMBO-k, VMBO-b, HAVO, VWO	2100	Limburg	South
VMBO-t, VMBO-k, VMBO-b	1000	Drenthe	North
VMBO-t, VMBO-k, VMBO-b	530	Gelderland	Centre
VMBO-t, HAVO, VWO	1600		
VMBO-t, VMBO-k, VMBO-b, HAVO, VWO	1650	Noord-Holland	North
HAVO, VWO	1500	Noord-Holland	North
VMBO-t, HAVO, VWO	1325	Utrecht	Centre
VMBO-t, VMBO-k, VMBO-b, HAVO, VWO	2460	Utrecht	Centre
VMBO-t, VMBO-k, VMBO-b, LWOO	611	Utrecht	Centre
HAVO, VWO	1500	Utrecht	Centre
VMBO-t, HAVO, VWO	1800	Utrecht	Centre
HAVO, VWO, VWO-plus	1500	Utrecht	Centre
VMBO-t, VMBO-k, VMBO-b, HAVO, VWO, Praktijkonderwijs	5300	Zuid-Holland	Centre
VMBO-t, VMBO-k, VMBO-b	510	Gelderland	Centre
VMBO-t, VMBO-k, VMBO-b, HAVO, VWO	2.025	Zuid-Holland	Centre
VMBO-t	433	Friesland	North
VMBO-t, HAVO, VWO, TVWO	667	Flevoland	North
VWO, gymnasium	1170	Zuid-Holland	Centre
VMBO-k, VMBO-b, vmbo gl	n/a	Noord-Holland	North
Gymnasium	1863	Zuid-Holland	Centre
VWO	825	Noord-Holland	North
VMBO-t, VMBO-k, VMBO-b, HAVO, VWO	1850	Utrecht	Centre
VMBO-t, HAVO, VWO	n/a	Noord-Brabant	South
VMBO-t, VMBO-k, VMBO-b, HAVO, VWO	1400	Flevoland	North
VMBO-t, HAVO, VWO	n/a	Noord-Brabant	South
VMBO-t	350	Zuid-Holland	Centre
HAVO, VWO	1200	Noord-Brabant	South
VMBO-t, VMBO-k, VMBO-b, HAVO, VWO	1850	Gelderland	Centre

4.4.2. General Response Analysis

The first analysis performed is to see the average score of the survey respondents in general. For each CSF, an average score is calculated from the total response received with the result as shown in Table 5. For each CSF the Cronbach's Alpha value is calculated using SPSS 17 to test inter-item reliability, which means assuring that individual items would produce results consistent with the overall score. Cronbach's Alpha value is calculated for the KPI constructing each CSF. A value of Cronbach's Alpha around 0.7 and greater indicates a reliable scale (Field, 2009). Since the values of Cronbach's Alpha for all items are in the range, it is acceptable and all factors are considered reliable.

A bar graph is presented in Figure 5 to give an overview of the average scores of the CSFs. It could be seen that each CSF is scored quite highly – around 4 in a scale of 1-5. This is quite expected as the CSF list was derived based on interviews with experts in the education quality field, and the most important factors and components were chosen. Therefore, respondents might find every factor to be important in assuring education quality. From test descriptive, the two most important CSFs listed are 'Teacher Attitude' and 'Delivery Method'.

4.4.3. Analysis per School Type

Further analysis is done on different school type groups. For this purpose, respondents are differentiated into two groups based on their school type: theoretical and practical schools. Schools that have VMBO-t, HAVO, and VWO levels in their school are included in the theoretical group. As well as schools that only have HAVO and VWO levels. All VMBO schools are included in the practical group. VMBO-t is included in either theoretical or practical group, depending on what other levels are in that school. Based on this differentiation, the theoretical group has 17 schools assigned to it and the remaining 18 schools is included in the practical group.

Summary of the score average from both groups is summarized in a bar graph shown in Figure 6. Because all scores are quite high (above 3.5), this graph uses the minimum value of 3 to give a clearer view of the differences between both groups.

Table 5. General response

Item Statistics				Cronbach's Alpha
	Mean	**Std. Deviation**	**N**	
Average score for Teacher Competence CSF	4.0000	.57522	35	.659
Average score for Teacher Attitude CSF	4.3571	.70525	35	.865
Average score for Curriculum Organization CSF	3.8000	.66642	35	.711
Average score for Delivery Method CSF	4.1214	.67348	35	.789
Average score for School Infrastructure CSF	3.8214	.70076	35	.805
Average score for Organizational Support CSF	3.7143	.66183	35	.736
Average score for Student Achievement CSF	3.9071	.54262	35	.627
				.916

Figure 5. General response

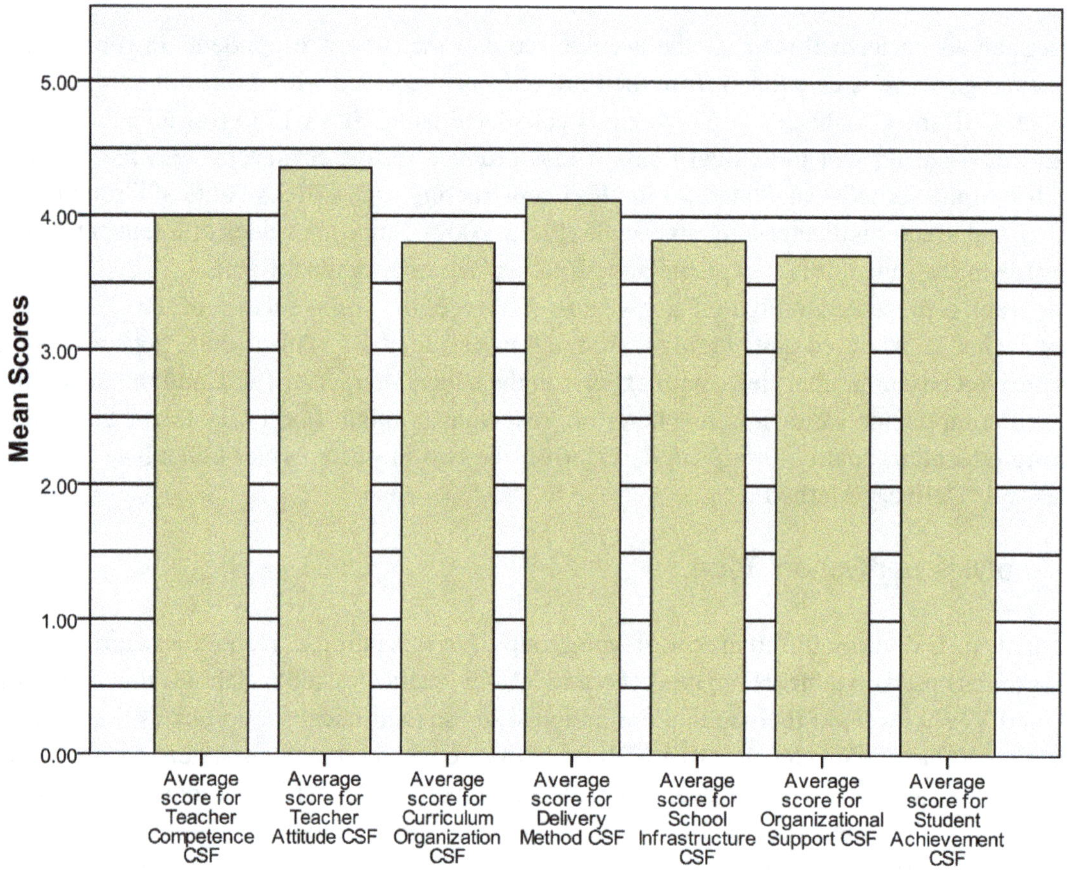

A comparison of the average scores of the two groups is presented in Figure 7. It could be seen that for both groups the CSFs 'Teacher Attitude' and 'Delivery Method' are listed as the two most important CSFs. A difference is seen in the third CSF for the different groups, which are 'Student Achievement' and 'Teacher Competence' – equally – for theoretical group and 'School Infrastructure' in the practical group. This could be affected by the fact that practical schools focus more on developing a student's practical skills which require good quality of the provided school facilities.

4.4.4. Analysis Based on a School's Definition of Quality

Our next analysis investigates the differences in score average based on how the respondent views quality in education. In the questionnaire, definitions of five different dimensions of education quality (Harvey & Green, 1993) as explained in Section 3.2, were firstly explained, and then respondent was asked to give their definition of education quality. Respondents could use their own wording in giving the definition, and it is then translated so it could be grouped into one of the five dimensions. From 35 respondents, 33 provide their view on education quality. The analysis is continued with these answers.

Figure 6. School type analysis

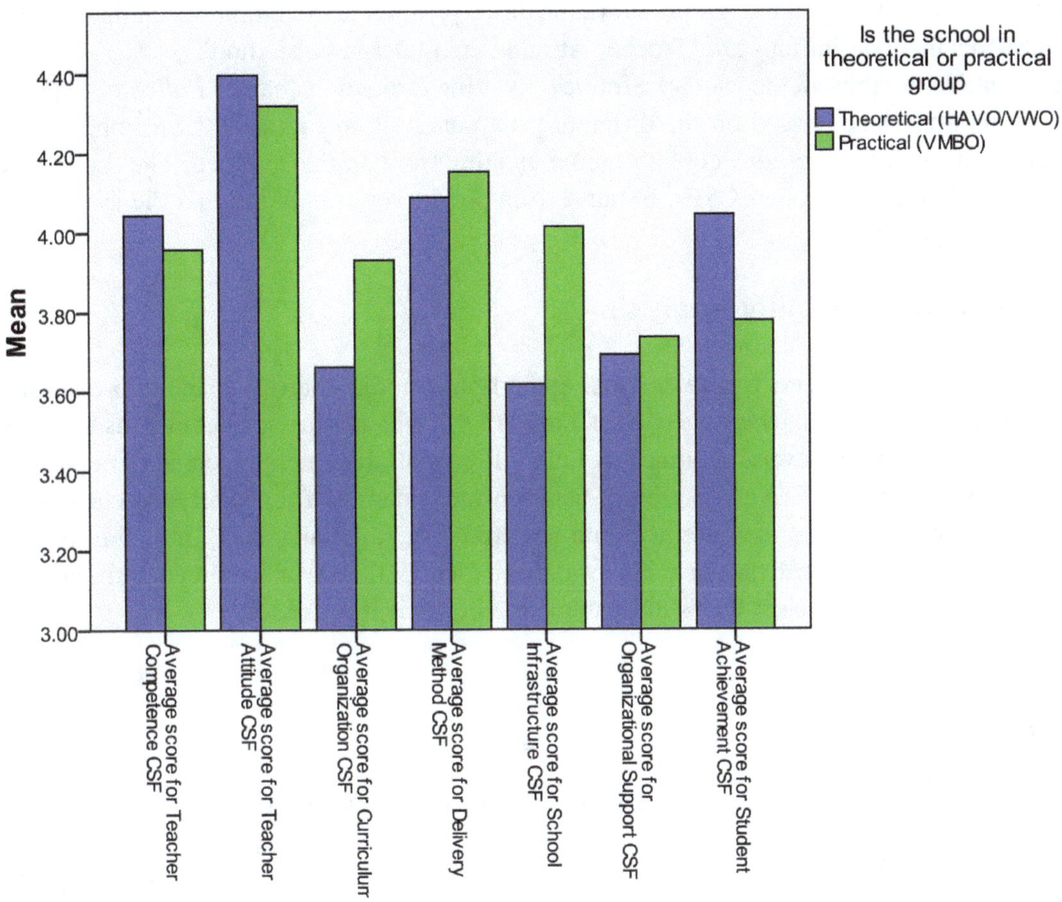

Figure 7. Theoretical and practical comparison

	Theoretical Group Mean Score
Average score for Teacher Attitude CSF	4.3971
Average score for Delivery Method CSF	4.0882
Average score for Student Achievement CSF	4.0441
Average score for Teacher Competence CSF	4.0441
Average score for Organizational Support CSF	3.6912
Average score for Curriculum Organization CSF	3.6618
Average score for School Infrastructure CSF	3.6176

	Practical Group Mean Score
Average score for Teacher Attitude CSF	4.3194
Average score for Delivery Method CSF	4.1528
Average score for School Infrastructure CSF	4.0139
Average score for Teacher Competence CSF	3.9583
Average score for Curriculum Organization CSF	3.9306
Average score for Student Achievement CSF	3.7778
Average score for Organizational Support CSF	3.7361

Some respondents would answer by choosing one of the definitions, and some would form a sentence that could be aligned with one of the definitions. 14 of the respondents view on education quality are aligned with 'Quality as Transformation'. Some examples of the definition in this group include 'Quality as equipment for life', 'Education allows a student to shape their future with knowledge and confidence'. Further, 8 respondents view 'Quality as Exceptional', 7 answer 'Quality as fitness for purpose', and 4 select 'Quality as Perfection'.

The average score for each definition group is presented in Table 6, while Figure 8 gives an overview of the answers through a line graph. From the descriptive table, it could be seen that the two most important CSFs in all definitions are 'Teacher Attitude' and 'Delivery Method'.

To summarize, we present the validated framework—the *Education Quality Indicator (EQI) Framework*—and its importance based on the different group analysis in Figure 9. CSF importance in the framework is presented in a gradient color scheme, ranging from orange to green. The 'Less important' scale is used relative to the other CSFs, because from our survey it is found that the average score of every CSF is bigger than 3.

4.5. Framework Feasibility Analysis

The next step in this research is to relate the findings and generated framework to the Information System (IS) it will be implemented in, which we will refer to as EQIS, which is in use in numerous Dutch secondary schools. EQIS handles several modules including financial planning, personnel data management, and students' study results. The compatibility between the generated framework and current IS could be analyzed by looking at the measurement and required data summarized in Table 5 in the previous chapter, and by matching it with the currently available data in EQIS. Furthermore, identification of data that is still needed to satisfy each KPI's measurement requirement is needed.

Table 6. Definition quality analysis

	What Is Their Definition of Education Quality											
	Quality as Exceptional			Quality as Perfection			Quality as Fitness for Purpose			Quality as Transformation		
	Mean	Std. Dev	Count	Mean	Std. Dev.	Count	Mean	Std. Dev.	Count	Mean	Std. Dev.	Count
Average score for Teacher Competence CSF	3.81	.97	8	3.94	.31	4	3.96	.57	7	4.13	.38	14
Average score for Teacher Attitude CSF	4.13	1.29	8	4.38	.25	4	4.46	.49	7	4.50	.43	14
Average score for Curriculum Organization CSF	3.66	.74	8	4.13	.60	4	4.00	.38	7	3.75	.77	14
Average score for Delivery Method CSF	4.06	1.11	8	4.25	.54	4	4.11	.45	7	4.16	.59	14
Average score for School Infrastructure CSF	3.94	.90	8	4.13	.32	4	4.07	.61	7	3.66	.66	14
Average score for Organizational Support CSF	3.84	.95	8	3.88	.14	4	3.39	.52	7	3.84	.57	14
Average score for Student Achievement CSF	3.75	.86	8	4.00	.35	4	3.71	.49	7	4.11	.38	14

Figure 8. Definition quality analysis

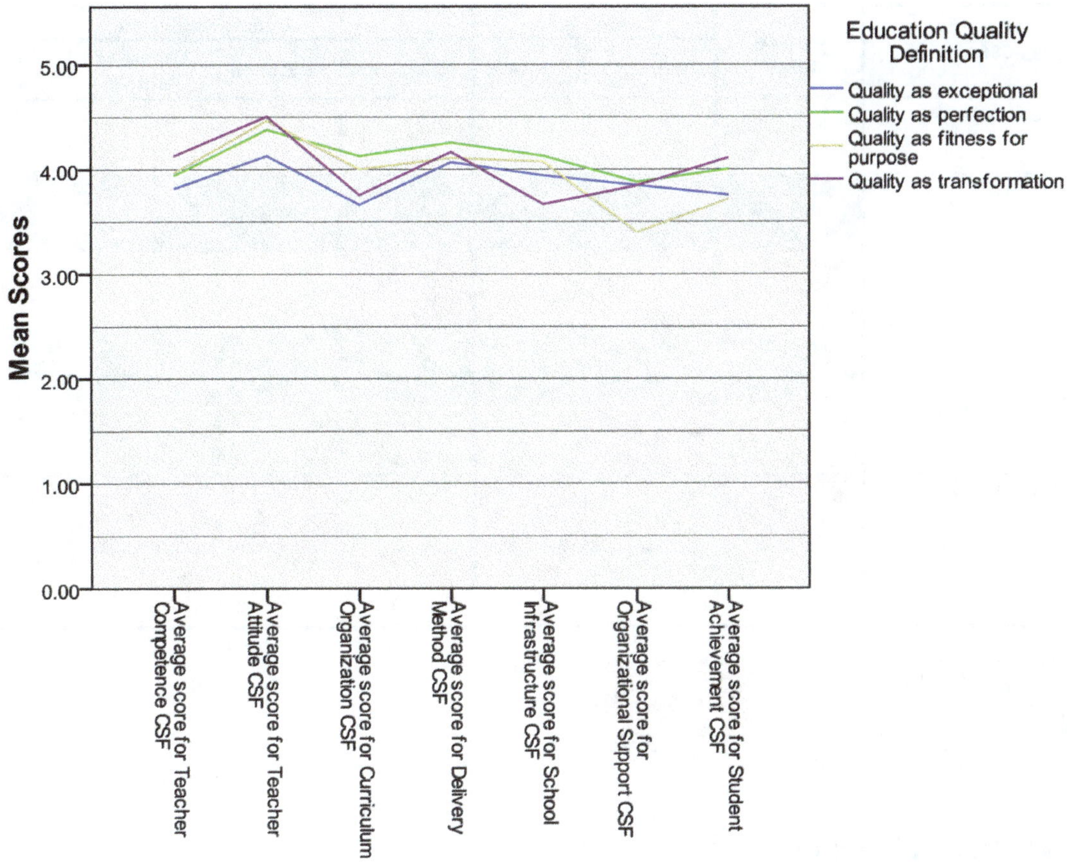

4.5.1. Current Data Model

In its data model, EQIS identifies several different components and uses different terms which are related to this research and its data needs. The detailed data model could be found in Appendix B, while Figure 11 shows the visualization of it.

4.5.2. Data and Framework Association

The next step is to relate the framework developed to the current EQIS system. This is done through an interview conducted with key experts from EQIS-CORP, who developed the system. The main goal of the interview is to identify what data are available for measuring the components identified in the framework, and what data are still needed. The interview lasted for 90 minutes by going through each item in the framework. The result of this process is summarized in Appendix C, which shows the association between currently available data in EQIS and the required data for the framework.

Figure 9. The Education Quality Indicator (EQI) framework

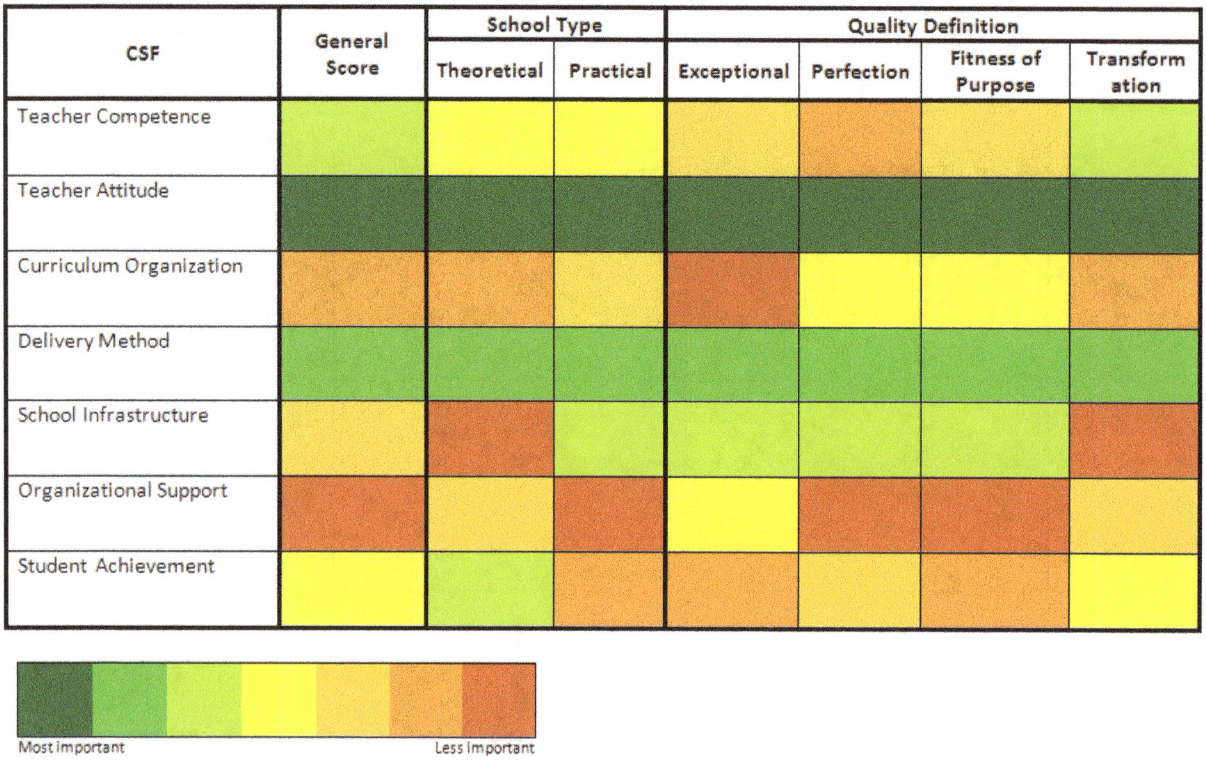

4.6. Dashboard Mockup

Figure 10 shows a mockup of the dashboard for the KPI Teacher Competence. Each CSF is measured by a combination of data which will give an insight about the quality of that CSF.

Data are presented with a comparison of last year's result as the benchmark. Further, a plus (+) and/or minus (-) indicator concludes each component measured, so a user can have a quick look at the overall

Figure 10. Dashboard mockup for the EQI KPI: teacher competence

	This Year	Previous Year	Objective	Satisfaction
Degree of Competence			To have more teacher closer to the highest qualification (i.e., 1st degree teacher)	
1st degree Teacher	30%	26%		
2nd degree Teacher	37%	32%		
Under Qualified Teacher	26%	29%		
Unqualified Teacher	7%	13%		
Investment in Teacher Learning (percentage of:)			Having teacher involved in continuous learning, from external activities such as seminars and also from internal discussions with other teachers	
Teacher going to seminars per year	63%	60%		
Financial allocation for teacher seminar	5%	5%		
Teacher conducting:				
Quarterly peer evaluation per course	76%	71%		
Quarterly peer evaluation per group	68%	68%		
Quarterly peer evaluation per study	84%	77%		

result, enabling identification and prioritization of the components to focus on. Spruit & Lammertink (2017) notably provide an extensive compilation of design guidelines for effective BI dashboards from a Gestalt theory perspective.

5. DISCUSSION AND CONCLUSION

This research tries to answer the research question and sub-questions through a literature review, explorative expert interviews, data analysis, and an online survey. Research findings show that through business

Figure 11. EQIS data model

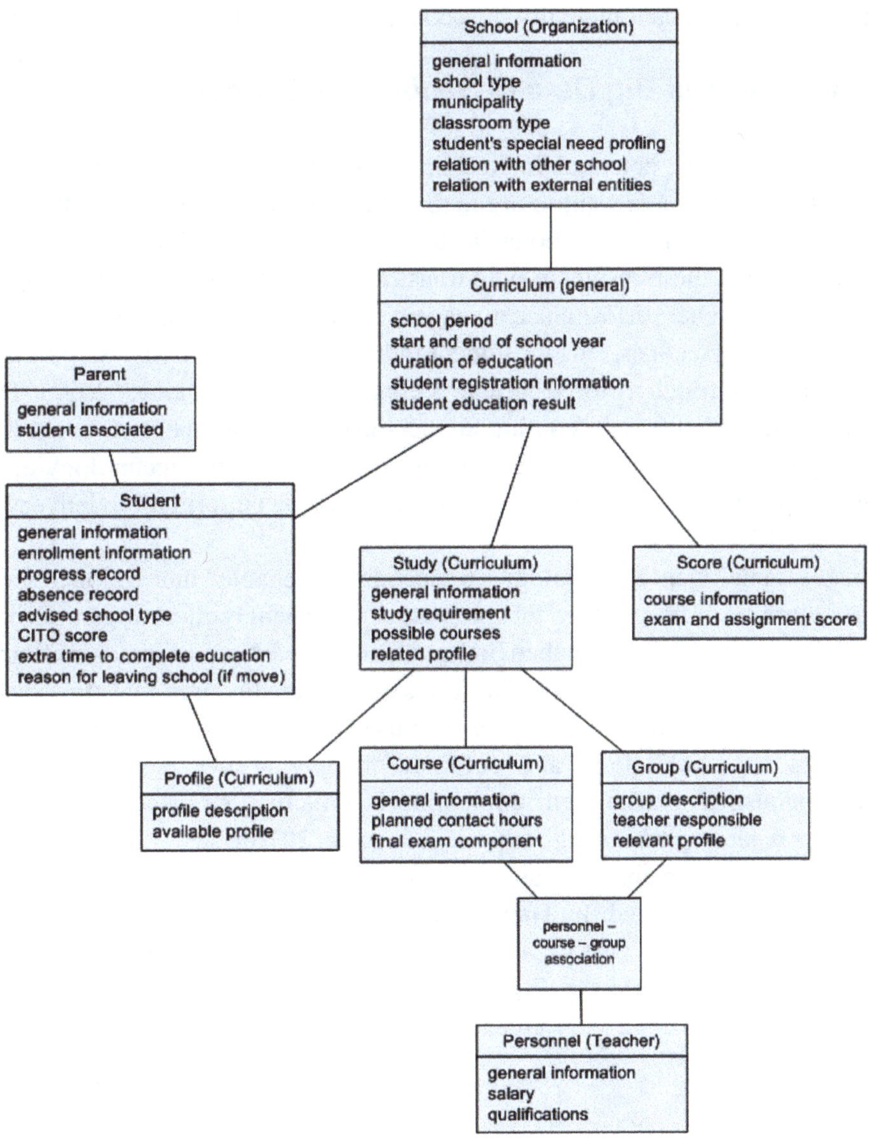

intelligence technologies provides a guideline as to what layers should be made available throughout this research. In implementing these layers into practice, business intelligence process steps are followed and associated to each layer of the framework. By doing so, this research is able to translate a vision of education quality into a practical visual tool – a dashboard – to help school management in monitoring their school quality and direct their decision making to achieve good quality education.

The process steps performed in this research yield the Education Quality Indicator (EQI) framework for secondary education quality assessment. This framework provides a well-grounded starting point in further developing a tangible multi-perspective measurement to assure education quality to be implemented at different levels of education and different settings of education schemes, in a generic manner yet paving the way for more personalized student performance mangement.

In every group analysis it was found that Teacher Attitude and Delivery Method are always the two most important CSFs. This shows that a teacher's ability to communicate with students is viewed to be most important in assuring education quality in secondary education.

5.1. Next Steps: Towards Big Data in Secondary Education

This study showcases the high potential for technology-enabled innovation in secondary education which is currently still nascent. We want to argue that it is not only quite feasible to take the next step by making availabe information more actionable through business intelligence technologies, but even more so, further build upon these results to help transform secondary education towards a much more personalized student and teacher performance management environment. Analogous to Business Performance Managment (BPM) practices, current student monitoring information systems can be connected to organizational strategy through a closed-loop process (*e.g.* Taylor & Baines, 2012). The information system's architecture should integrate continuous personalized assessments to support personalized performance management by design (Bekkers & Spruit, 2010). Such a technology-enabled environment will, in turn, improve workforce mobilization and continuous information delivery, among others (Verkooij & Spruit, 2013).

Deploying business intelligence technologies for technology-enabled innovation in secondary education also provides a proven infrastructure for integrating increasingly more organisation-specific data sources which may help to further personalize both student and teacher performance. Example variables include environmental sensors to monitor noise levels and air quality, and real-time datastreams from wearable technologies to optimally understand each individual student's and teacher's needs (*e.g.* Eskes et al., 2016; Heeringa *et al.*, 2007). Preferably, receipes for applying such variables in analytical models are formulated and published as meta-algorithmic models to facilitate transparant communication with students and teachers regarding their usage (Spruit & Jagesar, 2016).

On a final note, we need to remain aware and think ahead strategically regarding the seemingly endless potential of Business Intelligence and Big Data technologies in education. It is our strategic aim to work towards Big Data for Personalized Performance Management, not Big Brother for Privacy Invasion & Control. The Education Quality Indicator (EQI) framework for secondary education quality assessment, as presented in this work, provides a relevant and transparant step towards this goal.

REFERENCES

Becket, N., & Brookes, M. (2005). Analysing quality audits in higher education. *Brookes eJournal of Learning and Teaching, 1*(2), 1-12.

Bekkers, W., & Spruit, M. (2010). *The Situational Assessment Method Put to the Test: Improvements Based on Case Studies.* 4th International Workshop on Software Product Management, Sydney, Australia. doi:10.1109/IWSPM.2010.5623871

Berk, R. A. (2005). Survey of 12 strategies to measure teaching effectiveness. *International Journal of Teaching and Learning in Higher Education, 17*(1), 48–62.

Borahan, N. G., & Ziarati, R. (2002). Developing quality criteria for application in the higher education sector in Turkey. *Total Quality Management, 13*(7), 913–926. doi:10.1080/0954412022000017021

Card, D., & Payne, A. A. (2002). School finance reform, the distribution of school spending, and the distribution of student test scores. *Journal of Public Economics, 83*(1), 49–82. doi:10.1016/S0047-2727(00)00177-8

Chua, C. (2004). Perception of quality in higher education. In *Proceedings of the Australian Universities Quality Forum 2004.* AUQA Occasional Publication.

Darling-Hammond, L. (1999). *Teacher quality and student achievement: a review of state policy evidence.* Seattle, WA: Center for the Study of Teaching and Policy.

de Haan, M. (2012). *The effect of additional funds for low-ability pupils: A nonparametric bound analysis.* CESifo Working Paper (no. 3993). Munich, Germany: CESifo Group.

DiCicco-Bloom, B., & Crabtree, B. F. (2006). The qualitative research interview. *Medical Education, 40*(4), 314–321. doi:10.1111/j.1365-2929.2006.02418.x PMID:16573666

Dutch Eurydice Unit. (2007). *The education system in the Netherlands 2007.* The Hague, The Netherlands: Ministry of Education, Culture and Science.

Earthman, G. I. (2002). School facility conditions and student academic achievement. Los Angeles, CA: UCLA's Institute for Democracy, Education, and Access.

Eskes, P., Spruit, M., Brinkkemper, S., Vorstman, J., & Kas, M. (2016). The Sociability Score: App-based social profiling from a healthcare perspective. *Computers in Human Behavior, 59*, 39–48. doi:10.1016/j.chb.2016.01.024

Field, A. (2009). *Discovering statistics using spss* (3rd ed.). Sage Publications Ltd.

Gangadharan, G. R., & Swami, S. N. (2004). Business intelligence systems: Design and implementation strategies. In V. Lužar-Stiffler, & V. H. Dobrić (Eds.), *Proceedings of the 26th International Conference on Information Technology Interfaces (ITI 2004)* (pp. 139-144). Zagreb: SRCE University Computing Centre, University of Zagreb.

Gatfield, T., Barker, M., & Graham, P. (1999). Measuring student quality variables and the implications for management practices in higher education institutions: An Australian and international student perspective. *Journal of Higher Education Policy and Management, 21*(2), 239–252. doi:10.1080/1360080990210210

Ghazanfari, M., Rouhani, S., Jafari, M., & Akhavan, P. (2011). Association rule approach for evaluation of business intelligence for enterprise systems. *IUP Journal of Computer Sciences, 5*(2), 21–38.

Gibbs, G. (2010). *Dimension of Quality*. York, UK: Higher Education Academy.

Gilad, B., & Gilad, T. (1985). A systems approach to business intelligence. *Business Horizons, 28*(5), 65–70. doi:10.1016/0007-6813(85)90070-9

Guest, G., Bunce, A., & Johnson, L. (2006). How many interviews are enough? An experiment with data saturation and variability. *Field Methods, 18*(1), 59–82. doi:10.1177/1525822X05279903

Harvey, L., & Green, D. (1993). Defining quality. *Assessment & Evaluation in Higher Education, 18*(1), 9–34. doi:10.1080/0260293930180102

Heeringa, W., Nerbonne, J., Bezooijen, R. van, & Spruit, M. (2007). Geografie en inwoneraantallen als verklarende factoren voor variatie in het Nederlandse dialectgebied. *Tijdschrift voor Nederlandse taal- en letterkunde, 123*(1), 70–82.

Herring, J. P. (1999). Key intelligence topics: A process to identify and define intelligence needs. *Competitive Intelligence Review, 10*(2), 4–14. doi:10.1002/(SICI)1520-6386(199932)10:2<4::AID-CIR3>3.0.CO;2-C

Hevner, A. R., March, S. T., Park, J., & Ram, S. (2004). Design science in information systems research. *Management Information Systems Quarterly, 28*(1), 75–105.

Horsburgh, M. (1999). Quality monitoring in higher education: The impact on student learning. *Quality in Higher Education, 5*(1), 9–25. doi:10.1080/1353832990050102

Howard, G. S., Conway, C. G., & Maxwell, S. E. (1985). Construct validity of measures of college teaching effectiveness. *Journal of Educational Psychology, 77*(2), 187–196. doi:10.1037/0022-0663.77.2.187

Longhurst, R. (2010). Semi-structured interviews and focus groups. In N. Clifford, S. French, & G. Valentine (Eds.), *Key methods in geography* (2nd ed.; pp. 103–115). London: SAGE Publications Limited.

Lönnqvist, A., & Pirttimäki, V. (2006). The measurement of business intelligence. *Information Systems Management, 23*(1), 32–40. doi:10.1201/1078.10580530/45769.23.1.20061201/91770.4

Mergen, E., Grant, D., & Widrick, S. M. (2000). Quality management applied to higher education. *Total Quality Management, 11*(3), 345–352. doi:10.1080/0954412006865

Negash, S. (2004). Business intelligence. *Communications of the Association for Information Systems, 13*, 177–195.

Negash, S., & Gray, P. (2008). Business intelligence. In F. Burstein & C. W. Holsapple (Eds.), Handbook on decision support systems 2: Variations (pp. 175-193). Berlin: Springer-Verlag. doi:10.1007/978-3-540-48716-6_9

Owlia, M. S., & Aspinwall, E. M. (1996). A framework for the dimensions of quality in higher education. *Quality Assurance in Education*, *4*(2), 12–20. doi:10.1108/09684889610116012

Owlia, M. S., & Aspinwall, E. M. (1998). A framework for measuring quality in engineering education. *Total Quality Management*, *9*(6), 501–518. doi:10.1080/0954412988433

Pirttimäki, V. (2007). *Business intelligence as a managerial tool in large finnish companies* (Doctoral dissertation). Retrieved from TUT DPub, Tampere University of Technology, Publication 646. Retrieved from http://URN.fi/URN:NBN:fi:tty-200810021126

Power, D. J. (2007, March 10). *A brief history of decision support systems*. Retrieved from http://dssresources.com/history/dsshistory.html

Ramsden, P. (1991). A performance indicator of teaching quality in higher education: The course experience questionnaire. *Studies in Higher Education*, *16*(2), 129–150. doi:10.1080/03075079112331382944

Ranjan, J. (2009). Business intelligence: Concepts, components, techniques and benefits. *Journal of Theoretical and Applied Information Technology*, *9*(1), 60–70.

Roekel, H. v., Linders, J., Raja, K., Reboullet, T., & Ommerborn, G. (2009). *The BI framework: How to turn information into competitive asset*. Reading, UK: Logica.

Rouhani, S., Asgari, S., & Mirhosseini, S. V. (2012). Review study: Business intelligence concepts and approaches. *American Journal of Scientific Research*, *50*, 62–75.

Salonen, J., & Pirttimaki, V. (2005). Outsourcing a Business Intelligence Function. *Frontiers of E-Business Research*, 661-675.

Sangar, A. B., & Iahad, N. B. A. (2013). Critical factors that affect the success of business intelligence systems (BIS) implementation in an organization. *International Journal of Scientific & Technology Research*, *2*(2), 176–180.

Scheerens, J., Luyten, H., & Ravens, J. (2011). *Perspective on educational quality: Illustrative outcomes on primary and secondary schooling in the Netherlands*. Dordrecht: Springer; doi:10.1007/978-94-007-0926-3

School Choice International. (2008). *Education in the Netherlands: An overview*. White Plains, NY: The Plain White Press LLC.

Sharda, R., & Delen, D. (2013). *Business Intelligence: A Managerial Perspective on Analytics* (3rd ed.). Upper Saddle River, NJ: Pearson Prentice Hall.

Spruit, M., & Adriana, T. (2015). Quantifying education quality in secondary schools. *International Journal of Knowledge Society Research*, *6*(1), 55–87. doi:10.4018/IJKSR.2015010104

Spruit, M., & Jagesar, R. (2016). Power to the People! Meta-algorithmic modelling in applied data science. In *Proceedings of the 8th International Joint Conference on Knowledge Discovery, Knowledge Engineering and Knowledge Management* (pp. 400–406). Porto, Portugal: ScitePress. doi:10.5220/0006081604000406

Spruit, M., & Lammertink, M. (2018). Effective and efficient business intelligence dashboard design: Gestalt theory in Dutch long-term and chronic healthcare. In M. Lytras & P. Papadopoulou (Eds.), *Applying Big Data Analytics in Bioinformatics and Medicine* (pp. 243–271). IGI Global. doi:10.4018/978-1-5225-2607-0.ch010

Spruit, M., Vroon, R., & Batenburg, R. (2014). Towards healthcare business intelligence in long-term care: An explorative case study in the Netherlands. *Computers in Human Behavior*, *30*, 698–707. doi:10.1016/j.chb.2013.07.038

Tam, M. (2001). Measuring quality and performance in higher education. *Quality in Higher Education*, *7*(1), 47–54. doi:10.1080/13538320120045076

Taylor, J., & Baines, C. (2012). Performance management in UK universities: Implementing the Balanced Scorecard. *Journal of Higher Education Policy and Management*, *34*(2), 111–124. doi:10.1080/1360080X.2012.662737

Uline, C., & Tschannen-Moran, M. (2008). The walls speak: The interplay of quality facilities, school climate, and student achievement. *Journal of Educational Administration*, *46*(1), 55–73. doi:10.1108/09578230810849817

UNESCO. (2004). *Education for all – the quality imperative*. Paris: The EFA Global Monitoring Report Team.

UNESCO. (2012). *Netherlands (IBE/2012/CP/WDE/NE)*. Retrieved from http://www.unesco.org/ulis/cgi-bin/ulis.pl?catno=218669

Verkooij, K., & Spruit, M. (2013). Mobile Business Intelligence: Key considerations for implementation projects. *Journal of Computer Information Systems*, *54*(1), 23–33. doi:10.1080/08874417.2013.11645668

Vleugel, A., Spruit, M., & van Daal, A. (2010). Historical data analysis through data mining from an outsourcing perspective: The three-phases method. *International Journal of Business Intelligence Research*, *1*(3), 42–65. doi:10.4018/jbir.2010070104

Wasmann, M., & Spruit, M. (2012, April-June). Performance management within social network sites: The Social Network Intelligence Process method. *International Journal of Business Intelligence Research*, *3*(2), 49–63. doi:10.4018/jbir.2012040104

Watson, H. J., & Wixom, B. H. (2007). The current state of business intelligence. *Computer*, *40*(9), 96–99. doi:10.1109/MC.2007.331

Widrick, S. M., Mergen, E., & Grant, D. (2002). Measuring the dimension of quality in higher education. *Total Quality Management*, *13*(1), 123–131. doi:10.1080/09544120120098609

APPENDIX A: INITIAL FRAMEWORK

Table 7.

Component	CSF	KPI	Measurement	Data
Teacher	Teacher Competence	Teacher's education and training	• Teacher has received training and education in pedagogic and didactic field • 75% teachers are in the group of highly qualified teachers (1st degree)	• Teacher's education background record • Teaching level qualifications
		Teacher holds a diploma aligned with the subject they teach	85% teachers teach the subject with particular diploma they hold	• Teacher's education background record • Teacher's course record
		Teacher's teaching expertise	Number of years teacher has taught a particular subject	Teacher's teaching history record
		Teachers are involved in continuous learning	Teachers go to regular (yearly or half-yearly) conferences about their field	• Number of days teachers go conference in their field • Amount of money spent allocated for teacher learning and improvement
	Teacher Attitude	Highly motivated teachers	Teacher's attendance rate> 90%	• Teacher's absence frequency • Teacher's absence duration • Teacher and student survey
		Teachers have the ability to understand student's need	20% teachers has this ability, which allows peer group learning	Teacher and student survey on teacher's performance
		Teachers have the ability to encourage and motivate student	Student has high attendance rate	• Student survey on teacher performance • Student's absence record (frequency and duration)
		Teachers are emotionally involved with students	• 80% students opine so • Teachers receive good assessment from school management	• Student survey on teacher performance • Teacher's performance review from management
Curriculum	Curriculum Organization	School curriculum meets government standard	Government targets and standards are fulfilled	• Teacher survey • External assessment
		Teaching materials are up to date	Textbooks and study guides are from the last 5 years, or the most recent available	• Teacher survey • Course description
		Curriculum should contain primary knowledge	Materials necessary for aptitude (CITO) test should be covered in the curriculum	• Teacher survey • Management survey • External assessment
		Curriculum are properly designed and planned	Teaching and assessment plan are detailed into hours and should be available before each quarter starts	• Teacher survey • Course description associated to teaching plan
	Delivery Method	Usage of effective presentation method	At least 80% of students understood the material at the end of study hour	- Student survey • External assessment • Student quiz result at the end of contact hour
		Actively involving student into the process of pursuing knowledge	Classroom average of 7 or higher in assignments that require independent study and decision making	• Course description (explains the nature of the course) • Student test results
		Pay attention to the logical structure of teaching material	Monthly checkpoints on teaching plan that assures there is a build-up on the knowledge	• External assessment • Student and teacher survey • Yearly review
		Usage of methods that improve students' communication skill and team-working	Classroom average of 7 or higher in presentation and group assignments	• Course description (explains the nature of the course) • Student test results • External assessment

continued on following page

Table 7. Continued

Component	CSF	KPI	Measurement	Data
Organization	School Infrastructure	Sufficient space and available classroom	• School has sufficient space for every student • School has extra room available for unscheduled splitting of class	• Average student per classroom • Average square meter each student has in the classroom (enough space to move) • Classroom occupational rate
		Reasonable teacher to student ratio	1:20 teacher to student ratio	• Teacher record • Student record • Course planning
		School facilities and building are of good quality	Yearly school restoration and monthly maintenance control	School maintenance record
		Availability of guidelines for students	Students provided with a contact person (study guide advisor) that is available when facing a problem	• School guide • Personnel record • Student survey
	Organizational Support	Attention given by school to students in accordance to their socio-economic status	Students with lower socio-economic status receives extra financial subsidy	• Student record • School profile (percentage of student that requires special attention)
		Quality management policy regarding Human Resource of the school	Availability of guideline that assures the well being of both students and staff, which include addressing the support provided for students with special needs	• School regulation • Teacher and student survey • External assessment
		Clear evaluation of students' development progress	• Quarterly exams with monthly routine tests • CITO test	• Curriculum and academic calendar planning • CITO test score
		Well recognized school and reputation	• School receives award in the last 5 years • School achieve a positive review	• Excellente scholen • Elsevier's de beste scholen
Student	Student Achievement	The initial level of student's knowledge meets the school's entrance requirement	Student's CITO exam result should match the entrance requirement	• CITO scores • School level entry requirement • Advice from primary school
		High pass rate of student in each school level without having to re-sit a certain level	80% of students progress smoothly in their education continuation	Student profile record
		Students shows retention and persistence in their performance	Students has increasing test result throughout the year, or at least are in the same level with previous test	Student exam result (CITO, central exam, school exam)
		Students are able to continue to the next level after finishing their education	90% of students has a final exam score that is sufficient for them to be accepted in the higher education level	Student exam result

APPENDIX B: EQIS DATA MODEL

In its data model, EQIS identifies several different components and uses different terms which are related to this research and its data needs. The following explanation describes the definition of each term and how it relates to this research:

1. **School:** In EQIS, the term school is used to describe the data about each school. This could be related to the component 'Organization' used in this research. School has information about the school as a physical building and the organization of the school itself.
2. **Personnel (*personeel*):** EQIS stores information about all personnel working in the school, including teaching and non-teaching staff. This allows the availability of information about 'Teacher' component used in this research.
3. **Student (*leerling*):** The same term is used both in EQIS data model and this research with regards to the student. EQIS has various information available related to students which are relevant to this research.
4. **Group (*groep*):** The term group (or could also be associated to the commonly known term 'class') is related to the component 'Curriculum' of this research. Group is the term used to describe one class which has one teacher responsible for it and has a number of students registered to a group (e.g. group 8 is the last year of primary school, which is attended by students with the age of 11-13).
5. **Course (*vak*):** Another relevant term to the component 'Curriculum' of this research is course which describes the relevant information to courses offered in the school.
6. **Study (*studie*):** Study is also related to the component 'Curriculum', where study describes the specific level of the education structure. Study is related to group in a way where each group can only be associated to one study, while one study has several groups related to it.
7. **Profile (*profiel*):** Profile is treated as a separate entity in the data model. It holds the definition of the different profiles available for students to follow as explained in chapter 3.1. Further this entity also holds the information about the education type students follow. It is relevant to give a separate explanation of the term 'profile' here, as it affects the related course.
8. **Score (*cijfer*):** Score is a separate component – represented in a separate table in EQIS database – that holds all exam and assignment data of every course that have been registered. It also holds records from past school years as well.
9. **Curriculum (general):** The relationships between different points related to 'Curriculum' are summarized in this portion. It is not explicitly stated as a single component in the data model, but for the sake of clarity and ease of identification for this research, they are grouped here.
10. **Parent (*ouder*):** Another component which data is available in EQIS is regarding parent. This includes general information about parent's identity, which student they are related to, and necessary information about financial aspect related to tuition fee debit system.

The data available for each component are summarized in the following Table 8. Further detail of each actual table used in EQIS could be found in Appendices C and D. Further, Figure 11 summarizes the correlation between each component with a visual presentation of the data model.

Table 8. Correlation between available data and component

Component	Derived Data
School (Organization)	• School general information (name, address, bank account) • School type (education level) • Municipality where the school is registered • Classroom type relevant to registered course • Profiling of students with regards to their special need • Relations school has with other schools and/or other external entities
Teacher	• Teacher (personnel) general information (name, date of birth, nationality) • Teacher (personnel) salary • Teacher (personnel) qualifications (indicates the level of teacher's expertise based on their previous education and experience)
Student	• Student general information (name, date of birth, address, nationality) • Student enrollment information: o Education profile student takes o School type student is in o School year/level student is in o Associated courses (primary and elective) o Start and end date of each course associated to student o Student study information • Student progress record • Student absence record • Advised school type to student • CITO score • Extra time student require to complete education • Reason student leave school (in case of moving)
Curriculum (group)	• Description of class (group) • Teacher responsible for a class • Education profile relevant to a class
Curriculum (course)	• Course general information (name, code, relevant education type, duration) • Planned contact hours • Final exam components
Curriculum (study)	• Study general information (name, period, duration) • Study requirement • Possible courses to follow in a study
Curriculum (profile)	• Description of profile • Different profiles available for student
Curriculum (score)	• Course information • Exam result • Assignment result
Curriculum (general)	• School period • Start and end of school year • Duration of education • Student enrollment information (association between profile, course, study, group)
Parent	• Parent general information (name, address, nationality) • Associated student(s) to registered parent

APPENDIX C: EQI FRAMEWORK WITH DATA ASSOCIATIONS

Table 9.

Component	KPI	Data		Description
		Available	Not Available	
Teacher	Teacher's education and training	Teacher (personnel) qualifications		Personnel qualifications show the education history record of teachers. It also gives information about the profiling of teachers based on their teaching degrees.
	Teacher holds a diploma aligned with the subject they teach	• Teacher (personnel) qualifications • Association between personnel, group and course		Comparing between personnel qualifications and group and course record that they teach to determine if the subject they teach is aligned with their education history.
	Teacher's teaching expertise	Teacher (personnel) qualifications		Personnel qualification shows the teaching history and other related work experience of a teacher.
	Teachers are involved in continuous learning		• Teacher's conference log • Financial allocation record	These data could show how much is invested in assuring that teachers are involved in continuous learning.
	Highly motivated teachers	• Teacher's absence frequency • Teacher's absence duration	• Teacher survey • Student survey	Combining information gathered from teacher's absence frequency and duration, could give an insight on the attitude of teachers. Further, survey could give good justification of the information.
	Teachers have the ability to understand student's need		• Teacher survey • Student survey	Getting student's opinion on how teacher perform could measure how much teacher could understand their students. Further, peer evaluation also adds value to this information.
	Teachers have the ability to encourage and motivate student	• Student's progress in a course • Student's absence record	Student survey	Student survey shows how student feel about their teacher. This combined with student's progress report and their absence record give insight to how much teachers encourage them.
	Teachers are emotionally involved with students		• Student survey • Teacher's performance review (from management)	Combining teacher's performance review by management with student survey give an overview of how much teacher engage themselves emotionally with their students.

continued on following page

Table 9. Continued

Component	KPI	Data		Description
		Available	Not Available	
Curriculum	School curriculum meets government standard	• Scheduled contact hours • Actual contact hours	• Management review • Teacher survey (peer review) • External assessment	Qualitative measurement measure curriculum design best. Combination of external assessment result, management review, and discussion between teachers from the same subject provide this information.
	Teaching materials are up to date		• External assessment • Teacher survey • Course description	Course description gives information about the material used in teaching, external assessment and teacher survey confirms whether or not these materials are relevant and up to date.
	Curriculum should contain primary knowledge	• Scheduled contact hours • Exam components	• External assessment • Teacher survey • Management survey	Scheduled syllabus and exam components give information about the subjects that will be taught, and assessment from external assessor, teacher, and management evaluates the validity of this curriculum.
	Curriculum are properly designed and planned	Scheduled contact hours	• Teacher survey • Course description	Teacher survey and peer learning gives confirmation about the correctness and completeness of the scheduled courses.
	Usage of effective presentation method		• External assessment • Student survey • Student quiz result (end of contact hours) • Course planning	Course planning gives information about the method used for different material, which is then evaluated through external assessment and student survey. Furthermore, quiz result shows how much students understand the given material, which implicates the effectiveness of how teacher presents it.
	Actively involving student into the process of pursuing knowledge	Student test (assignment) result	• External assessment • Teacher survey • Course planning	Course planning explains the nature of the course, i.e. assignment that requires independent study and decision making, which are reviewed by external assessor and through peer review. Student assignment of the relevant task confirms how involved students are.
	Pay attention to the logical structure of teaching material		• Course description • Course planning • External assessment • Teacher survey • Student survey • Yearly review	Course description and planning give overview of how the teaching material is built, which is validated through external assessment, teacher and student survey, and yearly peer review.
	Usage of methods that improve students' communication skill and team-working	Student test results	• Course description • External assessment	Course description provides information about the nature of the course, i.e. teaching method type, which is validated by external assessor. Student test result show how student cope with the method.

continued on following page

Table 9. Continued

Component	KPI	Data		Description
		Available	Not Available	
Organization	Sufficient space and available classroom	• Course schedule • Student enrolled in a course • Classroom list	• Classroom occupational rate • Classroom size information	• Information about student listed in a course and which room a course will be conducted in, show the space each student will have during course. • Classroom occupational rate show the availability of classroom, in case of unscheduled class splitting (e.g. practicum that requires small groups)
	Reasonable teacher to student ratio	• Teacher record (number of) • Student record (number of) • Association between personnel, group, and course		List of student, teacher, and course planning shows how many students a teacher would handle in one course.
	School facilities and building are of good quality	School general information	School maintenance record	Record of maintenance work and routine check on school building gives an overview of the condition of the school.
	Availability of guidelines for students	Personnel qualifications	• School guide • Student survey	Information of qualified person and availability of school guide for students in case of problem are confirmed through student survey.
	Attention given by school to students in accordance to their socio-economic status	• Number of students needing extra assistance • Student record		School profiling based on the number of students needing assistance show how school should allocate the extra funding they receive.
	Quality management policy regarding Human Resource of the school		• External assessment • School regulation • Teacher survey • Student survey	Assessments and survey show the environment of the school, and makes sure that school regulations create a safe environment for teaching and learning activities.
	Clear evaluation of students' development progress	• Final exam components • Student progress report (CITO test score)	• External assessment • Curriculum and academic calendar planning	External assessors assure that the development of students is well planned and measured.
	Well recognized school and reputation		• School position in external assessment rank (e.g. Elsevier's de beste scholen) • Awards received by school (e.g. Excellenet Scholen)	School awards and appraisal give a general view of how a school is perceived by external parties.

continued on following page

Table 9. Continued

Component	KPI	Data		Description
		Available	Not Available	
Student	The initial level of student's knowledge meets the school's entrance requirement	• CITO score • Advised school type to student (from primary education) • Study requirement		End of primary education CITO score and advised school type compared to required level of a specific school type, gives an overview of compatibility between student knowledge and requirements.
	High pass rate of student in each school level without having to re-sit a certain level	• Student enrollment information • Extra time student require to complete education • Association between student and course • Student progress report		Student result record shows how students are progressing with their studies.
	Students shows retention and persistence in their performance	• CITO score • Exam result (school exam, central exam) • Association between student and course • Student progress report		Steady or increasing results of student exams show that students are performing in an expected level.
	Students are able to continue to the next level after finishing their education	• Exam result • Association between student and course • Final exam components	Requirements of the following education	Student's final exam score shows in what level they are, and whether it is sufficient for continuing to the following education.

Chapter 5
Impact of Accreditation on Engineering Education

Tayeb Brahimi
Effat University, Saudi Arabia

Akila Sarirete
Effat University, Saudi Arabia

Sajid Khalifa
Effat University, Saudi Arabia

ABSTRACT

The objective of this study is to investigate the impact of accreditation on engineering education including student learning outcomes and innovation based on two accreditation bodies the NCAAA in KSA, and the ABET in USA. The article explores the approach of constructionism with emphasis to makerspace by delivering engineering and design courses with opportunities for innovation, creativity, and the ability to design a system, component, or process to meet desired needs. This innovative approach shifts the active learning strategies from Do-It-Yourself to Do-It-With-Others culture. Makerspace is one of the integral parts of modern education system that brings together and facilitates the community of interdisciplinary individuals. Results from courses in engineering and design shows the benefit of the accreditation in terms of enhancing the overall program quality and the importance of re-evaluating strategies and methodologies of learning which help in delivering innovative solutions and educating tomorrow's leaders to address the most pressing issues facing our societies.

INTRODUCTION

The development and easy access to new technology continue to have an impact on teaching and learning methodologies, in particular in engineering education. Universities moved from the traditional approach focusing on education to the second generation universities focusing on education and research, and now to the third generation universities focusing on learning, innovation, and entrepreneurship. In the context of the third generation universities, accreditation supports innovation in both the delivery and the content,

DOI: 10.4018/978-1-5225-4191-2.ch005

and there is a continuous call to support innovation in engineering education and how to deal with the challenge of contemporary engineering design problems. Today, education is rapidly changing into a global activity that is reached by millions of people as reported at the IMF-World Bank Spring Meetings Symposium "Learning for All Symposium, Investing in a Brighter Future," in April 2014 (http://live.worldbank.org/learning-for-all). With the rapid increase use of information technologies educational institutions is changing the way faculty and students learn, work, and establish collaboration (Beetham et al., 2013, Clough, 2004). The learning cycle is an ongoing process that is designed to improve the quality of, as well as collaboration among learners especially when considering a non-traditional form of learning. In the traditional transfer learning model the instructor serves as the repository and transmitter of knowledge, however, in the distributed transfer learning environment the learner interacts with other students, peers, and has flexible access to all information and resources around him (Sarirete, 2009). In this context, accreditation is considered as the primary process for assuring and improving the quality of higher education institutions to boost their ongoing performance efforts for the benefit of their students and the society. Each college or university student wants to ensure that the selected institution is "accredited" and students will have the assurance of receiving the quality of education needed by employers or by other institution to pursue research (US Department, 2005). As reported by Fredericks et al. (2007), throughout the history of the accreditation, accreditation bodies have acted in response to academic and non-academic pressure to modify and improve their accreditation process however they were rarely visible to the students and the public in general. Today, accreditation bodies expect evidence from institution regarding student learning outcomes including innovation by implementing a continuous improvement process and engaging in quality assurance through internal and external review (http://www.abet.org/, http://www.ncaaa.org.sa/). All regional or international accreditation bodies have similar processes and practices: i) a self-review by the institution or program, ii) an on-site visit by external peer experts reviewers, and finally iii) a decision by the accrediting body to award or deny the accreditation. The review is actually repeated every three to ten years, in this process all accreditation bodies expect learning outcomes to be "well defined, articulated, assessed, verified, and used as a guide for future improvement" as reported by ABET. The accreditation process requires from institutions not only to critically evaluate their vision, mission, and strategies but also how well all these educational elements work together to meet the needs of all students. This is considered as "essential to the future of nations, their well-being, and the world economy" as reported by different organizations such as the United Nations Educational, Scientific and Cultural Organization (UNESCO), the World Bank, the Organization for Economic Co-operation and Development (OECD), and the Council for Higher Education Accreditation (CHEA, http://www.chea.org). According to UNESCO's 2009 World Conference (goo.gl/ZN7gK1) there is a considerable focus on the importance of student achievement with an important trend towards quality evaluation since institutions are now evaluated against their own self-defined mission and vision not against an institution model as previously required. Another trend reported by UNESCO is that "government agencies are now focusing more on whether institutions have adequate mechanisms in operation to support this dynamic process." In this paper two accreditation bodies and their impact on student outcomes will be discussed: The National Commission for Academic Accreditation and Assessment (NCAAA) established by the Higher Council of Education in Saudi Arabia (http://www.ncaaa.org.sa/), and the Accreditation Board for Engineering and Technology Inc. (ABET) (http://www.abet.org/), a US non-profit and non-governmental accrediting agency for academic programs in the disciplines of applied science, computing, engineering, and engineering technology. Today, researchers recognize that learning has three essential components: knowledge, skills, and understanding. According to the learning pyramid, developed by the National Training Laboratory, the first three level of learning, mainly group discussion, practice by doing, and teaching others are associated with active learning while the last four levels of learning, lecture, reading, audiovisual, and demonstration, are associated with passive learning. The domain of learning is based on four approaches (Bransford, 2000, Siemens, 2005): i) behaviorist learning which teaches the "what" through positive and negative reinforcement where learner react to external stimulus; ii) cognitive learning which teaches the "how", including procedures and principles, and considers the learner as an organized processor of knowledge and information; iii) constructivist learning which teaches the "why" and considers learning as a process of knowledge construction, the learner is considered active, and meaning is created by the learner from the experience gained; iv) connectivism learning emerged as a result of learner ability to acquire and share knowledge not only inside as traditional learning theories but outside using technology through communications, nodes and connections, Figure 1.

The key point in all the above methodologies is "learning." Learning is traditionally viewed as a vertical process, and practice is seen as an application of the theory that follows learning. The constructivism learning approach focuses more on the individual understanding of knowledge, but it also stresses the importance of social connection, as discussed in the social learning theory of Wenger (Wenger et al., 2002) where learning is positioned in the context of social participation in the world. In recent years we have witnessed the emergence of new models of teaching and learning where learning is practiced not only in the classroom but also in the community through social learning in the workplace (Wenger et al., 2002, Sarirete et al., 2009, Cohen, 2007). A more horizontal view emerged from the vertical process involving negotiation among learning partners, is accomplished through the application Community of Practice (CoPs) (Wenger et al., 2002). CoPs are structures that enable peer-to-peer learning among practitioners where the internet is one of the main factors of the "horizontalization". Communities of Practices (CoPs) are (Wenger and al., 2002): "…groups of people who share a concern, a set of problems, or a passion about a topic, and who deepen their understanding and knowledge of this area by interacting on an ongoing basis." These are considered as a group of "practitioners" who are sharing similar chal-

Figure 1. Learning theory timeline

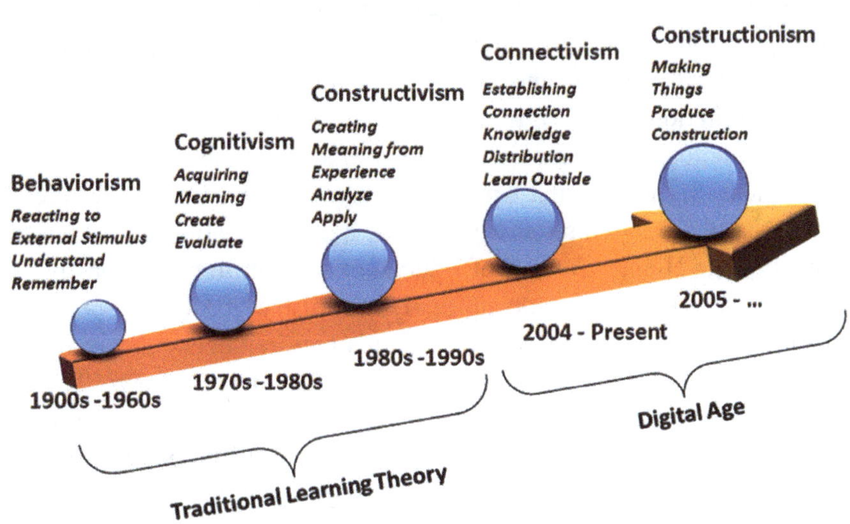

lenges, interact regularly to overcome these challenges while helping and learning from each other. In the context of makerspace environment (Hatch, 2013, Anderson, 2012), where students learn creative ways in problem-solving and engage through creative experimentation and more hands-on projects, the maker movement in engineering education is built upon the foundation of constructionism theory (experiential learning: learning-by-making) developed by Seymour Papert (Papert et al, 1991) where it is believed that people learn effectively through making things. The instructor role becomes a facilitator who coaches and help students in attaining their own goals, produce a construction that other learners can see, improve, or criticize (Martinez et al., 2013), Figure 1.

The objective of this work is to explore the approach of learning-by-making with emphasis to makerspace and the effect of accreditation on engineering education, in particular, student learning outcomes through two case studies, a course in Mathematics and a product design studio course. This innovative approach shifts the active learning strategies from Do-It-Yourself (DIY) to Do-It-With-Others (DIWO) culture.

NCAAA and ABET Accreditation Bodies

Accreditation is the primary process for assuring and improving the quality of higher education institutions by providing assurance that a program or institution meets established quality standards. The Council for Higher Education Accreditation (CHEA, http://www.chea.org) defines accreditation as "the process of external quality review created and used by higher education to examine colleges, universities, and programs for quality assurance and quality improvement." It is the process by which educational programs or institutions are reviewed by an accreditation body to verify if they meet certain standards of quality. Accreditation engages the institution in meeting high-quality standards, implementing a continuous not periodic improvement process, and engaging in quality assurance though internal and external review (US, 2007; ABET, 2015a, 2015b; Barbara, 2004).

In most countries accreditation is conducted by a government organization, such as a ministry of education, in other countries however accreditation bodies are independent of government and performed by private non-profit organizations (Marjorie, 1992). Many organizations provide accreditation of programs in engineering, engineering technology, and computing. Other accreditation bodies are limited to institutions in a single country, while others engage in international accreditation. By attending an accredited university, you would expect to receive a level of quality education that would be recognized by employers, professional associations, and other universities. The more important accreditors in the United States are i) Accreditation Board for Engineering and Technology – for applied science, computing, engineering, and technology programs, ii) Association to Advance Collegiate Schools of Business – for business schools, and iii) the National Architectural Accrediting Board – for architecture schools. In Saudi Arabia, the National Commission for Academic Accreditation and Assessment (NCAAA, 2003) was established by the Higher Council of Education in order to be responsible for accreditation and quality assurance in post-secondary education. The Ministry of Higher Education is responsible for supervising, planning and coordinating the Kingdom's requirements concerning higher education. The responsibilities of NCAAA are set out in the Higher Education By-Laws. The NCAAA mission is to encourage, support and evaluate the quality of post-secondary institutions and the programs they offer to ensure that: i) the quality of student learning outcomes, ii) the management and support services provided within institutions, iii) and the contributions to research and the communities served by post-secondary institutions, are all equivalent to high international standards. Among the most common accreditation is the Institutional Accreditation, certifying that its resources, as well as their processes and students learning outcomes, meet required standards for an institution of its type and the level of qualifications it offers. The NCAAA accreditation and quality assurance are based on 11 standards that cover different aspects of activities carried out by any academic entity where students' learning and teaching is considered of primary importance (Figure 2). The eleven general areas of activity are: 1) mission goals and objectives, 2) program administration, 3) management of program quality assurance, 4) learning and teaching, 5) student administration and support services, 6) learning resources, 7) facilities and equipment, 8) financial planning and management, 9) employment processes, 10) research, 11) relationships with the community.

The NCAAA (http://www.ncaaa.org.sa/) has five broad categories or types of learning outcomes: 1) knowledge, the ability to recall, understand, and present information including knowledge of specific facts, 2) cognitive skills, the ability to apply understanding of concepts, principles, theories and procedures in critical thinking and creative problem solving, both when asked to do so and when faced with unanticipated new situations, 3) interpersonal skills and responsibility, the ability to take responsibility for their own learning and continuing personal and professional development, work effectively in groups and exercise leadership when appropriate, act responsibly in personal and professional relationships, and act ethically and consistently with high moral standards in personal and public forums, 4) communication, information technology and numerical skills, including the ability to communicate effectively in oral and written form, use information and communications technology, and use basic mathematical and statistical techniques, and 5) psychomotor skills, involving manual dexterity is the fifth domain that applies to only some programs.

Figure 2. Standards of the National Commission for Academic Accreditation and Assessment

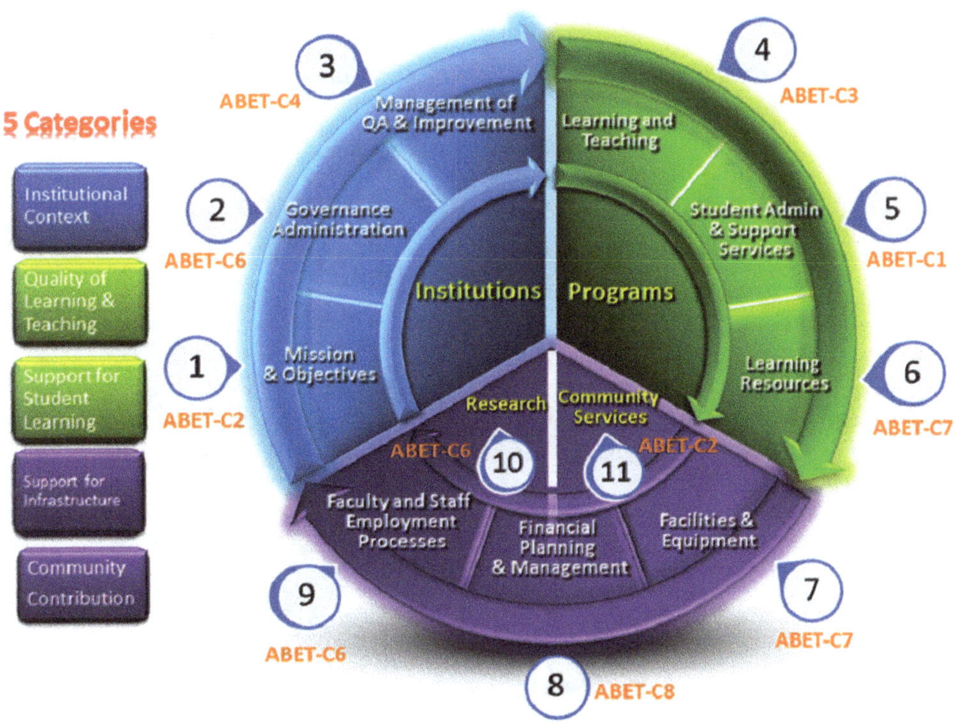

As for any accreditation body, ABET accreditation (http://www.abet.org/) provides assurance that a college or university program meets the quality standards established by the profession for which the program prepares its students. ABET serves the public through the promotion and advancement of education in applied science, computing, engineering, and technology. ABET accredits educational programs, promotes quality and innovation in education, consults and assists in the development and advancement of education worldwide in a financially self-sustaining manner, communicates with constituencies and the public regarding activities and accomplishments, anticipates and prepares for the changing environment and the future needs of constituencies, and manages the operations and resources to be effective and responsible. Compared to NCAAA, ABET has eight general criteria for Baccalaureate Level Programs, Figure 3.

For BET (http://www.abet.org/), student outcomes are outcomes (a) through (k) plus any additional outcomes that may be articulated by the program. These student outcomes are defined as: (a) an ability to apply knowledge of mathematics, science, and engineering (b) an ability to design and conduct experiments, as well as to analyze and interpret data (c) an ability to design a system, component, or process to meet desired needs within realistic constraints such as economic, environmental, social, political, ethical, health and safety, manufacturability, and sustainability (d) an ability to function on multidisciplinary teams (e) an ability to identify, formulate, and solve engineering problems (f) an understanding of professional and ethical responsibility (g) an ability to communicate effectively (h) the broad education necessary to understand the impact of engineering solutions in a global, economic, environmental, and societal context (i) a recognition of the need for, and an ability to engage in life-long learning (j) a knowledge of contemporary issues (k) an ability to use the techniques, skills, and modern engineering tools necessary for engineering practice. The student outcomes are divided into two categories, a set of five "hard" skills: (a), (b), (c), (e), and (k), and a second set of six "Soft professional" skills: (d), (f), (g), (h), (i), (j). Hard skills refer to student outcomes associated with applying mathematics, science,

Figure 3. ABET eight general criteria for Baccalaureate level programs

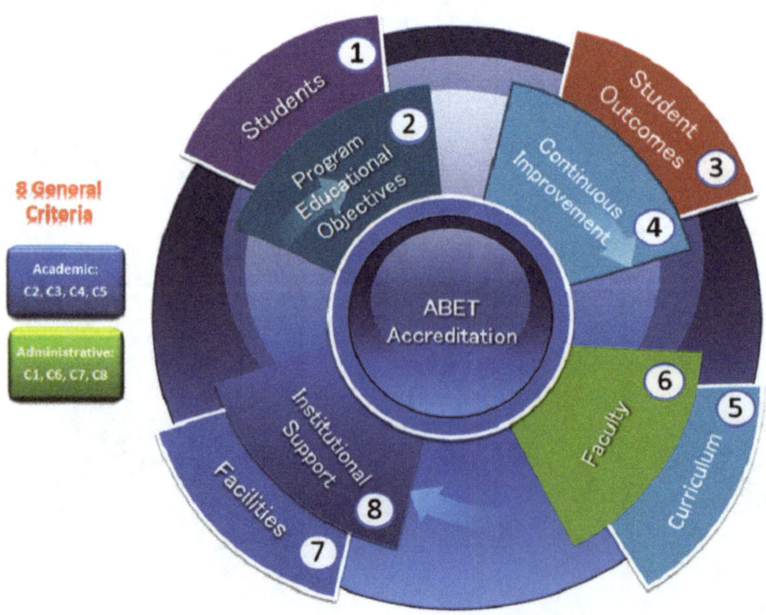

engineering and technology to solve technical problems including experimental design, analysis and interpretation. On the other hand, soft skills refer to student outcomes associated with team work, ethics and professionalism, communication, impact of Engineering solution, life-long learning, and knowledge of contemporary issues. These student ouctomes requirements show that ABET accreditation is more outcome oriented compared to NCAAA standard 3.

Accreditation and Student Learning Outcomes (SOs)

Accrediting organizations play a significant role in advancing the assessment of learning outcomes. As reported in ABET Training documentation (http://www.abet.org/) outcome-based accreditation focuses now on: "Learning, not teaching; Students, not faculty; and Outcomes, not inputs or capacity." Accreditation has emphasized student learning and development as an important criterion of effectiveness and quality (Maki, 2002, Fredericks, 2007, Mee, 2004, Staci, 2010, Taj 2007, Brahimi, et al., 2016). Table 1 shows NCAAA domains of learning mapped to ABET SOs.

The philosophy of accreditation became strongly oriented toward outcomes-based accreditation and continuous quality improvement (CHEA, 2015). According to ABET, outcomes are "what a student knows or can do by the time of graduation and student outcomes describe what students are expected to know and be able to do by the time of graduation. These relate to the skills, knowledge and behaviors that students acquire as they progress through the program". Faculty members must be part of accreditation process on a continuous basis and focus on how to assess student outcomes and explore new pedagogical strategies of best practice and best learning. Accreditation standards developed and used by national and international accreditors incorporate the assessment of student learning as a central process in evaluating institution program effectiveness. For ABET, each program must show how they are meeting the 13 outcomes: the ABET a-k. Also, the method used to assess these outcomes must be explained, documented including tangible results. For the program, the key outcome is to make sure that institution courses programs and courses incorporate these outcomes and their assessments in order to

Table 1. NCAAA domains of learning mapped to ABET student outcomes (a-k)

NCAAA Domains of Learning	ABET Student Outcomes (a - k)
Knowledge	(a) an ability to apply knowledge of mathematics, science, and engineering (h) the broad education necessary to understand the impact of engineering solutions in a global, economic, environmental, and societal context (j) an understanding of contemporary issues
Cognitive skills	(a) an ability to apply knowledge of mathematics, science, and engineering (b) an ability to design and conduct experiments, as well as to analyze and interpret data (c) an ability to design a system, component, or process to meet desired needs within realistic constraints such as economic, environmental, social, political, ethical, health and safety, manufacturability, and sustainability (e) an ability to identify, formulate, and solve engineering problems
Interpersonal skill & responsibility	(d) an ability to function on multidisciplinary teams (f) an understanding of professional and ethical responsibility (i) a recognition of the need for, and an ability to engage in life-long learning
Communication and Information Technology skills	(g) an ability to communicate effectively (k) an ability to use the techniques, skills, and modern engineering tools necessary for engineering practice.

improve teaching, learning, and decision-making. Data about what students know and can do are critical for improving student learning, their success, and their ability to promote and improve curricular and co-curricular learning experiences. Staci (Staci, 2010) reported that no institution appears to have lost an accreditation due to student learning outcomes assessment deficiencies and increasing numbers of institutions are being required to address such issues. A strategy to improve student learning outcomes is based on i) commitment to the standards set by the accreditation organization, ii) collecting evidence, iii) analyzing and documenting evidence, iv) using evidence for improvement, and v) demonstrating that students achieve the intended learning outcomes and that the institution improves it over time.

Makerspace: A Novel Approach to Creative Learning

Makerspaces, hackerspaces, hack labs, or fab labs are gathering point for learning, innovation, and sharing tools and knowledge in an innovate and a creative environment (Hatch, 2013, Anderson, 2012). Makerspaces are considered as one of the most important developments in educational technology for higher education where students learn creative ways in problem-solving and engage in more hands-on projects to improve creativity, innovation, and stay competitive in an economy with ever growing needs (Clough, 2004, Bates, 2015, Duderstadt, 2008). Today "Makerspace" has emerged in engineering education as a new space in providing engineers with opportunities for innovation, creativity, and the ability to design a system, component, or process to meet desired needs within realistic constraints as prescribed by accreditation bodies such as ABET. A quick search in Google trends shows the term "makerspace" increased four times between Marsh 2015 and January 2017. These makerspaces expand beyond offering classical services to the community by supporting innovation, invention, tinkering, and enhancing student's learning in an interdisciplinary environment and entrepreneurial spirit. In the design program, traditionally the learners are exposed to 2D technical drawing and at a later stage, to Computer Aided Design (CAD) for the production of manufacturing drawing. However, this method does not provide effective learning environment due to the learners' elementary knowledge to realize and comprehend the complex movements and dynamics of the product system. 3D CAD modeling application such as SolidWorks (http://www.solidworks.com/) allows learners to visualize the product function beyond their fundamental imagination. This is where, after designing the product in a virtual environment, it can be tested for the interference and functions, before proceeding to make the porotype. Another benefit SolidWorks offers to the learners is to convert the 3D model into STL file type that can be transferred to a 3D printer to print the product prototype.

The maker movement in engineering education is built upon the foundation of constructionism that is hands-on learning through making things. Hatch (Hatch, 2013), CEO and cofounder of the first makerspaces TechShop, suggests "Maker Movement Manifesto" with makers' activities and mind-sets articulated around nine key ideas, mainly make, share, give, learn, tool up, play, participate, support, and change. The growth of Maker Faires has been seen in different countries with over 400 Maker Faires organized around the world since 2012, and 1.4 million in attendees at the National Maker Faire from 2000 to 2016 (Noonoo, 2015). These platform spaces for learning and innovation have a broad range of maker equipment and tools, including 3D printers, 3D scanners, laser cutters, Arduino and micro-controllers, Raspberry Pi's and microprocessors, virtual reality and augmented reality, etc. According to the NMC Horizon Report 2016 (Johnson et al, 2016), makerspace and wearable technology will be adopted as a new way of learning within two to three years, while the Internet of Things technology is expected to be mainstream in universities and colleges within four to five years.

RESULT AND DISCUSSION

To show the importance of student outcomes and innovation through makerspace two case examples have been conducted at Effat University (http://www.effatuniversity.edu.sa). The first one is a course on Calculus for first year engineering students and the second one is a course in the design program, studio 3. The study uses direct and indirect assessment methods (Allen, 2004). In the direct student assessment samples of student work using final exams questions, assignments, quizzes, and student projects presentations are examined. In the indirect assessment, we gather information about student learning by looking at indicators of learning other than student work output such as students' feedback and surveys through Blackboard management system (BB). Both direct and indirect assessment approaches provided useful information in improving student learning. The first step of the analysis starts with course learning outcomes (CLOs) as defined in the course syllabi. For the Calculus course, the main purpose is to introduce students to the concepts of limit, continuity, and the related concepts of derivative and integral with emphases on conceptual understanding and applications. Students will apply these concepts to a wide range of practical problems including the equations of motion, related rates, and curve sketching. At the end of the course students will be able to i) Recognize the properties of a function from an algebraic, numerical, and graphical perspective (CLO1), ii) Evaluate the limits and test the continuity of a function graphically, numerically, and algebraically (CLO2), iii) Apply the basic rules of differentiation to various types of functions (CLO3), iv) Sketch graphs using first and second derivatives and solve problems involving rate of change (CLO4), Evaluate integrals by using different integration techniques (CLO5). The second step of the analysis defines the mapping matrix between the assessments (direct or indirect) and the course learning outcomes. The third step uses a statistical model to determine CLOs coverage, CLOs attainment percentages that are more than 75%, and CLOs attainment percentages that are more than 70%, and finally the average attainment value as shown in Figure 4. Results allow for comparison of data from different categories for easier and more effective decision-making. Figure 5 shows the coverage of each CLO for the specific course learning outcomes. This is helpful in selecting

Figure 4. Distribution of CLO attainment percentage, average, >75%, and >70%
Calculus I, spring 2017.

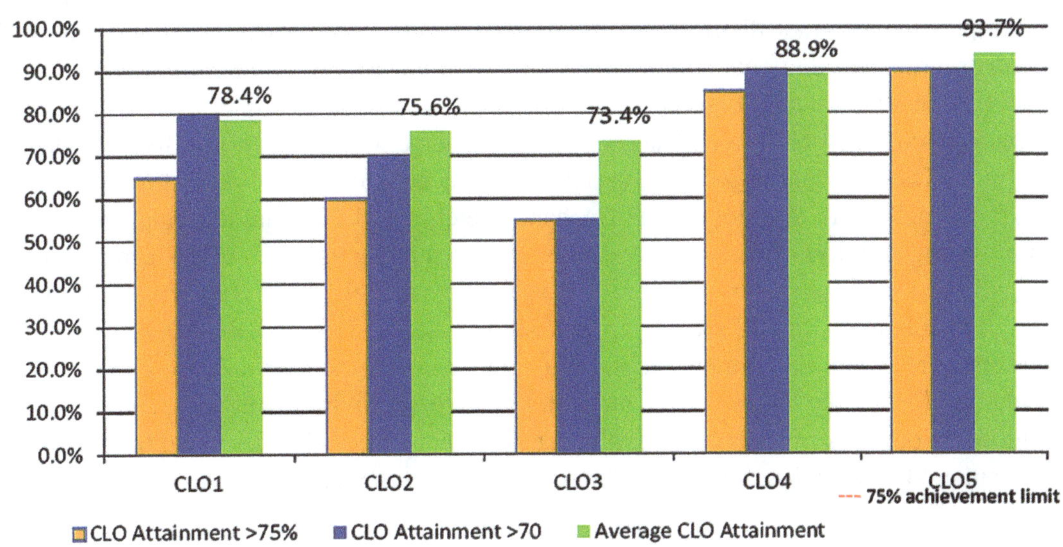

Figure 5. Course learning outcomes percentage coverage
Calculus I, spring 2017.

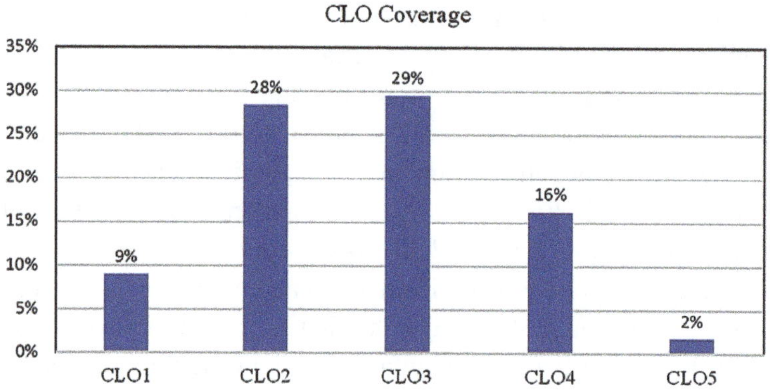

the more appropriate content of the assessments for students. It is clear from Figure 4 that CLO2, CLO3, and CLO4 are the most important components of this course. Indeed these CLOs are related to limits, continuity, differentiation, and graphing various types of functions. The 2% showed for CLO5 indicates less stress on assessment of integration for this course. This is because another course on integration (Calculus II) comes next to Calculus I and this has no effect on student learning outcomes. If this is not applicable then, in the next semester, this CLO needs to be adjusted by increasing its percentage coverage. In the present analysis, for CLO5 there are 90% of students who scored better than 75% while the average was 93%. For other CLOs the overall result shows acceptable CLO distribution. However, CLO3 (Apply the basic rules of differentiation to various types of functions) shows only 55% of students achieving more than 75%%; this is somehow low despite having an average of 73%. Hence it is advised to improve this learning outcome in the next cycle of this course. CLO distributions result can also be compared with previous semesters, hence the importance of re-evaluating the methodology used for each learning outcome. Data helps the instructor to improve material posted in Blackboard, analyze student interest for coming semester, propose and implement solutions, then repeated the process in the next cycle, till problems tracked are resolved. Individual course reports (CR) are used for evaluation of the course as well as the program. This process is conducted to ensure quality assurance through analyses of course completion rate, grade distributions, assessing student performances, types and nature of these assessments, program learning outcome tracking, and plans for improvements. The overall continuous improvement process is shown in Figure 6.

In the design studio 3 (sophomore), learners enter the course with minimum skills in product design and prototyping. They are challenged with varieties of projects pushing them to think outside the box scenario. Traditionally, after developing the freehand sketches and 2D hand drawings, learners would start with modeling activity, where soft models are prepared using varieties of craft materials such as cardboard and polystyrene as shown in Figure 7. However, the model quality is poor and not comparable with those produced using Rapid Prototyping Techniques such as Fused Deposition Molding (FDM). When learners were put into the traditional learning environment, the resultant product was limited in the functionality. Hence, the learners were put in a Makerspace environment with access to computer stations and some design software. After exploring a number of possibilities of adding functions, the ideas were gathered and finalized based on the feedback from the teammates, and the instructor who

Figure 6. Continuous improvement process

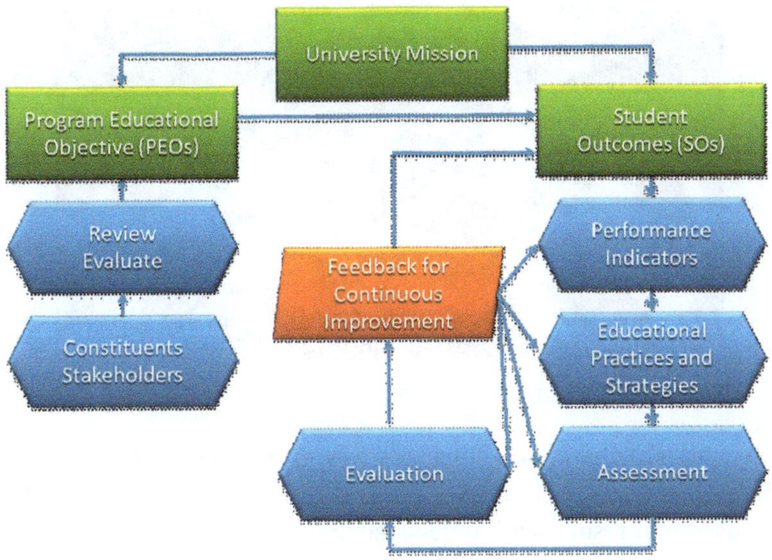

Figure 7. Polystyrene soft prototype

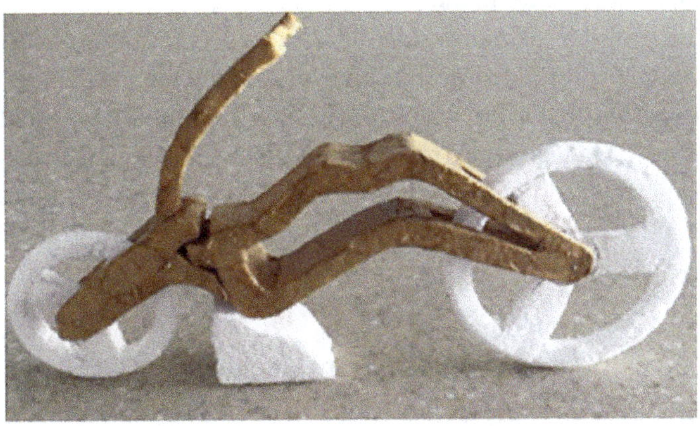

was only acting as a facilitator. Using hand sketches and 2D representations learners were unable to understand the behavior of the product system. This type of scenario is difficult to predict, specifically for learners with elementary knowledge and experience. This is where comprehensive and user-friendly application such as SolidWorks (http://www.solidworks.com/) will prove to be a very useful tool where learners can test their models without making prototypes. This unique learning experience will be the first exposer to the best industry practice for learners. After converting the 3D model into STL files, learners transferred the data to a 3D printer that processed and produced the model. The output using Fused Deposition Molding (FDM) produce a better design as shown in Figure 8. When learners were put into the traditional learning environment, the resultant product was limited in the functionality where few attempts of moving the functional parts would make the prototype obsolete and loos the function, such as wheels and handle whereas maker space consisting of 3D printers produced a robust prototype

Figure 8. FDM 3D printed prototype

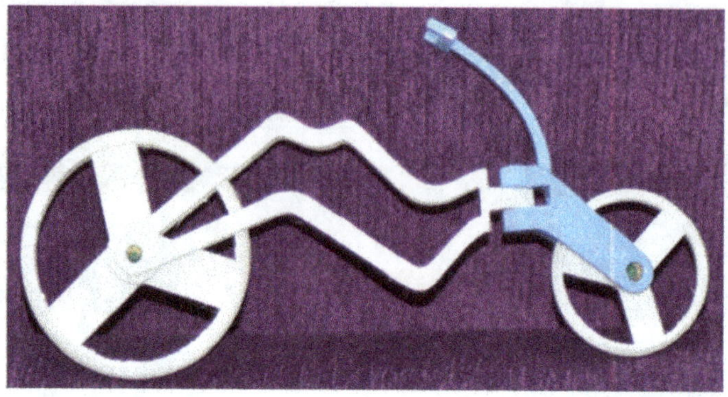

allowing appropriate joining method that withstands various types of tests and impacts. The porotypes and study models developed using traditional approach were from craft materials such Cardboard and Polystyrene which caused end results with defects such as improper surface texture and poor quality of Craftsmanship. On the other hand in a makerspace equipped with technologies, such as 3D printers, Laser cutter, and hand tools, the model quality was improved by 30% while development time has greatly reduced by 50%. The makerspace has proven to be an effective medium to impart the knowledge that created the experiential leaning environment.

Figure 9 shows the distribution of the average CLOs for the following learning outcomes: i) Create proof of concept (CLO1), ii) Produce design control drawings for entry into product development (CLO2), iii) Visual processing and perception (CLO3), iv) Comparative analysis of alternatives to design problems (CLO4), v) Manage time, respect deadlines and complete projects on time (CLO5), vi) Development of collaborative skills (CLO6), vii) Effective communication of product design ideas through verbal, graphic and written methods (CLO7), viii) Describing and defending design solutions and approaches in a professional manner (CLO8), ix) Craftsmanship demonstrated in the construction

Figure 9. Distribution of the average CLO attainment percentage
Studio 3, spring 2017.

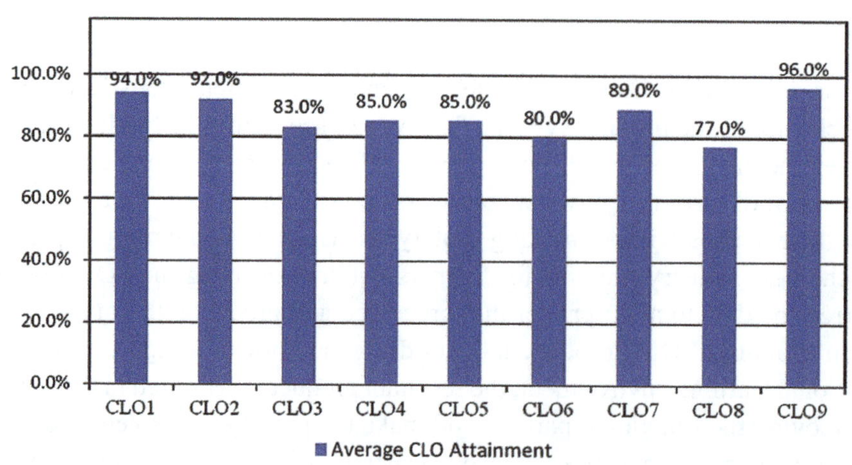

of study models and presentation models (CLO9). The overall distribution shows a satisfactory result. In Figure 10 we were interested in comparing the effectiveness measure based on grading criteria with traditional learning method and with makerspace environment model. Some evaluation criteria were used, such as learners' comprehension, an ability to prepare design documentation, model quality, and cycle time. These are the same criteria that are used to evaluate learners assessed work. From Figure 10, it is clearly evident that there is an improvement in all the area of design curriculum. The percentage increase of learners' design comprehension reached 50%, while accuracy in design documentation increased by 25%; both of these factors are directly related to the use of SolidWorks, which facilitates the virtual inspection and produces automatic standard views for technical drawing. The model quality has also improved by 46% while model development time has decreased by 50%; both of these factors are directly related to 3D printing.

CONCLUSION

Delivering design courses and providing engineers with opportunities for innovation, creativity, and the ability to design a system, component, or process to meet desired needs within realistic constraints is the goal of today's engineering accreditation bodies. Accreditation organizations emphasized student learning and development as an important criterion of effectiveness and quality of an institution. In the context of the third generation universities, accreditation supports innovation in both the delivery and the content, and there is a continuous call to support innovation and entrepreneurship in engineering education and how to deal with the challenge of contemporary engineering design problems. Faculty members are increasingly becoming a part of the accreditation process focusing on how to assess student

Figure 10. Effectiveness measure based on grading criteria in traditional and makerspace learning design approaches
Studio 3 course, spring 2017.

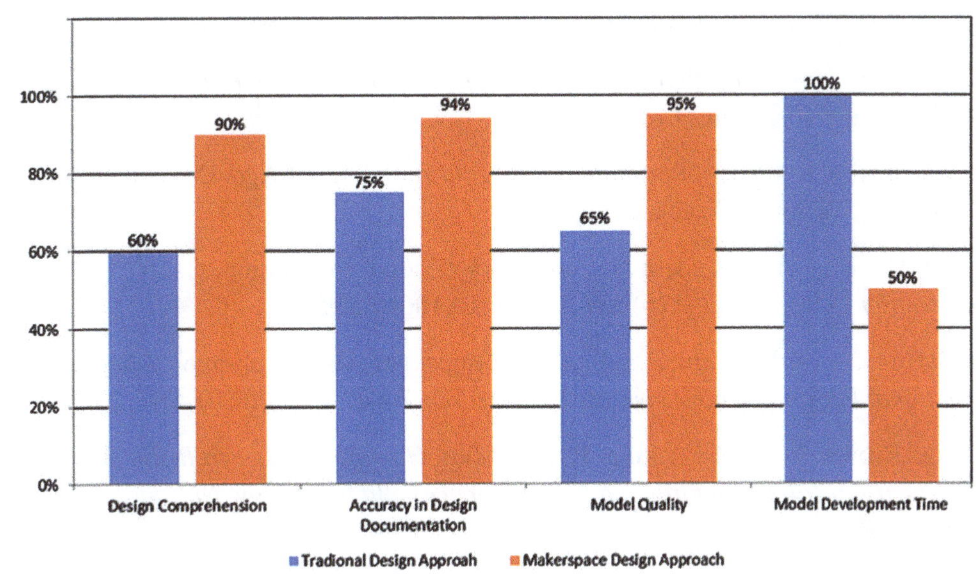

outcomes and explore new pedagogical strategies of best practice and optimal learning such as makerspace and learning through constructionism model. Results from courses in Engineering showed how important the learning outcome is in the process of re-evaluating strategies and methodologies used in the course learning process. In product design case-study it is revealed that SolidWorks and 3D printer application builds the Makerspace environment and accelerates the learning process through virtual product realization. Faculty members agree that the accreditation process has been beneficial in terms of enhancing the overall program quality and consider that accreditation, standards, self-study reports, external visiting team, have a positive change in the student outcome, assessment, and innovation. Students perform better when working in a makerspace environment where students learn creative ways in problem-solving and engage through creative experimentation and more hands-on projects. Makerspace is one of the integral parts of a modern education system that brings together and facilitates the community of interdisciplinary individuals.

ACKNOWLEDGMENT

The authors gratefully acknowledge the support of the College of Engineering and the Graduate Studies & Research at Effat University.

REFERENCES

ABET. (2015a). *Why Accreditation Matters.* Retrieved from http://www.abet.org/accreditation/why-abet-accreditation-matters/

ABET. (2015b). *Accreditation Outside of the US.* Retrieved from http://www.abet.org/accreditation/new-to-accreditation/accreditation-outside-the-u-s/

Allen, M. (2004). *Assessing Academic Programs in Higher Education.* Bolton, MA: Anker Publication Co.

Anderson, C. (2012). *Makers: The New Industrial Revolution.* New York: Crown Business.

Bates, T. (2015). *Teaching in a Digital Age, Guidelines for Designing Teaching and Learning for a Digital Age.* Tony Bates Associates Ltd.

Beetham, H., & Sharpe, R. (2013). Rethinking Pedagofy for a Digital Age. Designing for 21st Century Learning. Routledge, Taylor & Francis Group, UK.

Beno, B. A. (2004). The role of student learning outcomes in accreditation quality review. *New Directions for Community Colleges, 126*(126), 65–72. doi:10.1002/cc.155

Brahimi, T., Sarirete, A., & Ibrahimi, R. (2016). The Impact of Accreditation on Student Learning Outcomes. *International Journal of Knowledge Society Research, 7*(4), 51–62. doi:10.4018/IJKSR.2016100105

Bransford, J. D., Brown, A. L., & Cocking, R. R. (2000). *How People Learn Brain, Mind, Experience, and School. Commission on Behavioral and Social Sciences and Education, National Research Council, National Academy Press.*

Clough, G. W. (2004). *The Engineer of 2020: Visions of Engineering in the New Century*. Washington, DC: National Academy of Engineering.

Cohen, L. L., Manion, L., & Morrison, K. (2007). *Research Methods in Education*. London: Routledge.

Duderstadt, J. J. (2008). Engineering for a Changing World a Roadmap to the Future of Engineering Practice, Research, and Education. Ann Arbor, MI: University of Michigan.

Ewell, P. T. (2001). *Accreditation and Student Learning Outcomes: A Proposed Point of Departure. Council for Higher Education Accreditation*. CHEA Occasional Paper. Council for Higher Education Accreditation.

Hatch, M. (2013). The Maker Movement Manifesto. Rules For Innovation. In *The New World of Crafters. Hackers, and Tinkerers*. McGraw-Hill Education.

HETL. (2013). Exploring Spaces for Learning. *HETL Review*.

Hiemenz, J. (2011). *3D printing with FDM: How it Works*. Stratasys Inc. Retrieved from http://www.stratasys.com/3d-printers/technologies/fdm-technology

Johnson, L., Adams Becker, S., Cummins, M., Estrada, V., Freeman, A., & Hall, C. (2016). *NMC Horizon Report: 2016 Higher Education Edition*. Austin, TX: The New Media Consortium. Retrieved from https://library.educause.edu/~/media/files/library/2016/2/hr2016.pdf

Kalaani, Y., & Haddad, R. J. (2014). Continuous Improvement in the Assessment Process of Engineering Programs. *Proceedings of the 2014 ASEE South East Section Conference*.

Lenn, M. P. (1992). Global Trends in Quality Assurance in Higher Education. *World Education News and Reviews*, *5*(2), 20–21.

Maki, P. L. (2002). Developing an Assessment Plan to Learn about Student Learning. *Journal of Academic Librarianship*, *28*(1), 8–13. doi:10.1016/S0099-1333(01)00295-6

Martinez, S. L., & Stager, G. (2013). *Invent to learn: Making, Tinkering, and Engineering in the Classroom*. Torrance, CA: Constructing Modern Knowledge Press.

Mee, G. (2004). *Assessment of Student Learning in General Education: A Case Study*. Presentation at Building Learner-Centered Institutions: Developing Strategies for Assessing and Improving Student Learning, Western Association of Schools and Colleges and American Association of Higher Education Workshop.

NCAAA. (2013). *Orientation Handbook for NCAAA Review Teams*. Riyadh: National Commission for Academic Accreditation and Assessment.

Noonoo, S. (2015). *The Maker Mouvement Inforgrapgy*. Retrieved from https://www.eschoolnews.com/2015/11/20/maker-movement-614/

Papert, S., & Harel, I. (1991). Constructionism. Ablex Publishing Corporation.

Provezis, S. (2010). *Regional accreditation and student learning outcomes: Mapping the territory* (NILOA Occasional Paper No. 6). Urbana, IL: University of Illinois and Indiana University, National Institute for Learning Outcomes Assessment (NILOA). Retrieved from http://www.learningoutcomeassessment.org/occasionalpapersix

Sarirete, A., Noble, E., & Chikh, A. (2009). Knowledge and learning issues related to engineering education: A constructivist approach. *International Journal of Teaching and Case Studies*, *2*(1), 17–28. doi:10.1504/IJTCS.2009.026296

Siemmens, G. (2005). *A Learning Theory for the Digital Age*. Retrieved from http://www.elearnspace.org/Articles/connectivism.htm

Tanner, T. (2015). Accreditation and Student Learning Outcomes Progress and Challenges. *Proceedings of the CHEA 2015 Annual Conference*.

U.S. Department of Education. (2007). *Accreditation in the United States*. Retrieved from https://www2.ed.gov/admins/finaid/accred/index.html

Volkwein, J. F., Lattuca, L. R., Harper, B. J., & Domingo, R. J. (2007). Measuring the impact of professional accreditation on student experiences and learning outcomes. *Research in Higher Education*, *48*(2), 251–282. doi:10.1007/s11162-006-9039-y

Wenger, E., McDermott, R., & Snyder, W. (2002). Cultivating Communities of Practice. Harvard Business Press.

Yamayee, Z. A., & Albright, R. J. (2008). Direct and Indirect Assessment Methods: Key Ingredients for Continuous Quality Improvement and ABET Accreditation. *International Journal of Engineering Education*, *24*(5), 877–883.

Chapter 6
An Analysis of Student Performance in a Digital Electronics Design Course

Maria Vargas-Vera
Universidad Adolfo Ibanez, Chile

ABSTRACT

The main purpose of this research was to find relations between activities in Dees (Digital Electronics Education and Design Suite) and student performance in an undergraduate course of Digital Electronics. In our case of study, we used a dataset which contains examples of students using Dees toolkit. Firstly, we performed an analysis of the attributes of the dataset, to find correlations between student performance and activities developed during six sessions of the course. Secondly, we performed clustering using the algorithm k-means. Then, we concluded that, there is a relation between Dees activities performed by a student and student performance. This result opens the possibility of further analysis and perhaps the use of similar software toolkit in different courses of the Engineering curricula.

INTRODUCTION

Learning analytics has been used in educational settings to gain understanding of students, instructors and other stakeholders involved in the education process. As a result, Technology Enhanced Learning (TEL) has improved dramatically during the last decades. Currently, learning tools are more personalized and adaptive. This allows that the learning can be more optimized and therefore, learning is tailored to the need of each student (Chatti et al., 2012). We have classified the learning tools in three different categories. Firstly, we have the inquiry-guided learning tools. These tools focus in contexts where learners are to discover knowledge instead of passively memorizing concepts (Kruse & Pongsajapan, 2012). Secondly, we have the simulation-based environments. In these tools the data gathered from these educational environments has special features of student-performed actions. Thirdly, we have the data mining-based tools which find patterns in the data. These patterns can be used to improve the student learning. In fact, in recent years has been an interest in the use of Data Mining in the Education sector, in

DOI: 10.4018/978-1-5225-4191-2.ch006

particular, among researchers in the field of Technology Enhanced Learning. The objective is to gain an understanding of the behaviour of learners by building models based in collected data (Siemens, 2012). To clarify to the reader, data mining techniques are used to extract patterns from raw data. Then, later these patterns are found in un-seen data.

Summing up, advances in information technology have made possible to store, manage and process big datasets. In particular, Data Mining has an important role by helping users to understand their data and find relevant patterns on the data. Data mining techniques aim at extracting high-level knowledge from raw data. However, the use of the Data Mining methods requires that we perform a selection of variables and model selection which are critical issues in the data mining process. Variable selection is useful to discard irrelevant inputs, leading to simpler models that are easier to interpret and that usually give better performance. Complex models may over-fit the data, losing the capability to generalize, while a model that is too simple could present limited learning capabilities. These issues have represented a problem for educators as they find difficult to use Data Mining tools.

Our case of study uses collected data from students attending an undergraduate course. The experiments presented in this paper were carried out using the student dataset which can be found in UCI machine Learning Repository (Lichman, 2013). The dataset contains data of a digital design course at the University of Genoa. The course assessment consisted of 6 sessions with the exception of one session (session 1) all the remaining sessions contributed to the final evaluation of the course. A hundred and fifteen students participated in evaluation. However, according to the grades only 62 were evaluated by the instructors. We selected the student dataset for two reasons a) the first reason is that we want to assess if the use of a suite like Dees could help instructors to understand student behaviour and then to improve students' performance and b) the second reason is that we have the dataset to our disposal (Lichman, 2013). The software used in our data mining experiments is WEKA, an open source, which contains several algorithms for Data Mining. Our main contribution is to perform an analysis on student performance and to identify the correlations between activities and students grades. In fact, to detect exercises which were difficult for mostly all students so forth. Therefore, we believe that research on student performance (finding relationships between activities and grades) could benefit in great deal the Technology Enhanced Learning (TEL). The correlations (between student performance and grades) presented in this paper are based in the analysis of the UCI dataset for a digital electronics design course. Another kind of assessment like, gaining skills by a student in a Computing MPhil program at the Open University can be found in Barroca et al. (Barroca et al., 2010).

The rest of the paper is organized as follows: firstly it provides an overview of related work. Secondly, it presents a brief description of the clustering algorithm, used in our solution to student performance analysis, namely k-means. Fourthly, it shows experiments carry out and finally, it gives our conclusions and future work.

RELATED WORK

Data mining algorithms were originally developed in the area of Machine Learning under the umbrella of the Artificial Intelligence field. Later, these algorithms were adopted by the Database community as powerful techniques for discovering patterns in raw data. The main applications of the database community were in the business sector (Shaw et al., 2001). Successful applications in business are for example, the use of data mining techniques in supermarkets data for directing publicity campaigns. However, in the education sector there is recent interest in the use of data mining methods due that Educational Data Mining offers opportunities and potentials to understand learning process and to optimize learning through educational systems. In fact, educators had seen the benefit of applying data mining algorithms to find information about students and then, improve the learning process. There are several applications of data mining applied to the Education sector (Papamitsiou & Economides, 2014), for example, in online assessment data, for analysing the process of answering the questions or requesting feedback by students. A study described in (Bannert et al., 2014) analyses student processes of self-regulated learning and shows the differences of learning behaviour between successful students and less successful ones from their temporal patterns. In fact, it shows that successful students perform regulatory activities with a higher frequency and in a different order than the less successful ones. A framework for integrating domain knowledge in educational Process Mining is introduced in (Trcka & Pechenizkiy, 2009). This facilitates interactive process mining and help educators to analyse educational processes based on formal modelling. A work using a dataset of students of a Digital Design course (Lichman, 2013) is reported in (Vahdat et al., 2014). This work used a tool called Disco and a fuzzy mining algorithm for data mining of models. The objective of this work was to understand student's behaviour when interacting with Technology Enhanced Learning tools. In short, the work showed that is possible to gain insight into the learning process of students from the interaction with data.

ALGORITHM

Clustering is one of the techniques which are concerned with the partitioning of similar objects into clusters such that objects in the same cluster share common properties. Some algorithms use computational power of computing to automatically find groups or clusters. However, clustering algorithms often shown limited performance in high dimensional space due to the inherent sparsity of the data. In our research, we used a clustering algorithm called k-means which is briefly described below.

ALGORITHM K-MEANS

Given xi observations or characteristics with i=1,2,…,n. The algorithm creates k partitions or centroids from the observations ($k \leq n$) where k is given by the user randomly. The algorithm form the set of clusters $S = \{S_1, S_2, \ldots, S_k\}$. Then, computes the Euclidean distance from all the points to the centroids and selects the minimum distance from the points to the clusters using the formula below (Hartigan 1975; Mitchell, 1995; Nasser et al, 2006).

$$MSE = \sum_{i=1}^{k} \sum_{xj \in Si} \left\| xj - \mu i \right\|^2$$

where MSE (stands for Means Squared Error distortion), μi is the centroid vector consisting of the points in cluster Si and xj is the vector of characteristics to be assigned to a cluster. Once the Euclidean distances are computed then, the vectors of characteristics are assigned to a cluster according to the minimum distance. Then, the centroids of each cluster are re-calculated and the algorithm iterates again. The algorithm finishes when the centroids do not change and all the vectors of characteristics are associated to a cluster.

EXPERIMENTS

Dataset Analysis

The Dees dataset contains 29,059 examples of student laboratory sessions (Vahdat et al., 2014; Vahdat et al., 2015). The dataset does not contain null values. The data set contains 13 attributes which are as follows: session, student_Id, exercise, activity, start_time, end_time, idle_time, mouse_wheel, mouse_wheel_click, mouse_click_left, mouse_click_right, mouse_movement and keystroke.

We used software called WEKA (Hall et al., 2009; Witten et al, 2005; Witten et al, 2011) in the analysis of the dataset and a clustering algorithm already offered in WEKA. As a first step, we started our dataset analysis by performing a statistical analysis such as minimum, maximum, mean, standard deviation in each of the attributes.

Session

The session attribute shows the number of laboratory sessions to be recorded in the experiment, in our case 6 sessions, one of them (session 1) is not evaluated (see Figure 1 and Figure 2).

Student_Id

The attribute student_id shows the Id of student from 1 to 115. The name of student is anonymized for ethical reasons. The attribute Student_Id is shown in Figure 3 and Figure 4.

Exercise

Exercise shows the Id of the exercise the student is working on. Each session contains roughly from 4 to 6 exercises, shown as “Es_# of the session_# of the exercise” (e.g. Es_1_2: exercise 2 of session 1).

Figure 1. Session

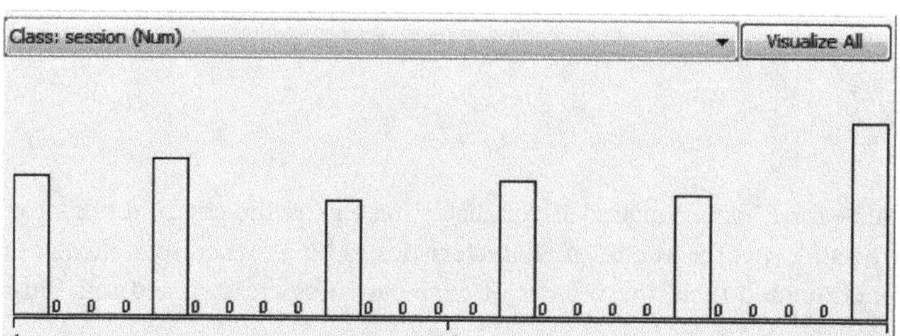

Figure 2. Session attribute

Selected attribute
Name: session — Type: Numeric
Missing: 0 (0%) — Distinct: 6 — Unique: 0 (0%)

Statistic	Value
Minimum	1
Maximum	6
Mean	3.616
StdDev	1.791

Figure 3. Student_id

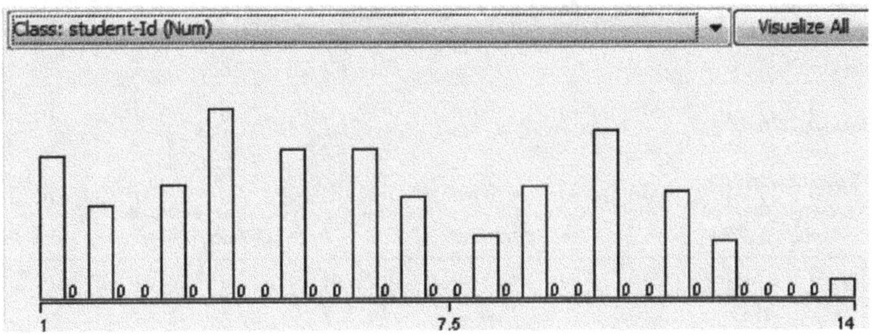

Figure 4. Student_id attribute

Selected attribute
Name: student-Id — Type: Numeric
Missing: 0 (0%) — Distinct: 13 — Unique: 0 (0%)

Statistic	Value
Minimum	1
Maximum	14
Mean	6.212
StdDev	3.4

'Es' with no number means the student has not started the exercise yet. The attribute Exercise is shown in Figure 5 and Figure 6.

Activity

The activities are labelled based on the title of web pages that are on focus. The abbreviation of each of the activities is: Es: Exercise; #: Number; Deeds: Digital Electronics Education and Design Suite; Diagram: Simulation Timing Diagram and FSM: Finite State Machine Simulator. The attribute Activity is shown in Figure 7 and Figure 8.

A description of the activities is given as follows:

Figure 5. Exercise

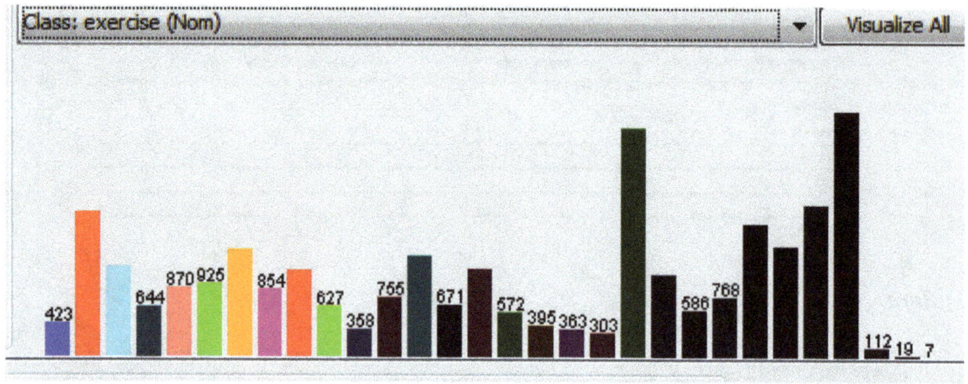

Figure 6. Exercise attribute

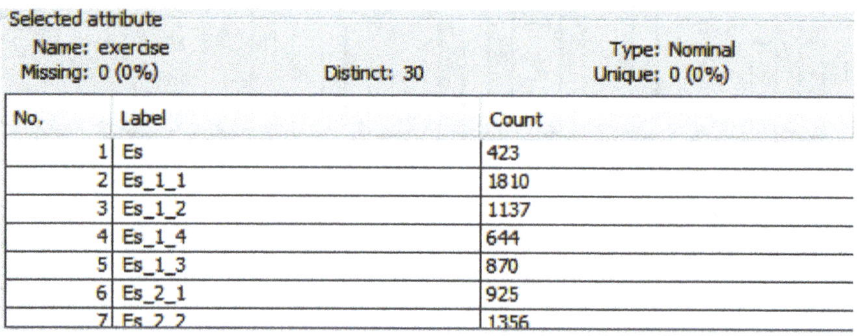

Selected attribute
Name: exercise
Missing: 0 (0%)
Distinct: 30
Type: Nominal
Unique: 0 (0%)

No.	Label	Count
1	Es	423
2	Es_1_1	1810
3	Es_1_2	1137
4	Es_1_4	644
5	Es_1_3	870
6	Es_2_1	925
7	Es_2_2	1356

Figure 7. Activity

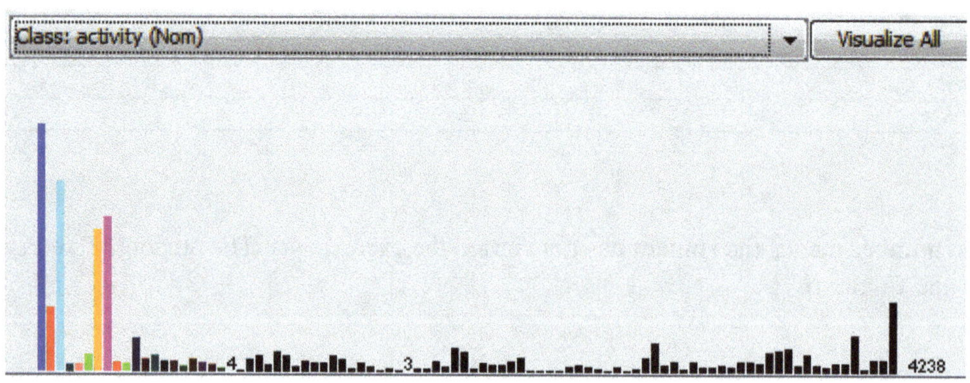

- **Study_Materials_Es_# of Session_# of Exercise:** It indicates that a student is studying/viewing the content of a specific exercise (i.e. Study_Es_6_1).
- **Deeds_Es_# of Session_# of Exercise:** It indicates that the student is working on a specific exercise inside the Deeds simulator (Digital Circuit Simulator), for example, Deeds_Es_6_1.

Figure 8. Activity attribute

Selected attribute
Name: activity — Type: Nominal
Missing: 0 (0%) — Distinct: 96 — Unique: 0 (0%)

No.	Label	Count
1	Other	4192
2	Aulaweb	1072
3	Blank	3238
4	Deeds	112
5	Study_Es_1_1	114
6	Deeds_Es_1_1	302
7	Properties	2384

- **Deeds_Es:** This shows when the student is on Deeds simulator but it is not clear what exercise he is working on. The "exercise" feature (the third feature) is considered from the moment the student study the content of an exercise to the moment he changes to another exercise; this can be estimated for assigning the number of exercise to Deeds as well.
- **Deeds:** It contains other activities related to Deeds, for instance, when the students save the circuit image or export it to VHDL.
- **TextEditor_Es_# of Session_# of Exercise:** This activity occurs when the student is writing the results of his work to submit later to the instructor. The students use a text editor (Word, Office) to answer to the questions and explain the solution they found through Deeds simulator (i.e. TextEditor_Es_6_1).
- **TextEditor_Es:** This activity indicates that the student is working on an exercise in the text editor but it is not clear which exercise it is. This happens due to change of file names by the student, so it cannot recognize automatically which exercise he/she is working on. Again, the note given above on Deeds_Es holds.
- **TextEditor:** This activity shows that the student is using the text editor but not on exercises, this can contain other activities related to the text editor, for instance when they just open it.
- **Diagram:** This activity occurs when the students use "Simulation Timing Diagram" to test the timing simulation of the logic networks, while using the Deeds simulator. It also contains these components: "Input Test Sequence" and "Timing Diagram View Manager ToolBar".
- **Properties:** Deeds simulator, Simulation Timing diagram, and FSM contain the properties window, which allows setting all the required parameters of the component under construction. For instance, the Properties can contain: "Switch Input", "Push-Button", "Clock properties", "Output properties", "Textbox properties". The data is labelled as "Properties". In order to understand if "Properties" refer to Deeds simulator or Simulation Timing diagram, it is necessary to look at the previous activity.
- **Study_Materials:** The student is viewing some materials relevant to the course (i.e. material provided by the instructor).
- **FSM_Es_# of Session_# of Exercise:** This activity occurs when the student is working on a specific exercise on "Finite State Machine Simulator" (e.g. FSM_Es_6_1).
- **FSM_Related.:** This activity occurs when the student is handling the components of Finite State Machine Simulator.

- **Aulaweb:** Students are using Aulaweb as a learning management system (based on Moodle) which is used for the course of digital electronics at the University of Genoa. In Aulaweb, the students might access the exercises, download them, upload their work and check the forum news.
- **Blank:** This activity occurs when the title of a visited page is not recorded.
- **Other:** This activity occurs when the student is not viewing any pages related to the course, then; the activity is assigned "Other". This includes, in the majority of the cases, activities which the student is performing but they are irrelevant activities to the course (i.e. if the student is on Facebook).

Start_Time

The start_time attribute shows the start date and time of a specific activity with the format: dd.mm. yyyy hh:mm:ss

End_Time

The end_time attribute shows the end date and time of a specific activity with the format: dd.mm.yyyy hh:mm:ss.

Iddle_Time

The attribute iddle_time shows the duration of idle time between the start and end time of an activity in milliseconds. The attribute Iddle_time is shown in Figure 9 and Figure 10.

Figure 9. Iddle_time

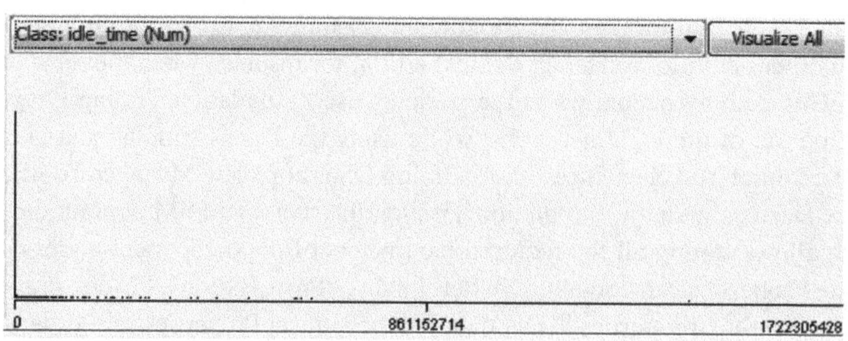

Figure 10. Iddle_time attribute

Selected attribute
Name: idle_time
Missing: 0 (0%)
Distinct: 8912
Type: Numeric
Unique: 7788 (27%)

Statistic	Value
Minimum	0
Maximum	1722305428
Mean	853594.561
StdDev	17162528.364

Mouse-Wheel

The attribute mouse_wheel shows the amount of mouse wheel during an activity. The attribute mouse_wheel is depicted in Figure 11 and Figure 12.

Mouse_Wheel_Click

The feature mouse_wheel_click shows the number of mouse wheel clicks during an activity. The Mose_wheel_click attribute is shown in Figure 13 and Figure 14.

Figure 11. Mouse-wheel

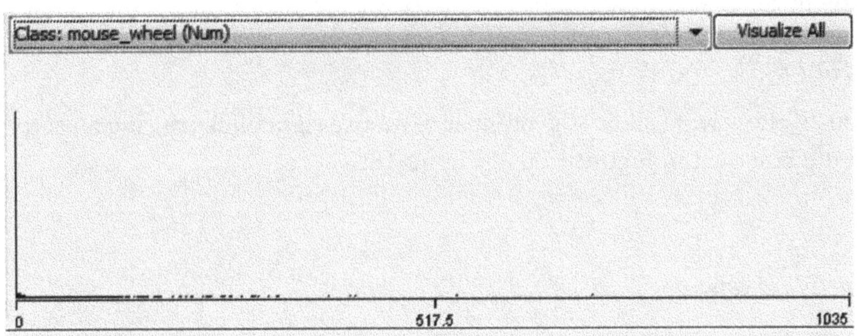

Figure 12. Mouse-wheel attribute

Selected attribute
Name: mouse_wheel
Missing: 0 (0%)
Distinct: 183
Type: Numeric
Unique: 65 (0%)

Statistic	Value
Minimum	0
Maximum	1035
Mean	2.451
StdDev	15.961

Figure 13. Mouse_wheel_click

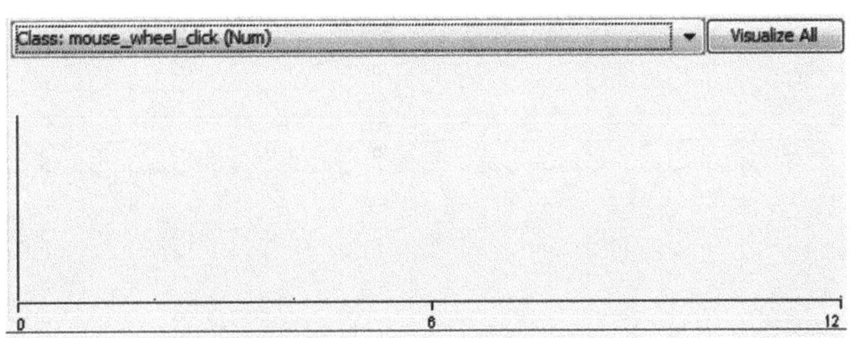

Figure 14. Mouse_wheel_click attribute

Selected attribute
Name: mouse_wheel_click — Type: Numeric
Missing: 0 (0%) — Distinct: 4 — Unique: 1 (0%)

Statistic	Value
Minimum	0
Maximum	12
Mean	0.001
StdDev	0.087

Mouse_Click_Left

The attribute mouse_click_left shows the number of mouse left clicks during an activity. The mouse_click_left attribute is depicted in Figure 15 and Figure 16.

Mouse_Click_Right

The attribute mouse_click_right shows the number of mouse right clicks during an activity. The mouse_click_right attribute is shown in Figure 17 and Figure 18.

Figure 15. mouse_click_left

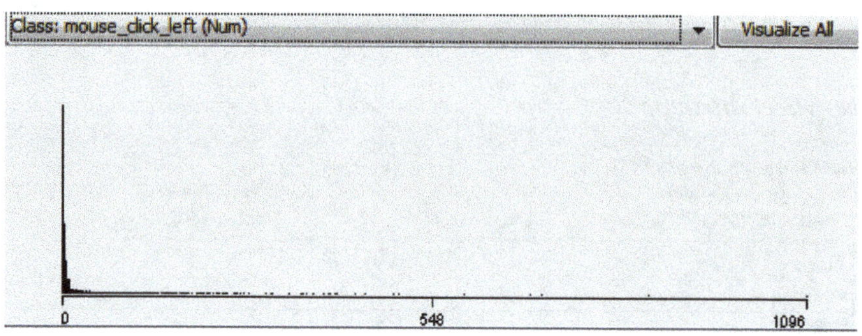

Figure 16. mouse_click_left attribute

Selected attribute
Name: mouse_click_left — Type: Numeric
Missing: 0 (0%) — Distinct: 206 — Unique: 66 (0%)

Statistic	Value
Minimum	0
Maximum	1096
Mean	6.888
StdDev	21.77

Figure 17. mouse_click_right

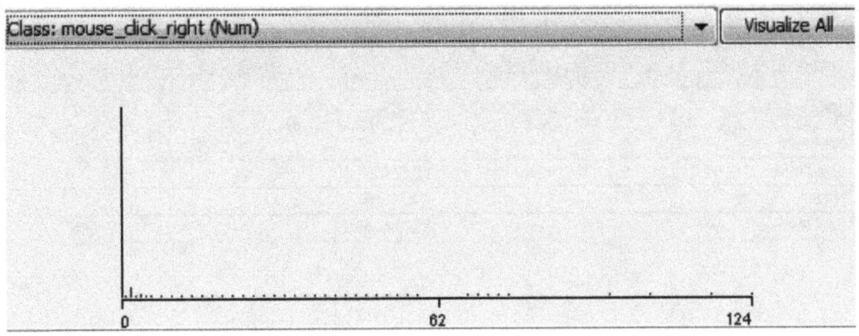

Figure 18. mouse_click_right attribute

Selected attribute
Name: mouse_click_right
Missing: 0 (0%)
Distinct: 42
Type: Numeric
Unique: 9 (0%)

Statistic	Value
Minimum	0
Maximum	124
Mean	0.349
StdDev	2.939

Mouse_Movement

The attribute mouse_movement shows the distance covered by the mouse movements during an activity. The mouse_movement attribute is shown in Figure 19 and Figure 20.

Keystroke

The keystroke attribute shows the number of keystrokes during an activity. The keystroke attribute is presented in Figure 21 and Figure 22.

Figure 19. Mouse_movement

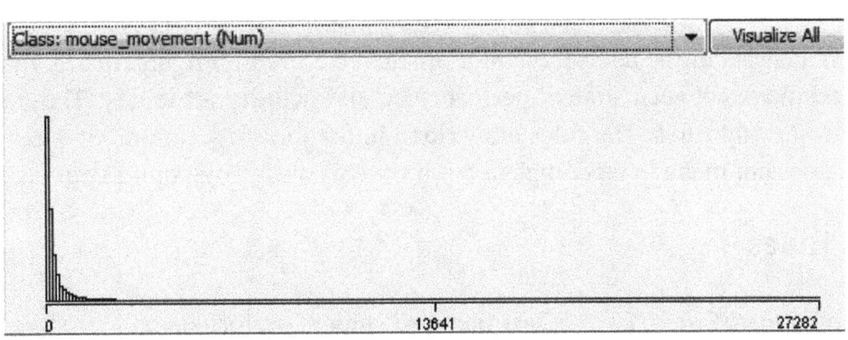

Figure 20. Mouse_movement attribute

Selected attribute
Name: mouse_movement
Missing: 0 (0%) Distinct: 2569 Type: Numeric Unique: 1113 (4%)

Statistic	Value
Minimum	0
Maximum	27282
Mean	401.16
StdDev	1028.466

Figure 21. Keystroke

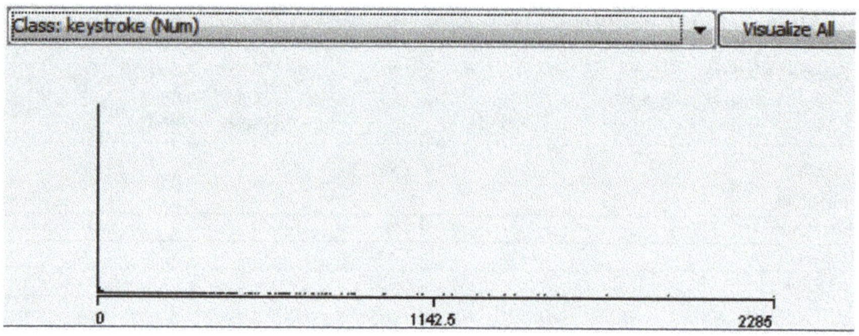

Figure 22. Keystroke attribute

Selected attribute
Name: keystroke
Missing: 0 (0%) Distinct: 327 Type: Numeric Unique: 151 (1%)

Statistic	Value
Minimum	0
Maximum	2285
Mean	6.07
StdDev	49.889

CORRELATIONS BEETWEEN ATTRIBUTES

We performed an analysis in the dataset (using statistics like minimum, maximum, mean, stddev) and found some correlations between student performance and activity attributes. These correlations are expressed in the following rules. The rules are written in the form **if** <condition> **then** <conclusion>. This set of rules does not mean to be complete but it gave us a starting point in our case of study.

Correlations Rules

- **If** amount of *activity Study_Es_#* is **low** then bad student performance
- **If** amount of *activity Deeds_Es_#* is **low** then bad student performance

- **If** amount of *activity Deeds_Es* is **low** then bad student performance
- **If** amount of *activity Deeds* is **low** then bad student performance
- **If** amount of *activity TextEditor_Es_#* is **low** then bad student performance
- **If** amount of *activity* TextEditor_Es is **low** then bad student performance
- **If** amount of *activity Diagram* is **low** then bad student performance
- **If** amount of *activity Properties* is **low** then bad student performance
- **If** amount of *activity Study_Materials* is **low** then bad student performance
- **If** amount of *activity FSM_Es_#* is **low** then bad student performance
- **If** amount of *activity FSM_Related* is **low** then bad student performance
- **If** amount of *activity Aulaweb* is **low** then bad student performance
- **If** amount of *activity Blank* is **high** then bad student performance
- **If** amount of *activity Other* is **high** then bad student performance
- **If** the amount of *mouse_wheel* is **low** then bad student performance
- **If** the amount of *keystroke* is **low** then bad student performance
- **If** the amount of *mouse_wheel_click* is **high** then maybe students are solving exercises
- **If not** Es_#_# then likely bad grade (students did not solve any exercise)

Each rule uses linguistic variables (high, medium and low) which have a specific value for each of the activities performed by students. For example, *activity* has the definition given below. Note that, in the *activity* definition we use the following notation.

Notation:

1→Study_Es_# of session_# of exercise, 2→Deeds_Es_# of session_# of exercise, 3→ Deeds_Es,

4→ Deeds, 5→ TextEditor_Es_# of session_# of exercise, 6 →TextEditor_Es, 7→ TextEditor,

8→Diagram, 9→Properties, 10→Study_Materials, 11→FSM_Es_# of session_# of exercise, 12→FSM_Related, 13→Aulaweb, 14→Blank, 15→Other

The linguistic variable activity is defined as follows:

activity is **high** if *activity* includes activities in set [1,2,3,4,5,6,7,8,9,10,11,12,13]
activity is **medium** if *activity* includes activities in set [1,2,3,4,5,6,7,8]
activity is **low** if *activity* includes activities in set [1,5,14,15]

In a similar fashion, the rest of the attributes could be analysed.

To remain to the reader according to Zadeh, a linguistic variable is a variable whose values are words or sentences in a natural or artificial language. In more specific terms, a linguistic variable can be characterized by a quintuple (H, T(H), U,G,M) in which H is the name of the variable; T(H) is the term-set of H, that is the collection of its linguistics values; U is the universe of discourse; G is a syntactic rule which generates the terms in T(H), M is the semantic rule which associates with each linguistic value X its meaning M(X) where M(X) denotes a fuzzy subset of U. The meaning of a linguistic value X is characterised by a compatibility function c: U → [0,1] which associates with each u in U its compatibility with X. A detailed explanation of a linguistic variable could be found in (Zadeh, 1975a; Zadeh 1975b; Zadeh 1976; Zadeh 1996).

Summing up, we believe that the best way to model the student activities is by using linguistic variables due the fact that, we could model more realistically the problem of student performance. For instance, we could define that *activity* in set [1,2,3,4,5,6,7,8,9,10,11,12,13] with high might be 0.7 while that of *activity* in set [1,5,14,15] might be 0.2.

CLUSTERING EXPERIMENTS

In our experiment, we used the software WEKA (WEKA, 2015) and a dataset consisting of 29,058 examples from the UCI repository (Lichman, 2013). The examples are part of a collection of data from session 1 to session 6 of an undergraduate Digital Design course. We considered a sample of 10 students for our experiment. We divided the dataset in two parts (60% for training and 40% for testing) and performed clustering on the data. The selected clustering algorithm k-means executed 5 iterations, within cluster sum of squared error were 108497.9657 and missing values globally replaced with mean/mode. The model and evaluation in the training set is given in Table 1 and Table 2.

Summing up, some conclusions can be drawn after performing clustering and studying the respective graphs. We observed that, there is a relation between student performance and the activity registered in deeds suite We used k-means with 80% of the dataset for training and 20% for testing (using data from all sessions S1 to S6 and sample of 10 students). In our experiment, we observed that, in the learning phase two clusters were formed. Cluster 0 shows the activity registered in solving Es_6_3 & Activity

Table 1. Cluster outputs

Attribute	Cluster Centroids		
	Full Data (29048)	**Cluster #0 (13987)**	**Cluster #1 (15071)**
Session	3.6156	5.0807	2.2559
Studen_Id	6.2116	5.96	6.4452
Exercise	Es_6_3	Es_6_3	Es_1_1
Activity	Other	Properties	Other
Start_time	13.11.2014 12:4:28	13.11.2014 12:4:28	2.10.2014 12:26:34
End_time	2.10.2014 12:26:33	16.10.2014 13:2:8	2.10.2014 12:26:33
Iddle_time	853594.5612	620880.7927	1069570.1089
Mouse_wheel	2.4511	2.512	2.3945
Mouse_wheel_click	0.0014	0.0013	0.0016
Mouse_click_left	6.8877	6.8346	6.9371
Mouse_click_right	0.3489	0.2012	0.486
Mouse_movement	401.16	409.5835	393.3423
Keystroke	6.0704	4.9743	7.0876

Within cluster sum of squared errors:108497.9657. Missing values globally replaced with mean /mode.

Table 2. Cluster outputs

Attribute	Cluster Centroids		
	Full Data (17434)	Cluster #0 (10172)	Cluster #1 (7262)
Session	3.6205	2.4611	5.2444
Studen_Id	6.2397	6.3533	6.0806
Exercise	Es_6_3	Es_4_5	Es_6_3
Activity	Other	Other	Properties
Start_time	20.11.2014 11:24:29	2.10.2014 12:1:59	20.11.2014 11:24:29
End_time	2.10.2014 11:50:25	2.10.2014 11:50:25	20.11.2014 11:57:0
Iddle_time	864493.3406	1154350.8262	458485.3065
Mouse_wheel	2.5092	2.4023	2.659
Mouse_wheel_click	0.0015	0.0016	0.0014
Mouse_click_left	6.9834	7.1843	6.702
Mouse_click_right	0.3755	0.515	0.1801
Mouse_movement	406.0573	402.2549	411.3834
Keystroke	6.1143	6.6773	5.3257

Within cluster sum of squared errors: 64868.8563. Missing values globally replaced with mean /mode.

properties while cluster 1 shows activity registered in solving exercise Es_1_1 & Activity Other. In the testing phase also two clusters were formed. Students solved Es_4_5 & Activity Other and Es_6_3 &Activity Properties. Further research, aims to determine which attributes are more relevant when assessing student performance.

A second set of experiments consisted in the analysis of the data of each session. Then, we obtained the following results.

Session 1: We observed that students solved mainly Es_1_1, Es_1_2 and Es_1_3 and fewer students solved Es_1_4.

Session 2: We observed that students solved exercises Es_2_1, Es_2_2, Es_2_3 and Es_2_4 and fewer students solved exercises Es_2_5 and Es_2_6.

Session 3: We noticed that students solved all the exercises namely Es_3_1, Es_3_2, Es_3_3 and Es_3_4. However, we noticed that there were more amount of students solving exercises Es_3_2 and Es_3_4.

Session 4: We observed that many students solved exercise Es_4_5 (data obtained from analysing the cluster of exercise 5 in session 4) and fewer students solved exercises Es_4_1, Es_4_2, Es_4_3 and Es_4_4.

Session 5: We observed that many students solved exercise Es_5_4. Also, we observed that no many students solved exercise Es_5_1 and very few students solved exercises Es_5_2 and Es_5_3.

Session 6: We observed that students solved exercises Es_6_1, Es_6_2 and Es_6_3 and no many solved exercise Es_6_4 and almost nobody solved exercises Es_6_5 and Es_6_6.

A third set of experiments consisted in analysing activities in each session.

Session 1

The majority of the student focused in activities Other and Aulaweb. In Aulaweb, the students might access the exercises, download them, upload their work, and check news. Then, we observed, but in lower proportion, activities such as Blank, Dees, Study_Materials_Es_1_1, Dees_Es_1, Properties, Diagram, Study_Materials_Es_1_2, Study_Materials_Es_1_4, TextEditor, TextEditor_Es, Dees_Es_2, TextEditor, TextEditor_Es, Study_Materials_Es_1_3, Dees_Es_1_4, TextEditor_Es, Dees_Es_1_4, TextEditor_Es and TextEditor_Es. In short, students basically were familiarizing with the problem and deeds suite by building a diagram and using editor to report answers.

Session 2

The set of activities performed in higher concentration at the beginning of session 2 are defined as follows: Study_Materials, Dees_Es_2, TextEditor, Blank, Diagram, Properties, Other, TextEditor, Aulaweb, Study_Materials_Es_2, Dees_Es_2,TextEditor, Study_Materials,Dees_Es_2,TextEditor, Study_Materials_Es_2, TextEditor, Dees_Es_2, Dees, Study_Materials_Es_2,TextEditor and Dees_Es_2. Finally, we found less concentration (at the end of session 2) of students performing activities like Study_Materials, TextEditor, Dees_Es_2, FSM and Study_Materials. The conclusion is that students did not solved exercises related to finite state machine exercises.

Session 3.

The set of activities performed in higher concentration (from the beginning of session until ¾ of the session 3) were activities such as Other, Blank, Study_Materials_Es_3_1, Dees_Es_3_1, TextEditor_Es, Properties, Diagram, Aulaweb, Study_Materials_Es_3_2, TextEditor_Es, Dees_Es_3_2 and Study_Materials_es_3_3. However, it was noticed less concentration of activities (in the last quarter of the session) on activities like TextEditor_Es, Dees_Es_3_3, Study_Materials_Es_3_4, Dees_Es_3_4, TextEditor_Es, Dees, TextEditor and Study_Materials_Es_2. In short, we observed that students worked in all the exercises of the session 3.

Session 4

We observed high concentration of activities Other, Study_Materials_es_4, Blank, Study_Materials_Es_4 in the first 1/5 of session 4. Then, we observed less concentration of activities (in the 2/5 of session 4) such as Study_Material_Es_4, Study_Materials_Es_4, Dees_Es_4, Additionally, we observed higher concentration of activities (3/5 of session 4) such as TextEditor, TextEditor_Es, Diagram, Aulaweb. Also, we observed less concentration (4/5 of session 4) such as TexEditor_Es, Dees_es_4, Dees_Es_4, Texteditor, Dees_Es_4, Dees_Es_4 and TextEditor. Finally, we observed higher concentration of activities (in the last 1/5 of session 4) such as TextEditor, Dees_Es_4, Properties, Study_Materials_Es_4, FSM, TextEditor and Study_Materials_Es_4. In short, we observed that many students solved exercise Es_4_5.

Session 5

We observed (in the first quarter of session) high concentration of activities such as Other, TextEditor, TextEditor_Es_5 and Study_Materials_Es_5_2. Then, we observed less concentration of activities (in the second quarter of session 5) such as Dees_Es_5_1, Aulaweb, Study_Materials_Es_5_1, and Blank. In the third quarter of session 5, we observed high concentration of activities such as Properties, Diagram, Dees_Es_5_2, TextEditor_Es, Study_Materials_Es_5_3 and TextEditor_Es. Finally, we observed high concentration of activities (in the last quarter of session 5) such as Dees_Es_5_3, Study_Materials_Es_5_4, Dees_Es_5_4, TextEditor_Es and Dees. In conclusion, we could say that students primarily were concentrated in solving exercise Es_5_4.

Session 6

We observed high concentration of activities (in the first 1/6 of session 6) such as Other, FSM, Blank, Study_Materials_Es_6_1, Properties, FSM, Aulaweb. We noticed less concentration of activities (in the 2/6 of session 6) such as TextEditor_Es, Dees_Es_6_1, Diagram, Study_Materials_Es_6_2, TexEditor and TextEditor. Also, we observed high concentration (in the 3/6 of session 6) such as FSM_Es_6_2, Dees_Es_6, Study_Materials_Es_6_3, TextEditor, FSM_Es_6_3, Dees_Es_6_4 and Study_Materials_Es. Finally, we observed low concentration (in the 4/ of session 6) of activities like Study_Materials_Es, Study_Materials_Es, Dees_Es, TextEditor and Study_Materials_Es. In conclusion, we can say that students did not solve all the exercises of the session 6.

Summary

Summing up, our experiment results are coherent with the grades that students obtained in the final evaluation of the course. These grades indicate that few students did well (22 out of 62) i.e. 35% while a bigger proportion of students did not perform well i.e. 40 out 62 (65%). According to our analysis, students did not solve all exercises in several sessions. Furthermore, from our data sample, mostly all students did not performed well enough in session 6. Finally, a four experiment consisted in comparing pattern of activities between a good students and bad students. The experiment showed that a good student (student with high score in the course) made use more frequently of the Dees suite while a bad student did not use the Dees suite frequently during each of the 6 sessions of the course. In other words, the pattern of a good student (in the dataset) shows a high concentration of activity Dees_Es, Dee_Es_# and Dees_Es while a bad student has a low concentration of activities Dees_Es, Dee_Es_# and Dees_Es.

CONCLUSION AND FUTURE WORK

We presented a study of the relation between activities performed by students and student performance. In our analysis, we used 29,059 examples of students from a digital design undergraduate course. Firstly, we did an analysis of each of the attributes in the dataset. From our analysis, we derived a set of rules, which correlates the performance of the student with Dees activities carried out by students. Secondly, we applied a clustering algorithm k-means implemented in WEKA, an open source framework for Data Mining (WEKA, 2015) in order to observe student activities patterns. The main contribution of this work was to perform an analysis and find relationships between student performance and activities carried out in Dees Suite. Preliminary results are encouraging as we found some correlations between attributes. Future work is concerned with the acquisition of a dataset of different Engineering courses at the undergraduate level. Additionally, we plan to carry out experiments of clustering performing a selection of the attributes in order to determine which attributes are more relevant to be considered in the model. Furthermore, an analysis of each student activities could be performed in order to determine the level of learning of each student and then, target tutorials/lectures to most difficult topics of the course.

REFERENCES

Bannert, M., Reimann, P., & Sonnenberg, C. (2014). Process mining techniques for analysing patterns and strategies in students self-regulated learning. Metacognition and Learning, 9(2), 161–185. doi:10.1007/s11409-013-9107-6 doi:10.1007/s11409-013-9107-6

Barroca, L., Rapanotti, L., Petre, M., & Vargas-Vera, M. (2010). *Developing Research Degrees Online.* International Conference of Education, Research and Innovation (ICERI), Madrid, Spain.

Chatti, M. A., Dyckhoff, A. L., Schroeder, U., & Th¨us, H. (2012). A reference model for learning analytics. International Journal of Technoogy Enhanced Learning, 4(5), 318–331. doi:10.1504/IJTEL.2012.051815 doi:10.1504/IJTEL.2012.051815

Hartigan, J. A. (1975). Clustering algorithms. New York: John Wiley.

Kruse, A., & Pongsajapan, R. (2012). Student-centered learning analytics. CNDLS Thought Papers.

Lichman, M. (2013). UCI Machine Learning Repository. Irvine, CA: University of California, School of Information and Computer Science.

Mitchell, T. M. (1997). Machine Learning. New York: McGraw Hill.

Nasser, H., Hamad, D., & Nasr, C. (2006). K-means Clustering Algorithm in Projected Spaces. *The 9th International Conference FUSION 2006*, 1-6.

Papamitsiou, Z., & Economides, A. (2014). Learning analytics and educational data mining in practice: A systematic literature review of empirical evidence. Journal of Educational Technology & Society, 17(4), 49–64.

Shaw, M., Subramaniam, M. C., Tan, G., & Welge, M. (2001). Knowledge management and data mining for marketing. Decision Support Systems, 31(1), 127–137. doi:10.1016/S0167-9236(00)00123-8 doi:10.1016/S0167-9236(00)00123-8

Siemens, G. (2012). Learning analytics: envisioning a research discipline and a domain of practice. *International Conference on Learning Analytics and Knowledge*. doi:10.1145/2330601.2330605 doi:10.1145/2330601.2330605

Trcka, N., & Pechenizkiy, M. (2009). From local patterns to global models: Towards domain driven educational process mining. *International Conference on Intelligent Systems Design and Applications.* doi:10.1109/ISDA.2009.159 doi:10.1109/ISDA.2009.159

Vahdat, M., Ghio, A., Oneto, L., Anguita, D., Funk, M., & Rauterberg, M. (2015). Advances in learning analytics and educational data mining. *European Symposium on Artificial Neural Networks, Computational Intelligence and Machine Learning.*

Vahdat, M., Oneto, L., Ghio, A., Donzellini, G., Anguita, D., Funk, M., & Rauterberg, M. (2014). A learning analytics methodology to profile students behaviour and explore interactions with a digital electronics simulator. In S. de Freitas, C. Rensing, T. Ley, & P. J. Munoz-Merino (Eds.), EC-TEL 2014. LNCS (Vol. 8719, pp. 596–597). Springer Verlag.

WEKA. (2015). *Data Mining Software in Java.* Retrieved from http://www.cs.waikato.ac.nz/ml/weka/index.html

Witten, I. H., Frank, E., & Hall, M. A. (2005). Data Mining: Practical Machine Learning Tools and Techniques (2nd ed.). Morgan Kaufmann Publishers.

Witten, I. H., Frank, E., & Hall, M. A. (2011). Data Mining: Practical Machine Learning Tools and Techniques (3rd ed.). Morgan Kaufmann Publishers.

Zadeh, L. A. (1975a). The concept of a linguistic variable and its applications to approximate reasoning. Part I. Information Sciences, 8(3), 199–249. doi:10.1016/0020-0255(75)90036-5 doi:10.1016/0020-0255(75)90036-5

Zadeh, L. A. (1975b). The concept of a linguistic variable and its applications to approximate reasoning. Part II. Information Sciences, 8(4), 301–357. doi:10.1016/0020-0255(75)90046-8 doi:10.1016/0020-0255(75)90046-8

Zadeh, L. A. (1976). The concept of a linguistic variable and its applications to approximate reasoning. Part III. Information Sciences, 8, 43–80.

Zadeh, L. A. (1996). Fuzzy Logic Computing with words. IEEE Transactions on Fuzzy Systems, 4(2), 103–111. doi:10.1109/91.493904 doi:10.1109/91.493904

Chapter 7
Perceived Innovative Teaching Procedures in Higher Education From Students' Perspectives From a Sentiment Analysis Approach

Ernesto D'Avanzo
University of Salerno, Italy

Miltiadis Demetrios Lytras
American College of Greece, Greece

Jose Picatoste
Universidad Autónoma de Madrid, Spain

Isabel Novo-Corti
Universidade da Coruña, Spain

Paola Adinolfi
University of Salerno, Italy

ABSTRACT

In the fourth revolution era talking innovation is not only necessary for improving and forwarding all social and economic activities, but also is it an exigence of those who are demanding high-quality goods or services. This is important for knowledge services, and becomes a core issue for educative issues designed for the millennials or digital natives. Sometimes, these exigencies are no shown directly, but it is possible assessing them by means of the analysis of sentiments, which reflects a range of feelings which are not clearly verbalized and even self-recognized. This paper analyzes sentiments for assessing the importance of innovative procedures in higher education, from the point of view of the students. A prototype architecture – LADEL (Learning Analytics Dashboard for E-Learning) - is introduced, for dealing with the diverse e-learning domains. Some experiments are conducted. This demonstrated the necessity of innovative procedures in higher education, since it is a widespread, multidisciplinary and transversal demand, even it is not always explicit.

DOI: 10.4018/978-1-5225-4191-2.ch007

1. SENTIMENTS AND INNOVATIVE FRAMEWORKS IN HIGHER EDUCATION: THE ERASMUS STUDENTS INFLUENCES IN CITIES AND VICE VERSA

According the "El Pais" (the most relevant Spanish newspaper in the country which is higher receptor of Erasmus Studients: Spain), states on May, 27th, 2007, that the Erasmus program has been, first and foremost, the most notable marketing exercise of that idea called 'Europe' in the last 30 years, undoubtedly the greatest illusion (in the sense of 'hope' and also of 'artifice') The now battered Union is able to offer its citizens. If nobody remembers the European Constitution and many doubt the solvency and intentions of the Monetary Union, everyone praises the benefits of Erasmus mobility. This is particularly clear for countries like Spain, which is the most important receptor of Erasmus students.

It is commonly known that the Erasmus program surpasses the academic environments where young people develop their university learning activity. This European program has served to change the lives of those who are involved in it. In addition, the life of these young people in other European cities during one or two semesters of their studies of degree, takes place in a moment of full personal boil, where the feelings are intense and, often, in evolution.

The Erasmus program is innovative in itself, however, it is necessary to disregard two fundamental aspects:

On the one hand, Erasmus are represented as the embodiment of the European project, successful polyglots whose transnational experiences would have served to refine and enhance their professional competences within the framework of that ideal, competitive and sophisticated Europe.

On the other hand, some forums talk about their stays with a certain disdain (and some envy), pointing out their tendency to participate in all kinds of parties and unrest, including high doses of alcohol and sex, which would result in the dilapidation of the time of Dedication to class and study.

Then, the innovative procedure of this program, which is now thirty years old and has been supporting more than 4.4 million students, is not only on mobility, but also in the conformance of new teaching environments and new urban geographies.

Rankings order universities, allowing them to be compared by condensing heterogeneous information about their characteristics and results into one indicator. Rankings simplify complexity, but offer a simple ordering, with some advantages and some disadvantages: they facilitate their assessment to users who do not have the time or the preparation to analyze in depth the performance of a university institution but conceal differential features of The universities which could be relevant. The students' mobility by means of Erasmus programs or other alternatives influences the mark on the ranking in an indirect way and, at the same time, the position on this ranking is a factor influencing the chosen university for the international mobility. Hazelkorn (2013) claims that *university rankings mechanisms* in use are subject to several drawbacks such as, for example, *measurement accuracy*, measuring the *university as a whole institution*, and the way data is being collected for measuring specific indicators at universities. For instance, only the *average quality* of a university is measured, while individual subjects are not considered in the computation. And different compilers have adopted different methods to produce these rankings (Berbegal-Mirabent & Ribeiro-Soriano, 2015). Moreover, indicators such as *university reputation* have a higher influence value than some others (Olcay & Bulu, 2016), especially on social media (Bunzel, 2007; Kietzmann, Hermkens, McCarthy & Silvestre, 2011). In this sense it appears unsurprising that Higher Education institutions turned to social media strategies to target and attract new students (Constantinides & Zinck Stagno, 2012). Furthermore, relevant educational factors such as *quality of teaching* or the *quality of student experience* are taken into account but only marginally (Hazelkorn, 2013), even if students use social media daily and, as such, they are well acquainted with their use (Westerman, Daniel & Bowman, 2016; Siamagka & Christodoulides, 2016). Not surprisingly, therefore, there haven't been new attempts of constructing rankings mechanisms that seek to incorporate student satisfaction (Vidal, 2016) and content analysis of news media coverage (Friedrichsmeier & Marcinkowski, 2016). For instance, some findings indicated that instructors, from any discipline or culture, could deliver courses through social media platforms thanks to different features provided by social media tools that encourage, for their part, students' participation (Kilis, Gülbahar, & Rapp, 2016). Other inquiries show how numbers of instructors are turning to social networking sites to communicate with students, since instructor credibility seems to increase when students are engaged with his social posting with respect to the only scholar posting activity of the teacher (Johnson, 2011).

The MOOCs (Massive Open Online Courses) could be considered a form of indirect contact between students and teachers of different countries that can foment the intentions of mobility of the students. A chief role in this context is played by MOOCs. According to *Class Central*[1], the popular search engine for online courses, MOOCs doubled on 2015. Always in 2015, the number of students enrolled in MOOCs was equal to the total number of students enrolled in the three previous years, when the first MOOC was launched at Stanford, and the total number of courses is 4,200.

According to data provided by *Class Central*, the number of students that, on 2015, have been enrolled at least in one course achieved 35 million. For instance, *coursera.org*, that is the world's leading provider of MOOCs, alone, in 2015, increased its subscribers up to 17 million, increasing its subscribers of 7 million in one year. *FutureLearn* became the third largest MOOC provider in the world, just behind *coursera* and *edX*, approaching about 3 million users. The competition among MOOCs allows new ways to convey traditional content, but on a grand scale, just as *FutureLearn* did launching the world's largest single session of a MOOC, with 440,000 students enrolled for one session of the Understanding IELTS[2], which, traditionally, was taught by the British Council. Indeed, MOOCs changed other traditional high educational habits, such as, for instance, the way courses' certificates are issued, in other words not anymore on the basis of the individual courses attended but earned by completing a given sequence of courses. This novelty changes also the way other MOOCs and traditional High Educational institutions. Whereas this could be more difficult to do for traditional universities programs, that are constrained by ministerial regulations which, in turn, require precise time slots to make changes and be approved, such user and/or labor oriented settings are adoptable by new programs (e.g. at Master or Ph.D. level) and conveyed either through brick and mortar channels or through MOOCs. A schematic example of the interrelation can be seen in Figure 1, the plausibility of such an approach. And the revenues gained by *coursera* and *udacity*, after adopting these new credentials policies, bode well in this respect.

Looking at emerging analytics strategies can help to make many decisions and policies that can be drawn. For instance, Acevedo & Marín (2015) show how Learning Analytics functionalities, such as the employing of *hidden patterns* in educational data, can be integrated in a Decision Support System (Power, Sharda, & Burstein, 2015; Moja, Friz, Capobussi, Kwag, Banzi, Ruggiero & Kunnamo, 2016; Chou, Tien, Lin & Chiu, 2016) to produce a Learning Decision Support System. In the global framework described in the previous paragraphs, this work has a double objective. First, reviewing a specific *learning analytics* method (Siemens & Long, 2011; Baker & Inventado, 2014; Merceron, Blikstein & Siemens, 2016), that is *sentiment analysis* (Shum & Ferguson, 2012; Siemens, 2013), in Higher Education, showing how it is employed to monitor student satisfaction on different platforms: *learning diaries,*

Figure 1. Innovative teaching by means of MOOCs, university rankings and Erasmus Students' sentiments

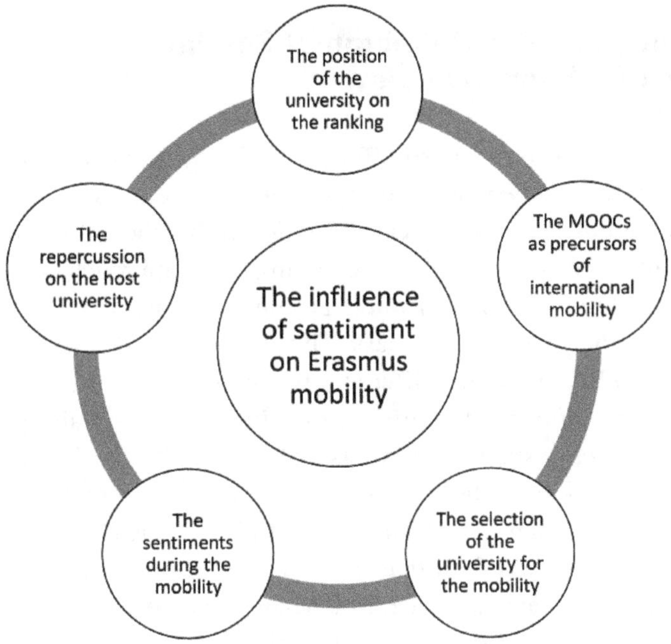

Twitter and *MOOCs*. Second, introducing an architecture that, using the platforms of the previous step, is capable to observe and support the modeling of students' and teachers' behaviors (Pursel, Zhang, Jablokow, Choi & Velegol, 2016; Wang, Yang, Wen, Koedinger, & Rosé, 2015), giving an overall view of their mutual activity. To our opinion, such a platform would be beneficial for both *decision makers*, and, in general, *policy makers*. A positive "side effect" from the availability of such a kind of approach would be its employment for the labor market. For instance *lifelong learning programs* (LLP) could be set by exploiting what unemployed people feel as important topics of their interest, ORANGE the *ZPD* Vygotsky (1980), and Herbert Simon's *bounded rationality* (Simon, 1991) and *satisficing* (Simon, 1956) theory. Our approach will ease both the learning and the teaching task. And the communication channel, among teachers and students, will also benefit by capturing emerging *attitudes*, identified as constructs, in batch, through structural equation modeling applied to data available from different platforms. In this sense, we adopt a cognitive perspective as already claimed elsewhere (D'Avanzo & Lytras, 2016). As regards Simon's theory, its discussion, even minimal, is outside the scope of this work. However, one of the most notable aspects in this context concerns the cognitive overload that students may face.

Next section reports on recent and relevant *sentiment analysis* literature with particular emphasis on MOOC's domain. Section 3 introduces the first contribution of this paper, reviewing 3 case studies where *sentiment analysis* is applied for Higher Education purposes (i.e., *learning diaries, Twitter* and *MOOCs*). Section 4 introduces LADEL, a SA prototype with a twofold objective: 1) monitoring *learning diaries*, *students blogs*, *social networks* and *MOOCs*, in order to obtain quantitative insights that can support Higher Education decision makers; 2) exploiting platform analytics for policy makers purposes, such as experimenting mechanisms able to match *lifelong learning* needs emerging from labor markets with the Higher Education programs. Section 5 discuss the approach in the light of its further development.

2. ANALYZING FEELINGS

2.1. Starting with an Operative Definition of Sentiment Analysis by Means of a Short Overview

In one of his last editorial and well managed effort, Liu (2015) defines *sentiment analysis* (hereafter SA) as "the computational study of people's opinions, sentiments, emotions, and attitudes", claiming its increasingly importance for business and society. After describing the algorithms employed for Twitter sentiment analysis, the authors categorized them according to the approach employed, identifying 4 different classes from the literature: *machine learning*, *lexicon-based*, a mixture of the previous two classes named *Hybrid*, and, finally the *Graph-based* class. The authors, besides specific aspects related to the four different approaches to SA, highlight different open issues about the task, such as *data sparsity*, *lack of benchmarks*, *multilingual content*, *sentiment tracking over time*. Paltoglou (2015) examined the plausibility of using SA to identify significant events that occur in the world (i.e. *event detection*), a task that, usually, is addressed by looking at the increasing or spikes of term frequency on the social platform. The authors, instead, look for sudden changes in the *positivity* or *negativity* that keywords are typically associated with. Experiments reported show that an important factor for *event detection* is the number of tweets analyzed. This implies that any approach is dependent on the coverage that an event receives on the media, while the number of days used to extract sentiment does not have significant weight on the task. Mamgain et *al.*. (2016) did an analysis of people's sentiment in top colleges in India, by exploiting three different kinds of machine learning algorithms (i.e., *Naïve Bayes*, *Support Vector Machine* and a *Multilayer Perceptron*), giving a special emphasis at the *SVM*, that are analyzed using different kernels (*RBF*, *linear*, *polynomial* and *sigmoid*). Experiments show that Multilayer Perceptron surpassed other algorithms because of its highly accurate approximation of the cost function, ideal number of hidden layers and learning the relationship among input and output variables at each step. Support Vector Machine result outperformed by the Naïve Bayes approach for polarity classification of the text because, as supported by the author, the model used by Naïve Bayes is based on the assumption of using independent probabilities. Litton (2015) proposes an approach to predict Internet Movie Database (IMDB) television ratings by crowdsourcing Twitter, in order to to capture instant feedback for television shows. To the author, SA employed to identify attitudes and emotions of each tweet captures the audience's' natural reactions with respect to the reviews, and, as such, might be more honest. Experiments have been performed doing SA on tweets for five different shows, considering from four to seven episodes for each show, and with two different types of statistical model on approximately 1,000 to 100,000 tweets per episode. Among variables included in the model, *mean score*, *show title*, and *vote count* result for significant predictors in the model.

Various kinds of texts have applied SA, included those coming from e-learning platforms (Adinolfi, D'Avanzo, Lytras, Novo-Corti & Picatoste, 2016). And more and more universities, claiming innovative teaching methods, encourage their instructors to exploit social media as platforms for student discussions, project works and assessment. For instance, Menkhoff et *al.* (2015) inquired the employment of live Twitter conversations, proposing four hypotheses about its deployment in higher education, as a social awareness stream in the classroom. The authors first hypothesized if students' desire to learn more about the positive relation between the subjects matter and the frequency of tweeting. Secondly, they postulated that social presence is positively related to the degree to which the tweeting experience stimulates students' desire to learn more about the respective subject matter. Third, the authors verified if the exchanging of tweets among students and instructor stimulates the desire to learn more about the respective subject matter. Finally, as a final working hypothesis the authors hope the implementation of a system to organize and categorizes tweets, allowing students to increase students' motivation for learning more their subject matter. The last hypothesis contains also a mechanism to reduce the cognitive overload which is caused by the large number of tweets learners have to deal with.

2.2. The Emotions as a key Factor

Literature on emotion analysis spreads over different field of inquiry[3]. The results of Augusto, Pulido & López (2011) show that people who are better able to regulate their own and others' emotions can better cope with difficulties and stress situations. To perform this study, collective samples subjected to high levels of stress were used, such as health personnel and teaching staff. For instance, in neuroscience, Brooks et *al.* (2016), through a neuro-imaging analysis, inquired the role played by emotion words on the neural representation of emotional experiences and perceptions across studies. Psychological literature on emotions generates an increasing body of knowledge. Houben et *al.* (2015) demonstrate how fluctuations of feelings across time is crucial for the psychological health of people. The results of the inquiry of Frijda et *al.* (1989) support that "emotions can be regarded both as experiences of forms of appraisal and as states of action readiness, showing how they can be analyzed in terms of sets of components, in which action readiness components take an important share". In his work Ekman, P. (1992) views emotions as a product of the evolution, where each of them has its own individual features (i.e., signal, physiology, and antecedent events) and some other in common with other emotions (i.e. rapid onset, short duration, unbidden occurrence, automatic appraisal, and coherence among responses). As well as Plutchik (1980), in his seminal work on the subject, provides an evolutionary foundation to conceptualize the emotion domain, both for human and animals. Shaver et *al.* (1987) explores the organization of emotion concepts, specifying the prototypes of five basic emotions, showing how the prototype approach might be employed to inquiry the processing of information about emotional events and the development of emotion knowledge. Shaver et *al.* (1987) and Ortony et *al.* (1990) compiled a list of primary emotions, where the basic categories are *anger*, *sadness*, *joy*, *love*, *surprise*, *happiness*, *fear* and *disgust*. However, in the literature, there is no unanimous agreement, as we will see in the following pages. For instance, Munezero & Montero & Mozgovoy & Sutinen (2013), in their approach, described in Section 3, employ Plutchik's eight emotions (i.e., *joy*, *sadness*, *fear*, *anger*, *anticipation*, *surprise*, *disgust* and *trust*) because they allow to derive *frustration* and *anxiety*, two emotions that play a fundamental role in the learning domain (Kort, Reilly & Picard, 2001), since their presence may hinder the learning process (Munezero & Montero & Mozgovoy & Sutinen, 2013; Plutchik, 1980).

2.3. Interaction Between Emotion and Sentiment

In social sciences, Burnap, et *al.* (2015) investigated how to forecast *spikes* in social tension analyzing social media data, showing that a combination of conversation analysis methods, along with text mining, outperforms a number of machine learning approaches to classify tension levels in individual tweets. However, it is in the social media where emotion analysis receive more and more attention, both from a theoretical and an applicative point of view (Cambria, 2016; Mohammad, 2015; Khandelwal, Mishra & Mishra, 2016). To this end, Santos et *al.* (2013) carried out a laboratory experiment gathering emotional information and exploring emotions detection from traditional methods. Then an expert labeled the reports obtained by combining analysis of user behavior, while they were typing a report, employing sentiment analysis on the written text. Then, machine learning algorithms used all data gathered to infer users' emotions. Rodriguez et *al.* (2012) analyzed a case study containing twelve essays written by a fresher student, along her first semester in college, with the aim of extracting emotions (*joy*, *anger*, *sadness* and *fear*) and use them in an adaptive e-learning system, supporting recommendations and collaborative activities to be accomplished by students, according to their preferences, needs, previous actions, as well "as the achievement of the activities employing individual or collaborative workspaces, generated dynamically according to the user features and the task to be accomplished". In such sense, user emotions, allow to recommend the most suitable activities for a given student, at that time according, not only to his features, preferences, actions, location, available time and device, but also to his/her emotional state at that time, allowing dynamic recommendation of activities according to the student emotions at each time. Rodriguez et *al.* (2012) claim the benefits of monitoring students' emotions during the learning process, looking at their evolution over a period of time. Alvarez et al. (2015) tested theories on collective emotions and social interaction in collective actions employing data from micro-blogs during the active phases of the anti-austerity movement in Spain. Findings show that activity and information cascades in the movement are strictly proportional to the increasing of negative collective emotions, as well as, taken individually, activists' social integration in the movement increases with their level of engagement and of expression of negativity. Overall, the experiments demonstrate the chief role played by "non-rational" factors in the formation and activity of social movements through online media. In general, feedback on motivation and self-esteem, related to the student's emotional state, is also encouraged in the e-learning, even when it concerns negative content such as, for example, bad students' performances (Hattie & Timperley, 2007). Tian, et *al.* (2009) discuss an approach to identify e-learner emotion, creating patterns to find which words are associated more with emotions, abstracting, from corpus, Chinese metaphors employing sentence meaning and structure. Furthermore, the authors exploited a case based reasoning recommendation strategy to improve emotion communication between two interacting sides.

3. CASE ANALYSIS

3.1. Sentiment Analysis of Learning Diaries

Munezero, Montero, Mozgovoy & Sutinen (2013) proposed an approach for analyzing and visualizing students' *sentiments*, *emotions* and *attitudes* contained in their learning diaries. Learning diaries represent, more and more, a tool useful both for the student and his teacher. The former, through the attitudes expressed in their diary during the course, can better understand both their progress and the *self-awareness* of their goal. For the latter, on the other hand, learning diaries represent a source of feedback to be acquainted with the student's emotional state. Unfortunately the number of diaries born during a course, also those of medium number of students, is becoming a significant drawback. The system proposed allows instructors to automatically extract and monitoring emotions. As a matter of fact, some emotional states can represent an obstacle during the learning experience. Students that feel *joy*, *satisfaction*, *gratification* and so forth, learn and perform better about their subject[4]. Furthermore, Järvenoja & Järvelä (2005) also claim the role played by emotional states towards the learning experience and how they may influence learning outcomes.

To achieve their objective, students' emotional states and attitudes towards their learning timeline are analyzed, Munezero, Montero, Mozgovoy & Sutinen (2013) implemented a SA system in order to capture sentiments and emotions contained in students' diaries for identifying students that are in need of "immediate and personalized feedback". In the following pages, the approach proposed is described, highlighting some key technical aspects of the system, and the experimental settings.

The SA system accepts learning diaries as input and, after that, splits them on the basis of the date entry. Afterward the system performs three fundamental steps: emotion extraction from the diary, negative/positive attributes' identification, topics' extraction. As for the output, the system returns charts that visualize the emotional states identified and their respective evolution over time.

As regards the identification of emotions, that is one of the most important tasks faced by the system, it compares each sentence, obtained during the splitting pre-processing step, against the NRC word-emotion lexicon (Mohammad & Turney, 2013), that was manually annotated into eight emotion categories, according to Plutchik's eight basic emotions (i.e., *joy*, *sadness*, *fear*, *anger*, *anticipation*, *surprise*, *disgust* and *trust*) (Plutchik, 1980). More in detail, when a word of the learning diary matches one of the NRC-lexicon, the system assigns a score of 1 within the matched emotion category, otherwise the score is 0. Based on this, the system calculates an overall emotional $eScore_{(category)}$, representing each Plutchik's category for each individual diary. The $eScore_{(category)}$ is calculated by dividing the number of words in the uploaded learning diary, that have nonzero emotional score for the category according to the NRC lexicon, and the number of words in the uploaded learning diary that have nonzero emotional score for any category according to the NRC lexicon. The system is also able to calculate *frustration* and *anxiety* emotional states (Plutchik, 1991) where the former results by the average *eScore* of *anger*, *surprise* and *sadness* (i.e., $eScore_{(anger,\ surprise,\ sadness)}$), while the latter is made by the average *eScore* of *anticipation* and *fear* (i.e., $eScore_{(anticipation,\ fear)}$). All Plutchik's emotion categories, calculated as described above, are visualized on a radar chart for each diary entry and summed up. Another visualization module reports on the average polarity attribute scores (i.e., *positive* vs. *negative*), directly obtained from the NRC lexicon, for a range of diary entries. Diaries' topics are visualized through *words clouds* modules, allowing the identification of frequent topics treated by individual students. A further visualization module displays the temporal flow of emotions in the learning diaries. Users have different visualization options to display either all the emotions or selecting a combination of them. The dataset is a sample from the corpus of Newman *et al.* (2008). The corpus of diaries is the composition of 35 first year college students (18 female and 17 male), that described their learning experience, for a total of 54 entries written by females and 51 entries written by males. The system architecture allows the visualization over time in all the emotions, including *frustration* and *anxiety*, and the proportionality between *anxiety* and *frustration* that the students are experiencing. For instance, the authors report about experiments where for 27 students (13 female and 14 male) anxiety increased while frustration decreased or vice versa. Employing the same dataset they also found that 30 participants, their three diary entries contained more anxiety than frustration.

Munezero *et al.* (2013) support that their system could provide many pedagogical insights as requested from the Programme for International Student Assessment (PISA[5]). For instance, one of PISA's claim is that students that have higher levels of performance in their scores are less anxious about the learning process, showing a positive correlation between interest and enjoyment of a subject and the students' PISA achievements. The authors claim many other pedagogical observational abilities about their system.

3.2. Social Media Sentiment Analysis for Universities' Evaluation

Tummel & Richert (2015) propose an approach for the analysis of opinions published on Twitter, as a complementary source for evaluating universities that, on their side, expect to improve performance measurement mechanisms and/or adjust their plans. To this end, the authors gathered social media data related to 9 German Institutes of Technology, a consortium known as TU9[6]. The authors choose Twitter as the source of their social media data, collecting all tweets matching word from a list of keywords containing combinations of the universities names and titles belonging to TU9. For a time spanning on German winter semester, it has been collected a dataset made of 16488, both in German and English. The dataset has been processed in three steps: *filtering*, *feature extraction* and *sentiment analysis* out-and-out. The *filtering* process is a canonical, even not trivial, task that takes care of cleaning the tweets (e.g., lower case, hyperlink removing, emoticon replacement, and so forth). *Feature extraction*, as known, correlates tweets properties to its respective sentiment, that in the case subject of matter is *positive* or *not positive*, in other words the two way sentiment classification (Agarwal, Xie, Vovsha, Rambow, & Passonneau, 2011). Among several feature selections methods available, ranging from the employing of *n-grams*, usually up to four or three consecutive words (Agarwal & Mittal, 2016), to the use of part-of-speech tags and lexicons (McKeown, K., Daume, H., Chaturvedi, Paparrizos, Thadani, Barrio, & Gravano, 2016), without forgetting the employing of emoticons (Collins, May, Weinthal, & Wicentowski, 2015), the authors adapted the criterion experimented by Pak & Paroubek (2010) according to a combination of unigrams and bigrams is beneficial for the task since the former are able to increase the coverage of data, while the latter capture the sentiment expression patterns. Moreover, following the approach proposed by Go, Bhayani, & Huang (2009), the authors also considered emoticons as n-grams, first because they allow the classifier to learn from other words the n-grams and, secondly, Kouloumpis, Wilson, & Moore (2011) showed that including the emoticons improves the classifier performance, as it has also been claimed by Barbosa & Feng (2010) and Davidov, Tsur, & Rappoport (2010). As for the classification of tweets, as *positive* or *not positive*, it has been employed a Naïve Bayes supervised learning machine that has been proven effective and efficient for several sentiment analysis tasks, ranging from the analysis of medical texts (Denecke & Deng, 2015; Noll, Mahon, Shroff, Carrico, & Lindauer, 2016) to E-commerce product reviews (Singh, Gill, Sharma, & Goel, 2016), from customer behavior modeling (Yadav, Feeroz & Yadav, 2012) to stock market prediction (Bhardwaj, Narayan, & Dutta, 2015). The underlying assumption behind a Bayes classifier is the conditional independence of features from each other, given a certain class. In the case, for each tweet, it is computed the probability that a tweet has a sentiment (i.e., *positive* or *not-positive*) when it contains a given set of features (i.e., a combination of n-grams). The whole classification has been carried out employing the NLTK toolkit[7], a free python implementation for natural language processing and machine learning purposes. The Bayes classifier was trained on a set of 3000 manually annotated tweets and tested on 1000 tweets, showing to correctly classify, as *positive* or *not-positive*, about 74% of them. The remainder of the dataset, which together contains 16,000 tweets, has been classified using the the model extracted from the training step. The authors found an unbalanced distribution of tweets per university that represents an issue to address since it is make difficult the comparison among the different institutions. For instance, Karlsruher Institut fur Technologie got 78% of *positive* tweets out of its total 767 tweets, scoring as the first institution of the ranking, while RWTH Aachen University, despite having the highest number of tweets within the dataset, has only 54% of *positive*. TU Dresden scored as the last institution of the ranking, since only 37% of tweets were *positive*. A second analysis allowed the authors to monitor sentiments about daily events and activities at each university. To carry on this task, all classified tweets are divided on daily basis, in order to analyze specific temporal points, either *positive* or *non-positive*, using word frequencies estimates for each point. For instance, turning to this monitoring task, the author estimated that the highest number of *positive* tweets emerged at the beginning of the semester, when orientation sessions and welcoming event took place and where new and old students express their positive attitude about the institution. Other similar event can be detected in a similar manner, either *positive* or *not-positive*, and used, for example, by the university to get sentiment about ongoing sentiments and schedule new ones.

3.3. Case Study: MOOC's Sentiment Analysis

Although their diffusion and popularity as well as their broad approval, MOOCs suffer in terms of satisfaction of students' needs whose most direct consequence is the high dropout rate (Diver & Martinez, 2015). Scholars from different disciplines have tried to find solutions to this issue but they did not find a solution yet (Zheng, Rosson, Shih, & Carroll, 2015; Freitas, Morgan, & Gibson, 2015; Gamage, Fernando, & Perera, 2015). For instance, Adamopoulos (2013) proposed an interdisciplinary approach based on the *grounded theory method* suggesting that the causes of student drop-out are of a different nature A predominant part of the analysis, it seems, however, to postpone the analysis of sentiment that falls in the scope of this paper (Ramesh, Kumar, Foulds, & Getoor, 2015; Crossley, Paquette, Dascalu, McNamara, & Baker, 2016).

Shen & Kuo (2015) introduced an approach to draw descriptive statistics which analyzes public sentiment in Twitter towards MOOC learning and positive and negative MOOCs related retweets, the approach identifies influencers of these retweets in order to allow MOOCs analysts recommending MOOC related messages to the influencers. Because at the time of this writing the approach of Shen & Kuo (2015) seems to be one of the most exhaustive, and methodologically well founded, we review it in the following pages as regard the SA for MOOCs. The authors, through a Twitter API, collected tweets containing the word "MOOC", referring to messages related to MOOCs, and the words "MOOC" and "learning", referring to messages about learning through MOOCs. The API search routine gathered 402,812 tweets from June 1, 2013 and May 31, 2014.

The approach proposed employs line charts depicting some statistics calculated in advance, such as the daily, weekly, and monthly tweet activities related to MOOCs and learning through MOOCs. These tools aim at showing the trends of MOOCs and learning through MOOCs. Furthermore, MOOC practitioners can identify the daily, weekly, and monthly peak and off-peak periods to learn the MOOC-related posting behaviors of Twitter users. Afterwards, on the collected data, it has been carried out the sentiment analysis, adopting *OpinionFinder*[8]. The aim was classifying subjective sentences, speech events and direct subjective expressions, as well as identifying opinion sources and sentiment expressions. All the results are displayed on line charts depicting the daily, weekly, and monthly activity of sentimental tweets related to MOOCs as well as those about learning through MOOCs. The charts work from fledged tools to support decision makers who wish identifying big news stories about MOOCs on certain dates, and/or evaluating public opinion toward these news topics.

The proposed approach took also care of identifying top influencers of both positive and negative information dissemination and learning related to MOOCs. Influencers of information dissemination on Twitter are identified looking at the numbers of their posts retweeted by other users, counting the number of times their username appears after "RT" or "via" tags. Thanks to social network diagrams of these retweets, the authors are able to display tweets' sentiments, about MOOCs for instance, are widespread from the top influencers and, among them, their role at various stages.

4. EVALUATION OF TEACHING THROUGH A MULTI-LEVEL SENTIMENT ANALYSIS APPROACH

Some preliminary experiments are introduced for tracing and unifying what has been introduced in the literature review above outlined. In particular, our aim is to create a SA prototype with a twofold objective: 1) monitoring *learning diaries*, *students blogs*, *social networks* (i.e., Twitter and Facebook) and *MOOCs*, in order to obtain quantitative insights that can support Higher Education decision makers for their daily activity, as stated above (e.g., monitoring student *satisfaction*, *anxiety*, *frustration*, *efficiency*, *dropout*, and so forth); 2) exploiting platform analytics for policy makers purposes, such as experimenting mechanisms able to match *lifelong learning* needs emerging from labor markets with the Higher Education programs, or running new weighting strategies that can be exploited as complementary components for existing universities ranking algorithms. The prototype is made of several dashboards that support the decision maker in his daily activity. Hence the name LADEL (*L*earning *A*nalytics *D*ashboard for *E*-*L*earning) chosen for the prototype.

4.1. LADEL Architecture

At least in this prototype phase LADEL consists of four main tunable modules: a) *collection module*, b) *cleaning module*, c) *word cloud module* and d) the *sentiment opinion module*. At the time of this writing we are experimenting two additional modules: e) the *timeline module* and f) the *social visualization module*. An important role in the architecture of LADEL is played by the employing of *dashboards* (from which it derives its name) that can be tuned depending on the task we are dealing with. Evidence from literature demonstrates the importance of employing *dashboards* in order to to inform decision makers about strategies to address their tasks (Robertson, McKiernan, & Holmes, 2015; Fernandez, McClain, Brown Williams & Ellison, 2015; Dolan & Veazie, 2015; Bera, 2016), especially for social analytics in distance learning (Hernández-García, González-González, Jiménez-Zarco & Chaparro-Peláez, 2015; Roberts, & Pakkiri, 2016), and human resource management (Lal, 2015).

Figure 2 shows the *sentiment dashboard* (SD) produced by analyzing the sentiment about MOOCand related terms[9] among the population of 4 Higher Education Institutions. Besides the chart displaying the overall sentiment, grouped on an increasing scale value (from the most negative value, -2, to the most positive value, +6), the SD reports details about each chart, such as an interactive table containing individual tweets with its sentiment score, offering the possibility of re-ranking displayed tweets using some filters visible at the top of the table. Indeed, the SD reports also other useful information about descriptive statistics of the analysis that, at the moment, do not appear in Figure 2 because of lack of space on the sheet. The *word cloud dashboard* shown in Figure 2 represents another kind of displaying module produced by LADEL, for text analytics purposes. Whereas the WCD display aggregated variables to provide an overall view, such as in Figure 2, it also allows, at the same time, to analyze its individual components through specific tables as those in the four corners (one for each institution).

Figure 2. Sentiment dashboard (SD): The SD visualizes sentiment about MOOC and related terms (#MOOCs, "learning MOOC", "e-learning") at four Higher Education institutions. The left column of the SD allow the decision maker to get a rapid insight about the sentiment subject of matter (e.g. MOOC) as well as a friendly comparison among the population at involved institutions. The right column allow a more specific analysis for each sentiment degree (from -2 to 6).

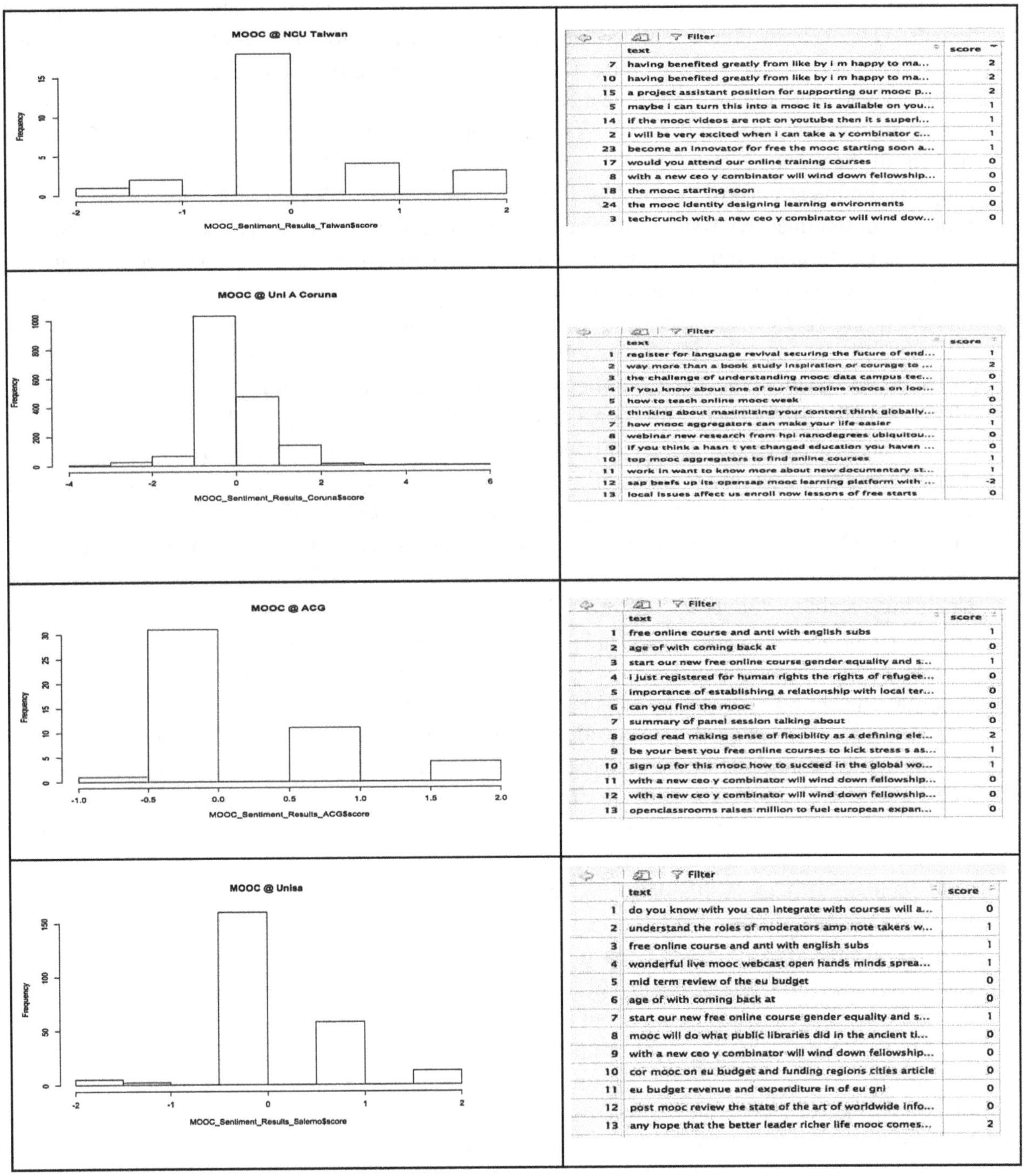

1. **Collection Module:** The main component of this module is the *searchTwitter()* function that returns tweets containing the searched string, along with different meta parameters/options such as *language*, *date*, *geocode* and so forth.
2. **Cleaning Module:** The corpus of tweets collected through the previous step, and stored in object data, is processed in this step employing a canonical cleaning procedure as discussed in the literature review of Section 3. In doing so, we took care of different issues contained in the corpus of tweets: 1) a lots of meta information that may be fundamental for other analysis we are interested in, such as those we are experimenting for the *social visualization module*; 2) punctuation marks, numbers, and unnecessary spaces must be removed; 3) we would not consider retweets (RTs). On the whole, we addressed all these issues building intermediate data object to store all information and recall them upon request, to deal with the different tasks. As a canonical cleaning process, only for sentiment purpose, we followed the sequence: first removing html links, which are not required for sentiment analysis; second, removing retweet entities; third, removing all #Hashtag and all "@people"; finally, removing all the punctuation, numbers and unnecessary spaces. A number of data objects contain all the information removed for the sentiment analysis phase. *Word cloud module* of the Figure 2 analyzes tweets with respect to the four universities under examination. In our case, it is accompanied by a set of tables that allow to explore the content of each component of the cloud. To implement our *Word cloud module* we started from the data objects containing all tweets collected for each institution, considering their cleaned version. Then, using a canonical text mining procedure, through an intermediate vector space model of the corpus we build a *term x document* matrix putting together all vectors of tweets coming from the four universities. As a final step, the matrix so obtained is displayed on the *word cloud dashboard* (WCD).
3. **Sentiment Opinion Module:** As already claimed in Section 2 and Section 3 there are several approaches for sentiment analysis. Liu (2015) provides a formal definition of a *belief* or *sentiment*, easily translatable in computational terms. The definition considers the *belief/sentiment* as an object **B** in a five dimensional space $B=(\mathbf{O}_j, \mathbf{f}_{jk}, \mathbf{SO}_{ijkl}, \mathbf{h}_i, \mathbf{T}_l)$ where $\mathbf{O}_j$ is the object, $\mathbf{f}_{jk}$ is the feature of $\mathbf{O}_j$, $\mathbf{SO}_{ijkl}$ is the sentiment value of the opinion of the opinion holder $\mathbf{h}_i$ on feature $\mathbf{f}_{jk}$ of the object $\mathbf{O}_j$ at the time $\mathbf{T}_l$. Ravindran et al. (2015) provide an exhaustive description and some examples of this formalism, as well as all steps needed to obtain the sentiment value $\mathbf{SO}_{ijkl}$. Currently, we are employing three machine learning algorithms (i.e., Naive Bayes classifiers, SVMs and decision trees) to classify sentiments, using different kinds of feature selection methods as well, both *syntactic* and *statistical* inspired (i.e., *PoS* and *Mutual Information*). However, in this paper we report on experiments obtained employing a baseline algorithm (Nakov, Ritter, Rosenthal, Sebastiani, & Stoyanov, 2016), as shortly described in the following pages, useful to compare further ongoing experimental settings. The baseline is grounded on the exploitation of a score that counts the number of times a *positive* (e.g., amazing, good, great, and so on) or a *negative* (e.g., nightmare, sucks, and so forth) word occurs in a given sentence/tweet. The sentiment word lexicon employed for the first experiment is made of about 68,000 English words. Based on this, the *score*() function is able to identify the raw sentiment employing a very easy matching algorithm. After the canonical cleaning process described above, each sentence is splitted by the space delimiter. The core of this step is represented by the boolean match of each words w.r.t. the positive or negative opinion-lexicon that is obtained by summing up the total positive sentiment to which must be subtracted the total negatives. The number of tweets returned by the *search* API call is different for the four universities and some tweets are lost during the processing because meaningless. Since the number

of tweets is not equal for each of the four organizations, we calculate a mean and standard deviation for each institution, as reported in the following table. Table 1 shows always a positive sentiment, in average 0.2142857< *Mean sentiment score* < 0.3845714, for all 4 institutions, with a *standard deviation* always in the same magnitude of the score 1.

4.2. Using LADEL to Evaluate MOOCs

As for the first battery of experiments, we wanted to highlight how the prototype works for the task carried out by Shen & Kuo (2015), probably with several lacks with respect to to the departure approach. Proposing a closed inquiry, that is analyzing *MOOC* and *learning MOOC* tweets but paying attention to the areas where the four hub universities are located.

As for the first experiment, we run LADEL to create a *sentiment dashboard*, as reported in Figure 2, where all sentiment charts are aligned, one under the other, to give the decision/policy maker an overview of the trend in sentiment, looking at all four institutions simultaneously.

Figure 3 shows the WSD w.r.t. institutions instead of using, as usual, the emotions. As for this presentation the WSD is improvable since we are processing for the work in progress a key-phrase extraction algorithm that identifies key-phrases instead of single terms to be represented on the cloud.

5. SOME REFLECTIONS, DISCUSSION, AND FUTURE WORK

The psychological profile of students who intend to participate in mobility programs such as Erasmus, has been analyzed in several studies that have proven the benefits of studying abroad gives young people regarding their self-esteem, flexibility and sensitivity cultural.

This work was undertaken with a double aim: 1) reviewing a specific *learning analytics* method, that is *sentiment analysis*, in Higher Education, showing how it is employed to monitor student satisfaction on different platforms: *learning diaries, Twitter* and *MOOCs*; 2) introducing an architecture that is capable to observe and support the modeling of students' and teachers' behaviors, giving an overall view of their mutual activity.

Regarding to the first objective we reviewed a large body of knowledge, certifying the existing interest of the communities, of both scholars and practitioners, towards *sentiment analysis* for Higher Education purposes. Moreover, as proved by the number of scientific references published during the last two/three years, this interest is constantly increasing. In carrying on this review we highlighted three different e-learning domains (i.e., *learning diaries, Twitter* and *MOOCs*;) showing the attempts to address them. These attempts have been proposed by different research groups but a unifying approach

Table 1. Descriptive statistics about the dataset[10]

Institution	Mean Sentiment Score	Standard Deviation	# of Tweets Collected
Mooc sentiment @ NCU Taiwan	0.2142857	0.8758971	28
Mooc sentiment @ Coruna	0.3845714	0.8311349	1750
Mooc sentiment @ ACG	0.3829787	0.6773732	47
Mooc sentiment @ Salerno	0.302521	0.6819508	238

Figure 3. The word cloud dashboard (WSD). The WSD displays, in this case, word clouds w.r.t. institutions. For each institution is represents the "basin" of its words identified on Twitter.

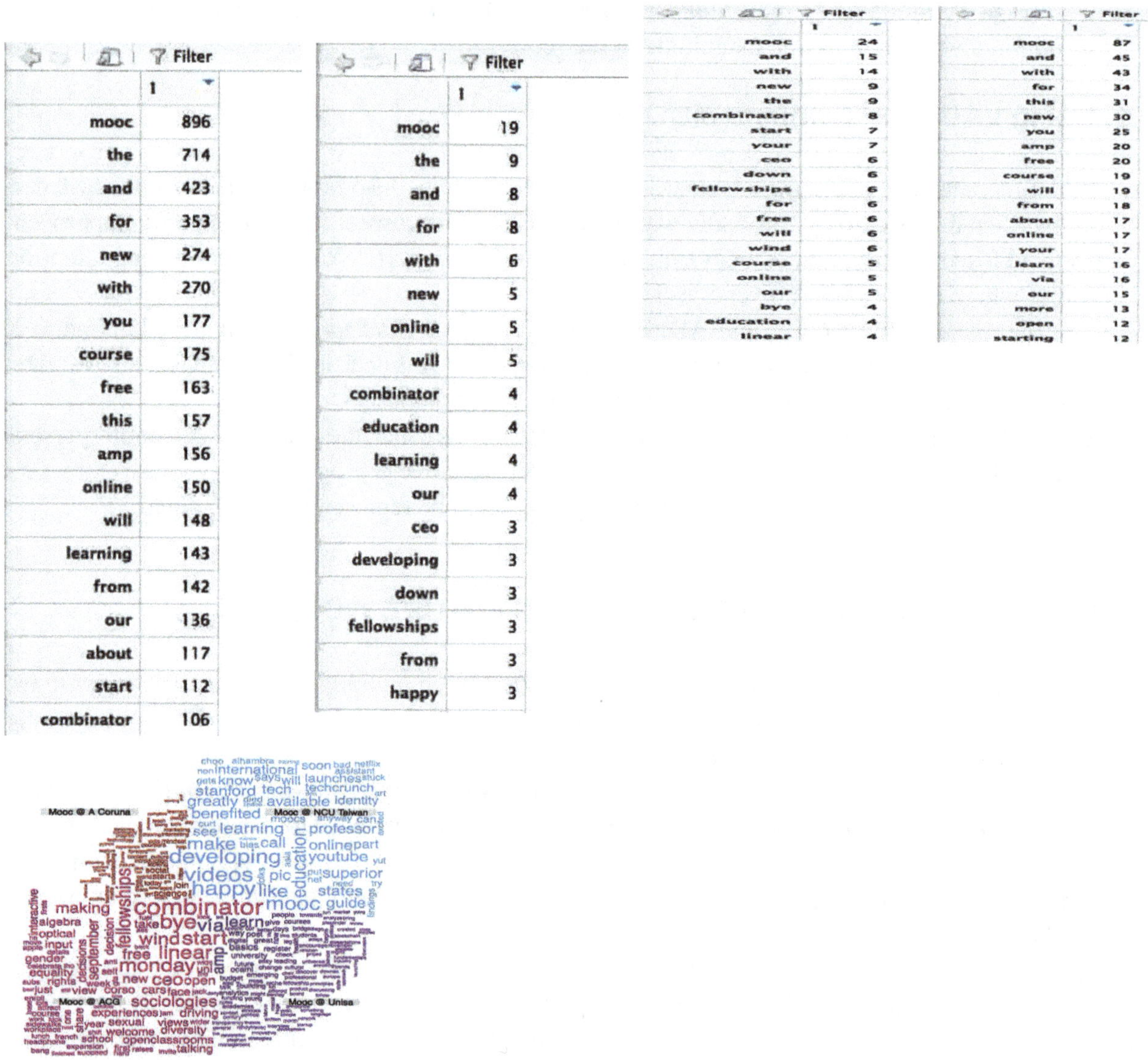

that can deal with all of them is still lacking. To our opinion, such a unifying approach is desirable since it could benefit the monitoring of the single Higher Education institutions and contribute to the definition of additional parameters for university ranking mechanisms. To this end we introduced LADEL, a prototype architecture of SA for Higher Education purpose. In section 4 we introduced the architecture and some preliminary experiments. There are a lot of limitations, some inherent to the prototype itself, some other deriving from the tasks it deals with (e.g. how to evaluate the platform). All these open issues are a stimulus to continue the development of the platform.

About the prototype, the development of the *timeline module* (a work in progress) will reports on the trends over time. Such a development requires a broader analysis (Calude & Longo, 2016). Moreover, experimentation concerns the role played by the emotional and cognitive states (e.g. attitudes). As said in Section 1, addressing their modelling will ease "learners" task, on the one hand, and the decision maker task, on the other hand. To this end we planned a series of experiments that would allow us to better understand how specific cognitive states can cause or block some learning path or decisions.

ACKNOWLEDGMENT

The authors sincerely thank Prof. Chien-wen Mark Shen from National Central University of Taiwan and to Mara Gruber.

REFERENCES

Acevedo, Y. V. N., & Marín, C. E. M. (2015). Towards a decision support system based on learning analytics. *Advances in Information Sciences and Service Sciences*, *7*(1), 1.

Adinolfi, D'Avanzo, Lytras, Novo-Corti, & Picatoste-Novo. (2016). Sentiment Analysis to Evaluate Teaching Performance. *International Journal of Knowledge Society Research, 7*(4), 86-107.

Agarwal, A., Xie, B., Vovsha, I., Rambow, O., & Passonneau, R. (2011). Sentiment analysis of twitter data. In *Proceedings of the workshop on languages in social media* (pp. 30-38). Association for Computational Linguistics.

Agarwal, B., & Mittal, N. (2016). Prominent feature extraction for review analysis: An empirical study. *Journal of Experimental & Theoretical Artificial Intelligence*, *28*(3), 485–498. doi:10.1080/0952813X.2014.977830

Alvarez, R., Garcia, D., Moreno, Y., & Schweitzer, F. (2015). Sentiment cascades in the 15M movement. *EPJ Data Science*, *4*(1), 1–13. doi:10.1140/epjds/s13688-015-0042-4

Augusto, J. M., Pulido, M., & López, E. (2011). Does Perceived Emotional Intelligence and Optimism/Pessimism predict psycological Well-being? *Journal of Happiness Studies*, *12*(3), 463–474. doi:10.1007/s10902-010-9209-7

Baker, R. S., & Inventado, P. S. (2014). Educational data mining and learning analytics. In *Learning analytics* (pp. 61–75). Springer New York.

Barbosa, L., & Feng, J. (2010). Robust sentiment detection on twitter from biased and noisy data. In *Proceedings of the 23rd International Conference on Computational Linguistics: Posters* (pp. 36-44). Association for Computational Linguistics.

Bera, P. (2016). How colors in business dashboards affect users decision making. *Communications of the ACM*, *59*(4), 50–57. doi:10.1145/2818993

Berbegal-Mirabent, J., & Ribeiro-Soriano, D. E. (2015). Behind league tables and ranking systems: A critical perspective of how university quality is measured. *Journal of Service Theory and Practice*, *25*(3), 242–266. doi:10.1108/JSTP-04-2013-0059

Bhardwaj, A., Narayan, Y., & Dutta, M. (2015). Sentiment Analysis for Indian Stock Market Prediction Using Sensex and Nifty. *Procedia Computer Science*, *70*, 85–91. doi:10.1016/j.procs.2015.10.043

Brooks, J. A., Shablack, H., Gendron, M., Satpute, A. B., Parrish, M. H., & Lindquist, K. A. (2016). The Role of Language in the Experience and Perception of Emotion: A Neuroimaging Meta-Analysis. *Social Cognitive and Affective Neuroscience*, nsw121. doi:10.1093/scan/nsw121 PMID:27539864

Bunzel, D. L. (2007). Universities sell their brands. *Journal of Product and Brand Management*, *16*(2), 152–153. doi:10.1108/10610420710740034

Burnap, P., Rana, O. F., Avis, N., Williams, M., Housley, W., Edwards, A., & Sloan, L. (2015). Detecting tension in online communities with computational Twitter analysis. *Technological Forecasting and Social Change*, *95*, 96–108. doi:10.1016/j.techfore.2013.04.013

Calude, C. S., & Longo, G. (forthcoming). The Deluge of Spurious Correlations in Big Data. *Foundations of Science*. doi:10.1007/s10699-016-9489-4

Cambria, E. (2016). Affective computing and sentiment analysis. *IEEE Intelligent Systems*, *31*(2), 102–107. doi:10.1109/MIS.2016.31

Chou, W. Y., Tien, P. T., Lin, F. Y., & Chiu, P. C. (2016). Application of visually based, computerised diagnostic decision support system in dermatological medical education: A pilot study. *Postgraduate Medical Journal*.

Collins, R., May, D., Weinthal, N., & Wicentowski, R. (2015). SWAT-CMW: Classification of Twitter Emotional Polarity using a Multiple-Classifier Decision Schema and Enhanced Emotion Tagging. *SemEval*, *2015*, 669.

Constantinides, E., & Zinck Stagno, M. (2012). Higher Education Marketing: A Study on the Impact of Social Media on Study Selection and University Choice. *International Journal of Technology and Educational Marketing*, *2*(1), 41–58. doi:10.4018/ijtem.2012010104

Crossley, S., Paquette, L., Dascalu, M., McNamara, D. S., & Baker, R. S. (2016). Combining click-stream data with NLP tools to better understand MOOC completion. In *Proceedings of the Sixth International Conference on Learning Analytics & Knowledge* (pp. 6-14). ACM. doi:10.1145/2883851.2883931

D'Avanzo, E., & Lytras, M. D. (2016). From Big Data to Smart Business: Some Philosophical Remarks - Revealing the new Era of Smart Data, Deep Learning and Cognitive Computing. *International Journal of Knowledge Society Research*, *7*(2), 125–135.

Davidov, D., Tsur, O., & Rappoport, A. (2010). Enhanced sentiment learning using twitter hashtags and smileys. In *Proceedings of the 23rd international conference on computational linguistics: posters* (pp. 241-249). Association for Computational Linguistics.

Denecke, K., & Deng, Y. (2015). Sentiment analysis in medical settings: New opportunities and challenges. *Artificial Intelligence in Medicine*, *64*(1), 17–27. doi:10.1016/j.artmed.2015.03.006 PMID:25982909

Diver, P., & Martinez, I. (2015). MOOCs as a massive research laboratory: Opportunities and challenges. *Distance Education*, *36*(1), 5–25. doi:10.1080/01587919.2015.1019968

Dolan, J. G., & Veazie, P. J. (2015). Balance Sheets Versus Decision Dashboards to Support Patient Treatment Choices: A Comparative Analysis. *The Patient-Patient-Centered Outcomes Research*, *8*(6), 499–505. doi:10.1007/s40271-015-0111-6 PMID:25618789

Ekman, P. (1992). An argument for basic emotions. *Cognition and Emotion*, *6*(3-4), 169–200. doi:10.1080/02699939208411068

Fernandez, M., McClain, D., Brown Williams, B., & Ellison, P. (2015). PBIS in Georgia Department of Juvenile Justice: Data Dashboard and Radar Reports Utilized for Team Data-Based Decision-Making With Facility Team Leader Perspectives. *Residential Treatment for Children & Youth*, *32*(4), 334–343. doi:10.1080/0886571X.2015.1113459

Freitas, S. I., Morgan, J., & Gibson, D. (2015). Will MOOCs transform learning and teaching in higher education? Engagement and course retention in online learning provision. *British Journal of Educational Technology*, *46*(3), 455–471. doi:10.1111/bjet.12268

Friedrichsmeier, A., & Marcinkowski, F. (2016). The mediatisation of university governance: A theoretical and empirical exploration of some side-effects. *Policy and Politics*, *44*(1), 97–113. doi:10.1332/030557315X14431876145728

Frijda, N. H., Kuipers, P., & Ter Schure, E. (1989). Relations among emotion, appraisal, and emotional action readiness. *Journal of Personality and Social Psychology*, *57*(2), 212–228. doi:10.1037/0022-3514.57.2.212

Gamage, D., Fernando, S., & Perera, I. (2015). Quality of MOOCs: A review of literature on effectiveness and quality aspects. In *Ubi-Media Computing (UMEDIA), 2015 8th International Conference on* (pp. 224-229). IEEE. doi:10.1109/UMEDIA.2015.7297459

Go, A., Bhayani, R., & Huang, L. (2009). Twitter sentiment classification using distant supervision. CS224N Project Report, Stanford, 1:12–18.

Hattie, J., & Timperley, H. (2007). The power of feedback. *Review of Educational Research*, *77*(1), 81–112. doi:10.3102/003465430298487

Hazelkorn, E. (2013). *World-Class Universities or World Class Systems?* Rankings and Higher Education Policy Choices.

Hernández-García, Á., González-González, I., Jiménez-Zarco, A. I., & Chaparro-Peláez, J. (2015). Applying social learning analytics to message boards in online distance learning: A case study. *Computers in Human Behavior*, *47*, 68–80. doi:10.1016/j.chb.2014.10.038

Houben, M., Van Den Noortgate, W., & Kuppens, P. (2015). The relation between short-term emotion dynamics and psychological well-being: A meta-analysis. *Psychological Bulletin*, *141*(4), 901–930. doi:10.1037/a0038822 PMID:25822133

Järvenoja, H., & Järvelä, S. (2005). How students describe the sources of their emotional and motivational experiences during the learning process: A qualitative approach. *Learning and Instruction*, *15*(5), 465–480. doi:10.1016/j.learninstruc.2005.07.012

Johnson, K. A. (2011). The effect of Twitter posts on students perceptions of instructor credibility. *Learning, Media and Technology, 36*(1), 21–38. doi:10.1080/17439884.2010.534798

Khandelwal, D., Mishra, M., & Mishra, V. K. (2016). *A Survey on Subjective Sentiment Analysis from Twitter Corpus*. Academic Press.

Kietzmann, J. H., Hermkens, K., McCarthy, I. P., & Silvestre, B. S. (2011). Social media? Get serious! Understanding the functional building blocks of social media. *Business Horizons, 54*(3), 241–251. doi:10.1016/j.bushor.2011.01.005

Kilis, S., Gülbahar, Y., & Rapp, C. (2016). Exploration of Teaching Preferences of Instructors use of Social Media. *European Journal of Open, Distance and E-learning, 19*(1), 1–18. doi:10.1515/eurodl-2016-0001

Kort, B., Reilly, R., & Picard, R. W. (2001). An Affective Model of Interplay between Emotions and Learning: Reengineering Educational Pedagogy-Building a Learning Companion. In Icalt (Vol. 1, pp. 43-47). Academic Press.

Kouloumpis, E., Wilson, T., & Moore, J. D. (2011). Twitter sentiment analysis: The good the bad and the omg! *Icwsm, 11*, 538–541.

Lal, P. (2015). Transforming HR in the digital era: Workforce analytics can move people specialists to the center of decision-making. *Human Resource Management International Digest, 23*(3), 1–4. doi:10.1108/HRMID-03-2015-0051

Litton, I. (2015). *#TwitterCritic: Sentiment Analysis of Tweets to Predict TV Ratings*. Academic Press.

Liu, B. (2015). *Sentiment analysis: Mining opinions, sentiments, and emotions*. Cambridge University Press. doi:10.1017/CBO9781139084789

Mamgain, N., Mehta, E., Mittal, A., & Bhatt, G. (2016). Sentiment analysis of top colleges in India using Twitter data. In *2016 International Conference on Computational Techniques in Information and Communication Technologies (ICCTICT)* (pp. 525-530). IEEE. doi:10.1109/ICCTICT.2016.7514636

McKeown, K., Daume, H., Chaturvedi, S., Paparrizos, J., Thadani, K., Barrio, P., & Gravano, L. (2016). Predicting the impact of scientific concepts using full-text features. *Journal of the Association for Information Science and Technology.*

Menkhoff, T., Chay, Y. W., Bengtsson, M. L., Woodard, C. J., & Gan, B. (2015). Incorporating microblogging (tweeting) in higher education: Lessons learnt in a knowledge management course. *Computers in Human Behavior, 51*, 1295–1302. doi:10.1016/j.chb.2014.11.063

Merceron, A., Blikstein, P., & Siemens, G. (2016). Learning Analytics: From Big Data to Meaningful Data. *Journal of Learning Analytics, 2*(3), 4–8. doi:10.18608/jla.2015.23.2

Mohammad, S., & Turney, P. (2013). Crowdsourcing a Word-Emotion Association Lexicon. *Computational Intelligence, 29*(3), 436–465. doi:10.1111/j.1467-8640.2012.00460.x

Mohammad, S. M. (2015). *Sentiment analysis: Detecting valence, emotions, and other affectual states from text.* Emotion Measurement.

Moja, L., Friz, H. P., Capobussi, M., Kwag, K., Banzi, R., Ruggiero, F., & Kunnamo, I. (2016). Implementing an evidence-based computerized decision support system to improve patient care in a general hospital: The CODES study protocol for a randomized controlled trial. *Implementation Science; IS*, *11*(1), 89. doi:10.1186/s13012-016-0455-x PMID:27389248

Molins-Ruano, P., Rodriguez, P., Atrio, S., & Sacha, G. M. (2016). Modelling experts behavior with e-valUAM to measure computer science skills. *Computers in Human Behavior*, *61*, 378–385. doi:10.1016/j.chb.2016.03.044

Munezero, M., Montero, C. S., Mozgovoy, M., & Sutinen, E. (2013). Exploiting sentiment analysis to track emotions in students' learning diaries. In *Proceedings of the 13th Koli Calling International Conference on Computing Education Research* (pp. 145-152). ACM. doi:10.1145/2526968.2526984

Nakov, P., Ritter, A., Rosenthal, S., Sebastiani, F., & Stoyanov, V. (2016). SemEval-2016 task 4: Sentiment analysis in Twitter. *Proceedings of the 10th international workshop on semantic evaluation (SemEval 2016)*. doi:10.18653/v1/S16-1001

Newman, M. L., Groom, C. J., Handelman, L. D., & Pennebaker, J. W. (2008). Gender differences in language use: An analysis of 14,000 text samples. *Discourse Processes*, *45*(3), 211–236. doi:10.1080/01638530802073712

Noll, D. A., Mahon, B. E., Shroff, B., Carrico, C., & Lindauer, S. J. (2016). *Twitter analysis of the orthodontic patient experience with braces versus Invisalign.* Academic Press.

Olcay, G. A., & Bulu, M. (2016). Is measuring the knowledge creation of universities possible?: A review of university rankings. *Technological Forecasting and Social Change*. doi:10.1016/j.techfore.2016.03.029

Ortony, A., Clore, G. L., & Collins, A. (1990). *The cognitive structure of emotions*. Cambridge university press.

Pak, P., & Paroubek, P. (2010). Twitter as a corpus for sentiment analysis and opinion mining. *Proceedings of the Seventh Conference on International Language Resources and Evaluation*, 1320–1326.

Paltoglou, G. (2015). Sentiment-based event detection in Twitter. *Journal of the Association for Information Science and Technology*.

Plutchik, R. (1980). A general psychoevolutionary theory of emotion. *Theories of Emotion*, *1*, 3-31.

Plutchik, R. (1991). *The emotions*. University Press of America.

Power, D. J., Sharda, R., & Burstein, F. (2015). *Decision support systems*. John Wiley & Sons, Ltd. doi:10.1002/9781118785317.weom070211

Pursel, B. K., Zhang, L., Jablokow, K. W., Choi, G. W., & Velegol, D. (2016). Understanding MOOC students: Motivations and behaviours indicative of MOOC completion. *Journal of Computer Assisted Learning*, *32*(3), 202–217. doi:10.1111/jcal.12131

Ramesh, A., Kumar, S. H., Foulds, J., & Getoor, L. (2015). Weakly supervised models of aspect-sentiment for online course discussion forums. *Annual Meeting of the Association for Computational Linguistics (ACL)*. doi:10.3115/v1/P15-1008

Ravindran, S. K., & Garg, V. (2015). *Mastering Social Media Mining with R*. Packt Publishing Ltd.

Roberts, D., & Pakkiri, R. (2016). *Decision sourcing: Decision making for the agile social enterprise*. Routledge.

Robertson, R. D., McKiernan, A. G., & Holmes, E. A. (2015). *DWI dashboard report: A tool to monitor impaired driving progress*. Academic Press.

Rodriguez, P., Ortigosa, A., & Carro, R. M. (2012, July). Extracting emotions from texts in e-learning environments. In *Complex, Intelligent and Software Intensive Systems (CISIS), 2012 Sixth International Conference on* (pp. 887-892). IEEE. doi:10.1109/CISIS.2012.192

Santos, O. C., Salmeron-Majadas, S., & Boticario, J. G. (2013). Emotions detection from math exercises by combining several data sources. In *International Conference on Artificial Intelligence in Education* (pp. 742-745). Springer Berlin Heidelberg. doi:10.1007/978-3-642-39112-5_102

Shaver, P., Schwartz, J., Kirson, D., & OConnor, C. (1987). Emotion knowledge: Further exploration of a prototype approach. *Journal of Personality and Social Psychology*, *52*(6), 1061–1086. doi:10.1037/0022-3514.52.6.1061 PMID:3598857

Shen, C. W., & Kuo, C. J. (2015). Learning in massive open online courses: Evidence from social media mining. *Computers in Human Behavior*, *51*, 568–577. doi:10.1016/j.chb.2015.02.066

Shum, S. B., & Ferguson, R. (2012). Social Learning Analytics. *Journal of Educational Technology & Society*, *15*(3), 3–26.

Siamagka, N. T., & Christodoulides, G. (2016). Social Media in Higher Education: An Investigation into UG Marketing Education in the UK. In Marketing Challenges in a Turbulent Business Environment (pp. 19-23). Springer International Publishing.

Siemens, G. (2013). Learning analytics: The emergence of a discipline. *The American Behavioral Scientist*.

Siemens, G., & Long, P. (2011). Penetrating the Fog: Analytics in Learning and Education. *EDUCAUSE Review*, *46*(5), 30.

Simon, H. A. (1956). Rational choice and the structure of the environment. *Psychological Review*, *63*(2), 129–138. doi:10.1037/h0042769 PMID:13310708

Simon, H. A. (1991). Bounded rationality and organizational learning. *Organization Science*, *2*(1), 125–134. doi:10.1287/orsc.2.1.125

Singh, R., Gill, J. S., Sharma, T., & Goel, G. (2016). Product Aspect Ranking, Sentiment Analysis and Classification of Product Reviews on E-Commerce Sites-A Review. *Journal of Network Communications and Emerging Technologies*, *6*(5). www. jncet. org

Stacey, E. (2007). Collaborative learning in an online environment. *International Journal of E-Learning & Distance Education*, *14*(2), 14–33.

Tian, F., Zheng, Q., Zhao, R., Chen, T., & Jia, X. (2009). Can e-Learner's emotion be recognized from interactive Chinese texts? In *Computer Supported Cooperative Work in Design, 2009. CSCWD 2009. 13th International Conference on* (pp. 546-551). IEEE.

Tummel, A. A. D. J. C., & Richert, S. J. A. (2015). Sentiment Analysis of Social Media for Evaluating Universities. *The Second International Conference on Digital Information Processing, Data Mining, and Wireless Communications (DIPDMWC2015).*

Vidal, P. (2016). *World university rankings: use of quantitative indicators and results from student surveys*. Academic Press.

Vygotsky, L. S. (1980). *Mind in society: The development of higher psychological processes.* Harvard University Press.

Wang, X., Yang, D., Wen, M., Koedinger, K., & Rosé, C. P. (2015). *Investigating How Student's Cognitive Behavior in MOOC Discussion Forums Affect Learning Gains.* International Educational Data Mining Society.

Westerman, D., Daniel, E. S., & Bowman, N. D. (2016). Learned risks and experienced rewards: Exploring the potential sources of students attitudes toward social media and face-to-face communication. *The Internet and Higher Education, 31*, 52–57. doi:10.1016/j.iheduc.2016.06.004

Yadav, M. P., Feeroz, M., & Yadav, V. K. (2012). Mining the customer behavior using web usage mining in e-commerce. In *Computing Communication & Networking Technologies (ICCCNT), 2012 Third International Conference on* (pp. 1-5). doi:10.1109/ICCCNT.2012.6395938

Zheng, S., Rosson, M. B., Shih, P. C., & Carroll, J. M. (2015). Understanding student motivation, behaviors and perceptions in MOOCs. In *Proceedings of the 18th ACM Conference on Computer Supported Cooperative Work & Social Computing* (pp. 1882-1895). ACM. doi:10.1145/2675133.2675217

ENDNOTES

1 https://www.class-central.com/report/moocs-2015-stats/

2 Techniques for English Language Tests course

3 At the time of this writing, a search on Google Scholar using the keyword "emotion analysis" produced about 43,000 results.

4 Lawson, C. 2005. The connections between emotions and learning. Center for Development and Learning. Available at http://www.cdl.org/resourcelibrary/articles/connect_emotions.php.

5 https://www.oecd.org/pisa/keyfindings/

6 An incorporated society of the nine oldest, and largest universities, focusing on engineering and technology in Germany: RWTH Aachen University, TU2 Berlin, TU Braunschweig. TU Darmstadt, TU Dresden, Leibniz Universitat Hannover, Karlsruher Institut fur Technologie, TU Mu'nchen and Universitat Stuttgart.

7 http://www.nltk.org/

8 http://mpqa.cs.pitt.edu/opinionfinder/

9 Section 4.1 contains more details about the task.

10 The number of tweets collected (last column) represents the tweets returned by the *search call* of Twitter, which had been requested 5000 tweets for each institution.

Chapter 8
The Development of a Virtual University Campus Using Second Life

Maria Vargas-Vera
Adolfo Ibanez University, Chile

ABSTRACT

This paper presents the development of a virtual campus named DeepThink designed to support a post-graduate program named MPhil (Master in Philosophy) at The Open University. The MPhil is a formal Open University degree delivered to a distance. The virtual campus integrates second life, moodle and several Web 2.0 technologies like elluminate (online conferencing tool), MyStuff (e-Portfolio), Skype and Ning (Social network). This integration between second life and web 2.0 technologies has caused enthusiasm in tutors at the Open University who saw the benefit of using DeepThink in their courses. This campus is an innovative project which brings new ways of supervision. Our campus DeepThink in general promotes higher Education using technologies like second life, which has shown to be useful in supervision and teaching undergraduate courses. Finally, we discuss our experiences on second life and its limitations.

INTRODUCTION

During the past few years we have observed that immersive environments have becoming popular for social gathering and for educational environments. The Open University has a long tradition of using technology to support Education; therefore, a virtual campus was in its own landscape. Traditionally, the Open University worked with the model where students do the courses in their own time. The problem with this model is that students face isolation and lack of resources. Then, the Open University decided to change its model of learning in a Computer Science program of studies. In order to accomplish this objective, the Computing Department launched a project called MPhil (see Appendix) to support the idea of non-isolated learning (i.e. constructivist, social and distributed learning). Three academics from the Open University formed the MPhil team (the author of this paper included) which have as a goal to

DOI: 10.4018/978-1-5225-4191-2.ch008

develop a virtual campus named DeepThink (Rapanotti et al., 2010, Rapanotti & Hall 2010; Minocha & Morse 2010; Minocha & Hardy 2011). This virtual campus was originally designed exclusively for supporting the MPhil program of studies (Barroca et. al, 2010). However, it has been used by lectures teaching undergraduate courses in the Open University. For example, Minocha discussed Geology field trips (Minocha 2010; Minocha, 2014).

To give some background to the reader, we should say that the project DeepThink (at the Computing Department, Open University) started in 2008 and evolved into an Educational framework consisting of synchronous and asynchronous internet and web technologies. In 2009, the Virtual university campus was released. Early October 2009, a group of students enrolled in an MPhil program of studies. The virtual campus (DeepThink) comprises second life (immersive environment), Moodle, Elluminate, My-Stuff (EPortfolios), Skype and Ning. Synchronous and asynchronous internet web technologies are the backbone for an integrated learning environment to support the part time MPhil Computing program at the Open University. The MPhil program is a recognised degree in UK and it is entirely delivered a distance. Also, the programme fits within the overall university approach to research student induction and training. The MPhil program complies with national standards that the University is subscribed to (UKGrad, 2015). To clarify to the reader, research skills training is part of most research degrees in the UK In order to satisfy with this requirement; the Open University has developed a repository of resources accessible to all research students, through the university's intranet. The resources consist of activities for developing and gathering evidence of each research skill. In our view, the Virtual MPhil has complemented the resources (offered by the Open University) with a series of online activities that help students develop and assess some of their research skills. For example, one skill is the development of communication skills, in particular, academic presentations. There are many resources that students could use to develop the communication skills. These resources are available from the University Intranet, the Library and the Virtual MPhil website. Additionally, supervisors play an important role helping on the development of the student skills by providing them with specific advice and feedback.

Summing up, the motivation behind DeepThink development was the knowledge that educators have found that web 2.0 technologies offer good possibilities of use in Education. Therefore, we wanted to support educators even further with the DeepThink integration. Our main contribution is to describe our experiences in the integration of second life with web 2.0 technologies. Additionally, we present our reflections on the second life platform.

This paper is organized as follows: firstly, it presents a related work section. Secondly, it gives the virtual campus architecture. Thirdly, presents a brief description of the DeepThink integrated technologies. Fourthly, discusses DeepThink design decisions. Fifthly, it gives an analysis of the client/server model offered in second life. Sixthly, it presents a categorization of questions used in the pilot, seventhly, the Appendix presents a description of the project and finally the last part of this paper, gives our conclusions and future work.

RELATED WORK

The use of avatars in virtual environments for social networking and entertainment purposes is well-stablished. While, the use of avatars in an education context is in an early stage (De Freitas, 2006). The applications have been limited to simulation games and activities such the Sim series and specialist use in Sciences and Mathematics. In fact, the literature on supporting research programs at distance using technology has its origin a few years ago. However, after an exhaustive literature review, we find that there is work dedicated in part to some issues on supporting degrees online by the use of a virtual campus. For example, a virtual campus to support a doctoral program for Education is described in (Stacey, 1997). However, the technology offered in this virtual campus is limited to an online conferencing FirstClass (conferencing voice/fax services and bulletin-board system). Harbon and England (Harbon & England, 2009) have looked at the practice of a research degree at a distance; however, they main focus of concern was on the development of the relationship between student and supervisor. The idea of supporting students and providing the means for skills development was not discussed by Harbon & England. Unwin (Unwin, 2009) reports on his experiences of using information and communication technologies to deliver a supportive distance-based model of supervision. His approach was to include distance students in face-to-face peer supervisory meetings through audio and video-conferencing. Induction and training was limited to sending those copies of handouts of face-to-face meetings or arranging meetings that students could also attend. As we can see it was not support for training (i.e. students acquiring skills). An Australian project called the Ancient History Virtual Campus (AHVC) (Keegan, 2010) has been addressed online induction and enhanced learning experiences by providing students with an immersive induction and student support program which could make possible to counter the feelings of isolation and lack of resources which are major problems for distance-education students and often discourage them from continuing their studies. Falloom (Falloom, 2010) explores the potential of avatar environments to act as powerful communication medium for students to display knowledge, understanding and engage in the development of thinking skills (interpreting, analysing, evaluating, synthesising and solving complex problems). It also, introduces and discusses the avatar-based authoring program MARVIN. Finally, Falloom identifies potential for the use of MARVIN as a digital storytelling tool to assist students in communicating outcomes from units of learning, and in supporting the development of a range of key learning competencies identified in the New Zealand Curriculum Framework (Ministry of Education, 2007).

VIRTUAL CAMPUS ARCHITECTURE

Deep|think is a large Second Life development, made of two Sims which have been modelled into distinct, but interconnected small islands each with a well-defined function, these functions are described below.

1. A welcome area for orientation purposes. Everybody can visit the welcome area and send a request message to join as member. As can be seen in Figure 1, there are some maps showing the different regions of the virtual campus. The avatar (physical representation of the person in the campus) can be transported to the desired region if the person has the required permissions.
2. A study area with meeting spaces, common rooms and exhibition facilities. The main intention of this area is to be used by staff and students.
3. A main auditorium and related smaller theatres for large events, such as conferences, workshops and lectures. Major events, like conferences and workshops, are supported by a large auditorium able to host up to 140 avatars at any one time, with video stream capabilities and slide presentation screens. For smaller groups, selections of meeting spaces are available, from little pods in the sky to underwater theatres (see Figure 2).

Figure 1. Welcome area

Figure 2. Under-water lecture theatre

4. A library area for access to a variety of resources for study and research (see Figure 3). The resources can be consulted as in the real Open University library (Scantlebury et. al, 2008).
5. A recreation space is provided for relaxation and recreational activities, like playing pool or listening music and even dancing modern music.
6. A sandbox, for rezzing objects and scripting activities. In this area users have a complete freedom to design and create objects. However, these objects are deleted overnight by the garbage collector.

Additionally to second life, DeepThink integrates several technologies like moodle, mystuff, skype and Ning. We describe each of these technologies in turn.

Second Life

Second life is an online virtual world platform developed by Linden Lab in San Francisco USA and it was launched in 2003 (www.secondlife.com).The main characteristics offered by second life are the follows:

Figure 3. Library area

- Second life is a 3D virtual world in which users are embodied as avatars. This feature is quite important in second life as allow users to have presence.
- Second life can be used for entertainment, business, education, military applications, and medicine among others.
- Second life let users to be creative and customise the environment to a large extent and finally second life offers its own scripting language.

Given the characteristics of second life described above. We thought that second life was the ideal platform for the Open University 3D virtual campus. This decision was due to the fact that we consider that second life allowed supervision sessions, training sessions, presentation of lectures, workshops, peer collaboration and to hold social events. Additionally, in second life is relatively straightforward to have a quest. Quests are widely used in virtual settings to keep students interested and motivated. For example (Boit et al., 2008) use quests and challenges in a game setting to teach users network security across a broad range of scenarios. As students proceed through their challenges, they learn new skills and gain the same experience levels as more competent students. Then, we decided to have a quest which in DeepThink was called *Mary quest*. The quest is a motivational avatar included in DeepThink to learn second life scripting. Mary, a student avatar, presents each location with some challenges to visitors. A full description of Mary quest can be found in (Rapanotti et al, 2009).

Moodle

Moodle is a learning management system used by tutors to create their own courses. Our Deepthink, 3D-virtual campus, included the VLE (Virtual Learning Environment) customized version of Moodle which was developed at Open University (OUVLE, 2015). This VLE was used to provide relevant information about the MPhil program of studies. The organization was done by research topics. Each potential supervisor contributed with technical material in his/hers research area. Then, the MPhil team organized this material in the VLE.

Elluminate

Elluminate is a synchronous online conferencing tool. Elluminate enables to talk in real time with a tutor or other students over the internet. The main features of the Elluminate tool are described as follows: synchronous communication and collaboration technology; it allows multiple users to talk to and see each other, while text chatting, sharing a whiteboard and other applications like word documents; sessions can be recorded and supports various moderation models. Analysing, the main characteristics offered by Elluminte we decided to include it in the virtual campus. Currently, Elluminate is used in DeepThink for supervision sessions, training sessions, interviews, technical presentations, lectures/workshops, peer collaboration and mini-viva.

Skype

Skype is telecommunications application software that supports video chat and voice calls from computers, tablets, and mobile devices via the Internet.We choose Skype to be integrated in DeepThink due to the main features. Skype is a synchronous communication tool, supports calls and chat i.e. conference calls up to 5 users and also, file sharing is supported. This application was included in the virtual campus due that, sometimes, the voice in second life was not working in-world as we expected. So, Skype was selected as an auxiliary tool in case of any problem with voice in the second life platform.

MyStuff

MyStuff is a private space for users to upload and organise their online materials. In MyStuff users control access to their own materials (i.e. users could share only portions of their own materials with peers or supervisors). To clarify to the reader, MyStuff is Open University in-house E-Portfolio system. MyStuff is used in DeepThink to collect evidence of PhD skills development (OUResSkills, 2015). MyStuff was attempted to be used for reporting, to Research School, the progress of the student when a report is shared between the student and their supervisor(s). MyStuff supports peer collaboration, when material is created and/or shared by collaborators. A growing number of commercial tools have come to market in the last years as an answer to institutional needs to meet accreditation and assessment requirements. Many of these systems promise support for student portfolios (Tosh et. al, 2005) and aggregated assessment data to meet reporting requirements. However, there are challenges in meeting these two diverse needs with a single product. That is because these products are combining two different paradigms of portfolios, which by their very nature, are in conflict with each other. Pearl and Leon Paulson (1994) outlined these differences by defining two types of portfolio. The main differences between them are summarized as follows:

- **Positivist Portfolios:** "The purpose of the portfolio is to assess learning outcomes and those outcomes are, generally, defined externally. Positivism assumes that meaning is constant across users, contexts, and purposes. The portfolio is a receptacle for examples of student work used to infer what and how much learning has occurred".
- **Constructivist Portfolios:** "The portfolio is a learning environment in which the learner constructs meaning. It assumes that meaning varies across individuals, over time, and with purpose.

> The portfolio presents process, a record of the processes associated with learning itself; a summation of individual portfolios would be too complex for normative description".

We adopted the constructivism Portfolio paradigm as we aimed to improve student learning by providing a structure for students to reflect systematically over time on the learning process and to develop the aptitudes, skills and habits that come from critical reflection. This opinion coincides with the expressed by Zubizarreta in (Zubizaretta, 2004).

Ning

It is a free platform which gives the tools to build a social network. In this case, the idea is to facilitate the creation of research groups (research students with similar interests). Also, to allow students socialization in a similar manner like they socialize with peers in Facebook or in another social network.

DESIGN DECISIONS

In this section we present some of the decisions taken when building DeepThink. In the first phase of DeepThink development several educational support aspects were covered. These aspects were student registration; support to students; group creation and security and privacy. Each of these aspects is described in turn.

Student Registration

A database of avatars was constructed in DeepThink. In this way, we have a list of registered students and their registered avatar's names. This database also registers members which are not enrolled in the MPhil program. The database was needed as the avatar's names are pre-defined names offered by second life and they do not correspond to the real student name.

Groups and Permissions

It was decided to create two groups namely DeepThinkers and DeepThink Admin. For each group there are several predefined roles. The roles allow admin members to set different privileges for members within the group. The Deepthinkers group comprises the following roles: Member, Supervisor and Admin. Only Supervisors and Admin can send out invitations to the group. The DeepThink Admin group comprises a person or a group of people who can perform administrative roles like updating the avatar database, sending invitations, adding new members among other activities.

Support Students

We defined the educational objects needed to support students within the MPhil program. These objects are for example, projectors, whiteboards, meeting room among others. The virtual campus has the possibility of displaying videos. The most popular and most widely used in second life is .mov and mp4 file formats. Videos are streamed into second life from a server location. However, the video needs to be in the correct format. Additionally, students are to be able to upload power-point presentations so students can present progress in their studies to their supervisors.

Security and Privacy

As in a real campus privacy and security were two aspects considered during the DeepThink development. Therefore, DeepThink handles security procedures to make sure that the discussions (in private meeting rooms) are not heard for other people inside the virtual campus.

DEPTHINK EVALUATION

This section is divided in two sections, firstly, a question categorization is outlined and secondly, a pilot is discussed.

Questions Categorization

We identified and built our questions categorization (depicted in Table 1) to be used in the pilot. The identified categories of questions include *opinion, multiple choice, usability, navigation, visualization, platform requirements and documentation.*

Table 1 contains ID question, Type of question, general template of the question and an example of the question. This categorization does not mean to be complete but it gave us a starting point in the evaluation.

Pilot

An evaluation prior to the student's enrolment (a pilot) was organized. The participants in the pilot were Associated Lecturers from the Open University. The pilot consisted in a tour to DeepThink to assess the

Table 1. Questions categorization

ID Question	Question Type	General Template Question	Example
1	Opinion	What do you think about X and Y?	What do you think about DeepThink and Second Life?
2	Multiple choice	Do you think that you could use X for Y?	Do you think that you could use DeepThink for your courses?
3	Usability	Did you find X easy to use?	Did you find DeepThink easy to use?
4	Navigation	Did you find the navigation from one region to another easy?	Did you find the navigation from one region to another easy?
5	Visualization	Does the resolution in X was good enough?	Does the resolution in DeepThink was good enough?
6	Platform requirements	Does your computer have the minimum requirements for the installation of Y?	Does your computer have the minimum requirements for the installation of second life?
7	Documentation	Did you find enough information on X?	Did you find enough information on DeepThink?

feasibility of use in their own teaching. At the end of the tour these Associated Lectures gave a feedback from the tour. Examples of questions that were asked to the tutors are shown below.

Question ID 1: What do you think about DeepThink and second life?

The overall impression has been encouraging and positive as everybody liked the design of the virtual campus and stated that it is a user-friendly environment.

Question ID 2: Do you think that you could use DeepThink for your courses?

Tutors expressed their wiliness to try to incorporate this campus in their teaching.

Question ID 3: Did you find DeepThink easy to use?

The tutors expressed their perception of a steep learning curve for students and tutors.

Question ID 4: Did you find the navigation from one region to another easy?

Tutors agree that the navigation was straightforward and that DeepThink has a good signalization. They could find each of the places in the tour.

Question ID 5: Does the resolution (graphics visualization) in DeepThink was good enough?

Tutors described DeepThink as visual and inviting campus and they stated that the campus offers possibilities of usage for teaching and learning.

Question ID 6: Does your computer have the minimum requirements for the installation of second life?

Tutors answered to have a computer satisfying the minimum requirements like the ones shown in Table 2. But, the main concern for the tutors during the tour was that the platform second life requires high specification computer and a reasonably fast broadband connection. Although, it was clear in principle that there is a benefit on the integration of second life in DeepThink.

Question ID 7: Did you find enough information on DeepThink?

Tutors answered that they found enough information in the website of the MPhil program and in the second life website.

Summing up, we think that transferring the virtual environment to real users is not always straight forward or easy. Trainees are not always willing to use the virtual environment for a number of reasons, such as the difficulty of the e-learning environment, the non-intuitive nature of the environment, among others. However, in our case, the response of the tutors during the evaluation (trip in the virtual campus) was positive. After the pilot, we really believed that tutors were inclined to use of new technology in their courses. To our knowledge Minocha has used the 3D-virtual campus, DeepThink, on Geology field trips (Minocha, 2014). Also, DeepThink has been used in courses of Software Engineering by colleagues from the Software Engineering group at the Computing Department, Open University, UK.

LIMITATION ON THE SECOND LIFE CLIENT/SERVER MODEL

Second Life is designed using the client/server model. Each region is managed by a server called simulator and users use the client which render the 3-D model. However, the Second Life client/server protocol is not public as the company Linden have a complete control of the Second Life platform. The information provided to us is the number of regions, registered accounts and online avatars.

In this section, we analyze in more detail the client/server model. The model client/server has the following characteristics: communication takes the form of a request message from the client (user) to the server asking for some work that needs to be done. The client/server model has become one of the central ideas of network computing. In fact, many business applications being written today use the client/server model. However, client/server model has advantages and disadvantages. The advantages of a client/server are that all data in servers have greater security; data storage is centralized so, updates to this data is easier; and many mature client/server technology is easy to use. While, the disadvantages of the client/ server model are: traffic congestion on the network and under client/server model if the server fails then client request are not fulfilled.

We concluded that scalability is the main problem in our virtual campus as a congestion of second life may occur slowing down the virtual campus response's time. This issue remains unsolved yet, but, it is an important parameter to consider in the long term plan as we aim to support a good number of research students. For the short term, the response time of the virtual campus is acceptable.

CONCLUSION AND FUTURE WORK

The major contribution of this work was to conceive a framework to support an MPhil program of studies to a distance. The framework uses second life, Moodle and web 2.0 technologies suitable for Education. We designed the campus defining the objects needed to support MPhil students like in a real campus, students goes thought the registration process and they are organized in groups according with the research

Table 2. Minimum requirements for Second Life

Windows platform	Minimum requirements
Operating system	Vista, windows 7, windows 8
Computer processor	CPU with SSE2 support, including Intel Pentium 4, Pentium M, Core or Atom, AMD Athlon 64 or later.
Computer memory	1 GB or more
Screen resolution	1024 X 768 pixels
Graphics card for Vista, Windows 7, Windows 8 (requires latest drivers)	NVIDIA GeForce 6600 or better OR ATI Radeon 9500 or better OR Intel 945 chipset

topic. Students groups are given permissions to use the objects in the campus. Also, supervisors are assigned to each student and they are given permissions for the use of the objects in the virtual campus. The most important aspect of the virtual campus DeepThink is that like in a real campus, offers support for students to acquire skills during the entire MPhil program (Vargas-Vera 2016; Minocha & Hardy 2011; Rapanotti et al., 2010, Rapanotti & Hall 2010; Minocha & Morse 2010). This is in fact, the main difference with other approaches discussed in the related work section. So far, the results are encouraging in two aspects a) the use of the virtual campus (DeepThink) in a real scenario i.e. supporting an approved officially program of studies at the Open University and b) in terms of people interested in the use of DeepThink in their courses. To my knowledge, there are people who like to try new technologies. Then, we envisage that more departments at the Open University could use DeepThink in the near future. The evaluation involving tutors showed encouraging results as they are very enthusiastic on trying new technology for their courses at undergraduate and graduate level.

As future work, we plan to explore how to support effectively students in DeepThink. For example, add to the library island, a librarian avatar which remembers the fields of individual interest and research. This functionality is similar to the functionality of the Amazon portal which remembers the previous purchases of clients and makes recommendations based on their profile.

ACKNOWLEDGMENT

We thank to colleagues of the MPhil Team Lucia Rapanotti and Leonor Barroca. Also, we give special thanks to Darrel Ince, former Head of the Computing Department at the Open University UK. Also, many thanks to Non Scantlebury and James McNulty, who helped to organise the library services and Graham Roberts for his assistance in the maintenance of the virtual campus (DeepThink). Finally, we would also like to acknowledge the development team at Two Four Communications, UK, particularly Andrew Jinman.

REFERENCES

Barroca, L., Rapanotti, L., Petre, M., & Vargas-Vera, M. (2010). Developing Research Degrees Online. *International Conference of Education, Research and Innovation (ICERI)*, Madrid, Spain.

Boit, A., Eirund, H., Geimer, T., Mendonca, J., Ott, A., & Sethmann, R. (2008). NetS-X - The Network Security Experience. *Proceedings of the 7th European Conference on i-Warfare (ECIW 2008).*

De Freitas, S. (2008). Serious Virtual Worlds. A scoping guide. Technical report. The Joint Information Systems Committee (JISC).

Falloon, G. W. (2010). Using avatars and virtual environments in learning: What do they have to offer? *British Journal of Educational Technology, 41*(1), 108-122.

Harbon, L., & England, N. (2009). The Cultural Practice of Research Higher Degree Supervision over Distance: A Case in Progress. University of Sydney Papers in TESOL, 2009(2006), 87-107.

Keegan, P. (2010). The Ancient History Virtual Campus: a model for online student induction and support in higher education. *Proceedings of the 1st International Australasian Conference on Enabling Access to Higher Education*, 175-186.

Ministry of Education. (2007). *The New Zealand curriculum framework*. Wellington: Learning Media Ltd.

Minocha S. (2010). Introducing Second Life, a 3D virtual world, to students and educators. *T4E*, 206-208.

Minocha, S. (2014). Developing a 3D virtual geology field trip in Unity 3D: reflection of our experiences. In Virtual Worlds - Best Practices in Education (VWBPE), Connections. Second Life and OS (Open Simulator Grid).

Minocha, S., & Hardy, C. L. (2011). *Designing navigation and wayfinding in 3D virtual learning spaces*. OZCHI.

Minocha, S., & Morse, D. (2010). Supporting distributed team working in 3D virtual worlds: A case study in Second Life. *Interactive Technology and Smart Education*, *7*(4), 200–219. doi:10.1108/17415651011096021

OUResSkills. (2015). *Research Degree Skills*. The Open University Web site: http://phdskills.open.ac.uk

OUVLE. (2015). *OU Virtual Learning Environment Program*. The Open University Web site: http://conclave.open.ac.uk/dev-ouvle

Paulson, F. L., & Paulson, P. (1994). Assessing Portfolios Using the Constructivist Paradigm (R. Fogarty, Ed.). Academic Press.

Rapanotti, L., Barroca, L., Vargas-Vera, M., & Minocha, S. (2009). deep|think: a Second Life campus for part-time research students at a distance. Computing Department, UK, TR2009-01.

Rapanotti, L., Barroca, L., Vargas-Vera, M., & Reeves, A. (2010). deep|think: A Second Life environment for part-time research students at a distance. *The 10th IEEE International Conference on Advanced Learning Technologies (ICALT 2010)*, 200-201.

Rapanotti, L., & Hall, J. (2010). *Lessons Learned in Developing a Second Life Educational Environment*. Valencia, Spain: CSEDU.

Rymaszewski, M., Wagner, J., & Wallace, M. (2008). *Second Life: The Official Guide*. Academic Press.

Scantlebury, N., McNulty, J., & Dowson, N. (2008). Developing sustainable library services within the context of a parallel universe. Proceedings of Researching Learning in Virtual Environments (ReLIVE 08).

Stacey, E. (2009). *A virtual campus: The experience of postgraduate students studying through electronic communication and resource access*. Victoria: Deakin University.

Tosh, D., Light, T.P., Fleming, K., & Haywood, J. (2005). Engagement with Electronic Portfolios: Challenges from the Student Perspective. *Canadian Journal of Learning and Technology, 31*(3).

UKGrad. (2015). *Joint Skills Statement of Skills Training Requirements*. The Vitae Web site: http://grad.ac.uk/jss/

Unwin, T. (2007). Reflections on supervising distance-based PhD students (Vol. 2009). Academic Press.

Vargas-Vera, M. (2016). Reflections on the Second Life Platform used in the Development of a Virtual University Campus. *IJKSR Journal, 7*(4).

Weber, A., Rufer-Bach, K., & Platel, R. (2007). *Creating Your World: The official Guide to Advanced Content Creation for Second Life*. Academic Press.

Zubizarreta, J. (2004). *The Learning Portfolio*. Bolton, MA: Anker Publishing.

APPENDIX

The MPhil program called DeepThink was a project developed at the Computing Department Open University UK. It started in 2008 and evolved into an Educational framework consisting of synchronous, asynchronous internet and web technologies. The inclusion of second life platform (3D immersive virtual environments) has brought benefits for two important reasons. Second life has becoming popular due to the notion of presence (users are represented as avatars). This enhances the sense of participation as opposed to traditional 2D internet-based technology.

The Virtual university campus was released and the first generation of postgraduate students was enrolled in 2009. The Virtual MPhil is a par-time course of studies at the Open University, almost; all the postgraduate student related processes (like supervision) are carried out remotely with exception of the viva which is carried out at the Open University premises. The MPhil was designed to take minim of 2 years and maximum of 6 years of studies. The student data used in the development of the campus DeepThink was anonymized and ethics permissions for the development of DeepThink were granted by the Open University's ethics committee.

Chapter 9
Use of Presentations in the Classroom:
How Innovative Can It Be?

Vassilia Stefanou
The American College of Greece, Greece

Maira Kotsovoulou
The American College of Greece, Greece

ABSTRACT

The use of electronic presentations in the classroom has become a controversial subject, as the innovative educational value of electronic presentation tools such as MS-PowerPoint or Prezi is being questioned. This study uses the participatory research approach to investigate how college instructors feel about the use of PowerPoint presentations when teaching an introductory course of computer information systems. Nine college instructors participated in this research project by exchanging their views through an online discussion forum. The findings revealed that PowerPoint presentations are perceived by instructors as valuable only when combined with other teaching techniques. Moreover, it became evident that the instructors perceived that although students' attention and participation is affected by the use of electronic presentations, their actual performance is not.

INTRODUCTION

The launching of MS-PowerPoint in the late eighties is considered by many educators a milestone in the history of Technology Enhanced Learning. One of the main uses of PowerPoint presentations is to support face-to-face teaching in classrooms. Nevertheless, there is a considerable number of instructors who feel that the use of electronic presentations, especially when they are not combined with other teaching techniques, may not be as effective as it appears to be.

A significant amount of research has been done on this subject. Various studies demonstrate how powerful PowerPoint presentations can be; at the same time, an impressive number of studies call for our attention to the weaknesses of this same method. Parker (2001, p. 76) points out that "PowerPoint

DOI: 10.4018/978-1-5225-4191-2.ch009

can be an impressive antidote to fear—converting public-speaking dread into moviemaking pleasure", but at the same time warns the users that "It helps you make a case, but it also makes its own case: about how to organize information, how much information to organize, how to look at the world". Criticizing PowerPoint, Waller & Gove (2007, p. 2) cite a communication specialist: "It [PowerPoint] provides a comforter, really. It would be more sensible just to talk (…) With PowerPoint, people feel they can get away with practicing less, if they have the words in front of them".

The aim of this study is not to take sides on this debate about the usefulness of PowerPoint presentations; rather, it is to investigate how instructors feel about the use of PowerPoint presentations. In particular, the research question that this paper attempts to answer is:

How do college instructors feel about the use of PowerPoint presentations when teaching an introductory course of computer information systems?

This issue was raised in a recent departmental meeting in my college; while discussing problems that were related to student motivation, participation, and performance, the possibility of the existence of a relationship between these and the in-class use of PowerPoint presentations was mentioned. In the context of that discussion it became apparent that not all colleagues used PowerPoint presentations in the same way, and not all of them shared the same feelings for the use of PowerPoint; consequently, the idea of investigating this further was born, since the findings would have a practical application in the teaching and learning in our department.

The interest in the college-level instructors stems from the authors college-level professor status. The reason for the interest in the introductory course level is that the majority of students attending introductory classes are college freshmen, thus quite young and usually lacking the maturity of older students; consequently, it is crucial for their professors to make use of the most enticing methods in their disposal in order to manage to attract their students' interest and actively engage them in an effective learning process.

The reason for choosing to investigate the use of PowerPoint presentations in the context of a computer information systems course is that instructors from the computer information systems discipline, given their background, are very well acquainted with PowerPoint and its 'magic'; in several cases, training students to use PowerPoint as a tool to create successful presentations may be one of the responsibilities of these same instructors. As a result, it is safe to assume that the preparation of their presentations is achieved rapidly and effortlessly, overcoming the disadvantage identified by Bartsch & Cobern (2003) related with the excessive time some instructors have to spend in the preparation of presentations.

The participatory research methodology was employed in this study. Nine professors, including the authors, participated in an online forum discussion in which their views about the use of PowerPoint presentations in our classrooms were exchanged.

METHODOLOGY

Finn (1994) identified three main features that differentiate participatory research from the other methodologies: people, power, and praxis. Participatory research emphasizes the importance of the involvement of the people-subjects in the whole research process (data collection, analysis, interpretation, etc). This shifts part of the power from the researcher to the participants: they are no longer just the research subjects; instead, they are empowered by their own active participation. The last feature, praxis (act) dictates exactly this active participation: no results can be derived unless the participants-subjects contribute their own input (Sohng, 1996).

Another principal difference between participatory research and traditional research paradigm is that in the latter, the focus is on *generating* knowledge; in participatory research, this is extended to include the utilisation and the application of knowledge (Pant, 2009). As Pant points out, this difference is also reflected in the role of the researcher - as perceived by the research subjects - and also in the tools that can be employed:

... survey and interview questions, consciously or otherwise, reflect the researcher's own values and ideology. Professional researchers know all and they control the entire process of research. Therefore, respondents often experience survey research as alienating, dominating, or oppressive in character. (Pant, 2009, p. 93)

The nature of this methodology makes it ideal for working with under-privileged or deprived communities; nevertheless, participatory research applicability is not limited in such communities. It can be used by any group of people when a problem is identified, or even when there is no particular problem, but the people wish to improve a process or a procedure. As Sohng (1996, p. 87) states, "participatory research is premised on the principle that the people with a problem carry out the investigation themselves".

The participatory research methodology borrows elements from critical theory methodology, since critical questions are raised and existing theories may be challenged during the process of the collaborative identification and analysis of the problem in a specific context (Wadsworth, 1998). However, participatory research has its main roots in participatory design, an approach to systems design that promotes active user participation in all stages of the design process and not just in the data collection part. The strength of this approach lies in the principle that the roles of users and designers are equally important (Kapoor, 2006; Sanders, Brandt, & Binder, 2010). The origins of participatory design are traced back in the 1970s in Norway, when Nygaard and Bergo worked with the Norwegian Iron and Metal Workers Union, and later in Sweden and Denmark (Bødker, 2010; Ehn, 1993). This systems design alternative is sometimes referred to as the "Scandinavian Challenge"; the philosophy behind it being that "involving users during system development is thought to lead to greater user commitment, acceptance, usage, and satisfaction with the system" (Zaphiris & Zacharia, 2001, p. 272). Blomberg & Henderson (1990, p. 359) have determined three tenets that are promoted by the participatory design approach, namely:

1. The goal should be the improvement of the quality of work life of the users
2. The orientation should be toward collaborative development
3. The process should be iterative.

Bannon (1991), a human-computer interaction specialist and an advocate of participatory design, in his paper "From human factors to human actors" described the transition from a passive, de-motivated individual-subject (factor) to an active participant-subject (actor). Kapoor (2006, p. 35) claims that when the participatory design strategy is employed, "The experiences of the users and their interests in the design outcome improve the work life of the users through collaborative development".

Given its roots, the successful application of participatory design in research areas related to work settings is not surprising. However, in the 1990s it started gaining popularity for other, non-work related settings, so although the main principle underlying user participation remained, various disciplines adapted participatory design to suit their own practices. As a result, today, participatory design can have a variety of connotations (Bødker, 2010). It has become an interdisciplinary approach, with the common denominator being that "design is neither done for, or by, the users, but with the users" (Lemmergaard, Gersbo-Møller, & Povlsen, 2005, p. 3).

It is worth mentioning at this point that there is a variety of research methods that stem from the participatory research paradigm, one of the most popular being the participatory action research; it's not uncommon to see the two terms (Participatory Research and Participatory Action Research) to be used interchangeably, however several researchers distinguish between the two. PAR combines the principles and goals of PR with the ones of Action Research, consequently the emphasis is not only in the collaborative process that shares with PR; PAR dictates that the implementation of the knowledge generated through the participants' collaboration should be part of the research process (Bell et al, 2004; Wadsworth, 1998). As Wadsworth (1998, p. 9) states, in PAR "... there are countless tiny cycles of participatory reflection on action, learning about action and then new informed action which is in turn the subject of further reflection."

Description of the Study

Taking into consideration the authors' personal interest in the use of PowerPoint presentations to support teaching at a college level and since the authors wished to be included in the contributing instructors instead of acting as external researchers-observers, the participatory research methodology was deemed as most appropriate for this study. While describing the participatory research methodology, Sohng (1996, p. 84) states that "In the ideal situation, the researcher already lives in the community and partakes in its affairs". Following the same line of thought, Pant (2009) explains that in a participatory research paradigm the researcher isn't expected or even supposed to be value-neutral. The participatory research methodology dictates that the role of the researcher is to act as a facilitator of the group (Lemmergaard, Gersbo-Møller, & Povlsen, 2005; Krishnaswamy, 2004; Evaluating Socio Economic Development, 2003). The participatory action research was also considered as an alternative methodology; however, given the small-scale nature of this project and the limited time frame, PAR was not a feasible methodology; the participants would have to exchange their views in the forum, apply the knowledge gained from the online discussion in class, then again discuss their feedback through the forum, and so on. Nevertheless, PAR may be considered as a candidate for any larger-scale studies in the areas identified in the last section of this paper as potential areas for further research.

The authors assumed the role of the group facilitators by creating an online discussion forum which remained open for nine days and by inviting fourteen instructors to participate. All the people who were invited were the authors' colleagues, teaching in the Computer Information Systems department of the same college. These instructors were selected on the basis of having taught the "Introduction to Information Systems" course in the last five years, regardless of seniority or level of experience. It is worth mentioning that the authors' seniority and experience were neither the highest nor the lowest in the group; all colleagues were peers, and the only colleague who had some additional administrative responsibilities along with the teaching ones was the Head of the department (Instructor 7). Eight colleagues responded to this invitation and participated in the online forum, so, including the authors, the total number of participants in the forum was nine. The following table shows the number of posts per participant:

Table 1. Number of posts per participant

Instructors	Number of Posts
Instructor 1 (Author)	7
Instructor 2 (Author)	2
Instructor 3	1
Instructor 4	3
Instructor 5	1
Instructor 6	1
Instructor 7	1
Instructor 8	1
Instructor 9	2
Total	19

All seven instructors gave their consent for the forum's posts to be used for the purposes of this study, by signing consent forms which were prepared for this purpose and which explained that the participants' names and personal data would not be revealed to any third party.

This asynchronous type of meeting in the form of an online discussion forum is quite common in participatory research design; other popular tools that can be employed to support both the participatory design and the participatory research methodology include semi-structured and open interviews, workshops, meetings, storytelling, role play, community seminars, fact finding tours, photo story, popular theatre, education camps, observation, etc. (Evaluating Socio Economic Development, 2003; Kapoor, 2006; Katsui & Koistinen, 2008; Krishnaswamy, 2004; Pant, 2009; Sanders, Brandt, & Binder, 2010; Sohng, 1996). In this particular study the choice of the online discussion forum can be justified not just by the short timeframe of this project -participants could contribute to the discussion asynchronously, at their convenience-, but also by the fact that all participants were quite familiar with this tool; it was not the first time that such a forum was used in the authors' department in order to collaboratively reach solutions to problems related to teaching and learning. The only drawback was the limited time availability of the forum combined with the busy schedule of the participants, since the nine-day period that the forum was available coincided with the second-grading period of coursework and exams in our department.

All participants were familiar with the use of PowerPoint presentations, therefore one of the main requirements of the participatory research methodology, i.e. that the researchers and the participants should have a common knowledge of the social model, was met (Stone, 1997). Katsui and Koistinen (2008) have identified two more requirements: accessibility of the research and meeting the needs of the participants. This study satisfied both requirements: information about the research could be accessed at any time by any participant; there was no hidden or secret agenda since all participants were explicitly informed in advance about the purpose of the online forum and they willingly chose to contribute. The second requirement - meeting the participants' needs - was also met. All of the participants were genuinely interested in the subject since they were all using PowerPoint presentations in their classrooms and the online discussion allowed them to exchange opinions and ideas about this technique; abiding with Pant's view (2009), the focus of this study was not just to generate a theory, but to apply in our teaching practices the knowledge gained through the online forum.

The instructors who chose to contribute to the forum were provided with certain guidelines through the forum's description, formulated based on my own experience of the use of PowerPoint presentations in my classes and on previous discussions we had with my colleagues about this in departmental meetings. These guidelines defined the framework of the discussion; the participants were not obliged to comment on all these aspects, and they were encouraged to discuss any other points they felt that they were related to the use of PowerPoint presentations in their classrooms. The following excerpt of the forum's description quotes these guidelines:

1. Continuous vs selective use: Do you use them throughout the year, i.e. during all semesters? For all your class sections? For all class meetings of a section? For the whole period of a lecture?
2. Factors that influence your decision towards using/avoiding PowerPoint Presentations.
3. Alternative methods/teaching aids.
4. Comparing lectures that you employ PowerPoint Presentations and lectures that you don't make use of such aids, have you identified any differences in the students' participation/interactivity/concentration in the classroom?
5. Have you observed an impact of PowerPoint Presentations on the student's performance and grades?
6. Any other thoughts/concerns you have related to the use of PowerPoint presentations in your classrooms.

LITERATURE REVIEW

A number of studies have been conducted investigating the impact of electronic presentations on teaching and learning. However, the study presented here does not aim to replicate or summarize their findings; rather, its intention is to investigate how the instructors perceive this impact. Consequently, this section will focus to the aspects that are related to the findings of this study.

A general conclusion drawn from the majority of the aforementioned studies is that despite the fact that students have a positive attitude and seem to prefer lectures conducted with electronic presentations, their performance does not exhibit any significant improvement (Craig & Amernic, 2006; Rankin & Hoaas, 2001; Bartsch & Cobern, 2003; Apperson, Laws, & Scepansky, 2006; Savoy, Proctor, & Salvendy, 2009; Susskind, 2005; Sugahara & Boland, 2006; Chou, Chang & Lu, 2015). In fact, in a study conducted by Sugahara & Boland (2006) testing the effectiveness of PowerPoint presentations in the Accounting classroom, it was suggested that using electronic presentations not only does not improve the accounting students' performance, but may even be responsible for reducing it.

Another interesting issue raised by Craig & Armenic (2006, p. 151) is related to the impact of PowerPoint presentations on the dynamics of classrooms; the researchers, reflecting upon the role of the instructor, discussed two conflicting views, the one supporting that the instructor is still viewed as the main actor in the classroom whereas the other supports that the instructor gets demoted to a "stagehand" and is viewed by the students as "a necessary, but annoying distraction". Moreover, the same researchers question the intended use of the PowerPoint presentations, by investigating whether the presentations, instead of supporting the message to be transferred to the students, are becoming the message themselves. Supporting this, Parker (2001, p. 80) cites Cathleen Belleville, a former product planner / graphic designer at Microsoft who has contributed to the design of PowerPoint software, describing her frustration about the preparation of presentations:

... we've got highly paid people sitting there formatting slides—spending hours formatting slides—because it's more fun to do that than concentrate on what you're going to say. It would be much more efficient to offload that work onto someone who could do it in a tenth of the time, and be paid less. Millions of executives around the world are sitting there going, 'Arial? Times Roman? Twenty-four point? Eighteen point?'

ANALYSIS

The findings are grouped based on the provided guidelines:

1. **Continuous vs. Selective Use of PowerPoint Presentations:** Instructors may employ PowerPoint presentations only for one particular semester, or use them continuously. They may use PowerPoint presentations for all their sections of the particular introductory course; or, they may use PowerPoint presentations only for some sections. In the sections where PowerPoint presentations are used, it is possible for an instructor to employ these presentations only for some lectures, or use PowerPoint for all lectures throughout a semester. Finally, PowerPoint presentations may be used only for a part of a lecture, or for the whole time a lecture takes place.

The online discussion forum showed that all participants make use of PowerPoint presentations, but the majority choose to use them selectively, i.e. not in all their lectures and/or not for the whole class time. It is worth mentioning that even the instructors who stated that they use PowerPoint presentations all the time, pointed out that PowerPoint is not the only supporting tool they employ, but that they combine electronic presentations with other teaching techniques.

2. **Factors That Influence the Instructors' Decision Towards Using PowerPoint Presentations:** Several arguments in favour of PowerPoint presentations emerged in the discussion forum. It was mentioned in several posts that the use of PowerPoint presentations facilitates the instructor since the time needed to prepare for a lecture gets minimized; PowerPoint presentations may function as tips for the instructor. Another advantage, also identified by several researchers (Susskind, 2005, 2008; Apperson, Laws, & Scepansky, 2006; Savoy, Proctor, & Salvendy, 2009) was that PowerPoint presentations can demonstrate the concepts to be taught in a highly structured manner, along with diagrams and other graphical elements. Almost all instructors mentioned that they always use PowerPoint presentations when they want to explain a concept that requires an image, diagram, picture, or video. However, it was also mentioned in the forum as a counter-argument that an image viewer could replace PowerPoint presentations for this particular context.

Another factor identified by the participants which justifies the use of PowerPoint presentations was the efficiency of lectures, as far as the time spent by the instructor to teach the material needed. However, the instructors also mentioned that they have to be careful not to move too fast between slides so that the students will have the time to keep notes and absorb the concepts taught – also commented in Apperson, Laws, & Scepansky's paper (2006). Instructors feel that when they have to cover specific material in order to prepare their students for their exams in a pre-determined amount of time, Power-

Point presentations can be of assistance, since the alternative of writing on the traditional whiteboard or blackboard is rather time consuming. Nonetheless, this point raised some shared concerns among the forum's contributors. Instructor 5 wrote

I prefer to use PPT only for lectures that illustrating an image is required for the best understanding of the students on the subject … Lately however, I need to use PPTs more and more to keep the pace in courses where the teaching time has been compressed due to new deadlines. As far as I am concerned this is a side effect use of PPTs and is not the best way for students.

Instructor 1's reply to this post raised a point about the role of the instructors:

… do you think that, when ppt presentations are used in this context, the students manage to grasp the concepts taught? Personally, when I use the presentations mainly because of time pressure, I feel that the students simply "observe" the lecture, and they don't really get involved … isn't this almost the same with going through the material from the textbooks by themselves? what is the role of the instructor in that case?

Instructor 4 replied by saying:

When I use the presentations simply because there is a time pressure and I need to cover specific material for the exams, I feel that the students are not really grasping the concepts. They don't have enough time to fully comprehend and absorb the material taught, so my role is minimal at that point: they could as well read these from the textbook or visit the textbook site and watch videos and figures from there … or, I could simply give them my presentations and ask them to view them at their own time, without a time pressure..

I don't like it when this happens, since I feel that I become redundant!

Finally, Instructor 1 wrote:

I share the same concern about becoming "redundant" the whole idea of using these presentations is that they should be supporting our lecturing; but when these are shown slide after slide and the instructor's elaboration on the bullets is ignored by the students (mainly because there is no time to go over the concepts with more examples … then what is the point of the instructor being there? The students could as well download these same presentations and go over them by themselves!

It is clear from the above quotes that there are cases where the instructors would prefer to support their teaching with other techniques (not PowerPoint presentations), but they feel that, unless they use PowerPoint they will run out of time; in one of my posts, I referred to PowerPoint as the "necessary evil", similarly to Craig & Amernic's (2006, p. 151) comparison of PowerPoint to a "crutch" for the instructor. This appears to be a lose-lose situation. If the instructors don't use PowerPoint presentations then they may not be able to teach the required material on time; on the other hand, when they do resort to PowerPoint because of time pressure, they worry that they could become redundant and that they have to find a way to justify the significance of their own role to the students.

3. **Alternative Methods/Teaching Aids:** All participants declared that they don't rely solely on PowerPoint presentations to support their teaching. Besides the old-fashioned whiteboard / blackboard, they also employ a variety of other techniques, including mind maps, case study discussions, videos, on line games, on line tests, forums, tech chats, web links, SCORMs, glossaries, wikis, and in-class exercises. Most instructors stated that they usually employ a combination of these techniques, according to the context of the material to be taught.
4. **Impact on Students' Participation/Interactivity/Concentration:** Most instructors agreed that the excessive use of PowerPoint presentations negatively affects students' participation. Instructor 5 claimed that "*PPTs seem to have both students and teachers locked within the boundaries of the PPT*" and that when PowerPoint presentations are not employed,

... the lecture becomes a dialogue ... The more experienced the instructor the better the lecture without a PPT. What I do not know and maybe worth checking is if an instructor has never delivered a lecture without a PPT, will they ever get experienced enough to enjoy the benefits of a pure class discussion?

Craig & Amernic (2006, p. 152) support this argument: "When we taught without PowerPoint or led a case discussion without PowerPoint or acted Socratic-like without PowerPoint, our relationship with students was unmediated and more human, more direct, less pre-meditated and less structured".

However, Instructor 3 supported that "Student's concentration degrades without PPT. If I write a lot, they focus on writing and they don't participate. If I wait I am running out of time. If I don't write much they cannot comprehend."

This second view, that students' concentration declines when PowerPoint presentations are not used, appears contradictory. However, Instructor 3 points out that when PowerPoint presentations are not used, then a lot of writing on the board has to take place. As a result, students may get tired and eventually lose their interest. Naturally, this may happen even when PowerPoint presentations are employed; the key, as Instructor 2 states, is to use PowerPoint presentations "... jointly with other teaching methods in order to encourage student interactivity." This is also evident in a post by Instructor 8:

... the slides I present are complemented by my notes on the whiteboard. These notes mainly provide with clarifications, examples and new market data that do not appear on slides. Also, students' attention is risen since they have to also read and/or note down what I write on the whiteboard...

As it became evident from several posts, this enhancement of student participation, enabled by a balanced use of PowerPoint presentations and other techniques, allows students to cultivate their critical thinking and their analytical skills.

5. **Impact on Students' Performance:** Most instructors felt that when PowerPoint presentations are used, the students tend to believe that their study material is automatically narrowed down to the handouts of the presentations, which naturally may result in lower performance. This was particularly apparent when the presentations, instead of listing the main points of the concepts taught, included a lot of text.

Student performance was also linked to the note-taking process, as it can be seen in one of Instructor 1's posts:

I value note taking as one of the most important aspects of learning, so I decided to try to minimize the use of PowerPoint in my CS1070 classes, and I get to use it now for some specific cases (for example, to show a video or pictures) and not all the time. I'm experimenting with this since last last year, and I actually switched back to the old-fashioned whiteboard; I've noticed that a lot of students now get to keep notes, and this time they don't simply copy what I have on the board … they get to write down their own notes as well – last semester, I was pleasantly surprised while grading short essay questions in their final exams, and I saw that a lot of students actually quoted me, and also referred to examples that were discussed in class … which means that these students had actually kept good notes, and this improved their performance.

6. **Other Thoughts/Concerns:** A shared concern which was raised had to do with the content of the presentations. Most instructors stated that they favoured PowerPoint presentations when a concept required the use of visual aids (pictures, diagrams, charts, videos). As Instructor 2 stated "… associating a term with an image enhances memorability. Moreover, I have figured out that effects such as animations, keep students alert". However, other instructors claimed that animations along with sound effects may have the opposite effect, since students may get distracted. A lot of research has been conducted related to the use of multimedia and graphics in PowerPoint presentations. Bartsch & Cobern's study (2003) indicates that both the instructors and the students do not prefer the "expanded" presentations, whereas the positive effects of adding graphics to a presentation are evident in several studies (Apperson, Laws, & Scepansky, 2006 & 2008; Bartsch & Cobern, 2003). An interesting finding is described by Savoy, Proctor, & Salvendy (2009, p. 866): "People tend to pay attention to what is presented on the slides as opposed to what is verbalized".

Another point mentioned was that although the combination of PowerPoint presentations with notes on the whiteboard was considered to be the optimum technique, this combination was not always feasible. It was stated that some classrooms had a limited whiteboard space since the projected presentation took most of it, and also that the dark lights required by PowerPoint presentations in some other classrooms did not allow for note-writing on the whiteboard. Fortunately, these technical problems are not impossible to solve.

CONCLUSION, LIMITATIONS, AND REFLECTIONS

This study was conducted as part of the authors' research towards a PhD in Technology Enhanced Learning, within the context of identifying tools and techniques that may contribute to innovative teaching and learning pedagogies, not only in traditional face-to-face teaching environments, but also in blended learning courses. The broader scope of the authors' research is to explore prevailing teaching and learning tools and techniques, in order to determine opportunities and areas of potential improvement, with further goal the development of more efficient and effective pedagogies that could be implemented in either traditional face-to-face settings, or blended ones. The use of electronic presentations was chosen to be studied here, as it is a technique that has been used for several decades – and it is considered a foremost innovative milestone in the history of teaching technologies and Information and Communication Technologies (ICTs) in general.

The contribution of this study lies in describing how college instructors feel about using PowerPoint presentations when teaching an introductory computer course. By exchanging opinions and views, the participants identified and shared possible PowerPoint presentations uses in their classrooms.

As it became obvious from the online discussion, the teaching method that all instructors considered as being the most effective was the combination of PowerPoint presentations with other techniques (writing notes on the whiteboard, videos, games, etc.). Savoy, Proctor, & Salvendy (2009) share the same view, stating that the choice of a teaching technique varies according to the material that needs to be taught; traditional presentations work better for concepts that require dialogue or verbal explanation, PowerPoint presentations are better when graphs and figures need to be communicated to the students, whereas in the case of concepts that appear both in text and in numeric form, either or both types of presentations can be used.

An emerging issue that worried several participants was the changing role of instructor when PowerPoint presentations were used. Moreover, the importance of encouraging students to keep notes was pointed out, as was the impact on student participation and interactivity. Finally, most instructors claimed that they did not find any positive association between the use of electronic presentations and the students' performance.

As with all studies, this one too has a number of limitations. A problem that became apparent even from the very beginning of the study was the short time frame in which the research was to be conducted. This created two conflicts; one with the instructors' busy schedule and a second one with the nature of the participatory research design which is by default rather time consuming (Katsui & Koistinen, 2008).

From the original fourteen instructors who were invited to the study, six did not contribute to the forum, and from these six, four stated - in the context of an informal conversation - that they would have been able to participate if the forum's availability had been extended. In fact, the original plan was for the forum to be available for a period of seven days, but responding to the authors' colleagues' request it was extended to nine days. Nevertheless, it is worth mentioning that three of the colleagues who did not contribute accessed and read the forum after the nine-day period. All three stated that their feelings about the use of PowerPoint presentations in their classrooms were represented by the posts of the other colleagues.

The second conflict, related to the time-consuming nature of the participatory research methodology, affected the data analysis and interpretation stages. Through the forum, the participants had the chance to exchange their opinions and ideas, and to perform some degree of reflection and analysis upon their teaching. Ideally, after the nine-day period for which the forum was available, a meeting with all nine instructors would have enabled a higher degree of participatory analysis of the data. However, setting up a meeting for nine instructors with conflicting time schedule proved to be impossible within the available time frame. Consequently, the degree of the other seven instructors' participation in the analysis and the interpretation of the findings was minimal.

Another notable point is that this study was narrowed down to investigate the feelings of instructors about the use of PowerPoint presentations. It is quite obvious that, along with instructors, students are also important stakeholders. Krishnaswamy (2004), in his paper "Participatory Research: Strategies and Tools", states that an essential aspect of participatory research methodology is to involve all stakeholders who will be affected by the research. Besides the fact that there is an extensive amount of research on this subject, it needs to be made clear that the reason that this study does not explore the students' perspective is not because the student's feelings on the matter are not considered as important as the instructors' ones; on the contrary, it is exactly because the students are considered stakeholders of equal value with the instructors that the students' views were not investigated here; this study could justifiably serve as the basis for further research on this topic: investigation of how students feel about PowerPoint presentations in their classrooms could be seen as a natural continuation and extension of this study.

Another potential area open for further research is to compare student performance when using different combinations of the various teaching techniques identified in this study.

Craig & Amernic (2006) claim that it's not wise for lecturers to unquestioningly adopt any new technology, thus PowerPoint users should be critical about the effect that a technology can have in their teaching. The same researchers state that PowerPoint "… is not merely a benign means of facilitating what educators have always done. Rather, it is changing much (perhaps most) of how we engage with our students and the disciplines which we profess. We should be curious as to why this is so." (2006, p. 158).

It is worth mentioning at this point that PowerPoint is no longer the only prevailing presentation software tool; other tools, such as Prezi, are also extensively used for several years, and recent studies similar to the one presented here reveal similar findings (Chou et al, 2015; Špernjak, 2014; Afar, 2015; Kiss, 2016).

Concluding, as it is common with research studies, rather than trying to give an answer, new questions are formed: How do students feel when they are on the receiving end of electronic presentations combined with other teaching techniques? What is the impact of the combined use of electronic presentations and other techniques on student performance? What could be an "optimum" combination of teaching techniques that can be used along with electronic presentations to maximize teaching and learning effectiveness? How is the role of the instructor changing when electronic presentations are employed?

REFERENCES

Afar, H. S. (2015). Educating With Prezi: A New Presentation Paradigm For Teaching, Learning, And Leading In The Digital Age. *College Student Journal*, *49*(4), 491–512. Retrieved from http://content.ebscohost.com/ContentServer.asp?T=P&P=AN&K=111986883&S=R&D=a9h&EbscoContent=dGJyMNLe80SeqLA4yOvsOLCmr0%252BeprVSrq64TK6WxWXS&ContentCustomer=dGJyMPGns0qxp7NJuePfgeyx44Dt6fIA

Apperson, J., Laws, E., & Scepansky, J. (2006). The impact of presentation graphics on students experience in the classroom. *Computers & Education*, *47*(1), 116–126. doi:10.1016/j.compedu.2004.09.003

Apperson, J., Laws, E., & Scepansky, J. (2008). An assessment of student preferences for PowerPoint presentation structure in undergraduate courses. *Computers & Education*, *50*(1), 148–153. doi:10.1016/j.compedu.2006.04.003

Bannon, L. (1991). From human factors to human actors: The role of psychology and human-computer interaction studies in system design. In J. Greenbaum & M. Kyng (Eds.), Design at work (pp. 25-44). Hillsdale, NJ: Lawrence Erlbaum Associates.

Bartsch, R. A., & Cobern, M. K. (2003). Effectiveness of PowerPoint presentations in lectures. *Computers & Education*, *41*(1), 77–86. doi:10.1016/S0360-1315(03)00027-7

Bell, J., Cheney, G., Hoots, C., Kohrman, E., Schubert, J., Stidham, L., & Traynor, S. (2004). *Comparative Similarities and Differences between Action Research, Participative Research, and Participatory Action Research*. Antioch University Seattle.

Blomberg, J. L., & Henderson, A. (1990). Reflections on participatory design: lessons from the trillium experience. In *Proceedings of the SIGCHI conference on Human factors in computing systems Empowering people - CHI '90* (pp. 353-360). New York: ACM Press. doi:10.1145/97243.97307

Bødker, S. (2010). A short review to the past and present of participatory design. Introduction to debate section. *Scandinavian Journal of Information Systems*, *22*(1), 45–48.

Chou, P.-N., Chang, C.-C., & Lu, P.-F. (2015). Prezi versus PowerPoint: The effects of varied digital presentation tools on students learning performance. *Computers & Education*, *91*, 73–82. doi:10.1016/j.compedu.2015.10.020

Craig, R. J., & Amernic, J. H. (2006). PowerPoint Presentation Technology and the Dynamics of Teaching. *Innovative Higher Education*, *31*(3), 147–160. doi:10.1007/s10755-006-9017-5

Ehn, P. (1993). Scandinavian Design: On participation and skill. In D. Schuler & A. Namioka (Eds.), *Participatory design: principles and practices* (pp. 41–70). Hillsdale, NJ: Lawrence Erlbaum Associates.

Evaluating Socio Economic Development. (2003). *SOURCEBOOK 2: Methods & Techniques - Participatory approaches and methods*. European Commission Documents.

Finn, J. (1994). The promise of participatory research. *Journal of Progressive Human Services*, *5*(2), 25–42. doi:10.1300/J059v05n02_03

Kapoor, K. (2006). *A multidimensional scaling and participatory design approach to classify open ended aircraft maintenance data* (Doctoral dissertation). Clemson University.

Katsui, H., & Koistinen, M. (2008). The participatory research approach in non-Western countries: Practical experiences from Central Asia and Zambia. *Disability & Society*, *23*(7), 747–757. doi:10.1080/09687590802469248

Kiss, G. (2016). Ms Power Point vs Prezi in Higher Education. *TOJET: The Turkish Online Journal of Educational Technology*, *15*(3), 126–130. Retrieved from https://search-proquest-com.ezproxy.lancs.ac.uk/docview/1833764605?rfr_id=info%253Axri%252Fsid%253Aprimo

Krishnaswamy, A. (2004). Participatory research: Strategies and tools. *Practitioner: Newsletter of the National Network of Forest Practitioners*, *22*, 17–22.

Lemmergaard, J., Gersbo-Møller, C., & Povlsen, L. B. (2005). The Scandinavian school revisited: a case study on new roles in the ISD process. *Proceedings of the 13th European Conference on Information Systems, Information Systems in a Rapidly Changing Economy*.

Pant, M. (2009). Participatory Research. In *Course 01 Participatory Lifelong Learning and Information and Communication Technologies* (Unit 08). PALDIN project, ALADIN-INDIA. Retrieved from http://www.unesco.org/education/aladin/paldin/courses.html

Parker, I. (2001, May 28). Annals of Business - Absolute Powerpoint: Can a software package edit our thoughts? *The New Yorker*, 76. Retrieved May 22, 2011, from http://www.newyorker.com/magazine/2001/05/28/absolute-powerpoint

Rankin, E. L., & Hoaas, D. J. (2001). Does the use of computer-generated slide presentations in the classroom affect student performance and interest? *Eastern Economic Journal, 27*(3), 355–366.

Sanders, E. B.-N., Brandt, E., & Binder, T. (2010). A framework for organizing the tools and techniques of participatory design. *Proceedings of the 11th Biennial Participatory Design Conference.* doi:10.1145/1900441.1900476

Savoy, A., Proctor, R.W., & Salvendy, G. (2009). Information retention from PowerPoint™ and traditional lectures. *Computers & Education, 52*(4), 858-867. doi: .10.1016/j.compedu.2008.12.005

Sohng, S. S. L. (1996). Participatory research and community organising. *Journal of Sociology and Social Welfare, 14*(4), 77–97.

Špernjak, A. (2014). Usefulness of Prezi and PowerPoint presentation. In *37th International Convention on Information and Communication Technology, Electronics and Microelectronics, MIPRO 2014 Proceedings*, 762–764. doi:10.1109/MIPRO.2014.6859667

Stefanou, V., & Kotsovoulou, M. (2016). Use of Powerpoint in the classroom: A participatory research project. *International Journal of Knowledge Society Research, 7*(3).

Stone, E. (1997). From the research notes of a foreign devil: Disability research in China. In C. Barnes & G. Mercer (Eds.), *Doing disability research* (pp. 207–227). Leeds, UK: Disability Press.

Sugahara, S., & Boland, G. (2006). The Effectiveness of PowerPoint presentations in the Accounting Classroom. *Accounting Education, 15*(4), 391–403. doi:10.1080/09639280601011099

Susskind, J. E. (2005). PowerPoints power in the classroom: Enhancing students self-efficacy and attitudes. *Computers & Education, 45*(2), 203–215. doi:10.1016/j.compedu.2004.07.005

Susskind, J. E. (2008). Limits of PowerPoints Power: Enhancing students self-efficacy and attitudes but not their behavior. *Computers & Education, 50*(4), 1228–1239. doi:10.1016/j.compedu.2006.12.001

Wadsworth, Y. (1998) What is Participatory Action Research? In *Action Research International, Paper 2*. Retrieved from: http://www.aral.com.au/ari/p-ywadsworth98.html

Waller, M., & Gove, M. (2007, April 18). PowerPointless. *The Sunday Times.*

Zaphiris, P., & Zacharia, G. (2001). Participatory Design of an Online Greek Language Course. *Abridged Proceedings of the 9th International Conference on Human Computer Interaction,* 272-274.

Chapter 10
Using Recommendation Systems in MOOC:
An Innovation in Education That Increases the Profitability of Students

Youssef Jdidou
Abdelmalek Esaadi University, Morocco

Mohamed Khaldi
Abdelmalek Esaadi University, Morocco

ABSTRACT

Massive Open Online Courses (MOOC) is a model of educational delivery that is, to varying degrees, massive, with theoretically no limit to enrollment; open, allowing anyone to participate, usually at no cost; online, with learning activities typically taking place over the web; and a course, structured around a set of learning goals in a defined area of study. The MOOCs (Massive Online Open Course) are online courses, which are mainly for higher education level. These courses present an interesting evolution in the distance learn methods. The MOOCs do not replace the current universities, but they can be an innovative proposal to the curriculum. In this chapter, the authors present the algorithm they are creating. The main purpose of this algorithm is to create automatic mechanisms as the recommendation system to give such assistance and personalized guidance to students. They will also discuss the integration of this algorithm in MOOCMAROC which is a MOOC platform powred by Open edX.

1. INTRODUCTION

Massive Open Online Courses (MOOCs) represent a change in educational paradigm and perhaps point towards the future of course deliverance, (MOOCs) are Open Educational Resources (OER) which provide a strategic opportunity to improve the quality and outreach of education The success of a MOOC is then related to the satisfaction of participants who find interest in its content and commits to follow it as long as it corresponds to their expectations.

DOI: 10.4018/978-1-5225-4191-2.ch010

A growing number of institutions have been involved in engaging and experimenting with MOOCs for the purpose of expanding access, marketing and branding, as well as the potential of developing new revenue streams. Motivations for learners to participate in MOOCs are varied, and many struggle to engage with courses and keep motivated in the context of an online learning environment (Yuan & Powell, 2013).

Some important platforms of current MOOCs already include recommendation systems, for example Coursera, however, we cannot know its operation because it is not an open source platform. The recommendation systems are increasingly present in our day-to-day virtual life, and in particular the recommendation systems applied to education are the subject of numerous studies (Manouselis, Drachsler, Vuorikari, Hummel, & Koper, 2011), trying that its inclusion can improve learning.

2. GROWTH OF MOOCs

More people signed up for MOOCs in 2015 than they did in the first three years. For example, Coursera the largest online course provider in the world, added 7 million new students to its user base which comprised 17 million students in total.

Around 1,800 new courses were announced in 2015, taking the total number of courses announced since the inception of MOOCs to 4,200. Explosive growth like this means the number of courses is still rising. And it's doing so daily. The number of MOOCs listed on Class Central grew at a rate of greater than 15 courses per day. But this kind of growth, like that associated with Coursera, is "faster than Facebook," specifically in terms of having a user growth rate greater than 2,000%. That's growth from roughly 160,000 learners at one university in 2011 to 35,000,000 learners at 570 universities and twelve providers in 2015 according to ONLINE COURSE REPORT.

Figure 1. Growth of MOOCs
According to Class Central (2015).

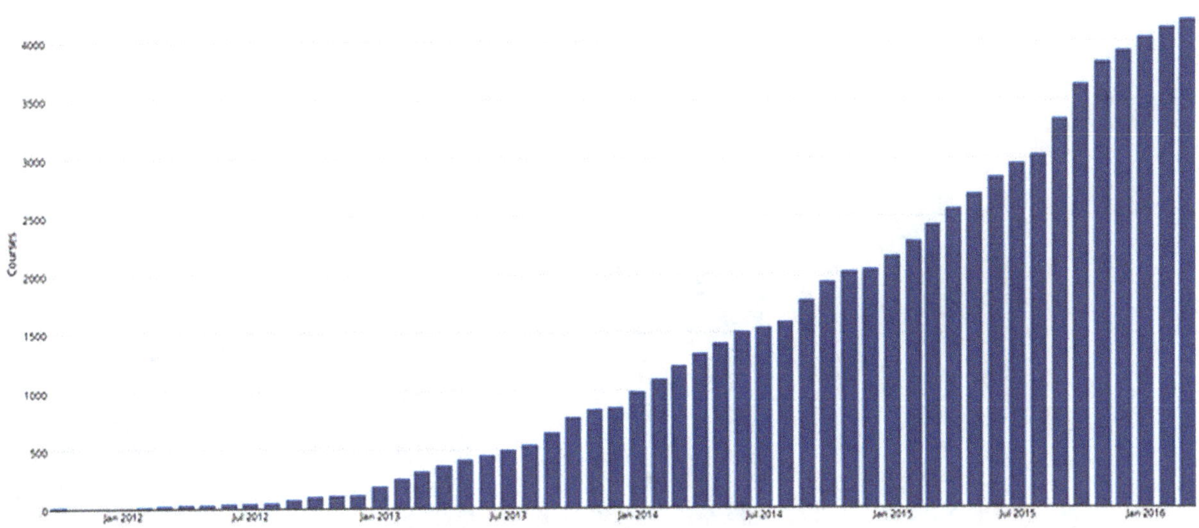

Business & Management, Science, Social Sciences, Computer Science, Humanities, Education & Teaching, Health & Medicine, Programming, Art & Design, Engineering and Mathematics, all of these subjects have seen substantial growth in the number of courses offered in their disciplines over the past three years. Meanwhile, subjects with lower earning potential that do not teach technical skills have sustained decay over the past three years, with Humanities courses declining rapidly from 20 percent of overall subject distribution in 2013 to less than 10 percent in 2015. This shifting distribution shows a pattern of prioritizing career outcomes for learners who are either on the job market or already in the workforce, specifically, that of technology.

This is the most comprehensive list of MOOC courses providers:

- **Coursera:** The most popular provider of massive open online courses globally, Coursera has more than 17 million users in more than 1000 courses from 117 institutions.
- **edX:** Owned by MIT & Harvard University. It's one of the largest providers of MOOC education internationally. Topics include biology, business, chemistry, computer science, economics, finance, electronics, engineering, food and nutrition, history, humanities, law, literature, mathematics, medicine, music, philosophy, physics, science, statistics and more.
- **Canvas Network:** It offers open, online courses taught by educators anywhere in the world. It collaborates with educators, institutions and technologists to cut educational barriers.
- **FutureLearn:** Owned by The Open University, England which provides step-by-step free online courses from topics such as science, technology, art, humanity, spiritual science and business.

English is the most common language in MOOCs platforms by 80% in 2014 and by 75% in 2015. After English, Spanish and French are the biggest languages in which courses are offered. Courses are currently being offered in 16 different languages, including Arabic in Jordan and Morocco.

Figure 2. Course distribution by subjects
According to Class Central (2015).

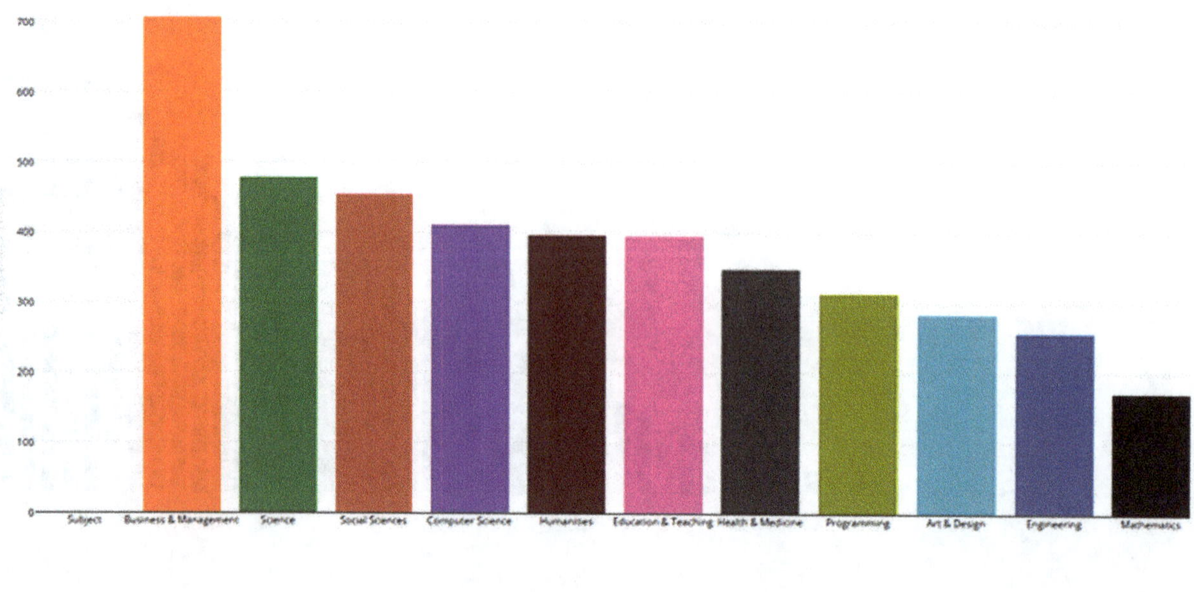

Figure 3. Course distribution by providers
According to Class Central (2015).

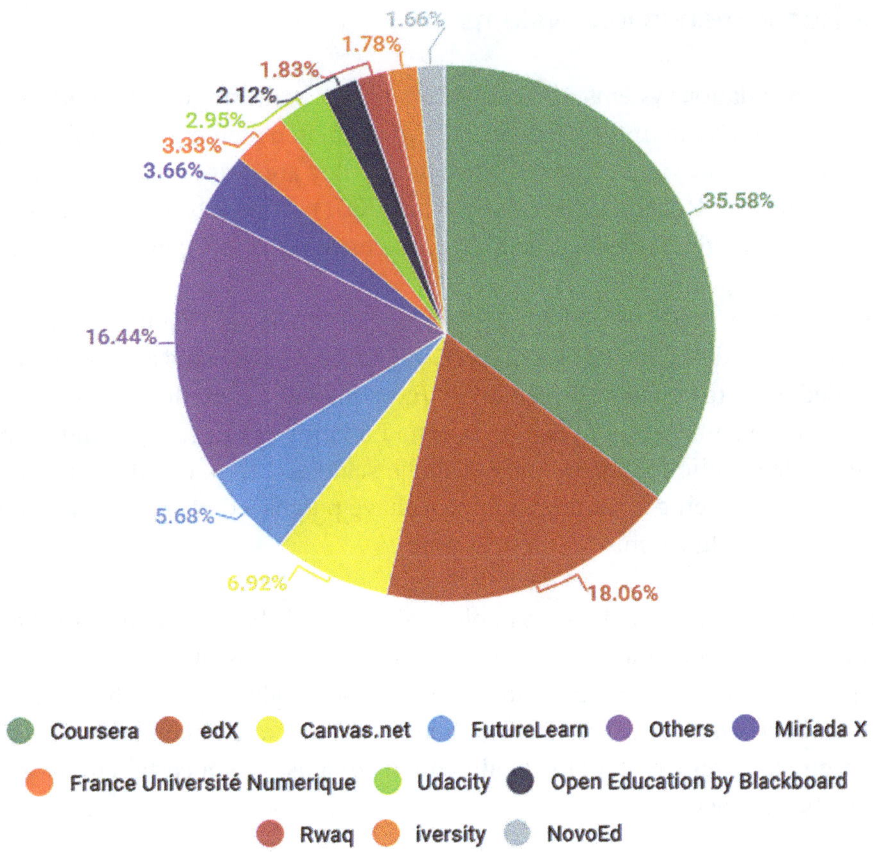

3. RECOMMENDATION SYSTEMS

Definition

The systems, platforms or engines of recommendation, are a type of filtering systems of information that are responsible to predict the user preference for an item (Ricci, Rokach, & Shapira, 2011) or those elements that could be better for that user. One way to make the recommendation is to look at those individuals who have similar tastes to the user or items with features common to other items that the user has purchased, seen or by those who have shown interest in the past, and the recommended.

In a generalized manner, we can speak of three types of systems of main recommendation, which will be explained in more detail in the following sections: recommendation systems, collaborative recommendation systems based on content and recommendation systems hybrids. However, we can also highlight other systems, such as those based on the demographics, which used the demographic characteristics obtained from the data of the user profile (Krulwich, 1997); the recommendation systems based on utility, that require information on how an item meets the needs of the user (Burke, 2002; Guttman, 1998) and the recommendation systems based on knowledge, that depart from the knowledge which gives the user about their needs.

Types of Recommendation Systems

Collaborative Recommendation Systems

Collaborative recommendation systems, also called collaborative filtering or Collaborative Filtering (CF), are based on the assumption that if the users X and Y punctuate n elements of similar way or behave in a similar way (for example, buying, viewing or listening), they are going to behave with other elements in a similar way (Goldberg, Roeder, Gupta, & Perkins, 2001). That is to say, makes predictions about the interests of a user through the collection of preferences or tastes of many users, converted into collaborators.

It could be said that the recommendation is performed in two steps, first looking for users who share the same patterns of evaluation with the user that is going to recommend and after you use the evaluations of these like-minded users to calculate a prediction. Explained in a more formal way, we can imagine a scenario in which we have m users, $\{u_1, u_2, \ldots, u_m\}$, and n items $\{i_1, i_2, \ldots, i_m\}$, and each user has a list of items, Iu_i, punctuated explicitly, for example, using a scale of 1 to 5, or inferred from their behavior implicitly, for example by seeing what other elements have purchased or in what has shown interest.

There are two types of algorithms for these systems:

- **Based in Memory:** Are used all or a sample of the data of the assessments of the users to calculate the similarity between the same. The algorithm of the closest neighbor is the most frequent and takes place in two steps: calculate the similarity or weight, $w_{i,j}$, which represents the distance or correlation between two users or items, i and j; and generate a recommendation to the user by taking the weighted average of all the qualifications of a user for a certain item or user, or using a simple weighted average.

In the case of algorithms based on elements, to calculate the similarity between the element i and the j, is looking for users who have qualified the two elements and then using a technique of calculation of similarities is determined the similarity $w_{i,j}$ between the two elements. In the case of algorithms based on user, first calculates the similarity, $w_{u,v}$, between users u and v, which have qualified the same elements.

Between techniques for the calculation of similarities, we can highlight the similarity based in the correlation (Pearson's correlation and its variations (Mclaughlin & Herlocker, 2004), the correlation by ranges of Spearman correlation and Kendall (Herlocker, Konstan, Terveen, & Riedl, 2004; Salton & Mcgill, 1983)), the similarity based on the cosine between vectors and the similarity based on probability.

- **Based on Models:** To design and development of models, as in the case of the machine learning algorithms or data mining, allow the system to find patterns based on some training data and then make smart predictions with actual data. In this type of algorithms are Bayesian classifiers (Mclaughlin & Herlocker, 2004), neural networks, genetic algorithms, clustering models (Han & Kamber, 2001), regression-based approach (Vucetic & Obradovic, 2005), models based on Markov decision, SVD (Singular Value Decomposition).

This type of algorithms has an advantage over those based in memory and is that better handled the dispersal of data and therefore enhances the scalability; however the construction cost of the model is high.

However, the increase in the use of this type of systems has led to the emergence of numerous problems that had not previously been taken into account and that currently pose a great challenge:

- **Scarcity of Data:** Occasionally the matrix user-element is very large and scattered and it is difficult to make a recommendation. When a user is new you can give the typical problem of cold start, in which the system cannot draw inferences as the user still has not evaluated the sufficient number of elements to allow the system to collect their preferences with precision and be able to make reliable recommendations. Equally, when new elements are added, have to be assessed by the sufficient number of users before being recommended (Adomavicius & Tuzhilin, 2005; Yu, Schwaighofer, Tresp, Xu, & Kriegel, 2004).
- **Scalability:** When the number of users and items is very high, for example, of the order of the tens of millions, many algorithms suffer serious problems of scalability so that infer recommendations is something practically impossible.
- **Synonymies:** Is the tendency to give different names to items that are identical or very similar. The majority of the recommendation systems do not have the capacity to discover the association between them and therefore are treated as if they were different elements.
- **Grey Sheep:** Refers to users whose views are not clear agreement or disagreement with any group of users. At the other end, a user whose tastes idiosyncratic make the task of recommendation is something almost impossible will be a Black Sheep.
- **Shilling Attacks:** Sometimes in systems where the entire world can give their views, users assess their own articles of positively and negatively to those of their competitors. It is advisable to take precautions to avoid this kind of manipulation.
- **Diversity:** The algorithms cannot recommend items with limited historical data, so that instead of helping to discover new products always will tend to recommend the most popular products. It enters in a loop, in which the new products are sections due to their low sales or qualifications, phenomenon that leads to a decrease in the diversity.

Recommendation Systems Based on Content

The recommendation systems based on content analyzed the content of the texts, such as documents, URLs, news, weblogs, descriptions of articles and the profiles of users to learn their preferences and needs (Pazzani, 1999). Subsequently, the system automatically, it is trying to recommend items that the user had already acquired or consumed in the past based on your profile.

In a more concrete form, when a user finds interesting a document or item, the system can provide similar content depending on the weights that are assigned to the words that describe the content of the document or as to the characteristics of the item within the user profile, i.e. you can access your user profile to recommend other elements that may be to your liking. This process is known as feedback by relevance.

This type of systems also have their drawbacks, the most important is that only certain types of content can be analyzed, mainly text. For other media sources, such as video or audio, the prediction is much more complicated. On the other hand, have the problem of commissioning, there must be enough information to get a recommendation reliable and not all users are willing to score the information they are offered by what is not always gets a appropriate feedback. It is also important to the problem of excessive specialization of certain users, i.e. only recommended articles with a high rating in the user profile or in its history of qualification, by what the user would see restricted its recommendations to that type of elements.

Recommendation Systems Hybrids

Hybrid recommendation systems combine collaborative filtering techniques with other techniques of recommendation, usually with systems based on content, with the goal of minimizing weaknesses.

In more detail, we can find hybrid systems in which they are added features of filtering systems based on content to a model of collaborative filtering, others in which they are added features of collaborative filtering systems to a model based on content, a combination of both or systems as a combination of different collaborative filtering algorithms.

Evaluation of the Recommendation Systems

According to (Mclaughlin & Herlocker, 2004) the metrics of evaluation of the recommendation systems are classified into: accuracy of prediction, such as the mean absolute error (MAE), the normalized median absolute error (NMAE) and the mean square error (RMSE), accuracy of classification as the receiver operational characteristic or ROC curve, and precision of range as the correlation of Pearson, the Kendall tau or the normalized distance of the performance metrics (NDPM) (Yao, 1995).

The most used is the mean absolute error, MAE, which calculates the average of the absolute difference between the forecasts and the correct qualifications. The smaller the error the better the prediction:

$$MAE = \frac{\sum_{\{i,j\}} \left| p_{i,j} - r_{i,j} \right|}{n}$$

$p_{i,j}$: prediction for the user j on the article i
$r_{i,j}$: Correct rating for the user j on the article i
n: The total number of qualifications of all users

As a solution to the variety of rating scales we can normalize the mean absolute error and express it as a percentage:

$$NMAE = \frac{MAE}{r_{max} - r_{min}}$$

r_{max}: upper limit of the rating scale
r_{min}: lower limit of the rating scale

Another measure, very popular now is the mean quadratic error:

$$RMSE = \sqrt{\frac{1}{n} \sum_{\{i,j\}} \left(p_{i,j} - r_{i,j} \right)^2}$$

n: The total number of qualifications of all users
$p_{i,j}$: prediction for the user j on the article i
$r_{i,j}$: Correct rating for the user j on the article i

However, the measure of the quality of a recommendation system in learning is one of the main research challenges as it is not limited to technical calculations, but that it is necessary to take into account the context in which it is carried out by the teaching-learning process. The evaluation of these systems is much more complex than that of general recommendation systems because, being adaptive systems, involved many more variables and you must choose appropriately the evaluation criteria.

4. RECOMMENDATION ALGORITHM

This section shall provide a detailed explanation of the algorithm of recommendation that we hope implement and will be a specification of the requirements for the achievement of our goal, obtain reliable recommendations for the students of the courses of the MOOC platform.

The algorithm implemented in this research is based on collaborative filtering systems, since it makes predictions about the problems more appropriate for a student at a certain time of course based on the experience of the colleagues with similar patterns of performance.

The companions of course are the collaborators; however, instead of sharing the same patterns of evaluation with the user that is going to make the recommendation, in this case, the similarity between the student and his companions is calculated on the basis of the number of matching problems made in a satisfactory manner. To explain the algorithm in detail we have the following assumptions:

- We assume that we have m+ 1 students registered in a course and n problems in the same, $\{p_1,p_2, \dots, p_n\}$.
- The student s_0 is the student logged into the MOOC platform and requires a recommendation at a certain time of course.
- The rest of the students, $\{s_1,s_2, \dots,s_m\}$, are the companions of course of a_0 to serve as collaborators.

We illustrate through an example the mechanism of the algorithm. We define (see Figure 4) some matrix and vectors that collect the similarities and differences of the student s_0 with their classmates in the moment in which he makes use of recommender.

In our example we took m= 15 and n=15 (see Figure 5)

- m=10 ➔ the student s_0 has 15 companions in the course.
- n=10 ➔ There are 15 type modules problem in the course.

Compares the problems made by each partner of the course with the problems made by the student s_0 and gets the number of problems that approved in the match. In this case, we note that the greatest number of problems matching approved is 5 and that are 5 companions that match in 5 issues approved: $\{s_1, s_3, s_6, s_9, s_{10}\}$. From now on we will refer to them as 'companions more matched.'

Figure 4. Mathematical model for our algorithm
Jdidou, Khaldi, & Chami, 2016.

For student a_0

$$PMA = [p_1 \quad \cdots \quad p_n] \qquad PMS = [p_1 \quad \cdots \quad p_n] \qquad PNP = [p_1 \quad \cdots \quad p_n]$$

For student s_1 to s_m

$$PMA = \begin{bmatrix} p_1 s_1 & \cdots & p_1 s_m \\ \vdots & \ddots & \vdots \\ p_n s_1 & \cdots & p_n s_m \end{bmatrix}$$

Problem made and approved

$$PMS = \begin{bmatrix} p_1 s_1 & \cdots & p_1 s_m \\ \vdots & \ddots & \vdots \\ p_n s_1 & \cdots & p_n s_m \end{bmatrix}$$

Problem made and suspense

$$PNP = \begin{bmatrix} p_1 s_1 & \cdots & p_1 s_m \\ \vdots & \ddots & \vdots \\ p_n s_1 & \cdots & p_n s_m \end{bmatrix}$$

Problem not performed

$$N_{MAP} = [s_1 \quad \cdots \quad s_m]$$

Number of matching approved Problems

Figure 5. Matching problems at the time of the course
Jdidou et al., 2016.

For student a_0

PMA	p_1	p_2	p_3	p_4	p_5	p_6	p_7	p_8	p_9	p_{10}
	1	1	1	0	1	1	1	1	0	0

PMS	p_1	p_2	p_3	p_4	p_5	p_6	p_7	p_8	p_9	p_{10}
	0	0	0	1	0	0	0	0	0	0

PNP	p_1	p_2	p_3	p_4	p_5	p_6	p_7	p_8	p_9	p_{10}
	0	0	0	0	0	0	0	0	1	1

For student s_1 to s_m

PMA	s_1	s_2	s_3	s_4	s_5	s_6	s_7	s_8	s_9	s_{10}
p_1	1	1	1	0	1	1	0	1	1	1
p_2	1	0	1	0	1	0	1	0	1	1
p_3	1	1	0	0	0	1	0	1	0	0
p_4	1	0	1	1	1	1	0	1	1	0
p_5	0	1	1	1	0	1	0	1	0	1
p_6	0	1	1	1	0	1	0	0	1	1
p_7	1	0	1	1	0	1	0	0	1	1
p_8	1	0	0	0	0	0	0	1	1	0
p_9	1	0	0	0	0	0	0	1	1	1
p_{10}	0	0	0	0	0	0	0	1	1	1

PMS	s_1	s_2	s_3	s_4	s_5	s_6	s_7	s_8	s_9	s_{10}
p_1	0	0	0	1	0	0	1	0	0	0
p_2	0	1	0	1	0	1	0	1	0	0
p_3	0	0	1	1	1	0	0	0	1	1
p_4	0	1	0	0	0	0	0	0	0	1
p_5	1	0	0	0	1	0	0	0	1	0
p_6	1	0	0	0	1	0	0	1	0	0
p_7	0	0	0	0	1	0	0	1	0	0
p_8	0	0	1	1	0	0	0	0	0	1
p_9	0	0	1	0	0	0	0	0	0	0
p_{10}	1	0	0	0	0	0	0	0	0	0

PNP	s_1	s_2	s_3	s_4	s_5	s_6	s_7	s_8	s_9	s_{10}
p_1	0	0	0	0	0	0	0	0	0	0
p_2	0	0	0	0	0	0	0	0	0	0
p_3	0	0	0	0	0	0	1	0	0	0
p_4	0	0	0	0	0	0	1	0	0	0
p_5	0	0	0	0	0	0	1	0	0	0
p_6	0	0	0	0	0	0	1	0	0	0
p_7	0	1	0	1	0	0	1	0	0	0
p_8	0	1	0	1	1	1	1	0	0	0
p_9	0	1	0	1	1	1	1	0	0	0
p_{10}	0	1	0	1	1	1	1	0	0	0

N_{MAP}	s_1	s_2	s_3	s_4	s_5	s_6	s_7	s_8	s_9	s_{10}
	5	4	5	3	2	5	1	4	5	5

In Figure 6 are represented the problems on which differs each of these companions more matched with the student s_0. Only take into account the problems that s_0 has not made, those who have made and suspended do not count as different problems.

At this point we discard the companions more matched do not differ in any problem because what we are looking for are companions who have problems likely to be recommended. Outside the study $\{s_1, s_6\}$ as they differ in 0 problems and we will continue with companions more matched differ to a lesser number of problems, $\{s_1, s_{10}\}$, from now on we will refer to them as 'companions more matched and least different'. The student s_9 also is excluded by the time.

In Figure 7 calculates the number of times that have been successfully each problem likely to be recommended by the companions more matched and less different. We note that the problems sorted according to their popularity are as follows $\{p_9, p_{10}\}$ being p_9 the problem most often repeated.

Figure 6. Companions more matched and least different
Jdidou et al., 2016.

PMA	s_0	s_1	s_3	s_6	s_9	s_{10}
p_1	1	1	1	1	1	1
p_2	1	1	1	0	1	1
p_3	1	1	0	1	0	0
p_4	0	0	0	0	0	0
p_5	1	0	1	1	0	1
p_6	1	0	1	1	1	1
p_7	1	1	1	1	1	1
p_8	1	1	0	0	1	0
p_9	0	1	0	0	1	1
p_{10}	0	0	0	0	1	1

PMS	s_0	s_1	s_3	s_6	s_9	s_{10}
p_1	0	0	0	0	0	0
p_2	0	0	0	1	0	0
p_3	0	0	1	0	1	1
p_4	1	0	0	0	0	0
p_5	0	1	0	0	1	0
p_6	0	1	0	0	0	0
p_7	0	0	0	0	0	0
p_8	0	0	1	0	0	1
p_9	0	0	1	0	0	0
p_{10}	0	1	0	0	0	0

PNP	s_0	s_1	s_3	s_6	s_9	s_{10}
p_1	0	0	0	0	0	0
p_2	0	0	0	0	0	0
p_3	0	0	0	0	0	0
p_4	0	0	0	0	0	0
p_5	0	0	0	0	0	0
p_6	0	0	0	0	0	0
p_7	0	0	0	0	0	0
p_8	0	0	0	1	0	0
p_9	1	0	0	1	0	0
p_{10}	1	0	1	1	0	0

Number of different problems	s_1	s_3	s_6	s_9	s_{10}
	2	0	0	4	2

Figure 7. Number of times to repeat each problem likely to be recommended
Jdidou et al., 2016.

PMA	s_0	s_1	s_{10}
p_1	1	1	1
p_2	1	1	1
p_3	1	1	0
p_4	0	0	0
p_5	1	0	1
p_6	1	0	1
p_7	1	1	1
p_8	1	1	0
p_9	0	1	1
p_{10}	0	0	1

PMS	s_0	s_1	s_{10}
p_1	0	0	0
p_2	0	0	0
p_3	0	0	1
p_4	1	0	0
p_5	0	1	0
p_6	0	1	0
p_7	0	0	0
p_8	0	0	1
p_9	0	0	0
p_{10}	0	1	0

PNP	s_0	s_1	s_{10}
p_1	0	0	0
p_2	0	0	0
p_3	0	0	0
p_4	0	0	0
p_5	0	0	0
p_6	0	0	0
p_7	0	0	0
p_8	0	0	0
p_9	1	0	0
p_{10}	1	0	0

PLR	s_1	s_{10}	Repetition
p_1	0	0	0
p_2	0	0	0
p_3	0	0	0
p_4	0	0	0
p_5	0	0	0
p_6	0	0	0
p_7	0	0	0
p_8	0	0	0
p_9	**1**	**1**	**2**
p_{10}	0	**1**	**1**

Problem likely to be recommended

Therefore, the problems recommended by some colleagues more matched and less different are: $\{p_9, p_{10}\}$

However, it considers that to be able to continue to make progress in the course it is necessary that the student s_0 has approved all of the above issues, so that, prior to recommending problems by their companions more matched and least different we recommend their own problems failed, in this case: $\{p_4\}$

At this time we have 3 recommendations, ordered: $\{p_4, p_9, p_{10}\}$

We can set up our application by default to store 3 recommendations for each student in the database, however, this is an editable parameter and it would only be necessary to change the value of the parameter number of the function set_recommendations(user_id, course_id, number) and make some more changes in the function get_recommendations(user_id, course_id, number) (Jdidou et al., 2016).

5. RESULTS AND DISCUSSION

MOOCMAROC

MOOCMAROC Is an initiative launched in late 2014 by professors of higher education and PhD students who belongs to LIROSA research unit at Abdelmalek Essaady University in Tetuan, MOROCCO. Since 2015 more than 3000 students benefited from courses at MOOCMAROC platform which is powered by Open edX, and because we seek innovation in our work we did choose Open edX for several reasons:

- Innovative content design in courses, representing world-class educational experiences delivered by edX partners.
- Innovations in the use of edX courses in residential, on-campus, and in-person teaching models, including blended learning, flipped classrooms, and seminars.
- Innovative research efforts undertaken by partners on the use of courses and the edX platform.
- Innovative uses of the edX platform, including extensions and inclusions of technology to enhance learning outcomes for learners.

Open edX

EdX is a nonprofit online initiative created by founding partners Harvard and MIT and composed of dozens of leading global institutions, the xConsortium. EdX offers interactive online courses and MOOCs from the world's best universities and institutions.

Open edX is the open source platform that powers edX courses. Through the commitment to the open source vision, edX code is freely available to the community. Institutions can host their own instances of Open edX and offer their own classes. Educators can extend the platform to build learning tools that precisely meet their needs. And developers can contribute new features to the Open edX platform.

Figure 8. MOOCMAROC logo design

The Open edX platform is a free--and open source--course management system (CMS) that was originally developed by edX. The Open edX platform is used all over the world to host Massive Open Online Courses (MOOCs) as well as smaller classes and training modules. Open edX basic components are:

Open Studio edX: is the tool to build edX courses. Access to teachers, it creates the course structure, and then add in the content: video, text, images, quizzes and other educational resources. It also helps manage the course schedule and program the publications content, add teachers, set scoring and more.

- **Open edX LMS:** The LMS is edX tool that participants use to access the course content, including videos, manuals, questionnaires and follow their progress. It provides a forum in lesquel learners and teachers can exchange. For teachers, a dashboard allows; register participants, produce reports and administer the courses.
- **Discussion Forums:** The edX forums are places for exchanges between participants and teachers. They are part of the course and can be added within the content. They also allow the vote on publications, sorting by date or subject categories filters on all topics and monitoring options and moderation.
- **XBlocks:** XBlock is the SDK for edX platform. It allows the community to expand and improve edX to meet future needs: from simple text to sophisticated collaborative learning systems or online laboratories, XBlock is one aspect of edX that makes it a tool such attractive.

Results

A total of 1200 students responded to the questionnaire about the effectiveness and feasibility of the platform. Majority of the respondents either indicated that they registered for the courses in MOOCMAROC because they have learning difficulties or frequently absent in the classroom, or personal interest, or for career advancement purposes. More than 70% of the respondents found the learning in the MOOC-

Figure 9. Open Studio edX

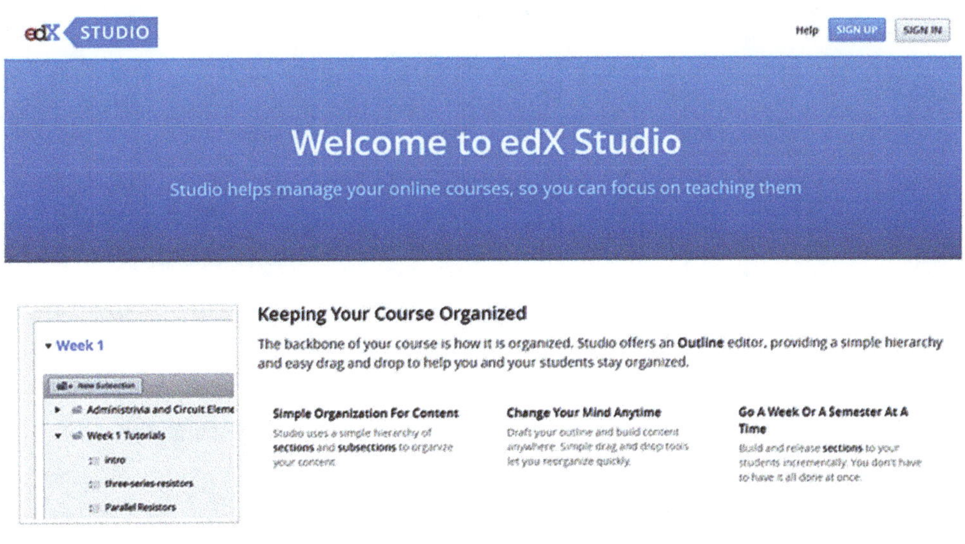

Figure 10. Open edX LMS (Learning Management System)

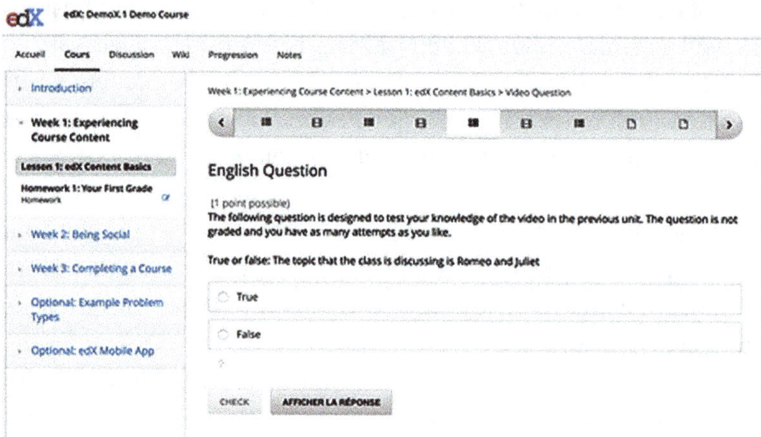

Figure 11. Discussion forums

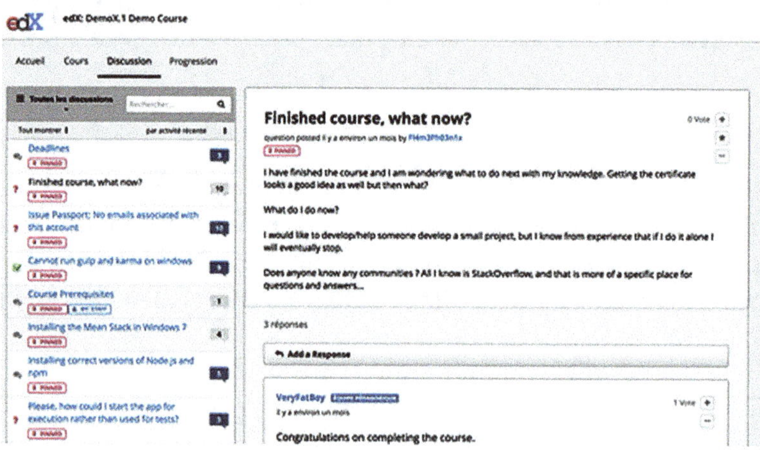

Figure 12. XBlocks

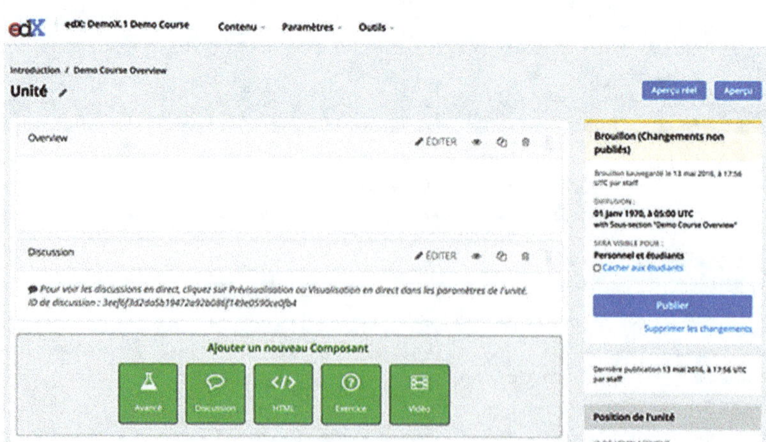

MAROC to be effective and indicated that they received feedback related to their work. Respondents indicate a high level of peer support. This is indicative of considerable level of students' collaboration.

In general, a very high level of satisfaction with the quality of the learning materials provided. This was corroborated by the students' qualitative feedback. Brain Rewiring exercises also received very good responses and were perceived as inspiring.

6. CONCLUSION

MOOCs are evolving and will be a part of the higher educational landscape for the foreseeable future. So it's very important to found innovative algorithm's and automatic mechanisms as the recommendation system to give assistance and personalized guidance to students.

To implement this algorithm we will work with an instance of MOOCMAROC platform. Subsequently, for the evaluation of the algorithm we will create two fictitious courses and save multiple fictitious students to make a series of tests and to be able to ensure the accuracy of the recommendations generated by the algorithm.

REFERENCES

Adomavicius, G., & Tuzhilin, A. (2005). Toward the next generation of recommender systems: A survey of the state-of-the-art and possible extensions. *IEEE Transactions on Knowledge and Data Engineering*, *17*(6), 734–749. doi:10.1109/TKDE.2005.99

Burke, R. (2002). Hybrid recommender systems: Survey and experiments. *User Modeling and User-Adapted Interaction*, *12*(4), 331–370. doi:10.1023/A:1021240730564

Goldberg, K., Roeder, T., Gupta, D., & Perkins, C. (2001). Eigentaste: A constant time collaborative filtering algorithm. *Information Retrieval*, *4*(2), 133–151. doi:10.1023/A:1011419012209

Guttman, R. H. (1998). *Merchant differentiation through integrative negotiation in agent-mediated electronic commerce* (M.S. thesis). School of Architecture and Planning, MIT.

Han, J., & Kamber, M. (2001). *Data Mining: Concepts and Techniques*. San Francisco, CA: Morgan Kaufmann.

Herlocker, J. L., Konstan, J. A., Terveen, L. G., & Riedl, J. T. (2004). Evaluating collaborative filtering recommender systems. *ACM Transactions on Information Systems*, *22*(1), 5–53. doi:10.1145/963770.963772

Jdidou, Y., Khaldi, M., & Chami, M. R. (2016). Recommendation Systems in MOOCs. *Proceedings of the 9th annual International Conference of Education, Research and Innovation*. doi:10.21125/iceri.2016.1540

Krulwich, B. (1997). Lifestyle finder: Intelligent user profiling using large-scale demographic data. *Artificial Intelligence Magazine*, *18*(2), 37–45.

Manouselis, N., Drachsler, H., Vuorikari, R., Hummel, H., & Koper, R. (2011). *Recommender systems handbook*. Academic Press.

Mclaughlin, M. R., & Herlocker, J. L. (2004). A collaborative filtering algorithm and evaluation metric that accurately model the user experience. *Proceedings of 27th Annual International ACM SIGIR Conference on Research and Development in Information Retrieval (SIGIR '04)*, 329–336. doi:10.1145/1008992.1009050

Pazzani, M. J. (1999). A framework for collaborative, content-based and demographic filtering. *Artificial Intelligence Review*, *13*(5-6), 393–408. doi:10.1023/A:1006544522159

Ricci, F., Rokach, L., & Shapira, B. (2011). *Introduction to Recommender Systems Handbook*. Springer. doi:10.1007/978-0-387-85820-3

Salton, G., & Mcgill, M. (1983). *Introduction to Modern Information Retrieval*. New York, NY: McGraw-Hill.

Vucetic, S., & Obradovic, Z. (2005). Collaborative filtering using a regression-based approach. *Knowledge and Information Systems*, *7*(1), 1–22. doi:10.1007/s10115-003-0123-8

Yao, Y. Y. (1995). Measuring retrieval effectiveness based on user preference of documents. *Journal of the American Society for Information Science*, *46*(2), 133–145. doi:10.1002/(SICI)1097-4571(199503)46:2<133::AID-ASI6>3.0.CO;2-Z

Yu, K., Schwaighofer, A., Tresp, V., Xu, X., & Kriegel, H. P. (2004). Probabilistic memory-based collaborative filtering. *IEEE Transactions on Knowledge and Data Engineering*, *16*(1), 56–69. doi:10.1109/TKDE.2004.1264822

Yuan, L., & Powell, S. (2013). *MOOCs and Open Education: Implications for Higher Education*. Academic Press.

Chapter 11
Knowledge Innovation Through Update Propagation in Collaborative Data Sharing Systems

Mehedi Masud
Taif University, Saudi Arabia

ABSTRACT

Innovative knowledge discovery comes through collaboration of knowledge in educational systems. In a collaborative educational system the heterogeneity of data in different learning management systems presents many difficulties for data sharing; some of these difficulties are how to integrate data, produce results for user queries, and find the correct data from heterogeneous learning management systems. In the past few years, various educational system architectures have been proposed; however, issues related to sharing data from different systems have been given less attention. Considering the lack of collaboration of knowledge this chapter investigates a problem of sharing of innovative knowledge among collaborative educational institutes. The knowledge is shared by propagation of updates. Updating innovative knowledge is done by propagating update from the originating source to other collaborative partners. The author examines update propagation in both cyclic and acyclic networks. Moreover, the authors considers cases where a source is temporarily unavailable or offline.

INTRODUCTION

Knowledge sharing deals with the knowledge exchange between heterogeneous Knowledge Base Systems (KBSs). Sharing of knowledge between knowledge base systems are different from the data integration systems (Lenzerini, 2003; Halevy, Ives, Suciu, & Tatarinov, 2003). Schema-level mapping and data-level mapping, a.k.a mapping tables are considered for creating acquaintances between knowledge bases systems, where the knowledge update between two systems is processed pair-wise. Schema-level mapping (Miller, Haas, & Hernandez, 2000) is used to resolve knowledge structure heterogeneity between two

DOI: 10.4018/978-1-5225-4191-2.ch011

knowledge sources and mapping tables are used as the form of data-level mappings (Kementsietsidis, Arenas, & Miller, 2003) for different knowledge vocabularies, which contains a set of data associations between data values in two sources. The use of mapping tables in the case of query answering or data updates introduces the following ideas. 1) Semantics of query answering or updates in autonomous knowledge base system which relies on the translation of queries or updates queries between sources through the mapping tables. 2) The notions of sound and complete translation are to characterize the relationship between translated queries or updates. 3) The definition of the mapping tables is not only the association between data values but also the association between pairs of translated queries and updates.

SYSTEM MODEL

The system architecture under consideration is shown in Figure 1. Our cooperative KBS consists of a set of sources with local knowledge base system $\{KBS_i, \text{for } 1 \leq i \leq m\}$, where each KBS_i is a pre-existing autonomous knowledge management system contains knowledge data source. Each system provides a set of services to share and access its knowledge locally and remotely. For example each system provides acquaintance services for creating acquaintances with other systems, query service for retrieving information over the network, and update service for updating local and remote knowledge. Once a system joins the network, it can establish acquaintances with other systems exchanging their schemas and use services exists in local system and its acquaintances. An acquaintance is a connection between two systems and is established by generating mapping tables (Kementsietsidis et al., 2003) on both systems. The acquaintances are transient since each system is fully autonomous and joins or leaves the network at its own will. Formally, we can define our collaborative KBS as follows.

Figure 1. System model

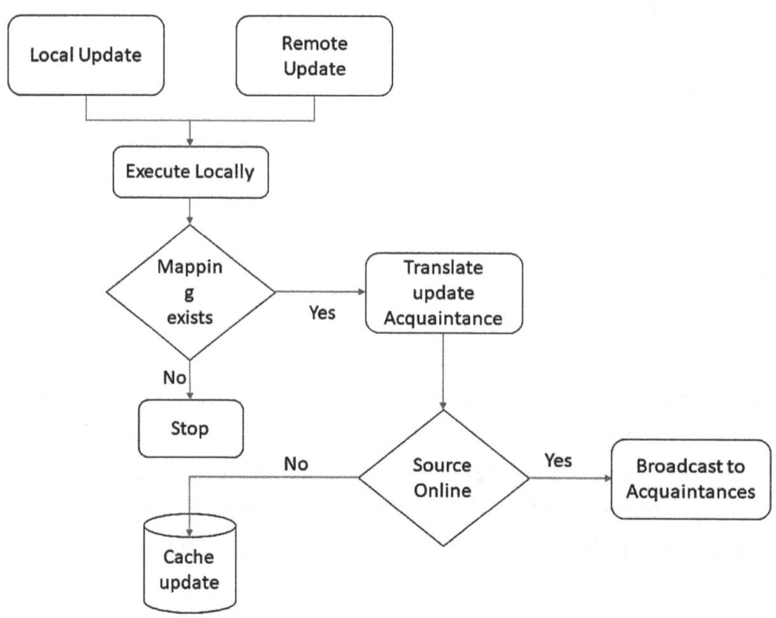

Definition 1: A collaborative KBS is a pair (N,M). Here, N = {(K,L})) is an undirected graph, where K = {KB_1, …,KB_n} is a set of knowledge base system or simply called sources, L = {(KB_i, KB_j) |KB_i, $KB_j \in$ K} is a set of acquaintances. Each source KB_i is associated with a knowledge database with schema $KDB_i[W_i]$, and each acquaintance (i,j) is associated with a set $M_{ij} \in$ M of mapping tables.

Topology Discovery and Knowledge Update

At the beginning, when a source joins a collaborative knowledge base system, it is only aware of its acquaintance. Compare to the discovery protocol (Kantere, Kiringa, & Mylopoulos, 2003), actual knowledge update is different from two perspectives. 1) Update algorithm continues its operation until it reaches a fixed point while discovery algorithm stops when a source is reached twice. 2) Actual queries and propagation is not performed by the discovery algorithm.

Mapping Tables and Its Characteristics

To support the knowledge sharing, it is required to translate the local query and update into the vocabulary of the other sources, which involves translating both the structure of the query to use the schema elements of the associated sources. It is often not possible to make this data conform to the local schema. For conformance the local knowledge base system must have anticipated the structure of all possible answers to the query. Mappings are required to fit the structures into the local schema (Kementsietsidis & Arenas, 2004). The basic algorithm (Kementsietsidis et al., 2003) has the following properties that has been developed to generate the mapping tables: Mapping tables are generated on demand which means entire tables are generated in each step from existing ones. Mapping tables represent expert knowledge that is typically created by domain specialists. Mapping table's creation is also time consuming and is performed manually by a set of experts (Kementsietsidis et al., 2003). In query translation algorithm (Kementsietsidis & Arenas, 2004), which supports select-project-join queries, queries are first expressed in terms of query, language and then it is transformed in some appropriate internal representation.

Mapping tables can be used to associate values both within and across domains. The table is an appropriate tool to use in collaborative systems because it respects the autonomy of the sources. It is required an alternative semantics in mapping tables and some of the motivated examples (Kementsietsidis et al., 2003) are mentioned for the reasoning capabilities which are desirable in an environment where mapping tables are used. To find out the valid set of all mapping tables over a specific set of attributes, it is required to combine the knowledge from the mapping tables available in a network of sources. A set of mapping tables, viewed as constraints, can often be used to infer additional mappings that not explicitly represented in any peer (Kementsietsidis et al., 2003).

KNOWLEDGE UPDATE SEMANTICS

Query or update execution process is initiated by the execution of a user-defined query locally in a source and then it is forwarded as is or it is translated to either or to a selected number of acquaintances of the current source. Execute and forward step is repeated in each of the forwarded source, which causes the further propagation of the query. After a fixed number of propagations of the initial user-defined query the propagation is terminated. It has been assumed that each query is defined with respect to the schema of a single peer. The user who issues the query or update is needed to be aware about the local schema.

In terms of execution, updates in are classified into two categories. A local update which is executed using only the data in the local peer. On the other hand, a global update uses the network to augment locally processed knowledge with knowledge that reside in other sources. We now formalize the above notions and explain the update semantics with emphasis on the semantics of global update.

Consider a set $KB = \{KB_1, KB_2, \ldots, KB_n\}$ of n sources. Each source KB_i, $1 \leq i \leq n$, is a knowledge database with its own schema and data.

Definition 2: A local update LU, hereafter just called an update, over a source KB_i $(1 \leq i \leq n)$ is defined with respect to the knowledge structure R_i of KB_i.

Definition 3: A global update GU over the sources in KB is a set of updates $\{LU^i_i, LU^i_{ij}, LU^i_{jk}, \ldots\}$ where LU^i_i is the originator of global update GU initiated at source KB_i; LU^i_{ij} is a set of updates translated from update LU^i_i at source KB_i for all acquainted sources KB_j, (where $1 \leq J \leq k$);LU^i_{jk} is a set of updates generated for all acquainted sources KB_k of source KB_j and so on.

In case of update operations (insert, update and delete), for a given source KB_i, the semantics for a remote update LU_i over local knowledge schema LS_i using the mapping tables between the source KB_i and KB_j. The translation of remote update LU_i to an update LU^i_{ij} using the mapping tables such that the set of affected rows by LU^i_{ij} only concerns those tuples which are related to the set of affected rows of LU_i through the mapping table.

There are three semantics associated with each mapping table in terms of the update. Those semantics are following: *CASCADE*: The update semantics will propagate along with the acquaintances by using associated mapping table. *NO ACTION*: Update will not propagate to the acquaintance. *SET DEFAULT*: It sets given attribute to a default value.

KNOWLEDGE UPDATE FRAMEWORK

In this section we describe some challenging issues regarding knowledge update operations in a collaborative knowledge sharing system. First, we describe the strategy to deal with processing of updates in a offline source. Due to unstructured topology of collaborative knowledge sharing networks a source may receive multiple copy of same update request through different paths. We also describe this issues and propose two solutions to resolve this issue. We also describe how to handle of conflicting updates. This situation arises when a source receives an update request from its acquainted source for adding knowledge, but at the same time the same source can receive an update or delete knowledge request from another source for the same knowledge.

Knowledge Update in Offline Sources

During the process of sending update query to the acquainted sources, any source could be unavailable in the network for any reason. It is important to keep track for those sources as well as the update queries and later on when the source becomes available, the source will receive the update request and will process it accordingly. Otherwise, knowledge integrity constraint will be violated in acquainted sources.

Figure 2 describes how update requests are propagated to a source when it becomes online from offline. When a source joins in the system and creates an input pipe for receiving messages. As update requests are stored into local system and after joining the new source offline updates are sent to the new source. Acquainted source also creates another pipe with the newly joined source. As result it can receive update message from newly joined source, i.e. bi-directional communication is established.

Update Processing Request Through Multiple Paths

In the knowledge update process a source can receive multiple update request for a unique update request through multiple path. When the receiving source is online then it will only process the first update request. Other update requests for the same query will be neglected.

However, if the receiving source is unavailable due to any reason then the update request will be stored into all the acquainted sources from where the update request comes from. As a result, for a single update request it will occupy multiple storage location and also it will create network traffic.

As mentioned earlier, for the offline source, update request is stored into the acquainted sources. There are two different approaches that can be applied to propagate the update request when offline source becomes online:

- **PUSH Method:** When a source becomes online, update request will be forwarded (if there exists a request for the source) to a source from the acquainted source. However, the update-query originating source needs to track continuously for the newly joined source.
- **PULL Method:** When a source becomes online, it will check with its acquainted sources for the update request. If found then the update query will be pulled out by the newly joined source. During the pulling process acquainted source may become offline.

Figure 2. Knowledge update for offline sources

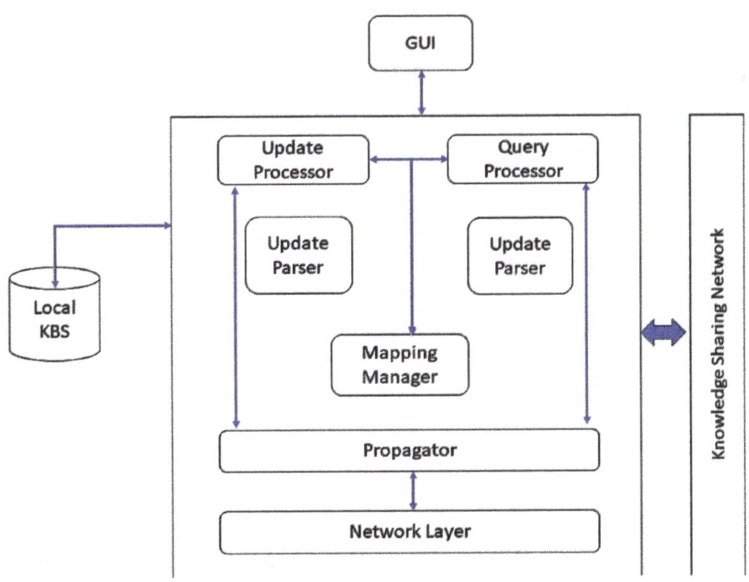

In a collaborative knowledge sharing system, offline data processing approaches also depend on the connectivity among the sources. In the network there may exist some sources, which are acquainted with most of the sources within the network. On the other hand some sources may have few acquainted source, as a result former needs to propagate more update request than later one. Some key points are discussed below for both PUSH and PULL methods:

If the number of acquainted source in the collaborative network is comparatively high and they frequently change their states (from one state to another i.e. online to offline) then the PUSH method will not be that much efficient. Because in one step it needs to continuously track for the online sources and during the PUSH process, source may changes its state. PULL method can also face the similar problem however it will not continuously look for the other sources.

Further comparison also depends on the network connectivity, number of acquainted sources, number of update request in a particular time, types of update request etc. As a result, it requires implementing a details testing environment where hundreds of source can continuously join and leave the source network and also it needs to apply simultaneously update request to each source for both PUSH and PULL method.

With respect to our implementation where JXTA pipes have been used for communication, PUSH method will be more useful due to the following reasons: 1) As there is only one input pipe to receive all the updates, it can create message overlapping when multiple updates will be pulled out simultaneously. 2) There exists separate output pipe for each acquainted source. As a result when a source will push the update requests, it will be distributed for accordingly.

There is another important issue that needs to consider in a collaborative network. As sources can change its state at any time or due to the mapping constraint such a situation may arise where an update request is stored for a offline source, but when the offline source become online, the online source may not be acquainted to the previous source where an update request is waiting for it and it may wait there forever if that source is not acquainted w.r.t. the update. These types of problem can be solved by two different approaches.

Solution 1

In an intensively connected collaborative knowledge sharing system, even if two sources are not acquainted with each other but it may exist an alternative path through which they can communicate with each other for any update request. In such a case, it is required to propagate through that path and multiple update conversation is required for each intermediate source to reach the destination source. It also needs to avoid multiple paths for the offline update request propagation. However, to find out a unique propagation path before forwarding the update request is the major concern in our case and it also needs to select the path in such a way that sources are in reachable distance. It is required to change the previously stored update according to the current path and corresponding mapping tables.

In Figure 3 there are three paths between source KB_1 to KB_6.

Route 1: $KB_1 \rightarrow KB_2 \rightarrow KB_3 \rightarrow KB_4 \rightarrow KB_6$
Route 2: $KB_1 \rightarrow KB_2 \rightarrow KB_4 \rightarrow KB_6$
Route 3: $KB_1 \rightarrow KB_5 \rightarrow KB_5$

Note that → (as well as an arrow in Figure 3) represents a one-way mapping in the direction of the arrow; and a dotted line in Figure 3 represents an existing acquaintance where one of the acquaintees is

Figure 3. Knowledge update processing through multiple paths

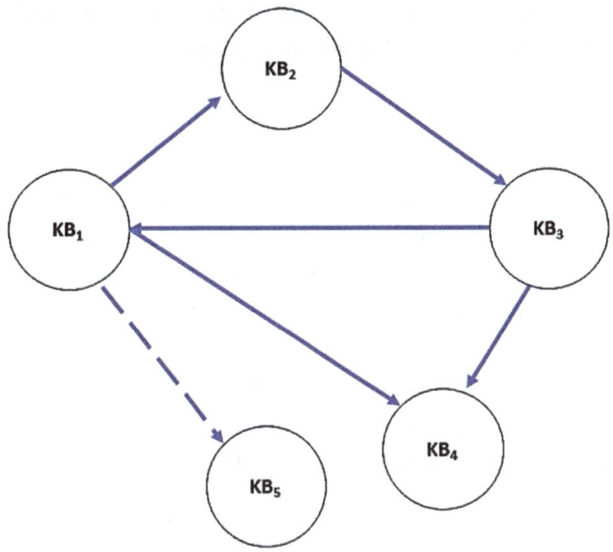

offline. For simplicity we are assuming messages are flowing through one direction i.e. mapping tables are unidirectional. In simple case, when all the sources are online, update request originating from KB_1 will be propagated through all three paths. However source KB_4 and KB_6 will only forward one request correspondingly. If KB_4 becomes offline then it needs to consider several points. 1) For KB_4 it is not required to store the update request to KB_2 and KB_3 i.e. request can be stored to any one location. 2) It needs to store the request in such a way that it can be deliverable through shortest path. It is also important to note that if any source is reachable through the alternate path, the system should take care for that source and later on if the offline source becomes online, it should not deliver the update request to the source that already processed the request. Otherwise it will create the network overhead as well as message overflow. For example, in Figure 3, source KB_6 is reachable through the path $KB_1 \rightarrow KB_5 \rightarrow KB_5$. So, it is not required for KB_4 (when it becomes online) to send the update request to KB_6. With respect to implementation additional attribute is requires (for indicating unique path), which will be included with the update request query. However, within that unique path any source can be offline.

Solution 2

Each source can maintain the state of other sources in the collaborative knowledge sharing system. When an acquainted source changes its state from offline to online state, then the update originating source or acquainted source (where update requests have been stored) will forward the update request accordingly. However such a solution may be feasible but not scalable w.r.t. implementation perspective. It will create an overhead for each source to maintain the state.

Acquaintance abolish: A source can abolish its acquaintance with another source without changing its state from online to offline. In such a case communication between two sources become inactive. However, it will maintain mapping with other acquainted sources. For example, in Figure 3, if *KB3* abolishes its mapping with source *KB4* i.e. two sources are not acquainted anymore but online. Now, any update request for *KB4* will be propagated through *KB2* (or other acquainted source if exists) rather than *KB3*. Source *KB3* will propagate the update request to other acquainted sources and any request for *KB4* will be deleted from its local database. If *KB4* is not acquainted with any source then it will be disconnected from the collaborative knowledge sharing system.

Conflicting Updates

If a source receives an update request from its acquainted source for inserting knowledge, but at the same time the same source can receive an update or delete request from another source for the same knowledge (i.e. both the request contains same primary key). The situation can also arise for offline sources. In that case it will create a conflict and knowledge integrity constraint will be violated since receiving source cannot decide which request needs to be executed first. In some cases, if delete request is executed first and then it receives update request then it will not be able to perform such a task. By inserting a timestamp to the update request the problem can be solved.

When an update originating source sends an update request to its acquainted source; it will attach a timestamp to the update query. In the update propagation path, it will always maintain original time stamp. As a result, if a source receives two conflicting update request simultaneously, it will compare the two time stamps and will select the request that was originated earlier. It needs to consider two major points in case of conflicting updates even the time stamp function is implemented:

1. In any case, if the receiving source executes the first update request and then it receives the conflicting request, which has the higher priority, then it needs to revert the previous update operation and then apply the other request. It may also require to propagate the previous update for the revert and apply the second update request.
2. In step 1, if the first update is a delete operation then it may not be possible to revert the previous operation easily. It is required to implement a mechanism to undo the delete operation before applying the second operation.

Above-mentioned problem can be minimized by using the delta optimization process. Once a source within a certain time frame has receives all the update requests, it will delete the conflicting update requests (which share the same key) and propagate the unique update as a single request.

Unique Query Id: Each source generates update query with a unique query *id*. Source can add a query prefix own query *id* to keep the global uniqueness property. For example, If Source 1 generates a query with prefix *A* and Source 2 with prefix *B* then even if the generated is query *id* is same but due to the prefix it will maintain global uniqueness property.

Query Propagation Cycle

Each source maintains its own prefix with the generated query *id*; as a result even if the query-originating source receives its own update query due the cyclic connection among the acquainted sources, by identifying the prefix, the cycle can be avoided. In the example depicted in Figure 4, there are five sources where arrow line 1represents the mapping table between two acquainted sources for one direction.

We have the mapping table like below: *KB1*→ *KB2, KB2*→ *KB3, P3*→ *KB1* and *KB1*→ *KB4*. As a result, in Figure 4 links are unidirectional.

Figure 4. Cyclically connected sources

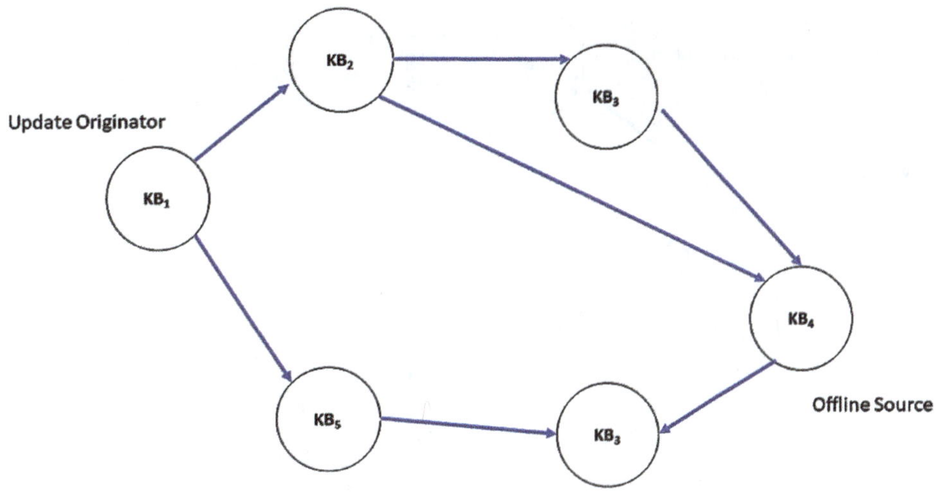

IMPLEMENTATION

The prototype of the architecture has been implemented on the top of JXTA (The JXTA Project, n.d.) using JAVA where JXTA provides services to create source groups, create sources and advertisements and communication pipe. Unicast pipes are effective but not efficient because two-way communication requires for the application. Bi-directional pipes are not considered part of JXTA specification, however by using two "unicast" pipe bi-directional pipe has been created.

The way bi-directional pipe works as follows:

1. A source publishes a unicast pipe advertisement.
2. Remote source discover the pipe advertisement and initiates a connection to the pipe.
3. Once the connection is made, the original source transmits information about a second pipe that is used for alternative way communication establishes a bi-directional pipe. These pipes have been used to communicate among PDMS network sources. The current prototype discovers sources in Hyperion (Arenas, Kantere, Kementsietsidis, & Kiringa, 2003), creates acquaintances, process updates and Select-Project-Join SQL queries.

Architecture

The prototype implementation of Hyperion source-to-source database management system architecture has been provided into Figure 5. A graphical user interface has been provided through which a user can set up acquaintances with new sources. Each source in the system manages its own collection of knowledge.

As the sources are autonomous with respect to the control and structure of the network, they can join or leave the network at any time. After joining to the network source establishes acquaintances with other sources and acquainted source can share and coordinate knowledge between each other. The "Servant" consists of four modules and is the main component of the architecture. Out of these four

Figure 5. Source architecture

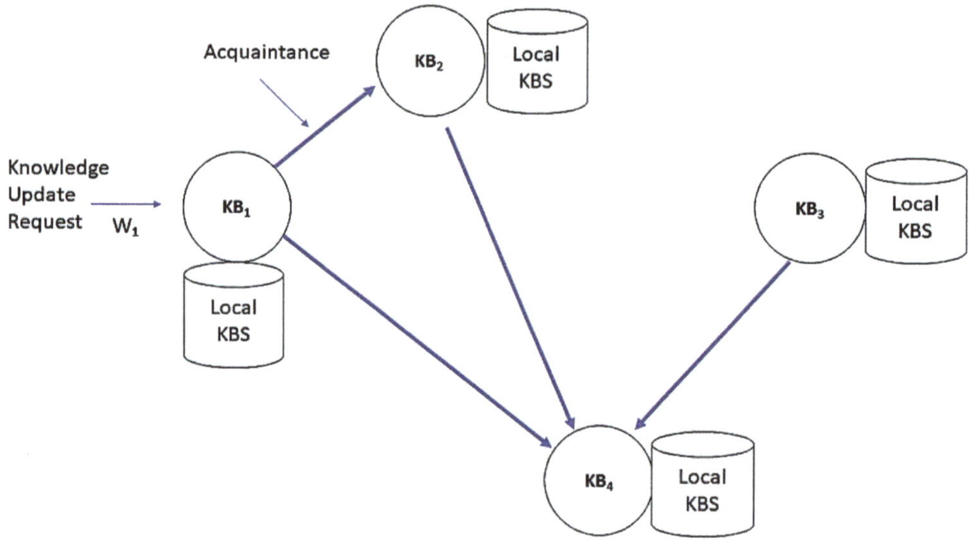

modules, Query processing unit which converts 1) Queries to their disjunctive normal form; 2) Queries to their T-queries and compute the complete translation of a query given a mapping table 3) Includes the algorithm for testing containment of T-queries and to test for a query whether it is sound translation of another w.r.t. mapping table (Kementsietsidis & Arenas, 2004).

A number of optimizations have been done to improve the efficiency of the algorithms. One of those optimizations is the representation of queries as T-queries, which allows to store in the databases both the query and the relationship with its sound translation. An interesting application of the optimization relies on the following observations: 1) In source-to-source systems usually users are often satisfies with incomplete answers as long as retrieved answers assures correctness. 2) Testing for T-query containment is a central approach because of the characteristics of the stored query.

Technical Description

Users are allowed to select three types of update queries (Insert, Update and Delete). At the present state users select the interested attribute from the list and inputs corresponding values for those attributes. After the selection is done, user can generate update query for local update and then translate the update query for remote sources. System will display the translated update query in the list for each acquainted sources according to the corresponding mapping tables. By clicking the Send Update button remote updates can be sent to the acquainted sources if they are available. Otherwise, the update query is saved to the database for further action.

Figure 6 represent the "knowledge update" flow for the implementation. Update request can be received by three ways. 1) User can input update query by using the interface. 2) User will be directly able to input update query into SQL format and 3) Remote update request (which will work as background) receive from other source also in SQL format.

Figure 6. Data update flow

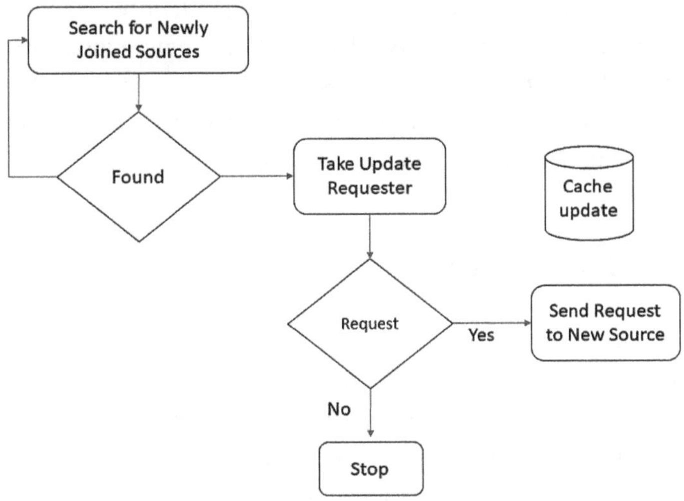

RELATED WORK

In distributed update algorithm, all the information is propagated to all the nodes that are distributed among all the databases. As a result queries can be answer locally. All nodes update their local databases by importing their neighbors by using coordination rules w.r.t. the neighbors. In their work, some super node starts the global procedure update. The super node sends the global request to its acquaintances and these acquaintances propagate request to their acquaintances neighbors and so on. In the process there may occurs some loops i.e. query result can go through some node and late on it can propagate through same node. In order to avoid the cycle or infinite loop they used they following procedure:

Node *N* stops the propagating of some result set *R* iff a) *N* is contained in the path *R* has passed through, and b) there is no new data in *R* for *N*. In this way in can be inferred that node *N* reaches a fixed point. However the algorithm is not a optimize solution. To achieve the optimize solution it required to know about the network topology. In order to minimize data transfer and duplication, it needs to allow for more fine-grained queries to acquaintances and answer from acquaintances i.e. delta optimization.

In coDB P2P database system (Franconi, Kuper, Lopatenko, & Zaihrayeu, 2004), network databases with different schemas are interconnected by means of GLAV coordination rules. For data, each node can be queried in its schema. The node can fetch from its neighbors if there is an involvement of coordination rules. The coordination rules can be also cyclic. To answer a query, it may require a fix-point computation among the rules (Franconi et al, 2004). A global update in P2P is started when some node sends to all of its acquaintance global update request that contains the definitions of appropriate coordination rules. The acquaintances execute the query, reposed with the query result and also propagate the query result to their acquaintances. The propagation process stops when the update request reaches to some node where there is no acquaintance for that node or the node received the update request earlier (Franconi et al, 2004). In our work, similar approach has been used to propagate the update query. In addition to it query id has been attached for each update query that generates at runtime.

In coDB (Franconi et al, 2004) query propagation is being done by using "diffusion computation" approach i.e. the moment node receives a query request it immediately answers by using the local data and forward it by using the outgoing links. It also does not propagate a query request its id is contained in the label of query request. Similar approach has also been used in our update algorithm however, we store the update query id in each source where it propagates and every time when it receives a new update request, before propagate the update query it checks its own database to eliminate the cycle.

CONCLUSION AND FUTURE WORK

To solve the problem of sharing between autonomous knowledge sources, mapping tables have been used in translation of structure queries and updates. Current knowledge update process mentioned in the paper has been implemented for system level user. However, it needs to extend the system into two levels. One for expert users and another for application users will be considered in next version. It also needs to implement interface for system performance for experimental data. The module should collect various information about global updates such as total execution time of an update, the volume of data in each message, longest update propagation path etc. It also needs to implement a log report for each source that can be used for administrative purposes. One of the major tasks of the system is to maintain the mapping table at each location. For example, if a source inserts a new knowledge and that may have new value for some attribute and it is essential to update mapping table before inserting that tuple. In some case it is also required to maintain mapping table, such as deleting a tuple may need to take some action to update mapping table. Maintaining the mapping table in real time is one of the main challenges for source database system to keep the system meaningful. The behavior of a source-to-source system in which each source continuously discovers alternative paths between itself and its acquaintances and it needs to use by the application to update its mapping tables. Furthermore, it needs to investigate the use of mapping tables in support of query answering and (Giunchiglia & Zaihrayeu, 2002) updates.

DISCUSSION

Internet has changed the pace at which knowledge and information are dispersed, opening up access to people around the globe of all socioeconomic levels. A movement for open and collaborative educational systems has taken shape so course materials can be shared broadly at no cost, revolutionizing collaborative education. These developments are especially promising for those who traditionally have not been able to access quality higher education. For example, recent research has shown a large share of Massive Open Online Courses' user base in developing countries are from low- and middle-income groups, and have a higher percentage of female users than elsewhere. Moreover, smart education, a concept that describes learning in digital age, has gained increased attention that has no boundaries. The development of new technologies and sharing of learning materials enables learners to learn more effectively, efficiently, flexibly and comfortably. In a collaborative knowledge sharing educational system learners utilize smart devices to access digital resources. The system that is proposed in this chapter allows educational partners to share knowledge with each other.

REFERENCES

Arenas, M., Kantere, V., Kementsietsidis, A., & Kiringa, I. (2003). The Hyperion Project: From data integration to data coordination. *Proceedings of the ACM SIGMOD RECORD*. doi:10.1145/945721.945733

Franconi, E., Kuper, G., Lopatenko, A., & Zaihrayeu, I. (2004). Queries and Updates in the coDB Peer to Peer Database System. *Proceedings of VLDB conference*. doi:10.1016/B978-012088469-8.50126-1

Giunchiglia, F., & Zaihrayeu, I. (2002). *Making peer databases interact-A vision for an architecture supporting data coordination. Cooperative Information Agents* (Vol. 2446, pp. 18–35). LNCS. doi:10.1007/3-540-45741-0_4

Halevy, A., Ives, Z., Suciu, D., & Tatarinov, I. (2003). Schema mediation in peer data management system. *Proceedings of ICDE*. doi:10.1109/ICDE.2003.1260817

Kantere, V., Kiringa, I., & Mylopoulos, J. (2003). Coordinating peer databases using ECA rules. Databases, information systems and peer-to-peer computing. *LNCS*, *2944*, 108–122.

Kementsietsidis, A., & Arenas, M. (2004). Data sharing through query translation in autonomous sources. *Proceedings of VLDB* (pp. 468–479). doi:10.1016/B978-012088469-8.50043-7

Kementsietsidis, A., Arenas, M., & Miller, R. J. (2003). Mapping data in peer-to-peer systems: Semantics and Algorithmic issues. *Proceedings of SIGMOD*. doi:10.1145/872757.872798

Lenzerini, M. (2003). Data Integration: A Theoretical Perspective. *Proceedings of PODS*. ACM.

Miller, R. J., Haas, L. M., & Hernandez, M. (2000). Schema Mapping as Query Discovery. *Proceedings of VLDB*.

The JXTA Project. (n. d.). Retrieved from http://www.jxta.org

Chapter 12
Strategic Digital City Projects:
Innovative Information and Public Services Offered by Chicago (USA) and Curitiba (Brazil)

Denis Alcides Rezende
Pontifícia Universidade Católica do Paraná (PUCPR), Brazil

ABSTRACT

In order to face numerous challenges, cities need innovative solutions. Offering innovative information and efficient public services is a permanent challenge for cities concerned with citizens' quality of life and effective municipal management. The objective of this study is to describe and assess the strategic digital city projects in Chicago (USA) and Curitiba (Brazil), using innovative information and public services offered to citizens by the website. The research methodology emphasizes a case study covering the city hall, municipal departments, and other municipal entities. The results show advantages for the citizens who have free communal access to public services on the internet. Chicago offers its citizens 281 public services distributed in 256 subjects or themes and Curitiba 508 public services distributed in 26 subjects or themes. In both cities, it resulted in benefits for citizens through access to innovative information and public services offered by the internet. The conclusion reiterated the importance of the implemented innovative strategic digital city projects.

1. INTRODUCTION

In order to face numerous challenges, cities need innovative solutions. One way to innovate the city is to create projects that have the strategies and information technology as concepts and precepts. Innovative information and public services, along with information technology (IT), are relevant resources to a proper smarter government. The use of information to provide public services is a constant challenge for cities concerned with planning and developing municipal affairs from the perspective of citizens' quality of life and effective municipal management. Such a challenge requires the involvement of the whole population of the city, including municipal employees and citizens, whether they are workers,

DOI: 10.4018/978-1-5225-4191-2.ch012

students, retired individuals, housewives, councilors or businessmen. Furthermore, the social, environmental, financial and political issues that cities constantly face mean that municipal managers are under pressure to adapt accordingly. At the same time, the participation of citizens in the affairs of a city is an inexorable requirement. One way of addressing these challenges is through collective information and public services at both city hall and municipality level, in which systematized information is a prerequisite for municipal organizational and management activities.

As an innovation, strategic digital city projects can contribute to the improvement of public policies and government programs through the provision of information and public services to citizens. The information can be an important resource that adds value to municipal management, facilitating the communications between the citizens and government to expand the credibility, trust and equality, while promoting accountability, transparency, and democracy. With the use of information technology it is possible to integrate the citizen to the government.

It is necessary to discuss and plan in advance for information and public services for effective integration between citizen and government. The planning of information and public services, like the municipal strategic planning, is one of the tools for managing city halls and towns of unquestionable relevance. These pressures for effectiveness can be minimized by the preparation and implementation of participative strategic planning in the cities, as it can propitiate the collective engagement of the citizens with their wishes and also can decentralize and share the local managers' decisions. Information and public services planning, like other municipal plans (e.g. Strategic Municipal Planning, Municipal Director Plan, Municipal Multi-Annual Plan, Governmental Plan and others) requires exhaustive practical exercises based on deep-seated theoretical fundaments. These exercises are related to dynamic intelligent daily activities of the city halls and the management actions of the cities. Such activities have to be prepared in an integrated and structured way, where personalized and timely information are utilized for suitable and participative management of the cities. Evidently, these activities will be more profitable to the cities if they have effective participation of their citizens.

Lack of innovative ideas causes citizens inquiries. Many cities have problems with the inexistence or inadequacy of information and public services, which enhances the difficulties of municipal management. Compounding this is the fact that citizen participation is uneven, creating sub-optimal democracy and a lack of full contribution to urban, rural and regional development.

The objective of this study is to describe the strategic digital city projects in Chicago (USA) and Curitiba (Brazil). The project emphasized innovative information and public services offered by website. Both projects covered city hall, municipal departments, and other municipal entities, such as schools, health centers and citizen-oriented municipal information offices. The reason for that is due to structuring, storage and availability of information and public services, which surely do not happen overnight and require short, medium and long-term action in the cities.

Essentially, what justifies this research is to observe the lack of innovative ideas in cities. In particular, the inexistence of strategic projects, taking into accounts the city information and the public services, preferably with the active participation of citizens.

2. LITERATURE REVIEW

In order to have the concepts debated and understood some pertinent legislations and culture of each country must be taken into consideration.

2.1. Public Services

Public service can be understood as any service provided by the government or by their delegates under state standards and controls to meet the essential needs of the community or secondary or simple convenience of the State. Examples of public services: public education, the police, the public health, the public transportation, telecommunications, and others (Meirelles, 2013). Also, public services can be understood as goods or services provided by the public sector for its constituents. Public services can be directly provided through the government or through financing the private sector provision of such services. The social rationale behind public services is that there are certain services that should be provided to all citizens, regardless of income (as defined by the market) or social standing. Concepts of deconcentration and devolution of public services delivery from the national to local governments and citizens have recently been applauded for their ability to see quicker gains than with centralized public services systems (Gfldr, 2010).

Scholars and administrators of municipal governments generally agree on four essential goals of public services: efficiency, effectiveness, equity and responsiveness (England, Pelissero & Morgan, 2012). Historically, the role of government in providing these services has led to a notion of government as bureaucratic, hierarchical and controlling. This relationship has led to calls from academia and the city to democratize the structure of public services and bring the citizen into the equation. It calls 'new public service' and define it as a structure where the citizen is at the center of the governance system and not on the outside (Denhardt & Denhardt, 2000).

Goods and services provisions are transferred from private to public when the private sector underprovides or when it is a necessity for the citizens to survive. If these services were left up to the market, the population would be affected and while there is no legal ruling on public services, they generally are popular within a country. Since most public services are paid for through the tax system, the citizens of those geographic areas have a vested interest in the types of services made available (Gruber, 2011).

A more important picture in this system is the role of information based public services. Since traditionally, governments have not had to compete with other vendors in their service provisions, they have not had to be concerned with disseminating adequate information about such services (Skelcher, 1992). This trend however has reversed in recent years with greater calls for complete transparency and full information of services.

2.2. Information, Information Model, Information System

The concept of information is any datum that creates consideration or warrants contemplation. It can be understood as an entity with a meaningful value attributed or added to it and having a natural and logical sense and application for its users (Rezende, 2012). Information, to be useful for decision-making, should have the following characteristics or premises: concrete, not to have verbs, and to be different from documents, programs, and files. Information and its respective systems serve crucial roles in the administrations of municipalities, presenting themselves as a strategic resource to help plan and manage city halls and towns in an intelligent, competitive, participative manner. To ensure this strategic connotation to information, the organization usually goes through an evolving cycle in stages that include: initiation, contact, control, integration, data administration, and maturity (Nolan, 1993).

The information acculturation process in the city halls and towns can be simple and effective if both public managers and residents (clients or information users) are participative, aware and thoroughly engaged in the utilization of information technological resources. The strategic information supported by information technology may occur in an evolving way, where information systems can be classified in various manners (Rezende & Abreu, 2013). Information has a highly significant value and can create greater power for those who own it, be it a person or a city. The information valorization process comprises certain logical phases and steps. At least three steps are fundamental to add value to information: understanding, selecting and using information. A badly prepared selection may cause major damages in the use of information (Weitzen, 1991).

In cities the information and the knowledge of people can contribute to municipal management. Information can enhance the roles and benefits of government and the citizen in any geographic area (Ekionea, Fillion & Koffi, 2012). Nowadays, the techno-social networks also allow citizen participation in municipal management, as a channel of communication, exchanging information as a citizen to government and from government to citizen (Flores & Rezende, 2013).

The information model describes all the necessary pieces of information for municipal management (Rezende, 2012). Such pieces of information can be structured in levels or types, *i.e,* strategic, managerial and operational information. They can be distributed according to their respective organizational functions or public issues. The information model is comprised of: strategic pieces of information (in a macro-related way with the external and internal environment), tactic and managerial pieces of information (grouped and synthesized) and operational pieces of information (in detail or analytical). Finally, the information model may contain integrated information, such as: conventional (trivial), personalized and timely.

All information can be classified as personalized information, either being a natural or legal person or a differentiated product or service. It may also be regarding a single characteristic of a citizen. All information of unquestionable quality, however, can be named ‘timely information’ (Rezende & Abreu, 2013).

An information system produces, as an output, data processing or resource transformation. For instance, information, can take the form of a computational resource of information (Marakas & O’Brien, 2011). Information systems within city government – whose primary purpose is to aid administrators in their decision-making processes and whose focus must be addressed to efficient municipal services – will be able to significantly contribute solutions to many municipal problems; to the extent that they effectively generate timely and personalized information. They must be seen as strategic tools to determine differential factors for city hall (Rezende, 2012). These systems of human and technical components accept, store, process, produce and transmit information, and can be used in conjunction with: human engagement, methodologies and information technology (Heeks, 2001). These are the ways by which people and organizations assemble process, store, use and disseminate information in a reciprocal relationship (Ward & Peppard, 2002).

An information system can positively influence operational effectiveness, municipal strategies and administrations, while benefiting any non-governmental actor that interacts with the municipality (Stair & Reynolds, 2007). The information system benefits are widely reported and justified in the pertinent literature and articles. They are presented as instruments for generating solutions to municipal problems (Laudon & Laudon, 2011). To facilitate these solutions, the information systems should be integrated and have an interdependent relation with the sub-systems, leading to the information exchange. This integration comes in many forms, including: systemic vision, systemic approach, forest view, municipal gear, information synergy and harmonic set of organizational functions. This way, the information systems show themselves to be sub-systems or organizational functions, divided into: production or services; commercial or marketing; material or logistics, financial, juridical-legal, human resources and their respective modules (Rezende & Abreu, 2013). Only through the integration of these sub-systems will it be possible to produce efficient public services.

The levels of information and decisions within city government mimic the pattern-hierarchy existing in most organizations (organizational pyramid). These levels are known as: strategic, tactic and operational. The decision made in each level requires varying degrees of information and data aggregation. The various decision levels call upon different information from their resulting products, such as screens, reports, etc. There is not any rigid classification to what allows people and administrations to classify their systems in different ways. All in all, the information system can be utilized in operational, managerial and strategic levels (Stair & Reynolds, 2007; Laudon & Laudon, 2011). The main difference amongst information systems in these classifications lays in the way the information is presented to users.

The operational information system provides detailed information. The managerial information system makes grouped or synthesized information available. The strategic information system enables the comparison of internal and external information flows within city hall, and intercity, and eventually generates indicators and knowledge. Another way to classify information systems is the city hall scope. In summation, there are systems at personal, group (or departmental), organizational, and inter-organizational levels where the global systems of information are framed, involving municipal governments of a multitude of geographic locations (Kroenke, 2011).

2.3. Information Technology and Electronic Government

The utilization of information technology (IT) or information and communication technologies (ICT) can be conceptualized as computational and technological resources for data storage, generation and use of information. IT is based on the following components: hardware and its devices and peripherals; software and its resources; telecommunications systems; data and information management (Stair & Reynolds, 2007; Turban, Mclean & Wetherbe, 1996; Rezende & Abreu, 2013). It can also be defined as telecommunications and computing technologies that supply automatic means and information handling, encompassing tangible hardware and intangible software (Heeks, 2001) and telecommunications networks (Ward & Peppard, 2002).

When information technology is applied in public administration (in the spheres of federal, state or municipal), it is called electronic government (e-gov). Thus, e-government can be seen as the application of the resources of information technology (IT) or information and communication technology (ICT) in public management and policies of federal organizations, state and local, including the city and municipal organizations. This may involve actions of government to government or government to society and its citizens (and vice versa), providing public information in an electronic media format (Rezende, 2012). Electronic government (e-gov) promotes efficient and cost-effective government; facilitates more convenient government services; allows greater public access to information and makes government more accountable to its citizens (Bhatnagar, 2004). Governments around the word have created websites that enhance citizen convenience in various projects within different levels of public services (West, 2005). E-gov involves the creation, development and interlinking of a variety of social, institutional and technological ecologies to deliver services which are perceived as legitimate, innovative, useful and welfare enhancing (Navarra & Cornford, 2005). The use of modern information and communication technologies, especially Internet and web technology, by a public organization to support or redefine the existing and/or future (information, communication and transaction) relations with 'stakeholders' in the internal and external environment has a tendency to create added value (Bekkers & Homburg, 2005). The uses of information technology in the public sector, covers a broad range of managerial issues: from high-level strategy to detailed tactics; from the technicalities of data flows and process mapping to the politics of e-government (Heeks, 2006). The strategic use of ICT, in and around public administrations, is for the purpose of creating a 'wired' or 'digital' government. Ideally, a wired government is more focused on and responsive to societal needs, and makes governments more efficient and democratic (Homburg, 2008).

2.4. Digital City

A digital city can be defined as a city that collects and organizes digital information, provides public information for person to person interaction online (Ishida, 2004) and can be lived in by digital citizens, who are able to participate in an online society (Mossberger, Tolbert & McNeal, 2008). As large cities become more fragmented physically, socially, and culturally, computer communications are seen to be a potentially integrative medium, tying the disparate fragments together into new threads of public discourse, in ways that few other media can manage (Graham & Aurigi, 2007). In this sense, the concepts of connectivity, accessibility and responsiveness must be covered (Duarte & Pires, 2011).

The concept of digital cities regards the gathering and organization of digital information to streamline the public services process and provide citizen/resident interaction (Besselaar & Beckers, 2009). It is the digital network environment, which interlinks advanced technological systems to public services, assets, brands, schools, non-profit organizations, enterprises, and micro and macro communities. This prototype makes information available in several patterns aiming to develop the information society's potential and transform the citizen into actor and protagonist of a virtual reality (Guerreiro, 2006).

The city's show concern about physical changes that are necessary to enable ICTs and to ease the functioning of digital cities and conceptual, cultural and urban impacts (Atkinson, 1997; Shiode, 2000). City's require new elements for organization and reproduction of the urban area, providing the shrinking of distances through the use of ICTs (Firmino, 2004) or like cities in network (Batten, 1995; Townsend, 2003).

For Lemos (2005) science and technology become important for urban development. The challenges of the urban area go beyond geographic boundaries in the virtualization of the cities or in the cyberspace and can bring the possibility of distance annulations amongst the dwellers of a city, even if the distance annulations be just symbolic, as it is through digital communication (Lefebvre, 1991). The city changes due to the advent of new communication technologies in a continuous move towards "de-territorization" of symbolic worlds and the break-up of frontiers between the ancient and modern, between local and global, between written and audiovisual culture, leading to fast urban modernization processes into the adequate environment for digital cities (Barbero, 1996). The exchange of telematics information help people emerge from the time-space confinement, traffic and other difficulties of physical places (Castells, 2005). It doesn't come to replace the real city with the virtual one; rather, the focus is on the enlargement of access for the citizens to activities of collective intelligence and on the occupation of the cyberspace, as in the geographic city, fulfilling thoroughly the citizens' needs (Lévy, 1999).

In the context of telecommunications, digital cities are also called "information highways", with a set of web applications, IP applications, services and equipment that provide citizens with a constantly present, ubiquitous, pervasive environment that not only is present everywhere at the same time but also spreads itself, infiltrates, penetrates and is spread. Digital cities, which are also known as, amongst other things, cybercities, virtual cities, electronic cities and intelligent cities represent projections into the digital world (Mendes, Bottoli & Breda, 2010).

The strategic digital city can be understood as an application of information technology resources in municipal management and in the availability of information and services to residents. It is a far-reaching project if compared to simply offering internet to citizens through telecommunications conventional resources. It goes beyond inclusion of citizens into the world network of computers, and into such ample projects as information systems for municipal management and citizen utilization, public services for the community and municipal safety systems. This project is based on the objectives and strategies of the city (Rezende, 2012). Brazilian government has been creating special programs to enhance and spread information technology and telecommunication infrastructure, disseminate access to the Internet, and stimulate web-based public services (Rezende et al., 2013).

2.5. Municipal Planning and Information Technology Alignment

Municipal Information Planning is a project that formalizes the necessary information for city hall and town management and, as a result, plans the municipal information systems and their respective needs of information technology assets and of human resources (Rezende, 2012).

Information Technology Strategic Planning (ITSP) is a dynamic and interactive process to, strategically, tactically and operationally, structure the organizational information, information systems, the information technology (and their resources: hardware, software, telecommunications systems and data and information management), the people involved, and the required infra-structure. This process positively assists all decisions, actions and respective processes of the organization (Turban, Mclean & Wetherbe, 1996; Lederer & Mahaney, 1996; Rezende, 2012).

The alignment between the ITSP and the municipal information planning is built from the vertical, horizontal, transversal, dynamic and synergetic relations of the municipal functions and the IT resources. Such alignment can promote the adjustment of strategic and operational suitability within the available technologies as a municipal management tool put together by quality concepts, productivity, effectiveness, continuity, competitive intelligence and municipal intelligence (Henderson & Venkatraman, 1993; Rezende; 2012).

3. RESEARCH METHODOLOGY

The research methodology employed here comprises an approach of applied work to a circumstantial reality, emphasizing the inductive method enhanced by professional experience achieved by the authors-researchers, both in advising projects for city halls and in academic projects for master and doctoral classes. It partially takes exploratory research concepts regarding documental and bibliographic raising (Nachmias & Nachmias, 2006). The methodology consisted of action-research case studies obtained from city hall. It has put together other approaches explained by the eclecticism and integration of inseparable methods (Yin, 2013).

The study sample consisted of two cities: Chicago (Illinois, USA) and Curitiba (capital of Paraná, Brazil).

Chicago has about 3 million inhabitants, and Curitiba 2 million. Chicago has been ranked the fourth best project and the fifth best project among all major U.S. cities in 2011 and 2010, respectively (Digital Communities, 2013).

Curitiba has been ranked number one in the Brazilian Index of Digital City (Cpqd, 2013).

The action-research protocol includes the analysis of specific criteria of the information and public services offered by the websites of City Hall

The observation unit included both websites.

The research was made in July 2013 until October 2015 and updating May 2017.

4. INFORMATION, PUBLIC SERVICES AND DIGITAL CITY PROJECT

In addition to strategies, Chicago offers its citizens 281 public services and Curitiba 508. All public services share their respective innovative information.

4.1. Innovative Strategies and Information and Public Services

On The City of Chicago Technology Plan, there are five foundational and innovative strategies of the strategic digital city project in Chicago: next-generation infrastructure; every community a smart community; efficient, effective, and open government; civic innovation; technology sector growth (Chicago, 2017). Each of these strategies is one public policy aimed at innovative information and public services offered through information technology resources

Curitiba has not formally published its strategies since there is no formal strategy project for the city. There are few and long-term projects.

4.2. Types of Information and Public Services Offered

The information and public services offered by Chicago are classified into the following types of 256 subjects or themes: abandoned; abandoned construction sites; abuse; accessibility; activity; adoption; advertising; alert; alley; alley light; animal; appeal; application; artist; assessment; assistance; backup; basement; benefit; bicycle; blood test; breast; brochure; building; calendar; care; career; caregiver; cart; cat; certification; check-up; Chicago; Chicago cultural center; child; citizen; city; city maintenance; city services; clean-up; clinic; code; communication; community; community services; complaint; compliment; construction; consultant; consultation; contract; contractor; corruption; counseling; crisis; cruelty; dca; damage; debris; development; disability; disabled; discrimination; district; doctor; dog; domestic; donation; drain; drivers; drug; dumping; educational resource; elderly; electrical; elevator; emergency; emergency response; engineer; environment; environmental; ethics; evaluation; event; exam; ex-offender; exposure; exterior; family; family planning; fare card; fees; filming; financial; assistance; fire; foia; food; forestry; form; garbage; grandchildren; grandparents; green; green building; gynecology; hand washing; health; health resource; health services; heat; help; hiv/aids; home visit; homeless; housing; illegal; illegal sale; impound; independent; infant; information; inspection; internship; intervention; issue; job training; kids; landfill; learning; license; light pole; liquid; local; location; maintenance; mammogram; map; mason; mbe/wbe/dbe/bepd; meals on wheels; mechanic; medical; medicine; mental health; minority; motorists; municipal; neighborhood; newsletter; no smoking; nutrition services; occupancy; online; park; parking; partnership; payment; pelvic; exam; permit; pet; physical; pick up; placement; planning; planting; plumbing; police; policy agenda; pothole; power; preschool; problem; procurement; program; project; property; protest; public; public health; pushcart; record; recycling; red-light; reentry; regional transit authority; registration; relief; rental; repair; report; residence; residential; resource; respite; restaurant; retail; review; rock; rodent; safety; sale; sanitary; sanitation; sanitation code; senior; services; sewer; shakman; shelter; sign; smoke; smoking; snow; sponsor; sponsorship; sports; status; sti; sti/hiv; sticker; storage tank; stray; street; street light; substance; summer job; support; tax; tax/fee/bill/ticket; taxi; testing; training; transportation; trash; tree; vacant lot; vehicle; vendor; vendor payment; venue; viaduct; violation; violence; violence prevention; waiver; wall; waste; water; weather; weeds; wellness; wheel chair; women's health; workshop; youth; zoning.

And Curitiba, 26 subjects or themes: capacity - training; citizenship; civil works; culture; education; emergencies; environment; food; formal business; funeral services; government procurement; health; housing and residence; information and publications; permits, certificates and licenses; prefecture - city hall; procurement and suppliers; security; social assistance; sport and leisure - recreation; taxes and fees; tourism; transit; transportation; urbanism; work – employment.

4.3. Analyses and Similarities of Information and Public Services

To analyze the similarities and differences of the strategic digital city projects were utilized different criteria among the literature (Holzer et al., 2005; Simão & Rodrigues, 2005; Middleton; 2007; Duarte & Pires, 2011; Rezende et al., 2013).

4.3.1. City Innovation

Innovation can be understood as doing something different and with added benefit or value, without necessarily being new (Rezende, 2012). And can be defined as the process of implementing new ideas to create value for an organization. This may mean creating a new service, system, or process, or enhancing existing ones. Innovation can also take the form of discontinuing an inefficient or out-of-date service, system, or process.

The world's cities are in dire need of innovation as they struggle to cope with unprecedented growth, which is expected to result in an extra two billion city-dwellers by the year 2050. In response to this need for better use of technology to improve urban environments, drive economic growth and inclusion and improve social cohesion, the World Economic Forum's Global Agenda Council on the Future of Cities publishes today its Top 10 Urban Innovations: (digitally) re-programmable space; the waternet: an internet of pipes; adopt a tree through your social network: connected trees that fight climate change; augmented humans; co-co-co: co-generating, co-heating, co-cooling; the sharing city: unleashing spare capacity; mobility-on-demand: a menu of personal mobility; Medellin revisited: infrastructure for social integration; smart array: intelligent street poles as a platform for urban sensing; urban farming: vertical vegetables (World Economic Forum, 2015).

In terms of innovative strategies, Chicago and Curitiba meet this criterion. Chicago has a unique, up-to-date, web-based project that engages citizens. Curitiba already has its strategies formalized in different and non-comprehensive projects in terms of long terms.

4.3.2. Communicability

Communicability is defined as the social and human components of Information Communication Technologies and is situated in the social sphere of information systems. For our purposes of more localized interactions, we can look at the efforts to incorporate diverse cultural and linguistic populations within the geographic boundaries of our observation units (Duarte & Pires, 2011).

Chicago's efforts at communicability are exemplified in the amount of services that entail filings of grievances and assistances. Both of these themes show an effort on City Hall to provide an arena for public discourse and participation in the allocation of city services. The former serves to provide a voice for populations that previously did not have one, specifically in the fields of police brutality and/or discriminatory housing policies. These areas of public service provide sites for the public to actively communicate with agencies and fellow citizens in efforts to enhance the functioning of government through the use of complete and full information and quality public services.

Although Curitiba has been ranked number one in the Brazilian Index of Digital City, in terms of communicability, it appears in second place (352 points out of the 2,250 possible points). The first, the city of Belo Horizonte, got 360 points. Furthermore, Curitiba has a Private Organization contracted to maintain and expand the communicability of the city. This demonstrates the effort that Curitiba has done to expand the communicability for its citizens.

4.3.3. Content

An analysis of content can be understood as the breadth of public information available on the website, the level of horizontal integration between government agencies and an estimate of the amount of information available about the dealings of such agencies (Middleton, 2007). Content can be one of the dimensions of accessibility, together with functionality and usability (Simon & Rodrigues, 2005).

In Chicago, information regarding each of the governmental agencies is clearly established on the website; with user friendly links at most points. Notably, in the field of job services, the website provides links to local, state and national agencies, showing a profound integration of information across geographic boundaries. The level of public information listed on the website is quite extensive, ranging from how to pay for parking tickets to obtaining FOIA (freedom of information act) documents (see list of themes, above). Furthermore, while not specifically stated by Middleton, the organization of the content on the website is admirable and enhances the ability of the citizen to access the information they are searching for with ease and speed.

In Curitiba content of information on public services is available primarily in two ways. The content in the first form is shown by subjects (or themes) and the second form is shown by Municipal Departments. The two ways seek to facilitate the understanding of citizen services offered and their content is user friendly and easy to access. The amount of information is extensive, ranging from basic institutional information, filling out forms, bill payments and other more complex information and services.

Frequency of updated information is also a primary concern of a content analysis for information and public services. In this respect, Chicago and Curitiba show a great effort for accuracy of useful information and efficient public services.

4.3.4. Functionality

The concept of functionality is best understood as how effectively a site/organization is designed in order to help the user navigate it. This is inclusive of how the services are organized and if there are summaries of the broader service structure. This indicator is the broadest in most evaluative lists and specific criterion can include readability, visual aesthetics ease of use and robustness of public services forms. As government services are intended for public use, broad accessibility is encouraged and must take into account disability access, and compatibility across advancements in ICT's (Middleton, 2007).

Chicago's overall functionality and interface of its city services website is clearly organized and easy to navigate. Subsuming the various services and information items into broader themes, allows the user of all levels to easily find what they are looking for. At the same time, it enables the interested user to scan the various thematic components of the website in a clear and concise manner. Additionally, the style is consistent on all pages, with its recognizable multi-shaded blue background and orange text/banners, signaling to the user that you are still within the City of Chicago's website.

In Curitiba the functionality of the site for navigation is organized properly. The possibility of finding the public service site is shown in two ways, which facilitates easy access by the citizen. The site works with all browsers and software icons are easy to see and handle.

Finally, it is worth noting that Chicago and Curitiba employ numerous interactive components through 'Online Service' icons. These are essential as they turn the passive user into an active user and they are clearly demarcated with a computer icon and are joined with a legend on the right hand side of the page in clear view.

4.3.5. Security and Privacy

With the advancement of information and communication technologies in the provision of public services, a primary concern lies in security and privacy. This indicator includes privacy policies and issues of authentication on the websites of city hall. Analysis must assess to what extent such policies appear on pages that accept sensitive data and the existence of the word 'privacy' on these pages. An additional concern is whether or not the privacy policies identify the agencies collecting the data and what data is collected, in the interests of the user (Holzer et al, 2005).

In Chicago, there is a 'privacy policy' link, although it is located and the bottom of each page visited, not always in clear view for the user. This link explains what data is collected and the process of collection. There are five sections of data collection: information gathering/cookies, on-line transactions, sending the City of Chicago and email, sale of data, and other web sites. This page notes repeatedly that sister web sites (Chicago Park District, Chicago Public Schools, Chicago Transit Authority, City Colleges of Chicago, Chicago Housing Authority, the Chicago Store, and the Metropolitan Exposition and Pier Authority have their own privacy policies and are not covered by the City of Chicago's policies.

In Curitiba the security and privacy of information and the public services is adequately controlled by specific software and managed for databases intended for these functions. There are specific policies for security and privacy to public services offered. The details are observed in each webpage and respective links.

For both websites (Chicago and in Curitiba), it is notable that the privacy policy link is posted on every page visited on the website, but it is not in clear view and perhaps may be suited better in a more prominent place for the beginning user. Additionally, navigating multiple privacy policies for each of the agencies listed above can be seen as problematic and complex from the standpoint of the citizen.

4.3.6. Public Services

Services can be best understood as within a two level approach: citizens and business. Within each of these levels, we measure availability of payment and registration and application services; for the citizen we look at online recruitment and for the business online tendering (Middleton, 2007).

In Chicago, these two levels of public services are not clearly separated, but are subsumed into the broad services list (organized in themes from A to Z). Within the advertising (partnership) section, there is no present online component, however there are phone numbers and email addresses to contact for further information. From the citizen perspective there are some online components of registration/application services (i.e. 'Inviting the Mayor to an event' can be applied for online) but other services simply provide registration applications that must be then printed/downloaded and emailed/faxed/mailed through the postal service. This can be seen as an area of improvement for the city services as enhanced technologies arise, as a means to increase efficiency and ease.

In Curitiba there are a significant number of public services, both for citizens (individuals) or specific companies (legal entities). The public services for citizens appear more online, as public services for companies mostly require filling out forms. Both public services provide ample information for Internet users (citizens or companies) in need of public services.

4.3.7. Citizen Participation

Citizen (public) participation is vital to the strategic digital city project as a complement to the innovative needs by the city managers; participation and innovation are needed to realize the full potentials of such projects (Rezende et al, 2013). Additionally, in their evaluation of eighty-four cities in the world, Holzer, et al found that citizen participation measurements had a mean of 3.26 and median of 2.18 (based on a weighted score of 20.0); clearly stressing the lack of political (citizen) participation in municipalities. In Holzer's study, the measurements used included: online civic engagement, internet based policy deliberation and citizen based performance measurements (Holzer et al, 2005).

Chicago employs a thematic section on policy agendas for the citizen to view. Within this category sits the Capital Improvement Program Advisory Committee, which was created from Executive order 90-2, sections one through three: (1) vest the powers to the Office of Budget and Management to annually develop a Capital Improvement Program, and decide the location, revenue source and name of all capital improvement projects undertaken by the City of Chicago; (2) establishes public meetings to debate on a Draft of the Program; (3) creates a Capital Improvement Advisory Committee (CIAC) to serve as an advisory body for the purpose of reviewing and making recommendations on the Capital Improvement Program and process. While it can be said that the public forum component seen in section two can work to increase citizen participation, it does so in a physical setting, which comes with its own sets of barriers; establishing a virtual forum for these debates might increase efficiency and efficacy of these services. Finally, the theme or category related to the 'citizen' houses information and services that are not participatory in nature or aimed at civic engagement. These items (i.e. extreme weather services, tips on pet care, and obtaining vital records) could be seen as solitary in nature and providing no assistance to the citizen participation component of the strategic digital city.

In Curitiba the citizen participation component is referenced in specific locations on the website, as there are several calls for it. In particular, we highlight the calling service (156 Contact Center) which receives requests for information and requests for public services. Also distinguished Brazilian financial law requires that in their "Municipal Multi-Annual Plan" citizen participation of at least three annual meetings.

5. DISCUSSION AND CONCLUSION

Currently only with innovative solutions will cities be able to face their many challenges. To perform smarter governance, it is necessary to have innovative information and adequate public services, and innovative information technology (IT) achieves this. This trend has become essential for the contemporary city, and it requires the participation of citizens and municipal managers to expand urban, rural and regional development. It can also contribute to municipal management by making planned information and the associated public services more streamlined. From the point of view of the citizen, municipal planning can also promote the practice of citizenship as citizens take part in the planning, structuring, storage and release of information for their use and benefit. This is particularly true insofar as the increase in public participation-based public services is concerned. Municipal planning also allows cities to extend their communications, education and social development activities. This is possible because a large number of cities face constant social, environmental, financial and political challenges promoting effective municipal management and an adequate quality of life for their citizens.

Undoubtedly, innovative information and public services planning, like municipal strategic planning, can become an inexorable participative instrument of management for municipal government. With the right modeling, planning and availability of information and municipal services, it makes possible the breakthroughs in citizenship building within the public space, municipal democratic governability, and transparency of management and in the urban, rural and regional development of the cities. Also, the information can facilitate communications between the citizens and govern to expand credibility, trust and equality, promoting accountability, transparency, and democracy.

The objective of describing the strategic digital cities projects in Chicago and Curitiba has been achieved as details of the innovative information and public services in these municipalities have been presented through their websites. Both projects covered the city hall, municipal departments and other municipal entities, such as schools, health centers and citizen-oriented municipal information offices.

In terms of innovative projects, Chicago by The City of Chicago Technology Plan formalized five foundational and innovative strategies of the strategic digital city project in Chicago while Curitiba has not formalized its strategies. In another way, Chicago offers its citizens 281 public services distributed in 256 subjects or themes and Curitiba 508 public services distributed in 26 subjects or themes. Despite numerical differences, the strategic digital city projects are very similar. The similarities were observed in the analysis of selected criteria (communicability; content; functionality; security and privacy; public services; and citizen participation). Despite of the numbers of information and public services offered as well as the similarities, both projects can be improved and should be further extended to citizens. Especially when the govern think of the citizens with low education and short familiarity with the use of the internet.

Still with regard to innovative ideas, also of note are the advantages for the citizens of Chicago and Curitiba, who have free communal access to public services on the internet.

Curitiba provides its citizens with a great deal more services, subsumed under more concise categories or themes. This fact informs the content indicator of Curitiba's services, in that navigation through the website is more streamlined. Notably, as with the literature on measurements, there are services within each city's website that is replicated. Additionally, of all (256) of Chicago's service themes, there is at least one online component for 176 (68%). Given the importance of citizen interaction and participatory behavior, this statistic is highly desirable. Curitiba also has a high percentage of replicated services.

In terms of benefits to cities, both projects provides it, notably innovative and modernization of municipal management activities improved access to information and public services as a result of increased internet use brought about by digital inclusion. With the use of the resources of information technology, in particular the Internet, it was observed that it is possible to integrate the citizen to the government. With this integration, it was possible to realize enhanced communications between the citizens and government, expanding the credibility, trust and equality while promoting accountability, transparency, and democracy.

Evidently there were many difficulties throughout the elaboration of this study to describe and assess the information and public services of the strategic digital city projects. The main limitation was the use of only the websites for research, without elaboration of services through interviews and meetings with managers and technicians of the City Hall in both cities.

These studies report the description and assessment of innovative information and public services of two urban centers with comparable strategic digital city projects. Such contributions are addressed to the academy, to the cities studied, and to other geographic areas. The case studies described facilitates further research applied to cities to understand and suggest alternatives for their challenges to urban, rural and regional development, and also for entities concerned with the quality of life of citizens. This work also contributes to the establishment of analogies among the cities.

There weren't website restrictions, or restrictions to information or public services of the city and of the City Hall. The main barrier to this work had to do with the research methodology itself as it reduces pertinent analyses and considerations to two cities and does not express the reality of American and Brazilian cities.

Innovations in cities are unquestionable. The analysis reiterates the importance of availability of information and the provision of public services to citizens through the Internet in their respective strategic digital city projects. Both, information and public services, allow citizens to plan and decide the most adequate use of such services. With the effective implementation of this kind of project, the democratic public space; transparency; effectiveness and governability of municipal services increase. As a result, social, urban, rural and regional development can be developed and, as a result, the quality of citizens' life can increase.

ACKNOWLEDGMENT

CNPq-Brasil and FA-Paraná.

REFERENCES

Atkinson, R. (1997). The digital technology revolution and the future of US cities. *Journal of Urban Technology*, *4*(1), 81–98. doi:10.1080/10630739708724548

Barbero, J. M. (1996). La ciudad virtual: transformationes de la sensibilidad y nuevos escenarios de comunicaión. Revista de la Universidad del Valle, 14, 26-38.

Batten, D. (1995). Networked cities: Creative urban agglomerations for the 21st century. *Urban Studies (Edinburgh, Scotland)*, *32*(2), 313–327. doi:10.1080/00420989550013103

Bekkers, V. J. J. M., & Homburg, V. (2005). *The information ecology of e-government: E-government as institutional and technological innovation in public administration*. Washington, DC: IOS Press.

Besselaar, P. V. D., & Beckers, D. (2009). *Demographics and sociographics of the digital city*. Retrieved from http://dl.acm.org/citation.cfm?id=701393

Bhatnagar, S. (2004). *E-government: From vision to implementation*. New Delhi: Sage Publications.

Castells, M. (2005). A sociedade em rede - a era da informação: economia, sociedade e cultura (8th ed.). São Paulo: Paz e Terra.

Chicago. (n.d.). *The City of Chicago Technology Plan*. Retrieved from http://techplan.cityofchicago.org

City of Chicago. (2013). *City services - service directory*. Retrieved from https://www.cityofchicago.org/city/en/svcs/servicedirectory.html

Cpqd. (2013). Centro de Pesquisa e Desenvolvimento em Telecomunicações. *Índice Brasil de Cidades Digitais*. Retrieved from https://www.cpqd.com.br

Curitiba. (2013). Prefeitura Municipal de Curitiba. *Serviços para o cidadão - serviços para empresas*. Retrieved from http://www.curitiba.pr.gov.br/servicos/cidadao

Denhardt, R., & Denhardt, J. (2000). The new public service: Serving rather than steering. *Public Administration Review*, *60*(6), 549–559. doi:10.1111/0033-3352.00117

Digital Communities. (2013). *Digital Cities Survey*. Retrieved from http://www.govtech.com/dc/digital-cities

Duarte, F. & Pires, H. F. (2011). Inclusión digital, tres conceptos clave: conectividad, accessibilidad, comunicabilidad. *Revista Electrónica de Recursos em Internet sobre Geografía y Ciencias Sociales*, *150*(1), 1-15.

Ekionea, J. B., Fillion, G., & Koffi, V. (2012). Improving municipal information and knowledge management capabilities: Case study. *Journal of Information & Knowledge Management*, *11*(4), 1250023-1250044. doi:10.1142/S0219649212500232

England, R. E., Pelissero, J. P., & Morgan, D. R. (2012). *Managing urban America* (7th ed.). Washington, DC: CQ Press.

Firmino, R. J. (2004). *Building the virtual city: The dilemmas of integrative strategies for urban and electronic spaces* (Doctoral thesis). University of Newcastle.

Flores, C. C., & Rezende, D. A. (2013). Strategic digital city: techno-social network twitter as communication channel for popular participation in city comprehensive plans. *Proceedings of the Nineteenth Americas Conference on Information Systems.*

Graham, S., & Aurigi, A. (2007). Virtual cities, social polarisation and the crisis in urban public space. *Journal of Urban Technology, 4*(1), 19–52. doi:10.1080/10630739708724546

Gruber, J. (2011). *Public finance and public policy* (3rd ed.). New York: Library of Congress.

Guerreiro, E. P. (2006). *Cidade digital: infoinclusão social e tecnologia em rede.* São Paulo: SENAC São Paulo.

Heeks, R. (2001). *Reinventing government in the information age: International practice in IT-enabled public sector reform.* London: Routledge.

Heeks, R. (2006). *Implementing and managing eGovernment: An international text.* Thousand Oaks, CA: Sage Publications.

Henderson, J. C., & Venkatraman, N. (1993). Strategic alignment: Leveraging information technology for transforming organizations. *IBM Systems Journal, 32*(1), 472–484. doi:10.1147/sj.382.0472

Holzer, M., Kim, C., Kim, S., Melitski, J., & Rho, S. (2005). Digital government worldwide: An e-government assessment of municipal Web sites. *International Journal of Electronic Government Research, 1*(1), 1–18. doi:10.4018/jegr.2005010101

Homburg, V. (2008). *Understanding e-government: Information systems in public administration.* London: Routledge.

Ishida, T. (2012). Activities and technologies in digital city Kyoto. *LNCS, 3081,* 166-187. Retrieved from https://link.springer.com/chapter/10.1007/11407546_8

Kroenke, D. (2011). *MIS essentials.* Prentice Hall.

Laudon, K. C., & Laudon, J. P. (2011). *Management information systems: Managing the digital firm. 12.* Prentice Hall.

Lederer, A. L., & Mahaney, R. C. (1996). Using case tools in strategic information system planning. *Information Systems Management Journal, USA, 13*(4), 47–51. doi:10.1080/10580539608907016

Lefebvre, H. (1991). *The production of space.* Oxford, UK: Basil Blackwell.

Lemos, A. (Ed.). (2005). Cibercidade 2: Ciberurbe: a cidade na sociedade da informação. Rio de Janeiro: Editora E-Papers.

Lévy, P. (1999). *Cibercultura.* São Paulo: Editora.

Marakas, G. M., & O'Brien, J. A. (2011). *Introduction to Information Systems* (15th ed.). Columbus, OH: McGraw-Hill.

Meirelles, H. L. (2013). Direito administrativo brasileiro (39th ed.). São Paulo: Malheiros.

Mendes, L. S., Bottoli, M. L., & Breda, G. D. (2010). Digital cities and open MANs: a new communications paradigm. *Proceedings of the 2010 IEEE Latin-American Conference on Communications, 8*(4), 1-8.

Middleton, M. R. (2007). Approaches to evaluation of websites for public sector services. *Proceedings IADIS Conference on e-Society*, 279-284.

Mossberger, K., Tolbert, C. J., & McNeal, R. S. (2008). *Digital citizenship: The internet, society, and participation*. Cambridge, MA: MIT Press.

Nachmias, D., & Nachmias, C. (2006). *Research methods in the social sciences*. New York: Worth Publishers.

Navarra, D. D., & Cornford, T. (2005). ICT, innovation and public management: governance, models & alternatives for e-government infrastructures. *Proceedings of the European Conference on Information Systems*.

Nolan, R. L. (1993). *Note on information technology and strategy*. Boston: Harvard Business School.

Rezende. (2012). *Planejamento de estratégias e informações municipais para cidade digital: guia para projetos em prefeituras e organizações públicas*. São Paulo: Atlas.

Rezende. (2014). *Information and Telecommunications Project for a Digital City: A Brazilian case study* (Vol. 31). Telematics and Informatics.

Rezende, D. A. (2015). Public Policy and a Strategic Digital City Project: A case study of the Brazilian Municipality of Vinhedo. *Journal of Urban Technology*, *22*, 1–21.

Rezende, D. A. (2012). *Planejamento de estratégias e informações municipais para cidade digital: guia para projetos em prefeituras e organizações públicas*. São Paulo: Atlas.

Rezende, D. A. (2016). Digital City Projects: Information and public services offered by Chicago (USA) and Curitiba (Brazil). *International Journal of Knowledge Society Research*, *7*(3), 16–30. doi:10.4018/IJKSR.2016070102

Rezende, D. A., & Abreu, A. F. (2013). *Tecnologia da informação aplicada a sistemas de informação empresariais: o papel estratégico da informação e dos sistemas de informação nas empresas. 9*. São Paulo: Atlas.

Rezende, D. A., Madeira, G. S., Mendes, L. S., Breda, G. D., Zarpelão, B. B., & Figueiredo, F. C. (2013). Information and Telecommunications Project for a Digital City: A Brazilian case study. *Telematics and Informatics*, *31*(1), 98–114. Retrieved from http://www.sciencedirect.com/science/article/pii/S0736585313000336

Shiode, N. (2000). Urban planning, information technology, and cyberspace. *Journal of Urban Technology*, *7*(2), 105–126. doi:10.1080/713684111

Simão, J. B., & Rodrigues, G. (2005). Acessibilidade às informações públicas: Uma avaliação do portal de serviços e informações do governo federal. *Revista Ciência da Informação*, *34*(2), 81–92.

Skelcher, C. (1992). Improving the quality of local Public services. *Service Industries Journal, 12*(4), 463–477. doi:10.1080/02642069200000059

Stair, R. M., & Reynolds, G. W. (2007). *Principles of information systems: A managerial approach* (8th ed.). Boston: Course Technology.

Townsend, A. (2003). Wired/unwired: the urban geography of digital networks. In *Urban Studies and Planning* (p. 206). Cambridge, MA: Massachusetts Institute of Technology.

Turban, E., Mclean, E., & Wetherbe, J. (1996). *Information technology for management: improving quality and productivity*. New York: John Wiley and Sons.

UNCDF. (2013). *Global Forum on Local Development Report*. Retrieved from http://www.cib-uclg.org/news/global-forum-local-development-report-pursuing-mdgs-through-local-government

Ward, J., & Peppard, J. (2002). *Strategic planning for information systems*. New York: John Wiley & Sons.

Weitzen, H. S. (1991). *O poder da informação: como transformar a informação que você domina em um negócio lucrativo*. São Paulo: Makron Books.

West, D. M. (2005). *Digital government: Technology and public sector performance*. Princeton University Press.

World Economic Forum. (n.d.). *Report 2015: Top 10 urban innovations of 2015*. Retrieved from https://www.weforum.org/agenda/2015/10/top-10-urban-innovations-of-2015

Yin, R. K. (2013). *Case study research: Design and methods* (5th ed.). London: Sage Publications Inc., USA.

APPENDIX: PONTIFÍCIA UNIVERSIDADE CATÓLICA DO PARANÁ – PUCPR, URBAN MANAGEMENT PROGRAM - PPGTU

Curitiba – Paraná – Brazil - www.pucpr.br/ppgtu

Research Project Protocol

Version: May 22, 2017.
Coordinator Professor: Denis Alcides Rezende, PhD <denis.rezende@pucpr.br>

Strategic Digital City Research (Smart City and Innovations)

Concepts

The Strategic Digital City Project is an application of information technology resources in municipal management (or city administration) and in the availability of public services and information to citizens or public managers. All these approaches (information for citizens and public managers, public services and information technology resources) are based on the cities strategies. It is a more comprehensive project that only offers internet for citizens through conventional telecommunication resources. It goes beyond digitally including data and citizens on the World Wide Web (REZENDE, Denis Alcides, 2012).

It is developing in four city subprojects:

- City Strategies Planning or Municipal Strategic Plan;
- City Information Planning;
- City Public Services Planning;
- City Information Technology Planning.

Those subprojects can contemplate strategies, information and public services in different municipal thematic (or city areas), such as: agriculture; science, technology and innovation; commerce; culture; education; sports; finance; government; housing; industry; legal affairs; leisure; environment; health; rural; sanitation; safety; municipal services; social; transit; transport; tourism; urban; etc.

City Strategies are means, forms, activities or paths to achieve cities objectives.

City Information's are any data worked or treated with significant value. It is useful for decisions and actions.

City Public Services are activities provided by the government under the norms and controls for the basic needs of citizens, society or the State. Unlike the information, which are only presented to citizens, public services require interactivity between citizens and electronic services offered by the city (using information technology resources).

Research Variables

1. City Strategies
2. City Information's
3. City Public Services
    a. Name; type; quantity;
    b. Analysis (qualitative and quantitative);
    c. Citizens influences;
    d. Public policies relations;
    e. Relations with smart city project;
    f. City innovations.
4. Information Technology Resources
    a. Hardware
        i. Name; type; quantity;
    b. Software
        i. Name; type; quantity;
        ii. Sites; portals; etc.;
    c. Telecommunications
        i. Name; type; quantity;
    d. Data and information management
        i. Name; type; quantity;
        ii. Analysis (qualitative and quantitative);
        iii. Citizens influences;
        iv. Public policies relations;
        v. Relations with city Strategies;
        vi. Relations with city Information's;
        vii. Relations with city public services;
        viii. Relations with smart city project;
        ix. City innovations.

Chapter 13
Innovation on User-Generated Content for Environmental Noise Monitoring and Analysis in the Context of Smart Cities

Juan Humberto Juárez Hipólito
Instituto Politécnico Nacional, Mexico

Marco Antonio Moreno Ibarra
Instituto Politécnico Nacional, Mexico

Miguel Torres-Ruiz
Instituto Politécnico Nacional, Mexico

Giovanni Guzmán
Instituto Politécnico Nacional, Mexico

Rolando Quintero
Instituto Politécnico Nacional, Mexico

ABSTRACT

This work presents an approach based on the concept of Volunteered Geographic Information (VGI) to monitoring environmental noise; it is a problem that specially affects people's quality of life in urban areas. In this work, mobile devices are used to massively collect environmental noise measurements, which are used to generate maps of a specific area and then make a forecast. The difference of this approach with respect to the traditional methods based on monitoring stations is that it is much less costly, which is a major innovation in developing countries. This approach is based on a GIS approach that consists of an application for mobile devices and a web mapping application; including Geospatial Analysis and Machine Learning methods for the acoustic noise prediction using contextual information. With this approach it will be possible to define actions to mitigate the effects of environmental noise, it is aligned in the context of the smart cities. The proposed case study is based on collecting noise data of the Mexico City.

DOI: 10.4018/978-1-5225-4191-2.ch013

1. INTRODUCTION

User-generated content from social networks and other kind of web and mobile applications have grown as quickly as expected. This has proven useful for diverse applications related to geographic phenomenon as monitoring and reporting activities and events on urban environments. It allows citizens to collaborate actively by sharing their observations on specific situations. A key aspect of smart cities is the analysis of contextual information, close to real-time, to enhance the operations and services in urban areas; in specific to sensing some city phenomena in order to detect how, when or where it occurs. This work presents a novel approach based on the concept of Volunteered Geographic Information (VGI) to monitoring environmental noise; it is a problem that specially affects people's quality of life in urban areas. In this work, mobile devices are used to massively collect environmental noise measurements, which are used to generate maps of a specific area and then make a forecast.

Environmental noise is not just a form of environmental pollution, but it is also a problem that affects the quality of life of people, generate them stress and cause them progressive hearing loss and other health problems, such as hypertension and other heart problems (Antón & Antón, 2012). It has been found, for example, that prolonged exposure to traffic is associated with a small increased risk of death from cardiovascular complications, especially in the elderly population (Halonen et al, 2015). According to the World Health Organization, noise is the second major cause of health problems, after the poor air quality. The high noise levels occur mainly in the most densely populated areas, such as Mexico City, one of the most populous countries in the world, so it is important to answer questions on where and when different levels of noise are generated.

Geospatial technologies have given citizens the opportunity to participate actively and intentionally in activities that were once relegated to the world of expert geographers and cartographers. This can be interpreted as the beginning of a new geography but without geographers. Neogeography is a social phenomenon that describes the use of geographic tools and techniques by ordinary people; that is to say, they are a subset of users who voluntarily produce their own information, which has the quality of being information with geographic content (Connors et al, 2012, Goodchild, 2009). This is kind of applications derive in concepts as Volunteered Geographic Information (VGI) by Goodchild (2007). VGI is content generated in an intentional and conscious effort by the users' community with little or no education, experience or training in geography or cartography, that is, by the neogeographers. This information helps expand the information from experts in the analysis of geographic information, such as the scientific community or private research organizations, so they can take advantage of both knowledge from expert and non-expert community (Connors et al, 2012; Elwood et al, 2012, Goodchild, 2009). Examples include Wikimapia, OpenStreetMap, GeoNames, GeoCommons and TierraWiki (Elwood et al, 2012, Goodchild, 2007 and Sui, 2008), crime and public safety, adventure and recreation activities (Parker et al, 2013) and timely response to natural disasters (Middleton et al, 2014).

VGI aims to reduce the gap between the work of the public, the researchers and the authorities responsible for taking decisions on environmental policies of public character (Connors et al, 2012), so it has been used in smart cities to optimize city operations to address environmental, social and economic issues (Nakano, 2015). Other methodologies have been developed to ensure the VGI's quality (Fonte, 2015).

Several environment projects that have been made taking into account the participation of citizens, are related to habitat restoration, public health, environmental planning, monitoring of water quality, health and preservation of forest and animal resources, management of forest fires, mapping and monitoring of crop fields (precision agriculture), humanitarian programs, etc. In fact, VGI establishes a new paradigm for socio-spatial research and the continuous monitoring of the changing landscape of social behavior and interaction in fast evolving urbanized societies, making VGI a big data phenomenon which cannot be conceived in isolation from other concepts of data science (Jiang and Thill, 2015). In addition, we point out that this work is based on Smart city concept, which has been used to making better use of Information and Communication Technologies (ICTs) to improve the services that support urban operations and services.

2. BACKGROUND

Rodriguez Manzo (2011) presented the first noise map of the Metropolitan Area of Mexico (ZMVM), to help authorities to issue policies to correct noise problems affecting the region and improve with them the quality of life of its inhabitants. In 2014, a system using ubiquitous computing for environmental noise monitoring in New York City was presented. The system analyzed historical data from noise complaints calls (including the address of the complaint, reported noise category, time, etc.), road networks and check-ins and points of interest from Foursquare. Some of the main distinctions of this project are its ability to infer the noise composition, as well as people's tolerance to noise at different times (Zheng et al, 2014a, Zheng et al, 2014b).

An application that consider models for predicting noise levels and for generating noise maps with an accuracy of 80.9% is presented in (Karolus, 2013). This application used ML techniques and geo-referenced voluntary measurements from NoiseMap. In addition, OpenStreetMap and LinkedGeoData were used in order to obtain information of streets, buildings and other noise sources. One of the major contributions of this work was the ability to predict noise levels in areas with a few or without measurements. Quintero (2013) presents an approach for generating environmental noise maps based on samples taken at different times by a system composed by calibrated microphone and a GPS. Sánchez (2011) presented acoustic maps based on real-time measurements, taking into consideration as a case study the area nearby an airport, using an array of four calibrated microphones to obtain noise measurements, which are analyzed for automatic location of the noise source. These results are used to generate noise maps based on simulation models specified in the ISO 9613 standard; the case study was the landing and aircrafts' take-of in the Mexico City International Airport, so the microphones were placed on streets around the airport.

In 2011, a scalable and parallel architecture which used the MapReduce programming paradigm for parallel processing of large data sets from different data flows and Machine Learning (ML) methods, particularly kernel methods for pattern recognition. With this project, its authors were able to create a map of environmental noise in real time, with data from a fixed sensors network and other mobile devices network, and they created predictive models to calculate noise levels from a traffic flow simulation (Kaiser 2013).

Laermometer collects audio signals from user's mobile devices and sends them to a server, allowing display noise maps generated with the noise measurements in a web interface. The purpose of this application is to help the user find quiet places to stay, or simply share sound levels in a certain area (Bilandzic et al, 2008). NoiseSPY contains a web portal where noise maps are displayed in real time (Kanjo, 2010). NoiseTube allows users to capture noise measurements using their own mobile device in order to create noise maps which are displayed on a website (Maisonneuve et al, 2009). Ear-Phone is a system that shows noise maps in a web portal, generated by the measurements that the users captured using their mobile devices and that were sent to a server. It has a single-point calibration system, which compares unknown values of the device with reference standards according to certain algorithms. The system includes reconstruction methods for missing measurements in order to improve the prediction of the generated noise maps (Rana et al, 2010). NoiseMap collects noise measurements, it consists of a mobile application supported on the web monitoring platform in order to encourage voluntary participation, this system rewards its users with ranks according to their activity level (Schweizer, 2011). NoiseWatch includes noise measurements from official scientific sources and VGI, volunteer users can be entered using the web platform or a mobile device (Jirka et al, 2012). There are also applications that use gamification techniques in order to motivate people to participate voluntarily, such as Noise Battle, a user's goal is to conquer the largest possible number of cells, which is achieved by taking more and better noise measurements in these areas than other players while avoiding loss them, which occurs when another user becomes who conquer the area in the same way (Karolus, 2013).

3. COLLABORATIVE MONITORING AND PREDICTION OF ENVIRONMENTAL NOISE

3.1 Issues

Most current environmental noise monitoring systems are based on an approach where a generally expensive metering station is used, in addition to the fact that their information is poorly shared, it is necessary to implement innovative solutions that are more appropriate, especially in developing countries, such as Mexico. According to the Background Section, Table 1 shows a comparison of the presented works to monitor environmental noise. Broadly speaking, it can be observed that the main difference in our work regarding the presented proposals is that it promotes VGI while using ML techniques to predict noise levels considering factors around the measurements. This approach integrates many of the functionalities to create a new contribution to environmental noise monitoring, particularly the features of VGI, existing in projects such as NoiseWatch, and the prediction of noise levels using ML techniques.

3.2 Methodology

In order to solve the problems described above, this paper presents a methodology. The methodology aims to take advantage of the VGI generated by the participation of people who, through an application on their mobile devices, capture the noise measurements where they are. Then, by using a ML approach, such as Support Vector Machines (SVM), we have to predict the noise levels on predefined places and create noise maps with booth the measurements and the predicted values, and present them to the user. This methodology is composed by the following phases: Data Acquisition, Analysis and Data Processing, and Visualization of the Information.

The methodology and its components are presented in Figure 1. In general, it can be observed that in the Data acquisition phase the users, acting voluntarily as sensors, capture environmental noise and their geospatial position using their mobile devices and send these measurements to a server where they are stored into a database. Then, in the Analysis and data processing phase the measurements and some contextual information (data about time intervals, nearby businesses, settlements and measurements) are used to train and test a ML model, in this case, a SVM, to describe the noise's behavior and predict

Table 1. Noise monitoring applications

Features	Laermometer	NoiseSPY	NoiseTube	NoiseBattle	NoiseQuest	Ear-Phone	Noise Watch	NoiseMap	Kernel stream Oracles	(Sánchez, 2011)	(Quintero, 2013	(Karolus, 2013)	Sheng, 2014	(Rodriguez Manzo, 2011	This approach
Promotes VGI	■	■	■	■	■	■	■	■				■			■
Mobile devices	■	■	■	■	■	■	■	■					■		■
Noise maps in a web site		■	■			■	■	■		■	■	■	■	■	■
Noise maps in mobile devices	■	■	■	■	■	■	■	■							■
Exchange measurements		■	■			■	■	■							■
Implements it own measure algorithms	■	■	■		■	■	■	■		■	■		■	■	■
Classifies the noise source and time			■				■			■			■	■	■
Consider factors around measurement												■	■	■	■
Prediction of noise levels									■			■	■	■	■

Figure 1. The conceptual diagram of the methodology

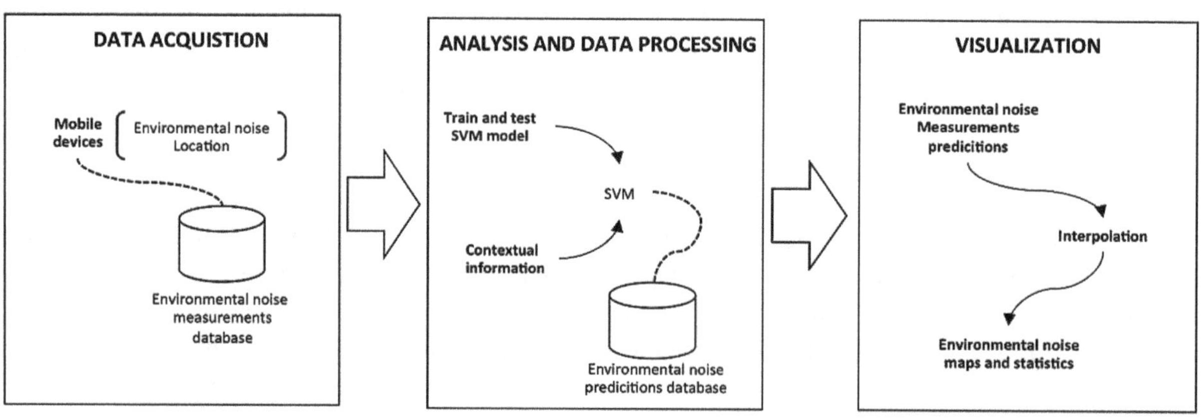

noise levels which are stored too into the database. Finally, in the Visualization of the information phase, both the measurements and the predictions are interpolated using a Web Processing Service (WPS), in this case, the Barnes algorithm with a standard color code; this layer is overlaid to other Web Map Service (WMS) layers, such as OpenStreetMap (OSM), resulting in an environmental noise map which is presented to the user, altogether with some relevant noise statistics, via a web browser. A system covering all these phases of the methodology corresponds to a client-server architecture, where the mobile device application and the noise web maps belong to the client side and all the rest to the server side.

- **Data Acquisition:** Data acquisition involves volunteer users who through their mobile devices are able to measure environmental noise levels that exist where they are, to send these measurements to a database server in order to store them. The steps covered in this phase are the follows: 1. Registration, 2. Capture of noise levels, 3. Temporary storage and 4. Server storage.

In Registration, each user is registered in the server via their mobile device, providing a user name and a brief description of the device. A single user can register for different mobile devices, and registration is a process which is necessary only once in each device. The microphone of the user device is used to capture the environmental noise in order to measure the noise level in a particular geographic location, the user must stop and remain still during the 10 seconds the sampling needs to prevent that the movement causes alterations in the reading. Each measurement is georeferenced by using the GPS radio or Wi-Fi radio of the user device. The georeferenced measurements are stored in a local database. In addition, for each measurement it is stored the date, time, the minimum and maximum value of noise. The purpose of using a local storage is to avoid the user have a permanent Internet connection.

Once the user has access to the Internet, the measurements stored in the device are sent to the server, where they are stored into a database. Once the server responds to the user device that it has received and stored the measurements, they are removed from the local storage of the mobile device.

- **Analysis and Data Processing:** In the phase of Analysis and Data Processing, a set of different noise levels are predicted, including some geographies where it is not likely to exist volunteer user's contributions, by using contextual information of those geographic points.

This phase covers several activities. First, the creation of a ML model, in this case, a SVM. Later, the training and evaluation of the model, which includes the random separation of measurements in a training set and a test set. Finally, the prediction of environmental noise in the area of interest, for which it is necessary the creation of the prediction set composed by a set of points of the union of a lattice of geographic points and the geometric centroids of the settlements, as well as the prediction of noise levels in the points of the prediction set.

Prediction is based on georeferenced measurements. We use the contextual information of the points where each measurement was performed and machine learning techniques for regression, in this case, Support Vector Machines (SVM), and particularly, Support Vector Regression (SVR). These methods are applied on the measured values to predict the noise levels at certain points, with both the measurements and the new predicted values in different geographic locations within the area of interest together.

Some factors around a noise measurement were considered as relevant to the prediction model, that is, factors in the geographic neighborhood of each measurement. We consider the following assumptions:

1. **Businesses Density:** Supposing that it is possible that a higher concentration of businesses with a lot of people in them around a geographic point, is equivalent to a greater movement of people, and therefore to higher levels of noise.

2. **Previous Noise Measurements:** Supposing that it is possible that noise measurements previously made in the same geographic area at similar time intervals, are somewhat similar to the current measurement value.
3. **Type of Settlements:** Supposing that it is possible that both the number and the type of settlements around a geographic area, partially determine the existing noise level in that regiόn.
4. **The Measurement Time:** Supposing that it is possible that the date and time the measurement was made partially determine the noise level recorded in the geographic area of that measurement.

An outline of the above factors is shown in Figure 2. The radius of the concentric circles represents the influence area of the respective factor around the point where it is desired to predict the noise level, that is, within the geographic neighborhood of the measurement. and the territorial division of Mexico from INEGI, which is an official source, adapting the names of some columns, turning the projection system to EPSG:4326, and populating the corresponding tables in the database. In a free space (with no obstacles), a sound emitted from a point source moves describing a spherical surface. Thus, with increasing distance r, the sound energy radiated from the r point source covers a larger area, so the sound pressure p decreases, that is, p ~1/r, which is known as the 1/r law, and indicates that the sound pressure p is inversely proportional to the distance r from the source. Then, since the noise intensity decays with distance and assuming a space with these characteristics, all the mentioned above numeric factors are calculated considering the distance from the geographic point of the measurement to the geographic point that represent each factor.

The algorithm for updating the prediction factors in the *universe set* (C_U) is defined as follows:
Input:

- The universe set composed by the geographic points where we will calculate the inuence of different factors: $C_U = \{p_1; p_2; \ldots p_{n1}\}$
- A set of radius of the geographic neighborhoods: {*businesses radius; settlements_radius; measurements_radius*}

Figure 2. Factors in the geographic neighborhood considered to predict noise level

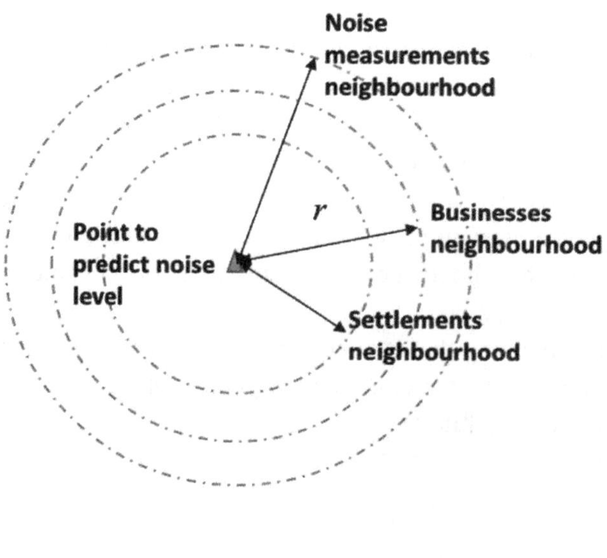

Output:

- The universe set $\mathbf{C}_U$ with the calculation of the affectation caused by different factors.

Data:

- A set of businesses from the DENUE database: *denue_set* = $\{d_1, d_2, \ldots d_{n2}\}$

```
foreach point ∈ C_U do
businesses_neighborhood ← circular geographic neighborhood with center at
point and radius businesses_radius
settlements neighborhood ← circular geographic neighborhood with center at
point and radius settlements_radius
measurements neighborhood ← circular geographic neighborhood with center at
point and radius measurements_radius
factor_1 ← 0
factor_2 ← 0
factor_3 ← 0
factor_4 ← 0
/* calculate the nearby businesses factor */
n ← 0
foreach business ∈ denue_set do
if business ∈ businesses_neighborhood then
business_point ← geographic point with the coordinates of business
people ← average people registered in business
distance ←  Euclidean distance between point and business_point
factor_1 ← factor_1 + people/(distance * distance)
n ← n + 1
end
end
factor_1 ← factor_1/n
/* calculate the nearby settlements factor */
n ←  0
foreach settlement ∈ settlements_neighborhood do
settlement_point ←  geographic point with the coordinates of the centroid of
settlement
type ←  numeric value registered for the type of place of the settlement
distance ← Euclidean distance between point and settlement_point
factor_2 ← factor_2 + type=(distance * distance)
n ← n + 1
end
factor_2 ← factor_2/n
```

```
/* calculate the nearby measurements factor */
n ← 0
foreach measurement ∈ measurements_neighborhood do
measurement_point ←  geographic point with the coordinates of measurement
noise ← average noise level captured in measurement
distance ← Euclidean distance between point and measurement_point
factor3 ← factor3 + noise/(distance * distance)
n ← n + 1
end
factor3 ←  factor3/n
factor4  ← n
/* update all the factors at the points in the universe set */
point[factor1] ← factor1
point[factor2] ← factor2
point[factor3] ← factor3
point[factor4] ← factor4
end
/* return the updated universe set */
return CU
```

The algorithm presents how the diverse factors are calculated around each point of C_U. As it was mentioned, the density of some geographic features around each measurement is considered, such as the businesses density, the kind of settlements surrounding, and other previously captured nearby measurements. Once knowing these densities, the influence of each feature is numerically calculated considering the distance from the respective measurement. All these numeric values are going to be used later by the ML algorithm to predict noise levels at any other geographic point.

It has been observed that the human body can not adapt to high and constant noise levels, that notall people are equally sensitive to noise and its effects and the sensitivity changes with factors such as time, making the noise more annoying at night than during the day (Ising and Kruppa 2014, Liu et al, 2014). Taking this into account, it is convenient to analyze noise using certain time intervals. Time intervals of the analyzes were performed considering the daily activities that in general, most of the population makes in the Mexico City. A different noise map can be obtained from each time interval. The proposal considers the following time intervals:

- **HL-00-Time Interval:** In the wee hours. From 00:00 to 06:00 hours, when most of the people sleep and there is usually less traffic.
- **HL-06-Time Interval:** In the morning. From 06:00 to 12:00 hours, when most of the people go to work or attend school in the morning shift.
- **HL-12-Time Interval:** In the afternoon. From 12:00 to 18:00 hours, when most of the people eat out or attend school in the afternoon shift.
- **HL-18-Time Interval:** At night. From 18:00 to 24:00 hours, when most of the people come back from work and go home to rest.

It is necessary to create, train, evaluate and use the learning model. For the construction of the model, it is necessary to obtain two sets: the learning set (C_A) and the prediction set (C_P). The unión of these sets of points makes the universe set (C_U) (Lantz, 2013). It can be seen in Figure 3.

The points of georeferenced measurements, that is, places where users have made noise measurements using their mobile devices, compose the C_A set. On the other hand, the C_P set is composed by the centroids of the settlements (in order to predict the noise level in each settlement, regardless of whether there is or not noise measurements inside it) and a lattice of points within the area of interest to make the prediction cover also areas where there are not settlements or few of them exist. The distance separating the arrangement of points in the lattice is arbitrary and can be configureured (increased or decreased) as preferred. The C_A is divided randomly into two subsets: the training set (C_{A1}) and the test set (C_{A2}). Using *k-fold cross validation* with $k = 10$ it is possible to define the proportion of C_{A1} as the 90% of C_A, and C_{A2} as the remaining 10%. With C_A it is possible to train and evaluate the ML model, in this case, a Support Vector Machine (SVM).

- **Visualization of Information:** The final phase in the methodology is the Visualization of Information. This uses a server for geospatial data, such as GeoServer, at this phase the measurements and the predicted values are integrated with the data from a map service (in this case OpenStreetMap). Then, using the standard color code for noise levels and the Barnes interpolation algorithm on the C_U points, the resulting noise maps, which describe the behavior of the noise in the area of interest, are generated and displayed, as well as relevant statistics about the data. The interpolation method (Barnes) is a geospatial interpolation algorithm that operates on a regular arrangement of cells covering a specific area in which there are measurements in irregularly distributed points (Weymouth et al, 1999 and Xia et al, 1999).

This phase includes the elaboration of noise maps that can be displayed in both desktop computers and mobile devices as well as reporting and statistics from noise in settlements belonging to municipali-

Figure 3. Sets of geographic points used to predict environmental noise

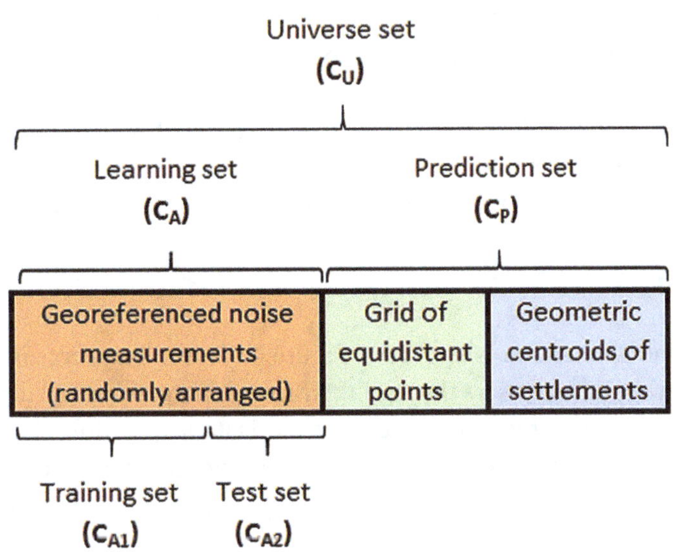

ties (or delegations) of interest and from noise in settlements in various time intervals. The basic unit of measurement for environmental noise, recommended by some international standards such as ISO 1996-1:2003, is the dB (A). The color code is defined by ISO 1996-2:2007. Most of the existing sounds are fluctuating by nature (and in some cases they are ephemeral), measures such as $L_{eq,T}$ and SEL allow to describe fluctuating sounds, that is, to move the corresponding fluctuating sound to a constant value. ISO 1996-1:2003 standard also recommends to use $L_{eq,T}$ and SEL as two basic noise levels descriptors. With regard to the categories in which noise measurements are grouped according to their intensity, using the classification presented in ISO 1996-2, which considers the range of sounds lower than 35 decibels, between 35 and 80 decibels at intervals of 5 decibels, and greater than 80 decibels.

4. SOLUTIONS AND RECOMENDATIONS

In order to verify the effectiveness of the methodology, as a study case the environmental noise monitoring in the Cuauhtémoc Delegation in Mexico City is considered, viewing it as a macro área level where it is possible to focus, at a micro level, in the environmental noise in streets around the Historic Center of Mexico City, in the Centro settlement. Two levels of detail are considered:

1. **Area of Study at Macro Level:** In this case the HL-12-time interval is considered to monitor the noise in the Cuauhtemoc Delegation in Mexico City. The reasons for choosing this area and this time interval as a study case are as follows:
   a. **Location:** The selected area includes the downtown of Mexico City.
   b. **Movement:** It is one of the most active areas in terms of population mobility,
   c. **Businesses:** It contains a high concentration of businesses, so it is expected that the measurement are most useful for the learning model.
   d. **Safety:** This place contains in general several of the settlements with greater security and better infrastructure, so it represents a lower risk during the measurement time intervals
2. **Area of Study at Micro Level:** For this level are considered the HL-06, HL-12, HNL-06 and HNL-12 time intervals to monitor the noise in the Historic Center of Mexico City. The reasons for choosing this place and its surroundings in these time intervals as a study case are as follows:
   a. **Noise:** It was determined that this is one of the regions with the highest generation of noise, because it is a place of broad commercial activity and transit of people.
   b. **Movement:** It is one of the most active areas in terms of population mobility.
   c. **Safety:** As one of the main tourist destinations in this city, this place offers constant surveillance, so it also represents the lowest risk during the noise measurements walks.

4.1 Implementation

A functional model of the application is shown in Figure 4. This system consists of an application for mobile devices that allow volunteer users through their microphone to perform georeferenced environmental noise level measurements; this module covers the Data acquisition phase of the methodology. These measurements are then sent to a server that receive them using an interface of synchronization services, there they are stored into a database and used by an analysis service to predict noise values,

Figure 4. Functional model of the system

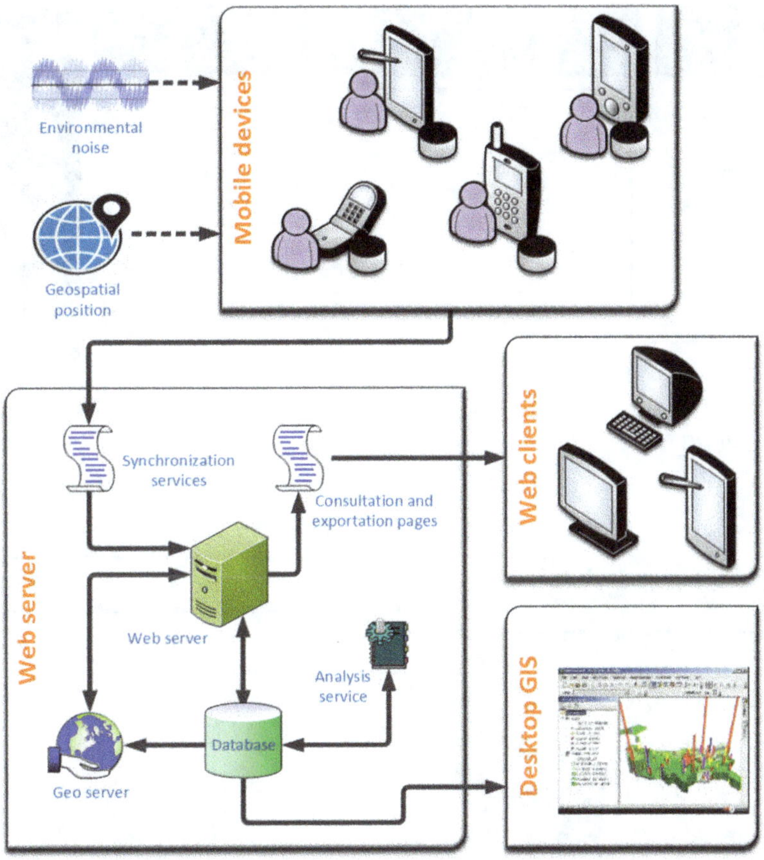

then a server for geospatial data, in this case, GeoServer, generates the noise maps; this module covers the Analysis and data processing phase of the methodology.

An application called NoiseMonitor was developed, to capture noise using mobile devices, in order to meet the needs of the Data acquisition phase; it is based on Android, with support for version 2.3.3 (API level 10) and higher; this application, which is shown in Figure 5, consists of a main screen, from which the user can move between three sections: the screen to capture the noise levels, the screen to visualize the noise map, and the screen to configureure data about the user and the device.

Using the R language, it was possible to perform a ML model, specifically, it was implemented a Support Vector Machine (SVM). A program designed to run periodically as a service was written in Python. This program first updates the prediction factors in the universe set, then it retrieves the required data from the database, and later it invokes another program, written in the R language, responsible for predicting the noise values in the prediction set points, which consists of the centroid of each settlement and municipality (or delegation) of interest, plus a lattice of points across the entire area of interest. After obtaining predictions, the program written in Python updates the corresponding predicted values in the database.

The web application for the Visualization of the information phase is shown in Figure 6, it is divided into four sections: the first tab shows the noise map, the second tab allows the user to search for geo-

Figure 5. Mobile application for environmental noise monitoring

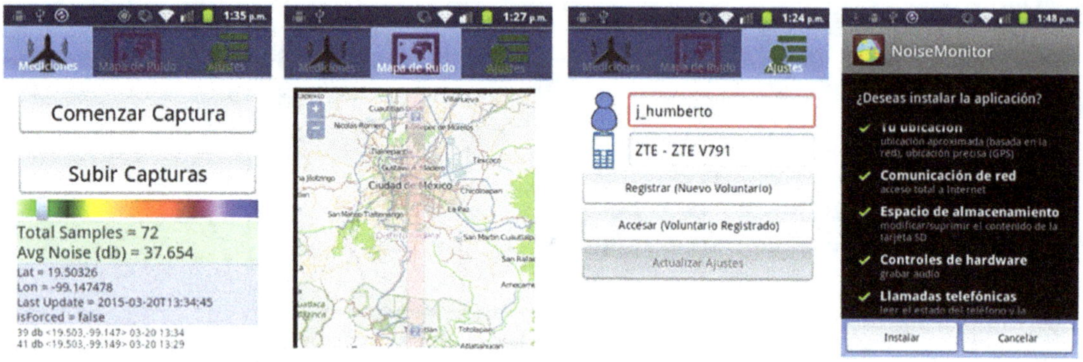

Figure 6. Web application

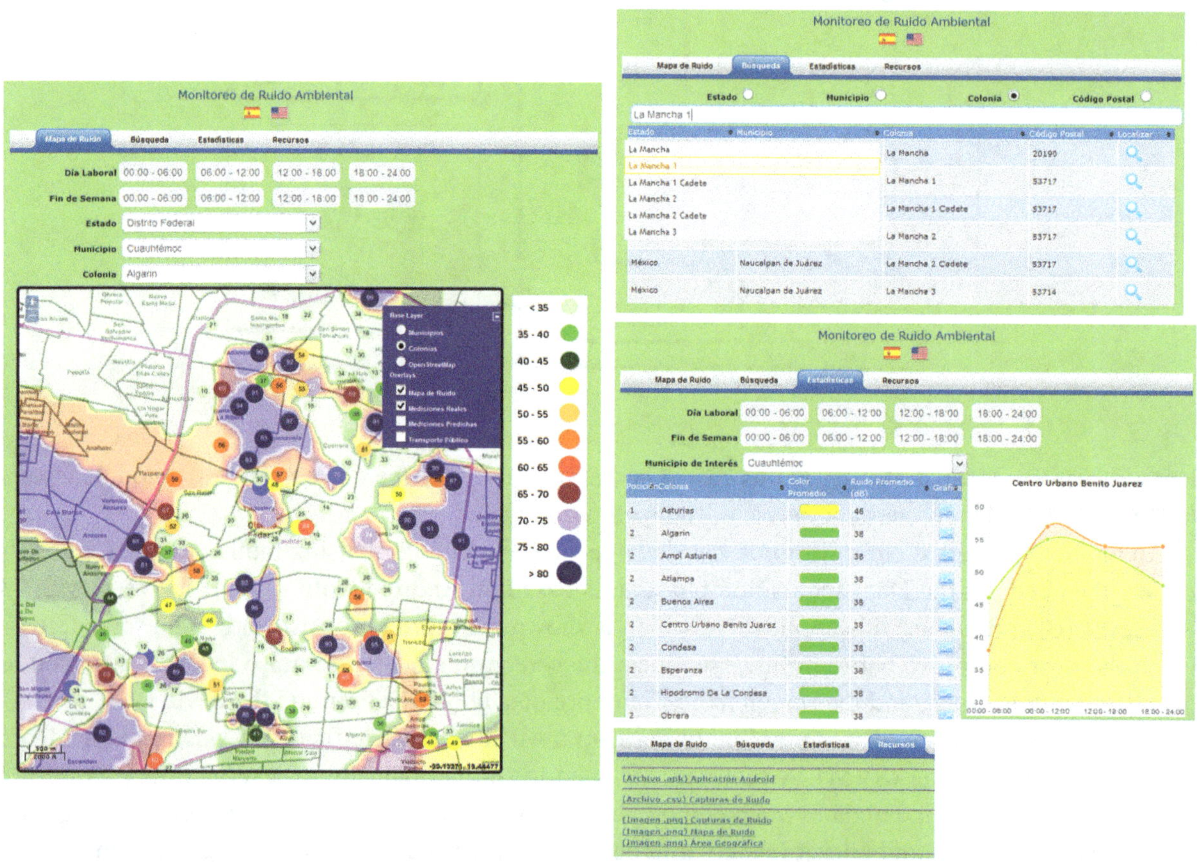

graphic places, the third tab shows some statistics about noise levels in different regions, and the fourth tab allows the user download some other resources. This application was developed using PHP, HTML5, CSS, JSON, JavaScript and AJAX. To display the map, the JavaScript framework OpenLayers, which reads data from the server for geospatial data, GeoServer, in WMS format was used. This transforms the data from the PostgreSQL database with the PostGIS extension.

The first group of samples was produced between July 6 and 10, 2015, on routes that attempted to cover at least a part of every settlement in the Cuauhtémoc Delegation, during the previously mentioned time intervals. Figure 7 shows the geographic distribution of measurements (left). The second group of samples was produced in the area of the Historic Center, following the path shown in Figure 8, at the time intervals mentioned above. In both groups of samples, capturing in total with the mobile device, 2,355 georeferenced environmental noise measurements in the area of interest, having traveled just over 83 km.

Some statistics on the distribution of the captured environmental noise measurements are shown in Figure 9, as a boxplot (left), a statistics table (center) and a histogram (right). The boxplot is shown in original scale (in dB(SPL) units) and in normalized scale (in a range between 0 and 1). It can be ap-

Figure 7. Measurement of environmental noise

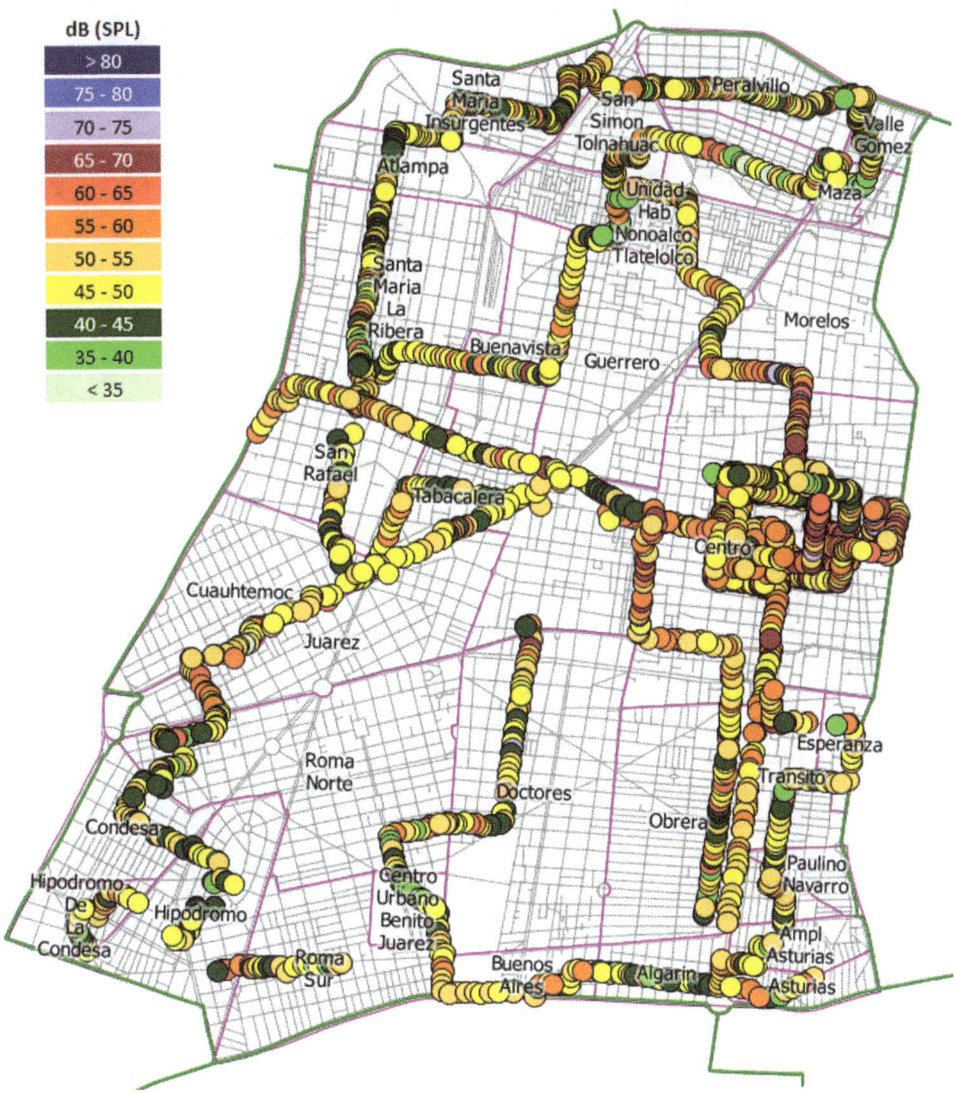

Figure 8. Measurements of environmental noise in the Historic Center

Figure 9. Statistics on the distribution of the noise measurements

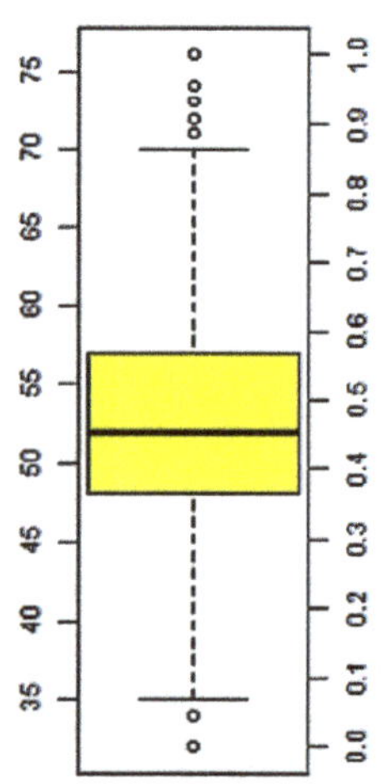

(a)

Statistic	Value
Count	2355
Minimum	32
Maximum	76
Mode	53
1st quartile	48
2nd quartile (Median)	52
3rd quartile	57
4th quartile	76
Average	52.45
Typical error	0.14
Standard deviation	7.03
Variance	49.38
Confidence level (95%)	0.28

(b)

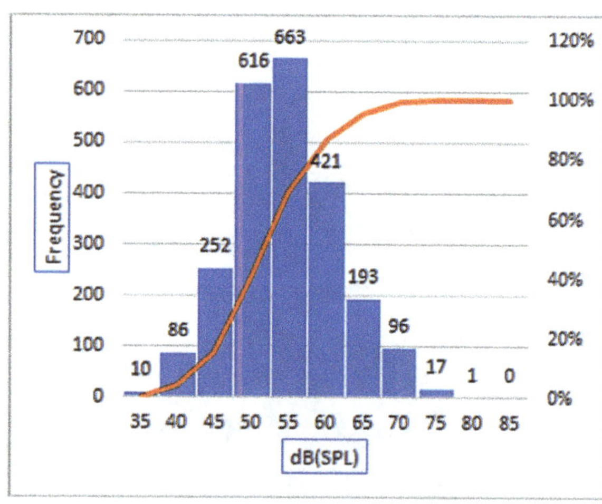

(c)

preciated that, using dB(SPL), even when the recorded measurements are in a range between 32 and 76, 50% of them are in the range between 48 and 57, with an average of 52.45. The histogram lets visually confirm previous observations as well as appreciate a similar to a normal distribution behavior of the data.

4.2 Noise Prediction Using Machine Learning

To find the right values to be used for the ML model, a program was developed in R language to evaluate the performance of support vector machines (SVM) under various parameter and compare it with other machine learning technique, specifically, against artificial neural networks (ANN).

From the set with 2355 noise measurements, 1871 (about 80%) were taken randomly to make the training set, and the remaining 484 (about 20%) to make the test set. These sets remained constant for evaluating both SVM and ANN. At the end of the training of each ML model, using the training set and every combination of the different parameters, and after predicting using the trained model and the noise levels of the test set, it was possible to compare the noise measurements (previously known) against the new noise levels (recently predicted by the model). Knowing the differences between both values it was possible to calculate the mean absolute error (MAE) and the correlation (CORR). With these results the accuracy of each model was determined, which is a necessary metric to compare the models, considering as a more accurate model when its MAE was the lowest and its CORR was the highest. For the geographic neighborhoods different radius lengths were evaluated and a radius of 200 m for DENUE businesses geographic neighborhood, 1000 m for the radius of the nearby settlements, and 1000 m for the radius of the nearby noise measurements.

In order to evaluate the ANN, the *neuralnet* function is considered. Different amount of nodes was used in the hidden layers, and the default algorithm, *rprop+* (resilient backpropagation with weight backtracking), was used. We built an ANN with 0 hidden nodes (ANN nod =0), other ANN with a hidden layer of 1, 2, 3, 4, 5 and 10 nodes, an ANN with two hidden layers of 5 nodes in each (ANN nod =5-5), an ANN with two hidden layers of 10 nodes in each (ANN nod=10-10), and finally an ANN with three hidden layers of 5 hidden nodes in each (ANN nod =5-5-5). Using a logarithmic scale, Figure 10 shows the performance of these different ANN configureurations. It can be appreciated the CORR increment, relative to other ANN with the same number of hidden layers, while increasing the number of nodes in the hidden layers. The MAE and the sum of squared errors (SSE) behave similarly, because the SSE only amplifies the effect of the MAE. The training time for the model (in seconds) depends directly on the number of steps performed by the algorithm, and generally grows exponentially as nodes in the hidden layers' increase. The best results concerning prediction accuracy were obtained with an ANN nod =10-10, although its training time was approximately 3.3 minutes, which is considerably high compared, for example, with an ANN nod =3, which took about 1.2 minutes to train, it had an average performance. Regarding training time, the worst results were obtained with an ANN nod =5-5 with about 7.7 minutes. However, this was one of the best ANN regarding the accuracy of prediction.

To evaluate the SVM performance was used the *ksvm* function from the kernlab library in the R language, and we also considered different kernel functions and parameters. The evaluated kernels were the radial basis or Gaussian kernel (rbfdot), the Laplacian kernel (laplacedot), the Bessel kernel (besseldot), the RBF Anova kernel (anovadot), the polynomial kernel (polydot), the linear kernel (vanilladot) and the hyperbolic tangent kernel (tanhdot). For every used kernel, the parameter C (used for the cost of restrictions violation) was evaluated in a range of 0.1 to 3.1 at intervals of 0.5. For each kernel and each value of C, the ξ parameter (used in the regression insensitivity loss function) was evaluated in a range

Figure 10. Performance of different ANN (MAE, CORR, training time, etc.)

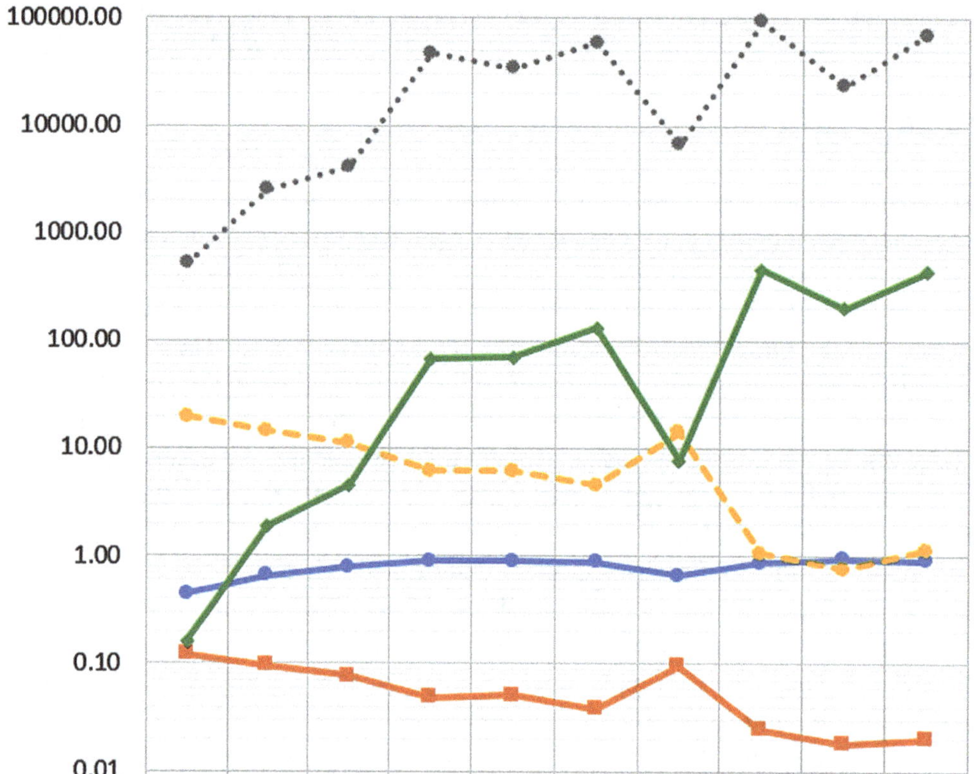

	NN 0	NN 1	NN 2	NN 3	NN 4	NN 5	NN 1-1	NN 5-5	NN 10-10	NN 5-5-5
CORR	0.441	0.645	0.774	0.887	0.885	0.869	0.651	0.853	0.929	0.910
MAE	0.119	0.095	0.076	0.048	0.051	0.038	0.095	0.024	0.018	0.020
SSE	19.248	14.228	10.998	6.121	6.146	4.514	13.988	1.064	0.748	1.117
Steps	520	2513	4109	46594	33854	59845	6714	94074	23404	70722
Training Time	0.2	1.9	4.5	67.1	69.8	130.6	7.7	463.2	199.9	434.3

of 0.1 to 2.6 at intervals of 0.5. Under these results 294 combinations were obtained. The value of the k parameter was 10 for performing *k-fold cross validation* with the training set in order to improve the model.

A comparison of the performance of the different kernels, considering the minimum MAE, the maximum CORR, and the minimum training time, is shown in Figure 11. Regarding the MAE and CORR, the best results were obtained with the rbfdot (Gaussian) kernel, followed by the laplacedot kernel, while the worst performance corresponded to the polydot (second degree) kernel, the tanhdot kernel and the vanilladot kernel. Regarding the minimum training time achieved, the best performance also corresponded to the rbfdot (Gaussian) kernel, with about 6 seconds, followed by vanilladot kernel and laplacedot kernel, with about 8 seconds; the polydot kernel obtained the worst performance, with about 3.8 minutes, even when it was configureured with grade 2, while higher degrees (not reported here) for the same kernel exceeded by far this time.

Figure 11. Performance of different SVM: (a) MAE and CORR; (b) Training time

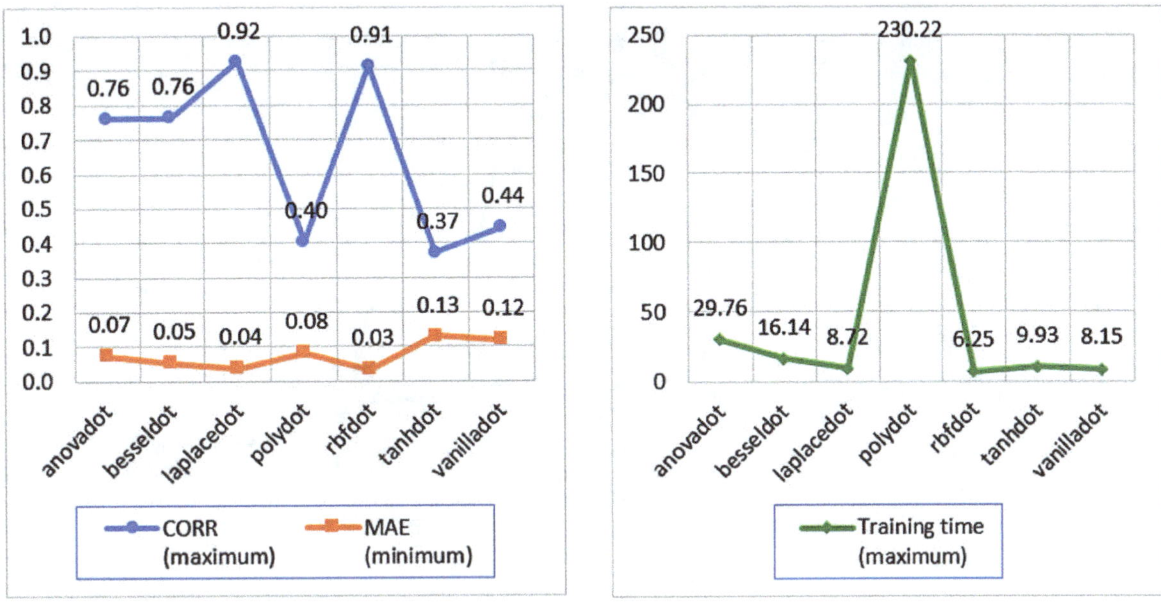

Once the ML models with ANN and SVM were analyzed, it was possible to compare them against each other to decide which one should be used for this particular data set. Using a logarithmic scale, Figure 12 shows a summary about the performance obtained with different ML models using SVM with different kernels, against using ANN with different amount of nodes in the hidden layers. In this case, the performance was determined in terms of CORR (maximum), MAE (minimum) and training time (minimum) achieved by each model. The columns are sorted according to the type of model (SVM or ANN) and the obtained MAE. For example, the MAE and CORR obtained with SVM *ker=vanilladot* proved to be comparable to an ANN nod=0, although this ANN took much less time training than that SVM.

The models that stand out are SVM *ker=rbfdot* and ANN nod=10-10, because they report the greater prediction accuracy in terms of the lowest MAE and the highest CORR for SVM and ANN, respectively. With the ANN nod=10-10 we obtained slightly better MAE and CORR results tan the ones were obtained with the SVM *ker=rbfdot*. However, regarding the model training time, the SVM took about 6 seconds while ANN required approximately 3.3 minutes (over 30 times the time taken by the SVM). A graphical comparison of the measurements and the predicted values of some of the above models are shown in Figure 13. It can be observed that the best results ((b) and (d)) correspond to cases where the graph of the predicted values stick much more to the measurements, which implies that the MAE decreases and the CORR increases. It can also be seen that the line of predicted values sticks much more to the line of measurements in the case of ANN ((d)) than in the case of SVM ((b)), which graphically reaffirms what is reported in Figure 13.

By contrast, some of the worst results ((a) and (c)) correspond to those models that predict almost always with a value around the average value of the test set, which means, contrary to the previous case, that the MAE increases and the CORR decreases.

As it already mentioned, the SVM ker=rbfdot produced the best results with our data (higher accuracy due to a smaller MAE and a greater CORR). In Figure 14 it is shown for this kernel in particular,

Figure 12. Performance comparison using SVM and ANN (MAE, CORR and training time)

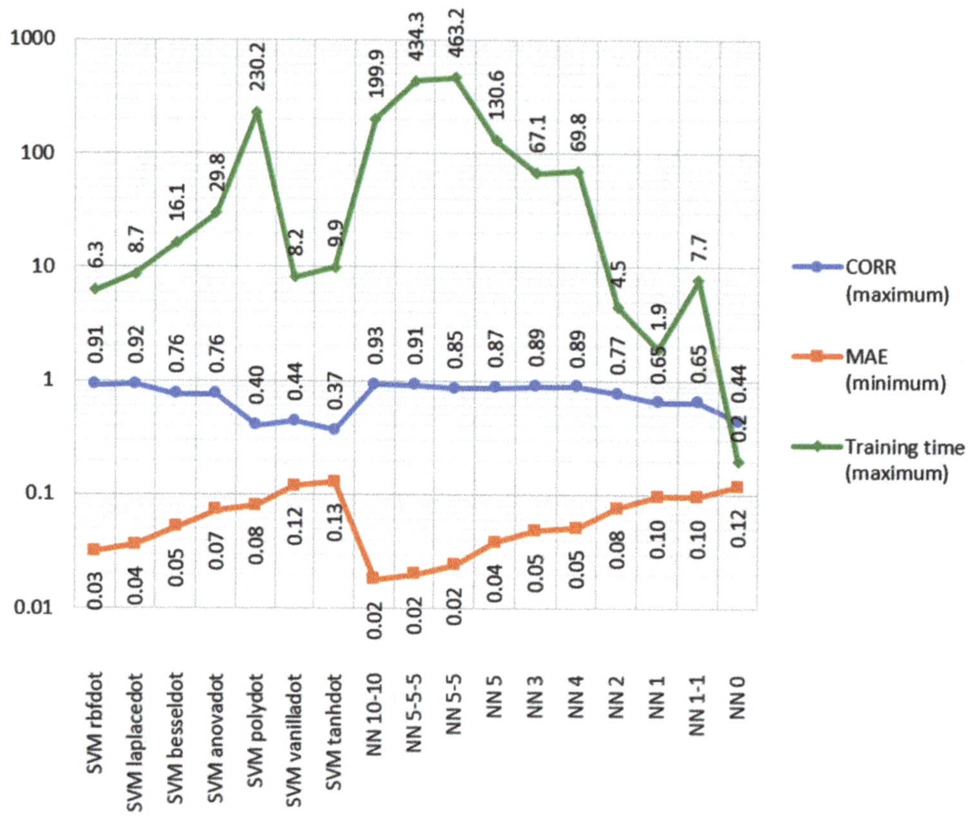

how is the changing trend for the training time, the MAE or test error, the training error, the CORR and the number of support vectors obtained during the parameters variation, C parameter (with the values 0.001, 0.01, 0.03, 0.05, 0.07, 0.09, 0.11, 0.5, 1.0, 1.5, 2.0, 2.5, 3, 4, 6, 8 and 10) and ξ parameter (with the values 0.001, 0.01, 0.03, 0.05, 0.07, 0.09, 0.1, 0.6, 1.1, 1.6, 2.1 and 2.6). Again, the k parameter remained constant with a value of 10. In general, the estimation of the kernel parameters allows to appreciate that when we increase the C parameter and decrease the ξ value, also the CORR and the training time increase, while the test error or MAE and the training time decrease. It can also be noted that the number of support vectors increases when C and ξ parameters decrease. Considering simultaneously the CORR and the MAE for the model prediction accuracy, as well as the training time for the performance during execution, consider the values of $C = 5.0$ and $\xi = 0.1$ as suitable for training a new SVM, while attempting to avoid overfitting and underfitting.

4.3 Environmental Noise Maps

An environmental noise map was developed using a QGIS, based on noise measurements in the Cuauhtémoc Delegation, which is shown in Figure 15. This map was obtained using the interpolation method IDW using the $C = 2$ parameter, and the color code defined in ISO 1996-2:1987 standard. It can be seen immediately that the highest noise levels recorded during the tours were located in the zone around the

Figure 13. Comparison of the measurements against the predicted values: (a) SVM ker=vanilladot, C=2.0, ξ=0.1 and k=10; (b) SVM ker=rbfdot, C=2.0, ξ =0.1 and k=10; (c) ANN nod=0; (d) ANN nod=5-5

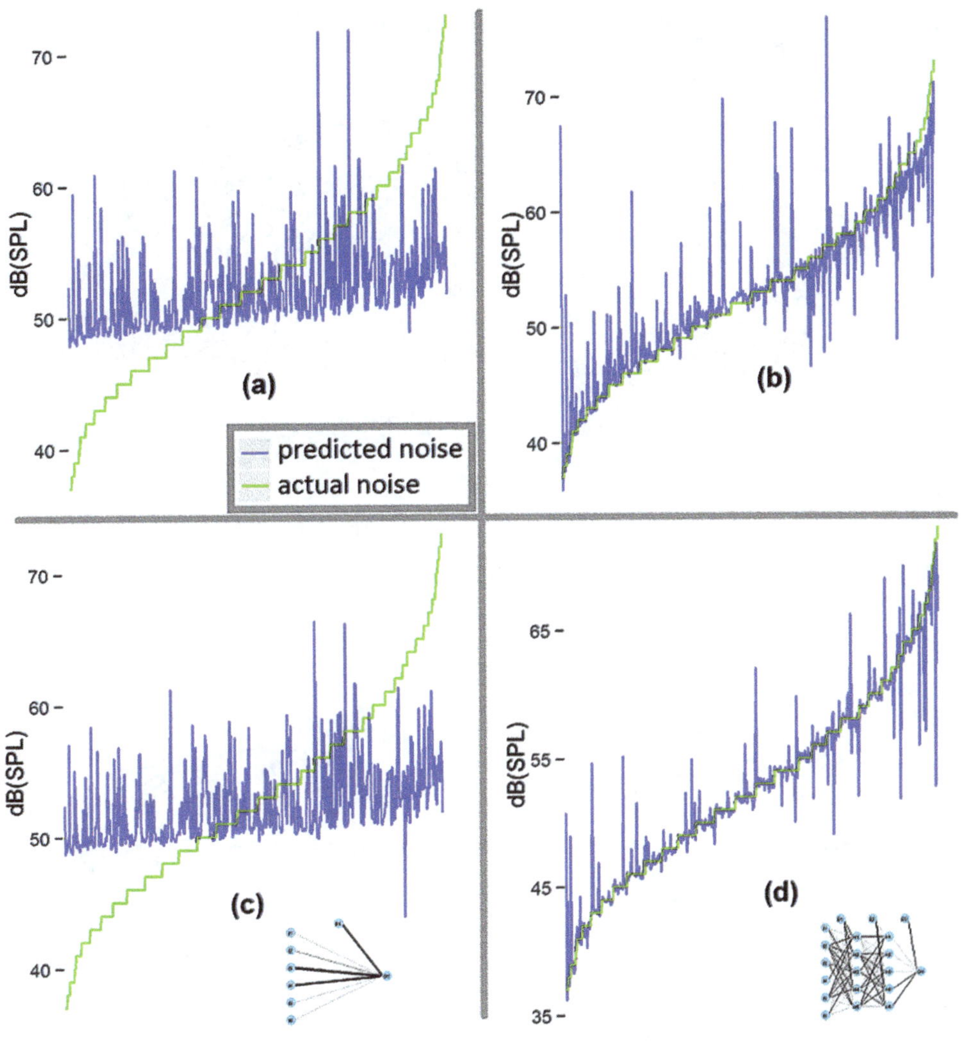

Historic Center. With the same interpolation method and the same color code, others noise maps were created using the measurements in the Historic Center within different time intervals. These maps are shown in Figure 16. Regarding the Cuauhtémoc Delegation, the highest noise concentration detected during the tours was in the Centro settlement (almost entirely) and in the Morelos settlement (near the Merced market zone), as can be seen in Figure 15. Moreover, particularly for the Centro settlement, Figure 16 shows that the highest noise concentration was found in streets around the National Palace (streets with high vendors' density, such as Corregidora, Correo Mayor, La Academia, Soledad and Venustiano Carranza). It also shows that, in general, the highest noise levels were registered in the *HNL-12*-time interval, while the lowest noise levels were registered in the HL-06-time interval. In general, we found that the highest average noise levels were caused by the constant noise of people (for example, the shout of street vendors and the continuous talk of crowds), followed by the noise caused by cars. Industrial

Figure 14. Results after varying the C and ξ parameters for SVM ker=rbfdot and k = 10: (a) training time; (b) MAE or test error; (c) training error; (d) CORR; (e) number of support vectors

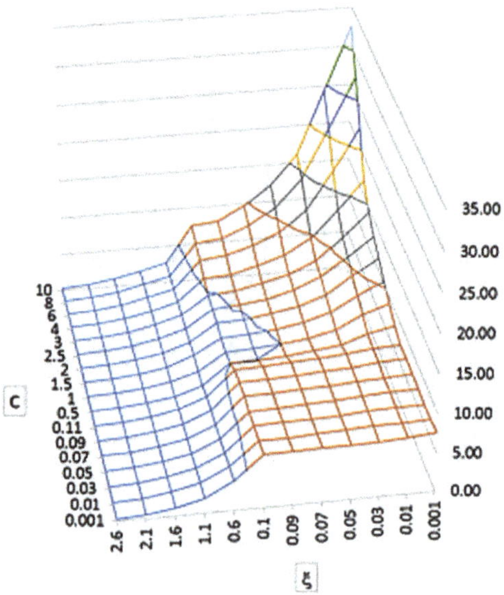

a)

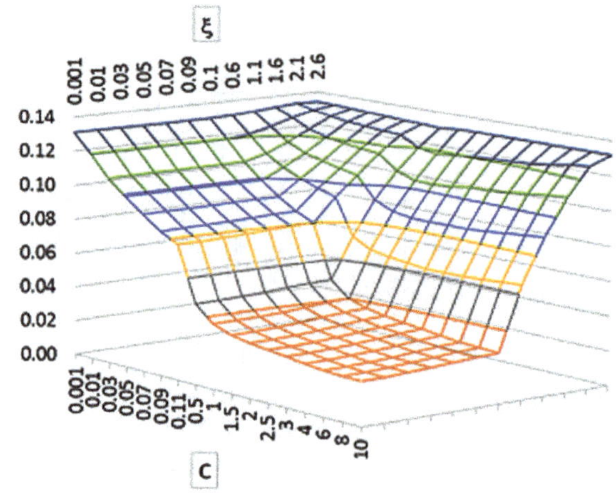

b)

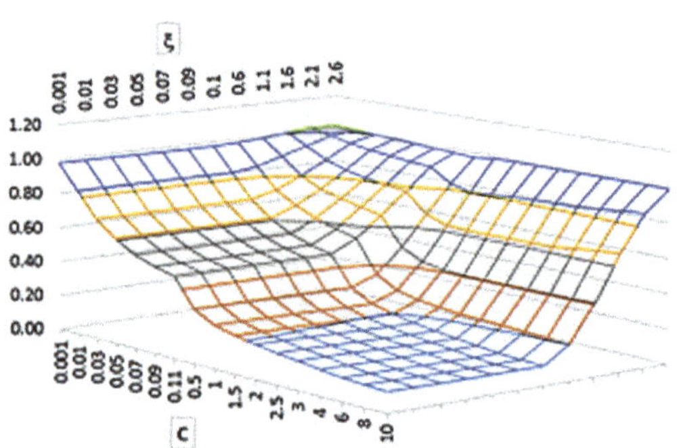

c)

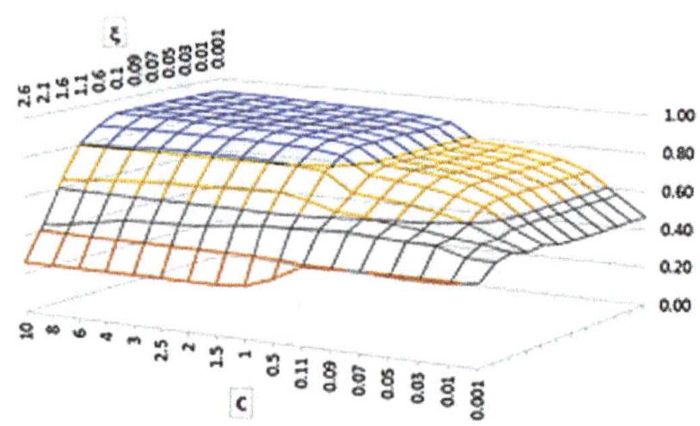

d)

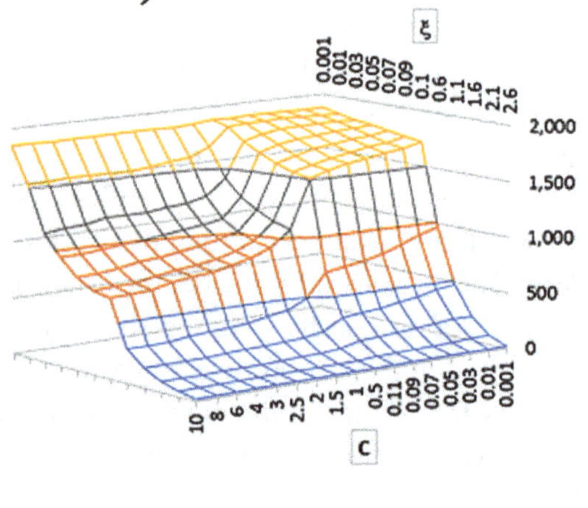

d)

Figure 15. Environmental noise map for Cuauhtémoc Delegation

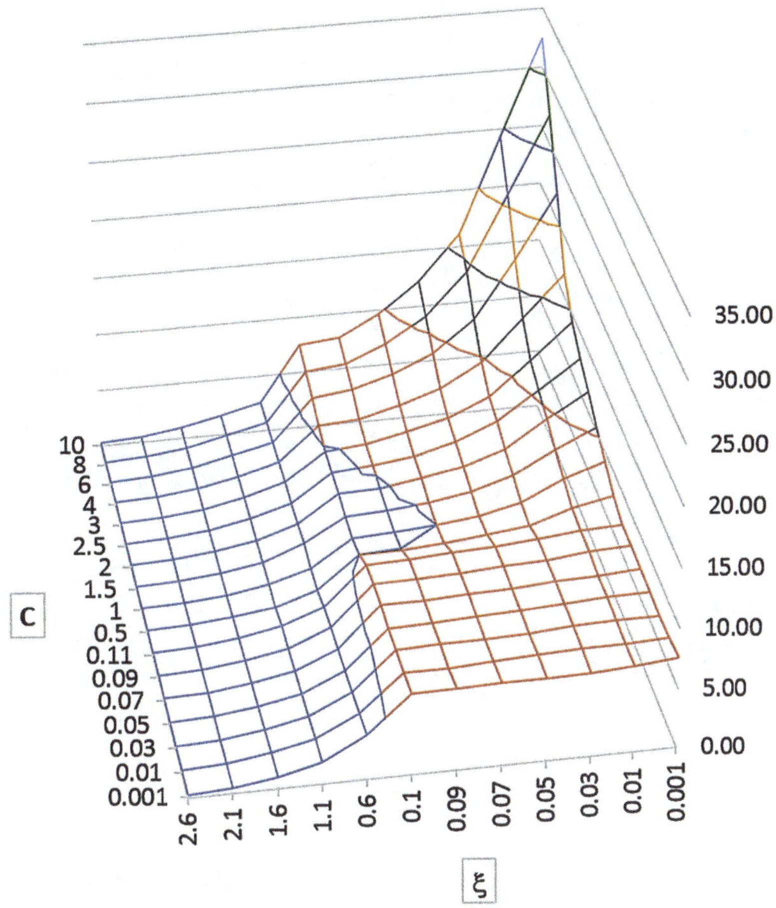

areas, such as in the Atlampla settlement, as opposite to what is expected, were found to be among the most peaceful and quiet areas, probably because those industries isolate inside the noise and the streets nearby them, they have few cars and people.

In general, the areas with the lowest noise levels were the inside of large parks and areas surrounded by trees, such as in the Hipodromo and the Tlatelolco settlements. Some of the most intense noises detected with the application, were impulsive sounds, such as the sneezing of people, the shout of a gas seller, the siren of a patrol or dogs barking. After predicting noise levels at various geographic points using ML and then applying an interpolation method with the Barnes algorithm using the GeoServer plug-in, it was possible to obtain the noise map, with measurements and predicted noise levels in the Cuauhtémoc Delegation.

Figure 17 shows a comparison between the noise map obtained by interpolation with Quantum GIS (left) on which points for the ML model are superimposed, and a noise map obtained using interpolation in GeoServer (right) for the *HL-12*-time interval. It is possible to compare the previously shown environmental noise maps against noise observations obtained by the NoiseWatch project, although they

Figure 16. Environmental noise maps for streets around the Historic Center

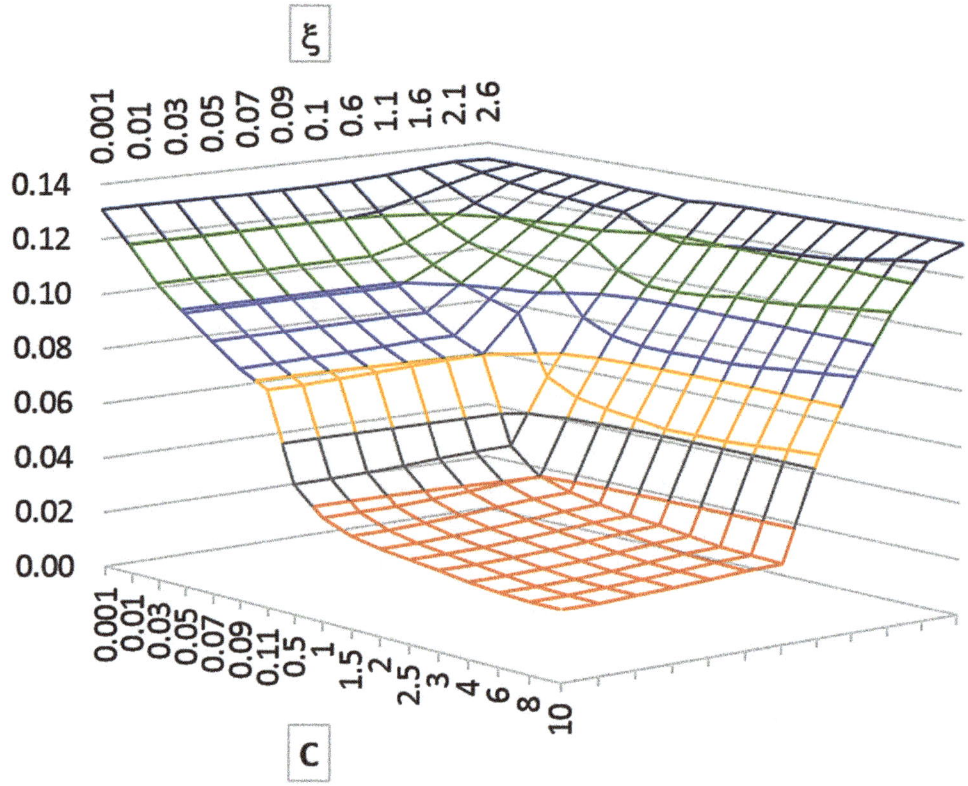

Figure 17. Noise map generated with measurements on which predicted values are superimposed (left) compared against a noise map generated with both measurements and predicted values (right)

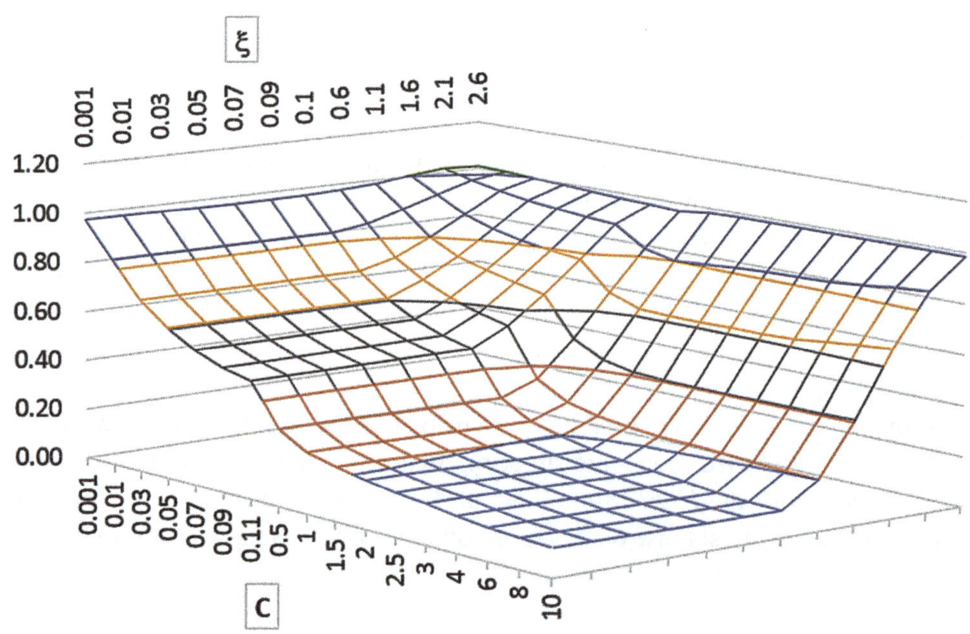

Figure 18.

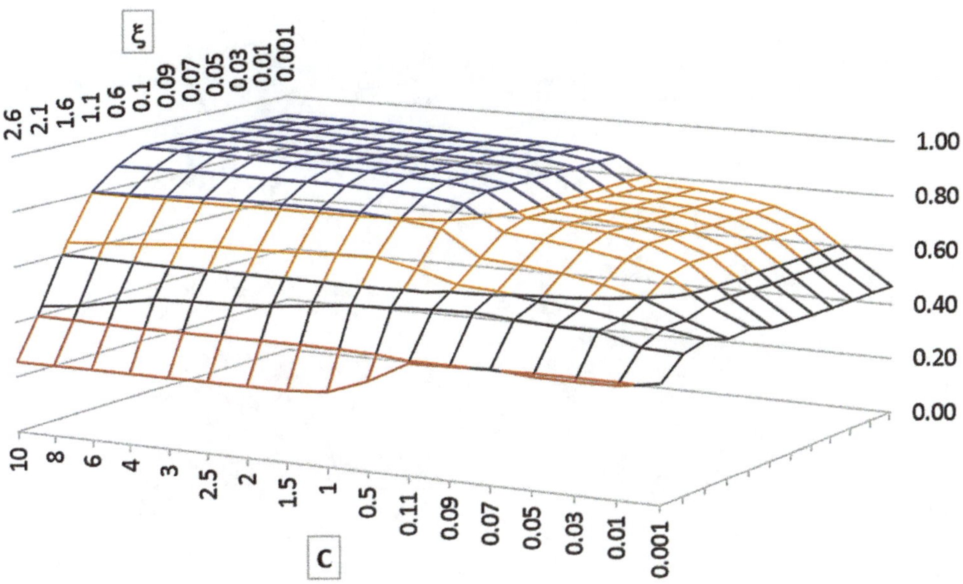

Figure 19.

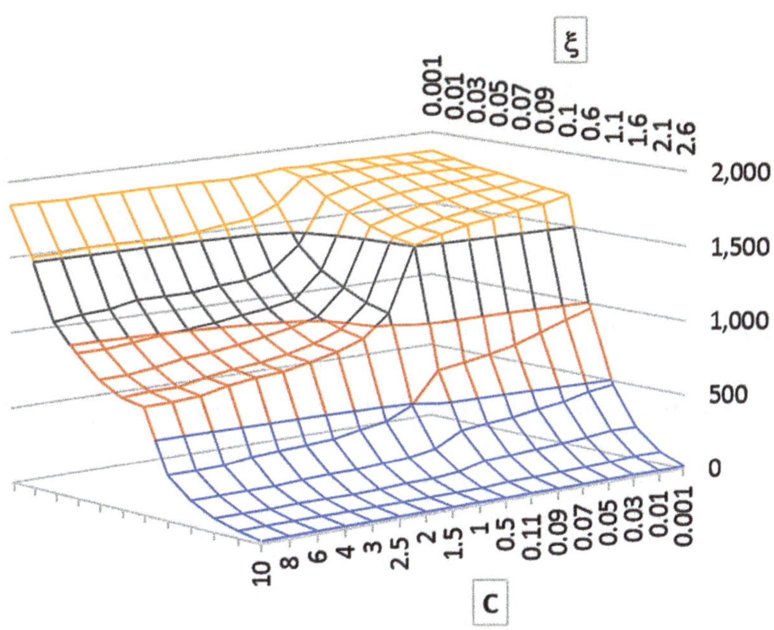

have a different subjective categorical scale, which includes the *Very Bad*, *Bad*, *Moderate*, *Good* and *Very Good* categories. The measurements in that project show good correlation. With this approach it is possible to obtain maps made with discrete points as NoiseWatch, as well as the continuous noise map made with interpolation covering the area of interest.

Figure 20.

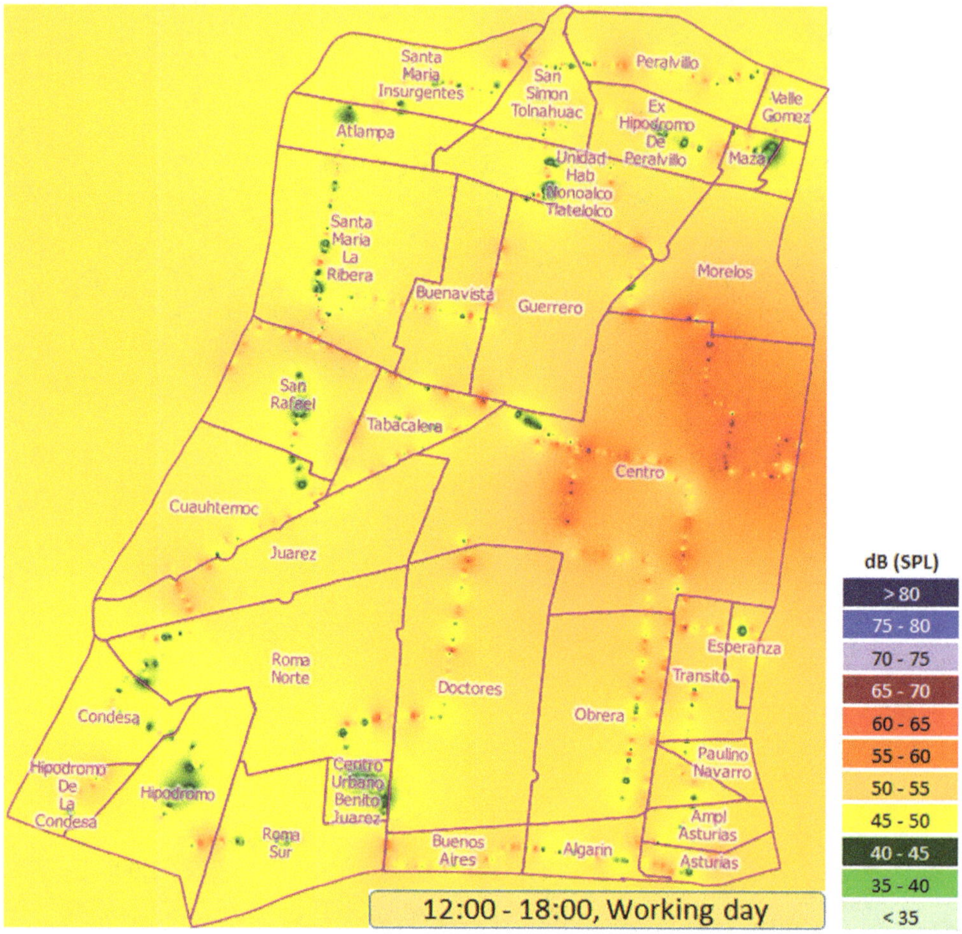

4.4 Considerations About the Results

Noise measurements were performed with a mobile device ZTE-V791. The geographic positions were obtained mainly using the GPS of mobile device, only a very small amount of them was obtained by WiFi positioning. Since the measurements correspond to sound pressure level, to get them the user had to remain immobile during the 10 seconds that the capture of noise lasted. Taking the measurement while moving was avoided to prevent the air hitting the device's microphone to cause more pressure on it, resulting in a higher noise level reading than the one actually existent. In addition, efforts were made to be impartial when making the measurements, not looking to record only events that showed a higher noise level, but trying to capture the sound at regular intervals (for example, each time the user had walked half a block) regardless of the noise level subjectively perceived there while looking for favorable weather conditions.

Figure 21.

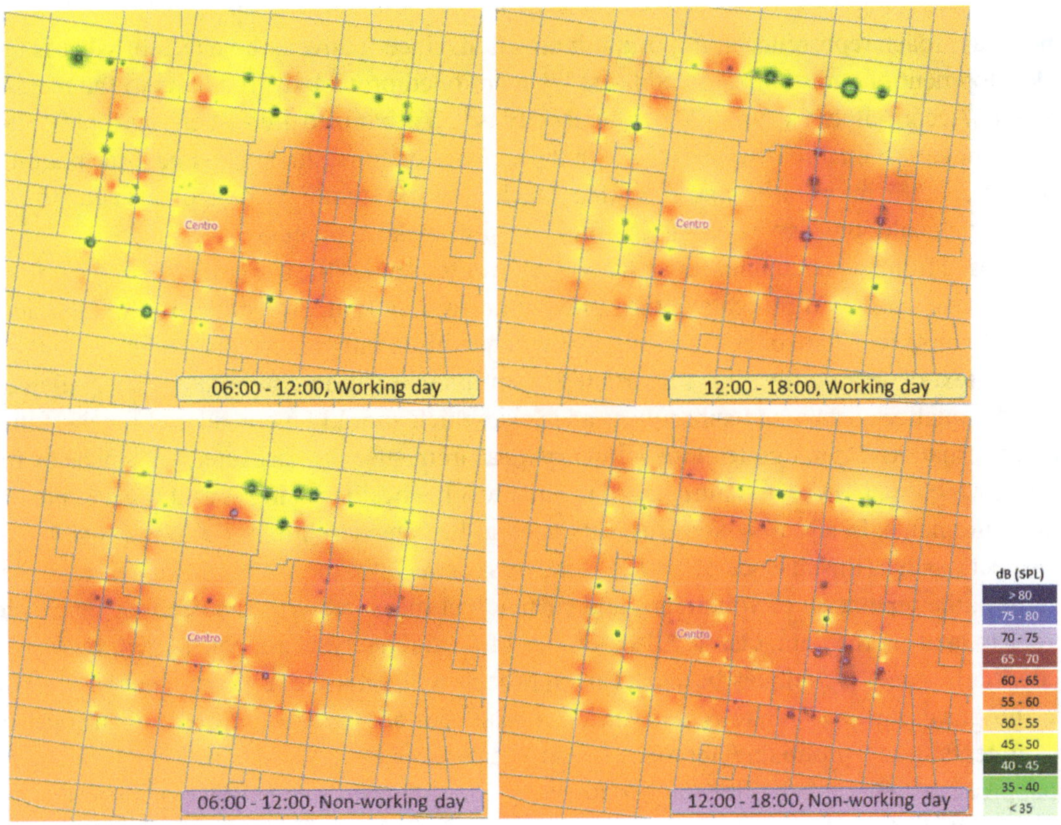

Figure 22.

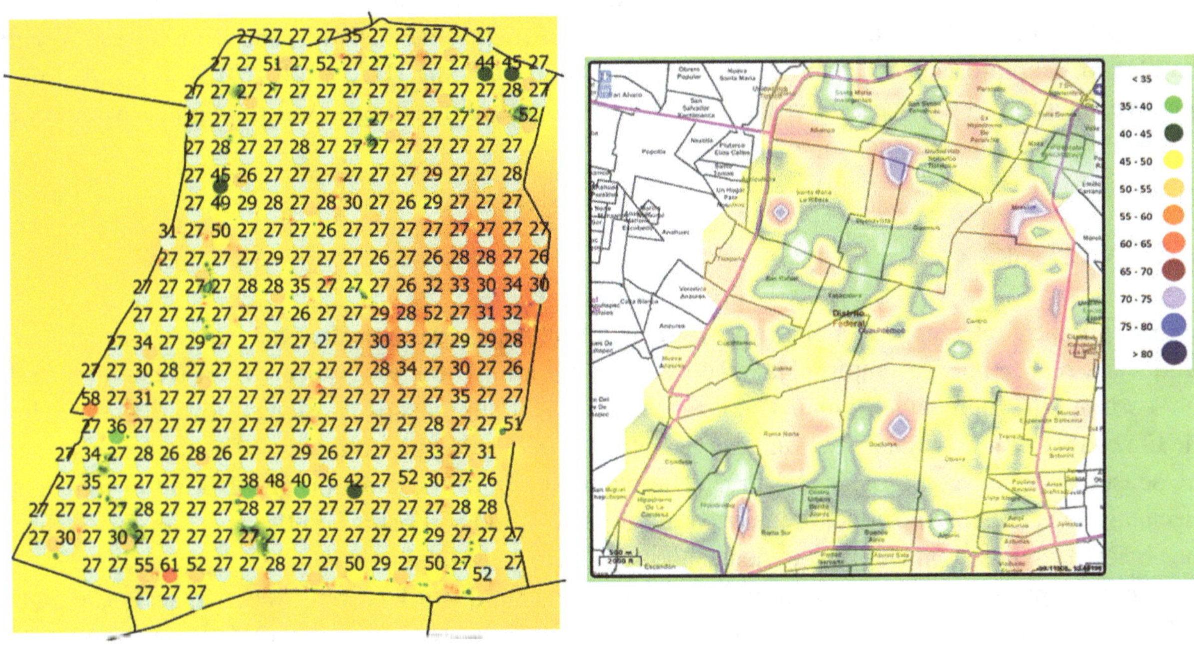

5. FUTURE RESEARCH DIRECTIONS

This kind of approach represents an important innovation, since it covers the needs of what is required for the development of smart cities, in addition, as mentioned previously, it adapts to the needs of the development. According to Gartner (2016), smart city is "an urbanized area where multiple sectors co-operate to achieve sustainable outcomes through the analysis of contextual real-time information shared among sector-specific information and operational technology systems". Governments need to establish links so that such solutions can be integrated into decision-making process.

The proposed framework contains the required features to support the use of data collected by citizens in order to define actions to mitigate and/or prevent noise pollution. According to this operation, the framework attempts to enhance the following tasks: acquisition, integration, presentation, analysis, and use in the context of smart cities. It is important to mention that validation of data is a key element that delineates the quality of data and subsequent analysis, which should be considered for the future. An interesting alternative is to integrate these voluntary measurements with measurements made by measuring stations, which will allow obtaining more refined results, besides using it as a criterion to validate citizen measurements. In addition, some aspects need to be considered in order to improve the quality of data, aspects such as the absence of quality standards for specific thematic, the lack of expert control in the capture, the reputation of volunteers, and currency of measurement data needs to be considered.

In order to analyze the data, classic GIS methods of spatial analysis are considered, but it is necessary to define big data techniques because this approach will generate a big amount of information. With this proposal, it is possible to build big data repositories and integrate data from various sources. For governments, it is a promising approach because it reduces the costs and time at difference to traditional approaches. On the other hand, big data techniques are proposed because this application aims to collect, to integrate and to analyze a very large set of data that cannot be treated using traditional methods (Jiang and Thill, 2015). According to Gartner, big data techniques have three properties: 1) it has a high-volume, 2) it is collected with high velocity, and 3) it includes variety asset information; it can be seen as the approach herein fit to this work. The big data approach has advantages of revealing individual characteristics rather than a general feature of traditional statistics, and it is consistent with the idea of people-oriented urbanization and urban–rural planning (Hao et al., 2015). From this perspective, data must be processed with advanced tools to reveal meaningful information by using tools as machine learning methods.

6. CONCLUSION

In this approach, citizens play a vital role, as their role changes dramatically from simple users to data producers, representing a major advantage over traditional approaches, especially in terms of speed, low cost and the high data volume. The use of this kind of approaches is oriented towards improving the life quality of inhabitants, providing services that incrementing the smartness of a city, because data are sensed and analyzed in near real-time. The main benefit of the creation of this kind of tools and mechanisms is to help inform and sensitize the population and authorities on the noise levels to which the society is exposed, in an effort to detect and stop, or at least to slow down.

The work presented here is one of those possibilities, and that it has some benefits, such as the use of VGI. This approach has found that, taking advantage of VGI, from a set of georeferenced noise measurements obtained voluntarily by people with their own mobile devices, for a subsequent analysis and predictions. The study of previous works relative to environmental noise monitoring has allowed us to define a methodology as well as to perform the analysis, design and development.

ACKNOWLEDGMENT

The authors whish to thank to the Instituto Politécnico Nacional (IPN), the Consejo Nacional de Ciencia y Tecnología (CONACyT) and the Secretaría de Investigación y Posgrado (SIP) projects 20171918 and 20171192, to support this research.

REFERENCES

Anton, D., & Anton, A. (2012). *Ecología y medio ambiente*. Mexico City, Mexico: ST Editorial.

Bilandzic, M., Banholzer, M., Peev, D., Georgiev, V., Balagtas-Fernandez, F., & De Luca, A. (2008, October). Laermometer: a mobile noise mapping application. In *Proceedings of the 5th Nordic conference on Human-computer interaction: building bridges* (pp. 415-418). ACM. doi:10.1145/1463160.1463208

Connors, J. P., Lei, S., & Kelly, M. (2012). Citizen science in the age of neogeography: Utilizing volunteered geographic information for environmental monitoring. *Annals of the Association of American Geographers*, *102*(6), 1267–1289. doi:10.1080/00045608.2011.627058

Elwood, S., Goodchild, M. F., & Sui, D. Z. (2012). Researching volunteered geographic information: Spatial data, geographic research, and new social practice. *Annals of the Association of American Geographers*, *102*(3), 571–590. doi:10.1080/00045608.2011.595657

Fonte, C. C., Bastin, L., Foody, G., Kellenberger, T., Kerle, N., & Mooney, P. et al.. (2015). VGI quality control. *Proceedings of the ISPRS Geospatial Week 2015*, 317-324.

Gartner. (2016). *Predicts 2016: IoT Technologies Optimize Smart City Operations*. Gartner.

Goodchild, M. F. (2007). Citizens as sensors: The world of volunteered geography. *GeoJournal*, *69*(4), 211–221. doi:10.1007/s10708-007-9111-y

Goodchild, M. F. (2009). Geographic information systems and science: Today and tomorrow. *Annals of GIS*, *15*(1), 3–9. doi:10.1080/19475680903250715

Halonen, J. I., Hansell, A. L., Gulliver, J., Morley, D., Blangiardo, M., Fecht, D., & Tonne, C. et al. (2015). Road traffic noise is associated with increased cardiovascular morbidity and mortality and all-cause mortality in London. *European Heart Journal*, *36*(39), 2653–2661. doi:10.1093/eurheartj/ehv216 PMID:26104392

Hao, J., Zhu, J., & Zhong, R. (2015). The rise of big data on urban studies and planning practices in China: Review and open research issues. *Journal of Urban Management*, *4*(2), 92–124. doi:10.1016/j.jum.2015.11.002

Ising, H. L., & Kruppa, B. (2004). Health effects caused by noise: Evidence in the literature from the past 25 years. *Noise & Health*, *6*(22), 5. PMID:15070524

Jiang, B., & Thill, J. C. (2015). Volunteered Geographic Information: Towards the establishment of a new paradigm. *Computers, Environment and Urban Systems*, *53*, 1–3. doi:10.1016/j.compenvurbsys.2015.09.011

Jirka, S., Brring, A., Kjeld, P., Maidens, J., & Wytzisk, A. (2012). A lightweight approach for the sensor observation service to share environmental data across Europe. *Transactions in GIS*, *16*(3), 293–312. doi:10.1111/j.1467-9671.2012.01324.x

Kaiser, C., & Pozdnoukhov, A. (2013). Enabling real-time city sensing with kernel stream oracles and mapreduce. *Pervasive and Mobile Computing*, *9*(5), 708–721. doi:10.1016/j.pmcj.2012.11.003

Kanjo, E. (2010). Noisespy: A real-time mobile phone platform for urban noise monitoring and mapping. *Mobile Networks and Applications*, *15*(4), 562–574. doi:10.1007/s11036-009-0217-y

Karolus, J. (2013). *Creating Noise Pollution Maps Based on User-generated Noise Measurements: Erstellung Von Lärmkarten Basierend Auf Nutzergenerierten Lautstärkemessungen* (Doctoral dissertation).

Lantz, B. (2013). *Machine learning with R*. Packt Publishing Ltd.

Liu, T., Zheng, Y., Liu, L., Liu, Y., & Zhu, Y. (2014). *Methods for sensing urban noises* (Tec. Rep. MSRTR- 2014-66). Academic Press.

Maisonneuve, N., Stevens, M., Niessen, M. E., & Steels, L. (2009). NoiseTube: Measuring and mapping noise pollution with mobile phones. In Information Technologies in Environmental Engineering (pp. 215-228). Springer Berlin Heidelberg.

Middleton, S. E., Middleton, L., & Modafferi, S. (2014). Real-time crisis mapping of natural disasters using social media. *IEEE Intelligent Systems*, *29*(2), 9–17. doi:10.1109/MIS.2013.126

Nakano, N., Tratz-Ryan, B., & Freeman, D. (2015). *Predicts 2016: IoT Technologies Optimize Smart City Operations*. Gartner.

Parker, C. J., May, A., & Mitchell, V. (2013). The role of VGI and PGI in supporting outdoor activities. *Applied Ergonomics*, *44*(6), 886–894. doi:10.1016/j.apergo.2012.04.013 PMID:22795180

Quintero, G. (2013). *Sistema móvil georeferenciado para la medición y análisis de ruido ambiental*. CIC-IPN.

Rana, R. K., Chou, C. T., Kanhere, S. S., Bulusu, N., & Hu, W. (2010, April). Ear-phone: an end-to-end participatory urban noise mapping system. In *Proceedings of the 9th ACM/IEEE International Conference on Information Processing in Sensor Networks* (pp. 105-116). ACM. doi:10.1145/1791212.1791226

Rodriguez Manzo, F. E. (2011). *Elaboración del primer mapa ruido y conformación de la red piloto de monitoreo de ruido para la ZMVM*. UAM.

Sánchez, L. (2011). *Modelo computacional para generar un mapa de ruido ambiental utilizando mediciones en tiempo real* (Ph.D. Doctoral Thesis). Centro de Investigación en Computación, IPN, México.

Schweizer, I., Bärtl, R., Schulz, A., Probst, F., & Muhläuser, M. (2011, November). NoiseMap-real-time participatory noise maps. *Proc. 2nd Int'l Workshop on Sensing Applications on Mobile Phones (PhoneSense'11)*, 1-5.

Sui, D. Z. (2008). The wikification of GIS and its consequences: Or Angelina Jolies new tattoo and the future of GIS. *Computers, Environment and Urban Systems*, *32*(1), 1–5. doi:10.1016/j.compenvurbsys.2007.12.001

Weymouth, G., Mills, G. A., Jones, D., Ebert, E. E., & Manton, M. J. (1999). A continental-scale daily rainfall analysis system. *Australian Meteorological Magazine*, *48*(3), 169–179.

Xia, Y., Winterhalter, M., & Fabian, P. (1999). A model to interpolate monthly mean climatological data at Bavarian forest climate stations. *Theoretical and Applied Climatology*, *64*(1-2), 27–38. doi:10.1007/s007040050108

Zheng, Y., Capra, L., Wolfson, O., & Yang, H. (2014). Urban computing: Concepts, methodologies, and applications. *ACM Transactions on Intelligent Systems and Technology*, *5*(3), 38. doi:10.1145/2629592

Zheng, Y., Liu, T., Wang, Y., Zhu, Y., Liu, Y., & Chang, E. (2014, September). Diagnosing New York city's noises with ubiquitous data. In *Proceedings of the 2014 ACM International Joint Conference on Pervasive and Ubiquitous Computing* (pp. 715-725). ACM. doi:10.1145/2632048.2632102

KEY TERMS AND DEFINITIONS

Environmental Noise Maps: Cartographic represention of environmental noise.

GIS (Geographic Information System): Information system developed to store, manipulate, analize and visualize geospatial data.

Machine Learning: An application of Artificial Intelligence (AI) that provides systems the ability to automatically learn and improve from experience without being explicitly programmed.

Smart Cities: Urban development vision to incorporate information and communication technology to manage a city's assets.

Support Vector Machines (SVM): An algorithm that performs classification by finding the hyperplane that maximizes the margin between the classes.

VGI (Voluntereed Geographic Information): User-generated content in the geographic context.

Chapter 14
Innovation Contests:
How to Engage Citizens in Solving Urban Problems?

Sarah Hartmann
Heinrich Heine University Duesseldorf, Germany

Agnes Mainka
Heinrich Heine University Düsseldorf, Germany

Wolfgang G. Stock
Heinrich Heine University Düsseldorf, Germany

ABSTRACT

Cities all over the world are challenged with problems evolving from increasing urbanity, population growth, and density. For example, one prominent issue that is addressed in many cities is mobility. To develop smart city solutions, governments are trying to introduce open innovation. They have started to open their governmental and city related data as well as awake the citizens' awareness on urban problems through innovation contests. Citizens are the users of the city and therefore, have a practical motivation to engage in innovation contests as for example in hackathons and app competitions. The collaboration and co-creation of civic services by means of innovation contests is a cultural development of how governments and citizens work together in an open governmental environment. A qualitative analysis of innovation contests in 24 world cities reveals this global trend. In particular, such events increase the awareness of citizens and local businesses for identifying and solving urban challenges and are helpful means to transfer the smart city idea into practicable solutions.

INTRODUCTION

Today, many governments as well as municipalities open up their data and make them available online on governmental open data portals. Such open data portals are available on the international level, e.g. http://data.europa.eu/euodp/en/data/ (European Union Open Data Portal), on the national level, e.g. https://www.data.gov/ (U.S.), https://data.gov.uk/ (United Kingdom), but also on the city level, e.g. https://open.

DOI: 10.4018/978-1-5225-4191-2.ch014

wien.gv.at/ (Vienna, Austria) or https://opendata.cityofnewyork.us/ (New York City, NY) and typically provide data that is available free of charge and possible to be re-used without any limitations or technical restrictions (Open Knowledge International, n.d.a). This data is often referred to as open government data and offers non-rivalrous, non-excludable as well as valuable information to citizens (Jetzek, Avital, & Bjørn-Andersen, 2013). Primarily on the municipal level, there are huge amounts of data generated e.g. by sensors which are relevant in citizens' everyday life and can referred to as open urban government data (Mainka, Hartmann, Meschede, & Stock, 2015a). By opening their data, governments aim at fostering participation, collaboration, and transparency, as well as economic and social values as citizens and companies can or will use the data to produce innovative products and services (Albano, 2013; European Commission, 2011). In particular, open data competitions (European Commission, 2011) or digital innovation contests are assumed to be helpful means to foster civic participation in the re-use of open data. Hjalmarsson & Rudmark (2012, p. 10) define such a contest as "an event in which third-party developers compete to design and implement the firmest and most satisfying digital service prototype, for a specific purpose, based on open data." This idea is taken one-step further by the concept of app competitions or hackathons (hack marathons) where governments and citizens develop new (mobile) applications in cooperation. These events are aimed at involving citizens to solve specific problems or address stated topics and are assumed to be a new way for civic engagement and participation. People from different backgrounds can come together at one table and try to create something value added to improve city life. The involvement of citizens in developing problem-solving innovation can be referred to as open government (Mainka et al., 2015a). However, do hackathons or similar contests help to develop value added services? Do all municipalities host the same events or are there differences? What are the outcomes of these events and how do governments accomplish them? This chapter aims at exploring the phenomenon of open innovation contests like hackathons and app competitions in more detail in order to figure out whether these events are indeed used by smart cities around the globe to engage citizens, to highlight differences between contests, and emphasize best practice examples. The analysis is based on informational world cities defined by Mainka et al. (2015a). Those cities are prototypical cities of the knowledge society and provide an enhanced ICT infrastructure. Hackathons and app competitions often take place in big cities, therefore a set of 24 cities was chosen as a starting point of a global investigation of innovation contests.

THE IDEA OF INNOVATION CONTESTS

More than the half of today's world population lives in urbanized areas. This evokes many problems for citizens, urban planners, and the government. In addition, smartphones and mobile connectivity have gained increasing importance in recent years and mobile exceeds fixed broadband subscriptions (Burger, 2012). In so-called "informational cities" (Castells, 1989) or "smart cities" (Castelnovo, Misuraca, & Savoldelli, 2015) citizens own and use mobile devices (Stock, 2011) and their demand for "services that increase their productivity, efficiency, communication skills, or create experiences that enhance their quality of life" (Walravens, 2015, p. 282) rises. Thus, especially in larger cities, governments are increasingly challenged to solve citizens' problems, improve their services and the quality of life. Data driven investigations and mobile apps that help citizens in everyday life could be a solution.

In informational cities not only a well-developed ICT infrastructure plays a crucial role in a city's growth and development but also human and social capital. Therefore, smart municipalities should aim at enhancing the quality of life in the city and boosting its economic growth in order to create a public social and economic value for all citizens (Caragliu, Del Bo, & Nijkamp, 2009). However, citizens' participation is required in order to fulfill their needs and provide services that indeed ease their everyday life. In our history citizens often have volunteered, e.g. as bodyguards in neighborhood safety patrols. According to Bellone & Goerl (1992), in some cases, citizens are able to provide better service than their government is able to. Since governments have opened their data and publish it on public data portals, citizens can help themselves and their community to transform open data into value-added services, for example through developing new smartphone apps. To take this one-step further, the data of smartphone applications can then again feed into governments' open data portals as for example in the case of the 311 service response system via which citizens can report issues or request city services via mobile apps. Thus, citizens do not necessarily have to be in the app development in order to create valuable services based on open government data, also citizens who do not have any programming skills may be asked to participate by using apps, "for example helping to redesign the park you're walking in" (Millard, 2010, p. 8). In this case, citizens are "data prosumers (both providers and consumers of data)" (Charalabidis, Loukis, & Alexopoulos, 2014). The data provided by the citizens, e.g. via 311 is also often published on governmental open data portals and can be used as a starting point for hackathons and app competitions (Hartmann, Mainka, & Stock, 2017). Hence, the data flow from the government to the citizens, who work with the data, has now changed into a bi-directional data exchange and even co-production becomes possible with the help of hackathons and app-competitions (Robinson & Johnson, 2016; Sieber & Johnson, 2015). It is not only the cities' government that plays an important part in transforming their city into a smart city but also the people within the city are a critical factor for success (Chourabi et al., 2012).

If citizens became developer of urban applications, the services are called 'citizen apps' (Desouza & Bhagwatwar, 2012). But designing mobile apps by end-users "can require significant technological innovation, and prizes can act as an inducement for innovation to such challenging development tasks" (Desouza & Bhagwatwar, 2012, p. 109). Therefore, innovation contests like app competitions or hackathons can be organized to develop mobile services collectively and motivate the public (Baraniuk, 2013; Briscoe & Mulligan, 2014). The concept of innovation contests refers to the use of these events in order to benefit from innovative ideas and solutions submitted by people outside of the organization that is hosting the contest (Hjalmarsson, Juell-Skielse, & Johannesson, 2017). However, hosting these events, which can last from one or two days up to several months, requires much support which in some cases is offered by governmental agencies like the Infocomm Development Authority (has now been renamed to Infocomm Media Development Authority) of Singapore, a supporter of the *AppVenture Challenge* (Chan, 2013). This is aggravated by the fact that still less is known about how to construct such events in order to achieve citizens' engagement as well as valuable and successful services. Juell-Skielse, Hjalmarsson, Johannesson, and Rudmark (2014) found out that fun and enjoyment, intellectual challenge, and status and reputation are the top three drivers of participation in innovation contests. By contrast, extrinsic motivation like money was stated to be less important for participants. In addition, Immonen, Palviainen, and Ovaska (2014) propose that the development of urban apps should be embedded in an "open data based business ecosystem" (p. 88), which consists of elements such as key partners, co-creation, revenue strategies, customers and markets, data structure, business development, and the value added. Such a business ecosystem is targeted at ensuring the sustainability of mobile apps (and not a quick development of an app followed by stopping the product some weeks later).

The question arises whether city governments in fact involve their citizens in the mobile app development process by hosting innovation contests and if they aim at creating successful and valuable solutions for their citizens, which can be assumed to be only seldom successful ad hoc, but to need further support in most cases. Furthermore, not only governments can be the initiators of these events, also citizens could organize them in order to build useful services based on the data that is available on governmental open data portals. The need for a long lasting support as well as the continuous development of the resulting apps might be only a few of the challenges that have to be met. Therefore, it is still unclear if these events are indeed useful, for example, to increase citizens-to-government communication and collaboration, or merely a hype with less effect (Johnson & Robinson, 2014; Hellberg & Hedström, 2015). For these reasons, an overview of innovation contests in 24 informational world cities will be given in the following and shall help explore different types of contests, their outcomes, organizers and supporters, as well as the challenges and opportunities that governments should consider before hosting such events.

METHOD

In order to answer the afore-mentioned issues, the innovation contest movement was analyzed through a web content research, since hackathons and app competitions are related to online available resources, i.e. promotions and reviews are hosted online, e.g. on government websites, blogs, as well as online news platforms. For this reason, an Internet search for announcements of hackathons and app competitions as well as experience reports using Google as a search engine was conducted. As it can be assumed that there is a greater need for these events in world cities, 24 informational world cities (as defined by Mainka et al. (2015a)) were used as the basis for the investigation (see appendix). To identify the respective competitions and events keywords like government data, open data, competition, contest, hackathon, and app in combination with the specific city name were used. The findings of this chapter have previously been published in the International Journal of Knowledge Society Research by Hartmann, Mainka, and Stock (2016) but were revised and updated extensively in June 2017.

INNOVATION CONTESTS AROUND THE GLOBE

For all 24 cities, hackathons or app competitions could be identified. Popular terms to describe open data contests are hackathon, app challenge, app competition, prototype-athon, appathon as well as hack or code festival which all can be summarized by the term ‘innovation contest’. The first events of this type presumably took place at Sun Microsystems and OpenBSD. Both used the term hackathon independently from each other for the first time in 1999 to announce a hack event for their employees. By using this term, they referred to events which were aimed at developing new software and not at committing computer crimes (Briscoe & Mulligan, 2014). However, differences between app competitions and hackathons can be found in their duration and setting. A hackathon is usually held offline, which means that people meet locally between one and three days, often at weekends, whereas app competitions take place for several months with a deadline till then the finished projects have to be handed in online. In addition, hackathons often allow for developing a new service in a small team whereas competitions in many cases call single persons or companies for submitting their applications. The initiative to host the event was found to come from the government (top-down) in most cases. Often they work in cooperation with local companies as well as NGOs and NPOs but also the hacker community hosted events in some cities (bottom-up). Additionally, several cities, e.g. Los Angeles, have already hosted specific hackathons (e.g. *Hack for LA*) several times (as in the case of LA every year since 2013) whereas others have only taken place once heretofore, e.g. the *Data in the City Hackathon* by Singapore in 2013.

Scope of Innovation Contests

Although it was searched for events in relation to cities, it turned out that hackathons and app competitions are not only a city-specific phenomenon. They can be hosted for different areas, for example, New York City (city level) or larger areas like New South Wales (state level), Finland (national level), the whole European Union (trans-national level), or all over the world (international level). Nowadays this concept of app development takes place in cities and regions all over the world, e.g. Boston, Amsterdam, and Paris, but it has its origins in the US were one of the first innovation contests called *Apps for Democracy*[1] was held in Washington in 2008 (Johnson & Robinson, 2014). The aim of this contest was to make the DC.gov's data catalog useful for everybody within the city. They managed to achieve 47 mobile applications with an estimated value of $2,300,000 by spending $50,000 on the contest (ISL, 2017).

An example of a nationwide competition is *Apps4Finland*, which is hosted in collaboration with the city of Helsinki since 2009 and was renamed in *Open Finland Challenge* in 2015. Often the resulting applications from other challenges, e.g. *Open Helsinki – Hack at Home* are handed in for competitions which address larger areas, as e.g. the *Open Finland Challenge*. Those competitions are organized, partnered, and sponsored by a wide range of institutions. In the case of the *Open Finland Challenge* the Open Knowledge Finland, the Forum Virium Helsinki as well as over a dozen additional partners support the event (Open Finland Challenge, n.d.). Some federal states, like New South Wales, use a concept named *apps4nsw* to call for applications based on the government data of NSW. This was the first competition in Australia which encouraged its participants to use state government data (N. S. W. Government, n.d.) and tries to bridge between government, citizens, and industry on the level of a federal state. Also the *Canadian Open Data Experience {CODE}* is a 48-hours hackathon on the federal level that invites participants to use open government data from all levels, i.e. provincial, territorial, municipal, and federal data to build applications (Canada.ca, n.d.).

Furthermore, there is a concept called *Apps for Europe*, which could be understood as an international network that hosts hackathons (among other events). They want to support valuable applications in their whole development process and "provide tools to transform ideas for data based apps into viable businesses" (Apps for Europe, n.d.a). Similar to *Apps for Europe* is the *National Day of Civic Hacking*. This concept started as a national one and has grown up by 2014 to be international, which is special as hackathons – usually – are held locally. However, although it is an international event by now, local meetings still take place but henceforth all over the world at the same time and aim at raising collaborations between residents, communities, and governments (DHMN Civic Hacks, April 09, 2015). An example of an international hackathon is also the *International Open Data Day* that is hold in the seventh year now (Open Data Day 2017, n.d.). This event takes place once a year at one single day all over the world and had more than 140 participating cities in 2014 (Weissman, February 24, 2014). In addition, it is one of the few examples which are not awarded but for fun. Instead of monetary awards, the support of open data usage and development of useful services for the neighborhood should be the main motivations to join these hackathons but also meeting new people, discussing ideas, and improving skills can be reasons why people attend the events. Some cities also use this international hackathon day as a starting point to set up a city-wide hackathon that addresses their specific issues as for example in the case of the *Democracy Hackathon Helsinki* that should bring together developers who like to develop new tools that enhance democracy and are based on open data (Forum Virium Helsinki, February 12, 2016).

The *Open Stockholm Award* is a noteworthy competition which not only allows Stockholm's residents to take part in the contest but calls for participants from all over the world (Stockholms stad, n.d.). Some originally national level competitions started to build broader networks by forwarding their contributions to an international competition like the *Smart City App Hack*. For example, participants of the *Open Finland Challenge* also took part in the *Helsinki Smart City App Hack* and competed with contributions from Barcelona, Dubai, and Phoenix at the *Smart City Expo* held in Barcelona in October 2015 (Appcircus, 2015). However, not only citizens can hand in their ideas and solutions in innovation contests, even city governments' themselves have a chance to compete with their ideas and innovations that are supposed to improve the quality of life in their cities and the work of their governments at the *Mayor's Challenge*. This competition is hosted by the Bloomberg Philanthropies, founded by Mike Bloomberg, and aims at improving civic life all over the world as well as it shall help city governments to get their innovative ideas implemented, earn recognition and learn from each other how they can overcome challenges as for example climate change, civic engagement in public problem solving, and aging populations (Bloomberg.org Group, n.d.).

Civic hackathons and app competitions do not only address people of different nationalities but also with very diverse skills. They primarily appeal on engaged and creative persons to join the events and not for developers and programmers exclusively. For example, Singapore invites "urban planners, architects, sustainability experts, technologists, researchers, developers, and designers to co-create new prototypes to help Singapore become a more livable, competitive and sustainable city" (Newton Circus Pte Ltd, 2017). In addition, Vienna states that the citizens are the most needed and emphasizes that especially statisticians, as well as librarians are wanted participants (OpenDataHackathon 2011, June 18, 2013). By contrast competitions like *apps4austria* also allow companies, institutions, and administrative organizations to participate (Digitales Österreich, n.d.).

Topics and Outcomes

Similar to the scope of competitions also the announced aims and topics can be various. The *Apps for Amsterdam* competition, for example, announced six general themes (vacancy, tourism & culture, democracy, mobility, security, and energy) to which contributions should be addressed (Waag society, Institute for art, science and technology, November 7, 2012) whereas others aim at solving specific problems like the *Safer Communities Hackathon*. This event was held by the Chicago Police Department in 2013 to see in which ways their new API could be used and to improve their interaction with residents (Whitaker, May 14, 2013). In addition, there are special series of hackathons, like the *Green Hackathon* or the *Open Energy Data Challenge* which aim at developing services for sustainability (Green Hackathon, n.d.; Vienna City Administration, n.d.). Another mentionable example is hosted by the citySDK project whose goal it is to harmonize application programming interfaces (APIs) of different cities so that they can be accessed by one common API, e.g. the issue reporting API Open311 (Forum Virium Helsinki, n.d.). This API could then be used for the *citySDK challenge* in 2014 to develop the "best cross-city Smart Participation app" (Hanna, April 17, 2014).

Beside topics also the preferred outcomes of innovation contests can vary. In most cases, hackathons are aimed at developing mobile applications and prototypes, although the *Open Data Day Helsinki Hackathon*[2] primarily focuses on teaching its participants about open data and how it can be used. In a few cases also ideas to solve problems are highly welcomed and awarded, e.g. for the Stockholm Award. With this award, Stockholm not only rewards apps or web services but also project plans which offer solutions within the stated categories (e.g. traffic and accessibility). Furthermore, they ask people who have an idea but do not want to participate to share them via their Twitter feed (Stockholms stad, n.d.). The Singapore government took the call for citizens' ideas one step further and established a platform called *eCitizenIdeas!* (Government of Singapore, 2017). It is supported and funded by a number of city agencies, e.g. Smart Nation and Digital Government Office (SNDGO), the Government Technology Agency (GovTech), Infocomm Media Development Authority (IMDA), National Environmental Agency (NEA), and shall enable citizens to share their ideas and solutions with their government. These ideas do not necessarily have to address hackathons. It is a platform for governmental challenges in general where citizens are asked to co-create innovation by sharing and voting for ideas and distribute the city's challenges in their social networks" (Government of Singapore, 2017). With this platform, the Singaporean Government outsources the generation of ideas to the public what is also known as "crowdsourcing". The term was introduced by Jeff Howe in 2006, who defines it as "the act of a company or institution taking a function once performed by employees and outsourcing it to an undefined (and generally large) network of people in the form of an open call" (Howe, June 02, 2006).

Organizers and Supporters

As the afore-mentioned examples show, lots of hackathons and competitions are organized by governmental agencies. San Francisco is reported to be one of the first cities that published datasets online (they started in 2009) and thus foster the use of open data (Franks, January 11, 2013). The first governmental hackathons and app competitions according to our study were found in Chicago, Helsinki, and New York. In addition, there are also new companies that emerged to host hackathons. One example is *AngelHack* which is operating since 2011 and organizes hackathons for other companies. Whereas their first hackathon was held at Adobe in San Francisco they are now operating internationally (Casecase, n.d.). Besides governmental agencies, NGOs, and companies that organize and support civic innovation contests, there are bottom-up initiatives as well. One example is a group of Chicago volunteers who name themselves *Open City*. Their goal is "to create apps with open data to improve transparency and understanding of our government" (Eder, May 15, 2017). In March 2012, they started to organize weekly hackathons for designing new mobile apps based on open data. These hackathons are open for everyone and have grown up to a group of more than 100 participants (e.g. developers, designers, researchers, journalists, policy wonks, and curious citizens) by now (Eder, May 15, 2017).

An outstanding example of governmental support for app competitions and hackathons is shown by the Infocomm Media Development Authority (IMDA). They are aimed at establishing a whole ecosystem where foreign companies, local enterprises, and start-ups collaborate and grow. They support this by setting up the necessary policies and regulations, infrastructure (e.g. by delivering ultra-high speed broadband access) as well as education for the required workforce (Info-communications Media Development Authority, November 28, 2016). Accordingly, they not only support a large number of innovation contests but also workshops to help people with the development of mobile applications, prototypes or open data visualizations. However, the IMDA is not the only supporter of such events, also a large number of enterprises, NGOs, and other governmental institutions, as well as citizen communities (Urban Prototyping (UP) Singapore and DEXTRA) have worked together to host dozens of hackathons. The Barcelona City Council shows similar ambitious work as it targets to foster innovative mobile applications and supports idea competitions and hackathons, but not only for the city itself. With hackathons like the *Smart City App Hack,* they want to establish "a global network of smart cities that face similar challenges and share one vision: to turn citizens into App Makers, empowering them to build apps and businesses that will make for a better city" (Dotopen S. L., 2015).

Many European hackathons and competitions are supported by a foundation called *Open Knowledge Foundation*, which is separated in single countrywide foundations. This non-profit organization is aimed at opening knowledge and information, supporting projects and collaborations in regard to open data (Open Knowledge International, n.d.b). Another non-profit group of volunteers on a city level is *BetaNYC*, which was founded with the aim of making its government more open, transparent, and participatory. They describe themselves as "a civic organization dedicated to improving lives in New York through civic design, technology, and data" (BetaNYC, n.d.) and organize monthly meetings, events, and support startups in order to create an "informed and empowered public that can leverage civic design, technology, and data to participate in the political process, and hold government accountable" (BetaNYC, n.d.). As members of the *Code for America's Brigade* they are part of a global network of volunteers, local governments, and community partners that aim at building new tools to solve urban problems, connecting people, and exchange about technologies and processes (Code for America Labs, n.d.).

Challenges

It is questionable which status the developed applications or services have. Are the winning services and prototypes indeed ready for use? In the case of *CodeAcrossNYC 2014* hackathon hosted by New York, most of the developed applications are web apps (BetaNYC, February 24, 2014). Whether web applications or smartphone apps, based on specific operating systems were developed most, is difficult to determine since not all events report about their success and publish the winning services. Nevertheless, organizers of hackathons and app competitions have to think not only about the issues and topics for which these events should find solutions but also about the users of the outcomes and their technical environments. Depending on the respective operating system various mobile applications could be needed, whereas mobile web apps would run notwithstanding the operating systems but with limited access options instead. One smartphone application which has become very successful is *Bike Citizens*[3] formerly known as *BikeCityGuide*. It has won nine awards since 2011 (e.g. *Apps for Amsterdam* and *Apps for Europe*) and the Android version has been downloaded between 100.000–500.000 times according to the Google Play Store. But also web applications can become successful, like the Chicago *Flu Shot App*, which was built by a civic hacker in cooperation with the Chicago Health Department and was then also adopted by the Cities of Boston and Philadelphia (Howard, January 17, 2013). The advantage of web apps is that they can be used by a broader range of people since they are independent of any device.

In order to bring a social or economic value out of the competition, the resulting ideas and products have to be accepted and used by citizens. In some cases, the developer gets some assistance from the city or the initiators of the hackathon. This can be in the form of financial, technical, as well as social support, e.g. to connect the developer with existing project groups. The *Apps for Europe* contest even brings it to the next level and not only looks for valuable open data based applications, the competition even aims at bringing the new apps into business (Apps for Europe, n.d.b). For this purpose also a *Business Lounge* event was established that shall give selected startups an opportunity to socialize with international experts (Waag society, Institute for art, science and technology, n.d.). In turn, this event offers the opportunity to win a pitch to the investors of *FutureEverything*[4] in Manchester which is a world leader in the digital and art sector. However, the literature has shown that extrinsic motivations are not among the top drivers of participation in open data competitions and participants seem to be aware of the low chances to enter the market and making a profit in the end (Juell-Skielse et al., 2014). In addition, these events are hosted with the aim to increase awareness and promote open data, which finally may lead to a collectively shared mission where everyone can make a difference (Hellberg & Hedström, 2015).

Similar to the outsourcing of ideas, also financial support can be outsourced to citizens which may "donate sums of money to support or finance a specific project" (Zogaj, Bretschneider, & Leimeister, 2014). Such an example of "crowdfunding" is the platform *citizenvestor* where citizens are invited to fund projects they like (Franks, January 11, 2013). The platform *ioby.org* takes this idea one step further and combines crowdfunding with resource-organizing. This means that they try to connect project organizers and supporters to make the projects successful also in the long term. They call this approach crowd-resourcing (Ioby, 2015). In most cases, the resulting services are aimed at solving specific issues with relevance for the city. Therefore, the challenge is not only to develop mobile apps but to make them successful and available to a broad range of citizens. The products of civic hacking or app competitions have to be promoted after these events so that they get recognition from a larger audience. For this purpose, Chicago provides a good example. They call for residents to become members of *The Civic User Testing Group* (CUTGroup) which is a project by the *Smart Chicago Collaborative*. The members of this group are paid with 20$ for testing new apps (Civic User Testing Group, n.d.). In addition, the *Smart Chicago Collaborative* offers free space for hosting new innovative applications and provides a good starting point for civic app projects (Whitaker, May 14, 2013).

The outcomes of hackathons and app competitions have shown that there is a need for financing and promoting the developed products. However, what if the hackathon is not only announced to develop a product for the market but also to develop tools for the whole city's engagement? This has happened at an international hackathon event in New York. They hosted a prototype-athon called *CodeAcross-NYC2014* which belonged to the international hackathon weekend *CodeAcross 2014* and was hosted under the slogan "Beyond Transparency. Let's take the open government movement one step further, by focusing on not only making data open, but actionable" (Bracy, January 13, 2014). This means that participants should work on datasets, portals, policies, and many other tools and topics concerning the provision and administration of open data and build prototype tools for city council members and community boards to help them to use and understand open data (BetaNYC, February 24, 2014). Thereby, the city officials' awareness was raised to the data they provide, since a lot of data has been published that was of poor quality. A major task at this event was to recognize how satisfied the participants are with the data provided by its government as well as to raise city officials' awareness for the importance and usefulness of open data (Weissman, February 24, 2014).

Potential for Change and Innovation

It still remains unclear whether hackathons are indeed able to make a difference and engage citizens in governmental processes. A survey conducted by the City of Vancouver was carried out to get more feedback from participants at hackathons (City of Vancouver, 2017). Vancouver's city government found out that participants demand further hackathon events and more support for the community. They like the exchange between participants and city officials. But there is also a claim for longer hacking sessions, faster Internet access, as well as more people with different backgrounds. In addition, participants prefer to be informed about upcoming events on the government's website, social media channels, as well as via emails (City of Vancouver, 2017). The city government should show that they strongly support these events and attach importance to participants' contributions. For instance, Vancouver's third *International Open Data Day* was accompanied by more than 20 city officials as well as the Federal Minister for Open Data at the national government. In addition, a meaningful location, like a city hall, is assumed to be helpful in order to underline that these events and their participants are highly welcomed by governments (Eaves, March 11, 2013). This confirms the government's aim for change to a more open and participative culture. Furthermore, the participants should be as much diverse as possible, since also people without programming skills can come up with great ideas (Eaves, March 11, 2013). This is one aspect that has changed over years. These events are not addressed to developers and computer programmers only, but allow everybody to participate and ask for a wide range of people with different skills. Innovation contests should be open to participants all over the world and cities should try to work in cooperation with each other. However, the analyzed cities perform very differently in doing so, e.g. in German and Italian cities innovation contests are scarcely available, whereas many other cities like e.g. Amsterdam, Barcelona, Chicago, Helsinki, and Singapore offer a wide range of competitions. Many cities tend to team up and host innovation contests jointly in order to build up global competitions which reach larger audiences. Although, not many contests seem to be well established as several ones were organized only once and only a few have been running yearly. In addition, not all of the apps and prototypes developed during these events can become successful in the long term, but to support some innovative ones, it might be helpful to build a whole innovation contest ecosystem, like it is targeted by IMDA of Singapore. Such an ecosystem could not only foster transparency and accountability but also participation in terms of the generation of ideas, services, and projects as well as their success. Similarly, Almirall, Lee, and Majchrzak (2014) claim that companies can learn from city governments' fast adaptation of open innovation and see a need for an integrated ecosystem approach to open innovation where initiatives, collaborations, and technologies are designed in order to be easily adopted by other cities and stakeholders. Furthermore, the focus should not be on developing solutions for one's own needs but to collaborate and interact with others and drive innovation proactively. A similar goal is pursued by the *Mayor's Challenge* hosted by the Bloomberg Philanthropies and also many other hackathons and app competitions that have been presented in this study show how governments already share their data and innovations with others.

More importantly than building successful applications, is to establish a community that aims at solving problems together regardless whether they are city officials or citizens. This could be achieved in cities like Chicago, Vancouver, and Singapore. Strong citizen communities, who organize visible events on their own, like in the case of Chicago, are in the minority and most hackathons and competitions are organized by governmental as well as non-governmental institutions and organizations. For this reason, still more governmental efforts seem to be needed to establish a culture of civic engagement and making citizens aware of the importance of open data, civic technologies, and innovations in general for the city. Citizens should recognize that they can benefit from these contests through making their city more livable and open. One group of citizens, who have recognized that, is *OpenDataBC*. They state on their website that governments should not have to do all of this alone, their citizens should help them so that they can "just concentrate on getting the data out there, in raw form, and we will help organize it, assemble it and tag it so it's more easily used by everyone" (OpenDataBC, n.d.). Thus, innovation contests can help to establish collaboration between citizens and governments as well as co-creation of public services that improve citizens' everyday life and address public issues. This also happens for example by means of the innovation competition *NYC BigApps* with which solutions for New York's three mayor challenges, i.e. "transportation, access to knowledge, and community resiliency" (NYC BigApps 2017, 2017) should be found.

CONCLUSION

This chapter contributes to the discussion on innovation contests as it shows how these events can be adapted to a wide range of different needs and issues within a city and offer a platform to generate ideas and solutions for city-specific problems. In particular, since the implementation of innovative projects and services is often too risky and resource consuming to be integrated into city departments' daily business (Almirall, Lee, & Majchrzak, 2014), innovation contests and the support of external partners and supporters can be valuable in order to find solutions for citizens' problems and improve governmental service provision. However, also more tangible results have already been achieved, for example the increasing popularity and re-use of open data has already led to enhanced data quality and new jobs have been created, e.g. a Chief Data Officer was proved for the city of San Francisco (San Francisco Mayor's Office of Civic Innovation, January 11, 2013). Hackathons and app challenges have even become so popular that guides, e.g. "How to run a hackathon"[5] and books, e.g. "Civic Apps Competition Handbook"[6] were published to support hosting these events. Furthermore, many governments started to work in cooperation when hosting innovation contests. Nevertheless, the scope, topics, outcomes, organizers, and supporters of hackathons and app competitions were shown to vary greatly between the analyzed cities and there are only a few concepts that take place in several cities in the same way, e.g. the *International Open Data Day*. Today's app challenges can range in size, e.g. from the city level up to an international level, in the addressed topics, from very broad themes, e.g. mobility up to specific solutions and tools for APIs, and the competitions' outcomes range from ideas up to market-ready mobile apps. In many cases, we see that the initiatives of opening data or initiating a hackathon or app competition come from the government but in some cities also the citizens build strong communities and are aimed at supporting their municipalities.

Among the cities' biggest challenges is the applications market launch. Only a small number of apps will be able to enter the market successfully and most of those will need much support. Therefore, especially the outcomes' financial support and competitive power are the biggest challenges. Also the success of the events' outcomes is still questionable. However, the great chance of these events is to bring people together as a community and develop city services, which could make the city smarter and enhance the quality of life. A great advantage is to solve urban problems collectively and foster the collaboration between governments and citizens. It can be concluded that innovation contests could have the potential to improve the government-to-citizen relationship since they call for civic engagement and help to overcome the cities' mayor challenges. Although it remains questionable if the potential of the crowd can be embedded into a successful ecosystem which helps to survive or even increase civic engagement to build value-added services for a livable future. At least, city governments should aim at cooperating with as many stakeholders as possible. They do not have to bear the burden of becoming a smart city alone. The example cases of many cities that have been described in this study show that hackathons and app competitions, i.e. innovation contests, can be helpful means in order to bring citizens, companies, and governments – also beyond the city level – together in order to discuss problems and find solutions in terms of specific services and tools but also in the form of financial, technical, or organizational support.

INFORMATIONAL CITY RESEARCH PROJECT

The investigation presented in this chapter is part of a research project on informational cities at the Department of Information Science of the Heinrich Heine University, Düsseldorf (Germany), started in 2010. Stock (2011) has laid the basic idea of how to analyse informational cities in the 21st century. His approach is multidisciplinary and joins urban studies, sociology as well as information science. In best practice investigations the cities Singapore and London have been analyzed (Khveshchanka, Mainka, & Peters, 2011; Murugadas, Vieten, Nikolic, & Mainka, 2015) and further regional investigations have been conducted in cities of the Gulf Region (Kosior, Barth, Gremm, Mainka, & Stock, 2015) as well as in Japanese cities (Fietkiewicz & Pyka, 2014; Fietkiewicz & Stock, 2015).

The increasing use of technology and the digital infrastructure have played a crucial role in the investigation of public services in informational cities. Thus, public libraries have been investigated according to their digital and physical services (Mainka, & Khveshchanka, 2012; Mainka et al., 2013; Orszullok, Peters, Stallmann, & Stock, 2013; Orszullok, Stallmann, Mainka, & Stock, 2012). Further, the integration of social media services as part of the digital library and in addition, as general digital service for governmental purpose (Mainka, Hartmann, Stock, & Peters, 2015) complemented the investigation of informational cities. One of the services used very frequently is the short messaging platform Twitter. As public libraries and governmental departments spread a lot of information through this service further investigation has focused on the information dissemination via Twitter (Förster, Lamerz, Mainka, & Peters, 2014, Förster & Mainka, 2015). Governments increasingly use e-services whereas the maturity of e-government services is on different levels in informational cities (Mainka, Fietkiewicz, Kosior, Pyka, & Stock, 2013). In some cases, the municipalities start to offer open data platforms and even present showcases of projects that reuse the available data (Mainka, Hartmann, Meschede, & Stock, 2015). However, municipalities are still looking for solutions and ideas how the digital transformation may lead to enhanced services and to solve urban problems. They are challenged by their own digital transformation of the administration (Hartmann, Mainka, & Stock, 2017). Thus, the increasing involvement of citizens in design thinking or open innovation processes has been introduced in some best practice examples (Mainka et al., 2016), but evidence of success factors are missing. Therefore, the chapter at hand contributes a qualitative study to this lack in research.

Investigations of the financial market, the labor market as well as the importance of entrepreneurship and creativity complement the research project (Dornstädter, Finkelmeyer, & Shanmuganathan, 2011; Murugadas, Vieten, Nikolic, Fietkiewicz, & Stock, 2015, Nowag, Perez, & Stuckmann, 2011). Recently, a conceptual framework of informational or smart cities has been developed by the researchers at the Department of Information Science which bridges the different aspects of the city, its society, economy, spaces, infrastructure, and problems (Barth et al., 2016). Furthermore, a qualitative investigation on the defined factors of an informational city has been scrutinised for 30 world cities around the globe (Mainka, 2017).

REFERENCES

Albano, C. S. (2013). Open government data: a value chain model proposal. *Proceedings of the 14th Annual International Conference on Digital Government Research, Association for Computing Machinery,* 285-286. doi:10.1145/2479724.2479775

Almirall, E., Lee, M., & Majchrzak, A. (2014). Open innovation requires integrated competition-community ecosystems: Lessons learned from civic open innovation. *Business Horizons*, *57*(3), 391–400. doi:10.1016/j.bushor.2013.12.009

Appcircus. (2015). *Helsinki smart city app hack*. Retrieved from http://helsinki.smartcityapphack.com/

Apps for Europe. (n.d.a). *About us*. Retrieved from http://live-appsforeurope.pantheonsite.io/about-us

Apps for Europe. (n.d.b). *Join the apps for Europe competition*. Retrieved from http://live-appsforeurope.pantheonsite.io/competition

Baraniuk, C. (2013). The civic hackers reshaping your government. *New Scientist*, *218*(2923), 36–39. doi:10.1016/S0262-4079(13)61625-5

Barth, J., Fietkiewicz, K. J., Gremm, J., Hartmann, S., Ilhan, A., Mainka, A., & Stock, W. G. et al. (2017). Informational urbanism. A conceptual framework of smart cities. In *Proceedings of the 50th Hawaii International Conference on System Sciences*. Washington, DC: IEEE Computer Society. doi:10.24251/HICSS.2017.340

Bellone, C., & Goerl, G. F. (1992). Reconciling public entrepreneurship and democracy. *Public Administration Review*, *52*(2), 130–134. doi:10.2307/976466

BetaNYC. (2014, February 24). *#CodeAcrossNYC 2014 wrap up*. Retrieved from https://beta.nyc/2014/02/24/codeacrossnyc-2014-wrap-up/

BetaNYC. (n.d.). *About BetaNYC*. Retrieved from https://beta.nyc/about/

Bloomberg.org Group. (n.d.). *Impact of the competition. Groundbreaking ideas are needed more than ever*. Retrieved from http://mayorschallenge.bloomberg.org/competition-impact/

Bracy, C. (2014, January 13). It's time to CodeAcross [Web log comment]. Retrieved from https://www.codeforamerica.org/blog/2014/01/13/its-time-to-codeacross/

Briscoe, G., & Mulligan, C. (2014). *Digital innovation: The hackathon phenomenon*. CreativeWorks London Working Paper, 6. Retrieved from http://www.creativeworkslondon.org.uk/wp-content/uploads/2013/11/Digital-Innovation-The-Hackathon-Phenomenon1.pdf

Burger, A. (2012, October 15). *ITU finds two times more mobile than broadband subscribers*. Retrieved from http://www.telecompetitor.com/itu-finds-two-times-more-mobile-than-fixed-broadband-subscribers/

Canada.ca. (n.d.). *Canadian Open Data Experience {CODE} 2015*. Retrieved from http://open.canada.ca/en/canadian-open-data-experience-code

Caragliu, A., Del Bo, C., & Nijkamp, P. (2009). Smart cities in Europe. In M. Buček, R. Capello, O. Hudec, & P. Nijkamp (Eds.), *Proceedings of the 3rd Central European Conference in Regional Science, Conference* (pp. 45-59). Academic Press.

Casecase. (n.d.). *AngelHack Series 7 Press Release*. Retrieved from http://angelhack.com/2014/03/13/angelhack-series-7-press-release/

Castells, M. (1989). *The informational city. Information technology, economic restructuring, and the urban-regional process.* Oxford, UK: Basil Blackwell.

Castelnovo, W., Misuraca, G., & Savoldelli, A. (2015). Smart cities governance: The need for a holistic approach to assessing urban participatory policy making. *Social Science Computer Review.* doi:10.1177/0894439315611103

Chan, C. M. L. (2013). From open data to open innovation strategies: Creating e-services using open government data. *Proceedings of the 46th Hawaii International Conference on System Sciences, IEEE Computer Science*, 1890-1899. doi:10.1109/HICSS.2013.236

Charalabidis, Y., Loukis, E., & Alexopoulos, C. (2014). Evaluating second generation open government data infrastructures using value models. *Proceedings of the 47th Hawaii International Conference on System Sciences*, 2114-2126. doi:10.1109/HICSS.2014.267

Chourabi, H., Nam, T., Walker, S., Gil-Garcia, J. R., Mellouli, S., Nahon, K., ... Scholl, H. J. (2012). Understanding smart cities: An integrative framework. *Proceedings of the 2012 45th Hawaii International Conference on System Sciences (HICSS '12)*, 2289-2297. doi:10.1109/HICSS.2012.615

City of Vancouver. (2017). *What you said about Vancouver open data day hackathon: Survey results.* Retrieved from http://vancouver.ca/your-government/open-data-hackathon-2013-survey-results.aspx

Civic User Testing Group. (n.d.). *Be a tester, get paid.* Retrieved from http://www.cutgroup.org/

Code for America Labs. (n.d.). *What are brigades?* Retrieved from http://brigade.codeforamerica.org/brigade/about/

Desouza, K. C., & Bhagwatwar, A. (2012). Citizen apps to solve complex urban problems. *Journal of Urban Technology, 19*(3), 107–136. doi:10.1080/10630732.2012.673056

DHMN Civic Hacks. (2015, April 09). National day of civic hacking [Web log comment]. Retrieved from http://dhmncivichacks.blogspot.de/2015/04/national-day-of-civic-hacking.html

Digitales Österreich. (n.d.). *apps4austria Wettbewerb. Teilnahmebedingungen.* Retrieved from http://www.oesta.gv.at/DocView.axd?CobId=49054

Dornstädter, R., Finkelmeyer, S., & Shanmuganathan, N. (2011). Job-Polarisierung in informationellen Städten [Job polarization in informational cities]. Information. *Wissenschaft & Praxis, 62*(2–3), 95–102.

Dotopen, S. L. (2015). *Smart city app hack. Terms and conditions.* Retrieved from http://smartcityapp.hackathome.com/rules/terms-and-conditions/

Eaves, D. (2013, March 11). Open data day 2013 in Vancouver [Web log comment]. Retrieved from https://eaves.ca/2013/03/11/open-data-day-2013-in-vancouver/

EderD. (2017, May 15). *About Derek.* Retrieved from http://derekeder.com/about

European Commission. (2011). *Open data an engine for innovation, growth and transparent governance.* Retrieved from http://eur-lex.europa.eu/LexUriServ/LexUriServ.do?uri=COM:2011:0882:FIN:EN:PDF

Fietkiewicz, K. J., Pyka, S., & Stock, W. G. (2015). Evaluating infrastructures of the 21st century city: Informational cities in Japan as case studies. *Advances in Research, 3*(3), 297–311. doi:10.9734/AIR/2015/12344

Fietkiewicz, K. J., & Stock, W. G. (2015). How "smart" are Japanese cities? An empirical investigation of infrastructures and governmental programs in Tokyo, Yokohama, Osaka and Kyoto. In *Proceedings of the 48th Hawaii International Conference on System Sciences* (pp. 2345-2354). Washington, DC: IEEE Computer Society.

Förster, T., Lamerz, L., Mainka, A., & Peters, I. (2014). The tweet and the city: Comparing Twitter activities in informational world cities. In *Proceedings of the 3. DGI 2014 Conference: Informationsqualität und Wissensgenerierung* (pp. 101-118). Frankfurt a.M.: DGI.

Förster, T., & Mainka, A. (2015). Metropolises in the Twittersphere: An informetric investigation of informational flows and networks. *ISPRS International Journal of Geo-Information, 4*(4), 1894–1912. doi:10.3390/ijgi4041894

Forum Virium Helsinki. (2016, February 12). *Democracy hackathon Helsinki.* Retrieved from https://forumvirium.fi/en/democracy-hackathon-helsinki/

Forum Virium Helsinki. (n.d.). *What is CitySDK?* Retrieved from http://www.citysdk.eu/about-the-project/

Government, N. S. W. (n. d.). *apps4nsw.* Retrieved from http://data.nsw.gov.au/apps4nsw

Government of Singapore. (2017). *About us.* Retrieved from https://ecitizen-ideas-uat.app.gov.sg/egp/process/EGOV/EideasAboutUs

Green Hackathon. (n.d.). Retrieved from http://www.greenhackathon.com/

Hanna. (2014, April 17). CitySDK challenge: Build best cross-city smart participation app - win 3000 euros [Web log comment]. Retrieved from https://www.citysdk.eu/citysdk-challenge-build-best-cross-city-smart-participation-app-win-3000-euros/

Hartmann, S., Mainka, A., & Stock, W. G. (2016). Opportunities and challenges for civic engagement: A global investigation of innovation competitions. *International Journal of Knowledge Society Research, 7*(3), 1–15. doi:10.4018/IJKSR.2016070101

Hartmann, S., Mainka, A., & Stock, W. G. (2017). Citizen relationship management in local governments: The potential of 311 for public service delivery. In A. A. Paulin, L. G. Anthopoulos, & C. G. Reddick (Eds.), *Beyond Bureaucracy* (pp. 337–553). Towards Sustainable Governance Informatisation; doi:10.1007/978-3-319-54142-6_18

Hellberg, A. S., & Hedström, K. (2015). The story of the sixth myth of open data and open government. *Transforming Government: People. Process and Policy, 9*(1), 35–51. doi:10.1108/TG-04-2014-0013

Hjalmarsson, A., Juell-Skielse, G., & Johannesson, P. (2017). *Open digital innovation. A contest driven approach.* Cham, Switzerland: Springer International Publishing AG. doi:10.1007/978-3-319-56339-8

Hjalmarsson, A., & Rudmark, D. (2012). Designing digital innovation contests. In K. Peffers, M. Rothenberger, & M. Kuechler (Eds.), *Design Science Research in Information Systems. Advances in Theory and Practice – Proceedings of the 7th International Conference DESRIST '12* (pp. 9-27). doi:10.1007/978-3-642-29863-9_2

Howard, A. (2013, January 17). Civic app for finding flu shots goes viral [Web log comment]. Retrieved from http://gov20.govfresh.com/civic-app-flu-shot-viral-open-government/

Howe, J. (2006, June 02). Crowdsourcing: A definition [Web log comment]. Retrieved from http://crowdsourcing.typepad.com/cs/2006/06/crowdsourcing_a.html

Immonen, A., Palviainen, M., & Ovaska, E. (2014). Requirements of an open data based business ecosystem. *IEEE Access*, *2*, 88–103. doi:10.1109/ACCESS.2014.2302872

Info-communications Media Development Authority. (2016, November 28). *What we do*. Retrieved from https://www.imda.gov.sg/about/what-we-do

Ioby. (2015). *About ioby*. Retrieved from https://www.ioby.org/about

ISL. (2017). *Apps for democracy. An innovation contest*. Retrieved from https://isl.co/work/apps-for-democracy-contest/

Jetzek, T., Avital, M., & Bjørn-Andersen, N. (2013). Generating value from open government data. In *Proceedings of the International Conference on Information Systems (ICIS 2013): Reshaping Society Through Information Systems Design* (*Vol. 2*, pp. 1737-1756). Academic Press.

Johnson, P., & Robinson, P. (2014). Civic hackathons: Innovation, procurement, or civic engagement? *Review of Policy Research*, *4*(31), 349–357. doi:10.1111/ropr.12074

Juell-Skielse, G., Hjalmarsson, A., Johannesson, P., & Rudmark, D. (2014). Is the public motivated to engage in open data innovation? In M. Janssen, H. J. Scholl, M. A. Wimmer, & F. Bannister (Eds.), *Proceedings 13th IFIP WG 8.5 International Conference EGOV '14, Dublin, Ireland, LNCS* (Vol. 8653, pp. 277-288). doi:10.1007/978-3-662-44426-9_23

Khveshchanka, S., Mainka, A., & Peters, I. (2011). Singapur: Prototyp einer informationellen Stadt. *Information. Wissenschaft & Praxis*, *62*(2-3), 111–121.

Kosior, A., Barth, J., Gremm, J., Mainka, A., & Stock, W. G. (2015). Imported expertise in world-class knowledge infrastructures: The problematic development of knowledge cities in the Gulf region. *Journal of Information Science Theory and Practice*, *3*(3), 17–44. doi:10.1633/JISTaP.2015.3.3.2

Mainka, A. (2017). *Informational world cities. An empirical investigation of cities in the 21st century* (Doctoral dissertation). Heinrich Heine University document server (document number 41536).

Mainka, A., Castelnovo, W., Miettinen, V., Bech-Petersen, S., Hartmann, S., & Stock, W. G. (2016). Open innovation in smart cities: Participation and co-creation of public services. *Proceedings of the 79th ASIS&T Annual Meeting (Vol. 53). Creating Knowledge, Enhancing Lives through Information & Technology.*

Mainka, A., Fietkiewicz, K., Kosior, A., Pyka, S., & Stock, W. G. (2013). Maturity and usability of e-government in informational world cities. In E. Ferrari & W. Castelnovo (Eds.), *Proceedings of the 13th European Conference on e-Government* (pp. 292-300). Reading, UK: Academic Conferences and Publishing International (ACPI).

Mainka, A., Hartmann, S., Meschede, C., & Stock, W. G. (2015a). Mobile application services based upon open urban government data. *Proceedings of the iConference 2015: Create, Collaborate, Celebrate.*

Mainka, A., Hartmann, S., Meschede, C., & Stock, W. G. (2015b). Open government: Transforming data into value-added city services. In M. Foth, M. Brynskov, & T. Ojala (Eds.), *Citizen's Right to the Digital City. Urban Interfaces, Activism, and Placemaking* (pp. 199–214). Singapore: Springer. doi:10.1007/978-981-287-919-6_11

Mainka, A., Hartmann, S., Orszullok, L., Peters, I., Stallmann, A., & Stock, W. G. (2013). Public libraries in the knowledge society: Core services of libraries in informational world cities. *Libri*, *63*(4), 295–319. doi:10.1515/libri-2013-0024

Mainka, A., Hartmann, S., Stock, W. G., & Peters, I. (2015). Looking for friends and followers: a global investigation of governmental social media use. *Transforming Government: People, Process and Policy*, *9*(2), 237–254.

Mainka, A., & Khveshchanka, S. (2012, June). Digital libraries as knowledge hubs in informational cities. *Libraries in the Digital Age (LIDA) Proceedings, 12*, 18–22.

Millard, J. (2010). Government 1.5: Is the bottle half full or half empty? *European Journal of ePractice*, *9*, 1-16.

Murugadas, D., Vieten, S., Nikolic, J., Fietkiewicz, K. J., & Stock, W. G. (2014). Creativity and entrepreneurship in informational metropolitan regions. In I. Filipovic, M. Kalcmer Calopa, & F. Galetic (Eds.), *Economic and Social Development. 7th International Scientific Conference* (pp. 142-151). Varazdin, Croatia: Varazdin Development and Entrepreneurship Agency.

Murugadas, D., Vieten, S., Nikolic, J., & Mainka, A. (2015). The informational world city London. *The Journal of Documentation*, *71*(4), 834–864. doi:10.1108/JD-06-2014-0090

Newton Circus Pte Ltd. (2017). *"Data in the city" hackathon*. Retrieved from http://www.upsingapore.com/events/data-city-hackathon/#hackathonhome

Nowag, B., Perez, M., & Stuckmann, M. (2011). Informationelle Weltstädte – Indikatoren zur Stellung von Städten im "Space of Flow" [Informational world cities - Indicators of the position of cities in the "space of flow"]. *Information. Wissenschaft & Praxis*, *62*(2–3), 103–109.

NYC Big Apps. (2017). *About*. Retrieved from http://www.bigapps.nyc/about/

Open Finland Challenge. (n.d.). *Open Finland challenge 2015*. Retrieved from http://openfinlandchallenge.fi/index.html%3Fp=371.html

Open Knowledge International. (n.d.a). *Why open data*. Retrieved from http://opendatahandbook.org/guide/en/what-is-open-data/

Open Knowledge International. (n.d.b). *About*. Retrieved from https://okfn.org/about//

OpenDataBC. (n.d.). *About*. Retrieved from https://www.opendatabc.ca/pages/about

OpenDataDay 2017. (n.d.). Retrieved from http://opendataday.org/

OpenDataHackathon 2011. (2013, June 18). Retrieved from http://www.barcamp.at/OpenDataHackathon_2011

Orszullok, L., Stallmann, A., Mainka, A., & Stock, W. G. (2012). Core services of digital and physical libraries in informational world cities - An empirical investigation. In *Smart City and Library Service. The Proceedings of the Sixth Shanghai International Library Forum* (pp. 288-301). Shanghai: Shanghai Scientific and Technological Literature Publishing House.

Robinson, P. J., & Johnson, P. A. (2016). Civic hackathons: New terrain for local government-citizen interaction? *Urban Planning*, *1*(2), 65–74. doi:10.17645/up.v1i2.627

San Francisco Mayor's Office of Civic Innovation. (2013, January 11). The civic innovation ecosystem blooms in 2012. What's next? [Web log comment]. Retrieved from https://medium.com/sfmoci/the-civic-innovation-ecosystem-blooms-in-2012-whats-next-70b685ab063b

Sieber, R. E., & Johnson, P. A. (2015). Civic open data at a crossroads: Dominant models and current challenges. *Government Information Quarterly*, *32*(3), 308–315. doi:10.1016/j.giq.2015.05.003

Stock, W. G. (2011). Informational cities: Analysis and construction of cities in the knowledge society. *Journal of the American Society for Information Science and Technology*, *62*(5), 963–986. doi:10.1002/asi.21506

Stockholms stad. (n.d.). *Open Stockholm award 2016*. Retrieved from https://www.openstockholmaward.se/?locale=en

Vienna City Administration. (n.d.). *Open Energy Data Challenge*. Retrieved from https://open.wien.gv.at/site/open-energy-data-challenge/

Waag society. Institute for art, science and technology. (2012, November 07). *Apps for Amsterdam: smart apps awarded*. Retrieved from https://waag.org/en/news/apps-amsterdam-smart-apps-awarded

Waag society. Institute for art, science and technology. (n.d.). *Apps for Europe first business lounge*. Retrieved from http://waag.org/en/event/apps-europe-first-business-lounge

Walravens, N. (2015). Mobile city applications for Brussels citizens: Smart city trends, challenges and a reality check. *Telematics and Informatics*, *32*(2), 282–299. doi:10.1016/j.tele.2014.09.004

Weissman, C. G. (2014, February 24). New York hackathon looks to use open data to assist with city governance [Web log comment]. Retrieved from https://pando.com/2014/02/24/new-york-hackathon-looks-to-use-open-data-to-assist-with-city-governance/

Whitaker, C. (2013, May 14). Using the new ClearPath API to help communities interact with the Chicago Police Department [Web log comment]. Retrieved from http://www.smartchicagocollaborative.org/using-the-new-clearpath-api-to-help-communities-interact-with-the-chicago-police-department/

Zogaj, S., Bretschneider, U., & Leimeister, J. M. (2014). Managing crowdsourced software testing: A case study based insight on the challenges of a crowdsourcing intermediary. *Journal of Business Economics*, *3*(84), 375–405. doi:10.1007/s11573-014-0721-9

ENDNOTES

1 https://isl.co/work/apps-for-democracy-contest/

2 https://forumvirium.fi/en/open-data-day-helsinki-hackathon/

3 https://play.google.com/store/apps/details?id=org.bikecityguide

4 http://futureeverything.org/about/

5 http://socrata.com/wp-content/uploads/2013/05/How-to-Run-a-Hackathon.pdf

6 http://govfresh.com/2012/12/civic-apps-competition-theres-a-book-for-that/'

APPENDIX: LIST OF STUDIED MUNICIPAL GOVERNMENTS

- Amsterdam (The Netherlands);
- Barcelona (Spain);
- Berlin (Germany);
- Boston (U.S.A.);
- Chicago (U.S.A.);
- Dubai (U.A.E.);
- Frankfurt (Germany);
- Helsinki (Finland);
- Hong Kong (China, SAR);
- London (United Kingdom);
- Los Angeles (U.S.A.);
- Melbourne (Australia);
- Milan (Italy);
- Montreal (Canada);
- Munich (Germany);
- New York City (U.S.A.);
- Paris (France);
- San Francisco (U.S.A.);
- Singapore; Stockholm (Sweden);
- Sydney (Australia);
- Toronto (Canada);
- Vancouver (Canada);
- Vienna (Austria).

Chapter 15
Innovation on Geo-Enrichment of Texts Using Gazetteers for Massive Open On-Line Courses

Vladimir Luna
Instituto Politécnico Nacional, Mexico

Rolando Quintero
Instituto Politécnico Nacional, Mexico

Miguel Torres-Ruiz
Instituto Politécnico Nacional, Mexico

Marco Moreno-Ibarra
Instituto Politécnico Nacional, Mexico

Imelda Escamilla
Instituto Politécnico Nacional, Mexico

ABSTRACT

Text documents available in the Web contain a large amount of geographic information. For instance, forum messages posted by students in Massive Open Online Courses (MOOCs) may contain references to places. Normally, this information is not exploited, although it can be useful to further understand the topics of courses. Therefore, we propose an approach to instantly provide additional information to MOOC students about geographic features found in publications at course forums (geo-enrichment). The results are displayed through our tool, called ORBIS, which automatically highlights the geographic entities in the texts, and provides access to additional information in the same environment, without disruption; interacting with maps and spatial relationships with other entities. Information on locations mentioned in text is obtained from queries posted to the gazetteer Linked OntoGazetteer. We applied our prototype to the students' posts in the forum space for the MOOC titled Maps and the Geospatial Revolution, offered by the Pennsylvania State University.

DOI: 10.4018/978-1-5225-4191-2.ch015

INTRODUCTION

Massive Open Online Courses (MOOCs) are an expansion of web-based resource mainly oriented to e-learning that offer students the possibility of distance education. One of the most important features in MOOCs are the discussion forums. These forums are the only way that students can interact with the instructors, allowing them to submit their work and share their knowledge and doubts, not only with instructors, but also with other students, forming what we can call an online community. A large amount of geographic information is contained in the messages posted by students in these forums and may contain references to places, points of interest or references to historical facts. MOOCs environments (i.e. Coursera, Udacity, Udemy, etc.) apply interactive discussion forums where instructors and students can ask questions, discuss ideas, provide help to or even socialize with other students (Yang et al., 2014). Unfortunately, this information is not exploited, although it can be useful to further understand the topics of the courses.

The higher education imposes serious challenges to diverse learners including students with racially, culturally, socioeconomically, intellectually and linguistically diverse backgrounds (Moriña, 2017). Inclusive education intends to address these challenges by enhancing dynamic but equal learning opportunities for all students regardless of their background and differences (Florian, 2015)

If forums could automatically highlight the geographic entities in the texts and gets access to additional information in the same environment, without disruption, interacting with maps, demographic data, and spatial relationships with other entities, it would make it more convenient to students to get additional information about an entity and even to encourage students and decrease the number of dropouts (Yang et al., 2013).

In (Duran et al., 2014) a proposal for managing educational resources produced by three high level educational institutions is described. By taking into account not only the meta-informations inside educational resources, but also the metadata extracted from linked open data in the web associated to massive open online courses (MOOCs). Thus, authors have visualized educational resources as a semantic corporate memory where semantic technologies and Linked Open Data approaches can improve the information integration task.

On the other hand, geospatial technologies and information have become ubiquitous nowadays (Goodchild, 2006; Riihelä and Mäki, 2015). The geospatial competences required to view and manipulate spatial data and to adequately use geospatial technologies are increasingly sought after by employers (Riihelä and Mäki, 2015). Given the growing importance and recognition of these competences, Geographic Information System and Technologies (GIS&T) concepts are taught in various education frameworks: (1) Traditional on-campus education offering academic GIS degrees; (2) on-line distance learning programs leading to academic degrees and certificates (Goodchild, 2006); and (3) open, mostly non-credit, geospatial education courses aiming at making GIS, concepts and technologies, accessible and understandable to as many people as possible for free.

The number of open courses designed to introduce GIS&T concepts to learners with different professional backgrounds, age and educations has increased tremendously over the last years, such is the case of MOOCs (Belgiu et al., 2015). By using the number of clicks on videos and the participation in discussion forums as control variables, Ferschke et al. (2015) found that the participation in chats lowers the risk of dropout by approximately 50%. Another recent research suggests the most positive impact when experiencing a chat with exactly one partner rather than more or less in a MOOC (Gaurav, et al.,

2016). The effect depends on how well the peer learning activities were incorporated into the curriculum. This effect relies also on whether sufficient support was offered to the groups.

In this work, we propose an approach to instantly provide additional information to MOOC students about geographic features found in publications at course forums to further understand the topics of the courses. To do this, we apply our prototype ORBIS, which is a web tool that automatically highlights the geographic entities in the texts. With this tool, the student gets access to additional information in the same environment, without disruption, interacting with maps, demographic data, and spatial relationships with other entities. Information on locations mentioned in text is obtained from queries posted to the gazetteer Linked OntoGazetteer (Moura, 2015a). The gazetteer Linked OntoGazetteer (LoG) is able to hold semantically rich relationships between places and other entities. The reference data used by LoG are obtained from online sources that publish data according to Linked Data (Sources of information like GeoNames, DBPedia, Freebase and Linked GeoData). Finally, we applied our prototype to the students' posts in the forum space for the Geo-MOOC titled Maps and the Geospatial Revolution course, offered by the Pennsylvania State University.

RELATED WORK

In recent years, several on-line approaches have been developed to support distance education, many of which have only been possible due to the development of semantic technologies and the adaption of existing tools to a dynamic hypertext environment. To cite a familiar example, the traditional highlighter pen was re-imagined as an on-line version to support students enrolled in on-line courses (Nunes et al., 2015a). This highlighter pen has several advantages over the original one: it can be shared between students, used to improve course contents and serve as an anchor to link to new resources on the Web. It can also help students to better understand course contents. Other e-learning tools (Nunes et al., 2015b) semantically analyze the content of posts on educational forums, many of which have hundreds of individual messages. Instructors can gain an overview of these discussions by the use of semantic technologies, which enable the summarizing of forum content into topics extracted from DBPedia. Another approach (Nunes et al., 2014a, b) uses extracted topics from forum posts to recommend other discussions that may enrich the current one. ISCOOL (Nunes et al., 2015a), an interactive educational platform that helps users develop their skills for objective text analysis and interpretation, uses similar methods to retrieve images from search engines to help and support students in text interpretation and analysis. These innovative tools for on-lone courses are very important for MOOCs, due to, as Fernandez and Mariño (2016) mentioned, the enrichment of contents improves the acceptation of materials by the students and decreases their desertion.

O'Reilly & Veeramachaneni (2014) developed an open source online platform where users would post their tagging projects and a crowd of helpers can participate in MOOC data science by selecting a project and tagging the content based on some instructions. It works in the following ways: Users requiring annotation of natural language can create an annotation project by providing a csv file for the content, instructions and examples for tagging; taggers can participate by selecting a project, following the instructions and tagging the content; a database consisting of tags for the content for the project is initialized and populated as taggers work. A number of analytic services are provided around this database such as evaluation of inter rater reliability, summary of tags, and summary of activity for a project (how many taggers helped, time series of number of tags); a service can be called upon to filter the tagged data based on the reliability measures just mentioned. It also uses methods based upon latent semantic analysis to learn a tagging model.

On the other hand, inclusive education has been the focus of educational reform for the last years. Research has shown that access to inclusive education leads to higher skill acquisition, increased achievement, inclusion in future environments as well as higher self-efficacy and self-determination among diverse learner (Stodden, Abhari, & Kong, 2015). To support diverse learners, higher education systems deal with three groups of challenges, namely learning process, learning environment, and learning media. In order to address these challenges using social technologies, educators need new strategies aligned with the needs of diverse learners (Quinton & Allen, 2014; Redecker et al., 2010). Using the technologies without changing the instructional strategies can limit the benefits to diverse learners. For example, if educators have limited knowledge in utilizing social networking sites as alternative learning environments or implementing network learning as the center of instructional practice, they may use these networks merely for information-seeking activities without considering the possible applications for engaging marginalized students in the learning process.

MOOC is an umbrella term referring to on-line courses that engage a large number of participants (Hew and Cheung, 2014). By contrast to traditional on-line learning courses, MOOCs are open to enrollment by everyone with an Internet connection, with no costs incurred and with no formal education pre-requisites. Although, van de Oudeweetering and Agirdag (2017) mentioned that MOOCs benefit the socially privileged in comparison to unprivileged groups. MOOCs facilitate participants exploring new topics or strengthening their skills within a professional field without enrolling in formal degree or certificate programs. As demonstrated in a recent study (Hew and Cheung, 2014), MOOC participants indicate professional development as the primary motivation to take the course. Several institutions are offering MOOCs in the geospatial domain to attract learners from different background into this field (Robinson et al., 2015). MOOCs designed to introduce GIS or GIS&T concepts and principles are referred to as GeoMOOCs throughout this paper. The first GeoMOOC, titled "Maps and Geospatial Revolution" was launched in 2013 and attracted tens of thousands of students from around the world (Robinson et al., 2015). Since then, GeoMOOCs offerings have been constantly growing (see Table 2). These courses take advantage of the increasing availability of open web services hosted on cloudbased platforms, open social media tools such as discussion forums, wikis, open learning materials including tutorials, textbooks, scientific publications and open spatial data and Free and Open Source (FOSS) initiatives (Sui, 2014).

Serious games have begun to emerge as complementary or alternative approaches to traditional learning activities. The combination of entertainment and educational tasks engages learners and encourages them to achieve learning goals, consequently impacting on their academic performance in a positive manner (Derbali and Frasson, 2012). Serious games have been able to captivate and engage students for a specific purpose such as developing new knowledge or acquiring specific skill sets. Moreover, Kurkovsky (2009) shows that games can also contribute to improve retentions rates: difficult subjects often experience high dropout rates, but these have been observed to decrease when games are used to supplement the course material (Morrison and Preston, 2009). Several works have discussed identifying the optimal balance of learning and entertainment that a game must have in order to be most effective (Green and McNeese, 2007; Squire and Jenkins, 2003; Johnson et al., 2005). So, MOOCs have become in an emerging research area, where new developments are necessary (Zancanaro and de Souza Domingues, 2017).

The contribution by Andogah et al. (2012) is about how this scope is important for more relevant web document retrieval and to resolve the problem of toponyms resolution. Recognizing place names in documents such as Web pages, news, and forum space in MOOCs can be doing with a Gazetteer. Another approach presented by Zhuhadar et al. (2015), use Collaborative Semantic Filtering technologies to enrich MOOC materials, thus enabling collaborative labeling and indexing.

Gazetteers play an often understated role in our contemporary informationalized lives. In containing a dictionary of place names, they offer the informational canvas from which a huge variety of geographic meaning is made, thus playing "a vital role in information systems" Goodchild and Hill (2008). Gazetteers are often tools used by several applications that work with geographic data. So an API that supports operations commonly used are fundamental piece for utilization in a gazetteer.

Linked Data refers to data published and reusable on the Web and readable by a machine. Its meaning defines that are linked to external data sets (Bizer et al., 2009; Bauer & Kaltenböck, 2011). Open Data refers to the legal interoperability of data (Baker et al., 2011). So, keeping in mind that the use of linked data approach does not require the use of open data; however, in order to obtain a potential profit, it is necessary to publish data as Linked Open Data good practices. (Duran et al., 2014). The open data format for publication is the Resource Description Framework (RDF) (Hjelm, 2001). In 2006 Berners-Lee established four rules for publishing data on the Web; these rules are known as "Open Data Principles" (Berners-Lee, 2006) and they consist of: 1. Use URIs to identify resources published on the Web; 2. Use HTTP URIs and so people can find those names; 3. When someone looks for a URI, provide useful information, using the standards (RDF, SPARQL, etc.); 4. Include links to other URIs, so that they can discover more things. The process for looking for a Web URI in order to obtain information on a referenced resource is called dereferenced (Bizer, 2007). URIs can identify resources which could be (Salazar, 2011): a) a resource that can be transmitted through the Web, b) concrete or abstract entities that cannot be transmitted through the Web.

The gazetteer Linked OntoGazetteer Moura (2015b) combine Linked Data sources to create a gazetteer that combines a broad coverage of places with urban detail, including content on geographic and semantic relationships involving places, their multiple names and related non-geographic entities. This gazetteer is accessible through Web services by applications and research initiatives on GIR, text processing, named entity recognition and others. The gazetteer currently contains over 13 million places, 140 million attributes and relationships, and 4.5 million non-geographic entities. Data sources include GeoNames, Freebase, DBPedia and LinkedGeoData, which is based on OpenStreetMaps.

Forums play a key role in the creating knowledge process, providing the ways for users to exchange ideas and collaborations. However, educational forums, and other online educational environments, often they suffer disruption issues. Due the contents are mainly produced by the participants (in our case the students), one or a few individuals can change the course of the discussions. Therefore, the alignment of the topics discussed in forums is a task performed by a moderator. In order to support students and teachers enriching geographic information forum discussions that are relevant to a course map or the like, in this paper, we propose an approach to instantly provide additional information to MOOC students about geographic features found in publications at course forums to further understand the topics of courses.

3. ORBIS: A FORUM ENRICHMENT TOOL

As it was mentioned, we propose an approach to enrich information to MOOC students about geographic features, by instantly providing additional data. The results are displayed through our tool, ORBIS, which automatically highlights the geographic entities in the texts. With this tool, the student gets access to additional information in the same environment, without disruption, interacting with maps and spatial relationships with other entities. ORBIS consists of 3 stages: i) collection and preparation of data, ii) finding named entities, get additional information from Linked OntoGazetteers (LoG) and iii) Visualization.

3.1 Collection and Preparation of Data

Mainly in this stage a standardize database is built with the information from discussion forums like posts and comments. This is done since the data can be presented in different formats and could come 3 from multiple data sources.

The data set used for the experiments was provided by data discussion forums from the Geo-MOOC course "Maps and the Geospatial Revolution". The dataset consists of 46 forums, 3656 threads, 16710 posts and 5842 comments.

3.2 Finding Named Entities

In this stage, countries, cities, rivers, monuments, organizations (mentioned in forum posts) are identified through named entity recognition techniques. The Named Entity Recognition (NER) functionality involves the processing of discussion texts and identifying occurrences of certain words or expressions which belong to a particular set of categories referred as Named Entities (NE). Examples of name entities could be: locations, organisms, organizations, name of persons.

Geo-parsing is a subset of named entity recognition, which identifies entities in text and classifies them into categories such as agent, organization and location. Geo-parsing is performed automatically based on language rules. A model based on these rules is then applied to unseen instances in order to find location words in unprocessed text. The text of a discussion forum is unstructured. If not supplemented with metadata, it is potentially difficult to parse due to lack of context (Gutierrez et al., 2015).

The following example shows how this stage works, the entry in forum is the post: "Used to 'change matters' website to explore vegetation changes in the Royal National Park area, south of Sydney, Australia, before and after, a bushfire there in the mid 90s?". In this text, the entities founded are as an Organization: "Royal National Park"; as Location: "Sydney" and "Australia". Figure 1 shows a highlighted entities retrieved as locations and organizations.

GeoNames is one of the largest gazetteers available on the web. It keeps information about more than 8 million places, and its main data sources are official cartographic agencies. Since GeoNames only stores data from real world places, ORBIS first queried this service for recovery the type of geographic entity. For the example above, the results are that "Royal National Park" is an entity from the Park class; "Sydney" is an entity of a Seat of a First-Order Administrative Division, and "Australia" is an Independent Political Entity. Figure 2 illustrates how the results are displayed in ORBIS interface.

Figure 1. Named entity recognition of locations from a forum post

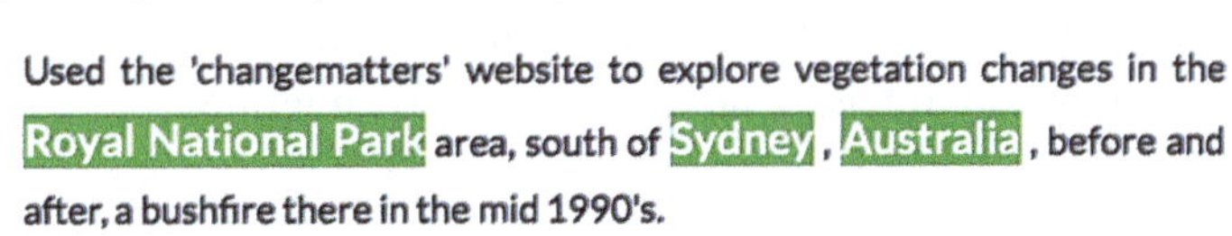

Figure 2. Type of geographic entity defined by GeoNames

3.3 Additional Information from LoG (Linked OntoGazetteer)

Once entities related to locations and organizations are identified, and after obtaining the type of geographic entity, given by GeoNames, each of them is enriched with more geographic information. To do this, the service retrieve *PlacesByName*() from the gazetteer Linked OntoGazetter is consumed. This service search for all the places that are associated with the given name.

- **Parameters:** Name that places should be associated.
- **Return:** List of places withal existing attibutes in this kind of vertices.

The list of locations can be obtained from DBPedia, GeoNames, Freebase, Wikipedia, among others.

3.4 Other Places With Similar Name

The list of places found by Linked OntoGazetteer in the first term are the most representative places and in second term they are the places with similar names but nevertheless do not necessary correspond with the mentioned place in the discussion forum.

Another example, suppose that the topic of forum is about California, first this entity is a state of the United States. Then, the enrichment with geographic information using the Linked OntoGazetteer indicate that California is also the name of an Institute of Technology, a street in Michigan, a town in Birmingham, in Missouri, in Pennsylvania, Ohio and Kentucky; it is also the name of a metro station in Chicago. Even outside the United States, California is a town in Trinidad and Tobago or in Santander, Colombia.

This is the main objective of our proposal, the student gets access to additional information in the same environment, without disruption, interacting with maps and spatial relationships with other entities. The student gets access to additional information of each geographic entity, for example, the demographic information about a country, the map with the location of a town, a detail description of a place, to cite some examples. Figure 3 shows the ORBIS interface with the geographic entities highlighted and the maps and description of all the similar entities founded. The student can click each of them and retrieve additional information as shown in Figure 4 and in Figure 5.

4. CONCLUSION AND FUTURE WORK

In this chapter, an approach to geo-enrich MOOC contents by instantly provide additional information to students about geographic features found in publications at course forums is presented. For this purpose, we presented our tool ORBIS, which automatically highlights the geographic entities in the texts. With this tool, the student get access to additional information in the same environment, without disruption, interacting with maps, demographic data, and spatial relationships with other entities. Information on locations mentioned in text is obtained from queries posted to the gazetteer LoG (Linked OntoGazetteer).

Experiments conducted on the Geo-MOOC titled Maps and the Geospatial Revolution dataset show that the additional information that the students gets with ORBIS, can be useful to further understand the topics of the courses. In the future, we plan to develop a web plugin to show geographic information in any web site, not only for discussion forum spaces in on-line courses, but also for news pages or blogs.

Most current environmental noise monitoring systems are based on an approach where a generally expensive metering station is used, in addition to the fact that their information is poorly shared, it is necessary to implement innovative solutions that are more appropriate, especially in developing countries, such as Mexico. According to the Background Section Table 1 shows a comparison of the presented works to monitor environmental noise. Broadly speaking, it can be observed that the main difference in our work regarding the presented proposals is that it promotes VGI while using ML techniques to predict noise levels considering factors around the measurements. This approach integrates many of the

Figure 3. ORBIS interface

functionalities to create a new contribution to environmental noise monitoring, particularly the features of VGI, existing in projects such as NoiseWatch, and the prediction of noise levels using ML techniques to integrate and to analyze a very large set of data that cannot be treated using traditional methods (Jiang and Thill, 2015).

According to Gartner, big data poses three properties: 1) it has a high-volume, 2) it is collected with high velocity, and 3) it includes variety asset information; it can be seen as the approach herein fit to this work. The big data approach has advantages of revealing individual characteristics rather than a general feature of traditional statistics, and it is consistent with the idea of people-oriented urbanization and urban–rural planning (Hao et al., 2015). From this perspective, data must be processed with advanced tools to reveal meaningful information by using tools as machine learning methods as well as defining a methodology as well as to perform the analysis, design and development.

Figure 4. Additional information on maps

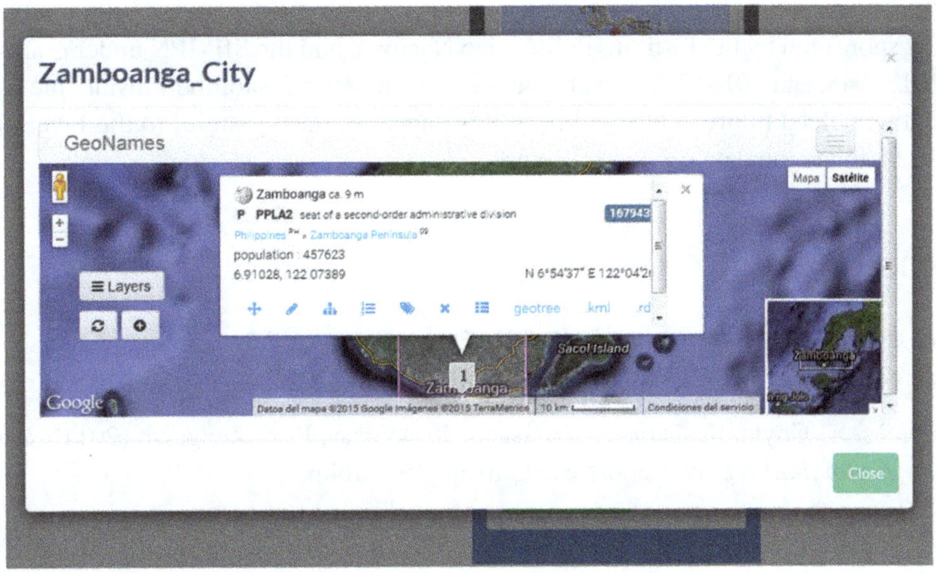

Figure 5. Information about the place from DBPedia

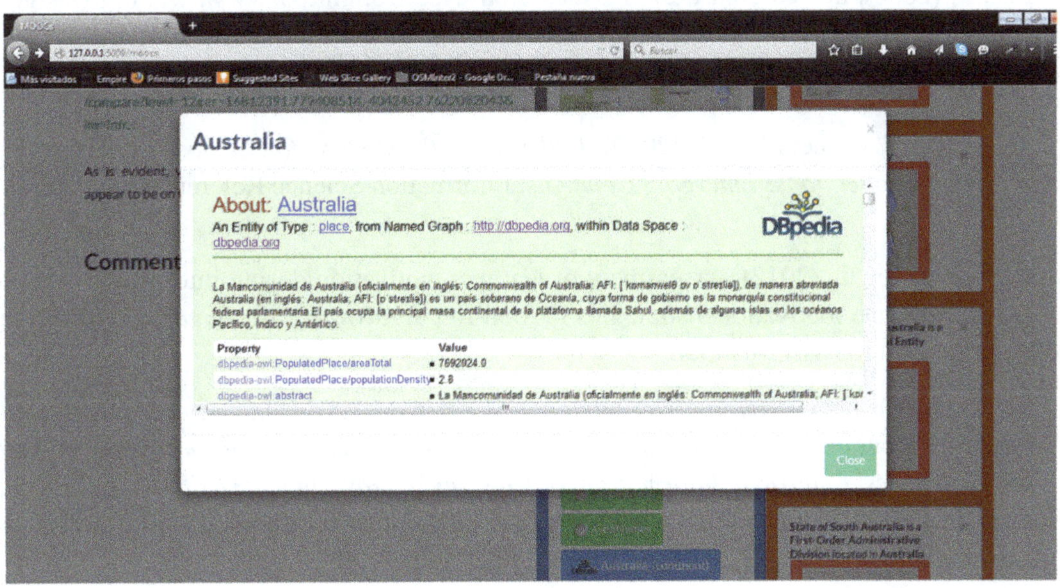

This chapter considers the MOOCs to bring into learning science in view of the novelty of the data collected. It identifies certain technology challenges that need to be resolved before we can exploit the big data in MOOCs to its full potential. By this reason, we call for enabling technology and setting a course towards standardization and web-based platforms that help a large community of people to collaborate on developing analytics. We advocate frameworks that are deliberately open source so that when they are released, everyone will be able to customize, refine and advance them.

ACKNOWLEDGMENT

Work partially sponsored by the Instituto Politécnico Nacional and the SIP-IPN under grants 20170330, 20171918, 20170048, and 20161219. We are thankful to the reviewers for their invaluable and constructive feedback that helped improve the quality of this paper. We also grateful to the Pennsylvania State University for facilitate the data used in this work.

REFERENCES

Andogah, G., Bouma, G., & Nerbonne, J. (2012). Every document has a geographical scope. *Data & Knowledge Engineering*, *81*, 1–20. doi:10.1016/j.datak.2012.07.002

Baker, T., Bermès, E., Coyle, K., Dunsire, G., Isaac, A., Murray, P., & Zeng, M. (2011). *Library linked data incubator group final report.* Report, W3C Incubator Group.

Bauer, F., & Kaltenböck, M. (2011). Linked open data: The essentials. Edition mono/monochrom, Vienna.

Belgiu, M., Strobl, J., & Wallentin, G. (2015). Open geospatial education. SPRS International. *Journal of Geo-Information*, *4*(2), 697–710.

Berners-Lee, T. (2006). *Linked data-design issues.* Retrieved from http://www. w3. org/DesignIssues/LinkedData. html

Bizer, C., Cyganiak, R., & Heath, T. (2007). *How to publish linked data on the web.* Academic Press.

Bizer, C., Heath, T., & Berners-Lee, T. (2009). *Linked data-the story so far. Semantic Services, Interoperability and Web Applications: Emerging Concepts*. Information Science Reference (an imprint of IGI Global).

Derbali, L., & Frasson, C. (2012). Assessment of learners motivation during interactions with serious games: A study of some motivational strategies in food-force. *Advances in Human-Computer Interaction*, *2012*, 5. doi:10.1155/2012/624538

Duran, C. K. G., Medina-Ramírez, R. C., & Juganaru-Mathieu, M. (2014, January). Using Linked Open Data to Enrich a Corporate Memory of Universities. In *Proceedings of the International Conference on e-Learning, e-Business, Enterprise Information Systems, and e-Government (EEE)* (p. 1). The Steering Committee of The World Congress in Computer Science, Computer Engineering and Applied Computing (WorldComp).

Fernandez, G., & Mariño, O. (2016). *State-of-the-Art and Future Directions of Smart Learning*. Springer Singapore.

Ferschke, O., Yang, D., Tomar, G., & Rosé, C. P. (2015, June). Positive impact of collaborative chat participation in an edX MOOC. In *International Conference on Artificial Intelligence in Education* (pp. 115-124). Springer. doi:10.1007/978-3-319-19773-9_12

Florian, L. (2015). Inclusive Pedagogy: A transformative approach to individual differences but can it help reduce educational inequalities. *Scottish Educational Review*, *47*(1), 5–14.

Goodchild, M. F. (2006). The fourth R? Rethinking GIS Education. *ESRI ArcNews*, *28*(3), 1.

Goodchild, M. F., & Hill, L. L. (2008). Introduction to digital gazetteer research. *International Journal of Geographical Information Science*, *22*(10), 1039–1044. doi:10.1080/13658810701850497

Green, M., & McNeese, M. N. (2007). Using edutainment software to enhance online learning. *International Journal on E-Learning*, *6*(1), 5.

Gutierrez, C., Figureuerias, P., Oliveira, P., Costa, R., & Jardim-Goncalves, R. (2015). Twitter mining for traffic events detection. In *Science and Information Conference (SAI)* (pp. 371–378). IEEE.

Hew, K. F., & Cheung, W. S. (2014). Students and instructors use of massive open online courses (moocs): Motivations and challenges. *Educational Research Review*, *12*, 45–58. doi:10.1016/j.edurev.2014.05.001

Hjelm, J. (2001). *Creating the semantic Web with RDF: Professional developer's guide*. John Wiley & Sons, Inc.

Johnson, W. L., Vilhjálmsson, H. H., & Marsella, S. (2005). Serious games for language learning: How much game, how much ai? *AIED*, *125*, 306–313.

Kurkovsky, S. (2009). Engaging students through mobile game development. *ACM SIGCSE Bulletin*, *41*(1), 44–48. doi:10.1145/1539024.1508881

Moriña, A. (2017). Inclusive education in higher education: challenges and opportunities Inclusive education in higher education: challenges and opportunities. *European Journal of Special Needs Education*, *32*(1), 3–17. doi:10.1080/08856257.2016.1254964

Morrison, B. B., & Preston, J. A. (2009). Engagement: Gaming throughout the curriculum. In *ACM. SIGCSE Bulletin*, *41*(1), 342–346. doi:10.1145/1539024.1508990

Moura, T. (2015a). *Enriquecimento de dados de referência para recuperaçao de informaçao geográfica utilizando linked data* (Master's thesis). Universidade Federal de Minas Gerais, Belo Horizonte, Brazil.

Moura, T. (2015b). Reference data enhancement for geographic information retrieval using linked data. In *ACM SIGSPATIAL'15*. ACM.

Nunes, B. P., Kawase, R., Fetahu, B., Casanova, M. A., & de Campos, G. H. B. (2014a). Educational forums at a glance: Topic extraction and selection. In S. I. Publishing (Ed.), *Web Information Systems Engineering–WISE 2014* (pp. 351–364). doi:10.1007/978-3-319-11746-1_25

Nunes, B. P., Mera, A., Kawase, R., Fetahu, B., Casanova, M. A., & de Campos, G. H. B. (2014b). A topic extraction process for online forums. In *IEEE 14th International Conference on Advanced Learning Technologies (ICALT)* (pp. 541–543). IEEE. doi:10.1109/ICALT.2014.158

Nunes, B. P., Nurmikko-Fuller, T., Lopes, G. R., & Renso, C. (2015a). A serious game powered by semantic web technologies. In *Proceedings of the 24th International Conference on World Wide Web Companion* (pp. 227–230). Wide Web Conferences Steering Committee. doi:10.1145/2740908.2742840

Nunes, B. P., Tyler-Jones, M., de Campos, G. H., Siqueira, S. W., & Casanova, M. A. (2015b). Fat: A real-time (f) orum (a) ssessment (t) ool to assist tutors with discussion forums assessment. In *Proceedings of the 30th Annual ACM Symposium on Applied Computing*. ACM.

O'Reilly, U. M., & Veeramachaneni, K. (2014). Technology for Mining the Big Data of MOOCs. *Research & Practice in Assessment, 9*, 29–37.

Quinton, S. R., & Allen, M. M. (2014). The social processes of web 2.0 collaboration: Towards a new model for virtual learning. In *Curriculum models for the 21st century* (pp. 35–53). Springer New York. doi:10.1007/978-1-4614-7366-4_3

Redecker, C., Ala-Mutka, K., & Punie, Y. (2010). *Learning 2.0-The impact of social media on learning in Europe.* Policy brief. JRC Scientific and Technical Report. EUR JRC56958 EN, available from: http://bit. ly/cljlpq

Riihelä, J., & Mäki, S. (2015). Designing and implementing an online gis tool for schools: The finnish case of the paikkaoppi project. journal of geography. *The Journal of Geography, 114*(1), 15–25. doi:10.1080/00221341.2014.897362

Robinson, A. C., Kerski, J., Long, E. C., Luo, H., DiBiase, D., & Lee, A. (2015). Maps and the geospatial revolution: Teaching a massive open online course (mooc) in geography. *Journal of Geography in Higher Education, 39*(1), 65–82. doi:10.1080/03098265.2014.996850

Salazar Argonza, J. (2011). Estado actual de la Web 3.0 o Web Semántica. *Tema del mes.*

Squire, K., & Jenkins, H. (2003). Harnessing the power of games in education. *Insight (American Society of Ophthalmic Registered Nurses), 3*(1), 5–33. PMID:12703249

Stodden, R. A., Abhari, K., & Kong, E. (2015). Secondary School Preparation and Transition of Youth with Disabilities. In *Transition of Youth and Young Adults* (pp. 7–30). Emerald Group Publishing Limited. doi:10.1108/S0735-004X20150000028002

Sui, D. (2014). Opportunities and impediments for open gis. *Transactions in GIS, 18*(1), 1–24. doi:10.1111/tgis.12075

Tomar, G. S., Sankaranarayanan, S., Wang, X., & Rosé, C. P. (2017). *Coordinating collaborative chat in massive open online courses.* arXiv preprint arXiv:1704.05543

van de Oudeweetering, K., & Agirdag, O. (2017). MOOCs as accelerators of social mobility? A systematic review. *Journal of Educational Technology & Society*, 1–12.

Yang, D., Piergallini, M., Howley, I., & Rose, C. (2014). Forum thread recommendation for massive open online courses. *Proceedings of 7th Conference on Educational Data Mining 2014.*

Yang, D., Sinha, T., Adamson, D., & Rosé, C. P. (2013). "turn on, tune in, drop out": Anticipating student dropouts in massive open online courses. Workshop of NIPS.

Zancanaro, A., & de Souza Domingues, M. J. (2017). Analysis of the scientific literature on Massive Open Online Courses (MOOCs). *Ried-Revista Iberoamericana de Educacion a Distancia, 20*(1), 59–80. doi:10.5944/ried.20.1.15910

Zhuhadar, L., Kruk, S. R., & Daday, J. (2015). Semantically enriched massive open online courses (moocs) platform. *Computers in Human Behavior, 51*, 578–593. doi:10.1016/j.chb.2015.02.067

Chapter 16
Internal Branding as Innovation Tenet:
A Transformational Paradigm Shift

Maria Matiatou
The American College of Greece, Greece

ABSTRACT

Innovation as a core value for most organizations is not simply the application of new technology to achieve a business goal: it must be directly expressed through brand experience. Brand driven innovation is human centric. New ideas require a welcoming organizational culture, positive mindsets and internal advocacy to grow. Businesses can really innovate when employees become their brand evangelists. In this chapter, we initially explore internal branding values and tactics. We assess its role as critical bridge over vision, culture and image gaps in case studies to bring awareness on success and risk factors. Employee perceptions of communication practices are captured and matched to aspiration, missions and organizational values. From this premise, we establish internal branding as practice that affects the company's ability to innovate effortlessly and organically. The strong liaison between diffusion of innovation and brand endorsement is confirmed, consolidating the vital role of internal branding in the implementation of an organization's business strategy.

INTRODUCTION

Internal Branding is rooted in the philosophy that we are all stakeholders in creating sustainable futures. A participatory brand culture inside the organization builds a mandate for the effective delivery of the brand to its constituents. This employee engagement is mobilized by the acceptance and wide adoption of a corporate citizenship across every functional level of the company. Employees are no longer considered peripheral stakeholders; as brand ambassadors they are made central to the protection and the development of the company's image and reputation, delivering a promise that is consistent with the organization's mission and values (Berry, Tom, Carson, &White, 2003).

DOI: 10.4018/978-1-5225-4191-2.ch016

Effective internal branding requires aspiration, meaningful relationships of trust, and clear communication lines across departments and hierarchy from top to bottom. Alignment of personal and corporate values does not occur behind closed doors, nor can brand faith be instilled on the grounds of ignorance, guessing or improvisation. Where there is a vision-culture gap, there is first and foremost lack of awareness, understanding and organizational identification.

If we want to exceed the trust of our customers, then we first have to build trust with our people. – Howard Schultz, Chairman of Starbucks

THE CONCEPT

There is no commonly accepted definition for internal branding so far except a descriptive sum of words used to depict the functional approach of the term: it is often perceived as the activities that build the bridge between strategy and execution. While people individually use words such as "living the corporate values", "leveraging the corporate brand strategy", "reinforcing brand requirements internally", staying true to the brand promise is not done consistently and unanimously across organizational levels. The typical format is for senior management to decide on the strategy while the actual brand experience is communicated by the least informed and lowest paid associates.

The Canadian Marketing Association defines internal branding as

... the set of strategic processes that align and empower employees to deliver the appropriate customer experience in a consistent fashion. These processes include, but are not limited to, internal communications, training support, leadership practices, reward & recognition programs, recruitment practices and sustainability factors. (MacLaverty et al, 2007)

Internal Branding is the glue that holds together what the company *says* about the brand and what employees actually *do*, by applying the external brand to internal vehicles. This greater call to action boosts engagement and drives business outcome (Grossman, 2008).

Much like brand, corporate reputation spreads across business territories and mirrors itself in constituents' brand perceptions. As Fombrun states (2005)

... a company's reputational capital is the excess market value of its shares—the amount by which the company's market value exceeds the liquidation value of its assets.

Internal branding works in three consecutive layers:

- Effective communication of the brand to employees
- Demonstration of its relevance and worth
- Link with every job in the organization to ensure successfully delivery of the brand essence

Through internal branding the organization links its culture and values to the personal values of its internal stakeholders in ways that enable both the organization and the individuals to achieve their goals in consistent ways.

Internal branding:

- Nurtures the organizational identity. It reinforces *who we are* and *what we do* by offering a clear view of the net result.
- Drives organizational clarity through message communication and meaningful associations.
- Initiates change. Successful transformational process is boosted by alignment across functions and employees committed to the brand.

THE FIVE Ws

Internal branding is the "who" and "why" beyond the "how" and is rooted in the need for meaningful engagement of key stakeholders, moving from an arm's length relationship to a multi-level dialog that can influence company decisions. The roadmap to brand validation is radically transformed to reflect the changing dynamics from linear employee management to active collaboration at the following levels:

- Integrated approach replaces fragmentation among departments
- Shift of focus from managing to building relations
- Emphasis on bridging and creating mutual benefits rather than buffering the organization from its internal stakeholders
- Common view of the bigger picture in space and time, linked to long term objectives instead of short term goals
- Coherent unanimous approach is embraced by everyone and replaces departmental idiosyncrasies

Companies that disregard internal branding deprive themselves from a critical asset: the missing link between promise and delivery. By focusing solely on external efforts and not sufficiently infusing internal brand with the time, budget and energy it deserves, they should not be surprised that employees don't deliver as promised.

Rarely is one individual exclusively assigned to internal branding; usually the task it is piled up together with a stack of other responsibilities, such as advertising, branding or direct marketing, and more often than not claimed by overlapping authorities of the marketing and human resources departments. These blurred lines of responsibilities are partly due to the cross functional nature of internal branding, but nevertheless challenge the clarity, linearity and univocity required for the task.

Internal branding needs to be embedded in the corporate strategy even more so in times of significant changes, challenges, or industry hardships that require rallying employees around a key initiative. Because they are the ones to deliver the brand, they need to believe in the product or service, to live the brand and stand 100 percent behind its mission (Grossman, 2008).

THE HOW FACTOR

Ideally Building the Internal Brand

By adopting an internal branding strategy the organization allows itself to communicate its identity to stakeholders in clear and consistent ways. Stakeholders' perceptions in turn are favorably shaped over time because they emerge from the company's transparent and consistent responses to their needs and interests. As per Melcrum's Special Report on Internal Branding (2008), the resumptive eight-step model devised by DG&A reflects this continuum and can be adapted for use in organizations of every size, culture or industry.

1. **Identify the Business Outcome:** If we know what success looks like, we can focus on bringing along the specific business results. The branding landscape helps articulate two types Of outcomes: a broader, vision-and-culture-related, that strengthens the emotional bond between employees and the organization; and an initiative-bound, focused on inducing specific behaviors around a new project.
2. **Engage Key Audiences by Determining Where They Come From:** To identify audience perceptions, key audiences need to be prioritized and analyzed on the basis of their demographics, status, educational qualifications, time and position within the organization. Their mindset, concerns, hopes and needs, as well as the job realities they face and their source of information also must be identified and assessed. Once this is done, the organization gets a strong grasp of where they stand and where we want them to be led so they can drive the desired business outcome.
3. **Define Communication Goals:** With business outcomes and audience mindset at hand, next level is to assign communication goals such as:
    a. Raise awareness about a product/service or initiative
    b. Provide audience with relevant and timely information
    c. Drive understanding of mission and values
    d. Increase employee participation and foster enthusiasm
    e. Build support for change and calm fears about impending change

Goals should follow the SMART model and be Specific, Measurable, Achievable, Realistic, Time-bound.

4. **Create and Develop Core Messages:** Develop a message map based on the anatomy of an elevated key speech that trickles down to supporting messages, proof points and anecdotal illustrations. Meaningful and interesting messages engage people, relieve them from overwhelming pressure, connect the outcome and purify communication.
5. **Develop an Internal Theme With Visual Identity**: In other words how to get the message across in a strategic and memorable way. A theme has to resonate with and inspire audiences, embrace the business goal, be memorable, unique, and complementary to the external brand. Brainstorming is essential during the first phase—scanning for quality will follow.
6. **Initiate a Communication Plan and Align Management:** Once the theme and identity are in place, the overall plan will be tailored on employee needs, using the best vehicles –personal meetings, newsletters, letter from the CEO—and taking into account roles and appropriate timing. Repeating the message in a regular pace will reinforce understanding, adoption and behavioral shifts. Management support is crucial to the success of the plan; validation and alignment need to happen before communication. As soon as the brand is introduced to the organization, employees are ready to engage themselves in becoming the new brand ambassadors.

7. **Select Tools and Tactics to Implement the Plan:** Tools such as e-mails, intranet, internal/external publications, podcasts and employee surveys, all encapsulate the crux of communication through different arteries and work best across different platforms. Tactics needed to implement the plan include leader training, team accountability and measurement of delivery results, which in turn will allow the monitoring and adjustment of strategy if needed be.
8. Evaluation will determine the success of the brand initiation by connecting the outcome to the goals determined in steps 1 and 3. Measurement can focus on employee engagement, understanding of messages, leadership communication, behavioral changes and bottom line impact.

Custodians of Corporate Reputation

For the company identity to reflect positive expectations of key stakeholders and these expectations in return to mirror the company identity, internal perception and external image need to be carefully harmonized.

It starts with vision, carries on with culture and ends up with image. If a central thread doesn't hold them together, emerging gaps impact company reputation in direct and obvious ways. Senior management aspirations and organizational values relate to human perceptions and feelings; they can greatly jeopardize impressions of external stakeholders when not working together under a shared scheme. Ideally, the company identity underlying a corporate brand is transparent and consistent to what the organization stands for in the minds of customers.

Gaps inevitably occur where there is communication deficit: misunderstanding, insufficient listening or selective, one-way flow of information. Opportunities to speak out, be heard and taken into account must not be left to chance; when individuals are made part of decisions concerning their environment, they identify more readily with this environment, integrating it into their value systems. A customer whose request has been fulfilled, an employee whose insight has been picked up, a leader whose aspiration has penetrated management layers to reach everyone on board, are all results of superior, transparent stances headed towards the same direction.

Figure 1. Corporate branding
Source: Hatch & Schultz, 2003.

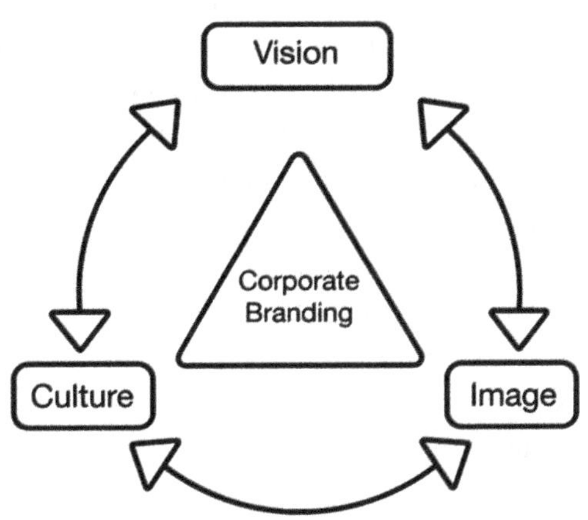

Key Behaviors

Internal Branding is an investment in the development of corporate image that induces the strategic advantage of distinctiveness through employee awareness, recognition and confidence. Projection of a consistent and inspiring image in internal as well as external environments safeguards the company's integrity and raises employee motivation and morale by allowing people to identify with their organization. It is the senior management's responsibility to transfuse its aspirations into a corporate culture through a set of organizational values felt and shared by all employees. Elevation of the internal identity held by employees will in turn reflect expectations of key stakeholders and influence them positively towards the organization (Cornelissen, 2011).

To make sure internal practices and processes are aligned to create the desired customer experience, an organization needs to step on the following stones: (BrandXpress Blog, 2005; MacLaverty, McQuillan, & Oddie, 2007).

- Follow a specific set of rules but beyond that, trust people to get things done.
- Be different and unique rather than formulaic and generic. Endorse the initiation of ideas to keep the message fresh, simple and relevant. Keeping things traditional within a changing environment will not help the organization move forward.
- Expand the frontiers outside the head office. Decentralizing emission centers reinforces the message and helps the organization speak in one voice.
- Let employees know *before* customers. Bypassing the very people who deliver the brand promise will undermine understanding, trust, and consistency of the message.
- Operate across functions. A brand is not in custody of a sole department; it's adopted, consumed and guarded across all departments who work in a networked way to build class within the brand.
- Think long-term as a requisite for brand building and a tool for success.
- Evaluate by measuring the things that really matter to the brand against current behaviors. Feedback obtained from such measurements should be actively fed to employees instead of resting in a file cabinet.

Setting the Right Context

In order to indoctrinate staff into the brand cult, practice of due diligence on behalf of leadership is the sine qua non that sets the wheels in motion within the right context. Careful selection of people willing to go the extra mile—walk out of their comfort zone to live up to the brand— can make a world of difference in how the brand will be experienced by customers. Skills can be improved, whereas preexisting attitudes are much harder to change.

From the viewpoint of a brand strategist, indoctrination to the brand culture starts with leadership (Van Anken, 2007). By helping senior management achieve their performance targets, tying objectives to their compensation system, appealing to their mentorship aspirations, involving them in cross-functional brand teams and enlisting their overall support, corporate officers are willing to act as brand champions while being accountable for other corporate functions. Other out-of-the-box tactics can be applied to obtain the support and involvement of employees in brand initiatives: brainstorming sessions, brand contests, achievement awards, performance appraisals, promotions, customer testimonials and compensation, all tied to delivery of the brand promise.

Figure 2. Internal branding model, topsail group

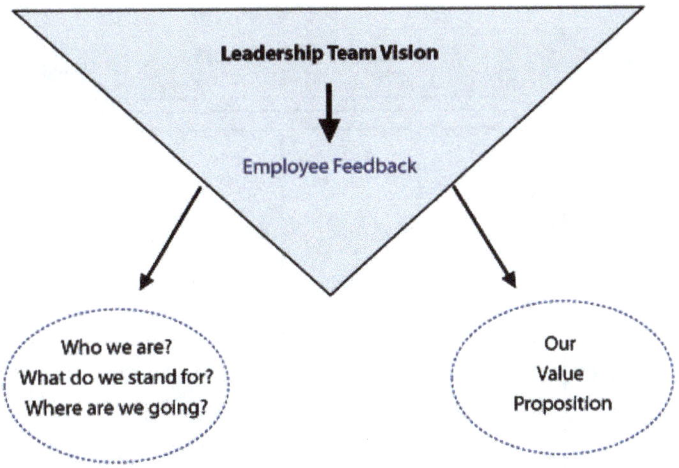

Jobs, Roddick, Branson, Dyson, are surrounded by devoted staff who is passionate about the brand; such leaders go out their way to encourage critical thinking, innovation, risk taking and curiosity—everything that mobilizes the creation of lasting brand value. From genuinely caring about people's lives, sharing their success stories, keeping them satisfied and interested, companies obtain all sorts of spillover benefits; employees feel they matter and this is directly proportional to the quality of services customers enjoy. Brands are held to higher account when values expand above the anticipated buzz and marketing spin (Hatch & Schultz, 2008).

A powerful brand house as per the Novo Nordisk model is visible from the roof (vision) and sustained by four pillars: people with values, science for people, care for people, and healthy communities, which align the multiple activities behind the brand. Real, imperfect leaders build a corporate brand memory by playing a very visible role in day-to-day activities and setting the example of brand engagement (Beverland, 2009, pp. 159-74). The undisputable modus operandi that leads to brand loyalty is '*show, don't tell*'.

STAKEHOLDERS BETWEEN PROMISE AND DELIVERY

Modern stakeholder theory (Mitchell, Agle, and Wood, 1997, pp.853-86) and innovative, visionary leadership identify employees as crucial to the company's successful brand delivery, placing them in quadrant D of the power-interest matrix —key players—because of their power to internalize and disseminate the company's values and invigorate its brands. The second four-field matrix depicts the two dimensions of brand strength, internal and external. While brands with high internal value are potential winners, those with high external affirmation but thin internal substance are eventually threatened. Internal brand substance is of paramount importance for overall brand strength; market penetration alone is not sufficient to sustain and boost an elusive brand. Corporate identity does not necessarily reflect brand identity, which in turn may not coincide with the brand image (Temporal, 2002). The harder a company works on the customer experience as nurtured by a dedicated and well informed staff the closer is customer perception to brand reality.

Figure 3. Stakeholder power-interest matrix
Conellissen, 2011, p.48.

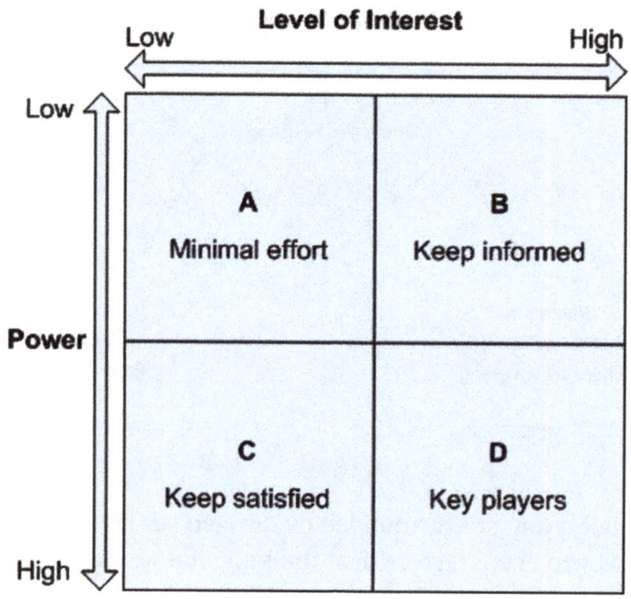

Figure 4. Brand strength categorization scheme
Burmann, Jost Benz, & Riley, 2009, pp. 390-97.

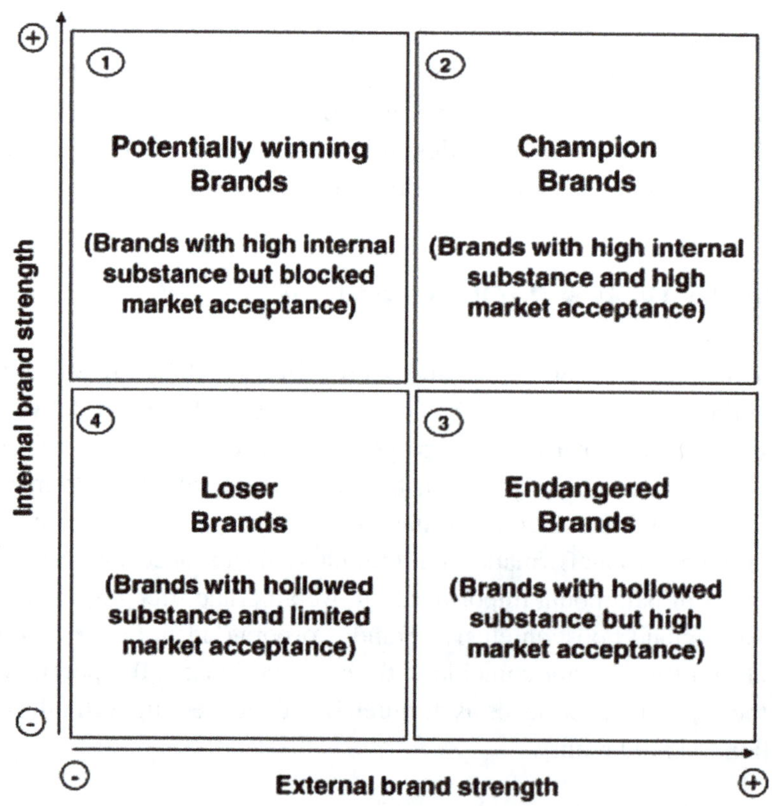

Yet in most companies employee status of high legitimacy and power is still underestimated and internal branding is either done poorly or not done at all. Senior management often fails to instill faith in the brand power, taking it as a given among employees. Possessing and utilizing the appropriate internal marketing tools and choosing the right turning points—moments of natural corporate change—to evoke the desired behavioral shifts, are key drivers with intrinsic value as ideal opportunities for an internal branding campaign. In times of a fundamental challenge or change, employees are more receptive to such initiatives as they enhance their sense of belonging to the new era and contribution to the advancement of the brand in its new endeavors. By creating messages that resonate with staff, the brand becomes part of their everyday experiences and on-brand behavior becomes instinctive.

Beliefs are far more valuable and inspiring than intentions—they are all about caring and they don't change over time. It is the brand essence that produces beliefs whereas intentions stick to the achievement of short term objectives and do not engage people in a timeless commitment. Evoking and sustaining a sense of pride for the company through mediums that become the message themselves, such as in the case of BP's *The Scroll*—a huge document with hard facts about the company—provides employees with the energy and the faith that are vital to energize them and help them embrace the brand vision (Colin, 2002). Of course, employees received a strong blow to their pride in 2009 when the oil spill destroyed most of the US east coast while BP shifted publicly the blame to contractors; the way a company handles a crisis has a direct impact on the staff's sense of dignity.

FACTS AND FIGURES

As per the global consulting firm Watson Wyatt Worldwide, Inc. ("Branding Internal Branding Topsail Group", n.d.) high levels of employee trust, understanding and belief in their brand result in 186 percent better performance in company earnings than low levels.

According to a study published by the American Marketing Association, while 8 percent of customers switching brands are enticed by competition, 68 percent are turned away by an employee's indifferent attitude.

Melcrum's Special Report on Internal Branding (2008) brings up a gallup of 2007 according to which companies with high engagement levels have 12 percent higher customer advocacy, 18 percent higher productivity and 12 percent higher profitability than those with average engagement levels.

Conversely, those with low engagement levels have 31 to 51 percent more employee turnover, 51 percent more inventory shrinkage and 62 percent more accidents than companies with average engagement levels.

ALIGNING CULTURE AND IMAGE BEHIND THE NEW VISION

Notorious Players

In the case of General Motors' attempt to fight small car brands with the new product line of Saturn, the "business as usual" attitude had no chance. Instead the company chose to start from the beginning, unconventionally launching the new brand from the inside out. The campaign was a film titled "*Spring. In Spring Hill.*" It was only after GM' image was *detached* from Detroit and *relocated* in the Spring Hill,

Tennessee plant that the internal experience was widely felt across retailers, white collar workers, suppliers and other internal constituents. And it was well after this internal experience had been articulated and evangelized by everyone in the company that the consumer brand was implemented.

Cisco was traditionally perceived as a place of hardware; somehow this perception had to be replaced by a new vision and perspective that would reflect the company's integral placement at the crossroad of all internet trajectories. This grand vision was communicated in an inspirational and empowering way by internally making it a call to action: "*The Internet is here: Are you ready?*"

The iconic Cadillac also had to undergo a major brand lifting when it lost pace of the significant shift from large, soft cars of marginal quality to high class, state-of-the-art design, luxury entries that addressed a much younger and more sophisticated customer group. Employees were hesitant and doubtful of the new project, so the company's ideas had to change in a radical and integral way. Aside from the lucrative new design, a whole new vocabulary was created and adopted to verbalize the bold, confident, forward-looking attributes in harmony with the timeless values of an iconic brand. Internal skeptics were repowered and re-oriented towards the new vision that would help the company recapture its iconic status. To foster attitude change films were created, linking the glorious days of the past to the new strategies and products and the profile of the new affluent buyer. Not long after, domestic doubters had become a dedicated team of brand ambassadors.

When Levis Strauss & Company decided to move beyond the traditional denim and launch the Dockers for Men line, initially wanted to target a slightly older male group without giving up its key brand attributes with the 501 brand. Dockers would be sold in different department stores hitting on the more sophisticated target group and would forever change perception on how man's clothing was sold. To succeed this, inside partners such as employees and retailers had to be convinced that the new strategy was not only possible but highly beneficial. Everyone was involved in the change of culture through innovative sessions and meetings that focused on consumer behavior and highlighted the new brand's shining possibilities. A radical new imagery was brought to life through the "store within the store" concept that demonstrated the entire scope of growth opportunities and benefits for customers and retailers (Sherwood & O'Neil, 2011).

The Saab Case

Although Saab is an example of successful brand re-ignition communicated through the value of its people, it is also a case in point that manifests the historic loss of a corporate identity which led to its inevitable demise.

In order to deal with declining sales during the 1990s, Saab assessed its brand according to the five Cs approach – Clarity, Commitment, Communication, Culture, Compensation. The uniqueness of the brand—comfort, security, individuality and personal focus—was captured and embedded in internal and external communications. Product development was redesigned to reflect the key brand features: safety, high class taste and unconventionality. Customers were surrounded by reception areas in a symbolic move that placed them at the epicenter of corporate consciousness. Finally, organizational culture shifted from the business-centered to the customer-centered approach through extensive staff training. At times of a relatively flat car market and under the shared ownership of General Motors, the company returned to an impressive growth of 40 percent (Bergstrom, Blumenthal, & Crothers, 2002, pp. 133-42).

Ironically, it was that same re-ignition that marked Saab's sharp decline and fatal bankruptcy in 2011. Much of the blame is laid at General Motors, which according to skeptics disrupted Saab's corporate identity by dismantling the brand integrity and melting it into their production system. It was not possible to reinvigorate Saab by degenerating it to an Opel clone with little left from its famous idiosyncratic vibe. Whatever made Saab a unique selling proposition, including its tradition and heritage, was diluted and suffocated without proper managerial or financial support. From a more pragmatic point of view, Saab most likely had concluded its corporate life cycle way before General Motors took over to extend its life expectancy for another 15 years. 140,000 cars per year is a fatally low production in an industry largely defined by economies of scale; a company with such a narrow identity was doomed to remain small and eventually die. New model engineering with all the safety and environmental issues that come along requires sales volumes in the hundreds of thousands. On top of it all, the privileged Swedish workforce model—high wage, low output—led to poor productivity and abysmal quality. In an era where consolidation through mergers and acquisitions had started to backpedal towards more streamlined business ventures, Saab was probably a consumable asset, also known as collateral damage.

Even if General Motors started off with the best of intentions and helped produce some of the finest 9-lines ever, acquiring Saab was the wrong move with the wrong company at the wrong time. Cash-stripped Saab required funding and support that GM was not adequate to provide, given its automation schemes and investment plans with Opel, Fiat, Lancia and Alfa Romeo. The narrow market of Saab devotees never fully accepted the innovations introduced in Saab 9000. Despite GM's good intentions, implementation was defective exactly because it attempted to fuse incompatible elements from different value systems which simply would not add up: US funding, German engineering, Swedish production systems. Such an amalgamation of corporate cultures could only blur Saab's identity and remove distinctiveness and impact from its corporate personality (Taylor, 2011; Pollard, 2011; Malmberg, 2008).

What could have saved Saab? Probably nothing since GM refused to fund the Youngman takeover and the company was insolvent beyond hope. Its excellent rebranding initiative never transformed its image in radical ways to reach massive target markets. But most likely two life jackets, *respect* of its unique identity and *faith* in the brand, could have led to better financial resolutions in the first place. A narrow, eclectic identity can be enhanced if it is carefully upgraded to a more salient status, reaching out to wider, more geographically dispersed market segments that share the same values and preferences. It will remain unknown if Saab's stellar reputation among its insane followers could have been magnified as a trend with the contribution of more appealing message strategies and less reluctant funding decisions.

LIVING THE BRAND

The 'We' Philosophy

Maritz Research and the Chartered Institute of Marketing, who worked together under the *Living-the-Brand* bandwagon project, discovered that 70 percent of customer perceptions of their brand experience tend to be driven by people-to-people moments. "Making the promise" and "keeping the promise" seems to be the paramount evidence of brand equity in the longer term.

Clearwater was the name given to HSBC bank's philosophy of ensuring alignment between every practice and process and this desired customer experience. HSBC was temporarily acquired by the Midland Bank brand and at the time was scoring very poorly in terms of image in the banking sector. It was only after HSBC decided to reposition its focus from organizational, marketing-oriented and company-centered jargon, to plain, measurable, consumer-centered talk that the bank got its act together and reacquired its status as a star performer.

Still, brand repositioning doesn't always succeed. Changes on the inside of the company often do not keep pace with the new messages about the brand sent to external constituents; without keeping the staff on board, without advancing organizational culture messages will fail to get across in consistency with the company's mission and values. When Barclays decided to reposition its brand for the first time in thirty years, it took care to coordinate its pace internally as well as externally, by setting an infrastructure to communicate with staff and help it to deal with negative public relations in the outside world. As a result, Barclays was then voted the world's most improved bank in a survey by Euromoney banking magazine (*Euromoney*, 2001; Gretchen, 2012). Currently it is interesting to observe how the bank works its way out of the crisis recently emerged from manipulating the Libor benchmark rates: settling out of court, waiving executive bonuses and cooperating with the Justice Department.

In the case of British Airways, the brand seemed to have a powerful internal reference and an overlooked role inside the organization that functioned solely on the inside without sufficient outward-facing manifestation. Physical reminders such as the introduction of a cellar on board were integrated in the brand promise to remind customers and cabin crews of what the brand was really about.

Mark Waller, Manager and Brand Specialist for Renault UK says: "*Brand Management is essentially about culture change.*" Changing the culture does not exclude anyone in any capacity or functional level if the company wants to speak in one voice to its customers.

Not everyone agrees that increased empowerment leads to better performance, especially with brands that are highly formulaic and don't give staff the sufficient latitude to deliver them. McDonalds' for one deals with standardization of their products and services across the world relying heavily on their consistency of standards and thus not allowing customization or flexibility. On face value, such cases evaluate increased empowerment of staff as running counter to the principles of brand management. Yet, even standardized products or services will eventually be in need of change, and real change can only happen when people across the company can connect with the customer experience (Brooke, 2002).

Ford Motor Company is a well-known case of sharpened focus and clarity through internal branding. Their message "Quality is Job 1" highlights their priority of commitment to quality using their brand as a communications vehicle.

Ritz Carlton, the epitome of brand consistency, is a legend in exceptional customer service among hotel customers and serves its reputation brilliantly through the message "*we are ladies and gentlemen serving ladies and gentlemen*", which highlights that corporate and internal brand are one and the same. Such level of brand equity does not occur by happenstance; it is taught in workshops, absorbed by personal and professional cultures and constantly reinforced at work (Baldoni, 2004).

A Corporate Culture of Sharing

A deeply rooted culture of outstanding service, such as the case of Ritz-Carlton, becomes second nature for the staff. A company benefits from employee loyalty because of their strong brand affinity, longer stay and valuable institutional knowledge that saves valuable resources needed for training of new staff. The American College of Greece has a long history of loyal employees acknowledged through initiatives such as the 25-year Associates—people who are part of the College's extensive history and carry its brand tradition and values for over two decades to the next generations.

According to findings from a study by the Canadian Marketing Association (Groom, MacLaverty, McQuillan, & Oddie, 2008), to the extent that internal branding requires cross-functional teams and multi-disciplinary practice, employees bridge strategy and implementation when their key drivers are understood and integrated in the process. Such drivers include pride, reward and consistency. Brands are associated with sets of values, such as passion, creativity, excellence, team work, integrity, or innovation, some of which are smoothly applied to the external whereas others to the internal brand promise.

Values are developed through the following stages:

- Quest for meaning through competitive analysis, best practices, external research and employees' experiences.
- Benchmarking and identification of gaps between best practices and internal protocol
- Development of values into themes tested against corporate brand
- Behavioral shifts to communicate messages associated with the values
- Maintenance programs to keep the plan going and the values fresh and relevant

Overall motivation, involvement of senior management, possibly an internal branding budget and individual advertising are means for inducing pride and confidence. The study claims that evaluation of employee intake and suitability, formal training and intensive brand orientation are key factors leading to desired behaviors. This overly structural and utilitarian approach tends to leave out the much necessary emotional and experiential components that lie at the root of a brand's relationship to its internal constituents. It takes much more than formal training and superficial orientation to adopt a brand and speak for it. It takes time, an ongoing relationship built on mutual trust and respect. The brand is a living thing that evolves and develops by virtue of the people who uphold its values.

According to a brand consultant, companies don't realize that internal brand advocacy is much more than a marketing tactic to get the buzz going; it is rather a strategic imperative to be immersed in the company culture (Gunelins, 2010). Employees rarely move from talking about their company to advocating it, defending it against negativity, and eventually evangelizing it. Yet this word-of-mouth marketing they are capable of generating is so powerful it is astonishing that only some companies realize its value and decide to jump on board the brand advocacy train.

It works like a pebble tossed into a pond: it sends out ripples in concentric circles that last long after the pebble sinks. Building a sustainable place for the brand should not under-consider the work force of the company and subsequently everyone else these people know and influence. Employees are a goldmine of information ready to offer their unique perspectives if only they are asked: they recognize flaws in procedure, identify barriers to purchase, spark innovation, obtain customer feedback. Listening to them is like putting a stethoscope to the company heartbeat. It is imperative that this type of information not only is collected but also tabulated to gain valuable, relevant and timely insight, and acted upon for the company to be true to its brand promise.

Branding within each of these people is tapping into the valuable living assets who live and breathe the brand and truly want to be part of something bigger than them. Holding the company flags carries little meaning without the tools that establish internal brand culture: mentorship programs, career development training, fringe benefits, alignment between HR and Marketing and a leadership that walk the talk. This higher purpose and meaning makes employees move to a larger space and infuse their "job" with a mission essence, shielding it from the shallowness and the vulnerability inherent to anything perfunctory (Rast, 2010). On the flip side, several tactics raise red flags within the work culture: if authority micromanage, if inequity is encouraged or tolerated, if there is disproportionate leniency or strictness to some, people will eventually talk and derogate, inside and outside the company.

A VEHICLE FOR INNOVATION

Brands are built by companies but they are owned by people and grown by experiences.

Engaging internal communication nurtures creativity because it activates employees and keeps them motivated. A corporate culture that fulfills this purpose motivates personnel to generate ideas. Employees will accept and respond to an innovation culture when their company demonstrates credibility, trust, consistency in its decisions, guidance, support, respect as well as a certain freedom of choice (Mast, 2009).

Innovation cultures are implemented through appropriate communication channels and change management frameworks. Employees who have a line-of-sight between their job and the organization's vision are more likely to be engaged in the innovation cycle. There are three domains where internal communication can impact employee engagement and build an effective communication culture:

- Interdepartmental relations, between peers and supervisors
- Alignment between the employee's values and the company's mission
- Creation of effective, multi-directional channels of communication (top to bottom, side to side, bottom up)

Diffusion (Rogers, 1995) is the process by which an innovation is communicated through certain channels over time among the members of a social system. In social systems members depend on each other to make innovation related decisions. Early adopters, the 10-25% of system members on the rapid adoption side of an innovation profoundly affect the decisions of later adopters. Each member of the social system follows his/her own innovation-decision cycle with a 5-stage process:

1. **Knowledge:** Awareness of the innovation and general purpose
2. **Persuasion:** Positive or negative attitude toward the innovation
3. **Decision:** Engagement in action that leads to adoption or rejection choice
4. **Implementation:** Putting innovation into effect
5. **Confirmation:** Evaluation of innovation-decision results

To be functional within an organization, this chain needs open and effective communication channels. It also requires an organizational culture that supports side-to-side, interdepartmental collaborations where flow of information is unhindered and knowledge is perceived as collective asset. People adopt an innovation when they are convinced that it will not disrupt normal functionalities and it will yield significant advantages compared to the idea it supersedes. Innovations may encounter resistance when they require significant adjustments and people are not convinced that rewards from adoption are imminent. Embracing the unfamiliar comes with awareness, persuasion and understanding of the new options.

Four additional variables complement the above to indicate varied rates of adoption and the context of an organization (Perez et al., 2017):

1. The type of decision for innovation: optional, collective or authoritarian. The more people involved in the decision-making process of an innovation, the slower its adoption rate.
2. The types of communication channels used in the diffusion process: individual or mass.
3. The nature of the social system or organization: leadership, standards, internal network connection that facilitate the diffusion of an innovation.
4. The personality and role of the promoter: idiosyncratic perspective and cognitive base of decision makers that determine their relevance as change promoters and innovation disseminators.

The conceptual model by Pfeffermann (2011) places dynamic capability for innovation communication at the center of a cyclical system of cross-functional elements. The model relies on information management, the function that permeates each of the interacting components for appropriate transmission of the innovation within the company. Innovative capability depends among others on the strength of interrelation among innovation activities and organizational communication. Upholding corporate communication with key stakeholders is a fundamental function in the openness required for the adoption and promotion of an innovation in systemic environments.

Figure 5. Elements of the dynamic capability innovation communication based on the conceptual definition Pfeffermann 2011.

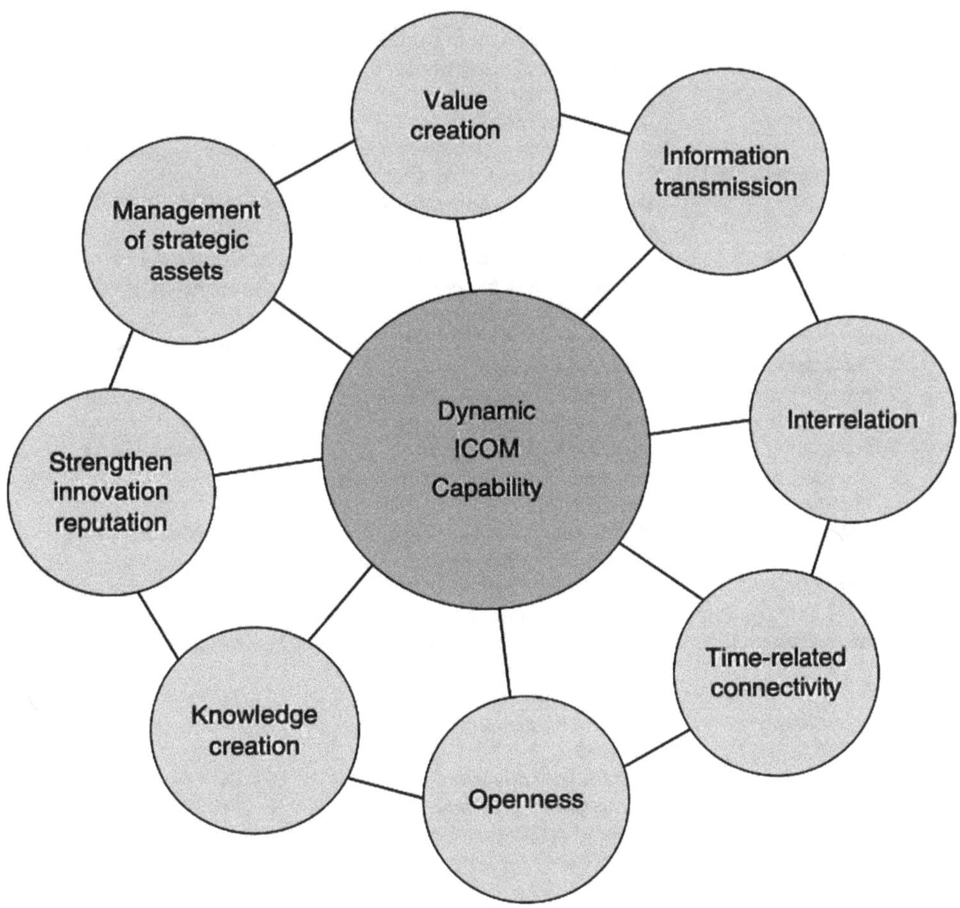

Innovation Communication as a Cross-Functional Dynamic Capability

The key to advancement of innovative ideas in a company is employee perception. Compatible, triable, observable, less complex innovations with greater relative advantage will be adopted more rapidly. Influencing employee perception comes with effective spread of the new idea in an environment of transparency, reliability, mutual trust and understanding. Hence, it is safe to assume that innovations are spread more rapidly in companies with a strong internal brand and an organizational culture of collaboration.

Damanpour (1991) in his seminal meta-analysis associates organizational innovation with 13 of its potential determinants, with statistically significant results among others in managerial attitude toward change and internal communication (Greenhalgh et al., 2004).

Table 1. Impact of structural determinants on organizational innovativeness from a meta-analysis of 23 studies of service and manufacturing

Potential Determinants	Definition	Association with Organizational Innovativeness
Administrative intensity	Indicator of administrative overhead.	Positive, significant
Centralization	Extent to which decision-making autonomy is dispersed or concentrated in an organization.	Negative, significant
Complexity	"Specialization," "functional differentiation," and "professionalism."	Positive, significant
External communication	Degree of organization members' involvement and participation in extraorganizational professional activities.	Positive, significant
Formalization	Reflects emphasis on following rules and procedures in conducting organizational activities.	No significant association
Functional differentiation	Extent to which divided into different units.	Positive, significant
Internal communication	Extent of communication among organizational units.	Positive, significant
Managerial attitude toward change	Extent to which managers or members of the dominant coalition favor change.	Positive, significant
Managerial tenure	Length of managers' service and experience within an organization.	No significant association
Professionalism	Professional knowledge of an organization's members.	Positive, significant
Slack resources	Reflects an organization's resources beyond minimal requirement to maintain operations.	Positive, significant
Specialization	Number of an organization's specialties.	Positive, significant
Technical capacity	Reflects an organization's technical resources and technical potential.	Positive, significant
Vertical differentiation	Number of levels in an organization's hierarchy.	No significant association

Damanpour, 1991.

Climate for Implementation

According to Klein and Sorra (1996) effective implementation of an innovation depends on two factors: the organizational environment for the implementation of a given innovation and targeted employees' perceptions of the innovation's suitability to their values.

What matters beyond the objective characteristic(s) of an innovation is how managers perceive and value them. To the same extent, the degree employees accept and use the said innovation wholeheartedly is an indicator of how aligned they are with their corporate brand and how they collectively perceive implementation policies and procedures.

Practices that encourage innovation adoption are training, user support, time to experiment, praise and incentives for innovation use (Spanos 2009). To the degree that employees expect support and reward within their organization for learning, adopting and implementing the innovation, internal communication as a facet of internal branding plays a key role in facilitating the transition.

It is not easy to achieve a reputation for innovation. In fact, most companies hope to be perceived as innovative but few really live up to this expectation. Demonstrating a line of innovations does not make an innovative company (Aaker 2007). Facts do not automatically translate into perception. It is hard to tell the innovation story to outside people if you don't have a task force of firm believers supporting the story. To break out of the clutter and establish yourself as a true innovator out there, you need to start from within.

Bold Moves Embraced by Organizational Culture

Taking the 'suggestion box' notion to another level, Ericsson brought the "inside the box" thinking into life. In 2008 the company started IdeaBoxes, its own internal innovation pipeline for people to get their own concepts noticed and developed (Paynter, 2013) (Sunderland, 2015). An online forum is available for employees to post their ideas for peer feedback and votes of approval. Box creators use this brainstorming space to spot weaknesses and recommend ideas for improvement. Employees from all kinds of disciplines and backgrounds (Karlsson, 2015) flock into the thread to contribute their ideas for which they always receive credit. Through discussion and feedback, the topic is transformed progressively into a concept with application potential.

In the same vein, IBM created a novel culture for social media innovation to bring together employees, customers and friends in a vibrant forum for powerful idea-sharing. The decentralized philosophy is a milestone in the history of the company—driving unprecedented collaboration and innovation: 100,000 employees are registered on the company platform and share their insight across 17,000 blogs. The company has its own internal tools to encourage discussion within its diverse and distributed culture, but does not regulate employees' social media activity in public. An internal wiki serves as a hub of information drawing millions of views and downloads every day. IBM innovative approach can be summarized in four pillars:

Stand Back, Involve Employees in SM Planning, Give Them Tools—and a Green Light, Use Crowd-Sourcing

Brands like Ericsson and IBM invest in a participatory culture that manifests a steadfast commitment to their knowledge-based human capital. Employees encouraged to voice their ideas or concerns and praised for their contribution are highly likely to uphold their brand and deliver on its promise wholeheartedly. Within the culture exist different identification levels indicating the type of perception: innovation culture, pioneers, mediocrity, standstill and refusal (Linke and Zerfass, 2011). Effective internal communication is the critical link between identification and positive action towards the innovation. In their highly regarded study *"Internal communication and innovation culture: developing a change framework"*, Linke and Zerfass (2011) measure the quality and degree of involvement within a company and propose a framework for implementing an innovation culture by means of internal communication. The table below highlights the rate of employee identification with a set of important messages associated with different phases in the innovation culture.

The study reveals that employees do not embrace innovation in similar ways, rates or time frames. Awareness, understanding, acceptance and action levels vary according to the message evaluated. Clearly acceptance stands out showing good penetration of the message and a culture encouraged to adopt innovation. Where responsibility is felt and employee initiative is supported across the organization there is higher level of commitment that leads to action.

LITERATURE REVIEW: ISSUES ADDRESSED AND QUESTIONS RAISED

Steyn's *Educational Model* of Corporate Communication Strategy (2003) shifts focus from the linear external approach 'from company to stakeholders' to the analysis of the internal environment as an integral slice of the corporate communication landscape. This open-eyed approach was the outcome of a longitudinal research project conducted by the University of Pretoria amongst non-profit organizations, government institutes and small to medium-sized companies in South Africa, and prioritizes the key role of stakeholders in strategy formulation via the alignment of their relationship issues with organizational goals. Internal branding enters the equation as the corporate strategy that will lead to resonance of the brand to inside stakeholders – an important thread woven inside Steyn's interactive model, which regards every functional micro-strategy as part of the larger strategic macro-picture.

Table 2. Messages of innovation philosophy and according phases of identification

	Phases of identification								
	Awareness		Understanding		Acceptance		Action		
Messages	*n*	%	*n*	%	*n*	%	*n*	%	Total
a) The management is interested in issues and ideas of its employees	143	26.7	130	24.3	198	37.0	64	12.0	535
b) The management is trying to implement proposals from the employees	130	27.9	90	19.3	180	38.6	66	14.2	466
c) The employees are proud of the company	125	24.3	142	27.6	126	24.5	121	23.5	514
d) Employee suggestions do not only come from departments whose primary task is the development of ideas	97	22.4	85	19.6	176	40.6	75	17.3	433
e) The employees are concerned with the future of the company	112	20.8	141	26.2	171	31.8	114	21.2	538
f) The employees try new and unknown ways in their field of work	92	18.7	98	19.9	183	37.2	119	24.2	492
g) The employees feel responsible for the company's success	107	19.1	142	25.3	164	29.2	148	26.4	561
h) My boss sounds interested in my ideas	94	17.8	99	18.8	135	25.6	200	37.9	528
i) I can try things without fear of negative consequences or failure	90	21.1	64	15.0	165	38.6	108	25.3	427
Total	990	22.0	991	22.1	1,498	33.3%	1,015	22.6	4,494

Linke & Zerfass, 2011.

Keller (1990) has developed the Mannheimer CI test to measure the internal effect of corporate identity and employee identification to their company. A corporate identity evokes reactions which in turn affect the culture and behavioral shifts within the organization. This diagnostic instrument can yield results that will point the way toward an effective internal branding strategy. Based on this model, five dimensions assess employee involvement: (Van Rier & Cees, 1995, pp. 56-57)

- **Identification Skill:** The need, willingness or fear to identify
- **Performance:** The willingness or motivation to perform
- Satisfaction with career or job
- Corporate climate: information, style of leadership and atmosphere in the company
- Evaluation of company

According to Benet et al (2009, pp. 126-43) paid communication is only the deliberate, structured part of brand communication; messages however are more often amplified or undermined by people within the business. The question raised is how much of what companies communicate is intentional. In a highly connected world, employees are brand ambassadors carrying the news all over the place: family, friends, social media. Knowledge brings power, so if a company lifts the veil of traditional management secrecy, makes brand values part of employees' everyday reality, expands the talent base and fosters the big-picture mindset, there is huge potential to stimulate and harness the energy of employees and engage the brightest talent in growing the corporate brand.

Bridging the gaps between mind-sharing to emotional branding and from there to cultural branding is an issue addressed by D.Holt in his book *How Brands Become Icons* (Holt, 2004, pp. 21-22). Marc Cobe argues for the need of a brand to be packed with emotion, personality and sensory experience, while Bedbury remains focused in the generic code and brand essence of the mind-share paradigm. Contemporary experts argue that internal branding is a magic tool that unites the entire organization in an emotive brand spirit which they express in everything they do. Communications build emotional linkages between brand and customers, mediated through employees who act as brand advocates and create long lasting bonds with loyal customers. It is this extra mile that managers are to walk that empowers employees so they in turn will trigger distinctive associations articulated through everything the brand does and forge an intimate connection with customers. The problem is to resist the impulse to restrict the brand in a mind-sharing, abstract-term typology, which necessarily overlooks what makes iconic brands valuable to both internal advocates and external consumers.

Often the terms *Internal Branding* and *Internal Marketing* are used interchangeably despite their differences at the semantic level and beyond. Internal Marketing is a forerunner that operates as an auxiliary facet of what is considered to be the overall endogenous corporate strategy, reinforcing the relationship between employee and customer satisfaction. The two strategies walk hand-in-hand but contrary to internal branding, which is about awareness and adoption of identity, image and reputation, internal marketing is about selling the concept of the product/service first to the employees and prioritizing their satisfaction. At the higher levels of Maslow's pyramid of needs, self-actualization and self-development are rooted in the high expectations held by both employees and customers in service environments.

According to Fisk et al. (1992) the employee is an internal customer who needs to be satisfied so that s/he is best prepared to serve the external customer. Motivated employees are crucial to the company's success even more so in times of thin margins and an elusive economic recovery. As pointed out by Mishra at the International Journal of Business and Management (2010), the objective of Internal

Marketing is to achieve service excellence through motivated and customer conscious employees. As per the two-step flow theory, employees are prepared to act as a powerful intercessory public of opinion leaders who will in turn pass their verdict to the people they serve. Service delivery relies primarily on people, so their actions have a major impact on customer acquisition, retention and erosion.

Scholarly work also detects linkage of internal branding and innovation. Baker et al. (1992), Goes and Park (1997) contend that communication structures and inter-organizational networks positively influence the company's aptitude to innovate with opportunities for shared learning, knowledge transfer and resource exchange (Baker et al., 1992; Goes and Park, 1997).

A CRITICAL VIEW

As a strategic choice, internal branding can be the vehicle to successful brand adoption but futile if not effectively implemented. Employees may not perform adequately because they don't experience properly the brand themselves, the management does not set the right tone, the training content is not engaging, or there is lack of post-training reinforcement that leads to a shift from the goals initially set forth. This deficit of momentum, backed up by absence of feedback and recognition derails the plan and undermines expected results (Bird, 2012).

It is therefore the emergence of experiential education rather than surface training that leads to alignment of corporate and personal values, memorable brand actualities and long-lasting relationships.

Challenges

- Overpromising through external branding without adequate preparation of employees to deliver on customer expectations. This situation is addressed by training and effective communications that help orient employees and adjust their behavior prior to external campaign launching.
- Failure to align internal branding with proactive brand-building strategy, thus compromising first-line support of organizational messages and their successful delivery to external stakeholders. Internal branding should not be the aftermath of a successful campaign; it needs to be integrated to strategic planning initiatives as a distinct individual brand behavior.
- Extensive relying on external communications to build internal brand awareness rather than training, peer-to-peer recognition, alignment of appraisal/assessments and rewards.
- On the flip side, extensive relying on internal communications where an integrated communications approach through internal and external media is necessary to inspire people and change their behaviors.
- Viewing internal branding as a tactic rather than a strategy. Support from senior management backed up with sufficient planning and resources are mandatory to sustain the project over time.
- Internal branding is not the big and splashy corporate brainwashing, so careful alignment of message and tactics should be used to get everyone on board.
- Employee motivation through feedback, appraisals or incentives is often overlooked. An attractive message can never get across if people carrying it are not inspired and motivated.
- Behaviors need time to change. Go slow before you can go fast, in other words allow time for expectations to turn into results (Steinmetz, 2009).

Risks and Threats

It is a paradox to assume that risks in the internal and threats in the external environments may occur because of adoption of an internal branding strategy. It is more likely that such disruptions occur because of defective implementation or rejection of the internal branding philosophy as a whole. Biases can be endemic in an organization and attitudes built up over the years are difficult to change. In big hierarchies orders trickle down from top but rarely make it beyond the first few layers of management. Without reinforcement of strategies and objectives clarity is blurred, the message hardly gets to the bottom, and managers are left to improvise. More often than not, traditional managers act as gatekeepers to vital information that needs to get across if they don't endorse the sharing culture that benefits the brand. This type of management feels threatened by shared knowledge; they believe that withholding information protects the organization, reinforces their sense of job security and downsizes competition dangers. Top-down approaches like *'Tell and Sell'* and *'Withhold and Uphold'* encourage buffering from the inside; they intentionally keep employees disengaged from dialogue or even uninformed, and thus skeptical or cynical about any change. In defensive corporate cultures employees are often excluded from crucial information and decision-making as a way for managers to avoid dissent and negative feedback (Cornelissen, 2011, pp. 221-22). These are serious impediments in the alignment of corporate and employee values. To a large extent open-mindedness and direct communication between senior management and the company workforce generates feedback that can lift such barriers and function as an assessment tool for the efficiency of communication channels within the organization.

Risks also stem from resisting innovation. To survive and thrive in times of limited resources and an ever-evolving technological context, companies intelligently adapt to the differentiated needs of their stakeholders. Forward-looking organizations see the necessity for departure from outdated managerial models, promote adoption of new technologies and support the creative involvement of employees as key strategies to advancement and growth. The pervasiveness of modern technology across all industries, the possibilities it offers for data management and enhanced experiences, and the ways these affect decision making and consumer behavior are the reasons why companies should embrace an innovative, horizon-view approach.

Trashing of brands occurs all the time in corporate history and causes shock waves all around the company. Powerful brands survive by infusing their proposals with more attractiveness, their products with more addictive ingredients, while spending time, money and energy to restore the company's image in the public sphere. Sustaining corporate pride within its internal constituents is only feasible through skilled intervention and is a key driver in successfully handling the crisis.

Although a national brand is much broader and historically significant than a corporate one, Greece is a typical example of a brand gone bad during the past three years, with total lack of rebranding initiatives and a deafening silence from the internal branding territory. Greek citizens more than ever need to be inspired and encouraged to restore belief in their country, the timeless values it represents and its potential to recover from the worst crisis it has faced since World War II. The serious blurring of identity and deficit of reputation based on a sequel of negative images spinned around by drama-seeking media are nurtured by the lack of consistent message and alignment strategy. Moreover, the chronic absence of a dignified leadership with the country's best interests at heart boosts suspicion and disbelief—two disastrous elements that are certainly echoed outside the borders and traumatize national reputation.

Opportunities

When corporate and personal values are aligned, the organization is at a place where it can advocate its brand(s) in one voice, bridging the gaps between what it projects to external constituents (image) and what these constituents perceive about the company (identity). It also brings into sharp focus corporate personality, the profound level in which the organizational spirit and culture is manifested, infusing it with integrity and credibility (Cornelissen, 2011, p. 48).

It is precisely this alignment that warrants the company's stability, coherence and distinctiveness in the eyes of stakeholders, elucidating where it comes from and where it aspires to be directed.

SUGGESTIONS FOR FURTHER RESEARCH

Like previously stated, internal branding has not always been successfully implemented and carried out for a number of reasons: misunderstandings, failure to align implicit and explicit brand image, or lack of the open-mindedness that removes barriers between functionalities and leads the way to awareness, acceptance and action. Behavioral shifts occur from an insightful strategic plan, hard work and an honest commitment; anything less will produce from zero to minimal results. A notion worthy of investigation is the extent to which employees are able to act as a homogeneous, stable and role-based group (Greenwood, 2008), whose shared values enable the brand to slide across organizational functions and radiate to external publics. In reality, group interests are not the sum of individual needs, which are often divergent and mitigated. In this context, alignment of values may be more easily said than done.

Striking cases of failures to internally promote the brand can be aggregated and tabulated in categories according to their level of penetration, length and intensity of effort, barriers raised, and reasons behind the failure as perceived at different operational environments within the organization. This type of research will require a combination of qualitative and quantitative methods, such as intensive interviews, focus groups or survey questionnaires over a certain period of time that will produce a wealth of information on each attempt for internal branding and the reasons why it did not produce the desired outcomes.

A different type of research that can yield a useful indicator of internal branding success is a *before—after* assessment of the ways employees perceive their brand and how this understanding reflects the true brand identity as perceived by customers. This parallel study could reveal stunning results on how perceptions on both sides are aligned and the extent to which customers actually receive what they have been initially promised. Again an amalgam of qualitative and quantitative tools exhausting both customer and employee feedback can help identify the vacuums that may exist at different stages of the branding journey and the outcomes that these disruptions may evoke.

Future studies should also be directed to develop a cross-cultural comparison of employees' perceptions as outcomes of internal brand commitment that support or mitigate innovation adoption and affect sustainability performance.

CONCLUSION

As a corporate strategy, internal branding is rooted in the concept of *oneness* that permeates every organizational function or discipline. It also stems from an inclusive worldview which finds a lot of resistance within traditionally fragmented and sheltered corporate structures that perceive shared knowledge as a high risk tactic. In the social era, reward comes to organizations that embrace change and create value by connecting people and ideas instead of building stereotypes; power stems from community and collaboration rather than ownership of direction by a few.

What If...Let's visualize the ideal scenario of a legit inside branding effort, one that brings together the best possible arrays of actions that can be taken towards this direction and see how it looks:

What if all insight obtained from external research on customer demographics, profiles, preferences, is spread across the company and ingrained in the minds of each employee?

What if management actually requests employee feedback *before* a campaign goes public?

What if they are the first to reflect on the brand experience and be armed to act as brand ambassadors?

Most likely they will deliver the brand as their personal experience—a powerful way to communicate the corporate persona to customers and impact their behavior.

And most likely this success will be the outcome of an insightful plan devised by Corporate Communications and Human Resources—a strategy that takes into full account the interfaces between corporate brand, VCI alignment and organizational identity.

Disney's mantra "*employees are our cast members*" comes to life because it places them where they belong: on stage. Internal branding initiates a virtuous circle of improvement by enabling employees to detect the job elements that are incompatible with the company orientation and thus improve customer experience. It's not just a matter of training—it's nurturing the brand internally to the point that it becomes part of the company's DNA.

REFERENCES

Σπανός, Γ. Ε., & Spanos, Y. E. (2009). Innovation adoption: an integrative model. *SPOUDAI-Journal of Economics and Business, 59*(1-2), 100-124.

Aaker, D. (2007). Innovation: Brand it or lose it. *California Management Review, 50*(1), 8–24. doi:10.2307/41166414

Baker, W., Nohria, N., & Eccles, R. G. (1992). The network organization in theory and practice. Academic Press.

Baldoni, J. (2004). Creating the Internal Brand. *Link and Learn Newsletter*. Retrieved from http://www.lc21.com/directions/articles_pdfs/creating_the_internal_brand.pdf

Benett, A. (2009). *Good for Business: The Rise of the Conscious Corporation*. New York, NY: Palgrave Macmillan.

Bergstrom, A., Blumenthal, D., & Crothers, S. (2002). Why Internal Branding Matters: The Case of Saab. *Corporate Reputation Review, 5*(2/3), 133–142. doi:10.1057/palgrave.crr.1540170

Berry, T., Carson, L., & White, S. (2003) *We Are All Stakeholders: Participatory Decision-making and Corporate Sustainability*. Paper presented at the Corporate Social Responsibility & Environment Conference, University of Leeds, UK

Beverland, M. (2009). *Building Brand Authenticity: 7 Habits of Iconic Brands*. Houndmills, UK: Palgrave Macmillan; doi:10.1057/9780230250802

Bird, J. (2012). Why Your Employees Don't Change after Training. International Success Academy [Blog]. Retrieved from http://internationalsuccessacademy.com/why-your-employees-dont-change-aftertraining/?goback=.gde_2586108_member_143989384

Branding Internal Branding Overview. (n.d.). Topsail Group [Blog]. Retrieved from http://www.topsail-group.com/branding/internal/index

BrandXpress Blog. (2005). Building an Internal Brand [Blog]. Retrieved from http://www.brandxpress.net/2005/09/building-an-internal-brand/

BrandXpress Blog. (2005). Internal Branding – 8 Principles [Blog post]. Retrieved from http://www.brandxpress.net/2005/09/internal-branding-8-principles/

Brooke, J. (2002). *The Brand Inside Maritz*. Retrieved from http://www1.cim.co.uk/filestore/resources/canons/brandinside.pdf

Burmann, C., Jost-Benz, M., & Riley, N. (2009). Towards an Identity-based Brand Equity Model. *Journal of Business Research*, *62*(3), 390–397. doi:10.1016/j.jbusres.2008.06.009

Cornelissen, J. (2011). *Corporate Communication: A Guide to Theory and Practice* (3rd ed.). Los Angeles, CA: SAGE.

Damanpour, F. (1991). Organizational innovation: A meta-analysis of effects of determinants and moderators. *Academy of Management Journal*, *34*(3), 555–590. doi:10.2307/256406

Euromoney. (2001). *Barclays Bank: The World's Most Improved Bank*. Retrieved from http://www.euromoney.com/Article/1009394/Article.html?Type=Article&ArticleID=1009394

Goes, J. B., & Park, S. H. (1997). Interorganizational links and innovation: The case of hospital services. *Academy of Management Journal*, *40*(3), 673–696. doi:10.2307/257058

Greenhalgh, T., Robert, G., Macfarlane, F., Bate, P., & Kyriakidou, O. (2004). Diffusion of innovations in service organizations: Systematic review and recommendations. *The Milbank Quarterly*, *82*(4), 581–629. doi:10.1111/j.0887-378X.2004.00325.x PMID:15595944

Greenwood, M. (2008). *Classifying Employees as Stakeholders*. Monash University, Australia. Department of Management working paper series. Retrieved from http://www.mngt.waikato.ac.nz/departments/Strategy%20and%20Human%20Resource%20Management/airaanz/proceedings/melbourne2008/ref/M.%20 Greenwood.pdf

Groom, S., MacLaverty, N., McQuillan, P., & Oddie, H. (2008). *Internal Branding -- A Human Resources Perspective*. Canadian Marketing Association.

Grossman, D. (2008). *Special Report on: Internal Branding*. Melcrum. Retrieved from http://www.slideshare. net/employerbrandingvn/internalbranding-8077975

Gunelius, S. (2010). *The Importance of Internal Brand Advocates*. Corporate-Eye [Blog]. Retrieved from http://www.corporate-eye.com/blog/2010/11/the-importance-of-internal-brand-advocates/

Hatch, M. J., & Schultz, M. (2008). *Taking Brand Initiative: How Companies Can Align Strategy, Culture, and Identity through Corporate Branding*. San Francisco, CA: Jossey-Bass.

Holt, D. (2004). *How Brands Become Icons: The Principles of Cultural Branding*. Boston, MA: Harvard Business School.

IBM Syndicated feeds [Web log post]. (2011). Retrieved from https://www.ibm.com/blogs/zz/en/

Karlsson, M. (2015, March 4). *IdeaBoxes: A management system for innovation with Magnus Karlsson. Interview by L. Sutherland*. Retrieved from http://www.collaborationsuperpowers.com/ideaboxes-a-management-system-for-innovation-magnus-karlsson/

Klein, K. J., & Sorra, J. S. (1996). The challenge of innovation implementation. *Academy of Management Review*, *21*(4), 1055–1080.

Linke, A., & Zerfass, A. (2011). Internal communication and innovation culture: Developing a change framework. *Journal of Communication Management*, *15*(4), 332–348. doi:10.1108/13632541111183361

MacLaverty, N., McQuillan, P., & Oddie, H. (2007). *Internal Branding Best Practices Study*. Canadian Marketing Association.

Malmberg, M. (2008). *Contributions of Internal Branding Practices to Corporate Brand Success*. Stockholm School of Economics, Department of Marketing and Strategy. Retrieved from http://arc.hhs.se/download.aspx?MediumId=658

Mast, C. (2009). Mitarbeiterkommunikation, Change und Innovationskultur – Balance von Informationen und Emotionen. In A. Zerfass & K. M. Mo¨slein (Eds.), *Kommunikation als Erfolgsfaktor im Innovationsmanagement* (pp. 271–288). Wiesbaden: Strategien im Zeitalter der Open Innovation, Betriebswirtschaftlicher Verlag Gabler. doi:10.1007/978-3-8349-8242-1_15

Matiatou, M. (2015). From Internal Branding to Cultural Transformation: A Virtuous Circle. *International Journal of Knowledge Society Research*, *6*(2), 1–19. doi:10.4018/IJKSR.2015040101

Mishra, S. (2010, January). Internal Marketing- A Tool to Harness Employees' Power in Service Organizations in India. *International Journal of Business and Management*, *5*, 1.

Mitchell, C. (2002, January). Selling the Brand Inside. *Harvard Business Review*. Retrieved from https://hbr.org/2002/01/selling-the-brand-inside

Mitchell, R. K., Agle, B. R., & Wood, D. J. (1997). Toward a Theory of Stakeholder Identification and Salience: Defining the Principle of Who and What Really Counts. *Academy of Management Review*.

Morgenson, G. (2012). FAIR GAME; The British, At Least, Are Getting Tough. *The New York Times*. Retrieved from http://www.nytimes.com/2012/07/08/business/barclays-case-opens-a-window-on-wallst-fair-game.html?_r=2

Paynter, B. (2013, April 16). To Boost Internal Innovation, Ericsson Thinks Inside The Boxes [Web log post]. Retrieved from https://www.fastcompany.com/3004745/boost-internal-innovation-ericsson-thinks-inside-boxes

Perez, G., Popadiuk, S., & Cesar, A. M. R. V. C. (2017). Internal factors that favor the adoption of technological innovation defined by information systems: A study of the electronic health record. *RAI Revista de Administração e Inovação*, *14*(1), 67–78. doi:10.1016/j.rai.2016.12.003

Pfeffermann, N. (2011). Innovation communication as a cross-functional dynamic capability: Strategies for organizations and networks. In *Strategies and communications for innovations* (pp. 257–289). Springer Berlin Heidelberg. doi:10.1007/978-3-642-17223-6_18

Pollard, T. (2011). *Saab Files for Bankruptcy: The End of the Swedish Saga*. CAR Magazine Site [Blog]. Retrieved from http://www.carmagazine.co.uk/News/Search-Results/Industry-News/Saab-files-for-bankruptcy-the-end-of-the-Swedish-saga/

Rast, H. (2010). *Three Dimensions of Internal Branding*. Social Media Explorer [Blog]. Retrieved from http://www.socialmediaexplorer.com/digital-marketing/the-three-dimensions-of-internal-branding/

Rogers, E. M. (1995). *Diffusion of innovations* (4th ed.). New York: Free Press.

Rogers, E. M. (2002). Diffusion of preventive innovations. *Addictive Behaviors*, *27*(6), 989–993. doi:10.1016/S0306-4603(02)00300-3 PMID:12369480

Rogers Everett, M. (1995). Diffusion of innovations. New York: Academic Press.

Sherwood, P., & O'Neill, B. (2011). *Brand Building Inside The Building*. Step 1 Branding LLC [Blog]. Retrieved from http://www.steponebranding.com/StepOneBranding/Step1_files/Cases%20.pdf

Steinmetz, A. (2009). *Internal Branding Challenges and How to Overcome Them*. Inward Consulting Blogspot [Blog]. Retrieved from http://inwardconsulting.blogspot.gr/2009/10/internal-branding-challenges-and-how-to.html

Steyn, B. (2003). From Strategy to Corporate Communication Strategy: A Conceptualization. *Journal of Communication Management*, *8*(2), 168–183. doi:10.1108/13632540410807637

Sutherland, L. (2015, March 4). IdeaBoxes: A management system for innovation [Web log post]. Retrieved from http://www.collaborationsuperpowers.com/ideaboxes-a-management-system-for-innovation-magnus-karlsson/

Taylor, A. (2011). *Saab without Tears*. CNNMoney [Blog]. Retrieved from http://money.cnn.com/2011/12/20/ autos/saab_general_motors.fortune/index.htm

Temporal, P. (2002). Corporate Identity, Brand Identity, and Brand Image [Blog]. Retrieved from http://www.brandingasia.com/columns/temporal10.htm

Van Riel, C. (1995). *Principles of Corporate Communication*. London, UK: Prentice Hall.

VanAuken, B. (2007). *70 Ideas for overcoming brand culture obstacles*. Branding Strategy Insider [Blog]. Retrieved from http://www.brandingstrategyinsider.com/2007/09/internal-brand-html.html

Compilation of References

Aaker, D. (2007). Innovation: Brand it or lose it. *California Management Review*, *50*(1), 8–24. doi:10.2307/41166414

ABET. (2015a). *Why Accreditation Matters*. Retrieved from http://www.abet.org/accreditation/why-abet-accreditation-matters/

ABET. (2015b). *Accreditation Outside of the US*. Retrieved from http://www.abet.org/accreditation/new-to-accreditation/accreditation-outside-the-u-s/

Acevedo, Y. V. N., & Marín, C. E. M. (2015). Towards a decision support system based on learning analytics. *Advances in Information Sciences and Service Sciences*, *7*(1), 1.

Adell, J., & Castañeda, L. (2010). Los entornos Personales de Aprendizaje (PLEs): una nueva manera de entender el aprendizaje. In R. Roig Vila, & M. Fiorucci (Eds.), *Claves para la investigación en innovación y calidad educativas. La integración de las Tecnologías de la Información y la Comunicación y la Interculturalidad en las aulas.* Alcoy: Marfil–Roma TRE Universita degli studi. Retrieved from https://digitum.um.es/jspui/bitstream/10201/17247/1/Adell%26Casta%C3%B1eda_2010.pdf

Adell, J., & Castañeda, L. (2013). La anatomía de los PLEs. In L. Castañeda & J. Adell (Eds.), *Entornos Personales de Aprendizaje: Claves para el ecosistema educativo en red* (pp. 11–27). Alcoy: Marfil. Retrieved from https://digitum.um.es/xmlui/bitstream/10201/30408/1/capitulo1.pdf

Adinolfi, D'Avanzo, Lytras, Novo-Corti, & Picatoste-Novo. (2016). Sentiment Analysis to Evaluate Teaching Performance. *International Journal of Knowledge Society Research, 7*(4), 86-107.

Adinolfi, P., DAvanzo, E., Lytras, M. D., Novo-Corti, I., & Picatoste, J. (2016). Sentiment Analysis to Evaluate Teaching Performance. *International Journal of Knowledge Society Research*, *4*(7), 86–107. doi:10.4018/IJKSR.2016100108

Adomavicius, G., & Tuzhilin, A. (2005). Toward the next generation of recommender systems: A survey of the state-of-the-art and possible extensions. *IEEE Transactions on Knowledge and Data Engineering*, *17*(6), 734–749. doi:10.1109/TKDE.2005.99

Afar, H. S. (2015). Educating With Prezi: A New Presentation Paradigm For Teaching, Learning, And Leading In The Digital Age. *College Student Journal*, *49*(4), 491–512. Retrieved from http://content.ebscohost.com/ContentServer.asp?T=P&P=AN&K=111986883&S=R&D=a9h&EbscoContent=dGJyMNLe80SeqLA4yOvsOLCmr0%252BeprVSrq64TK6WxWXS&ContentCustomer=dGJyMPGns0qxp7NJuePfgeyx44Dt6fIA

Agarwal, A., Xie, B., Vovsha, I., Rambow, O., & Passonneau, R. (2011). Sentiment analysis of twitter data. In *Proceedings of the workshop on languages in social media* (pp. 30-38). Association for Computational Linguistics.

Agarwal, B., & Mittal, N. (2016). Prominent feature extraction for review analysis: An empirical study. *Journal of Experimental & Theoretical Artificial Intelligence*, *28*(3), 485–498. doi:10.1080/0952813X.2014.977830

Ahumada, P. (2001). *La Evaluación una concepción de aprendizaje significativo.* Chile: Ediciones Universitarias de Valparaíso de la Universidad Católica de Valparaíso.

Albano, C. S. (2013). Open government data: a value chain model proposal. *Proceedings of the 14th Annual International Conference on Digital Government Research, Association for Computing Machinery,* 285-286. doi:10.1145/2479724.2479775

Alderete, M., & Formichella, M. (2016). Efecto de las TIC en el rendimiento educativo: el Programa Conectar Igualdad en la Argentina. *Revista CEPAL, 119,* 89-107. Retrieved from http://repositorio.cepal.org/handle/11362/40404

Allen, M. (2004). *Assessing Academic Programs in Higher Education.* Bolton, MA: Anker Publication Co.

Almirall, E., Lee, M., & Majchrzak, A. (2014). Open innovation requires integrated competition-community ecosystems: Lessons learned from civic open innovation. *Business Horizons, 57*(3), 391–400. doi:10.1016/j.bushor.2013.12.009

Alvarez, R., Garcia, D., Moreno, Y., & Schweitzer, F. (2015). Sentiment cascades in the 15M movement. *EPJ Data Science, 4*(1), 1–13. doi:10.1140/epjds/s13688-015-0042-4

Ames, C. (1990). Motivation: What teachers need to know. *Teachers College Record, 91*(3), 409–421.

Anderson, C. (2012). *Makers: The New Industrial Revolution.* New York: Crown Business.

Andogah, G., Bouma, G., & Nerbonne, J. (2012). Every document has a geographical scope. *Data & Knowledge Engineering, 81,* 1–20. doi:10.1016/j.datak.2012.07.002

Anta, R., El-Wahab, S., & Giuffrida, A. (2009). *Mobile Health: The potential of mobile telephony to bring health care to the majority. IDB Publications 8600.* Inter-American Development Bank.

Anton, D., & Anton, A. (2012). *Ecología y medio ambiente.* Mexico City, Mexico: ST Editorial.

Appcircus. (2015). *Helsinki smart city app hack.* Retrieved from http://helsinki.smartcityapphack.com/

Apperson, J., Laws, E., & Scepansky, J. (2006). The impact of presentation graphics on students experience in the classroom. *Computers & Education, 47*(1), 116–126. doi:10.1016/j.compedu.2004.09.003

Apperson, J., Laws, E., & Scepansky, J. (2008). An assessment of student preferences for PowerPoint presentation structure in undergraduate courses. *Computers & Education, 50*(1), 148–153. doi:10.1016/j.compedu.2006.04.003

Apps for Europe. (n.d.a). *About us.* Retrieved from http://live-appsforeurope.pantheonsite.io/about-us

Apps for Europe. (n.d.b). *Join the apps for Europe competition.* Retrieved from http://live-appsforeurope.pantheonsite.io/competition

Aranguiz, M. S., & Quintana, M. G. (2016). ICT Resources to Improve Learning in Higher Education. *International Journal of Knowledge Society Research, 4*(7), 1–11. doi:10.4018/IJKSR.2016100101

Arenas, M., Kantere, V., Kementsietsidis, A., & Kiringa, I. (2003). The Hyperion Project: From data integration to data coordination. *Proceedings of the ACM SIGMOD RECORD.* doi:10.1145/945721.945733

Assolombarda. (1994). *Ricerca ed innovazione tecnologica: Analisi del fabbisogno delle aziende.* Milano.

Atkinson, R. (1997). The digital technology revolution and the future of US cities. *Journal of Urban Technology, 4*(1), 81–98. doi:10.1080/10630739708724548

Augusto, J. M., Pulido, M., & López, E. (2011). Does Perceived Emotional Intelligence and Optimism/Pessimism predict psycological Well-being? *Journal of Happiness Studies, 12*(3), 463–474. doi:10.1007/s10902-010-9209-7

Badilla, M. G., Vera, A., Carripán, C., & Quilodrán, J. (2015). Experiencias y reflexiones sobre el aporte de los mundos virtuales inmersivos en las habilidades pedagógicas y tecnológicas de alumnos en Formación Inicial Docente: la experiencia del proyecto TYMMI en OpenSim. *Encuentro Internacional Virtual Educa*. Retrieved from http://reposital.cuaed.unam.mx:8080/jspui/handle/123456789/4073

Badilla, M. G., Carrasco, J. L., & Prats, M. A. (2014). Use of PLE-Portfolio to Assess the Competency-Based Learning through Web 2.0 in Technical Engineering Education. *International Journal of Engineering Education, 30*(3), 675–682.

Badilla, M. G., & Meza, S. (2015). A pedagogical model to develop teaching skills. The collaborative learning experience in the Immersive Virtual World TYMMI. *Computers in Human Behavior, 51*, 594–603. doi:10.1016/j.chb.2015.03.016

Badilla, M. G., Vera, A., & Lytras, M. (2017). Pre-service teachers skills and perceptions about the use of virtual learning environments to improve teaching and learning. *Behaviour & Information Technology, 36*(6), 575–588. doi:10.1080/0144929X.2016.1266388

Baker, T., Bermès, E., Coyle, K., Dunsire, G., Isaac, A., Murray, P., & Zeng, M. (2011). *Library linked data incubator group final report*. Report, W3C Incubator Group.

Baker, W., Nohria, N., & Eccles, R. G. (1992). The network organization in theory and practice. Academic Press.

Baker, R. S., & Inventado, P. S. (2014). Educational data mining and learning analytics. In *Learning analytics* (pp. 61–75). Springer New York.

Baldoni, J. (2004). Creating the Internal Brand. *Link and Learn Newsletter*. Retrieved from http://www. lc21.com/directions/articles_pdfs/creating_the_internal_brand.pdf

Bannert, M., Reimann, P., & Sonnenberg, C. (2014). Process mining techniques for analysing patterns and strategies in students self-regulated learning. Metacognition and Learning, 9(2), 161–185. doi:10.1007/s11409-013-9107-6 doi:10.1007/s11409-013-9107-6

Bannon, L. (1991). From human factors to human actors: The role of psychology and human-computer interaction studies in system design. In J. Greenbaum & M. Kyng (Eds.), Design at work (pp. 25-44). Hillsdale, NJ: Lawrence Erlbaum Associates.

Baraniuk, C. (2013). The civic hackers reshaping your government. *New Scientist, 218*(2923), 36–39. doi:10.1016/S0262-4079(13)61625-5

Barberá, E. (2006). Aportaciones de la tecnología a la e-Evaluación, RED: Revista de Educación a Distancia. *Monograph, VI*, 1–13.

Barbero, J. M. (1996). La ciudad virtual: transformationes de la sensibilidad y nuevos escenarios de comunicaión. Revista de la Universidad del Valle, 14, 26-38.

Barbosa, F. A. (Ed.). (2011). *ICT EDUCATION 2010 - Survey on the use of Information and Communication Technologies in Brazilian Schools*. Sao Paulo: Brazilian Network Information Center.

Barbosa, L., & Feng, J. (2010). Robust sentiment detection on twitter from biased and noisy data. In *Proceedings of the 23rd International Conference on Computational Linguistics: Posters* (pp. 36-44). Association for Computational Linguistics.

Barroca, L., Rapanotti, L., Petre, M., & Vargas-Vera, M. (2010). *Developing Research Degrees Online*. International Conference of Education, Research and Innovation (ICERI), Madrid, Spain.

Barroca, L., Rapanotti, L., Petre, M., & Vargas-Vera, M. (2010). Developing Research Degrees Online. *International Conference of Education, Research and Innovation (ICERI)*, Madrid, Spain.

Barroso, J., Cabero, J., & Vázquez, A. (2012). Formación desde la perspectiva de los entornos personales de aprendizaje. *Revista Apertura, 4*(1), 1-12. Retrieved from http://www.udgvirtual.udg.mx/apertura/ num16/1_formacion.html

Barth, J., Fietkiewicz, K. J., Gremm, J., Hartmann, S., Ilhan, A., Mainka, A., & Stock, W. G. et al. (2017). Informational urbanism. A conceptual framework of smart cities. In *Proceedings of the 50th Hawaii International Conference on System Sciences*. Washington, DC: IEEE Computer Society. doi:10.24251/HICSS.2017.340

Bartsch, R. A., & Cobern, M. K. (2003). Effectiveness of PowerPoint presentations in lectures. *Computers & Education, 41*(1), 77–86. doi:10.1016/S0360-1315(03)00027-7

Basso, M., & Badilla, M.G. (2016a). ICT resources to improve learning in Higher Education. *International Journal of Knowledge Society Research, 7*(4), 1-11. doi: 104018/IJKSR.2016100101

Basso, M., & Badilla, M. G. (2016b). Propuesta de modelo de innovación en evaluación con uso de TIC. *Proceedings of the IX Congreso Internacional y XV Nacional Investigadores en Educación (INVEDUC).*

Bates, T. (2015). *Teaching in a Digital Age, Guidelines for Designing Teaching and Learning for a Digital Age*. Tony Bates Associates Ltd.

Batten, D. (1995). Networked cities: Creative urban agglomerations for the 21st century. *Urban Studies (Edinburgh, Scotland), 32*(2), 313–327. doi:10.1080/00420989550013103

Bauer, F., & Kaltenböck, M. (2011). Linked open data: The essentials. Edition mono/monochrom, Vienna.

Becket, N., & Brookes, M. (2005). Analysing quality audits in higher education. *Brookes eJournal of Learning and Teaching, 1*(2), 1-12.

Beetham, H., & Sharpe, R. (2013). Rethinking Pedagofy for a Digital Age. Designing for 21st Century Learning. Routledge, Taylor & Francis Group, UK.

Bekkers, W., & Spruit, M. (2010). *The Situational Assessment Method Put to the Test: Improvements Based on Case Studies*. 4th International Workshop on Software Product Management, Sydney, Australia. doi:10.1109/IWSPM.2010.5623871

Bekkers, V. J. J. M., & Homburg, V. (2005). *The information ecology of e-government: E-government as institutional and technological innovation in public administration*. Washington, DC: IOS Press.

Belgiu, M., Strobl, J., & Wallentin, G. (2015). Open geospatial education. SPRS International. *Journal of Geo-Information, 4*(2), 697–710.

Bellavista, J. (1997). The Barcelona Science Park: a triple helix model in the Catalan and Spanish Research System. In H. Leydesdorff & H. Etzkowitz (Eds.), *A Triple Helix of University-Industry-Government relations. The future location of research*. Academic Press.

Bell, J., Cheney, G., Hoots, C., Kohrman, E., Schubert, J., Stidham, L., & Traynor, S. (2004). *Comparative Similarities and Differences between Action Research, Participative Research, and Participatory Action Research*. Antioch University Seattle.

Bellone, C., & Goerl, G. F. (1992). Reconciling public entrepreneurship and democracy. *Public Administration Review, 52*(2), 130–134. doi:10.2307/976466

Belsey, A. M. (2005). *AIDS and the Family: Policy Options for a Crisis in Family Capital*. UN Department of Economic and Social Affairs.

Benett, A. (2009). *Good for Business: The Rise of the Conscious Corporation*. New York, NY: Palgrave Macmillan.

Beno, B. A. (2004). The role of student learning outcomes in accreditation quality review. *New Directions for Community Colleges, 126*(126), 65–72. doi:10.1002/cc.155

Bera, P. (2016). How colors in business dashboards affect users decision making. *Communications of the ACM, 59*(4), 50–57. doi:10.1145/2818993

Berbegal-Mirabent, J., & Ribeiro-Soriano, D. E. (2015). Behind league tables and ranking systems: A critical perspective of how university quality is measured. *Journal of Service Theory and Practice, 25*(3), 242–266. doi:10.1108/JSTP-04-2013-0059

Bergstrom, A., Blumenthal, D., & Crothers, S. (2002). Why Internal Branding Matters: The Case of Saab. *Corporate Reputation Review, 5*(2/3), 133–142. doi:10.1057/palgrave.crr.1540170

Berk, R. A. (2005). Survey of 12 strategies to measure teaching effectiveness. *International Journal of Teaching and Learning in Higher Education, 17*(1), 48–62.

Berners-Lee, T. (2006). *Linked data-design issues*. Retrieved from http://www. w3. org/DesignIssues/LinkedData. html

Berry, T., Carson, L., & White, S. (2003) *We Are All Stakeholders: Participatory Decision-making and Corporate Sustainability.* Paper presented at the Corporate Social Responsibility & Environment Conference, University of Leeds, UK

Besselaar, P. V. D., & Beckers, D. (2009). *Demographics and sociographics of the digital city*. Retrieved from http://dl.acm.org/citation.cfm?id=701393

BetaNYC. (2014, February 24). *#CodeAcrossNYC 2014 wrap up*. Retrieved from https://beta.nyc/2014/02/24/codeacross-nyc-2014-wrap-up/

BetaNYC. (n.d.). *About BetaNYC*. Retrieved from https://beta.nyc/about/

Beverland, M. (2009). *Building Brand Authenticity: 7 Habits of Iconic Brands.* Houndmills, UK: Palgrave Macmillan; doi:10.1057/9780230250802

Bhardwaj, A., Narayan, Y., & Dutta, M. (2015). Sentiment Analysis for Indian Stock Market Prediction Using Sensex and Nifty. *Procedia Computer Science, 70*, 85–91. doi:10.1016/j.procs.2015.10.043

Bhaskaran, R. (2004). *Digital Gangetic Plains (DGP): 802.11-based Low-Cost Networking for Rural Areas - 2001-2004: A Report.* The DGP Media Labs Asia Team. Available: http://www.cse.iitk.ac.in/users/braman/papers/dgp-report.pdf

Bhatnagar, S. (2004). *E-government: From vision to implementation*. New Delhi: Sage Publications.

Bhusal, P., Zahnd, A., Eloholma, M., & Halonen, L. (2007). Energy-efficient innovative lighting and energy supply solutions in developing countries. *International Review of Electrical Engineering, 2*(5), 665-670.

Bilandzic, M., Banholzer, M., Peev, D., Georgiev, V., Balagtas-Fernandez, F., & De Luca, A. (2008, October). Laermometer: a mobile noise mapping application. In *Proceedings of the 5th Nordic conference on Human-computer interaction: building bridges* (pp. 415-418). ACM. doi:10.1145/1463160.1463208

Bird, J. (2012). Why Your Employees Don't Change after Training. International Success Academy [Blog]. Retrieved from http://internationalsuccessacademy.com/why-your-employees-dont-change-aftertraining/?goback=.gde_2586108_member_143989384

Bizer, C., Cyganiak, R., & Heath, T. (2007). *How to publish linked data on the web*. Academic Press.

Bizer, C., Heath, T., & Berners-Lee, T. (2009). *Linked data-the story so far. Semantic Services, Interoperability and Web Applications: Emerging Concepts.* Information Science Reference (an imprint of IGI Global).

Blomberg, J. L., & Henderson, A. (1990). Reflections on participatory design: lessons from the trillium experience. In *Proceedings of the SIGCHI conference on Human factors in computing systems Empowering people - CHI '90* (pp. 353-360). New York: ACM Press. doi:10.1145/97243.97307

Bloomberg.org Group. (n.d.). *Impact of the competition. Groundbreaking ideas are needed more than ever.* Retrieved from http://mayorschallenge.bloomberg.org/competition-impact/

Bødker, S. (2010). A short review to the past and present of participatory design. Introduction to debate section. *Scandinavian Journal of Information Systems, 22*(1), 45–48.

Boit, A., Eirund, H., Geimer, T., Mendonca, J., Ott, A., & Sethmann, R. (2008). NetS-X - The Network Security Experience. *Proceedings of the 7th European Conference on i-Warfare (ECIW 2008).*

Borahan, N. G., & Ziarati, R. (2002). Developing quality criteria for application in the higher education sector in Turkey. *Total Quality Management, 13*(7), 913–926. doi:10.1080/0954412022000017021

Bracy, C. (2014, January 13). It's time to CodeAcross [Web log comment]. Retrieved from https://www.codeforamerica.org/blog/2014/01/13/its-time-to-codeacross/

Brahimi, T., Sarirete, A., & Ibrahimi, R. (2016). The Impact of Accreditation on Student Learning Outcomes. *International Journal of Knowledge Society Research, 7*(4), 51–62. doi:10.4018/IJKSR.2016100105

Branding Internal Branding Overview. (n.d.). Topsail Group [Blog]. Retrieved from http://www.topsailgroup.com/branding/internal/index

BrandXpress Blog. (2005). Building an Internal Brand [Blog]. Retrieved from http://www.brandxpress. net/2005/09/building-an-internal-brand/

BrandXpress Blog. (2005). Internal Branding – 8 Principles [Blog post]. Retrieved from http://www. brandxpress.net/2005/09/internal-branding-8-principles/

Bransford, J. D., Brown, A. L., & Cocking, R. R. (2000). *How People Learn Brain, Mind, Experience, and School. Commission on Behavioral and Social Sciences and Education, National Research Council, National Academy Press.*

Brewer, E., Demmer, M., Du, B., Fall, K., Ho, M., Kam, M., & Surana, S. et al. (2005). The Case for Technology for Developing Regions. *IEEE Computer, 38*(6), 25–38. doi:10.1109/MC.2005.204

Briscoe, G., & Mulligan, C. (2014). *Digital innovation: The hackathon phenomenon.* CreativeWorks London Working Paper, 6. Retrieved from http://www.creativeworkslondon.org.uk/wp-content/uploads/2013/11/Digital-Innovation-The-Hackathon-Phenomenon1.pdf

Briscones, I., & Blázquez, J. (2008). Evaluación de los aprendizajes en la formación con TIC. *Tarbiya, Revista de Investigación e Innovación Educativa*, (39), 41-59. Retrieved from https://revistas.uam.es/tarbiya/article/view/7192

Brooke, J. (2002). *The Brand Inside Maritz.* Retrieved from http://www1.cim.co.uk/filestore/resources/ canons/brandinside.pdf

Brooks, J. A., Shablack, H., Gendron, M., Satpute, A. B., Parrish, M. H., & Lindquist, K. A. (2016). The Role of Language in the Experience and Perception of Emotion: A Neuroimaging Meta-Analysis. *Social Cognitive and Affective Neuroscience*, nsw121. doi:10.1093/scan/nsw121 PMID:27539864

Buckner, L., & Yeandle, S. (2011). *Valuing Carers.* Carers; doi:10.4018/IJKSR.2015070103

Bunzel, D. L. (2007). Universities sell their brands. *Journal of Product and Brand Management, 16*(2), 152–153. doi:10.1108/10610420710740034

Burbules, N. (2012). El aprendizaje ubicuo y el futuro de la enseñanza. *Encounters on Education, 13*, 3–14. Retrieved from https://ojs.library.queensu.ca/index.php/encounters/article/view/4472/4498

Burger, A. (2012, October 15). *ITU finds two times more mobile than broadband subscribers*. Retrieved from http://www.telecompetitor.com/itu-finds-two-times-more-mobile-than-fixed-broadband-subscribers/

Burke, R. (2002). Hybrid recommender systems: Survey and experiments. *User Modeling and User-Adapted Interaction, 12*(4), 331–370. doi:10.1023/A:1021240730564

Burmann, C., Jost-Benz, M., & Riley, N. (2009). Towards an Identity-based Brand Equity Model. *Journal of Business Research, 62*(3), 390–397. doi:10.1016/j.jbusres.2008.06.009

Burnap, P., Rana, O. F., Avis, N., Williams, M., Housley, W., Edwards, A., & Sloan, L. (2015). Detecting tension in online communities with computational Twitter analysis. *Technological Forecasting and Social Change, 95*, 96–108. doi:10.1016/j.techfore.2013.04.013

Bush-Brown, A., & Davis, D. (1992). *Hospitable Design for Healthcare and Senior Communities*. Van Nostrand Reinhold.

Cabero, J., & Vázquez, A. (2013). Los Entornos Personales de Aprendizaje: uniendo lo formal, informal y no formal para la construcción del conocimiento. In *Los Entornos Personales de Aprendizaje. Visiones y retos para la formación* (pp. 9-26). Editorial de la Universidad Metropolitana de Caracas. Retrieved from http://tecnologiaedu.us.es/tecnoedu/images/stories/ples_2014.pdf

Calude, C. S., & Longo, G. (forthcoming). The Deluge of Spurious Correlations in Big Data. *Foundations of Science*. doi:10.1007/s10699-016-9489-4

Cambria, E. (2016). Affective computing and sentiment analysis. *IEEE Intelligent Systems, 31*(2), 102–107. doi:10.1109/MIS.2016.31

Campodall'Orto, S., & Ghiglione, B. (1997). The Technology Transfer Process within the New Innovation Models, in Managing Technological Knowledge Transfer. EC-Social Sciences COST, A3 (Vol. 4). EC Directorate General, Science, research and Development, Brussels.

Canada.ca. (n.d.). *Canadian Open Data Experience {CODE} 2015*. Retrieved from http://open.canada.ca/en/canadian-open-data-experience-code

Caragliu, A., Del Bo, C., & Nijkamp, P. (2009). Smart cities in Europe. In M. Buček, R. Capello, O. Hudec, & P. Nijkamp (Eds.), *Proceedings of the 3rd Central European Conference in Regional Science, Conference* (pp. 45-59). Academic Press.

Card, D., & Payne, A. A. (2002). School finance reform, the distribution of school spending, and the distribution of student test scores. *Journal of Public Economics, 83*(1), 49–82. doi:10.1016/S0047-2727(00)00177-8

Casasbuenas, G. J. (2011). The contribution of Colombian Civil Society Organizations to e-government for the Improvement of Transparency through the Use of Information and Communication Technologies. In D. Piaggesi, K. J. Sund, & W. Castelnovo (Eds.), *Global Strategy and Practice of E-Governance: Examples from Around the World* (pp. 324–337). New York: IGI Global. doi:10.4018/978-1-60960-489-9.ch018

Casas, C., & Lajoie, W. C. (2006). *The Fortune at the Bottom of the Pyramid. The Voxiva Story*. Wharton School Publishing.

Casecase. (n.d.). *AngelHack Series 7 Press Release*. Retrieved from http://angelhack.com/2014/03/13/angelhack-series-7-press-release/

Castells, M. (2005). A sociedade em rede - a era da informação: economia, sociedade e cultura (8th ed.). São Paulo: Paz e Terra.

Castells, M. (1989). *The informational city. Information technology, economic restructuring, and the urban-regional process*. Oxford, UK: Basil Blackwell.

Castelnovo, W., Misuraca, G., & Savoldelli, A. (2015). Smart cities governance: The need for a holistic approach to assessing urban participatory policy making. *Social Science Computer Review*. doi:10.1177/0894439315611103

Castillo, R. L. (2011). Municipal Mobile SMS Services: An e-Government Initiative of the Municipality of La Paz, Bolivia. In D. Piaggesi, K. J. Sund, & W. Castelnovo (Eds.), *Global Strategy and Practice of E-Governance: Examples from Around the World* (pp. 24–33). New York: IGI Global.

Cataldi, Z., Méndez, P., Dominighini, C., & Lage, F. (2012). *Dispositivos móviles en educación superior y entornos personalizados de aprendizaje*. WICC 2012. Retrieved from http://sedici.unlp.edu.ar/bitstream/handle/10915/19437/Documento_completo.pdf?sequence=1

CESPRI. (1997). *Cambiamenti nella struttura industriale lombarda e politiche regionali per l'innovazione tecnologica, Rapporto di ricerca*. Milan: University Bocconi.

CETID. (2011). *The Center of Excellence for Technology and Innovation in Favor of Persons with Disabilities (CETID)*. Available: http://www.sedpcd.sp.gov.br

Chan, M. E. (2016). La virtualización de la educación superior en América Latina: entre tendencias y paradigmas. *Revista de Educación a Distancia, 48*(1). Retrieved from http://www.um.es/ead/red/48/chan.pdf

Chan, C. M. L. (2013). From open data to open innovation strategies: Creating e-services using open government data. *Proceedings of the 46th Hawaii International Conference on System Sciences, IEEE Computer Science*, 1890-1899. doi:10.1109/HICSS.2013.236

Charalabidis, Y., Loukis, E., & Alexopoulos, C. (2014). Evaluating second generation open government data infrastructures using value models. *Proceedings of the 47th Hawaii International Conference on System Sciences*, 2114-2126. doi:10.1109/HICSS.2014.267

Chatti, M. A., Dyckhoff, A. L., Schroeder, U., & Th¨us, H. (2012). A reference model for learning analytics. International Journal of Technoogy Enhanced Learning, 4(5), 318–331. doi:10.1504/IJTEL.2012.051815 doi:10.1504/IJTEL.2012.051815

Chicago. (n.d.). *The City of Chicago Technology Plan*. Retrieved from http://techplan.cityofchicago.org

Chih-Hung, C., & Hwang, G. (2017). Effects of the Team Competition-Based Ubiquitous Gaming Approach on Students' Interactive Patterns, Collective Efficacy and Awareness of Collaboration and Communication. *Journal of Educational Technology & Society, 20*(1), 87–98.

Chou, W. Y., Tien, P. T., Lin, F. Y., & Chiu, P. C. (2016). Application of visually based, computerised diagnostic decision support system in dermatological medical education: A pilot study. *Postgraduate Medical Journal*.

Chou, P.-N., Chang, C.-C., & Lu, P.-F. (2015). Prezi versus PowerPoint: The effects of varied digital presentation tools on students learning performance. *Computers & Education, 91*, 73–82. doi:10.1016/j.compedu.2015.10.020

Chourabi, H., Nam, T., Walker, S., Gil-Garcia, J. R., Mellouli, S., Nahon, K., … Scholl, H. J. (2012). Understanding smart cities: An integrative framework. *Proceedings of the 2012 45th Hawaii International Conference on System Sciences (HICSS '12)*, 2289-2297. doi:10.1109/HICSS.2012.615

Chua, C. (2004). Perception of quality in higher education. In *Proceedings of the Australian Universities Quality Forum 2004*. AUQA Occasional Publication.

Cisco. (2017). *Cisco Visual Networking Index: Global Mobile Data Traffic Forecast Update, 2016–2021 White Paper*. Retrieved from http://www.cisco.com/c/en/us/solutions/collateral/service-provider/visual-networking-index-vni/mobile-white-paper-c11-520862.pdf

City of Chicago. (2013). *City services - service directory*. Retrieved from https://www.cityofchicago.org/city/en/svcs/servicedirectory.html

City of Vancouver. (2017). *What you said about Vancouver open data day hackathon: Survey results*. Retrieved from http://vancouver.ca/your-government/open-data-hackathon-2013-survey-results.aspx

Civic User Testing Group. (n.d.). *Be a tester, get paid*. Retrieved from http://www.cutgroup.org/

Clough, G. W. (2004). *The Engineer of 2020: Visions of Engineering in the New Century*. Washington, DC: National Academy of Engineering.

Code for America Labs. (n.d.). *What are brigades?* Retrieved from http://brigade.codeforamerica.org/brigade/about/

Cohen, L. L., Manion, L., & Morrison, K. (2007). *Research Methods in Education*. London: Routledge.

Collins, R., May, D., Weinthal, N., & Wicentowski, R. (2015). SWAT-CMW: Classification of Twitter Emotional Polarity using a Multiple-Classifier Decision Schema and Enhanced Emotion Tagging. *SemEval*, *2015*, 669.

Connors, J. P., Lei, S., & Kelly, M. (2012). Citizen science in the age of neogeography: Utilizing volunteered geographic information for environmental monitoring. *Annals of the Association of American Geographers*, *102*(6), 1267–1289. doi:10.1080/00045608.2011.627058

Constantinides, E., & Zinck Stagno, M. (2012). Higher Education Marketing: A Study on the Impact of Social Media on Study Selection and University Choice. *International Journal of Technology and Educational Marketing*, *2*(1), 41–58. doi:10.4018/ijtem.2012010104

Cornelissen, J. (2011). *Corporate Communication: A Guide to Theory and Practice* (3rd ed.). Los Angeles, CA: SAGE.

Cpqd. (2013). Centro de Pesquisa e Desenvolvimento em Telecomunicações. *Índice Brasil de Cidades Digitais*. Retrieved from https://www.cpqd.com.br

Craig, R. J., & Amernic, J. H. (2006). PowerPoint Presentation Technology and the Dynamics of Teaching. *Innovative Higher Education*, *31*(3), 147–160. doi:10.1007/s10755-006-9017-5

Crossley, S., Paquette, L., Dascalu, M., McNamara, D. S., & Baker, R. S. (2016). Combining click-stream data with NLP tools to better understand MOOC completion. In *Proceedings of the Sixth International Conference on Learning Analytics & Knowledge* (pp. 6-14). ACM. doi:10.1145/2883851.2883931

Cuillier, D., & Piotrowski, S. J. (2009). Internet information seeking and its relation to support for access to government record. *Government Information Quarterly*, *26*(3), 441–449. doi:10.1016/j.giq.2009.03.001

Curitiba. (2013). Prefeitura Municipal de Curitiba. *Serviços para o cidadão - serviços para empresas*. Retrieved from http://www.curitiba.pr.gov.br/servicos/cidadao

D'Avanzo, E., & Lytras, M. D. (2016). From Big Data to Smart Business: Some Philosophical Remarks - Revealing the new Era of Smart Data, Deep Learning and Cognitive Computing. *International Journal of Knowledge Society Research*, *7*(2), 125–135.

Damanpour, F. (1991). Organizational innovation: A meta-analysis of effects of determinants and moderators. *Academy of Management Journal, 34*(3), 555–590. doi:10.2307/256406

Daniela, L., Kalniņa, D., & Strods, R. (2017). An overview on effectiveness of technology-enhanced learning (TEL). *International Journal of Knowledge Society Research, 8*(1).

Darling-Hammond, L. (1999). *Teacher quality and student achievement: a review of state policy evidence*. Seattle, WA: Center for the Study of Teaching and Policy.

Davidov, D., Tsur, O., & Rappoport, A. (2010). Enhanced sentiment learning using twitter hashtags and smileys. In *Proceedings of the 23rd international conference on computational linguistics: posters* (pp. 241-249). Association for Computational Linguistics.

De Freitas, S. (2008). Serious Virtual Worlds. A scoping guide. Technical report. The Joint Information Systems Committee (JISC).

de Haan, M. (2012). *The effect of additional funds for low-ability pupils: A nonparametric bound analysis*. CESifo Working Paper (no. 3993). Munich, Germany: CESifo Group.

De Miguel, M. (2005). *Modalidades de enseñanza centradas en el desarrollo de competencias. Orientaciones para promover el cambio metodológico en el Espacio Europeo de Educación Superior*. Oviedo: Universidad de Oviedo.

Denecke, K., & Deng, Y. (2015). Sentiment analysis in medical settings: New opportunities and challenges. *Artificial Intelligence in Medicine, 64*(1), 17–27. doi:10.1016/j.artmed.2015.03.006 PMID:25982909

Denhardt, R., & Denhardt, J. (2000). The new public service: Serving rather than steering. *Public Administration Review, 60*(6), 549–559. doi:10.1111/0033-3352.00117

Derbali, L., & Frasson, C. (2012). Assessment of learners motivation during interactions with serious games: A study of some motivational strategies in food-force. *Advances in Human-Computer Interaction, 2012*, 5. doi:10.1155/2012/624538

Desouza, K. C., & Bhagwatwar, A. (2012). Citizen apps to solve complex urban problems. *Journal of Urban Technology, 19*(3), 107–136. doi:10.1080/10630732.2012.673056

DHMN Civic Hacks. (2015, April 09). National day of civic hacking [Web log comment]. Retrieved from http://dhmn-civichacks.blogspot.de/2015/04/national-day-of-civic-hacking.html

Díaz, S. (2014). Desarrollo de una ficha de observación para el análisis y evaluación de experiencias educativas en mundo virtuales. *Revista Internacional de Investigación e Innovación Educativa, 2*, 69–82. Retrieved from http://www.upo.es/revistas/index.php/IJERI/article/view/1088

Díaz-Barriga, F., & Hernández, G. (2002). *Estrategias docentes para un aprendizaje significativo. Una interpretación constructivista*. Editorial Macgraw-Hill.

DiCicco-Bloom, B., & Crabtree, B. F. (2006). The qualitative research interview. *Medical Education, 40*(4), 314–321. doi:10.1111/j.1365-2929.2006.02418.x PMID:16573666

Digital Communities. (2013). *Digital Cities Survey*. Retrieved from http://www.govtech.com/dc/digital-cities

Digitales Österreich. (n.d.). *apps4austria Wettbewerb. Teilnahmebedingungen*. Retrieved from http://www.oesta.gv.at/DocView.axd?CobId=49054

Ditrendia. (2016). *Informe Mobile en España y en el Mundo 2016*. Retrieved from http://www.amic.media/media/files/file_352_1050.pdf

Diver, P., & Martinez, I. (2015). MOOCs as a massive research laboratory: Opportunities and challenges. *Distance Education*, *36*(1), 5–25. doi:10.1080/01587919.2015.1019968

Dolan, J. G., & Veazie, P. J. (2015). Balance Sheets Versus Decision Dashboards to Support Patient Treatment Choices: A Comparative Analysis. *The Patient-Patient-Centered Outcomes Research*, *8*(6), 499–505. doi:10.1007/s40271-015-0111-6 PMID:25618789

Dornstädter, R., Finkelmeyer, S., & Shanmuganathan, N. (2011). Job-Polarisierung in informationellen Städten [Job polarization in informational cities]. Information. *Wissenschaft & Praxis*, *62*(2–3), 95–102.

DOT-Force. (2001). *Digital Opportunities for All, Report of the G8 Digital Opportunities Task Force*. DOT-Force.

Dotopen, S. L. (2015). *Smart city app hack. Terms and conditions*. Retrieved from http://smartcityapp.hackathome.com/rules/terms-and-conditions/

Duarte, F. & Pires, H. F. (2011). Inclusión digital, tres conceptos clave: conectividad, accessibilidad, comunicabilidad. *Revista Electrónica de Recursos em Internet sobre Geografía y Ciencias Sociales*, *150*(1), 1-15.

Duderstadt, J. J. (2008). Engineering for a Changing World a Roadmap to the Future of Engineering Practice, Research, and Education. Ann Arbor, MI: University of Michigan.

Durall, E., Gros, B., Maina, M., Johnson, L., & Adams, S. (2012). *Perspectivas tecnológicas: educación superior en Iberoamérica 2012-2017*. Austin, TX: The New Media Consortium.

Duran, C. K. G., Medina-Ramírez, R. C., & Juganaru-Mathieu, M. (2014, January). Using Linked Open Data to Enrich a Corporate Memory of Universities. In *Proceedings of the International Conference on e-Learning, e-Business, Enterprise Information Systems, and e-Government (EEE)* (p. 1). The Steering Committee of The World Congress in Computer Science, Computer Engineering and Applied Computing (WorldComp).

Dutch Eurydice Unit. (2007). *The education system in the Netherlands 2007*. The Hague, The Netherlands: Ministry of Education, Culture and Science.

Dzidonu, C. (2010). *An analysis of the role of ICTs to achieving the MDGs*. UNDESA. Available: unpan1.un.org

Earthman, G. I. (2002). School facility conditions and student academic achievement. Los Angeles, CA: UCLA's Institute for Democracy, Education, and Access.

Eaves, D. (2013, March 11). Open data day 2013 in Vancouver [Web log comment]. Retrieved from https://eaves.ca/2013/03/11/open-data-day-2013-in-vancouver/

EderD. (2017, May 15). *About Derek*. Retrieved from http://derekeder.com/about

Ehn, P. (1993). Scandinavian Design: On participation and skill. In D. Schuler & A. Namioka (Eds.), *Participatory design: principles and practices* (pp. 41–70). Hillsdale, NJ: Lawrence Erlbaum Associates.

Ekionea, J. B., Fillion, G., & Koffi, V. (2012). Improving municipal information and knowledge management capabilities: Case study. *Journal of Information & Knowledge Management*, *11*(4), 1250023- 1250044. doi:10.1142/S0219649212500232

Ekman, P. (1992). An argument for basic emotions. *Cognition and Emotion*, *6*(3-4), 169–200. doi:10.1080/02699939208411068

Elwood, S., Goodchild, M. F., & Sui, D. Z. (2012). Researching volunteered geographic information: Spatial data, geographic research, and new social practice. *Annals of the Association of American Geographers*, *102*(3), 571–590. doi:10.1080/00045608.2011.595657

England, R. E., Pelissero, J. P., & Morgan, D. R. (2012). *Managing urban America* (7th ed.). Washington, DC: CQ Press.

Ericsson and Digital Health Initiative. (2011). *Challenges and Opportunities in Scaling UP Digital Health.* Author.

Eskes, P., Spruit, M., Brinkkemper, S., Vorstman, J., & Kas, M. (2016). The Sociability Score: App-based social profiling from a healthcare perspective. *Computers in Human Behavior, 59*, 39–48. doi:10.1016/j.chb.2016.01.024

Etzkowitz, H. (1997). The Triple Helix: Academy-industry-governement relations and the growth of neo-corporatist industrial policy in the U.S. In S. Campodall'Orto (Ed.), Managing Technological Knowledge Transfer. EC Social Sciences COST A3 (Vol. 4). EC Directorate General, Science, Research and Development.

Etzkowitz, H. (1994). Academic-Industry Relations: A Sociological Paradigm for Economic Development. In H. Leydesdorff & P. Van den Besselaar (Eds.), *Evolutionary Economics and Chaos Theory: New directions in technology studies*. London: Pinter.

Eurofound. (2004). *Health and care in an enlarged Europe.* European Foundation for the Improvement of Living and Working Conditions.

Eurofound. (2006). *Employment in social care in Europe.* European Foundation for the Improvement of Living and Working Conditions.

Euromoney. (2001). *Barclays Bank: The World's Most Improved Bank.* Retrieved from http://www.euromoney.com/Article/1009394/Article.html?Type=Article&ArticleID=1009394

European Commission. (2011). *Open data an engine for innovation, growth and transparent governance.* Retrieved from http://eur-lex.europa.eu/LexUriServ/LexUriServ.do?uri=COM:2011:0882:FIN:EN:PDF

Evaluating Socio Economic Development. (2003). *SOURCEBOOK 2: Methods & Techniques - Participatory approaches and methods.* European Commission Documents.

Ewell, P. T. (2001). *Accreditation and Student Learning Outcomes: A Proposed Point of Departure. Council for Higher Education Accreditation.* CHEA Occasional Paper. Council for Higher Education Accreditation.

Falloon, G. W. (2010). Using avatars and virtual environments in learning: What do they have to offer? *British Journal of Educational Technology, 41*(1), 108-122.

Fernandez, G., & Mariño, O. (2016). *State-of-the-Art and Future Directions of Smart Learning.* Springer Singapore.

Fernandez, M., McClain, D., Brown Williams, B., & Ellison, P. (2015). PBIS in Georgia Department of Juvenile Justice: Data Dashboard and Radar Reports Utilized for Team Data-Based Decision-Making With Facility Team Leader Perspectives. *Residential Treatment for Children & Youth, 32*(4), 334–343. doi:10.1080/0886571X.2015.1113459

Ferschke, O., Yang, D., Tomar, G., & Rosé, C. P. (2015, June). Positive impact of collaborative chat participation in an edX MOOC. In *International Conference on Artificial Intelligence in Education* (pp. 115-124). Springer. doi:10.1007/978-3-319-19773-9_12

Fiedler, S., & Väljataga, T. (2011). Personal learning environments: Concept or technology? *International Journal of Virtual and Personal Learning Environments, 2*(4), 1–11. doi:10.4018/jvple.2011100101

Field, A. (2009). *Discovering statistics using spss* (3rd ed.). Sage Publications Ltd.

Fietkiewicz, K. J., & Stock, W. G. (2015). How "smart" are Japanese cities? An empirical investigation of infrastructures and governmental programs in Tokyo, Yokohama, Osaka and Kyoto. In *Proceedings of the 48th Hawaii International Conference on System Sciences* (pp. 2345-2354). Washington, DC: IEEE Computer Society.

Fietkiewicz, K. J., Pyka, S., & Stock, W. G. (2015). Evaluating infrastructures of the 21st century city: Informational cities in Japan as case studies. *Advances in Research, 3*(3), 297–311. doi:10.9734/AIR/2015/12344

Finn, J. (1994). The promise of participatory research. *Journal of Progressive Human Services*, *5*(2), 25–42. doi:10.1300/J059v05n02_03

Firmino, R. J. (2004). *Building the virtual city: The dilemmas of integrative strategies for urban and electronic spaces* (Doctoral thesis). University of Newcastle.

Flores, C. C., & Rezende, D. A. (2013). Strategic digital city: techno-social network twitter as communication channel for popular participation in city comprehensive plans. *Proceedings of the Nineteenth Americas Conference on Information Systems*.

Florian, L. (2015). Inclusive Pedagogy: A transformative approach to individual differences but can it help reduce educational inequalities. *Scottish Educational Review*, *47*(1), 5–14.

Fondazione Rosselli-CES&T. (1995). *Analysis of the regional science & technology policies in Europe* (CE-DG XII, Grant Contract: PSS*0819). Fondazione Rosselli.

Fonte, C. C., Bastin, L., Foody, G., Kellenberger, T., Kerle, N., & Mooney, P. et al.. (2015). VGI quality control. *Proceedings of the ISPRS Geospatial Week 2015*, 317-324.

Förster, T., Lamerz, L., Mainka, A., & Peters, I. (2014). The tweet and the city: Comparing Twitter activities in informational world cities. In *Proceedings of the 3. DGI 2014 Conference: Informationsqualität und Wissensgenerierung* (pp. 101-118). Frankfurt a.M.: DGI.

Förster, T., & Mainka, A. (2015). Metropolises in the Twittersphere: An informetric investigation of informational flows and networks. *ISPRS International Journal of Geo-Information*, *4*(4), 1894–1912. doi:10.3390/ijgi4041894

Forum Virium Helsinki. (2016, February 12). *Democracy hackathon Helsinki*. Retrieved from https://forumvirium.fi/en/democracy-hackathon-helsinki/

Forum Virium Helsinki. (n.d.). *What is CitySDK?* Retrieved from http://www.citysdk.eu/about-the-project/

Franconi, E., Kuper, G., Lopatenko, A., & Zaihrayeu, I. (2004). Queries and Updates in the coDB Peer to Peer Database System. *Proceedings of VLDB conference*. doi:10.1016/B978-012088469-8.50126-1

Freitas, S. I., Morgan, J., & Gibson, D. (2015). Will MOOCs transform learning and teaching in higher education? Engagement and course retention in online learning provision. *British Journal of Educational Technology*, *46*(3), 455–471. doi:10.1111/bjet.12268

Friedrichsmeier, A., & Marcinkowski, F. (2016). The mediatisation of university governance: A theoretical and empirical exploration of some side-effects. *Policy and Politics*, *44*(1), 97–113. doi:10.1332/030557315X14431876145728

Frijda, N. H., Kuipers, P., & Ter Schure, E. (1989). Relations among emotion, appraisal, and emotional action readiness. *Journal of Personality and Social Psychology*, *57*(2), 212–228. doi:10.1037/0022-3514.57.2.212

Gamage, D., Fernando, S., & Perera, I. (2015). Quality of MOOCs: A review of literature on effectiveness and quality aspects. In *Ubi-Media Computing (UMEDIA), 2015 8th International Conference on* (pp. 224-229). IEEE. doi:10.1109/UMEDIA.2015.7297459

Gangadharan, G. R., & Swami, S. N. (2004). Business intelligence systems: Design and implementation strategies. In V. Lužar-Stiffler, & V. H. Dobrić (Eds.), *Proceedings of the 26th International Conference on Information Technology Interfaces (ITI 2004)* (pp. 139-144). Zagreb: SRCE University Computing Centre, University of Zagreb.

García, B. (2010). Modelos teóricos e indicadores de evaluación educativa. *Sinéctica, 35*, 1-17. Retrieved from http://www.scielo.org.mx/scielo.php?pid=S1665-109X2010000200005&script=sci_arttext&tlng=pt

García, L. M. (2014). Evaluación Formativa de los Aprendizajes en el Contexto Universitario: Resistencias y Paradojas del Profesorado. *Educación XX1, 17*(2), 35-54. Retrieved from http://revistas.uned.es/index.php/educacionXX1/article/view/11478/11418

García-Cabot, A., De-Marcos, L., & García-Lopez, E. (2015). An empirical study on m-learning adaptation: Learning performance and learning contexts. *Computers & Education, 82,* 450-459. 10.1016/j.compedu.2014.12.007

GarridoA. (2013). *Edmodo.* Retrieved from http://edmodo.antoniogarrido.es/

Gartner. (2016). *Predicts 2016: IoT Technologies Optimize Smart City Operations.* Gartner.

Gatfield, T., Barker, M., & Graham, P. (1999). Measuring student quality variables and the implications for management practices in higher education institutions: An Australian and international student perspective. *Journal of Higher Education Policy and Management, 21*(2), 239–252. doi:10.1080/1360080990210210

Gebhardt, C., & Etzkowitz, H. (1996). Regional innovation Organiser: a quasi-public role for transational corporations and universities. Management and New Technology, COST A3.

Ghazanfari, M., Rouhani, S., Jafari, M., & Akhavan, P. (2011). Association rule approach for evaluation of business intelligence for enterprise systems. *IUP Journal of Computer Sciences, 5*(2), 21–38.

Gibbs, G. (2010). *Dimension of Quality.* York, UK: Higher Education Academy.

Gilad, B., & Gilad, T. (1985). A systems approach to business intelligence. *Business Horizons, 28*(5), 65–70. doi:10.1016/0007-6813(85)90070-9

Giunchiglia, F., & Zaihrayeu, I. (2002). *Making peer databases interact-A vision for an architecture supporting data coordination. Cooperative Information Agents* (Vol. 2446, pp. 18–35). LNCS. doi:10.1007/3-540-45741-0_4

Go, A., Bhayani, R., & Huang, L. (2009). Twitter sentiment classification using distant supervision. CS224N Project Report, Stanford, 1:12–18.

Goes, J. B., & Park, S. H. (1997). Interorganizational links and innovation: The case of hospital services. *Academy of Management Journal, 40*(3), 673–696. doi:10.2307/257058

Goldberg, K., Roeder, T., Gupta, D., & Perkins, C. (2001). Eigentaste: A constant time collaborative filtering algorithm. *Information Retrieval, 4*(2), 133–151. doi:10.1023/A:1011419012209

Goodchild, M. F. (2006). The fourth R? Rethinking GIS Education. *ESRI ArcNews, 28*(3), 1.

Goodchild, M. F. (2007). Citizens as sensors: The world of volunteered geography. *GeoJournal, 69*(4), 211–221. doi:10.1007/s10708-007-9111-y

Goodchild, M. F. (2009). Geographic information systems and science: Today and tomorrow. *Annals of GIS, 15*(1), 3–9. doi:10.1080/19475680903250715

Goodchild, M. F., & Hill, L. L. (2008). Introduction to digital gazetteer research. *International Journal of Geographical Information Science, 22*(10), 1039–1044. doi:10.1080/13658810701850497

Government of Singapore. (2017). *About us.* Retrieved from https://ecitizen-ideas-uat.app.gov.sg/egp/process/EGOV/EideasAboutUs

Government, N. S. W. (n. d.). *apps4nsw.* Retrieved from http://data.nsw.gov.au/apps4nsw

Graham, S., & Aurigi, A. (2007). Virtual cities, social polarisation and the crisis in urban public space. *Journal of Urban Technology, 4*(1), 19–52. doi:10.1080/10630739708724546

Granados, L., & Mendoza, J. (2014). Construcción de Mundos Virtuales para el Desarrollo de Destrezas de Lateralidad basado en Web3D. *Revista Educación en Ingeniería, 9*(17), 13-25. Retrieved from https://www.educacioneningenieria.org/index.php/edi/article/view/352

Green Hackathon. (n.d.). Retrieved from http://www.greenhackathon.com/

Greenhalgh, T., Robert, G., Macfarlane, F., Bate, P., & Kyriakidou, O. (2004). Diffusion of innovations in service organizations: Systematic review and recommendations. *The Milbank Quarterly*, *82*(4), 581–629. doi:10.1111/j.0887-378X.2004.00325.x PMID:15595944

Green, M., & McNeese, M. N. (2007). Using edutainment software to enhance online learning. *International Journal on E-Learning*, *6*(1), 5.

Greenwood, M. (2008). *Classifying Employees as Stakeholders*. Monash University, Australia. Department of Management working paper series. Retrieved from http://www.mngt.waikato.ac.nz/departments/Strategy%20and%20Human%20Resource%20Management/airaanz/proceedings/melbourne2008/ref/M.%20 Greenwood.pdf

Groom, S., MacLaverty, N., McQuillan, P., & Oddie, H. (2008). *Internal Branding -- A Human Resources Perspective*. Canadian Marketing Association.

Grossman, D. (2008). *Special Report on: Internal Branding*. Melcrum. Retrieved from http://www.slideshare. net/employerbrandingvn/internalbranding-8077975

Gruber, J. (2011). *Public finance and public policy* (3rd ed.). New York: Library of Congress.

Guerreiro, E. P. (2006). *Cidade digital: infoinclusão social e tecnologia em rede*. São Paulo: SENAC São Paulo.

Guest, G., Bunce, A., & Johnson, L. (2006). How many interviews are enough? An experiment with data saturation and variability. *Field Methods*, *18*(1), 59–82. doi:10.1177/1525822X05279903

Gunelius, S. (2010). *The Importance of Internal Brand Advocates*. Corporate-Eye [Blog]. Retrieved from http://www.corporate-eye.com/blog/2010/11/the-importance-of-internal-brand-advocates/

Gutierrez, C., Figureuerias, P., Oliveira, P., Costa, R., & Jardim-Goncalves, R. (2015). Twitter mining for traffic events detection. In *Science and Information Conference (SAI)* (pp. 371–378). IEEE.

Guttman, R. H. (1998). *Merchant differentiation through integrative negotiation in agent-mediated electronic commerce* (M.S. thesis). School of Architecture and Planning, MIT.

Halevy, A., Ives, Z., Suciu, D., & Tatarinov, I. (2003). Schema mediation in peer data management system. *Proceedings of ICDE*. doi:10.1109/ICDE.2003.1260817

Halonen, J. I., Hansell, A. L., Gulliver, J., Morley, D., Blangiardo, M., Fecht, D., & Tonne, C. et al. (2015). Road traffic noise is associated with increased cardiovascular morbidity and mortality and all-cause mortality in London. *European Heart Journal*, *36*(39), 2653–2661. doi:10.1093/eurheartj/ehv216 PMID:26104392

Han, J., & Kamber, M. (2001). *Data Mining: Concepts and Techniques*. San Francisco, CA: Morgan Kaufmann.

Hanna. (2014, April 17). CitySDK challenge: Build best cross-city smart participation app - win 3000 euros [Web log comment]. Retrieved from https://www.citysdk.eu/citysdk-challenge-build-best-cross-city-smart-participation-app-win-3000-euros/

Hansen, H. (2005). Choosing evaluation models. A discussion on evaluation design. *Evaluation*, *11*(4), 447–462. doi:10.1177/1356389005060265

Hao, J., Zhu, J., & Zhong, R. (2015). The rise of big data on urban studies and planning practices in China: Review and open research issues. *Journal of Urban Management*, *4*(2), 92–124. doi:10.1016/j.jum.2015.11.002

Harbon, L., & England, N. (2009). The Cultural Practice of Research Higher Degree Supervision over Distance: A Case in Progress. University of Sydney Papers in TESOL, 2009(2006), 87-107.

Hartigan, J. A. (1975). Clustering algorithms. New York: John Wiley.

Hartmann, S., Mainka, A., & Stock, W. G. (2016). Opportunities and challenges for civic engagement: A global investigation of innovation competitions. *International Journal of Knowledge Society Research*, *7*(3), 1–15. doi:10.4018/IJKSR.2016070101

Hartmann, S., Mainka, A., & Stock, W. G. (2017). Citizen relationship management in local governments: The potential of 311 for public service delivery. In A. A. Paulin, L. G. Anthopoulos, & C. G. Reddick (Eds.), *Beyond Bureaucracy* (pp. 337–553). Towards Sustainable Governance Informatisation; doi:10.1007/978-3-319-54142-6_18

Harvey, L., & Green, D. (1993). Defining quality. *Assessment & Evaluation in Higher Education*, *18*(1), 9–34. doi:10.1080/0260293930180102

Hatch, M. (2013). The Maker Movement Manifesto. Rules For Innovation. In *The New World of Crafters. Hackers, and Tinkerers*. McGraw-Hill Education.

Hatch, M. J., & Schultz, M. (2008). *Taking Brand Initiative: How Companies Can Align Strategy, Culture, and Identity through Corporate Branding*. San Francisco, CA: Jossey-Bass.

Hattie, J., & Timperley, H. (2007). The power of feedback. *Review of Educational Research*, *77*(1), 81–112. doi:10.3102/003465430298487

Haworth, R. (2016). Personal learning environments: A solution for self-directed learners. *TechTrends*, *60*(4), 359–364. doi:10.1007/s11528-016-0074-z

Hazelkorn, E. (2013). *World-Class Universities or World Class Systems?* Rankings and Higher Education Policy Choices.

Heeks, R. (2001). *Reinventing government in the information age: International practice in IT-enabled public sector reform*. London: Routledge.

Heeks, R. (2006). *Implementing and managing eGovernment: An international text*. Thousand Oaks, CA: Sage Publications.

Heeringa, W., Nerbonne, J., Bezooijen, R. van, & Spruit, M. (2007). Geografie en inwoneraantallen als verklarende factoren voor variatie in het Nederlandse dialectgebied. *Tijdschrift voor Nederlandse taal- en letterkunde, 123*(1), 70–82.

Heflin, H., Shewmaker, J., & Nguyense, J. (2017). Impact of mobile technology on student attitudes, engagement, and learning. *Computers & Education, 107*, 91-99. 10.1016/j.compedu.2017.01.006

Heimerl, K., & Brewer, E. (2010). The Village Base Station. *Proceedings of the 4th ACM Workshop on Networked Systems for Developing Regions*. doi:10.1145/1836001.1836015

Hellberg, A. S., & Hedström, K. (2015). The story of the sixth myth of open data and open government. *Transforming Government: People. Process and Policy*, *9*(1), 35–51. doi:10.1108/TG-04-2014-0013

Henderson, J. C., & Venkatraman, N. (1993). Strategic alignment: Leveraging information technology for transforming organizations. *IBM Systems Journal*, *32*(1), 472–484. doi:10.1147/sj.382.0472

Herlocker, J. L., Konstan, J. A., Terveen, L. G., & Riedl, J. T. (2004). Evaluating collaborative filtering recommender systems. *ACM Transactions on Information Systems*, *22*(1), 5–53. doi:10.1145/963770.963772

Hernández-García, Á., González-González, I., Jiménez-Zarco, A. I., & Chaparro-Peláez, J. (2015). Applying social learning analytics to message boards in online distance learning: A case study. *Computers in Human Behavior*, *47*, 68–80. doi:10.1016/j.chb.2014.10.038

Herring, J. P. (1999). Key intelligence topics: A process to identify and define intelligence needs. *Competitive Intelligence Review*, *10*(2), 4–14. doi:10.1002/(SICI)1520-6386(199932)10:2<4::AID-CIR3>3.0.CO;2-C

HETL. (2013). Exploring Spaces for Learning. *HETL Review*.

Hevner, A. R., March, S. T., Park, J., & Ram, S. (2004). Design science in information systems research. *Management Information Systems Quarterly*, *28*(1), 75–105.

Hew, K. F., & Cheung, W. S. (2014). Students and instructors use of massive open online courses (moocs): Motivations and challenges. *Educational Research Review*, *12*, 45–58. doi:10.1016/j.edurev.2014.05.001

HfALA. (2007). *The Health for All in Latin America Project. Reference manual, theoretical and methodological framework, experiences and directory of best practices*. Perugia, Italy: Fondazione Angelo Celli.

Hiemenz, J. (2011). *3D printing with FDM: How it Works*. Stratasys Inc. Retrieved from http://www.stratasys.com/3d-printers/technologies/fdm-technology

Hjalmarsson, A., & Rudmark, D. (2012). Designing digital innovation contests. In K. Peffers, M. Rothenberger, & M. Kuechler (Eds.), *Design Science Research in Information Systems. Advances in Theory and Practice – Proceedings of the 7th International Conference DESRIST '12* (pp. 9-27). doi:10.1007/978-3-642-29863-9_2

Hjalmarsson, A., Juell-Skielse, G., & Johannesson, P. (2017). *Open digital innovation. A contest driven approach*. Cham, Switzerland: Springer International Publishing AG. doi:10.1007/978-3-319-56339-8

Hjelm, J. (2001). *Creating the semantic Web with RDF: Professional developer's guide*. John Wiley & Sons, Inc.

HM Government UK. (2004). *Carers (Equal Opportunities) Act 2004*. London: The Stationary Office.

Holt, D. (2004). *How Brands Become Icons: The Principles of Cultural Branding*. Boston, MA: Harvard Business School.

Holzer, M., Kim, C., Kim, S., Melitski, J., & Rho, S. (2005). Digital government worldwide: An e-government assessment of municipal Web sites. *International Journal of Electronic Government Research*, *1*(1), 1–18. doi:10.4018/jegr.2005010101

Ho, M. R., Smyth, T. N., Kam, M., & Dearden, A. (2009). Human-Computer Interaction for Development: The Past, Present, and Future. *Information Technologies and International Development*, *5*(3), 1–18.

Homburg, V. (2008). *Understanding e-government: Information systems in public administration*. London: Routledge.

Hornik, R. (2016). A strategy to counter propaganda in the digital era. *Yearbook of the Institute of East-Central Europe*, *14*(2), 61–74.

Horsburgh, M. (1999). Quality monitoring in higher education: The impact on student learning. *Quality in Higher Education*, *5*(1), 9–25. doi:10.1080/1353832990050102

Hosman, L. (2010). A National ICT-in-Education Initiative: Macedonia Connects. In *E-Strategies for Technological Diffusion and Adoption: National ICT Approaches for Socioeconomic Development* (pp. 1–18). New York: IGI Global. doi:10.4018/978-1-60566-388-3.ch001

Houben, M., Van Den Noortgate, W., & Kuppens, P. (2015). The relation between short-term emotion dynamics and psychological well-being: A meta-analysis. *Psychological Bulletin*, *141*(4), 901–930. doi:10.1037/a0038822 PMID:25822133

Howard, A. (2013, January 17). Civic app for finding flu shots goes viral [Web log comment]. Retrieved from http://gov20.govfresh.com/civic-app-flu-shot-viral-open-government/

Howard, G. S., Conway, C. G., & Maxwell, S. E. (1985). Construct validity of measures of college teaching effectiveness. *Journal of Educational Psychology*, *77*(2), 187–196. doi:10.1037/0022-0663.77.2.187

Howe, J. (2006, June 02). Crowdsourcing: A definition [Web log comment]. Retrieved from http://crowdsourcing.typepad.com/cs/2006/06/crowdsourcing_a.html

Huitt, W. (2011). *Motivation to learn: An overview. Edu. Psychol. Interactive.* Valdosta, GA: Valdosta State University Univ. Available http: //www.edpsycinteractive.org/topics/motivation/motivate.html

IBM Syndicated feeds [Web log post]. (2011). Retrieved from https://www.ibm.com/blogs/zz/en/

ICCC. (2002, April). Ageing Dialogues 2020: the Future of Ageing. *Proceedings of the Second World Assembly on Ageing*, 131-132.

ICCC. (n.d.). *International Student Design Competitions Retrospective – 1994-2005.* Retrieved from http://www.unpan.org/Regions/Global/Directories/Resources/tabid/456/ItemID/1836/language/en-US/Default.aspx

ICCC. (n.d.). *Music As A Natural Resource: Solutions for Social and Economic Issues – Compendium.* Retrieved from http://www.unpan.org/Regions/Global/Directories/Resources/tabid/456/ItemID/1836/language/en-US/Default.aspx

Immonen, A., Palviainen, M., & Ovaska, E. (2014). Requirements of an open data based business ecosystem. *IEEE Access*, *2*, 88–103. doi:10.1109/ACCESS.2014.2302872

Info-communications Media Development Authority. (2016, November 28). *What we do.* Retrieved from https://www.imda.gov.sg/about/what-we-do

International Longevity Center-USA and Schmieding Center for Senior Health and Education. (2006). *Caregiving in America.* International Longevity Center.

Ioby. (2015). *About ioby.* Retrieved from https://www.ioby.org/about

Ishida, T. (2012). Activities and technologies in digital city Kyoto. *LNCS*, *3081*, 166-187. Retrieved from https://link.springer.com/chapter/10.1007/11407546_8

Ising, H. L., & Kruppa, B. (2004). Health effects caused by noise: Evidence in the literature from the past 25 years. *Noise & Health*, *6*(22), 5. PMID:15070524

ISL. (2017). *Apps for democracy. An innovation contest.* Retrieved from https://isl.co/work/apps-for-democracy-contest/

ITU and UNESCO. (2010). *A 2010 Leadership Imperative: The future built on BROADBAND.* A Report of the Broadband Commission.

ITU. (2011). *Measuring the Information Society 2011.* Geneva, Switzerland: International Telecommunication Union.

Järvenoja, H., & Järvelä, S. (2005). How students describe the sources of their emotional and motivational experiences during the learning process: A qualitative approach. *Learning and Instruction*, *15*(5), 465–480. doi:10.1016/j.learninstruc.2005.07.012

Jdidou, Y., Khaldi, M., & Chami, M. R. (2016). Recommendation Systems in MOOCs. *Proceedings of the 9th annual International Conference of Education, Research and Innovation.* doi:10.21125/iceri.2016.1540

Jdidou, Y., & Khaldi, M. (2016). Increasing the Profitability of Students in MOOCs using Recommendation Systems. *International Journal of Knowledge Society Research*, *4*(7), 75–85. doi:10.4018/IJKSR.2016100107

Jenson, I., Leith, P., Doyle, R., West, J., & Miles, M. P. (2016, November). Innovation system problems: Causal configurations of innovation failure. *Journal of Business Research, 69*(11), 5408–5412. doi:10.1016/j.jbusres.2016.04.146

Jetzek, T., Avital, M., & Bjørn-Andersen, N. (2013). Generating value from open government data. In *Proceedings of the International Conference on Information Systems (ICIS 2013): Reshaping Society Through Information Systems Design* (*Vol. 2*, pp. 1737-1756). Academic Press.

Jiang, B., & Thill, J. C. (2015). Volunteered Geographic Information: Towards the establishment of a new paradigm. *Computers, Environment and Urban Systems, 53*, 1–3. doi:10.1016/j.compenvurbsys.2015.09.011

Jirka, S., Brring, A., Kjeld, P., Maidens, J., & Wytzisk, A. (2012). A lightweight approach for the sensor observation service to share environmental data across Europe. *Transactions in GIS, 16*(3), 293–312. doi:10.1111/j.1467-9671.2012.01324.x

Johnson, K. A. (2011). The effect of Twitter posts on students perceptions of instructor credibility. *Learning, Media and Technology, 36*(1), 21–38. doi:10.1080/17439884.2010.534798

Johnson, L., Adams Becker, S., Cummins, M., Estrada, V., Freeman, A., & Hall, C. (2016). *NMC Horizon Report: 2016 Higher Education Edition*. Austin, TX: The New Media Consortium. Retrieved from https://library.educause.edu/~/media/files/library/2016/2/hr2016.pdf

Johnson, P., & Robinson, P. (2014). Civic hackathons: Innovation, procurement, or civic engagement? *Review of Policy Research, 4*(31), 349–357. doi:10.1111/ropr.12074

Johnson, W. L., Vilhjálmsson, H. H., & Marsella, S. (2005). Serious games for language learning: How much game, how much ai? *AIED, 125*, 306–313.

Jones-Evans, D. (1997). Entrepreneurial Universities - Cases of Good Practices from the Republic of Ireland. *Proceedings of the International Conference: Technology Policy and Less Developed Research and Development Systems in Europe.*

Juell-Skielse, G., Hjalmarsson, A., Johannesson, P., & Rudmark, D. (2014). Is the public motivated to engage in open data innovation? In M. Janssen, H. J. Scholl, M. A. Wimmer, & F. Bannister (Eds.), *Proceedings 13th IFIP WG 8.5 International Conference EGOV '14, Dublin, Ireland, LNCS* (Vol. 8653, pp. 277-288). doi:10.1007/978-3-662-44426-9_23

Kaiser, C., & Pozdnoukhov, A. (2013). Enabling real-time city sensing with kernel stream oracles and mapreduce. *Pervasive and Mobile Computing, 9*(5), 708–721. doi:10.1016/j.pmcj.2012.11.003

Kalaani, Y., & Haddad, R. J. (2014). Continuous Improvement in the Assessment Process of Engineering Programs. *Proceedings of the 2014 ASEE South East Section Conference.*

Kanjo, E. (2010). Noisespy: A real-time mobile phone platform for urban noise monitoring and mapping. *Mobile Networks and Applications, 15*(4), 562–574. doi:10.1007/s11036-009-0217-y

Kantere, V., Kiringa, I., & Mylopoulos, J. (2003). Coordinating peer databases using ECA rules. Databases, information systems and peer-to-peer computing. *LNCS, 2944*, 108–122.

Kapoor, K. (2006). *A multidimensional scaling and participatory design approach to classify open ended aircraft maintenance data* (Doctoral dissertation). Clemson University.

Karlsson, M. (2015, March 4). *IdeaBoxes: A management system for innovation with Magnus Karlsson. Interview by L. Sutherland.* Retrieved from http://www.collaborationsuperpowers.com/ideaboxes-a-management-system-for-innovation-magnus-karlsson/

Karolus, J. (2013). *Creating Noise Pollution Maps Based on User-generated Noise Measurements: Erstellung Von Lärmkarten Basierend Auf Nutzergenerierten Lautstärkemessungen* (Doctoral dissertation).

Katsui, H., & Koistinen, M. (2008). The participatory research approach in non-Western countries: Practical experiences from Central Asia and Zambia. *Disability & Society*, *23*(7), 747–757. doi:10.1080/09687590802469248

Kaufman, J. C., Kaufman, S. B., & Lichtenberger, E. O. (2011). Finding creativity on intelligence tests via divergent production. *Canadian Journal of School Psychology*, *26*(2), 83–106. doi:10.1177/0829573511406511

Keegan, P. (2010). The Ancient History Virtual Campus: a model for online student induction and support in higher education. *Proceedings of the 1st International Australasian Conference on Enabling Access to Higher Education*, 175-186.

Kementsietsidis, A., & Arenas, M. (2004). Data sharing through query translation in autonomous sources. *Proceedings of VLDB* (pp. 468–479). doi:10.1016/B978-012088469-8.50043-7

Kementsietsidis, A., Arenas, M., & Miller, R. J. (2003). Mapping data in peer-to-peer systems: Semantics and Algorithmic issues. *Proceedings of SIGMOD*. doi:10.1145/872757.872798

Khandelwal, D., Mishra, M., & Mishra, V. K. (2016). *A Survey on Subjective Sentiment Analysis from Twitter Corpus*. Academic Press.

Khveshchanka, S., Mainka, A., & Peters, I. (2011). Singapur: Prototyp einer informationellen Stadt. *Information. Wissenschaft & Praxis*, *62*(2-3), 111–121.

Kietzmann, J. H., Hermkens, K., McCarthy, I. P., & Silvestre, B. S. (2011). Social media? Get serious! Understanding the functional building blocks of social media. *Business Horizons*, *54*(3), 241–251. doi:10.1016/j.bushor.2011.01.005

Kilis, S., Gülbahar, Y., & Rapp, C. (2016). Exploration of Teaching Preferences of Instructors use of Social Media. *European Journal of Open, Distance and E-learning*, *19*(1), 1–18. doi:10.1515/eurodl-2016-0001

Kimani, M. (2008). Better health at the click of a button: Information helps Rwandan clinics reach out. *Africa Renewal*, *22*(1), 5. doi:10.18356/48f5cee5-en

Kiss, G. (2016). Ms Power Point vs Prezi in Higher Education. *TOJET: The Turkish Online Journal of Educational Technology*, *15*(3), 126–130. Retrieved from https://search-proquest-com.ezproxy.lancs.ac.uk/docview/1833764605?rfr_id=info%253Axri%252Fsid%253Aprimo

Klein, K. J., & Sorra, J. S. (1996). The challenge of innovation implementation. *Academy of Management Review*, *21*(4), 1055–1080.

Kort, B., Reilly, R., & Picard, R. W. (2001). An Affective Model of Interplay between Emotions and Learning: Reengineering Educational Pedagogy-Building a Learning Companion. In Icalt (Vol. 1, pp. 43-47). Academic Press.

Kosior, A., Barth, J., Gremm, J., Mainka, A., & Stock, W. G. (2015). Imported expertise in world-class knowledge infrastructures: The problematic development of knowledge cities in the Gulf region. *Journal of Information Science Theory and Practice*, *3*(3), 17–44. doi:10.1633/JISTaP.2015.3.3.2

Kouloumpis, E., Wilson, T., & Moore, J. D. (2011). Twitter sentiment analysis: The good the bad and the omg! *Icwsm*, *11*, 538–541.

Krishnaswamy, A. (2004). Participatory research: Strategies and tools. *Practitioner: Newsletter of the National Network of Forest Practitioners*, *22*, 17–22.

Kroenke, D. (2011). *MIS essentials*. Prentice Hall.

Krulwich, B. (1997). Lifestyle finder: Intelligent user profiling using large-scale demographic data. *Artificial Intelligence Magazine*, *18*(2), 37–45.

Kruse, A., & Pongsajapan, R. (2012). Student-centered learning analytics. CNDLS Thought Papers.

Kurkovsky, S. (2009). Engaging students through mobile game development. *ACM SIGCSE Bulletin*, *41*(1), 44–48. doi:10.1145/1539024.1508881

Kusakabe, M. (2012). *Measuring Wellbeing for the City of Liverpool.* Open City Foundation Wellbeing Survey Series.

Lal, P. (2015). Transforming HR in the digital era: Workforce analytics can move people specialists to the center of decision-making. *Human Resource Management International Digest*, *23*(3), 1–4. doi:10.1108/HRMID-03-2015-0051

Lane, D., Malerba, F., Maxfield, R., & Orsenigo, L. (1991). Choice and Action. *Journal of Evolutionary Economics.*

Lantz, B. (2013). *Machine learning with R.* Packt Publishing Ltd.

Laudon, K. C., & Laudon, J. P. (2011). *Management information systems: Managing the digital firm. 12.* Prentice Hall.

Lavieri, E. (2014). *A Study of Adaptive Learning for Educational Game Design.* ProQuest UMI.

Leclercq, D., & Cabrera, A. (2014). *Ideas e Innovaciones. Dispositivos de evaluación de los aprendizajes en la educación.* Editorial Universitaria.

Lederer, A. L., & Mahaney, R. C. (1996). Using case tools in strategic information system planning. *Information Systems Management Journal, USA*, *13*(4), 47–51. doi:10.1080/10580539608907016

Lee, J., Lim, C., & Kim, H. (2017). Development of an instructional design model for flipped learning in higher education. *Educational Technology Research and Development*, *65*(2), 427–453. doi:10.1007/s11423-016-9502-1

Lefebvre, H. (1991). *The production of space.* Oxford, UK: Basil Blackwell.

Lehmann, C. A., Giacini, J. M., & Davis, D. (2012). *Innovative and Technology for the Ageing.* U.N. *Publications.*

Lemmergaard, J., Gersbo-Møller, C., & Povlsen, L. B. (2005). The Scandinavian school revisited: a case study on new roles in the ISD process. *Proceedings of the 13th European Conference on Information Systems, Information Systems in a Rapidly Changing Economy.*

Lemos, A. (Ed.). (2005). Cibercidade 2: Ciberurbe: a cidade na sociedade da informação. Rio de Janeiro: Editora E-Papers.

Lenn, M. P. (1992). Global Trends in Quality Assurance in Higher Education. *World Education News and Reviews*, *5*(2), 20–21.

Lenzerini, M. (2003). Data Integration: A Theoretical Perspective. *Proceedings of PODS.* ACM.

Lévy, P. (1999). *Cibercultura.* São Paulo: Editora.

Leydesdorff, H., & Etzkowitz, H. (1996). Emergence of a Triple Helix of University-Industry-Government Relations. *Science & Public Policy.*

Leydesdorff, H., & Etzkowitz, H. (Eds.). (1997). *A triple Helix of University-Industry-Government relations. The future location of Research, Book of Abstracts.* Science Policy Institute, State University of New York.

Leydesdorff, H., & Van den Besselaar, P. (Eds.). (1994). *Evolutionary Economics and Chaos Theory: New directions in technology studies.* London: Pinter.

Lichman, M. (2013). UCI Machine Learning Repository. Irvine, CA: University of California, School of Information and Computer Science.

Lidman, R. (2011). Is the Internet Mightier than the Sword: An Anti-Corruption Perspective. In D. Piaggesi, K. J. Sund, & W. Castelnovo (Eds.), *Global Strategy and Practice of E-Governance: Examples from Around the World* (pp. 340–358). New York: IGI Global. doi:10.4018/978-1-60960-489-9.ch019

Linke, A., & Zerfass, A. (2011). Internal communication and innovation culture: Developing a change framework. *Journal of Communication Management, 15*(4), 332–348. doi:10.1108/13632541111183361

Litton, I. (2015). *#TwitterCritic: Sentiment Analysis of Tweets to Predict TV Ratings*. Academic Press.

Liu, T., Zheng, Y., Liu, L., Liu, Y., & Zhu, Y. (2014). *Methods for sensing urban noises* (Tec. Rep. MSRTR- 2014-66). Academic Press.

Liu, B. (2015). *Sentiment analysis: Mining opinions, sentiments, and emotions*. Cambridge University Press. doi:10.1017/CBO9781139084789

Longhurst, R. (2010). Semi-structured interviews and focus groups. In N. Clifford, S. French, & G. Valentine (Eds.), *Key methods in geography* (2nd ed.; pp. 103–115). London: SAGE Publications Limited.

Lönnqvist, A., & Pirttimäki, V. (2006). The measurement of business intelligence. *Information Systems Management, 23*(1), 32–40. doi:10.1201/1078.10580530/45769.23.1.20061201/91770.4

López, M. (2013). *Aprendizajes, Competencias y TIC*. Editorial Pearson.

Lothridge, K., Fox, J., & Fynan, E. (2013). Blended learning: Efficient, timely, and cost effective. *Journal of Forensic Sciences, 45*(4), 407–416. doi:10.1080/00450618.2013.767375

Mace, J. C. (2007). *Powering up: Information Technology for Rural Schools in Latin America and the Caribbean*. Enersol Associates. Available: http://www.enersol.org/programs/docs/EduSol-Paper_Dec2007.pdf

MacLaverty, N., McQuillan, P., & Oddie, H. (2007). *Internal Branding Best Practices Study*. Canadian Marketing Association.

Maggio, L., Saltarelli, A., & Stranack, K. (2016). *Crowdsourcing the Curriculum: A MOOC for Personalized, Connected Learning EDUCAUSE Learning Initiative*. ELI.

Mainka, A. (2017). *Informational world cities. An empirical investigation of cities in the 21st century* (Doctoral dissertation). Heinrich Heine University document server (document number 41536).

Mainka, A., Castelnovo, W., Miettinen, V., Bech-Petersen, S., Hartmann, S., & Stock, W. G. (2016). Open innovation in smart cities: Participation and co-creation of public services. *Proceedings of the 79th ASIS&T Annual Meeting (Vol. 53). Creating Knowledge, Enhancing Lives through Information & Technology.*

Mainka, A., Fietkiewicz, K., Kosior, A., Pyka, S., & Stock, W. G. (2013). Maturity and usability of e-government in informational world cities. In E. Ferrari & W. Castelnovo (Eds.), *Proceedings of the 13th European Conference on e-Government* (pp. 292-300). Reading, UK: Academic Conferences and Publishing International (ACPI).

Mainka, A., Hartmann, S., Meschede, C., & Stock, W. G. (2015a). Mobile application services based upon open urban government data. *Proceedings of the iConference 2015: Create, Collaborate, Celebrate.*

Mainka, A., Hartmann, S., Meschede, C., & Stock, W. G. (2015b). Open government: Transforming data into value-added city services. In M. Foth, M. Brynskov, & T. Ojala (Eds.), *Citizen's Right to the Digital City. Urban Interfaces, Activism, and Placemaking* (pp. 199–214). Singapore: Springer. doi:10.1007/978-981-287-919-6_11

Mainka, A., Hartmann, S., Orszullok, L., Peters, I., Stallmann, A., & Stock, W. G. (2013). Public libraries in the knowledge society: Core services of libraries in informational world cities. *Libri, 63*(4), 295–319. doi:10.1515/libri-2013-0024

Mainka, A., Hartmann, S., Stock, W. G., & Peters, I. (2015). Looking for friends and followers: a global investigation of governmental social media use. *Transforming Government: People, Process and Policy*, *9*(2), 237–254.

Mainka, A., & Khveshchanka, S. (2012, June). Digital libraries as knowledge hubs in informational cities. *Libraries in the Digital Age (LIDA) Proceedings, 12*, 18–22.

Maisonneuve, N., Stevens, M., Niessen, M. E., & Steels, L. (2009). NoiseTube: Measuring and mapping noise pollution with mobile phones. In Information Technologies in Environmental Engineering (pp. 215-228). Springer Berlin Heidelberg.

Maki, P. L. (2002). Developing an Assessment Plan to Learn about Student Learning. *Journal of Academic Librarianship*, *28*(1), 8–13. doi:10.1016/S0099-1333(01)00295-6

Malmberg, M. (2008). *Contributions of Internal Branding Practices to Corporate Brand Success.* Stockholm School of Economics, Department of Marketing and Strategy. Retrieved from http://arc.hhs.se/download.aspx?MediumId=658

Mamgain, N., Mehta, E., Mittal, A., & Bhatt, G. (2016). Sentiment analysis of top colleges in India using Twitter data. In *2016 International Conference on Computational Techniques in Information and Communication Technologies (ICCTICT)* (pp. 525-530). IEEE. doi:10.1109/ICCTICT.2016.7514636

Manouselis, N., Drachsler, H., Vuorikari, R., Hummel, H., & Koper, R. (2011). *Recommender systems handbook.* Academic Press.

Marakas, G. M., & O'Brien, J. A. (2011). *Introduction to Information Systems* (15th ed.). Columbus, OH: McGraw-Hill.

Marín, V., Negre, F., & Pérez, A. (2014). Construction of the foundations of the PLE and PLN for collaborative learning. *Comunicar*, *21*(42), 35–43. doi:10.3916/C42-2014-03

Marqués, P. (2013). Impacto de las TIC en la educación: funciones y limitaciones. *3 c TIC: cuadernos de desarrollo aplicados a las TIC, 2*(1), 1-15. Retrieved from https://www.3ciencias.com/wp-content/uploads/2013/01/impacto-de-las-tic.pdf

Martinez, S. L., & Stager, G. (2013). *Invent to learn: Making, Tinkering, and Engineering in the Classroom.* Torrance, CA: Constructing Modern Knowledge Press.

Mast, C. (2009). Mitarbeiterkommunikation, Change und Innovationskultur – Balance von Informationen und Emotionen. In A. Zerfass & K. M. Mo¨slein (Eds.), *Kommunikation als Erfolgsfaktor im Innovationsmanagement* (pp. 271–288). Wiesbaden: Strategien im Zeitalter der Open Innovation, Betriebswirtschaftlicher Verlag Gabler. doi:10.1007/978-3-8349-8242-1_15

Matiatou, M. (2015). From Internal Branding to Cultural Transformation: A Virtuous Circle. *International Journal of Knowledge Society Research*, *6*(2), 1–19. doi:10.4018/IJKSR.2015040101

McKeown, K., Daume, H., Chaturvedi, S., Paparrizos, J., Thadani, K., Barrio, P., & Gravano, L. (2016). Predicting the impact of scientific concepts using full-text features. *Journal of the Association for Information Science and Technology.*

Mclaughlin, M. R., & Herlocker, J. L. (2004). A collaborative filtering algorithm and evaluation metric that accurately model the user experience. *Proceedings of 27th Annual International ACM SIGIR Conference on Research and Development in Information Retrieval (SIGIR '04)*, 329–336. doi:10.1145/1008992.1009050

Mee, G. (2004). *Assessment of Student Learning in General Education: A Case Study.* Presentation at Building Learner-Centered Institutions: Developing Strategies for Assessing and Improving Student Learning, Western Association of Schools and Colleges and American Association of Higher Education Workshop.

Meirelles, H. L. (2013). Direito administrativo brasileiro (39th ed.). São Paulo: Malheiros.

Mendes, L. S., Bottoli, M. L., & Breda, G. D. (2010). Digital cities and open MANs: a new communications paradigm. *Proceedings of the 2010 IEEE Latin-American Conference on Communications, 8*(4), 1-8.

Menkhoff, T., Chay, Y. W., Bengtsson, M. L., Woodard, C. J., & Gan, B. (2015). Incorporating microblogging (tweeting) in higher education: Lessons learnt in a knowledge management course. *Computers in Human Behavior, 51*, 1295–1302. doi:10.1016/j.chb.2014.11.063

Merceron, A., Blikstein, P., & Siemens, G. (2016). Learning Analytics: From Big Data to Meaningful Data. *Journal of Learning Analytics, 2*(3), 4–8. doi:10.18608/jla.2015.23.2

Mergen, E., Grant, D., & Widrick, S. M. (2000). Quality management applied to higher education. *Total Quality Management, 11*(3), 345–352. doi:10.1080/0954412006865

Middleton, M. R. (2007). Approaches to evaluation of websites for public sector services. *Proceedings IADIS Conference on e-Society*, 279-284.

Middleton, S. E., Middleton, L., & Modafferi, S. (2014). Real-time crisis mapping of natural disasters using social media. *IEEE Intelligent Systems, 29*(2), 9–17. doi:10.1109/MIS.2013.126

Millard, J. (2010). Government 1.5: Is the bottle half full or half empty? *European Journal of ePractice, 9*, 1-16.

Miller, R. J., Haas, L. M., & Hernandez, M. (2000). Schema Mapping as Query Discovery. *Proceedings of VLDB.*

Ministry of Education. (2007). *The New Zealand curriculum framework.* Wellington: Learning Media Ltd.

Minocha S. (2010). Introducing Second Life, a 3D virtual world, to students and educators. *T4E*, 206-208.

Minocha, S. (2014). Developing a 3D virtual geology field trip in Unity 3D: reflection of our experiences. In Virtual Worlds - Best Practices in Education (VWBPE), Connections. Second Life and OS (Open Simulator Grid).

Minocha, S., & Hardy, C. L. (2011). *Designing navigation and wayfinding in 3D virtual learning spaces.* OZCHI.

Minocha, S., & Hardy, C. L. (2011). Designing navigation and wayfinding in 3D virtual learning spaces. *Proceedings of OZCHI*, 211-220. doi:10.1145/2071536.2071570

Minocha, S., & Morse, D. (2010). Supporting distributed team working in 3D virtual worlds: A case study in Second Life. *Interactive Technology and Smart Education, 7*(4), 200–219. doi:10.1108/17415651011096021

Mishra, S. (2010, January). Internal Marketing- A Tool to Harness Employees' Power in Service Organizations in India. *International Journal of Business and Management, 5*, 1.

Misseyanni, A., Daniela, L., Lytras, M., Papadopoulou, P., & Marouli, C. (2017) Analyzing Active Learning Strategies in Greece and Latvia: Lessons Learnt and the Way Ahead. *INTED 11th International Technology, Education and Development Conference.* doi:10.21125/inted.2017.0940

Mitchell, C. (2002, January). Selling the Brand Inside. *Harvard Business Review.* Retrieved from https:// hbr.org/2002/01/ selling-the-brand-inside

Mitchell, T. M. (1997). Machine Learning. New York: McGraw Hill.

Mitchell, R. K., Agle, B. R., & Wood, D. J. (1997). Toward a Theory of Stakeholder Identification and Salience: Defining the Principle of Who and What Really Counts. *Academy of Management Review.*

Mohammad, S. M. (2015). *Sentiment analysis: Detecting valence, emotions, and other affectual states from text.* Emotion Measurement.

Mohammad, S., & Turney, P. (2013). Crowdsourcing a Word-Emotion Association Lexicon. *Computational Intelligence*, *29*(3), 436–465. doi:10.1111/j.1467-8640.2012.00460.x

Moissa, B., Gasparini, I., & Kemczinski, A. (2015). A Systematic Mapping on the Learning Analytics Field and Its Analysis in the Massive Open Online Courses Context. *International Journal of Distance Education Technologies*, *13*(3), 1–24. doi:10.4018/IJDET.2015070101

Moja, L., Friz, H. P., Capobussi, M., Kwag, K., Banzi, R., Ruggiero, F., & Kunnamo, I. (2016). Implementing an evidence-based computerized decision support system to improve patient care in a general hospital: The CODES study protocol for a randomized controlled trial. *Implementation Science; IS*, *11*(1), 89. doi:10.1186/s13012-016-0455-x PMID:27389248

Molins-Ruano, P., Rodriguez, P., Atrio, S., & Sacha, G. M. (2016). Modelling experts behavior with e-valUAM to measure computer science skills. *Computers in Human Behavior*, *61*, 378–385. doi:10.1016/j.chb.2016.03.044

Morgenson, G. (2012). FAIR GAME; The British, At Least, Are Getting Tough. *The New York Times*. Retrieved from http://www.nytimes.com/2012/07/08/business/barclays-case-opens-a-window-on-wallst-fair-game.html?_r=2

Moriña, A. (2017). Inclusive education in higher education: challenges and opportunities Inclusive education in higher education: challenges and opportunities. *European Journal of Special Needs Education*, *32*(1), 3–17. doi:10.1080/08856257.2016.1254964

Morrison, B. B., & Preston, J. A. (2009). Engagement: Gaming throughout the curriculum. In *ACM. SIGCSE Bulletin*, *41*(1), 342–346. doi:10.1145/1539024.1508990

Mossberger, K., Tolbert, C. J., & McNeal, R. S. (2008). *Digital citizenship: The internet, society, and participation*. Cambridge, MA: MIT Press.

Moura, T. (2015a). *Enriquecimento de dados de referência para recuperaçao de informaçao geográfica utilizando linked data* (Master's thesis). Universidade Federal de Minas Gerais, Belo Horizonte, Brazil.

Moura, T. (2015b). Reference data enhancement for geographic information retrieval using linked data. In *ACM SIGSPATIAL'15*. ACM.

Munezero, M., Montero, C. S., Mozgovoy, M., & Sutinen, E. (2013). Exploiting sentiment analysis to track emotions in students' learning diaries. In *Proceedings of the 13th Koli Calling International Conference on Computing Education Research* (pp. 145-152). ACM. doi:10.1145/2526968.2526984

Murugadas, D., Vieten, S., Nikolic, J., Fietkiewicz, K. J., & Stock, W. G. (2014). Creativity and entrepreneurship in informational metropolitan regions. In I. Filipovic, M. Kalcmer Calopa, & F. Galetic (Eds.), *Economic and Social Development. 7th International Scientific Conference* (pp. 142-151). Varazdin, Croatia: Varazdin Development and Entrepreneurship Agency.

Murugadas, D., Vieten, S., Nikolic, J., & Mainka, A. (2015). The informational world city London. *The Journal of Documentation*, *71*(4), 834–864. doi:10.1108/JD-06-2014-0090

Nachmias, D., & Nachmias, C. (2006). *Research methods in the social sciences*. New York: Worth Publishers.

Nakano, N., Tratz-Ryan, B., & Freeman, D. (2015). *Predicts 2016: IoT Technologies Optimize Smart City Operations*. Gartner.

Nakov, P., Ritter, A., Rosenthal, S., Sebastiani, F., & Stoyanov, V. (2016). SemEval-2016 task 4: Sentiment analysis in Twitter. *Proceedings of the 10th international workshop on semantic evaluation (SemEval 2016)*. doi:10.18653/v1/S16-1001

Nasser, H., Hamad, D., & Nasr, C. (2006). K-means Clustering Algorithm in Projected Spaces. *The 9th International Conference FUSION 2006*, 1-6.

Navarra, D. D., & Cornford, T. (2005). ICT, innovation and public management: governance, models & alternatives for e-government infrastructures. *Proceedings of the European Conference on Information Systems.*

NCAAA. (2013). *Orientation Handbook for NCAAA Review Teams.* Riyadh: National Commission for Academic Accreditation and Assessment.

Negash, S., & Gray, P. (2008). Business intelligence. In F. Burstein & C. W. Holsapple (Eds.), Handbook on decision support systems 2: Variations (pp. 175-193). Berlin: Springer-Verlag. doi:10.1007/978-3-540-48716-6_9

Negash, S. (2004). Business intelligence. *Communications of the Association for Information Systems*, *13*, 177–195.

Newman, M. L., Groom, C. J., Handelman, L. D., & Pennebaker, J. W. (2008). Gender differences in language use: An analysis of 14,000 text samples. *Discourse Processes*, *45*(3), 211–236. doi:10.1080/01638530802073712

Newton Circus Pte Ltd. (2017). *"Data in the city" hackathon.* Retrieved from http://www.upsingapore.com/events/data-city-hackathon/#hackathonhome

Nolan, R. L. (1993). *Note on information technology and strategy.* Boston: Harvard Business School.

Noll, D. A., Mahon, B. E., Shroff, B., Carrico, C., & Lindauer, S. J. (2016). *Twitter analysis of the orthodontic patient experience with braces versus Invisalign.* Academic Press.

Noonoo, S. (2015). *The Maker Mouvement Inforgrapgy.* Retrieved from https://www.eschoolnews.com/2015/11/20/maker-movement-614/

Nowag, B., Perez, M., & Stuckmann, M. (2011). Informationelle Weltstädte – Indikatoren zur Stellung von Städten im "Space of Flow" [Informational world cities - Indicators of the position of cities in the "space of flow"]. *Information. Wissenschaft & Praxis*, *62*(2–3), 103–109.

Nunes, B. P., Mera, A., Kawase, R., Fetahu, B., Casanova, M. A., & de Campos, G. H. B. (2014b). A topic extraction process for online forums. In *IEEE 14th International Conference on Advanced Learning Technologies (ICALT)* (pp. 541–543). IEEE. doi:10.1109/ICALT.2014.158

Nunes, B. P., Kawase, R., Fetahu, B., Casanova, M. A., & de Campos, G. H. B. (2014a). Educational forums at a glance: Topic extraction and selection. In S. I. Publishing (Ed.), *Web Information Systems Engineering–WISE 2014* (pp. 351–364). doi:10.1007/978-3-319-11746-1_25

Nunes, B. P., Nurmikko-Fuller, T., Lopes, G. R., & Renso, C. (2015a). A serious game powered by semantic web technologies. In *Proceedings of the 24th International Conference on World Wide Web Companion* (pp. 227–230). Wide Web Conferences Steering Committee. doi:10.1145/2740908.2742840

Nunes, B. P., Tyler-Jones, M., de Campos, G. H., Siqueira, S. W., & Casanova, M. A. (2015b). Fat: A real-time (f) orum (a) ssessment (t) ool to assist tutors with discussion forums assessment. In *Proceedings of the 30th Annual ACM Symposium on Applied Computing*. ACM.

NYC Big Apps. (2017). *About.* Retrieved from http://www.bigapps.nyc/about/

Ogata, H., Matsuka, Y., El-Bishouty, M. M., & Yano, Y. (2009). LORAMS: Linking physical objects and videos for capturing and sharing learning experiences towards ubiquitous learning. *International Journal of Mobile Learning and Organisation*, *3*(4), 337–350. doi:10.1504/IJMLO.2009.027452

Olcay, G. A., & Bulu, M. (2016). Is measuring the knowledge creation of universities possible?: A review of university rankings. *Technological Forecasting and Social Change*. doi:10.1016/j.techfore.2016.03.029

Open Finland Challenge. (n.d.). *Open Finland challenge 2015*. Retrieved from http://openfinlandchallenge.fi/index.html%3Fp=371.html

Open Knowledge International. (n.d.a). *Why open data*. Retrieved from http://opendatahandbook.org/guide/en/what-is-open-data/

Open Knowledge International. (n.d.b). *About*. Retrieved from https://okfn.org/about//

OpenDataBC. (n.d.). *About*. Retrieved from https://www.opendatabc.ca/pages/about

OpenDataDay 2017. (n.d.). Retrieved from http://opendataday.org/

OpenDataHackathon 2011. (2013, June 18). Retrieved from http://www.barcamp.at/OpenDataHackathon_2011

O'Reilly, U. M., & Veeramachaneni, K. (2014). Technology for Mining the Big Data of MOOCs. *Research & Practice in Assessment*, *9*, 29–37.

Orszullok, L., Stallmann, A., Mainka, A., & Stock, W. G. (2012). Core services of digital and physical libraries in informational world cities - An empirical investigation. In *Smart City and Library Service. The Proceedings of the Sixth Shanghai International Library Forum* (pp. 288-301). Shanghai: Shanghai Scientific and Technological Literature Publishing House.

Ortony, A., Clore, G. L., & Collins, A. (1990). *The cognitive structure of emotions*. Cambridge university press.

OUResSkills. (2015). *Research Degree Skills*. The Open University Web site: http://phdskills.open.ac.uk

OUVLE. (2015). *OU Virtual Learning Environment Program*. The Open University Web site: http://conclave.open.ac.uk/dev-ouvle

Owlia, M. S., & Aspinwall, E. M. (1996). A framework for the dimensions of quality in higher education. *Quality Assurance in Education*, *4*(2), 12–20. doi:10.1108/09684889610116012

Owlia, M. S., & Aspinwall, E. M. (1998). A framework for measuring quality in engineering education. *Total Quality Management*, *9*(6), 501–518. doi:10.1080/0954412988433

Pak, P., & Paroubek, P. (2010). Twitter as a corpus for sentiment analysis and opinion mining. *Proceedings of the Seventh Conference on International Language Resources and Evaluation*, 1320–1326.

Paltoglou, G. (2015). Sentiment-based event detection in Twitter. *Journal of the Association for Information Science and Technology*.

Pant, M. (2009). Participatory Research. In *Course 01 Participatory Lifelong Learning and Information and Communication Technologies* (Unit 08). PALDIN project, ALADIN-INDIA. Retrieved from http://www.unesco.org/education/aladin/paldin/courses.html

Papamitsiou, Z., & Economides, A. (2014). Learning analytics and educational data mining in practice: A systematic literature review of empirical evidence. Journal of Educational Technology & Society, 17(4), 49–64.

Papert, S., & Harel, I. (1991). Constructionism. Ablex Publishing Corporation.

Parker, I. (2001, May 28). Annals of Business - Absolute Powerpoint: Can a software package edit our thoughts? *The New Yorker*, 76. Retrieved May 22, 2011, from http://www.newyorker.com/magazine/2001/05/28/absolute-powerpoint

Parker, C. J., May, A., & Mitchell, V. (2013). The role of VGI and PGI in supporting outdoor activities. *Applied Ergonomics*, *44*(6), 886–894. doi:10.1016/j.apergo.2012.04.013 PMID:22795180

Patra, R., Pal, J., Nedevschi, S., Plauche, M., & Pawar, U. (2007). Usage Models of Classroom Computing in Developing Regions. *Proceedings of International Conference on Information Technologies and Development (ICTD2007)*, 158-167. doi:10.1109/ICTD.2007.4937401

Paulson, F. L., & Paulson, P. (1994). Assessing Portfolios Using the Constructivist Paradigm (R. Fogarty, Ed.). Academic Press.

Paynter, B. (2013, April 16). To Boost Internal Innovation, Ericsson Thinks Inside The Boxes [Web log post]. Retrieved from https://www.fastcompany.com/3004745/boost-internal-innovation-ericsson-thinks-inside-boxes

Pazzani, M. J. (1999). A framework for collaborative, content-based and demographic filtering. *Artificial Intelligence Review*, *13*(5-6), 393–408. doi:10.1023/A:1006544522159

Perez, G., Popadiuk, S., & Cesar, A. M. R. V. C. (2017). Internal factors that favor the adoption of technological innovation defined by information systems: A study of the electronic health record. *RAI Revista de Administração e Inovação*, *14*(1), 67–78. doi:10.1016/j.rai.2016.12.003

Pfeffermann, N. (2011). Innovation communication as a cross-functional dynamic capability: Strategies for organizations and networks. In *Strategies and communications for innovations* (pp. 257–289). Springer Berlin Heidelberg. doi:10.1007/978-3-642-17223-6_18

Piaggesi, D., & Davis, D. (2015). The Triple Helix Approach for the Creation of a Knowledge Society. *International Journal of Knowledge Society Research*, *6*(3).

Pirttimäki, V. (2007). *Business intelligence as a managerial tool in large finnish companies* (Doctoral dissertation). Retrieved from TUT DPub, Tampere University of Technology, Publication 646. Retrieved from http://URN.fi/URN:NBN:fi:tty-200810021126

Plutchik, R. (1980). A general psychoevolutionary theory of emotion. *Theories of Emotion*, *1*, 3-31.

Plutchik, R. (1991). *The emotions*. University Press of America.

Pohoryles, R. J. (2017). Social Innovation – a complex subject to deal with, Innovation. *The European Journal of Social Science Research*, *30*(2), 141–143. doi:10.1080/13511610.2017.1297019

Pollard, T. (2011). *Saab Files for Bankruptcy: The End of the Swedish Saga*. CAR Magazine Site [Blog]. Retrieved from http://www.carmagazine.co.uk/News/Search-Results/Industry-News/Saab-files-for-bankruptcy-the-end-of-the-Swedish-saga/

Power, D. J. (2007, March 10). *A brief history of decision support systems*. Retrieved from http://dssresources.com/history/dsshistory.html

Power, D. J., Sharda, R., & Burstein, F. (2015). *Decision support systems*. John Wiley & Sons, Ltd. doi:10.1002/9781118785317.weom070211

Prahalad, C. K. (2005). *The fortune at the bottom of the pyramid*. Wharton School Publishing.

Provezis, S. (2010). *Regional accreditation and student learning outcomes: Mapping the territory* (NILOA Occasional Paper No. 6). Urbana, IL: University of Illinois and Indiana University, National Institute for Learning Outcomes Assessment (NILOA). Retrieved from http://www.learningoutcomeassessment.org/occasionalpapersix

Pursel, B. K., Zhang, L., Jablokow, K. W., Choi, G. W., & Velegol, D. (2016). Understanding MOOC students: Motivations and behaviours indicative of MOOC completion. *Journal of Computer Assisted Learning*, *32*(3), 202–217. doi:10.1111/jcal.12131

Quintero, G. (2013). *Sistema móvil georeferenciado para la medición y análisis de ruido ambiental.* CIC-IPN.

Quinton, S. R., & Allen, M. M. (2014). The social processes of web 2.0 collaboration: Towards a new model for virtual learning. In *Curriculum models for the 21st century* (pp. 35–53). Springer New York. doi:10.1007/978-1-4614-7366-4_3

Ramesh, A., Kumar, S. H., Foulds, J., & Getoor, L. (2015). Weakly supervised models of aspect-sentiment for online course discussion forums. *Annual Meeting of the Association for Computational Linguistics (ACL).* doi:10.3115/v1/P15-1008

Ramsden, P. (1991). A performance indicator of teaching quality in higher education: The course experience questionnaire. *Studies in Higher Education*, *16*(2), 129–150. doi:10.1080/03075079112331382944

Rana, R. K., Chou, C. T., Kanhere, S. S., Bulusu, N., & Hu, W. (2010, April). Ear-phone: an end-to-end participatory urban noise mapping system. In *Proceedings of the 9th ACM/IEEE International Conference on Information Processing in Sensor Networks* (pp. 105-116). ACM. doi:10.1145/1791212.1791226

Ranjan, J. (2009). Business intelligence: Concepts, components, techniques and benefits. *Journal of Theoretical and Applied Information Technology*, *9*(1), 60–70.

Rankin, E. L., & Hoaas, D. J. (2001). Does the use of computer-generated slide presentations in the classroom affect student performance and interest? *Eastern Economic Journal*, *27*(3), 355–366.

Rapanotti, L., Barroca, L., Vargas-Vera, M., & Minocha, S. (2009). deep|think: a Second Life campus for part-time research students at a distance. Computing Department, UK, TR2009-01.

Rapanotti, L., Barroca, L., Vargas-Vera, M., & Reeves, A. (2010). deep|think: A Second Life environment for part-time research students at a distance. *The 10th IEEE International Conference on Advanced Learning Technologies (ICALT 2010)*, 200-201.

Rapanotti, L., & Hall, J. (2010). *Lessons Learned in Developing a Second Life Educational Environment.* Valencia, Spain: CSEDU.

Rast, H. (2010). *Three Dimensions of Internal Branding.* Social Media Explorer [Blog]. Retrieved from http://www.socialmediaexplorer.com/digital-marketing/the-three-dimensions-of-internal-branding/

Ravindran, S. K., & Garg, V. (2015). *Mastering Social Media Mining with R.* Packt Publishing Ltd.

Redecker, C., Ala-Mutka, K., & Punie, Y. (2010). *Learning 2.0-The impact of social media on learning in Europe.* Policy brief. JRC Scientific and Technical Report. EUR JRC56958 EN, available from: http://bit. ly/cljlpq

Reimers, F. M. (2015). Taking Action on Global Education. *Proceedings of the Special seminar at UNESCO Bangkok.* Retrieved from www.unescobkk.org/news/article/taking-action-on-global-education

Reynolds, K., Barnhill, D., Sias, J., Young, A., & Greer, F. (2014). Use of the QR Reader to Provide Real-Time Evaluation of Residents Skills Following Surgical Procedures. *Journal of Graduate Medical Education*, *6*(4), 738–741. doi:10.4300/JGME-D-13-00349.1 PMID:26140128

Rezende, D. A. (2015). Public Policy and a Strategic Digital City Project: A case study of the Brazilian Municipality of Vinhedo. *Journal of Urban Technology*, *22*, 1–21.

Rezende, D. A., Madeira, G. S., Mendes, L. S., Breda, G. D., Zarpelão, B. B., & Figueiredo, F. C. (2013). Information and Telecommunications Project for a Digital City: A Brazilian case study. *Telematics and Informatics*, *31*(1), 98–114. Retrieved from http://www.sciencedirect.com/science/article/pii/S0736585313000336

Rezende. (2012). *Planejamento de estratégias e informações municipais para cidade digital: guia para projetos em prefeituras e organizações públicas*. São Paulo: Atlas.

Rezende. (2014). *Information and Telecommunications Project for a Digital City: A Brazilian case study* (Vol. 31). Telematics and Informatics.

Rezende, D. A. (2016). Digital City Projects: Information and public services offered by Chicago (USA) and Curitiba (Brazil). *International Journal of Knowledge Society Research*, *7*(3), 16–30. doi:10.4018/IJKSR.2016070102

Rezende, D. A., & Abreu, A. F. (2013). *Tecnologia da informação aplicada a sistemas de informação empresariais: o papel estratégico da informação e dos sistemas de informação nas empresas. 9*. São Paulo: Atlas.

Rhodes, M. (1961). An Analysis of Creativity. *Phi Delta Kappan*, *42*(7), 306–307.

Ricci, F., Rokach, L., & Shapira, B. (2011). *Introduction to Recommender Systems Handbook*. Springer. doi:10.1007/978-0-387-85820-3

Riihelä, J., & Mäki, S. (2015). Designing and implementing an online gis tool for schools: The finnish case of the paikkaoppi project. journal of geography. *The Journal of Geography*, *114*(1), 15–25. doi:10.1080/00221341.2014.897362

Roberts, D., & Pakkiri, R. (2016). *Decision sourcing: Decision making for the agile social enterprise*. Routledge.

Robertson, R. D., McKiernan, A. G., & Holmes, E. A. (2015). *DWI dashboard report: A tool to monitor impaired driving progress*. Academic Press.

Robinson, A. C., Kerski, J., Long, E. C., Luo, H., DiBiase, D., & Lee, A. (2015). Maps and the geospatial revolution: Teaching a massive open online course (mooc) in geography. *Journal of Geography in Higher Education*, *39*(1), 65–82. doi:10.1080/03098265.2014.996850

Robinson, P. J., & Johnson, P. A. (2016). Civic hackathons: New terrain for local government-citizen interaction? *Urban Planning*, *1*(2), 65–74. doi:10.17645/up.v1i2.627

Rodriguez Manzo, F. E. (2011). *Elaboración del primer mapa ruido y conformación de la red piloto de monitoreo de ruido para la ZMVM*. UAM.

Rodriguez, P., Ortigosa, A., & Carro, R. M. (2012, July). Extracting emotions from texts in e-learning environments. In *Complex, Intelligent and Software Intensive Systems (CISIS), 2012 Sixth International Conference on* (pp. 887-892). IEEE. doi:10.1109/CISIS.2012.192

Rodríguez, R., Escribano, J., & Lara, P. (2009). Las TIC como herramienta para desarrollar competencias transversales en el aula. In A. Blanco (Ed.), Desarrollo y Evaluación de Competencias en Educación Superior (pp. 159-178). Madrid: Ediciones Narcea S.A.

Roekel, H. v., Linders, J., Raja, K., Reboullet, T., & Ommerborn, G. (2009). *The BI framework: How to turn information into competitive asset*. Reading, UK: Logica.

Rogers Everett, M. (1995). Diffusion of innovations. New York: Academic Press.

Rogers, E. M. (1995). *Diffusion of innovations* (4th ed.). New York: Free Press.

Rogers, E. M. (2002). Diffusion of preventive innovations. *Addictive Behaviors, 27*(6), 989–993. doi:10.1016/S0306-4603(02)00300-3 PMID:12369480

Rouhani, S., Asgari, S., & Mirhosseini, S. V. (2012). Review study: Business intelligence concepts and approaches. *American Journal of Scientific Research, 50*, 62–75.

Rubene, Z. (2006). *Topicality of Critical Thinking in the Context of Higher Education Reform in Pedagogy and Teacher Education*. University of Latvia.

Rymaszewski, M., Wagner, J., & Wallace, M. (2008). *Second Life: The Official Guide*. Academic Press.

Sabato, S., Vanhercke, B., & Verschraegen, G. (2017). Connecting entrepreneurship with policy experimentation? The EU framework for social innovation, Innovation. *The European Journal of Social Science Research, 30*(2), 147–167. doi:10.1080/13511610.2017.1282308

Salazar Argonza, J. (2011). Estado actual de la Web 3.0 o Web Semántica. *Tema del mes.*

Salonen, J., & Pirttimaki, V. (2005). Outsourcing a Business Intelligence Function. *Frontiers of E-Business Research*, 661-675.

Salton, G., & Mcgill, M. (1983). *Introduction to Modern Information Retrieval*. New York, NY: McGraw-Hill.

San Francisco Mayor's Office of Civic Innovation. (2013, January 11). The civic innovation ecosystem blooms in 2012. What's next? [Web log comment]. Retrieved from https://medium.com/sfmoci/the-civic-innovation-ecosystem-blooms-in-2012-whats-next-70b685ab063b

Sánchez, L. (2011). *Modelo computacional para generar un mapa de ruido ambiental utilizando mediciones en tiempo real* (Ph.D. Doctoral Thesis). Centro de Investigación en Computación, IPN, México.

Sanders, E. B.-N., Brandt, E., & Binder, T. (2010). A framework for organizing the tools and techniques of participatory design. *Proceedings of the 11th Biennial Participatory Design Conference*. doi:10.1145/1900441.1900476

Sangar, A. B., & Iahad, N. B. A. (2013). Critical factors that affect the success of business intelligence systems (BIS) implementation in an organization. *International Journal of Scientific & Technology Research, 2*(2), 176–180.

Santos, O. C., Salmeron-Majadas, S., & Boticario, J. G. (2013). Emotions detection from math exercises by combining several data sources. In *International Conference on Artificial Intelligence in Education* (pp. 742-745). Springer Berlin Heidelberg. doi:10.1007/978-3-642-39112-5_102

Sanz, C. V., Cukierman, U. R., Zangara, M. A., González, A. H., Santángelo, H. N., Rozenhauz, J. C., . . . Ibañez, E. (2007). Integración de la tecnología móvil a los entornos virtuales de enseñanza y de aprendizaje. *II Congreso de Tecnología en Educación y Educación en Tecnología*. Universidad Nacional de La Plata. Retrieved from http://sedici.unlp.edu.ar/handle/10915/19120

Sarirete, A., Noble, E., & Chikh, A. (2009). Knowledge and learning issues related to engineering education: A constructivist approach. *International Journal of Teaching and Case Studies, 2*(1), 17–28. doi:10.1504/IJTCS.2009.026296

Sattolo, I., Lipera, L., Romero, J. C., Cos, S., Figueroa, S., Cisneros, J. A., & Minutella, D. (2016). Elementos interactivos en los mundos virtuales 3 D. *XVIII Workshop de Investigadores en Ciencias de la Computación*. Retrieved from http://sedici.unlp.edu.ar/bitstream/handle/10915/53406/Documento_completo.pdf-PDFA.pdf?sequence=1

Savoy, A., Proctor, R.W., & Salvendy, G. (2009). Information retention from PowerPoint™ and traditional lectures. *Computers & Education, 52*(4), 858-867. doi: .10.1016/j.compedu.2008.12.005

Scantlebury, N., McNulty, J., & Dowson, N. (2008). Developing sustainable library services within the context of a parallel universe. Proceedings of Researching Learning in Virtual Environments (ReLIVE 08).

Scheerens, J., Luyten, H., & Ravens, J. (2011). *Perspective on educational quality: Illustrative outcomes on primary and secondary schooling in the Netherlands*. Dordrecht: Springer; doi:10.1007/978-94-007-0926-3

School Choice International. (2008). *Education in the Netherlands: An overview*. White Plains, NY: The Plain White Press LLC.

Schweizer, I., Bärtl, R., Schulz, A., Probst, F., & Muhläuser, M. (2011, November). NoiseMap-real-time participatory noise maps. *Proc. 2nd Int'l Workshop on Sensing Applications on Mobile Phones (PhoneSense'11)*, 1-5.

Sepúlveda, E., Badilla, M. G., & Careaga, M. (2014). Mobile devices for teaching English as a second– language in Higher Education, the case of DUOC in Chile. *Journal of Mobile Multimedia*, *10*(3 & 4), 234–243.

Sharda, R., & Delen, D. (2013). *Business Intelligence: A Managerial Perspective on Analytics* (3rd ed.). Upper Saddle River, NJ: Pearson Prentice Hall.

Shaver, P., Schwartz, J., Kirson, D., & OConnor, C. (1987). Emotion knowledge: Further exploration of a prototype approach. *Journal of Personality and Social Psychology*, *52*(6), 1061–1086. doi:10.1037/0022-3514.52.6.1061 PMID:3598857

Shaw, M., Subramaniam, M. C., Tan, G., & Welge, M. (2001). Knowledge management and data mining for marketing. Decision Support Systems, 31(1), 127–137. doi:10.1016/S0167-9236(00)00123-8 doi:10.1016/S0167-9236(00)00123-8

Shen, C. W., & Kuo, C. J. (2015). Learning in massive open online courses: Evidence from social media mining. *Computers in Human Behavior*, *51*, 568–577. doi:10.1016/j.chb.2015.02.066

Sherwood, P., & O'Neill, B. (2011). *Brand Building Inside The Building*. Step 1 Branding LLC [Blog]. Retrieved from http://www.steponebranding.com/StepOneBranding/Step1_files/Cases%20.pdf

Shiode, N. (2000). Urban planning, information technology, and cyberspace. *Journal of Urban Technology*, *7*(2), 105–126. doi:10.1080/713684111

Shum, S. B., & Ferguson, R. (2012). Social Learning Analytics. *Journal of Educational Technology & Society*, *15*(3), 3–26.

Siamagka, N. T., & Christodoulides, G. (2016). Social Media in Higher Education: An Investigation into UG Marketing Education in the UK. In Marketing Challenges in a Turbulent Business Environment (pp. 19-23). Springer International Publishing.

Sieber, R. E., & Johnson, P. A. (2015). Civic open data at a crossroads: Dominant models and current challenges. *Government Information Quarterly*, *32*(3), 308–315. doi:10.1016/j.giq.2015.05.003

Siemens, G. (2012). Learning analytics: envisioning a research discipline and a domain of practice. *International Conference on Learning Analytics and Knowledge*. doi:10.1145/2330601.2330605 doi:10.1145/2330601.2330605

Siemens, G. (2013). Learning analytics: The emergence of a discipline. *The American Behavioral Scientist*.

Siemens, G., & Long, P. (2011). Penetrating the Fog: Analytics in Learning and Education. *EDUCAUSE Review*, *46*(5), 30.

Siemmens, G. (2005). *A Learning Theory for the Digital Age*. Retrieved from http://www.elearnspace.org/Articles/connectivism.htm

Silva, J., & Salinas, J. (2014). *Innovando con TIC en la formación inicial docente: aspectos teóricos y casos concretos*. Santiago: Enlaces. Retrieved from http://www.grupotecnologiaeducativa.es/images/LIBROS/ticfid_2014.pdf

Simão, J. B., & Rodrigues, G. (2005). Acessibilidade às informações públicas: Uma avaliação do portal de serviços e informações do governo federal. *Revista Ciência da Informação*, *34*(2), 81–92.

Simon, H. A. (1956). Rational choice and the structure of the environment. *Psychological Review*, *63*(2), 129–138. doi:10.1037/h0042769 PMID:13310708

Simon, H. A. (1991). Bounded rationality and organizational learning. *Organization Science*, *2*(1), 125–134. doi:10.1287/orsc.2.1.125

Singh, R., Gill, J. S., Sharma, T., & Goel, G. (2016). Product Aspect Ranking, Sentiment Analysis and Classification of Product Reviews on E-Commerce Sites-A Review. *Journal of Network Communications and Emerging Technologies*, *6*(5). www. jncet. org

Skelcher, C. (1992). Improving the quality of local Public services. *Service Industries Journal*, *12*(4), 463–477. doi:10.1080/02642069200000059

Sohng, S. S. L. (1996). Participatory research and community organising. *Journal of Sociology and Social Welfare*, *14*(4), 77–97.

Šperjak, A. (2014). Usefulness of Prezi and PowerPoint presentation. In *37th International Convention on Information and Communication Technology, Electronics and Microelectronics, MIPRO 2014 Proceedings*, 762–764. doi:10.1109/MIPRO.2014.6859667

Sprague, A. (2016). Improving the ESL Graduate Writing Classroom Using Socrative: (Re) Considering Exit Tickets. *TESOL Journal*, *7*(4), 989–998. doi:10.1002/tesj.295

Spruit, M., & Adriana, T. (2015). Quantifying education quality in secondary schools. *International Journal of Knowledge Society Research*, *6*(1), 55–87. doi:10.4018/IJKSR.2015010104

Spruit, M., & Jagesar, R. (2016). Power to the People! Meta-algorithmic modelling in applied data science. In *Proceedings of the 8th International Joint Conference on Knowledge Discovery, Knowledge Engineering and Knowledge Management* (pp. 400–406). Porto, Portugal: ScitePress. doi:10.5220/0006081604000406

Spruit, M., & Lammertink, M. (2018). Effective and efficient business intelligence dashboard design: Gestalt theory in Dutch long-term and chronic healthcare. In M. Lytras & P. Papadopoulou (Eds.), *Applying Big Data Analytics in Bioinformatics and Medicine* (pp. 243–271). IGI Global. doi:10.4018/978-1-5225-2607-0.ch010

Spruit, M., Vroon, R., & Batenburg, R. (2014). Towards healthcare business intelligence in long-term care: An explorative case study in the Netherlands. *Computers in Human Behavior*, *30*, 698–707. doi:10.1016/j.chb.2013.07.038

Squire, K., & Jenkins, H. (2003). Harnessing the power of games in education. *Insight (American Society of Ophthalmic Registered Nurses)*, *3*(1), 5–33. PMID:12703249

Stacey, E. (2007). Collaborative learning in an online environment. *International Journal of E-Learning & Distance Education*, *14*(2), 14–33.

Stacey, E. (2009). *A virtual campus: The experience of postgraduate students studying through electronic communication and resource access*. Victoria: Deakin University.

Stair, R. M., & Reynolds, G. W. (2007). *Principles of information systems: A managerial approach* (8th ed.). Boston: Course Technology.

Stefanou, V., & Kotsovoulou, M. (2016). Use of Powerpoint in the classroom: A participatory research project. *International Journal of Knowledge Society Research*, *7*(3).

Steinmetz, A. (2009). *Internal Branding Challenges and How to Overcome Them.* Inward Consulting Blogspot [Blog]. Retrieved from http://inwardconsulting.blogspot.gr/2009/10/internal-branding-challenges-and-how-to.html

Steyn, B. (2003). From Strategy to Corporate Communication Strategy: A Conceptualization. *Journal of Communication Management*, *8*(2), 168–183. doi:10.1108/13632540410807637

Stockholms stad. (n.d.). *Open Stockholm award 2016.* Retrieved from https://www.openstockholmaward.se/?locale=en

Stock, W. G. (2011). Informational cities: Analysis and construction of cities in the knowledge society. *Journal of the American Society for Information Science and Technology*, *62*(5), 963–986. doi:10.1002/asi.21506

Stodden, R. A., Abhari, K., & Kong, E. (2015). Secondary School Preparation and Transition of Youth with Disabilities. In *Transition of Youth and Young Adults* (pp. 7–30). Emerald Group Publishing Limited. doi:10.1108/S0735-004X20150000028002

Stone, E. (1997). From the research notes of a foreign devil: Disability research in China. In C. Barnes & G. Mercer (Eds.), *Doing disability research* (pp. 207–227). Leeds, UK: Disability Press.

Sugahara, S., & Boland, G. (2006). The Effectiveness of PowerPoint presentations in the Accounting Classroom. *Accounting Education*, *15*(4), 391–403. doi:10.1080/09639280601011099

Sui, D. (2014). Opportunities and impediments for open gis. *Transactions in GIS*, *18*(1), 1–24. doi:10.1111/tgis.12075

Sui, D. Z. (2008). The wikification of GIS and its consequences: Or Angelina Jolies new tattoo and the future of GIS. *Computers, Environment and Urban Systems*, *32*(1), 1–5. doi:10.1016/j.compenvurbsys.2007.12.001

Susskind, J. E. (2005). PowerPoints power in the classroom: Enhancing students self-efficacy and attitudes. *Computers & Education*, *45*(2), 203–215. doi:10.1016/j.compedu.2004.07.005

Susskind, J. E. (2008). Limits of PowerPoints Power: Enhancing students self-efficacy and attitudes but not their behavior. *Computers & Education*, *50*(4), 1228–1239. doi:10.1016/j.compedu.2006.12.001

Sutherland, L. (2015, March 4). IdeaBoxes: A management system for innovation [Web log post]. Retrieved from http://www.collaborationsuperpowers.com/ideaboxes-a-management-system-for-innovation-magnus-karlsson/

Tam, M. (2001). Measuring quality and performance in higher education. *Quality in Higher Education*, *7*(1), 47–54. doi:10.1080/13538320120045076

Tanner, T. (2015). Accreditation and Student Learning Outcomes Progress and Challenges. *Proceedings of the CHEA 2015 Annual Conference.*

Taylor, A. (2011). *Saab without Tears.* CNNMoney [Blog]. Retrieved from http://money.cnn.com/2011/12/20/ autos/saab_general_motors.fortune/index.htm

Taylor, E. W., & Cranton, P. (2012). *The Handbook of Transformative Learning. Theory, Research, and Practice.* San Francisco: Jossey-Bass Inc., Publishers.

Taylor, J., & Baines, C. (2012). Performance management in UK universities: Implementing the Balanced Scorecard. *Journal of Higher Education Policy and Management*, *34*(2), 111–124. doi:10.1080/1360080X.2012.662737

Tejerina, L., & Westley, D. G. D. (2007). Financial services for the poor: household survey sources and gaps in borrowing and saving. Sustainable Development Department - Technical Papers Series, Inter-American Development Bank.

Tejerina, L., Bouillon, C., & Demaestri, E. (Eds.). (2006). *Financial Services and Poverty Reduction in Latin America and the Caribbean.* Washington, DC: Inter-American Development Bank.

Teknova. (1995). *Sistema di monitoraggio della ricerca scientifica e dellíinnovazione tecnologica in Lombardia*. Ricerca IRER cod. 93.64.

Temporal, P. (2002). Corporate Identity, Brand Identity, and Brand Image [Blog]. Retrieved from http:// www.brandingasia.com/columns/temporal10.htm

The JXTA Project. (n. d.). Retrieved from http://www.jxta.org

The Royal Society. (2006). *Digital Healthcare: The Impact of Information and Communication Technologies on Health and Healthcare*. The Royal Society.

Tian, F., Zheng, Q., Zhao, R., Chen, T., & Jia, X. (2009). Can e-Learner's emotion be recognized from interactive Chinese texts? In *Computer Supported Cooperative Work in Design, 2009. CSCWD 2009. 13th International Conference on* (pp. 546-551). IEEE.

Tomar, G. S., Sankaranarayanan, S., Wang, X., & Rosé, C. P. (2017). *Coordinating collaborative chat in massive open online courses*. arXiv preprint arXiv:1704.05543

Tosh, D., Light, T.P., Fleming, K., & Haywood, J. (2005). Engagement with Electronic Portfolios: Challenges from the Student Perspective. *Canadian Journal of Learning and Technology, 31*(3).

Tourón, J., & Santiago, R. (2015). Flipped Learning model and the development of talent at school. *Revista de Educación, 368*, 176-208. Retrieved from http://goo.gl/KYL3TX

Townsend, A. (2003). Wired/unwired: the urban geography of digital networks. In *Urban Studies and Planning* (p. 206). Cambridge, MA: Massachusetts Institute of Technology.

Trcka, N., & Pechenizkiy, M. (2009). From local patterns to global models: Towards domain driven educational process mining. *International Conference on Intelligent Systems Design and Applications*. doi:10.1109/ISDA.2009.159 doi:10.1109/ISDA.2009.159

Tummel, A. A. D. J. C., & Richert, S. J. A. (2015). Sentiment Analysis of Social Media for Evaluating Universities. *The Second International Conference on Digital Information Processing, Data Mining, and Wireless Communications (DIPDMWC2015)*.

Tur, G., Marín, V. I., & Carpenter, J. (2017). Using Twitter in Higher Education in Spain and the USA. *Comunicar, 25*(51), 19-27. 10.3916/C51-2017-02

Turban, E., Mclean, E., & Wetherbe, J. (1996). *Information technology for management: improving quality and productivity*. New York: John Wiley and Sons.

U.S. Department of Education. (2007). *Accreditation in the United States*. Retrieved from https://www2.ed.gov/admins/finaid/accred/index.html

UKGrad. (2015). *Joint Skills Statement of Skills Training Requirements*. The Vitae Web site: http://grad.ac.uk/jss/

Uline, C., & Tschannen-Moran, M. (2008). The walls speak: The interplay of quality facilities, school climate, and student achievement. *Journal of Educational Administration, 46*(1), 55–73. doi:10.1108/09578230810849817

UNCDF. (2013). *Global Forum on Local Development Report*. Retrieved from http://www.cib-uclg.org/news/global-forum-local-development-report-pursuing-mdgs-through-local-government

UNDESA. (2007, October). *Intergenerational Solidarity: Strengthening Economic and Social Ties*. Expert Group Meeting and Background Paper, UN Department of Economic and Social Affairs, Division of Social Policy and Development.

UNESCO. (2004). *Education for all – the quality imperative*. Paris: The EFA Global Monitoring Report Team.

UNESCO. (2005). *E-government toolkit for developing countries*. UNESCO. Available: http://unesdoc.unesco.org/images/0013/001394/139418e.pdf

UNESCO. (2012). *Netherlands (IBE/2012/CP/WDE/NE)*. Retrieved from http://www.unesco.org/ulis/cgi-bin/ulis.pl?catno=218669

United Nations Educational, Scientific and Cultural Organization (UNESCO) & ACNUR. (2017). *Mobile learning Week Policy Forum*. Retrieved from http://www.unesco.org/new/fileadmin/MULTIMEDIA/HQ/ED/pdf/mlw2017_PolicyForumOutcomes.pdf

United Nations Educational, Scientific and Cultural Organization (UNESCO). (2006). *Using ICT to Develop Literacy. UNESCO ICT in Education Programme*. Bangkok: Phongwarin Printing Ltd. Retrieved from http://unesdoc.unesco.org/images/0014/001464/146426e.pdf

United Nations Educational, Scientific and Cultural Organization (UNESCO). (2013a). *Directrices de la UNESCO para las políticas de aprendizaje móvil*. Retrieved from http://unesdoc.unesco.org/images/0021/002196/219662S.pdf

United Nations Educational, Scientific and Cultural Organization (UNESCO). (2013b). *Enfoques estratégicos sobre las TICS en educación en América Latina y el Caribe*. Santiago, Chile: UNESCO. Retrieved from http://www.unesco.org/new/fileadmin/MULTIMEDIA/FIELD/Santiago/images/ticsesp.pdf

United Nations Educational, Scientific and Cultural Organization (UNESCO). (2015). QINGDAO Declaration. *International conference on ICT and post-2015 education. Seize digital opportunities, lead education transformation*. Retrieved from http://unesdoc.unesco.org/images/0023/002333/233352E.pdf

Unwin, T. (2007). Reflections on supervising distance-based PhD students (Vol. 2009). Academic Press.

Vahdat, M., Ghio, A., Oneto, L., Anguita, D., Funk, M., & Rauterberg, M. (2015). Advances in learning analytics and educational data mining. *European Symposium on Artificial Neural Networks, Computational Intelligence and Machine Learning*.

Vahdat, M., Oneto, L., Ghio, A., Donzellini, G., Anguita, D., Funk, M., & Rauterberg, M. (2014). A learning analytics methodology to profile students behaviour and explore interactions with a digital electronics simulator. In S. de Freitas, C. Rensing, T. Ley, & P. J. Munoz-Merino (Eds.), EC-TEL 2014. LNCS (Vol. 8719, pp. 596–597). Springer Verlag.

van de Oudeweetering, K., & Agirdag, O. (2017). MOOCs as accelerators of social mobility? A systematic review. *Journal of Educational Technology & Society*, 1–12.

Van Riel, C. (1995). *Principles of Corporate Communication*. London, UK: Prentice Hall.

VanAuken, B. (2007). *70 Ideas for overcoming brand culture obstacles*. Branding Strategy Insider [Blog]. Retrieved from http://www.brandingstrategyinsider.com/2007/09/internal-brand-html.html

Vargas-Vera, M. (2016). Reflections on the Second Life Platform used in the Development of a Virtual University Campus. *IJKSR Journal, 7*(4).

Vargas-Vera, M. (2016). Reflections on the Second Life Platform used in the Development of a Virtual University Campus. *International Journal of Knowledge Society Research*, *4*(7), 12–23. doi:10.4018/IJKSR.2016100102

Vázquez, E., Martín, E., & Castrillo, M. (2016). Analysis of PLEs' Implementation under OER Design as a Productive Teaching-Learning Strategy in Higher Education. A Case Study at Universidad Nacional de Educación a Distancia. *Digital Education Review, 29*, 62-85. Retrieved from https://eric.ed.gov/?id=EJ1106187

Venne, R. (2005). *Mainstreaming the concerns of older people into the social development agenda*. United Nations Secretariat: Division for Social Policy and Development.

Verkooij, K., & Spruit, M. (2013). Mobile Business Intelligence: Key considerations for implementation projects. *Journal of Computer Information Systems*, *54*(1), 23–33. doi:10.1080/08874417.2013.11645668

Viale, R. (1998, March 4). *Tripla elica in Lombardia: evoluzione nel raccordo tra ricerca, impresa e governo*. Conferenza Regionale della Lombardia - Scenari dello Sviluppo, Milano, Italy.

Viale, R., & Ghiglione, B. (2005). *The Triple Helix model: a Tool for the Study of European Regional Socio Economic Systems*. Fondazione Rosselli Publication.

Vidal, P. (2016). *World university rankings: use of quantitative indicators and results from student surveys*. Academic Press.

Vienna City Administration. (n.d.). *Open Energy Data Challenge*. Retrieved from https://open.wien.gv.at/site/open-energy-data-challenge/

Visvizi, A. (2013). *Social Innovation in the EU and the Black Sea Region: Trends, challenges and opportunities*. Xenophon Paper no. 13. International Centre for Black Sea Studies (ICBSS).

Visvizi, A. (2015). Education, (the production of) knowledge and progress in context of the global public goods debate. In E. Latoszek et al. (Eds.), *Facing the Challenges in European Union: Re-thinking EU Education and Research for Smart and Inclusive Growth* (pp. 661–674). Warsaw: Warsaw University Press.

Vleugel, A., Spruit, M., & van Daal, A. (2010). Historical data analysis through data mining from an outsourcing perspective: The three-phases method. *International Journal of Business Intelligence Research*, *1*(3), 42–65. doi:10.4018/jbir.2010070104

Volkwein, J. F., Lattuca, L. R., Harper, B. J., & Domingo, R. J. (2007). Measuring the impact of professional accreditation on student experiences and learning outcomes. *Research in Higher Education*, *48*(2), 251–282. doi:10.1007/s11162-006-9039-y

Vota, W. (2010). Updated Quick Guide to Low-Cost ICT Devices for Educational Systems in the Developing World. infoDev, the World Bank.

Vucetic, S., & Obradovic, Z. (2005). Collaborative filtering using a regression-based approach. *Knowledge and Information Systems*, *7*(1), 1–22. doi:10.1007/s10115-003-0123-8

Vygotsky, L. S. (1962). Thought and language. Cambridge, MA: MIT Press. doi:10.1037/11193-000

Vygotsky, L. S. (1980). *Mind in society: The development of higher psychological processes*. Harvard University Press.

Waag society. Institute for art, science and technology. (2012, November 07). *Apps for Amsterdam: smart apps awarded*. Retrieved from https://waag.org/en/news/apps-amsterdam-smart-apps-awarded

Waag society. Institute for art, science and technology. (n.d.). *Apps for Europe first business lounge*. Retrieved from http://waag.org/en/event/apps-europe-first-business-lounge

Wadsworth, Y. (1998) What is Participatory Action Research? In *Action Research International, Paper 2*. Retrieved from: http://www.aral.com.au/ari/p-ywadsworth98.html

Wagner, D., Castillo, N., Murphy, K., Crofton, M., & Tuz, F. (2014). Mobiles for literacy in developing countries: An effectiveness framework. *Prospects*, *44*(1), 119–132. doi:10.1007/s11125-014-9298-x

Waller, M., & Gove, M. (2007, April 18). PowerPointless. *The Sunday Times*.

Walravens, N. (2015). Mobile city applications for Brussels citizens: Smart city trends, challenges and a reality check. *Telematics and Informatics*, *32*(2), 282–299. doi:10.1016/j.tele.2014.09.004

Walters, K. (1994). *Re-Thinking Reason: New Perspectives in Critical Thinking Albany*. State University of New York Press.

Wang, X., Yang, D., Wen, M., Koedinger, K., & Rosé, C. P. (2015). *Investigating How Student's Cognitive Behavior in MOOC Discussion Forums Affect Learning Gains*. International Educational Data Mining Society.

Ward, J., & Peppard, J. (2002). *Strategic planning for information systems*. New York: John Wiley & Sons.

Wasmann, M., & Spruit, M. (2012, April-June). Performance management within social network sites: The Social Network Intelligence Process method. *International Journal of Business Intelligence Research*, *3*(2), 49–63. doi:10.4018/jbir.2012040104

Watson, H. J., & Wixom, B. H. (2007). The current state of business intelligence. *Computer*, *40*(9), 96–99. doi:10.1109/MC.2007.331

Weber, A., Rufer-Bach, K., & Platel, R. (2007). *Creating Your World: The official Guide to Advanced Content Creation for Second Life*. Academic Press.

Weissman, C. G. (2014, February 24). New York hackathon looks to use open data to assist with city governance [Web log comment]. Retrieved from https://pando.com/2014/02/24/new-york-hackathon-looks-to-use-open-data-to-assist-with-city-governance/

Weitzen, H. S. (1991). *O poder da informação: como transformar a informação que você domina em um negócio lucrativo*. São Paulo: Makron Books.

WEKA. (2015). *Data Mining Software in Java*. Retrieved from http://www.cs.waikato.ac.nz/ml/weka/index.html

Wenger, E., McDermott, R., & Snyder, W. (2002). Cultivating Communities of Practice. Harvard Business Press.

West, D. M. (2005). *Digital government: Technology and public sector performance*. Princeton University Press.

Westerman, D., Daniel, E. S., & Bowman, N. D. (2016). Learned risks and experienced rewards: Exploring the potential sources of students attitudes toward social media and face-to-face communication. *The Internet and Higher Education*, *31*, 52–57. doi:10.1016/j.iheduc.2016.06.004

Weymouth, G., Mills, G. A., Jones, D., Ebert, E. E., & Manton, M. J. (1999). A continental-scale daily rainfall analysis system. *Australian Meteorological Magazine*, *48*(3), 169–179.

Whitaker, C. (2013, May 14). Using the new ClearPath API to help communities interact with the Chicago Police Department [Web log comment]. Retrieved from http://www.smartchicagocollaborative.org/using-the-new-clearpath-api-to-help-communities-interact-with-the-chicago-police-department/

Widrick, S. M., Mergen, E., & Grant, D. (2002). Measuring the dimension of quality in higher education. *Total Quality Management*, *13*(1), 123–131. doi:10.1080/09544120120098609

Wilson, M., & Warnock, K. (2007). *At the heart of change: the role of communication in sustainable development & the case for communication in sustainable development*. Panos Publications.

Witten, I. H., Frank, E., & Hall, M. A. (2005). Data Mining: Practical Machine Learning Tools and Techniques (2nd ed.). Morgan Kaufmann Publishers.

Witten, I. H., Frank, E., & Hall, M. A. (2011). Data Mining: Practical Machine Learning Tools and Techniques (3rd ed.). Morgan Kaufmann Publishers.

Woodill, G. (2011). *The mobile learning edge. Tools and Technologies for Developing your Teams*. EBSCO Publishing, Inc.

World Bank. (2004). Building blocks of e-government: lessons from developing countries. PREMnote, number 91, the World Bank.

World Economic Forum. (n.d.). *Report 2015: Top 10 urban innovations of 2015*. Retrieved from https://www.weforum.org/agenda/2015/10/top-10-urban-innovations-of-2015

WTIS. (2015). *World Telecommunication/ICT Indicators Symposium*. Retrieved from http://www.itu.int/en/ITU-D/Statistics/Pages/events/wtis2015/default.aspx

Xia, Y., Winterhalter, M., & Fabian, P. (1999). A model to interpolate monthly mean climatological data at Bavarian forest climate stations. *Theoretical and Applied Climatology*, *64*(1-2), 27–38. doi:10.1007/s007040050108

Yadav, M. P., Feeroz, M., & Yadav, V. K. (2012). Mining the customer behavior using web usage mining in e-commerce. In *Computing Communication & Networking Technologies (ICCCNT), 2012 Third International Conference on* (pp. 1-5). doi:10.1109/ICCCNT.2012.6395938

Yamayee, Z. A., & Albright, R. J. (2008). Direct and Indirect Assessment Methods: Key Ingredients for Continuous Quality Improvement and ABET Accreditation. *International Journal of Engineering Education*, *24*(5), 877–883.

Yang, D., Sinha, T., Adamson, D., & Rosé, C. P. (2013). "turn on, tune in, drop out": Anticipating student dropouts in massive open online courses. Workshop of NIPS.

Yang, D., Piergallini, M., Howley, I., & Rose, C. (2014). Forum thread recommendation for massive open online courses. *Proceedings of 7th Conference on Educational Data Mining 2014*.

Yannoukakoua, A., & Arakab, I. (2014). Access to Government Information: Right to Information and Open Government Data Synergy. *Procedia: Social and Behavioral Sciences*, *147*, 332–340. doi:10.1016/j.sbspro.2014.07.107

Yao, Y. Y. (1995). Measuring retrieval effectiveness based on user preference of documents. *Journal of the American Society for Information Science*, *46*(2), 133–145. doi:10.1002/(SICI)1097-4571(199503)46:2<133::AID-ASI6>3.0.CO;2-Z

Yeandle, S., Buckner, L. (2007). *Carers, Employment and Services: Time for a new social contract?* Carers, Employment and Services Report Series, 6.

Yin, R. K. (2013). *Case study research: Design and methods* (5th ed.). London: Sage Publications Inc., USA.

Yuan, L., & Powell, S. (2013). *MOOCs and Open Education: Implications for Higher Education*. Academic Press.

Yu, K., Schwaighofer, A., Tresp, V., Xu, X., & Kriegel, H. P. (2004). Probabilistic memory-based collaborative filtering. *IEEE Transactions on Knowledge and Data Engineering*, *16*(1), 56–69. doi:10.1109/TKDE.2004.1264822

Zadeh, L. A. (1975a). The concept of a linguistic variable and its applications to approximate reasoning. Part I. Information Sciences, 8(3), 199–249. doi:10.1016/0020-0255(75)90036-5 doi:10.1016/0020-0255(75)90036-5

Zadeh, L. A. (1975b). The concept of a linguistic variable and its applications to approximate reasoning. Part II. Information Sciences, 8(4), 301–357. doi:10.1016/0020-0255(75)90046-8 doi:10.1016/0020-0255(75)90046-8

Zadeh, L. A. (1976). The concept of a linguistic variable and its applications to approximate reasoning. Part III. Information Sciences, 8, 43–80.

Zadeh, L. A. (1996). Fuzzy Logic Computing with words. IEEE Transactions on Fuzzy Systems, 4(2), 103–111. doi:10.1109/91.493904 doi:10.1109/91.493904

Zancanaro, A., & de Souza Domingues, M. J. (2017). Analysis of the scientific literature on Massive Open Online Courses (MOOCs). *Ried-Revista Iberoamericana de Educacion a Distancia*, *20*(1), 59–80. doi:10.5944/ried.20.1.15910

Zaphiris, P., & Zacharia, G. (2001). Participatory Design of an Online Greek Language Course. *Abridged Proceedings of the 9th International Conference on Human Computer Interaction,* 272-274.

Zheng, S., Rosson, M. B., Shih, P. C., & Carroll, J. M. (2015). Understanding student motivation, behaviors and perceptions in MOOCs. In *Proceedings of the 18th ACM Conference on Computer Supported Cooperative Work & Social Computing* (pp. 1882-1895). ACM. doi:10.1145/2675133.2675217

Zheng, Y., Capra, L., Wolfson, O., & Yang, H. (2014). Urban computing: Concepts, methodologies, and applications. *ACM Transactions on Intelligent Systems and Technology*, *5*(3), 38. doi:10.1145/2629592

Zheng, Y., Liu, T., Wang, Y., Zhu, Y., Liu, Y., & Chang, E. (2014, September). Diagnosing New York city's noises with ubiquitous data. In *Proceedings of the 2014 ACM International Joint Conference on Pervasive and Ubiquitous Computing* (pp. 715-725). ACM. doi:10.1145/2632048.2632102

Zhuhadar, L., Coleman, P., & Marklin, S. (2016). Applicative Personalized Learning: How Gamification is Driving Learning. *International Journal of Knowledge Society Research*, *4*(7), 24–37. doi:10.4018/IJKSR.2016100103

Zhuhadar, L., Kruk, S. R., & Daday, J. (2015). Semantically enriched massive open online courses (moocs) platform. *Computers in Human Behavior*, *51*, 578–593. doi:10.1016/j.chb.2015.02.067

Zogaj, S., Bretschneider, U., & Leimeister, J. M. (2014). Managing crowdsourced software testing: A case study based insight on the challenges of a crowdsourcing intermediary. *Journal of Business Economics*, *3*(84), 375–405. doi:10.1007/s11573-014-0721-9

Zubizarreta, J. (2004). *The Learning Portfolio*. Bolton, MA: Anker Publishing.

Σπανός, Γ. E., & Spanos, Y. E. (2009). Innovation adoption: an integrative model. *SPOUDAI-Journal of Economics and Business,* *59*(1-2), 100-124.

About the Contributors

Miltiadis D. Lytras is Associate Professor at Deree- ACG with a research focus on semantic web, knowledge management and e-learning, with more than 100 publications. He has co-edited more than 45 special issues in International Journals (IEEE Transaction on Knowledge and Data Engineering, IEEE Internet Computing, IEEE Transactions on Education, Computers in Human Behaviour, Interactive Learning Environments, Journal of Knowledge Management, Journal of Computer Assisted Learning) and has authored/(co-)edited 42 books (e.g., Open Source for Knowledge and Learning Management, Ubiquitous and Pervasive Knowledge Management, Intelligent Learning Infrastructures for Knowledge Intensive Organizations, Semantic Web Based Information Systems, China Information Technology Handbook, Real World Applications of Semantic Web and Ontologies, Web 2.0: The Business Model, etc.). He (has) serves(ed) as the (Co) Editor in Chief of 8 international journals (e.g., International Journal on Semantic Web and Information Systems, International Journal of Knowledge Society Research, International Journal of Knowledge and Learning, International Journal of Technology Enhanced Learning).

Linda Daniela is a professor and senior researcher at the University of Latvia, Riga, Latvia; Chair of the Council for Promotion in Pedagogy of the University of Latvia; Head of the Scientific Institute of Pedagogy; Expert of Education at the Council of Sciences of the Republic of Latvia; co-operating expert with the Ministry of Education of the Republic of Latvia. Professor Daniela is an accomplished author and editor. Her works were published in Europe and in the US. At the same time, Professor Daniela is actively engaged with pedagogy, serving as a lecturer and scientific supervisor of doctoral and master theses. Professor's Daniela research interests include: ICTs' enhanced approaches to teaching and learning, virtual education, smart education, educational technologies for learning, educational robotics, educational processes and solutions for reducing social exclusion from the educational processes; active citizenship, EU. Professor Daniela is an author and co-author of publications about processes in all dimensions of education. She has been involved in several grants and projects in the fields of education and specifically related to improving the efficiency of teaching and learning across curriculum through the utilization of sophisticated information and communication technologies.

Anna Visvizi is a political scientist and economist, editor and research consultant with extensive experience in academia and the think-tank sector in Europe and the US. The author of more than 70 published works, she presented her work in many forums across Europe and the US, including Capitol Hill. A former DAAD fellow, former Marie Curie fellow, she was also awarded fellowships to conduct research at the London School of Economics and the New York University. A practiced team-worker, researcher, analyst and lecturer, her expertise spans four interrelated areas of research, i.e., the political economy of economic integration, including the EU and the euro area crisis as well as nascent integration schemes in emerging markets; international business; economy and security in Central Europe; and global safety, security and sustainable growth and development. Dr. Visvizi participated in several collaborative research projects funded by the European Commission under Framework Programs, incl. FP5, FP6, FP7; by the Polish National Centre for Science (NCN); Polish Ministry of Foreign Affairs; Faculty Resource Network (FRN); International Visegrad Fund (IVF), and other. Dr. Visvizi presented her academic work in more than 100 international conferences, while at the same time contributing to the global policy-debate through her participation in such events as CEPA Annual Forum 2016, Bled Strategic Forum 2016 and other high-level formats of political discussion and debate in Europe and in the US. Dr. Visivizi taught and/or conducted research at the University of Warwick (UK), Warsaw School of Economics (Poland), Aalborg University (Denmark), Polish Institute of International Affairs (PISM), Centre for the Study of Globalization and Regionalization (CSGR), German Institute for International and Security Affairs (SWP), Polish Academy of Sciences, Institute of East-Central Europe (IESW). She is the founder and Editor in Chief of a policy-briefs series, titled COMMENTARY IESW distributed electronically to the Polish administration and academic community. She serves as well as executive editor of the English version of the Yearbook of the Institute of East-Central Europe (YIESW), one of the most influential journals on the Polish market (listed in CEEOL and Index Copernicus).

* * *

Paola Adinolfi is a full professor of Organization Studies at the University of Salerno, Dept. of Management and Innovation Systems.

Matilde Basso Aránguiz received her Geologist Degree in Universidad de Concepción, Chile in 2001. Ever since 2011 she has been working as Assistant Professor in the Civil Engineering Department at Universidad Católica de la Santísima Concepción (UCSC). In 2015, she enrolled in the Master Program in Educational Technology and Knowledge Management offered by the Education Faculty at UCSC. Currently, she is the Head of the career of the Civil Geological Engineering, and she is working on her master thesis project linked to her projects granted to support teaching by UCSC (FAD 11/2016 and FAD 09/2017). Her area of interest is related to Education in Engineering and evaluation through the use of ICT.

Tayeb Brahimi, Assistant Professor at the Department of Electrical and Computer Engineering (ECE), at Effat University, Jeddah, Kingdom of Saudi Arabia, received his Ph.D. (1992) and Master Degree (1987) from Ecole Polytechnique, University of Montreal, Canada. He has worked as Research Scientist under Bombardier Chair/Canadair from 1992 to 1998. In 1998 he joined Jeppesen DataPlan in California as a Programmer Analyst, then Peregrine System (acquired by Hewlett-Packard in 2005), a B2B company in Concord (CA), as a technical Support Analyst, then as Quality Assurance Engineer and Consultant for Electronic data interchange (EDI) commercial software in Dallas, Texas, providing strategic support, guidance and technical resolution of problems related to EDI, ESD (Electronic Software Download), and online web application. Dr. Tayeb Brahimi is internationally recognized for his contribution to the development of teaching and research programs between university and government Institutions. He received internationally recognized awards and performed a leading role for a distinguished institution (Bombardier Chair/University of Montreal). He is consultant at IONPARA Inc. (http://www.

iopara.ca/team.shtml) for wind turbines and Aeronautics consulting, he published more than 80 articles in scientific journals, international conferences, and internal technical reports on aircraft icing, wind turbines, and methodologies of teaching and learning. Among other activities, Dr. Tayeb Brahimi is reviewer for many international journals, invited speaker by the Japan Society of Mechanical Engineering, Japan Turbo machinery Association (Ishikawajima-Harima Heavy Industries, Tokyo) as well as the International Conference on Engineering Education & Research 2015 (FICEER2015), and participated in Public Debate on Energy organized by the Government of Quebec, Canada (Public Debate on Energy).

Ernesto D'Avanzo is at the Department of Political, Social and Communication Sciences at the University of Salerno where he teaches Philosophy of Science and Decision Making and Data, Web and Social Analytics. He is Associate editor at the International Journal on Semantic Web and Information Systems (IJSWIS) and Associate researcher at the High Performance Computing and Networking Institute of the National Research Council (ICAR - CNR), Italy. decision models and decision support systems that make use of artificial intelligence methods and techniques (e.g., machine learning and natural language processing) and mathematical models such as path analysis, confirmatory factor analysis, latent growth modelling in order to build dynamic information systems prototypes based on analytical and quantitative skills and bias towards making data-based decisions.

Imelda Escamilla obtained his Ph. D. Degree by the Centro de Investigaci6n en Computaci6n, in the Intelligent Processing of Geospatial Data Laboratory. Her fields of interest include analytical methods for geographic information, ontology development, semantic geo-coding, Web-GIS, and machine learning.

Giovanni Guzman is a Researcher-Professor at the Center for Computing Research, IPN. He obtained his PhD and MSc in 2007 and 2003 from the Center for Computing Research. He has published about 70 scientific publications in journals and conferences. His research interests focus on raster data processing, image analysis and mobile devices applications for spatial information processing.

Sarah Hartmann has been working as a research assistant at the Department of Information Science at the Heinrich Heine University in Düsseldorf, Germany. Her research interests are in the area of e-government and smart cities with a main focus on citizen relationship management systems and services, civic participation, and the use of mobile applications, social media, and innovation contests to communicate, interact, and co-create with citizens.

Youssef Jdidou is a PhD candidate in Computer sciences. In research, his current interests include: E-learning, Adaptive Hypermedia Systems, MOOCs, and Recommendation Systems. He is the President of the Association of Scientific Research, Innovation and Technology and Founder of Tetuan International Conference on Education and Technology.

Juan Humberto Juárez Hipólito was a student of Computer Science in the Instituto Politécnico Nacional. His areas of interest include geographic information retrieval, mining the social media, geographic information systems, and machine learning approaches.

Mohamed Khaldi is a Professor at Abdelmalek Essaadi University since 1987, specialist in E-learning and Pedagogy.

Sajid Khalifa is an Assistant Professor of Product Design in Design Department, College of Architecture and Design at Effat University. Dr. Khalifa completed his PhD in Manufacturing Systems and a Masters in Rapid Product Development, both from De Montfort University, UK, and a BSc (Hns) in Industrial Design from Coventry University, UK. Dr. Khalifa's research areas include Innovative Product Design and Development, Material properties and applications, Computer Aided Design (CAD), Computer Aided Manufacturing (CAM), Rapid Prototyping (RP), Strategic Production Planning and Advanced Manufacturing Processes. Dr. Khalifa has spent more than a decade in industry as a practitioner on various assignments and projects, ranging from Aerospace, Defense and Domestic products. Before joining the Effat University, Dr. Khalifa worked in the UK Education Industry for prestigious Further and Higher Education Institutions.

Maira Kotsovoulou received her BSc in Business Administration with major in Computer Information Systems from The American College of Greece – Deree College (Athens, Greece, 1994), and her MSc in Human Computer Interaction from Heriot-Watt University (Edinburgh, U.K., 1995). She is also currently working part-time towards a distance learning PhD in e-research and Technology Enhanced Learning at Lancaster University, U.K. Moreover, she is a professor in the department of Information Technology at Deree – The American College of Greece. Her research interests include but are not limited to the areas of e-learning, blended learning, and technology enhanced learning (TEL) and more specifically in the area of teaching and learning computer programming using visual programming environments.

Vladimir Luna obtained his Ph. D. Degree by the Centro de Investigaci6n en Computaci6n, in the Intelligent Processing of Geospatial Data Laboratory. His areas of interest include geographic information system, user profiling, ontology development, and e-learning.

Agnes Mainka is a researcher at the Department of Information Science at the Heinrich Heine University in Düsseldorf, Germany. Her research interests are smart cities, social media, libraries and open government. As a lecturer, she works together with students on open data, smart cities, and e-government projects. As an active member of the OK Lab Düsseldorf, she participates in open government activities in her hometown.

Mehedi Masud received his PhD and Masters in Computer Science from the University of Ottawa, Canada. Currently, he is serving as an Associate Professor at the Department of Computer Science, Taif University, KSA. His research interests include issues related to P2P and networked data management, query processing and optimization, eHealth, information security, cloud data management, and big data. He has published several research papers at international journals and conferences. He also served as a member of the technical committees of several international conferences and workshops. I am also an editorial board member in some journals including Journal of Internet and Information Systems (JIIS), Journal of Engineering and Computer Innovations, and Journal of Software (JWS). He also served as a guest editor for Journal of Computer Science and Information Science (ComSIS).

Maria Matiatou is a Communications expert, Information Communication Technology specialist, Higher Education Administration and Academic Advising Module Manager.

Marco Moreno-Ibarra is a full time research professor at the Centre for Computing Research (CIC) of the Instituto Politécnico Nacional (IPN), PhD in Computer Science (2007) and member of the National Research System level 2. Former Director of the National Calculus Centre (CENAC), former Director of Systems, Informatics and Telecommunications of National Council of Research, Science and Technology (CONACYT) and former head of the Laboratory of Intelligent Processing of Geospatial Information. He has over 100 articles in journals, national and international conferences as well as being a reviewer for publications such as the International Journal of Geographical Information Science, Computers and Geosciences and Computers in Human Behavior, among others. He teaches the courses of Foundations of Geographic Information Science and Tools for the design and implementation of GIS within the master and doctorate programs in computer science at CIC-IPN. His research areas include GIS design, automatic generalization, volunteered geographic information and geospatial semantic similarity.

Isabel Novo-Corti has a PhD in economics (Universidade da Coruña). Professor (University School) of Economic Analysis at the Universidade da Coruña, in the faculties of Economics and Business, Law and Sociology. In addition, she is Professor-Tutor of the Associated Center of the UNED in A Coruña. She was director of the Department of Economic Analysis and Business Administration 2009-2017. Coordinator of the Economic Development & Social Sustainability (EDaSS) Research Group. Member of the University Institute of Maritime Studies of the University of Coruña and Member of the Economic Forum of Galicia. She has published her works in the most prestigious international scientific journals. Her research has been internationally recognized, proof of which are the prizes received. He has conducted research stays at the universities of Reading (United Kingdom), Washington (San Louis, Missouri, United States), Harvard (Massachusetts, United States), Tras dos Montes and Alto Douro (UTAD, Portugal) and Targu-Jui Romania.

Danilo Piaggesi is Managing Director of the FRAmericas (FRA) and a member of Fondazione Rosselli's Board. FRA focuses on Knowledge Society, ICT, and innovation for development. He founded and directs FRA's International Knowledge Economy Program (IKEP), working with multilateral and bilateral cooperation to support development projects where ICT, innovation and the principles of the Knowledge Economy can be instrumental for achieving socio-economic growth. He is also the founder of the "ICT for Development International School" or ICT4DEVIS a higher education summer programme. Between 2007 and 2009 he was Knowledge Economy Coordinator in the Vice Presidency of the Inter American Development Bank (IADB), in Washington D.C, after having started and run its Information and Communication Technology for Development Division at the same institution, as Division Chief from 1999 to 2007. The ICT Division was in charge of structuring and implementing the Bank's policy to introduce ICT in the Bank's project portfolio, providing technical assistance to IADB's borrowing member countries, and better informing Latin America & Caribbean government decisions regarding ICT and its applications. Prior to the IABD, from 1981 to 1991, Mr. Piaggesi worked for the United Nations Food and Agriculture Organization (FAO) at different duty stations in Africa and Latin America in the field of technology transfer for development. From 1992 to 1998 he was part of the technical staff of Telespazio, Telecom-Italia Group in Rome, where he was in charge of the Strategic Alliances and International Activities Division. Mr. Piaggesi also consulted for the European Union in Brussels, evaluating project proposals for funding in the field of telecommunications and environment. Mr. Piaggesi is a Physicist by training, with specialization in geophysics, cum laude, Diploma from the University of Rome (1980), and an Executive International Business Certificate from Georgetown University/ John Cabot University, in Washington D.C and in Rome (1996). Other professional training included remote sensing (1981); digital image processing and analysis (1986); technical cooperation project formulation and appraisal (1989); telecommunications management (1995-1996) and ICT, innovation and Knowledge Society for development (2005). Mr. Piaggesi's most recent publications published by IGI Global, USA, discuss trends, issues and challenges surrounding the deployment of ICT in a globalized, knowledge-based world.

Jose Picatoste holds a degree in economics and a master's degree in international migrations from the University of A Coruña (Spain). He also holds a master's degree in Secondary Education by the International University of La Rioja (Spain). At present, he is part of the teaching and research staff of the Autonomous University of Madrid, as a PhD student, in the Department of Economic Structure and Development Economics. He has received research awards and has published books and papers in prestigious journals at international level, as well as presented his work at numerous international conferences.

María Graciela Badilla Quintana is Assistant Professor at the Faculty of Education at Universidad Católica de la Santísima Concepción, Chile. She is a member of the CIEDE UCSC -Centro de Investigación en Educación y Desarrollo [Center for Research in Education and Development], Director of the Doctoral in Education in Consortium program and Editor in Chief of the REXE scientific Journal. Her research interests are focus on ICT integration on educational Innovation and include between others themes related with Immersive Virtual Worlds and Gamification in teaching and learning processes. Between 2016 and 2018 she is Visiting Researcher in the Laboratory for Embodied Cognition and Embodied Games Lab, at Arizona State University thanks to a postdoctoral fellowship granted by Becas Chile from Chilean Government.

Rolando Quintero, born in Mexico City in 1975, obtained a Ph.D. in Computer Science from the National Polytechnic Institute of Mexico. He is a researcher at the Center for Computing Research of the IPN. Author of around 80 scientific papers in conferences and journals. He is a member, level 1, of the National System of Researchers (SNI) from the Mexican Council of Science and Technology (CONACYT). He has conducted basic research projects and technological development with national institutions. He has directed about twenty graduate thesis in his areas of interest that include knowledge representation and processing of semantic information.

Denis Alcides Rezende is a Full Professor and Researcher in the Post-Graduate Program of Public Administration and Urban Management at PUCPR Catholic University (Pontifícia Universidade Católica do Paraná, Brazil). CNPq Brazil Research Fellow (2013-2019). Visiting Professor (Strategic Digital City) - Chaddick Institute for Metropolitan Development - School of Public Service - DePaul University - Chicago - USA (2013 - 2016). He has been involved with project coaching, and been a professor and thesis evaluator - Steinbeis University - School of International Business and Entrepreneurship – Germany (2015 - 2016). He holds his Post-Doctorate in Strategic Digital City, 2014, School of Public Service (DePaul University, Chicago - EUA). Post-Doctorate in Municipal Public Administration, 2006, USP University (Universidade de São Paulo, Brazil). He has a PhD in Information Technology and Public-Private Strategic Planning, 2002, UFSC University (Universidade Federal de Santa Catarina, Brazil). He has a Master of Science in Information Technology, 1999, UFPR University (Universidade Federal do Paraná, Brazil). He has a Bachelor in Administration, 1992, FADEPS University (Faculdade De Plácido e Silva, Brazil). Author and co-author of 21 books and more than 250 academic articles (papers) on strategic planning in public and private organizations, public management, information systems, strategic digital city and information technology management. Business and Public Sector Consultant in projects aiming the same issues of the books mentioned above.

Akila Sarirete received her bachelor's degree in Computer Science at Institut National d'Informatique in Algeria and her Master's degree from the University of Quebec (Montreal) and INI (Algeria). She worked as a Research Assistant and Software Engineer in Canada (Montreal) and as a Senior Software Engineer in the United States (California) before moving to Saudi Arabia to join the faculty at Effat University as a Lecturer in 2002 in the Computer Science (CS) department. She got her Cisco Regional Academy Instructor Certification in 2004 and worked as a Cisco Coordinator till 2011. She earned her PhD degree in Computer Science (Knowledge Management in CoPs of e-Learning) from ESI (Ecole Superieure Nationale d'Informatique). As a faculty member of the CS department at Effat University, she served as the Chair of the CS department and then from 2013 as a Dean for the College of Engineering. She is an active researcher and community member. Her current research interests are in Information Retrieval and Ranking Systems in Service Oriented Architecture. She is as well interested in Knowledge Management and Communities of Practice and Knowledge Sharing.

Marco Spruit is a researcher at the Information and Computing Sciences department of Utrecht University in the Netherlands. As principle investigator in the department's Applied Data Science Lab, Marco's research centres around Analytic Systems in an Applied Data Science context. Marco serves on the editorial boards of the international journals on Decision Analytics, Business Intelligence Research, Semantic Web and Information Systems, Autonomic Computing, and Computer Information Systems. Before 2007 Marco worked in industry as a software developer for fourteen years in the fields of Business Intelligence and Text Analytics.

Vassilia Stefanou received her BSc in Business Administration with major in Computer Information Systems from The American College of Greece – Deree College (Athens, Greece, 1994), and her MSc in Human Computer Interaction from Heriot-Watt University (Edinburgh, U.K., 1995). She is also currently working part-time towards a distance learning PhD in e-research and Technology Enhanced Learning at Lancaster University, U.K. Moreover, she is an assistant professor in the department of Computer Information Systems at Deree – The American College of Greece. Her research interests include but are not limited to the areas of Human Computer Interaction, e-learning, blended learning, and technology enhanced learning.

Wolfgang G. Stock is professor for information science and head of the Information Science Department of the Heinrich Heine University Düsseldorf, Germany. His research activities und lectures include information retrieval, knowledge representation, informetrics, smart cities, social media, and the markets of digital information. He is author of more than 300 articles and of some basic text books in information science. Additionally, he is editor of the book series "Knowledge & Information. Studies in Information Science" (De Gruyter Saur).

Miguel Torres-Ruiz is a Professor and Researcher of the Intelligent Processing of Geospatial Information Laboratory in the CIC-IPN. He has published around 90 papers in National and International Journals and Conferences. His research scopes are focused on developing approaches to conceptualize the geographic domain, design of intelligent GIS, ontology-driven information integration and methodologies oriented to the spatial reasoning. Additionally, he is member of the S.N.I. (level 1), ACM, IEEE, AMIICE, CONACOFI, and CONAVEF and he has participated as consultant in several projects for SENASICA-SAPARPA, CENAPRED, and IFE.

Maria Vargas-Vera received her PhD from the Artificial Intelligence Department at Edinburgh University in 1995 and she was awarded Fellow of the British Computer Society (FBCS) since November 2009. Dr. Vargas-Vera's current research focuses on Ontology Mapping, Question Answering and Applications using Semantic Web Technologies. Furthermore, Dr Vargas-Vera has published many research papers in international conferences and journals and she is also a member of program committees of international Conferences. Dr Vargas-Vera is an Associated Editor, the International Journal of Knowledge and Learning (IJKL) and the Journal of Emerging Technologies in Web Intelligence (JETWI).

Index

K

L

M

N

O

P

R

S

T

U

V

W

www.ingramcontent.com/pod-product-compliance
Lightning Source LLC
LaVergne TN
LVHW060302011026
849161LV00011B/2761